Strategic St

This new reader brings together key essays on strategic theory by some of the leading contributors in the field.

Filling a large gap in the market, it will guide students through both the theoretical and practical aspects of strategic studies. Including classic essays and works of contemporary scholarship, the volume provides a wide-ranging survey of the key ideas and themes in the field of strategic studies. It comprises six thematic sections, each of which has an editors' introduction and suggestions for further reading:

- uses of strategic theory
- interpretation of the classics
- instruments of war: land, sea, and air power
- nuclear strategy
- irregular warfare and small wars
- future warfare, future strategy.

Striking a balance between theoretical essays and case studies, *Strategic Studies* will be essential reading for all students of strategic studies, international security, and modern warfare, as well as for professional military students.

Thomas G. Mahnken currently serves as the US Deputy Assistant Secretary of Defense for Policy Planning. He previously served as a Professor of Strategy at the US Naval War College and a Visiting Fellow at the Philip Merrill Center for Strategic Studies at the Johns Hopkins University's Paul H. Nitze School of Advanced International Studies (SAIS). He is author of *Uncovering Ways of War: US Intelligence and Foreign Military Innovation, 1918–1941* (2002). He is co-editor of *The Journal of Strategic Studies*.

Joseph A. Maiolo is Senior Lecturer in War Studies at the Department of War Studies, King's College London. In 2005–06 he was Visiting Research Fellow at the Norwegian Institute of Defense Studies. He is author of *The Royal Navy and Nazi Germany, 1933–39* (1998) and co-editor (with Robert Boyce) of *The Origins of World War Two: The Debate Continues* (2005). He is co-editor of *The Journal of Strategic Studies*.

Strategic Studies

A Reader

Edited by
Thomas G. Mahnken
and Joseph A. Maiolo

Routledge
Taylor & Francis Group

LONDON AND NEW YORK

First published 2008
by Routledge
2 Park Square, Milton Park, Abingdon, Oxon, OX14 4RN

Simultaneously published in the USA and Canada
by Routledge
711 Third Avenue, New York, NY 10017

Routledge is an imprint of the Taylor and Francis Group, an informa business

Typeset in Baskerville by
RefineCatch Limited, Bungay, Suffolk

British Library Cataloguing in Publication Data
A catalogue record for this book is available from the British Library

Library of Congress Cataloging in Publication Data
Strategic studies : a reader / edited by Thomas G. Mahnken and Joseph A. Maiolo.
    p. cm.
Includes bibliographical references.
ISBN 978–0–415–77221–1 (hardback) – ISBN 978–0–415–77222–8 (paperback)
– ISBN 978–0–203–92846–2 (e book) 1. Strategy. I. Mahnken, Thomas G., 1965-
II. Maiolo, Joseph A.
U162.S672 2008
355.02–dc22

                                                                2007042137

ISBN10: 0–415–77221–4 (hbk)
ISBN10: 0–415–77222–2 (pbk)
ISBN10: 0–203–92846–6 (ebk)

ISBN13: 978–0–415–77221–1 (hbk)
ISBN13: 978–0–415–77222–8 (pbk)
ISBN13: 978–0–203–92846–2 (ebk)

Contents

Acknowledgments

The editors would like to thank S. Rebecca Zimmerman for her assistance in compiling this volume.

The publisher would like to thank the following for permission to reprint their material:

The Johns Hopkins University Press, for Brodie, Bernard, "Strategy as a Science," *World Politics* 1: 4 (1949), 467–488 © The Johns Hopkins University Press.

Oxford University Press, for Freedman, Lawrence, "Strategic Studies and the Problem of Power," from *War, Strategy, and International Politics* (1992), edited by Freedman, Lawrence *et al.*, 279–294.

Naval War College Press, for Fuller, William C., Jr., "What is a Military Lesson?," from *Strategic Logic and Political Rationality: Essays in Honor of Michael I. Handel* (Frank Cass, 2002), edited by Bradford A. Lee and Karl-Friedrich Walling, 38–59.

Oxford University Press, for Sun Tzu, *The Art of War* (Samuel B. Griffiths [trans.]) (1963).

David Higham Associates, for the estate of Basil Liddell Hart, for Liddell Hart, Basil, *Strategy: The Indirect Approach* (Faber & Faber, 1954).

Yale University Press, for Schelling, Thomas C., *Arms and Influence* (1966).

Taylor and Francis, for Holden Reid, Brian, "J.F.C. Fuller's Theory of Mechanized Warfare," *The Journal of Strategic Studies* 1: 3 (1978).

Naval Institute Press, for Corbett, Julian, *Some Principles of Maritime Strategy* (1988).

Taylor and Francis, for Overy, R.J., "Air Power and the Origins of Deterrence Theory Before 1939," *The Journal of Strategic Studies* 15: 1 (1992).

MIT Press Journals, for Byman, Daniel L., and Matthew C. Waxman, "Kosovo and the Great Air Power Debate," *International Security* 24: 4 (Spring, 2000) © 2000 by the President and the Fellows of Harvard College and the Massachusetts Institute of Technology.

Harcourt, Inc., for Brodie, Bernard, "War in the Atomic Age," from *The Absolute Weapon* (1946).

Foreign Affairs, for Wohlstetter, Albert, *The Delicate Balance of Terror*, 37 (2) (1959).

Encyclopaedia Britannica, Inc., for Lawrence, T.E. "Science of Guerrilla Warfare," from *Encyclopaedia Britannica*, 14th edn. © 1929 by Encyclopaedia Britannica, Inc.

Foreign Languages Press Service of the People's Republic of China, for Mao Tse Tung, *Selected Military Writings of Mao Tse Tung* (1968).

Greenwood Publishing Group, for Galula, David, *Counterinsurgency Warfare: Theory and Practice*, Praeger Security International Acad. (1964).

Princeton University Press, for Mack, Andrew, "Why Big Nations Lose Small Wars: the Politics of Asymmetric Conflict," in Klaus Knorr, *Power, Strategy, and Security* (1983) © 1983 Princeton University Press. Reprinted with permission of Princeton University Press.

Taylor and Francis, for Kilcullen, David J., "Countering Global Insurgency," *The Journal of Strategic Studies* 28: 4 (2005).

Taylor and Francis, for Neumann, Peter R. and M.L.R. Smith, "Strategic Terrorism: the Framework and its Fallacies," *The Journal of Strategic Studies* 28: 4 (2005).

The National Interest, for Krepinevich, Andrew F., "From Cavalry to Computer: The Patterns of Military Revolutions," *The National Interest* (Fall 1994).

Naval War College Press, for Evans, Michael, "Kadesh to Kandahar: Military Theory and the Future of War," *Naval War College Review* (Summer 2003).

National Defense University Press, for Gray, Colin S., "Why Strategy is Difficult," *Joint Force Quarterly* (Spring 2003).

Taylor and Francis, for Roberts, Adam, "The 'War on Terror' in Historical Perspective," *Survival* 47: 2 (2005).

Taylor and Francis, for Strachan, Hew, "The Lost Meaning of Strategy," *Survival* 47: 3 (2005).

General introduction

The events of recent years demonstrate that war will be a feature of international relations for the foreseeable future. The 2003 Iraq War and Israel's 2006 war in Lebanon against Hezbollah, as well as the continuing possibility of conflict on the Korean Peninsula, in the Persian Gulf, and across the Taiwan Strait, demonstrates that force remains an instrument of statecraft.

At the same time, war appears to be taking new forms. Since the early 1990s, theorists and practitioners have been arguing that we are in the early phases of a Revolution in Military Affairs brought on by the development and diffusion of information technology. The ongoing insurgencies in Iraq and Afghanistan, and the Global War on Terrorism more broadly, remind us that not all wars are fought among nation-states. North Korea's demonstration of its nuclear capability, and continued suspicion that Iran would like to follow suit, demonstrate that nuclear weapons (and nuclear strategy) remain a concern.

In a world in which so much about the character and conduct of war appears to be changing, an understanding of the theory of war reminds us that the nature of war does not change. Moreover, an understanding of the enduring nature of war can help us focus on its changing character and conduct.

Theory offers the student of strategy a conceptual toolkit to analyze strategic problems. An understanding of theory equips the student with a set of questions to guide further study. As Carl von Clausewitz wrote, the purpose of theory is not to uncover fixed laws or principles, but rather to educate the mind. As he put it:

> [Theory] is an analytical investigation leading to a close *acquaintance* with the subject; applied to experience – in our case, to military history – it leads to a thorough *familiarity* with it . . . Theory will have fulfilled its main task when it is used to analyze the constituent elements of war, to distinguish precisely what at first sight seems fused, to explain in full the properties of the means employed and to show their probable effects, to define clearly the nature of the ends in view, and to illuminate all phases of warfare in a thorough critical inquiry. Theory then becomes a guide to anyone who wants to learn about war from books; it will light his way, ease his progress, train his judgment, and help him to avoid pitfalls . . . It is meant to educate the mind of the future commander, or, more accurately, to guide him in his self-education, not to accompany him to the battlefield; just as a wise teacher guides and stimulates a young man's intellectual development, but is careful not to lead him by the hand for the rest of his life.[1]

In other words, we study strategic theory in order to learn how to think strategically.

Because the stakes in war are so high, strategy is a supremely practical endeavour. The most elegant theory is useless if it lacks practical application. Strategic theory thus succeeds or fails in direct proportion to its ability to help decision makers formulate sound strategy. As the twentieth century American strategist Bernard Brodie put it, "strategy is a field where truth is sought in the pursuit of viable solutions."[2]

On strategy

Because strategy is about how to win wars, any discussion of strategy must begin with an understanding of war. As Clausewitz famously defined it, "war is thus an act of force to compel our enemy to do our will."[3] Two aspects of this definition are notable. First, the fact that war involves force separates it from other types of political, economic, and military competition. Second, the fact that war is not senseless slaughter, but rather an instrument that is used to achieve a political purpose differentiates it from other types of violence.

Strategy is, or rather should be, a rational process. As Clausewitz wrote, "No one starts a war – or rather, no one in his senses ought to do so – without first being clear in his mind what he intends to achieve by that war and how he intends to conduct it."[4] In other words, success in war requires a clear articulation of political aims and the development of an adequate strategy to achieve them. Clausewitz's formulation acknowledges, however, that states sometimes go to war without clear or achievable aims or a strategy to achieve them. As Germany demonstrated in two world wars, mastery of tactics and operations counts for little without a coherent or feasible strategy.[5]

Successful strategy is based upon clearly identifying political goals, assessing one's comparative advantage relative to the enemy, calculating costs and benefits carefully, and examining the risks and rewards of alternative strategies. The purpose of strategy is ultimately to convince the enemy that he cannot achieve his aims. As Admiral J.C. Wylie wrote, "the primary aim of the strategist in the conduct of war is some selected degree of control of the enemy for the strategist's own purpose; this is achieved by control of the pattern of war; and this control of the pattern of war is had by manipulation of the centre of gravity of war to the disadvantage of the opponent."[6]

Military success by itself is insufficient to achieve victory. History contains numerous examples of armies that won all the battles and yet lost the war due to a flawed strategy. In the Vietnam War, for example, the US military defeated the Viet Cong and North Vietnamese Army in every major engagement they fought. The United States nonetheless lost the war because civilian and military leaders never understood the complex nature of the war they were waging. Conversely, the United States achieved its independence from Britain despite the fact that the Continental Army won only a handful of battles.[7]

It is worth emphasizing that the primacy of politics applies not only to states, but also to other strategic actors. As Ayman al-Zawahiri, Al Qaeda's chief theoretician, wrote in his book *Knights Under the Prophet's Banner*:

> If the successful operations against Islam's enemies and the severe damage inflicted on them do not serve the ultimate goal of establishing the Muslim nation in the heart of the Islamic world, they will be nothing more than disturbing acts, regardless of their magnitude, that could be absorbed and endured, even if after some time and with some losses.

Clausewitz would doubtless approve of Zawahiri's understanding of strategy, if not his goals.

Just as it would be wrong to view war as nothing more than slaughter, it would be misleading to believe that force can be used in highly calibrated increments to achieve finely tuned effects. War has its own dynamics that makes it an unwieldy instrument, more a bludgeon than a rapier. Interaction with the adversary makes it difficult to achieve even the simplest objective. As Clausewitz reminds us, "War is not the act of a living force upon a lifeless mass but always the collision of two living forces."[8] In other words, just as we seek to use force to compel our adversary to do our will, so too will he attempt to use force to coerce us. Effectiveness in war thus depends not only on what we do, but also on what an opponent does. This interaction limits significantly the ability to control the use of military force.

About this volume

This reader brings together works on strategic theory by some of the leading contributors to the field. It includes a mixture of hard-to-find classics as well as the latest scholarship. It is meant to be of use to both students and practitioners of strategy. It is also meant to be interdisciplinary, of interest both to historically-minded political scientists as well as theoretically-minded historians.

Our intention in assembling this collection is to guide readers through a wide-ranging survey of the key issues in strategy. In making our choices, we have attempted to strike a balance between theoretical works, which seek to discover robust generalizations about the nature of modern strategy, pertinent historical studies, which attempt to ground the study of strategy in the realities of modern war, and extracts from classic works from writers such as Sun Tzu and T.E. Lawrence. No doubt some readers will be surprised to see one of their favourites omitted and some issues neglected. Inevitably, for reasons of space, the editors could not include all the essays and issues they would have ideally wanted. Nonetheless, we feel that this collection offers students a balanced starting-point for the serious study of strategy.

All the essays, chapters and extracts appear in their original form. The editors agreed right from the start that heavily edited gobbets could never do justice to the originals, and that students would benefit most from reading the selections as their authors intended them to be read rather than in an abridged form.

Contributors to this volume come from a wide variety of backgrounds. They represent a diversity of academic disciplines: from mathematics to history, from economics to anthropology. As a result, students will encounter in this anthology a wide variety of writing styles and methodologies, which reflects the importance of strategy as scholarly discipline and real-world preoccupation.

The reader is divided into six sections. Each section begins with brief synopses of the included works and some background material to provide context, as well as suggestions for further reading. To help students focus while reading, we have also provided a list of study questions. Readers should also note that in addition to our suggestions for further reading, the notes of the works reproduced here are a valuable bibliographic source.

The collection begins with a section discussing the role of strategic theory and history for theorists, policymakers, and professionals. It also discusses the use and abuse of strategic theory and history.

The second section contains a set of essays that interpret, and reinterpret, classical strategic theory. It includes excerpts from some of the classic texts of strategic theory by Sun Tzu, Liddell Hart, and Schelling.

Having discussed strategic theory holistically, the third section contains essays that explore the traditional instruments of war: land, sea, and air power. They are meant to provide the reader with a better understanding of what each of these instruments can—and cannot—accomplish.

The fourth section builds on the previous two by exploring the extent to which the advent of nuclear weapons changed the theory and practice of strategy.

The fifth section explores irregular warfare, including limited wars, small wars, and terrorism.

The final section addresses issues of future warfare and strategy. The works included address the debate about revolutions in military affairs, and offer some insight into how strategists should approach the daunting challenge posted by the future. Are there enduring principles of strategy that future strategists neglect at their peril, or does the changing nature of warfare also transform the fundamentals of strategy?

Notes

1   Carl von Clausewitz, *On War*, edited and translated by Michael Howard and Peter Paret (Princeton, NJ: Princeton University Press, 1989), 141.
2   Bernard Brodie, *War and Politics* (New York: Macmillan, 1973), 452–3.
3   Clausewitz, *On War*, 75.
4   Ibid., 579.
5   David Stevenson, *1914–18: The History of the First World War* (London: Penguin Books, 2005); Karl-Heinz Frieser, *The Blitzkrieg Legend: The 1940 Campaign in the West* (Annapolis, MD: Naval Institute Press, 2005).
6   J.C. Wylie, *Military Strategy: A General Theory of Power Control* (Annapolis, MD: Naval Institute Press, 1989), 77.
7   Andrew F. Krepinevich, Jr., *The Army and Vietnam* (Baltimore: The Johns Hopkins University Press, 1986); Piers Mackesy, *The War for America, 1775–1783* (University of Nebraska Press, 1993).
8   Clausewitz, *On War*, 4.

Part I

The uses of strategic theory

INTRODUCTION

The three essays in this section offer readers an important point of departure for the exploration of strategic studies. All three authors share the view that strategy is much more than the practical application of a few common-sense rules of thumb; that strategy should be studied methodically; and that useful strategic knowledge demands that theorists think rigorously about "the lessons" of past wars.

In the first essay, Bernard Brodie (1909–1978), one of the most original strategic theorists of the nuclear age, argues that strategy should be studied "scientifically." For Brodie, contemporary (1949) strategic thought rarely amounted to more than the application of the allegedly "enduring" principles of war. Drawing on examples from World War II, Brodie shows how this sort of substitution of slogans for thought led strategists to squander resources and opportunities. To become a useful guide for action, Brodie argued, strategy must become a social science similar to economics. Strategy and economics both begin with common-sense propositions about human interactions. What makes economics different, however, is that economists have developed their propositions into well-defined concepts and generalizations that can be applied and tested systematically. A similar "theoretical framework" for strategy would provide a basis for weighing competing strategic choices. It would also provide a common language of well-thought-out concepts to ensure that strategic debates take place on a "rational and meaningful plane." Brodie does not suggest that this methodology will mechanically produce the right answers; instead, approaching "strategy as a science" will compel strategists to *ask the right questions*.

Brodie's call for a science of strategy set the agenda for much of the early thought on nuclear strategy, with its preoccupation with game theory and systems analysis. As Brodie later saw, the scientific approach had its limits, not the least of which was the neglect of the social and political context of the Cold War. Among those calling for a return to the classical approach to strategy, with its sensitivity to the social forces and human passions that drive war and politics, was the eminent British military historian Sir Michael Howard (see "Further Reading").

In an essay written in tribute to Howard's work, Sir Lawrence Freedman of King's College London shows how the classical approach too can accommodate a sophisticated understanding of key concepts within a theoretical framework. Drawing on insights from political science and sociology, he examines the concept of "power." Although power is often measured in terms of assets (men, money, hardware, etc.), power should be understood as a relationship between opposing wills. As Freedman defines it, "power is the *capacity to produce effects that are more advantageous than would otherwise have been the case*." To illustrate, Freedman turns to deterrence theory: A deters (or exercises power over) B, when B modifies its behavior in response to A's threats. As anyone familiar with international relations knows, however, deterrence relationships are in practice never straightforward. B may not *perceive* the threat or *respond* in the way intended by A. The complexities of politics and psychology conspire to frustrate the exercise of power, especially when it requires the continual application of force. Put simply, B will always seek ways to subvert A's control. Although for these reasons any exercise of power is inherently unstable, power at its most stable is achieved when B *accepts* A's will in the form of authority. What Freedman's analysis suggests is that an understanding of power relevant to strategic studies must encompass more than "control" through "force." Strategy, he writes, is "the art of creating power to obtain the maximum political objective using available military means."

While the first two essays reproduced here offer different insights into the methodology of strategic studies, the last one examines the way in which strategic thinkers have used and abused history. William C. Fuller, Jnr., of the US Naval War College disputes the accepted wisdom that armed forces routinely ignore the "lessons" of prior wars. Even the most cursory survey shows that nations and their armed forces have constantly striven to learn from past experience. The real problem, as Fuller sees it, is not a lack of interest in historical lessons, but instead the problem of knowing what "the lessons" are and how to embrace them. He sets out the typical styles of extracting military lessons and the pitfalls associated with them, specifically the fallacies of the "linear projection" and the "significant exception." Strategists fall for the first of these by rigidly predicting future military outcomes from those of the immediate past; strategists fall for the second when they explain away prior military experiences that do not conform to the existing model of war as "significant exceptions." These two fallacies occur because military organizations prefer steady incremental change to radical transformation, and because they often prefer to prepare for the wars they want to fight instead of the ones that they may actually be more likely to fight. What Fuller's analysis shows is that the whole concept of a "military lesson" is dubious and potentially dangerous. Although military organisations can learn much from wars of the past, useful "military lessons" are short-lived because of the interactive nature of war. After all, future adversaries may find a way to creatively exploit a strategy based on prior experience, or may simply learn precisely the same lesson, and so produce a frustrating strategic stalemate.

Study questions

1. Why does Brodie call for a science of strategy?
2. What is "power"? And how does the definition offered by Freedman shape your understanding of strategy?
3. Is strategy an "art" or a "social science"?
4. Are historical "lessons" a reliable guide for future strategy?

Further reading

Brodie, Bernard, *Strategy in the Missile Age* (Princeton, NJ: Princeton University Press, 1959).
Fearon, James, "Rationalist Explanations for War," *International Organization* (Summer 1995), pp. 317–414.

Fischer, David Hackett, *Historians' Fallacies* (London: Routledge, 1971).

Gat, Azar, *A History of Military Thought: From the Enlightenment to the Cold War* (Oxford: Oxford University Press).

Gooch, John, "Clio and Mars: The Use and Abuse of History," *The Journal of Strategic Studies* 3, 3, (1980) pp. 21–36.

Howard, Michael, *The Causes of War* (Ashgate: London, 1983).

Lanir, Zvi, "The 'Principles of War' and Military Thinking," *The Journal of Strategic Studies* 16, 1, (1992) pp. 1–17.

McIvor, Anthony D., ed., *Rethinking the Principles of War* (Annapolis, MD: US Naval Institute Press, 2005).

1   Strategy as a science

Bernard Brodie

The recent resignations from posts of high civil authority or ceremonial rank of former military officers will no doubt allay somewhat the suspicions current a year or more ago that the military were "moving in" where they did not belong. Although the original appointment to civil posts of such men as Generals George C. Marshall and Walter B. Smith was hardly due to design on the part of the armed services, being quite easily and plausibly explained on other and quite innocuous grounds, the military departments unquestionably do have a greater influence upon high policy decisions than was true before the recent war. It is therefore time to express concern not so much that that military will move in where they do not belong, but rather that in the process of moving in where in part, at least, they do belong, their advice will reflect their imperfections not as diplomatists but as soldiers.

That concern, besides receiving its immortal expression in the famous apothegm of Clemenceau that war was too important to be left to the generals, has often been expressed by soldiers themselves.[1] It is not simply that the waging of war or the preparation for it requires many skills to which the soldier makes no pretentions. It is that the skill which is peculiarly his own is in all but the rarest instances incomplete with respect to one of its fundamentals—a genuine understanding of military strategy.

That is hardly surprising, since the understanding would have to follow the development of a theoretical framework which as yet can scarcely be said to exist. Creating the mere foundations of such a framework would require a huge enterprise of scholarship, and the military profession is not a scholarly calling—as its members would be the first to insist. Nor, for various reasons, including good ones, does it wish to become so. The scholar who on rare occasions appears within its ranks can expect but scant reward for the special talents he demonstrates. It is for quite different accomplishments that the silver stars which are the final accolade of success are bestowed.

The soldier's rejection of the contemplative life would be of no concern to him or to us if the universally enduring maxims of war—the so-called "classical principles of strategy"— which are quite simply elucidated and easily understood, really did provide an adequate foundation upon which to erect precise strategic plans. The soldier has been trained to believe that they do. I shall try to demonstrate that on the contrary the theory contained in those maxims is far too insubstantial to enable one even to begin organizing the pressing problems in the field, that the bare core of theory which they do embody is capable of and demands meaningful elaboration, and that that elaboration and the mastery of it by military practitioners must require intensive, rigorous, and therefore prolonged intellectual application. If I succeed in doing that, there will be no difficulty in demonstrating that strategy is not receiving the scientific treatment it deserves either in the armed services or, certainly, outside of them. And it will also be quite easy to show that our failure to train our military leaders in the scientific study of strategy has been costly in war, and is therefore presumptively—perhaps even demonstrably—being costly also in our present security efforts.

There are, to be sure, certain basic ideas about fighting a war which over the centuries have been proved valid. These ideas have been exalted by various writers to the status of "principles," and have been distinguished from other elements in the art of generalship chiefly by their presumptive character of being unchanging. "Methods change, but principles are unchanging" is the often-quoted dictum of Jomini. These principles, while not often apparent to the uninitiated, are certainly not esoteric. They have the characteristic of being obvious at least when pointed out, and many generals, from Napoleon to Eisenhower, have stressed their essential simplicity.

However, it is also true that as generally presented, these "principles" are skeletal in the extreme. They not only contain within themselves no hints on how they may be implemented in practice, but their very expression is usually in terms which are either ambiguous or question-begging in their implications—a trait which has grown more marked since Jomini's day under the effort to preserve for them the characteristic of being unchanging. For example, in a recent list of ten "Principles of War" adopted by the Canadian Chiefs of Staff Committee for the use and guidance of the Canadian Armed Forces, we find "Economy of Effort" (traditionally called "Economy of Force") listed as No. 7, with the following explanation:

7. Economy of effort

Economy of effort implies a *balanced* employment of forces, and a *judicious* expenditure of all resources with the object of achieving an *effective* concentration at the *decisive* time and place.[2]

The four words I have italicized are obviously the points at issue. To give them genuine meaning in a way that would convert them to tools useful in the planning process would clearly require in each case a large amount of analytical elaboration. One must note, of course, that even as stated the principle is not without meaning. It argues that military resources should not be wasted either through failing to use them at all or through dispersing them among ill-chosen or ill-coordinated objectives.[3] Although the idea is thus reduced to a truism, the fact remains that its violation has often been advocated during war and sometimes practiced, and is also clear historically that in the main (though with conspicuous exceptions) the military leader has been somewhat less prone to reject or ignore the principle than the civilian leader who sometimes urges strategic views upon him. The soldier's indoctrination is thus not without value, since it tends to fix in the front of his mind a rule which might otherwise slip out of that place, but it amounts to little more than a pointed injunction to use common sense.

There have been a number of books—extraordinarily few in any one generation—which have attempted to add flesh to the bare bones of the orthodox principles by presenting historical examples both of their conspicuous violation and of their ideal observance.[4] These have been exceedingly useful contributions, and it would be a good thing if more professional soldiers read them. In a day when the techniques of war changed but little from one generation to the next, they were more than adequate. Napoleon, who often mentioned the simplicity of the principles by which he was guided, nevertheless admonished those who would emulate him: "Read over and over again the campaigns of Alexander, Hannibal, Caesar, Gustavus, Turenne, Eugene, and Frederick. Make them your models. This is the only way to become a great general and to master the secrets of war." It is still a good rule. It tempts one to indulge the fantasy that if Admiral Halsey had read over and over again the campaigns of Nelson and his colleagues in the wars of 1793–1815 (quite accessible in Mahan and elsewhere), he might have been a good deal more skeptical of the "Don't divide the fleet" doctrine that betrayed him at Leyte Gulf.

In the present day, with the techniques of war changing radically not only from generation to generation but from decade to decade, a list of theorems inherited almost intact from the early nineteenth century, however much embroidered by examples even from recent military history, can hardly serve the function generally reposed upon it. The modern officer accountable for strategic planning and decisions has a burden of which his counterpart of a century or more ago was quite free. Nelson could spend his lifetime learning and perfecting the art of the admiral without any need to fear that the fundamental postulates of that art would change under his feet. His flagship at Trafalgar was then forty years old, but in no wise inferior in fighting potentialities to the majority of the ships engaged. The modern admiral or general has no such assurance. Changes, even marginal ones, in the inherent potentialities or limitations of the machines with which war is waged may affect not merely the handling of those machines but a whole strategic concept. Principles may still survive those changes intact, but if they do it will be because they have little applicability or meaning for the questions that really matter. The rules fathered by Jomini and Clausewitz may still be fundamental, but they will not tell one how to prepare for or fight a war.

That the "enduring principles" have endured so long as a substitution for a body of live and flexible theory is due mainly to their exceptional convenience. Because they lend themselves so readily to "indoctrination," they are peculiarly well adapted to the traditional patterns of military education. They can be quickly learned as part of a brief course in a war college. And since the graduates of that college may then be presumed to have a common denominator of strategic knowledge, that knowledge can be disregarded in considering candidates for promotion to top rank. Moreover, the common denominator permits the assumption that in the crisis of battle the subordinate commander will readily understand and perhaps on occasion anticipate the intentions of his supreme commander. That it is desirable to achieve such rapport is beyond doubt; the only question is the price paid for it.

Closely related to the "principle" in inherent character, and often derived from it, is the aphorism or slogan which provides the premises for policy decisions. The military profession is by no means alone in its frequent recourse to the slogan as a substitute for analysis—certain scholarly disciplines, not excluding political science, have been more than a little untidy in this regard—but among the military we find some extreme examples of its ultimate development. The slogan may originate in fact or in fancy, it may have but a brief vogue or it may endure apparently forever, it may enthrall a particular service or the entire profession of arms, but in any case it provides in the area and in the moment of its ascendancy the key to the basic decisions. "The ram is the most formidable of all the weapons of the ship" was a dictum never genuinely substantiated in battle and basically untrue, but it dominated naval architecture for almost half a century.[5] "He will win who has the resolution to advance" was the maxim of du Picq which inspired the pre-World War I French school of the *offensive à outrance*. It might have better survived the battles of 1914 had not those battles inspired a slogan even more terse and homely: "Fire kills." Those latter two words, trenchant enough but scarcely incisive, had more to do with determining Allied strategy in World War I than any number of volumes could possibly have had.

The maxim may indeed be the supreme distillate of profound thought, but only at its first use—that is, when it is still an apt expression and not yet a slogan. No sooner does it become currency than it is counterfeit. The function of a slogan is to induce rigidity of thought and behavior in a particular direction, which in art may mean the development of a school having its own distinctive value. If the conduct of war is an art rather than a science, as is often alleged, at least it is not art for art's sake. The progress of strategy as a science will be roughly measurable by the degree to which it frees itself from addiction to the slogan.

Of late the armed services have, to be sure, devoted some care to analyzing the "lessons" of their campaigns. General Eisenhower, for example, shortly after V-E Day set up a commission under General L.T. Gerow to study the lessons of the European theatre in World War II. Despite the pre-occupation of such studies with tactics and especially administration, their value for stimulating strategic insights is potentially great. But unless the analysts are properly equipped intellectually to exploit such values, the net result of the studies is likely to be that of intensifying the military propensity to "prepare for the last war." With their traditional reverence for what they term the "practical," the military are inclined to dignify by the name of "battle experience" what is in fact an excessively narrow pragmatism. There is of course no substitute for the test of battle or experience in war, but there are at least three reasons why such experience is of limited usefulness and may even be positively misleading.

First, since great changes occur from one war to the next, military planners are obliged to make far-reaching decisions on issues concerning which there is little or no directly applicable experience. We certainly have no experience today with the mass use of atomic bombs. There is a good deal of experience which is in some manner relevant, but it must be sought out and applied with subtlety and discrimination and with constant concern for the qualifications enjoined by the elements of dissimilarity.[6] The incredible and sometimes disastrous lag of tactical and strategic conceptions behind developments in materiel, which Mahan regretfully regarded as inevitable in view of the ancient "conservatism" of the military profession, is due less to conservatism than to the absence of the habit of scientific thinking.

Secondly, the larger decisions of any war, or of the preparation for that war, cast the mold for the experience which ensues, so that the results often fail to provide a basis for judgment upon those decisions. The experience may be fortunate or unfortunate; but since the enemy's responses have a good deal to do with its being one or the other, and since his capacity for error may be no less than one's own, one cannot rely upon success or failure to provide the whole answer. Was a decision which turned out well rather than ill a good decision? From the pragmatic point of view, clearly yes! But the analyst who wishes to derive general lessons applicable to the future, who is anxious to find the solution which will minimize the appalling human costs of war, may not be so easily persuaded. He will be obliged to go beyond history—*i.e.*, beyond experience—to explore the feebly lit realm of "what might have been."

Thirdly, even within the scope of what our experience does illuminate, the lessons it affords are rarely obvious in the sense of being self-evident. Too many "analyses" of World War II experience remind one of the seven blind men who touched different parts of the elephant. The evidence which relates to a question is generally massive and many sided. Its examination requires not only thoroughness but also imagination. The examiner must be on the alert for rigidities of thought and action in the actors which vitiated the results of even repeated experiment.[7] He must look for the hidden jokers in a situation, the vagaries of circumstance which profoundly affected the outcome, and must clearly distinguish between the unique and the representative. In short, he must engage in a refined analytical operation involving a large element of disciplined speculation. The task requires a mind trained for analysis and for the rigorous scrutiny of evidence.

The strategist of the American armed forces has often in the past stressed the difficulty of his problems as compared with his opposite number of European military establishments. The latter has always been much less in doubt concerning the identity of the probable adversary and the probable theaters of operations. Although the Soviet Union has very conveniently narrowed the problem for us, the sets of circumstances which might govern a conflict with that country still cover an extraordinarily broad range. It is all the more necessary, therefore, that we develop a conceptual framework adequate not only as a base of departure for specific strategic plans but also as a means of weighing one plan against another. The planning operation goes on apace. There are divisions of the Military Establishment set up for that purpose which manage to keep themselves earnestly employed. All sorts of new paraphernalia, including electronic computer machines for solving logistics and mobilization problems, are brought into use. All that is lacking is a conceptual basis for determining whether the plan in hand is a good one—whether it is better than some conceivable alternative. It is an old military dogma that any decision is better than none; the same apparently holds true for strategic plans.

That strategic theory is reducible to a few common-sense propositions does not distinguish it from other social sciences, including the science of economics, which has undoubtedly enjoyed the most systematic and intensive development among the social sciences and which, as I shall shortly point out, bears other and more significant parallels to strategy. One of our leading economists, Professor Frank Knight, has characterized his discipline as follows: "Economic thought runs almost entirely in terms of the obvious and the common-place ... The most interesting feature of economic theory is that its larger and more important questions are generally self-answering when explicitly and correctly stated—in so far as they can be answered at all. Indeed, the problem of social action, from the economic standpoint, is chiefly that of getting people ... to act in accord with principles which when stated in simple and set terms are trite even to the man on the street."[8]

Whether or not other economists would entirely agree—and any process of reducing a large body of knowledge to a few simple propositions necessarily involves arbitrariness—the fact remains that one distinguished economist was able to see his field in that light and could presumably have produced the phrases necessary to implement his assertion. That he did not feel especially obligated to do so is itself revealing. Save for the purpose of persuading busy or simple people to a desired course of action, there is no profit in such an enterprise. The profit is all in the opposite direction, in refinement and retesting of one's conceptual tools in order that analysis of a particular problem may be more precise, that is, more correct. At any rate, in the effort to explore the ramifications or specific application of those questions which "are generally self-answering when explicitly and correctly stated," the economics profession has produced a tremendous body of literature of impressive quality. The far older profession of arms, content with mere reiteration of its wholly elementary postulates, which change not with the changing years, has yet to round out a five-foot book-shelf of significant works on strategy. The purpose of soldiers is obviously not to produce books, but one must assume that any real ferment of thought could not have so completely avoided breaking into print.[9]

The comparison drawn above between economics and strategy is especially telling in view of the similarity of objectives between the two fields. Although the economist sometimes disclaims responsibility for those community values which determine economic objectives, it is quite clear that historically he has been devoted mainly to discovering how the resources of a nation, material and human, can be developed and utilized for the end of maximizing the total real wealth of the nation. Even where somewhat different objectives are stressed, such as the maintenance of full employment, the character of his task is affected only marginally, because that task is fundamentally a study in efficiency. It is the study of the efficient allocation of the national (or other community) resources for the economic ends set down by the community, and the lists of ends presented will differ from one community to another and from one generation to the next more in the nominal priorities accorded specific items than in general content or basic structure.

Strategy, by comparison, is devoted to discovering how the resources of the nation, material and human, can be developed and utilized for the end of maximizing the total effectiveness of the nation in war. The end thus stated is of course also subject to various qualifications. During peacetime we are more interested in avoiding war than in winning one when it comes, and our military preparations will be affected thereby not only quantitatively but qualitatively as well. Also, we wish to minimize, both in peace and in war, the burden which our security efforts impose upon our pursuit of other values and objectives. Security is, after all, a derivative value, being meaningful only in so far as it promotes and maintains other values which have been or are being realized and are thought worth securing, though in proportion to the magnitude of the threat it may displace all others in primacy. For that reason there is a vast difference between peace and war in the proportion of the national resources made available for security purposes. But in any case we are dealing primarily with problems of efficiency in the allocation of limited resources and with measuring means against policies and vice versa.

In the narrower military sense, strategy deals only with mobilized resources and is concentrated upon achieving victory over a specific enemy under a specific set of political and geographic circumstances. But strategy must also anticipate the trails of war, and by anticipation to seek where possible to increase one's advantage without unduly jeopardizing the maintenance of peace or the pursuit of other values. This broader enterprise, which might be called "security policy,"[10] can be construed to cover the total preparation for war as well as the waging of it. It would thus deal—though with clearly defined and limited objectives—with political, social, and economic as well as military matters in both domestic and foreign contexts.

Security policy so defined can hardly be the province primarily of the soldier, though he should be able to offer pertinent advice concerning it based on his mastery of the military problem. A large number of other skills are more directly related. In matters concerning industrial mobilization, for example, the function of the military specialist is or should be confined to specifying the items needed and their respective orders of priority. The handling of the business must devolve upon the politician, the industrialist or the factory manager, and the social scientist. Similarly, in problems involving political relations with other states, the soldier's function is confined to pointing out the military advantage or disadvantage which might be expected to follow from a specific course of action. The question of offsetting costs, political and otherwise, and the consequent determination of net profit or loss in a proposed policy is not only a question of civilian responsibility but actually involves skills with which the soldier is normally not equipped, though it is desirable that he appreciate the limitations in freedom of maneuver which beset the politician and the diplomatist. Even in the matter of determining the overall size of the defense budget, the soldier has relatively little to contribute. He should be able to provide us with a rational plan for the allocation of whatever sums are accorded him, but the determination of how large those sums should be must depend upon consideration of a wide range of factors, many of which lie entirely outside his usual realm of discourse.[11] One can go still closer to the heart of the military problem—and point out that the strategy of strategic bombing is very largely a matter of target selection, where the economist (possibly also the psychologist) has at least as much to offer as the military specialist.

In any case, whether we are discussing security policy in the broad sense or more specific-ally military strategy—or even tactics—we are discussing problems involving economy of means, *i.e.*, the most efficient utilization of potential and available resources to the end of enhancing our security. One might expect to find, therefore, that a substantial part of classical economic theory is directly applicable to the analysis of problems in military strat-egy. One might further expect that if the highly developed conceptual framework which lies ready at hand in the field of economics were in fact so applied, or at least examined for the suggestive analogies which it offers, some very positive results would follow.

A good example is to be found in the military concept of the "balanced force," in the name of which all sorts of aggressions against good sense have been perpetrated. The concept has been applied to all levels of military organization, tactical and strategic, and has long been familiar in its distinctively naval form of the "balanced fleet." Almost too obvious to be worth recording, but nevertheless basic and all-too-often forgotten, is the point that "balance" can mean little or nothing except in relation to predictions or expectations con-cerning circumstances of future combat, including those circumstances created by one's own strategic plans. A force which is well "balanced" with respect to one set of circumstances is likely to be wholly unbalanced with respect to another, except in so far as the balance sought represents a compromise between different sets of possible or probable circumstances.[12]

Once this point were firmly grasped, and the effort made to establish orders of probability and of risk[13] for various sets of circumstances—in strategy we are always dealing with multiple-contingency analysis—we would have a context for resolving the issues of balance according to the well-known concept of *marginal utility*. That is, a balanced force could be defined as one in which the marginal utilities, tactically and strategically considered, of the last increments to each of the existing components were approximately equalized. To gauge marginal utilities among those components would be anything but easy, but at least the conceptual basis of balance would be clarified in a way that helped to indicate the scope and the direction of the analysis necessary to provide the answers. In that respect the situation would be immeasurably superior to reliance upon such tradition-charged abstractions as "homogeneous" and "symmetrical," to mention two adjectives frequently found in consort with "balanced force." In short, what we are discussing is the difference between thought and dogma.

It might of course be aesthetically abhorrent to discover gallant admirals and airmen discussing their common problems, or the occasional amiable debates between them, in terms like "marginal utility," "diminishing returns," or "opportunity costs." It happens, incidentally, to be quite abhorrent to this writer to find himself inadvertently pleading for a jargon in any discipline, though in this instance there is no danger of corrupting the pure; the military already have a quite substantial jargon of their own. But the advantage of using symbols which are tied to well-thought-out formulations has at least two advantages besides the obvious one of providing a short-hand for intra-discipline communication: first, it may help to assure that the fundamentals of a problem will not be overlooked, and secondly, it may offer economies in the process of thinking the problem through.

To persuade oneself that the fundamentals *can* be overlooked in a strategic problem dealing with the composition or balancing of forces, one need only study the arguments propounded by both sides in the recent inter-service controversy over the super-aircraft-carrier, the *United States*. Secretary Louis Johnson's decision of April 23, 1949 to abandon construction of the vessel seems to have been based on considerations of dubious relevancy, to say the least. It could scarcely have been otherwise, inasmuch as the issue was quite openly a jurisdictional dispute. The Air Force was exercised over an attempted invasion by another service of what it regarded as its exclusive domain, strategic bombing. Such a consideration is of course a basic irrelevancy, out of which all the others were bound to proceed.

For example, the Air Force argument that aircraft carriers were "vulnerable" and the Navy reply that "not a single large aircraft carrier was lost in the last three years of World War II" had in common the characteristic of conveying little illumination. We all know that any ship afloat can be sunk and any aircraft can be downed. We also know that both types of craft have had great utility in war in the past. The real issue is utility, and since every military unit or weapon is expendable in war, the question of relative vulnerability is significant only because it affects utility. This is another of those truistic assertions which somehow need to be repeated. What we need to know is the circumstances under which aircraft carriers have succeeded in their missions in the past and those under which they have failed, either through their own destruction or otherwise. We also need to know how current trends, technological and otherwise, are affecting those circumstances. And in so far as we are considering a carrier capable of launching large bombers as well as the types of planes traditionally carried by such vessels, we should have to investigate thoroughly the distinctive ways in which the performance of the ship–plane team would compare with or differ from the performance of long-range, land-based bombers. In such a comparison the question of relative cost for the two types of operation would obviously be important,[14] but costs can be compared only where functions are comparable. To the extent that the carrier was discovered to have distinctive functions and performance characteristics—the Navy insists it would need the large carrier even for strictly naval use—the real issue would be the importance of those distinctive functions and characteristics as weighed against their cost. In all this we would obviously be obliged to tie our analysis to a specific enemy and to sets of conditions which have at least the quality of being conceivable.

We can already see the extent of the research and analysis involved, but the marginal utility concept warns us also against static comparisons. The value of the proposed carrier in comparison with its rough equivalent (performance-wise) of long-range, land-based aircraft must vary with the number of such aircraft and of such carriers already in hand or planned for procurement. As numbers were added to either type (*e.g.*, B-36s), the onset of diminishing returns in further additions to that type would involve an increase in the relative value of the favorable qualities distinctive to the other type (carrier-aircraft team). At what point, if ever, that increase would be sufficient to cause us to shift production resources from the former type to the latter would be a question for which our research would seek answers. But to ask such questions is to put the issues of balanced force generally, and of B-36s *versus* large carriers in particular, on a rational and meaningful plane—which is to say an entirely different plane from the one on which such issues have thus far been fought out.

One thing is certain—that the cost of conducting such a research would amount to considerably less than the cost of one B-36, let alone one carrier. Whether the armed services have within their own ranks personnel who are equipped to ask the proper questions and to direct the relevant research is another matter. Of two things this writer is convinced: that they can have persons so equipped if they want to, and that they should want to.

We do, to be sure, find the services under the pressure of events acting as though they intuitively perceived the considerations involved in the principle of marginal utility. That is to be expected, since the principle reflects only a relatively modest refinement of common sense. For example, during 1944 the Navy severely cut back its production of submarines not because those in service in the Pacific had failed but because they had been too successful.

They had sunk so many Japanese ships that they were having difficulties finding new targets. The situation for submarines was described as one of "saturation." But the trouble with intuitive perception *in lieu of* conceptual understanding is that it is likely to be tardy and incomplete. Prior to our entry into World War II, the rough rule of thumb method of thinking implied by the word "saturation" was applied quite disastrously to another problem: how much antiaircraft armament should be installed on our combatant ships? The reasoning was entirely in terms of the minimum number of guns necessary to "cover" with defensive fire each of the ship's quadrants. The governing dogma was that offensive strength should not be sacrificed for greater defensive strength. The result was that our battleships on the day of Pearl Harbor were virtually naked with respect to antiaircraft defenses.[15] And it was not until more than a year after that attack that the principle was finally adopted that the amount of antiaircraft armament to be installed on an existing ship was to be limited only by the amount it was physically capable of carrying and servicing, and in order to raise that level a good deal of top hamper was removed. What was belatedly discovered, in other words, was that long after the four quadrants of the ship were "covered," the marginal utility of another antiaircraft gun remained much higher than the marginal utility of many other items of comparable weight or space consumption (including empty space itself) to be found on the decks of our warships.

There is of course a great hurdle between clear understanding of the principles applicable to a problem and the practical resolution of that problem. The antiaircraft problem just discussed might not have been solved any better on the basis of marginal utility theory— if the valuation applied to each antiaircraft gun had remained inordinately low—than it actually was in the absence of such theory. And we do frequently encounter that intuitive perception which effectively replaces conceptual understanding. But so frequently we do not. Besides, there is a great practical difference between that rule of thumb which is recognized to be the optimum feasible realization of correct theory and that much more common species of rule of thumb which simply replaces the effort of theorizing.

Moreover, one cannot forbear to add that some of the more glaring errors of our recent military history could not have been perpetrated by intelligent men who were equipped with even a modicum of theory. To tarry a moment longer with our "marginal utility" concept but to shift now to an operational example already alluded to above: could Admiral Halsey possibly have followed the "Don't divide the fleet doctrine" to the preposterous length of hurling ninety ships against sixteen at Leyte Gulf (the Japanese sixteen also being greatly inferior individually to their American counterparts) if he had had any inkling at all of marginal utility thinking? He had other and pressing tasks in hand besides the pursuit of the northernmost Japanese force, and surely many of those ninety ships, especially the new battleships, would have had a far greater utility on those other tasks—which were in fact completely ignored—than they could possibly have on that pursuit. We know that Halsey applied the doctrines he had been taught. It was not that he had failed his teachers but that they had failed to teach him much that could genuinely assist him.

But examples could be piled on indefinitely. Nor can one permit the inference that a single concept borrowed from economics could magically resolve the strategic problems which confront us. It does happen to be the conviction of this writer that a substantial part of economic theory could be very profitably adapted to strategic analysis, including analysis of operational plans, and that those responsible for such analysis would do well to acquaint themselves with that theory—but even that is not the essential issue. Whether this or that concept can be applied with profit is something which interests us only in passing. It is in the field of methodology that a science like economics has most to contribute, and the point which it is the whole purpose of this article to bring home is that what is needed in the approach to strategic problems is *genuine analytical method*. Formerly the need for it was not great, but, apart from the rapidly increasing complexity of the problem, the magnitude of disaster which might result from military error today bears no relation to situations of the past.

For evidence of the primitive development of strategic theory, it is not necessary to compose an ideal model of what can be as a contrast to what is. Historically, we have the case of Mahan as Exhibit A. The tremendous impact (furthered, it should be noticed, by the active interest of various highly placed civilians) of Mahan's writings upon the naval branch of the calling can be explained only, as the French strategist Admiral Castex explained it, by the fact that those writings filled "a vacuum." And since Mahan's theories were almost without exception gleaned from studious observation of the practice (and to some extent the writings) of the great naval leaders of a hundred years and more before his time, there is a rather persistent vacuum to account for. Mahan was, as a matter of fact, in some essential respects behind his own times.[16] Certainly he could not be called systematic. But he stood before his colleagues as one who seemed to know the purpose for which warships were built, and he carried all before him. Nor is it altogether irrelevant to point out that Mahan in his maturity felt obliged to regard himself as a misfit in the naval profession, and that the service in which he found himself put itself to few pains to encourage the development of his exceptional and indeed anomalous talents.[17]

Moreover, Mahan has remained, for the United States Navy at least, an isolated phenomenon. The groundwork which he laid for what might have become a science of naval strategy was never systematically developed by the profession. In the thirty-five years since his death—years of overwhelming technological and political change—the service from which he sprang has not produced his successor. Mahan's endowment was a high and rare one, to be sure, but his genius was hardly so resplendent as to paralyze any incipient will to emulate. There can be no doubt that the failure to develop what was so auspiciously begun has had its effects in the realm of strategic and policy decision on naval matters.

Nor is the Navy alone in this regard. Air power is still young, but it is certainly not new. Yet it is not possible to find in any language a treatise which explores in discerning and relatively objective fashion the role of air power in war, the factors governing its potentialities and limitations, its relation to other arms, and the chief considerations affecting its mode of operation. Sea power has at least had its Mahan; the literature of air power is all fragments and polemics. That the fact is reflected in the decision-making process can no doubt be demonstrated. It would indeed be amazing if it were not so reflected.

Having said thus much, I am now obliged to point to available remedies. The term "available" must perhaps be stretched a bit, because we are dealing fundamentally with a conflict in value systems. The profession of arms requires inevitably a subordination of rational to romantic values. Loyalty and devotion to heroism are necessarily the hallmark of the calling. Action, decisiveness, and boldness are idealized, though few professions have succeeded so well in building up bureaucratic inhibitions to their realization. The qualities bred into the senior military officer by his institutional environment thus include real and relatively rare virtues, but they also include an anti-theoretical bias which is in fact anti-intellectual. His talents, often real and pronounced, are undeveloped on the side of dialectics. The emphasis is on the so-called "practical," and on command, which is to say administration. "One learns by doing" is one of his favorite axioms; whatever requires a different approach to the learning process—reflection, for example—is suspect.[18] And in his eagerness to be doing, he does throughout his career a fantastically large amount of work of a sort which contributes nothing to his greater understanding of his art even on the technical level.

His training at one of the various war colleges—which he reaches at about the age of thirty-five to forty—is looked upon as an interlude in the more active phases of his career. The courses there are of survey type and of relatively short duration. The pressure upon the student is intense, but, partly for that reason, there is little encouragement to what one might call rumination, certainly not of a type which might carry over into the subsequent phases of his active duty.

At present the Military Establishment operates three war colleges: the Naval War College at Newport, Rhode Island, the Air War College at Maxwell Field, Alabama, and the National War College at Washington, D.C. The Army has no war college today (the National War College having taken over the plant formerly used for that purpose), but some attention is given to strategic problems at the Command and General Staff School at Fort Leavenworth, Kansas. At none of these institutions is the course which incorporates strategy of longer than eight to ten months duration, and the portion of the course actually devoted to strategy may be relatively small. It must be observed that the National War College provides a type of training which is somewhat different from that of the other two colleges. It devotes more attention to politics and international relations, and the half of the course given over to military studies surveys the problems of all three services rather than of only one.

These facts in themselves suggest an avenue of approach if reform is seriously to be furthered. We need to make of our war colleges genuine graduate schools in method and duration of training. The military staffs should be chosen for the special attainments of their members in the several fields of strategic analysis (a process which must await development of a corps of officers possessing the requisite competences), and at least for the more advanced courses (*i.e.*, the second and third years of a system which does not yet exist), the students should be selected according to standards which give due weight to the intellectual purpose of the institution. It would also be desirable to reach down into younger age levels than are presently to be found at the war colleges. Such reform in itself would really not be enough—some consideration would have to be given the whole basis of promotion, the system of duty assignments, and perhaps also methods of training at the military and naval academies—but it would be an important start.

The military will object that it is not their purpose to train scholars, that there are other besides intellectual qualities necessary in a military leader, and that their needs in strategic planners are after all very limited. They are of course right. The successful military leader must have something besides a good mind and a good education in strategy. But that is only to say that the military calling is more exacting than others. In what other profession does the individual affect or control directly not only the lives of thousands of his fellow citizens but also the destiny of the national community and perhaps also of western civilization as we know it? Analytical acumen need not be emphasized to the exclusion of those other qualities (*i.e.*, "leadership," *et al.*), but it has a long way to go to gain consideration even comparable to the latter.

So far as concerns the limited needs of the Military Establishment for strategic planners, those needs may not be as limited as appears on the surface. If some of those problems were seriously thought through which are now handled by a process often called "mature judgment," there might quickly develop a marked shortage of thinkers. In any case, we probably have here as in other branches of the military art a field for specialists who are selected and trained for the specialty. Thus far we have had specialization in everything else. And regardless of how limited was the actual need in such special skills as strategic analysis, we should have to have a respectably broad base for selecting those called to the task and an adequate means of training them.

Notes

1   One of the more recent instances is contained in the illuminating book *Operation Victory* (New York, Scribner's, 1947), by Major General Sir Francis de Guingand, former Chief of Staff to Marshal Montgomery. This author points out again and again that the World War II experiences of the British Army reflected a lack of training in high strategy on the part of the British armed services, which have in fact devoted at least as much attention to the subject as their American counterparts.
2   Reprinted from an article in the *Canadian Army Journal* for December 1947 by *Military Review*, vol. 28, no. 7 (October, 1948), pp. 88f. The Canadian list of principles, which I am selecting only because it happens to be one of the most recent official pronouncements on the subject, appears to be a somewhat revised version of an article published under the title "Principles of Modern Warfare" in the *Royal Air Force Quarterly* (Great Britain), January, 1948.
3   To the purist it must be acknowledged that this interpretation and indeed the original Canadian statement quoted somewhat scramble at least two of the traditional principles. As usually stated, the principle of "Economy of Force" confines itself to the dictum that all forces available should be effectively utilized. The rest of the statement belongs to the doctrine usually called the "Principle of Concentration." There is also more than a redolence of that fine old thought called the "Principle of the Aim." In that connection it is noteworthy that the Canadian list cited does give place to the latter two principles, as Nos. 6 and 1 respectively, and the authors seem to be unaware that in No. 7 they were largely repeating themselves. All of which may conceivably reflect the barrenness of the concepts.
4   One of the best modern examples is Major-General Sir Frederick Maurice's *Principles of Strategy*, New York, R.R. Smith, 1930. On the naval side we have, besides the works of Mahan, the excellent volume by Julian S. Corbett, *Some Principles of Maritime Strategy*, London, 1911. Corbett, incidentally, was a civilian and a professional historian, and the chief works of Mahan likewise are essentially and predominantly histories with only occasional analytical interjections.
5   See my *Sea Power in the Machine Age*, Princeton, Princeton University Press, 2nd ed., 1943, pp. 85–8, 237. This idea and its origin provide an interesting case study in the deriving of tactical "lessons" from the experience of battle.
6   Professor P.M.S. Blackett has demonstrated that even a person trained as a scientist may conspicuously fail to demonstrate proper discrimination in applying analogous experience to the military problem of the atomic bomb. See his *Fear, War, and the Bomb*, New York, Whittlesey, 1949. The only safeguard against such error, as in any field of scientific endeavor, lies in expanding the number of persons with similar competence. In this instance, Dean Louis Ridenour, among others, was able promptly to expose some of the fallacies in Blackett's analysis. See his review article in *Scientific American*, vol. 180, no. 3 (March, 1949), pp. 16–19 (reprinted in *World Politics*, vol. I, no. 3, under the title of "The Bomb and Blackett"). In the military profession the problem of criticism is greatly compounded by the institution of rank, with its extravagant rigidities not only of obedience but also deference. Through the process of promotion the individual is accorded, by fiat, wisdom as well as authority, the stage of infallibility being attained at approximately the fourth star.
7   The Battle for Leyte Gulf furnishes some interesting illustrations of the rigidities to which I refer, of which I shall here mention only one. Because it had been so in every previous major action in the Pacific War. Admiral Halsey erroneously assumed that in this instance too the enemy's principal force had to be where his carriers were. His conviction that battleships could only play a supporting role caused him to confine his own battleships to such a role. By keeping them with the fleet which he threw against a decoy force he deprived them of any chance of affecting the outcome. If his six modern battleships had been left off the mouth of San Bernardino Strait they would almost certainly have sunk the major force of the Japanese Fleet. An interesting question poses itself: had that happened, what would have been the popular (and professional) attitude today on the value of the battleship type? It might not have been a wiser attitude than the presently prevailing one— Leyte Gulf was after all a special case—but it would surely have been different. Since I am making several references to Leyte Gulf, I might refer the reader to my review article on the subject, "The Battle for Leyte Gulf," *Virginia Quarterly Review*, vol. 23, No. 3 (Summer, 1947), pp. 455–60.

8 Frank H. Knight, *Freedom and Reform*, New York, Harper, 1947, p. 130.

9 I am trying desperately here to restrain the bias of the academician that the effort of writing is an almost indispensable catalyst to the production of original thoughts. On the other hand, too many people have found that it is so to enable us quite to reject the idea.

10 The temptation to use the finer-sounding phrase "grand strategy" must be suppressed in deference to historic usage, though that term has sometimes been used to cover what I mean by "security policy." In traditional usage, "grand strategy" refers to the basic but all-embracing features of a plan of war, as distinct from either the details of a war plan or the strategy of a particular campaign.

11 All will agree that concerning military appropriations the soldier is not well situated to tell us what we can afford. But what is equally important, he lacks any objective criteria for telling us what he needs. Under pressure from Congress, he is accustomed to presenting his "minimum essential requirements" in quite precise terms; but if he were under equal pressure to be honest, he would admit the wholly illusory character of that precision. I am developing this point in another paper to be published shortly.

12 In a penetrating essay written during his imprisonment, Grand Admiral Karl Doenitz has analyzed Germany's failure on the seas in World War II. He argues convincingly that if Germany had concentrated her pre-war naval expenditures mainly or exclusively on the submarine arm—instead of dispersing her naval resources on a "symmetrically balanced" fleet—she would have been able to defeat Great Britain within a few months of the opening of hostilities. The error in judgment stemmed from Hitler's conviction that they would not have to fight the British and that a surface fleet would be useful for dominating the Baltic against the Soviet Union. Through Doenitz does not make the point, what he is in effect arguing is that a balanced fleet for a war against the Soviet Union alone was a wholly unbalanced one for a war against Britain, and that proper balance for the latter task would have entailed almost exclusive reliance on the submarine.

13 Clearly applicable in this connection is an idea which an economist in a high policy-making post in the government has called "the principle of the least harm," and which might be expressed as follows: Other things being equal, that policy should be selected which will do the least damage in case the prediction upon which it is based turns out to be wrong. Or, in other words, different sets of circumstances envisaged as possible for the future must be weighted for policy purposes not alone according to their presumed orders of probability but also according to the degree of risk inherent in the policy which each suggests. One can of course point to numerous instances in the military field where this principle has been more or less consciously followed. The only admonition necessary is that the "order of probability," while it must be qualified by considerations of risk, should not be lost sight of. Otherwise, the "principle of the least harm" will no doubt serve to incur the most harm. For those interested in mathematical systematization of this and related problems, the work of Professors John von Neumann and Oskar Morgenstern on the theory of games would be illuminating. See their *Theory of Games and Economic Behavior*, Princeton, Princeton University Press, 1947. However, for various reasons I do not share their conviction that their theory could be directly and profitably applied to problems of military strategy.

14 And exceedingly difficult to work out. The issue is confused by all sorts of differentials in related fixed and sunk capital, in rates of obsolescence, in multiple-use characteristics, and in operating as distinct from initial costs.

15 The explanation frequently offered by Navy spokesmen during and since the war, that our gross deficiencies in naval antiaircraft armament at the time in question was due chiefly to the unwillingness of Congress to appropriate sufficient funds to the purpose, seems not to withstand the test of the record. I can find little evidence that the Navy as a whole—and particularly the Bureau of Ships—came anywhere near predicting the needs of the war in that category of weapons, or that any concerted effort was made to persuade Congress of the urgency of the problem. Certainly one can find little to indicate that the Navy was eager to sacrifice other, less necessary things accorded it by Congress in order to remedy this glaring deficiency.

16 For example, his dogmatic insistence that the *guerre de course* (commerce raiding) could not be "by itself alone decisive of great issues" clearly contributed to the almost universal failure prior to World War I to anticipate the strategic significance of the submarine as a commerce destroyer. The submarine had become before Mahan's death in all essential respects the instrument it is today, but in any case his assertion was illogical on the face of it. Whether commerce destruction against a nation like Great Britain could be "decisive of great issues" depended entirely on the scale on

which it could be carried out. The submarine and later the airplane made it possible to carry it out on a large scale even under conditions of gross surface inferiority. See my *Sea Power in the Machine Age*, pp. 302–4, 328–32; also my *Guide to Naval Strategy*, Princeton, Princeton University Press, 3rd ed., 1944, pp. 137–40. The point remains interesting today because comparable considerations apply to the current controversy on the decisiveness of strategic bombing, especially with the atomic bomb.

17 See William E. Livezey, *Mahan on Sea Power*, Norman, University of Oklahoma Press, 1947, chap. 1. Mahan's elevation after retirement to Rear-Admiral had, it should be noticed, nothing to do with his services to his country and his profession as a thinker and writer. He was promoted along with every other captain on the retired list who had lived long enough to be a veteran of the Civil War.

18 Shakespeare, in introducing the dramatic contrast to Hamlet, uses the soldier, Fortinbras.

2 Strategic studies and the problem of power

Lawrence Freedman

I

> 'The strategic approach' is . . . one which takes account of the part played by force, or the threat of force in the international system. It is descriptive in so far as it analyses the extent to which political units have the capacity to use, or to threaten the use of armed force to impose their will on other units; whether to compel them to do some things, to deter them from doing others, or if need be to destroy them as independent communities altogether. It is prescriptive in so far as it recommends policies which will enable such units to operate in an international system which is subject to such conditions and constraints.[1]

Michael Howard has throughout his career served as one of the most eloquent and lucid exponents of the strategic approach. He was outlining his own creed when he described classical strategists as

> the thinkers who assume that the element of force exists in international relations, that it can and must be intelligently controlled, but that it cannot be totally eliminated.[2]

In that essay, first published in 1968, he concluded by wondering whether classical strategy as a self-sufficient study still had any claim to exist. The field was then dominated by the inputs of political scientists, physical scientists, systems analysts, and mathematical economists and a grasp of modern military technology appeared, above all, to be of central importance for those seeking to make sense of the great—and largely nuclear—strategic issues of the day. During the next decade, as the costs of allowing a preoccupation with technology to crowd out the traditional themes of strategic thought and as the limitations of the sophisticated methodologies developed in the United States become painfully apparent, Howard's confidence in a classical approach returned, suitably modified to take account of the rate of technological advance.[3]

It is only in recent decades that the study of strategy has become academically respectable. After the Great War, for many the only reason to study war was in order to design an international order in which disputes would be settled without resort to arms. It was only when Quincy Wright produced his monumental *The Study of War*, that the virtue of serious empirical analysis became acknowledged.[4]

Historians sustained the study of the ebb and flow of political life, with diplomatic historians undertaking this responsibility for international affairs. However, even here, until well into this century, the role of military force as a political instrument was studied only in the most general terms. Diplomatic historians were of course interested in the threat of force and its application in particular instances, but they rarely descended into issues of tactics and logistics.

Only those close to the military establishment saw virtue in the study of strategy. They produced campaign histories and tried to search for principles of strategy with which to educate the officer corps. At best, as with Clausewitz, practitioners understood the relationship between war and the character of the societies fighting them: at worst, there was little interest in anything other than tips on the conduct of battle. As Bernard Brodie observed, 'Some modicum of theory there always had to be. But like much other military equipment, it had to be light in weight and easily packaged to be carried into the field.'[5] Thus he noted the tendency to strip such theory as did emerge to its barest essentials and then convert it into maxims, or lists of the principles of war. Strategic theory, complained Brodie, thus became pragmatic and practical, unreflective of the framework in which the strategists were operating.

There was therefore prior to the start of the nuclear age no established framework for the academic study of military strategy. Diplomatic historians were aware of individual strategies; students of international relations understood why strategies were needed; military practitioners busied themselves with the design of strategies; political theorists and international lawyers sought to reorder the world so that strategy would be irrelevant.

The experience of the 1930s and 1940s knocked much of the idealism out of political and intellectual life. A world war followed so quickly by a cold war might have encouraged the study of strategy under any circumstances. The advent of nuclear weapons pushed questions of strategy right to the fore of political life, and once they were there it could not be long before the academic community would follow. Howard and Brodie were part of an emerging community of strategic thinkers who brought a variety of academic disciplines to bear on these great problems.

They, along with others generally drawn from the disciplines of history and politics, initially worried most as to the sense of nuclear strategy, doubting whether nuclear strength could be turned into a decisive military asset when faced with an adversary of some— even if inferior—nuclear strength. But East and West were acting and talking as if nuclear weapons had superseded all other types of weapons, and commitments to allies had been made on exactly this supposition. So the few classical strategists found themselves in a conundrum for which their intellectual traditions had left them unprepared. Into the breach stepped a new breed of strategists, often from schools of economics and engineering rather than politics and history, who sought to demonstrate how a wholly novel situation might be mastered by exploiting novel methodologies.[6]

Their approach derived its significance largely from their concentration on those features of the nuclear age which distinguished it from the exercise of military power in pre-nuclear times. This inevitably led to the neglect of the traditional sources of military power. In addition, because so much of the intellectual attraction of the new methodologies derived from their abstract nature, the scenarios of future conflict explored made only a slight attempt to relate decision-making to any recognizable social and political context.

Almost by definition, should anything remotely resembling these scenarios ever come to pass, the political and social context would be utterly transformed. But many of the new strategists argued that to the extent that social forces and human passions must inevitably be in play their role should be minimized, for there would be a premium on cool, rational decision-making if there was to be any satisfactory result to a nuclear confrontation. Formal rationality not mass emotion must govern decisions. At most, the prospect of mass emotion might be used by the calculating manager to persuade his opponent that the time had come to strike a bargain.

It was almost an attempt to transform the exercise of political power by making it subject to the managerial revolution and so turn states into rational decision-makers, maximizing utilities. This analytical approach illuminated aspects of strategy that had not always been appreciated in the classical approach but it lacked the broad, historically tuned insight of the classicist. Meanwhile the classical strategists lacked a theoretical framework to help integrate the new analyses. It is not surprising that there has been a constant return to Clausewitz.

Michael Howard has been unusual in his attention to the need for a conceptual framework if the study of strategy is to progress. My concern in this essay is to explore the possibility that strategic theory can be taken further by investigating what must be one of its central concepts—power.

The classical approach starts with the state as the central unit of the international system, reflecting sovereignty, a capacity for independent action, and certain value-systems. States need strategy because they are vulnerable: they can be created or destroyed by armed force. Howard has always insisted that a concern with this dark side of the international system could never provide a total approach to international politics, but it was necessary to take care of it in order that the lighter side could glow. He has stressed the adverse consequences of following it too slavishly, for this could provoke conflicts rather than prevent them. The strategic approach must only be used in conjunction with other, more positive, approaches to the conduct of relations among states. However, so long as armed force remains a feature of the system it cannot be ignored.

The fact that military strategy must come to terms with force distinguishes it from those other forms of planning which are often described as strategic but which do not involve 'functional and purposive violence'. In one pithy definition Howard describes military strategy as 'organized coercion'.[7]

The ideal for the strategist might be to achieve a condition of 'pure coercion', when his will becomes irresistible, but the opportunities for this have been diminishing in the modern international system and so a state resorting to force as an instrument of policy must overcome an opposing, and armed, will.[8]

Thus, along with Beaufre, Howard sees strategy as a 'dialectic of two opposing wills'.[9] The stress on 'will' in an analysis of the meaning of strategy is important because it provides a link with classic definitions of power, which Howard by and large follows, as referring to the ability to get one's way against a resistant opponent. In one essay he defines it as the ability of political units 'to organize the relevant elements of the external world to satisfy their needs'. As an attribute of a political unit this is normally described as a capacity. So strategic power becomes 'coercive capacity', which is elaborated elsewhere as 'the capacity to use violence for the protection, enforcement or extension of authority'.[10]

This understanding of power is central to the strategic approach. In this essay I wish to question whether it is adequate to the task. The elaboration of a satisfactory concept of power is a familiar endeavour among political theorists and the lack of an agreed definition has suggested that this is one of those 'essentially contested' concepts that defy definition because it can only be understood through a package of values and assumptions that are in themselves matters of fundamental dispute.[11]

In the first part of this essay I take a brief look at the concept of power in political theory as a means of raising some of the issues relevant to a discussion of how the concept has been and might be used in strategic theory. I then consider why this question has not been addressed as much as it might have been by the strategic studies community. Morgenthau's view of power provides a link between political theory and strategic theory, before a consideration of the insights that might be derived from contemporary strategic theory. In the final part I attempt to elaborate a concept of power relevant to strategic theory. Through this I seek to justify a definition of strategy as the art of creating power to obtain the maximum political objectives using available military means.

II

Although the intensive political science debate on this nature of power has been much more extensive and sophisticated than that in strategic studies it has still reached a dead end. This is not the place to survey the massive literature on power, but it is worth noting some features.

Much of the difficulty stems from the fact that the starting-point for most analyses of power—in political theory as much as strategic studies—is that it is an expression of the subject's will. This is reflected in different ways in three of the classic definitions of power: Thomas Hobbes, 'man's present means to any future apparent good';[12] Max Weber, 'the probability that one actor in a social relationship will ... carry out his own will';[13] and Bertrand Russell—'the production of intended effects'.[14]

One of the key questions is whether power is only realized through conflict. Talcott Parsons, for example, sees power as a generalized capacity to seek group goals, and he stresses the extent to which these goals can be consensual and achieved by an accepted authority.[15] Those who disagree insist that this neglects the inherently coercive and conflictual dimensions of power. They are concerned that insufficient stress is given to the 'power over' questions as opposed to the 'power to'.[16]

There are many problems with the analysis of power in terms of 'power over'. Pluralist theorists, such as Dahl, sought to measure power by looking at the processes of decision-making and tended to discover that no one group had a monopoly of power in terms of being able to get their way. This was vulnerable to the sort of critique developed by the more radical theorists such as Bachrach and Baratz, who pointed to the importance of successful non-decisions, that is the ability to get a set of interests enshrined in the unspoken and unchallenged consensus, as a critical indicator of power.[17] Power can be exercised by the creation of social and political institutions which ensure that only the most innocuous second-order issues ever come forward for decision. If the major questions relating to the distribution of resources and values in a society are successfully kept from political consideration then this is an effective exercise of power. So what is measured may not be very interesting.

Others have argued that power can be measured by looking at the distribution of resources and values, but that is open to the objection that the distribution may not have been intended and so cannot truly be said to be an exercise of power. Looking at the political hierarchy in search for 'power élites' also has its limitations, in that one élite may not always win on all issues, and that those in an apparently subordinate position may not be dissatisfied with the outcomes of the political process. Thus is it really an exercise of power if the effects were not intended? At the very least must one show that its exercise has made a difference?

Those who are most keen to find the sources of power have been those most anxious to seize them. The strategists with the most sensitive theories of power have been Marxist-Leninists because their theorizing has been closely linked with political action (praxis). Marxist theory has taken as its starting-point the existence of a conflict of interest between the ruling and working classes and seen its strategic task as being one of creating a consciousness of class oppression rather than using its own awareness of this to analyse inequality.

The difficulties of doing this have given Marxists a sense of the great variety of means by which people can be kept down. Concepts like hegemony, which are now so useful in understanding international relations, were first applied systematically by activist-theoreticians such as Gramsci[18] who were anxious to discover how it was that ruling groups could ensure passivity and compliance among the masses. The problem of seizing control of the state in conditions when all the odds were stacked in favour of the ruling group stimulated sustained strategic debate.

Marxists were least interested in decision-making in a bourgeois democracy, which they saw as part of the pretence by which ruling groups hid the realities of power from the masses. Rather they were interested in the processes by which mass consciousness became clouded by the ability of the ruling class to influence the way they saw political reality, and, at the other extreme, those historic, revolutionary moments when the masses rise to the challenge and attempt to take power.

From a variety of perspectives other political theorists have considered the relationship of power to authority on the one hand and force on the other. This link between power and authority is an important issue in much political theory, according to whether the two are considered to be exclusive or extensions of each other.[19] There is little doubt that the peaceful exercise of authority is much more satisfactory than the violent exercise of force when it comes to getting one's way. But how is that to be achieved? The trick of the powerful is to rule by encouraging the ruled to internalize the ruler's own values and interests.

III

Can strategists make a contribution to this debate? Strategic studies itself is not rich in theory. It appeals to the practical and the pragmatic. Much of the fascination of strategy is that it is concerned with politics at its most pure and raw—the pursuit of interests even where they conflict with those of others, the problems of anticipating the decisions of competitors or rivals when taking one's own, the attempt to manipulate and shape the environment rather than simply becoming the victim of forces beyond one's control.

As such it has long intrigued students of politics—Machiavelli is considered to be one of the founding fathers of modern strategy.[20] Arguably, it should be acknowledged as one of the central branches of political theory. Yet a preoccupation with strategy has often been considered slightly improper, perhaps because it requires regarding political life too much through the eyes of the practitioner. Academic political theory has been dominated by questions of order and justice. Even the study of power has often been about whether to exercise it can be moral, rather than how the concept can be refined to aid our understanding of the dynamics of political life.[21]

From a moral perspective strategy appears as subversive: it illuminates the means by which the drive for order is thwarted and the unjust can triumph. Meanwhile, more contemporary political analysis has sought to identify patterns and regularities in political systems that tend to deny the importance of the active element in political life.

The debate within political science on the concept of power which raged during the 1960s and 1970s[22] barely caused a ripple in the study of international politics, let alone strategic theory. Graham Allison's discovery of the limitations to rational decision-making in *Essence of Decision* mirrored without reference many of the arguments used by pluralist writers in their battle with the élite theorists.[23]

Yet there was a relevant intellectual tradition which influenced those coming to these questions from the broader study of international politics. Those working within the realist tradition had 'power' as the central concept and in general have defined it along established lines, stressing causation and the production of intended effects, and identifying it in terms of power over resources.[24]

Let us consider Hans Morgenthau's concept of power.[25] There is, with Morgenthau, as is often noted, a tension between his understanding of power as a means to ultimate ends, and power as an end in itself.[26] It must be to be some extent an end in itself. Unless one exercise of power is always different from another according to the ends being sought, the acquisition of power as a general capacity which can serve a variety of ends is a natural activity.

Power is directly related to political processes. Anything that can be achieved by natural means does not require power. Excluded from consideration are non-controversial inter-actions, such as extradition treaties. Morgenthau's concept of politics is thus very narrow— too narrow for most modern tastes. It is even more circumscribed in domestic affairs, where much more activity is shaped by non-political factors. In international affairs, without the social cement, much more is left to politics.

Yet while Morgenthau's understanding of politics is too narrow, his definition of power is intriguing:

> When we speak of power, we mean man's control over the minds and actions of other men . . .
>
> Thus the statement that A has or wants political power over B signifies always that A is able, or wants to be able, to control certain actions of B through influencing B's mind.

Thus the concept of power stresses 'the psychological element of the political relationship'. As such, it works through an expectation of benefits or a fear of disadvantage, or 'respect or love of a man or an office'. It involves orders, threats, and persuasion but also a recognition of authority or prestige, an aspect of international politics Morgenthau considered too often neglected.

This is distinguished from the actual exercise of physical violence. The threat of this violence is an intrinsic element of international politics, but when violence becomes an actuality, it signifies the abdication of political power in favour of military or pseudo-military power. Yet Morgenthau cannot separate the application of force from power because war has a political objective. War is a non-political means to a political end—the accumulation of power. 'The political objective of war itself is not per se the conquest of territory and the annihilation of enemy armies, but a change in the mind of the enemy which make him yield to the will of the victor.' Note here too the identification of realizing one's will as an expression of power.

There are obvious problems with the distinction between physical force and psychological power. The only time when one can truly enforce one's will is when one has achieved physical dominance. This is a problem to which I shall return.

What interests me for the moment is the consequence of the presumption that power is exercised through the mind of the target—it is in the mind of the beholder. This is a useful starting-point for any analysis of power, yet its immediate impact is to undermine two of the common assumptions with which many analyses start, and with which Morgenthau is often associated—that power is an asset to be accumulated and is achieved to the extent that one's will can be realized.

Once it is recognized that power can only be exercised through its impact on the subject's mind then it is accepted that it is relational and dependent upon the mental construction of political reality by the subject.

IV

This problem can be taken further by a consideration of deterrence theory, which, for strategic studies, has been the most thoroughly considered power relationship.[27] A standard definition is employed by George and Smoke: 'Deterrence is simply the persuasion of one's opponent that the costs and/or risks of a given course of action he might take outweigh its benefits.'[28] The definition makes it clear that the idea is to dissuade the opponent from initiating action rather than to *compel* him to do—or undo—something against his will, which distinguishes it from a more general definition of power.[29] However, it is by no means clear that the 'something' in question threatens the deterrer directly. The deterred may decide not to act in a particular way, even though this may have no direct bearing on the interests of the deterrer. The definition acknowledges that the success of deterrence depends on the opponent being persuaded. No matter how sincere the deterrer might be in his conditional threats, if the opponent does not take these threats seriously then deterrence will fail.

If deterrence is in the eye of the beholder then the opponent may simply misapprehend the message that he is being sent and fail to act accordingly. The problem with designing deterrence strategies has therefore been to find ways of ensuring that the opponent receives the threat, relates it to his proposed course of action, and decides as a result not to go ahead as planned. The use in the definition from George and Smoke of the phrase 'costs and/or risks' recognizes that the opponent need not be convinced that the costs will definitely be imposed, only that there is a significant probability of this being so.

This peculiar quality of deterrence, with the opponent being persuaded *not* to do something, makes it very difficult to know whether in practice a deterrence relationship is in being. If the opponent is inactive this may be because he has no inclination to act, or, if he has been persuaded not to act, then this may be for reasons quite unconnected with the deterrer or from the particular character of deterrent threats.

This is often discussed as a problem for the deterrer. Is he wasting his time by making an effort to deter something that cannot be deterred or does not need deterring? How can he make his threats sufficiently credible to penetrate the mind-set of his opponent? Does this credibility depend on really being prepared to carry out the threat or merely conveying a sufficient probability that he just might?

But it is also a problem for the deterred. Is he missing an opportunity because of mythical fears about the possible consequences? The condition of paranoia, which is much discussed in the deterrence literature, is an obvious example of being influenced by fear of another which has little basis in reality. A deterrer can remain innocent of his influence on an opponent's calculations without the opponent losing his grip on reality. It is possible, indeed quite normal, to be persuaded against a particular course of action by the thought of how the target might respond. Prudence might dictate caution without the potential target being aware that he had ever been at risk. A would-be aggressor may thus be effectively deterred by an accurate assessment of the likely form of his potential victim's response without the victim having to do very much.

The phrase 'self-deterrence' is sometimes used to denote an unwillingness to take necessary initiatives as a result of a self-induced fear of the consequences. But all deterrence is self-deterrence in that it ultimately depends on the calculations made by the deterred, whatever the quality of the threats being made by the deterrer. So while much of the discussion of deterrence revolves around the problem of adopting it as a strategy, analytically it is important to recognize that it is as interesting to examine it from the perspective of the deterred as much as the deterrer.

Moreover, deterrence can seem far less problematic when we start from the point of view of the deterred. Once certain courses of action have been precluded through fear of the consequences should they be attempted, this conclusion may be institutionalized. It requires little further deliberation.

I noted earlier the focus of strategic studies on military means rather than political ends. The political ends are normally described in terms of obtaining conformity to the 'will' of the political unit. With unconditional surrender at the end of total war this may be achieved, but with many conflicts where force is employed the outcome is much more messy and confused than this decisive objective would anticipate. Much of the strategic theory developed by such figures as Kahn and Schelling has discussed strategy in terms of an incomplete antagonism, by which elements of common interest can be influential even during the most intensive conflict, and has considered the conduct of the key players during the course of a conflict in terms of bargaining.

A bargain normally means an adjustment to ends. A less than perfect outcome is achieved but it is still the most that can be achieved. How then does this fit in with definitions of strategy which discuss it in terms of the search for appropriate means to achieve given ends—such as the much-used definition developed by Basil Liddell Hart, 'The art of distributing and applying military means to fulfil the ends of policy.'[30]

It is possible to discuss either military means or political ends in isolation from each other. That is what happens in much strategic studies, which turns into the most microscopic examination of means unrelated to any serious discussion of what ends might be served. Equally, many discussions of political ends are on a macroscopic scale and discussed without any consideration of whether they are at all feasible in practice.

A key aspect of strategy is the *interdependence* of decision-making. This does not only refer to the need to take the goals and capabilities of opponents into account. It must take in the need to motivate one's own forces by appealing either to their very personal goals of survival/ comfort/honour or to their broader values, as well as the need to appeal to allies to throw in their lot with you. Equally, with allies, there is co-operation to achieve the overriding goal of the containment or defeat of the enemy, but as with the grand alliance during the Second World War, this can be combined with confrontation over the shape of the post-war settlement or competition for the hearts and minds of the liberated territories. Again, this requires some adjustment of both means and ends. In practice, strategic relations are *all* mixtures of co-operation, confrontation, and competition.

The interdependence of the decision-making means that effective strategy is based on a sound appreciation of the structure of the relationships involved and the opportunities it provides the various actors. It is necessary to anticipate the choices faced by others and the way that your action shapes those choices.

V

Where does this leave us with the analysis of power and strategy? The view that strategy is bound up with the role of force in international life must be qualified, because if force is but one form of power then strategy must address the relationship between this form and others, including authority.

The analysis of power has been dominated by a sense of hierarchy, as a relationship between a super-ordinate and a sub-ordinate. This seems to be accepted in strategic theory yet it is contradicted by the anarchic character of the international system and the lack of a supreme locus of power. If power resources are decentralized then power relationships cannot be simply hierarchical. It is further assumed that the atomized nature of the system produces regular clashes between individual units which, because they are not mediated through a complex social structure, are more likely to be settled through force. While this Hobbesian view of the international system has been properly contradicted,[31] it does provide a contrary tendency to that in domestic politics in modern states with an authoritative government and many effective constraints against the regular use of force to settle conflicts.

It is hard to get away from a view of power as a capacity to produce effects. In my view, if it is insisted that these effects be 'intended and foreseen'[32] then in practice this is too restrictive. My definition of power is the *capacity to produce effects that are more advantageous than would otherwise have been the case.* How might this work as a concept?

A can oblige B to modify his behaviour through a successful application of force. In this case B's range of choice is physically restricted and his perceptions of A's power is reinforced through superior strength. However, it is normally preferable for A to encourage B to modify his behaviour through coercive threats (and also inducements). Best of all for A is if B does his bidding without question because he accepts A's authority. With all exertions of power other than *force majeure*, A's objective is to persuade B to change his preferred pattern of behaviour. In these cases an appreciation of power must start with B's understanding of his relationship with A.

Theorists normally give short shrift to the idea that power is an asset. Although we talk of the powerful, in practice we are talking of power resources. There is nothing automatic in their application: they can be squandered or exploited brilliantly. There is an art to politics. Yet if by looking at great strength we act cautiously with A then A has exerted power. *So power is a capacity that exists to the extent that it is recognized by others.* It is a perceived capacity that cannot be independent of what is perceived.

This does not require a distinction between power and brute force. Force is not something different, merely the most extreme case when recognition of A's power becomes inescapable. Nor does power dissolve into authority at the other extreme. Authority is a form of power. If people do what you want because of awe or respect then that is the best form of power.

The perception of B may bare scant resemblance to the intention of A. The identification of power with the ability to achieve a desired effect, that is with *will*, ignores the problem that many of the effects involved are unintended or partial. It is one thing to demonstrate mastery over nature—quite another to demonstrate mastery over other wilful beings. It is rare in any social system for an actor to be able to disregard pressure of one sort or another, positive and negative, from all others, which would imply a complete monopoly of power. Even when A is in an unassailable position *vis-à-vis* B, B may still have potentials that cause A to modify his behaviour. There is a fundamental difference between the exertion of 'power over' nature or physical objects, and over other individuals or groups who also have a capacity of sorts.

In most social systems, even those marked by a high degree of conflict, individual actors participate in a multiplicity of political relationships. B does not simply need to modify his behaviour because of A but also because of C and D as well. Most decisions are complex and involve a variety of considerations involving other actors. *The more dense and complex the social structure the more difficult the exertion of power because B cannot attend only to the pressures from A.*

The greater the coherence within a political community the more likely it is that power will be exercised through authority. In modern, complex structures this will mean that it has been institutionalized. For reasons that are familiar this is extremely difficult in international society but it has been achieved in some areas—for example Western Europe and North

America. Conflict will develop within a political community to the extent that institutional forms leave one group feeling disadvantaged, and to the extent that it sees itself to be a distinct community on its own. This is the natural state of the international community. But it is moderated by awareness of a shared fate resulting from the costs of conflicts and the benefits of interdependence.

The two-way character of most political relationships and the complex character of most political systems mean that any exercise of power is manifestly unstable. It is, however, possible to go further and argue that *any exercise of power is inherently unstable*.

Let us examine this last point more fully. The ideal type towards which most discussions of power tend is of A wholly controlling B's fate. Suppose that A has captured B. A's most complete exercise of power would be to execute B immediately. But then the power relationship would cease to exist. Let us assume that A wishes only to imprison B. To start with B may be hopelessly cowed. Gradually he may find ways of not doing A's bidding. This may be no more than time-wasting. He may become aware that he is something of a prize for A and that A will eventually wish to exhibit him in a reasonable physical condition. He will also know that A cannot cope with a complete challenge to his authority and so he will begin to seek the limits of A's tolerance.

All this may be quite trivial and petty. In essential terms it may not matter. Despite all the irritations imposed on his captors, B is still taken and displayed. But multiply this relationship and the individual assertions of freedom at the margins can have a cumulative effect. A cannot provide a warden for every prisoner. The fewer he has, the greater the opportunity for conspiracies and acts of defiance. If control is lost completely then there might be a mass break-out.

Absolute control requires a continual application of force. It needs continual renewal. While for hard cases this may be found when necessary, in practice a more relaxed relationship will often be sought. Occupying forces will seek to do bargains with the victim populations— material goods, respect for religious symbols, etc. That is, they seek to reduce the coercive aspects of the relationships and seek to develop durable structures which soften the impact of conflict.

VI

This analysis may be able to help clarify the character of strategic activity.

The focus of strategic thinking must be the ability of a state to sustain itself. Much writing on strategy and international politics distinguishes the problems of the state in its external relations from the requirements of internal order. This is a false dichotomy. A state with problems in internal order is more vulnerable to external pressure—it is a supplicant, requiring powerful friends to put down insurgency and provide economic assistance. It is vulnerable to an unfriendly opponent stirring the pot a little.

Often problems of internal order at most require local police action. The complexity of social interactions in a modern society ensures a coherence that in itself deters secessionists and insurrectionists. However, this is by no means always the case. Many modern states are still at an early stage of development and are not based on any natural social cohesion. They are agglomerations of nationalities or tribes who feel their greatest loyalty to the group rather than society at large.

We can thus distinguish between hard and soft states according to the degree of social cohesion and popular legitimacy which they enjoy. Hard states can be vulnerable externally. But strong national feeling is an important source of political strength.

The same distinction can be applied at the regional level. Western Europe is a strong sub-system, in that it is marked by a complex interdependence and shared values, while Eastern Europe may be weak. The potential for conflict tends to decline with the complexity of the social structure. None the less conflicts persist and strategy only comes into being when there is an antagonism of which all participants are aware. It is interesting to consider unconscious power relationships but they do not involve strategy.

While strategy may start with a visible conflict which will have to be decided by force the ideal resolution may be for A to turn his advantage into authority. The institutionalization of advantage so that it becomes reflected in consensus and procedure is the supreme achievement of strategy. Strategists specialize in situations in which force may be necessary, but a sole preoccupation with force misses the opportunities of authority. Although all power is unstable, that based on authority has a much longer half-life than that based on force.

Because in most cases, the power relationship between A and B is only one of a number in which both actors participate, B may have a variety of options as to how to respond to A's threats. In order to get B to produce the required behaviour A must gain B's attention and shape his construction of reality. This must depend on the coercive means at A's disposal, but to translate these means into effective power is an art rather than a science because of the need both to ensure that B does not use his own means to frustrate this effort and also to influence B's developing assessment of his own situation. This is always the case even in war. In the movement towards the decisive clash, B may be holding out all the time for a better peace settlement than unconditional surrender. Force may for a moment provide complete control but the instability of such control requires that either it is renewed continuously or else transformed, through the strategist's art, into authority.

In this sense *strategy is the art of creating power*. Power is unstable and subject to qualification. It does not always produce the preferred effects, but it produces more advantageous effects than would otherwise have been achieved.

Notes

1 Michael Howard, 'The Strategic Approach to International Relations', repr. in *The Causes of Wars* (London, 1983), 36.
2 Michael Howard, 'The Classical Strategists', repr. in *Studies in War and Peace* (London, 1970), 155.
3 See in particular 'The Relevance of Traditional Strategy' and 'The Forgotten Dimensions of Strategy', in *Foreign Affairs*, Jan. 1973 and Summer 1979 respectively. Both are reprinted in *The Causes of Wars*.
4 Quincy Wright, *The Study of War* (Chicago, 1942). (Abridged version edited by Louise Leonard Wright, Chicago, 1964.)
5 Bernard Brodie, *Strategy in the Missile Age* (Princeton, NJ, 1959) 21.
6 This is discussed in my *The Evolution of Nuclear Strategy* (London, 1981), esp. Section Five.
7 'The Relevance of Traditional Strategy', in *Causes*, 85.
8 Ibid. 86.
9 André Beaufre, *Deterrence and Strategy* (London, 1965), although he disagreed with Beaufre's tendency to extend the use of the term strategy.
10 'Morality and Force in International Politics', in *Studies*, 235; 'Ethics and Power in International Policy', in *Causes*, 61; 'Military Power and International Order', in *Studies*, 209.
11 W.B. Gallie, 'Essentially Contested Concepts', *Proceedings of the Aristotelian Society*, 56 (1955–6), 167–98. For a discussion of power along these lines see William E. Connolly, *The Terms of Political Discourse* (2nd edn.; Princeton, NJ, 1983).
12 Thomas Hobbes, *Leviathan*, parts 1 and II (Indianapolis, 1958), 78.
13 Max Weber, *Economy and Society*, ed. Guenther Roth and Claus Wittich (3 vols., New York, 1968), 53.
14 Bertrand Russell, *Power: A New Social Analysis* (London, 1938), 25.

15 Talcott Parsons, 'On the Concept of Political Power', *Proceedings of the American Philosophical Society*, 107 (1963), 232–62.
16 See Steven Lukes, *Power: A Radical View* (London, 1974).
17 Robert Dahl, *Who Governs? Democracy and Power in an American City* (New Haven, Conn., 1961); Peter Bachrach and Morton Baratz, 'The Two Faces of Power', *American Political Science Review*, 56 (Nov. 1962), 947–52.
18 A. Gramsci, *Selections from the Prison Notebooks* (London, 1971).
19 See John Hoffman, *State, Power and Democracy* (Sussex, 1988), pt. 2.
20 He is the first to be considered in Edward Meade Earle's *Makers of Modern Strategy* (Princeton, NJ, 1962).
21 This is one of the main preoccupations of Connolly, *Terms of Political Discourse*. It is interesting to note how much Howard has been preoccupied with this tension between 'morality and force' and 'ethics and power'. See n. 17.
22 For collections of materials on this debate see Marvin Olsen (ed.), *Power in Societies* (London, 1970) and Steven Lukes (ed.), *Power* (London, 1986).
23 Graham Allison, *Essence of Decision: Explaining the Cuban Missile Crisis* (Boston, Mass., 1971). For a critique along these lines see Lawrence Freedman, 'Logic, Politics and Foreign Policy Processes: A Critique of the Bureaucratic Politics Model', *International Affairs* (July 1976).
24 See for example Stanley Hoffman, 'Notes on the Elusiveness of Modern Power', *International Journal*, 30 (Spring 1975); David Baldwin, 'Power Analysis and World Politics', *World Politics*, 31 (Jan. 1979); Jeffrey Hart, 'Three Approaches to the Measurement of Power in International Relations', *International Organization*, 30 (Spring 1976).
25 I am basing this section largely on the excerpt from Hans Morgenthau, *Politics Among Nations*, repr. as 'Power and Ideology in International Politics', in James Rosenau (ed.), *International Politics and Foreign Policy* (New York, 1961), 170–2.
26 See Kenneth Waltz, *Man, the State and War: A Theoretical Analysis* (New York, 1959), 35.
27 This question is considered in more detail in Lawrence Freedman, 'In praise of general deterrence', *International Studies* (Spring, 1989).
28 Alexander George and Richard Smoke, *Deterrence in American Foreign Policy: Theory and Practice* (New York, 1974), 11.
29 A distinction is developed in the literature between *deterrence* and *compellance*—between 'inducing inaction and making someone perform'. It has been most fully elaborated by Thomas Schelling, *Arms and Influence* (New Haven, Conn., 1966), 175, 69 ff.
30 Basil Liddell Hart, *Strategy: The Indirect Approach* (London, 1967), 335.
31 Charles Beitz, *Political Theory and International Relations* (Princeton, NJ, 1979), 44.
32 Dennis Wrong, *Power: Its Forms, Bases and Uses* (London, 1988), 2.

3   What is a military lesson?

William C. Fuller, Jr.

'Those who do not learn the lessons of the past are condemned to repeat them.' This hackneyed statement, popularly but erroneously ascribed to George Santayana, ought of course to be paired with the comment of the German philosopher Hegel, which (in paraphrase) is that the one thing we learn from history is that nobody ever learns anything from history.[1] What can we or do we usefully learn from the experience of previous wars? This is a very important question, not least because if one contemplates the twentieth century, one notices almost immediately that a whole variety of military establishments compiled a dismal record at predicting the character of the next war – that is, at correctly forecasting the nature of the conflict they were to confront next.

Consider World War 1. Almost no one in Europe, with the exception of the obscure Polish-Jewish financier Ivan Bliokh, understood that World War I would be a protracted war of attrition and stalemate.[2] Nearly everybody else expected that the coming pan-European war would be short and decisive, over in a matter of months, if not weeks.[3] But the predictive skills of the leaders of the major powers did not improve later in the century. In 1940, for example, many Soviet leaders dismissed the idea that Germany could conduct a successful Blitzkrieg against the USSR, despite Hitler's campaigns in Poland and France.[4] Then, too, Japan, in preparing for a war against the United States in 1941 adopted a theory of victory that was utterly bizarre, that bespoke a fatal incomprehension of the US system of government and the temperament of its people.[5] Still later, the United States itself failed to anticipate the Vietnam War and arguably never grasped its essential character, even at its end.[6] Thus the Soviet Union also misunderstood the war on which it embarked in Afghanistan in 1979, with catastrophic results.[7] This list could be expanded almost effortlessly, although it would be both unedifying and depressing to do so.

The question naturally arises: *Why* was this the case? What explains why the military establishments of so many countries have been so badly wrong about the very thing that Clausewitz declared was their most important task? After all, in one of the best-known passages in *On War*, Clausewitz insisted that,

> the first, the supreme, the most far-reaching act of judgment that the statesman and commander have to make is to establish . . . the kind of war on which they are embarking; neither mistaking it for, nor trying to turn it into, something that is alien to its nature. This is the first of all strategic questions and the most comprehensive.[8]

Why, then, do military establishments get it wrong? An answer proposed by some is that the ability of the military to perceive the obvious is clouded over by an almost willful blindness. It has, for example, been maintained that the great European military powers contemptuously ignored the experience of the American Civil War, supposedly because, as Moltke apocryphally said, that war was merely a matter of two ragged militias chasing each other around a continent and consequently had no instructive value for the officers of the professional armies of civilized countries.[9] The 'lessons' of almost every war fought since are said to have been stupidly disregarded by one nation or another. This view – that military establishments have an uncanny capacity for overlooking the obvious – is still very much with us.

Take Colonel (Ret.) John Warden of the US Air Force, an important air power theorist of the past decade. In an influential essay he argues that:

> many vital lessons have flowed from isolated events in the past. The following are examples of lessons that should have been obvious at the time but were subsequently ignored, with great loss of life: the effect of the long bow on French heavy cavalry at Agincourt; the difficulty of attacking the trenches around Richmond; the carnage wrought by the machine-gun in the Russo-Japanese War; the value of the tank as demonstrated at Cambrai; and the effectiveness of aircraft against ships as shown by the sinking of the *Ostfriesland* in tests after World War I.[10]

Now Colonel Warden is, of course, trying to make a case for the importance of the lessons (or his version of the lessons) of the Persian Gulf War, which is the 'isolated event' to which he wants to call our attention. Yet his remarks here are problematic, not in the least because the examples he cites are not 'lessons' at all, but rather empirical observations (and frequently incorrect ones) about the efficacy of various weapons.[11] They are not prescriptive and tell us nothing about what to do (or what not to do), which a lesson *by definition* must. But a still greater objection can be made to Warden's implicit allegation that military establishments routinely ignore the experience of prior wars: it is demonstrably false.

For instance, it is simply not the case that Europeans dismissed the American Civil War; on the contrary, they studied it assiduously. G.F.R. Henderson's *Stonewall Jackson and the American Civil War* was a textbook at the British Staff College at Camberley for many years.[12] In Germany, there were a number of serving officers – among them Scheibert, Mangold, and Freydag-Loringhoven – who specialized in writing about the North American campaigns of 1861–65.[13] Even in Imperial Russia, at the beginning of the 1880s, the Tsar himself decreed a controversial (and extremely unpopular) reform of the entire Russian cavalry arm based upon his appreciation of the operations of 'Jeb' Stuart and Phil Sheridan.[14]

If European military elites did not ignore the American Civil War, they were even more eager to profit from the 'lessons' of their own recent conflicts. Consider the German Wars of Unification. The successes of Prussia and then Germany in 1866 and 1870, respectively, commanded the attention of the entire world. The armies of the other great powers, and even those of the smaller powers, attempted to analyze the factors that had produced German victory; there was an intense, even frenzied interest in studying and if possible copying the most important features of Germany's military system. For instance, the Prussian advantage in numbers *vis-à-vis* France in 1870 was clearly a function of the Prussian practice of conscription, which led to the creation of large reservoirs of trained men. After all, Germany had been able to put 1.1 million troops into the field, while France could initially muster no more than 560,000. One form or another of conscription was adopted after the Franco-Prussian war by defeated France, Italy, Holland, and Tsarist Russia. Even Britain, which recoiled from conscription as alien to its traditions, still wanted to remain militarily competitive; the reforming Secretary of State for War, Edward Cardwell, used fear of Prussia to ram through Parliament a series of laws overhauling the British Army and abolishing finally the purchase of commissions by officers.[15]

Indeed, the reverberations of Prussia's victories were felt in areas of European life not obviously connected to the performance of armies and fleets. Bismarck's cryptic remark that 'the battle of Königgrätz was won by the Prussian schoolmaster' was interpreted to mean that efficiency in modern war depended on the intelligence and initiative of the troops.[16] It was not enough any more to have soldiers who behaved like automata, who did exactly what they were told, and displayed neither independence nor ingenuity. It was also believed that education could develop these traits. If it was unrealistic to expect that every soldier would be a graduate of an elementary school, at a bare minimum the corporals and sergeants – non-commissioned officers in general – would have to be educated men. 'Literate non-commissioned officers are a burning necessity for contemporary armies', wrote one Russian commentator in 1873.[17] As a result of this insight, governments throughout Europe took steps to make schools more numerous and accessible. The notion that popular education was somehow indispensable to national security put down roots, and it did so precisely because of the wars of German unification. What was true of the American Civil War and Bismarck's wars of unification in the mid-nineteenth century is equally true of every major war fought since, for military organizations have scrutinized them all in the hope of ascertaining their lessons.

Far from spurning the lessons of the past, most nations and their military establishments have, by contrast, evidenced an insatiate desire to assimilate them. In the US armed forces, for example, there are 'lessons-learned' databases; the army has a center for the study of lessons learned; and there are 516 volumes in the Naval War College Library that have the word 'lessons' in the title. What is true of the US military is true of other militaries. Moreover, it has been true for an extremely long time. Once Frederick the Great of Prussia happened to overhear some officers denigrate the value of studying past wars and military theory, maintaining instead that personal experience was the only source of military excellence. The king was moved to remark to them that he knew of two mules in the army's commissary corps that had served through 20 campaigns. 'Yet', added Frederick 'they are mules still.'[18]

It is hardly surprising that military organizations evince such profound curiosity about the so-called 'lessons' of the past; knowledge of military history can be construed as an inoculation against error and mistake in war, which at worst can produce defeat and at the very best can exact an extremely high cost in blood. It was Bismarck, after all, who observed that 'fools say they learn from experience. I prefer to profit by others' experience.'[19]

There are two components to the question of military lessons. The first is the problem of knowing what the lessons are. In Bismarck's terms, how are we to comprehend what are the precise elements of other people's experience that we ought to absorb? To extract useable lessons from the past, we have to interpret it, and interpretation can be skewed by prejudice, pre-conceptions, and tacit assumptions. The second problem concerns the action taken in response to this process of learning. The issue is one of receptivity – that is, the degree to which a military organization actually embraces a lesson in practice and alters the way in which it conducts business as a result.

Extracting military lessons

Three styles of interpreting or reading military history are pertinent to determining what the lessons of experience are. We might describe these as the antique (or pre-modern), the positivist, and the pragmatic.[20] The antique or pre-modern style of interpretation was dominant virtually everywhere until the middle of the nineteenth century. It assumes that war is universal and fundamentally unchanging. In this view, what was true of war a thousand years ago is equally true today, for the reason that human nature is not malleable and people everywhere across time and space are very much the same. It is this attitude that lies behind the statement of Thucydides that he wished his book about the Peloponnesian War to endure forever and be a 'possession for all time'. After all, Thucydides believed that an important objective of his work was to expose profound truths about war and about human polities at war that would be of permanent value, since 'exact knowledge of the past' would be 'an aid to the understanding of the future'.[21] It is also this kind of thinking that explains Napoleon's famous comment that 'knowledge of the higher parts of war is acquired only through the study of history of the wars and battles of the Great Captains', by whom he meant Alexander, Hannibal, Caesar, Gustavus Adolphus, Marshal Turenne, and Frederick the Great.[22]

There is obviously something profound and true about this point of view, particularly at the level of strategy. As Michael Handel rightly noted: 'the basic logic of strategy . . . is universal'.[23] Much that is instructive and suggestive about strategy can indeed be gleaned from an analysis of past wars, even wars fought in antiquity – for which reason the Naval War College's strategy course gives Thucydides' work a prominent place. Yet even at the strategic level there is something missing from this style of interpretation, since to understand any war one must grasp its political as well as purely military characteristics. And while the logic of strategy does transcend history and geography, politics are earthbound, the product of specific circumstances, cultures, and institutions. The values, mores, preferences, and expectations of particular societies are often quite different, and these differences play a significant role in shaping the nature of war.

However, when the subject at hand is operations or tactics the pre-modern approach can be even more misleading, since history is by no means a perfect or exact guide to the future. It scarcely needs saying that the character of war has changed over the centuries. One of the more obvious instruments of that change has been technological advance.

By the middle of the nineteenth century, for example, new technologies – the telegraph, the railway, the rifle, and so forth – began to revolutionize the battlefield. It was the beginning of a period of extremely rapid military-technical innovation that continued unabated until the outbreak of World War I. Between 1870 and 1914, the great powers of the world scrambled to adopt the newest and latest technological improvements in weapons. Smokeless powder, magazine rifles, quick-firing (QF) artillery, machine-guns, the dreadnought, and the airplane – all were added to the arsenals of the powers.[24] However, despite all this rapid change, there were soldiers in Europe in whom the pre-modern view of war was so deeply engrained, and whose attachment to military tradition was so strong, that they denied that the new weaponry made any difference to the underlying logic of war.

Baron Jomini, famous theoretician of Napoleonic warfare, insisted that 'improvements in firearms will not introduce any important change in the manner of taking troops into battle'.[25] Colonel G.F.R. Henderson remained convinced until his death that the increased lethality and range of the new weapons had neither reduced the value of the cavalry, nor invalidated the massing of troops in close order for the bayonet charge.[26] And the colorful Russian General M.I. Dragomirov, war hero and influential military savant, was even blunter in his dismissal of the idea that modern technology could substantively change war: 'there is nothing to make a fuss about in all the pretended revelations of the science of war', he wrote. 'Modern tactics remain substantially what they were at the time of Napoleon.

Napoleonic tactics rest on a firm foundation, on principles that can never be affected by changes of armament.'[27]

Yet everyone did not share this extreme opinion. Other military leaders and thinkers, perhaps less conservative, less hidebound, recognized that war had indeed changed.[28] They disagreed, however, about how meaningful the changes had been. This leads us to the next style of interpreting military lessons and of war in general – what we might describe as the positivist approach.

Positivism was an intellectual system worked out by the French philosopher Auguste Comte (1798–1857). It was the contention of Comte that it was possible to construct a thoroughly scientific method for the study of history and society that would eventually result in the discovery of actual laws of human development. One found these laws by deducing the present condition from all probable antecedents. This process of deduction would give rise to generalizations, and generalizations, once tested, would lead to positive laws – hence 'positivism'. Positivism was one of the most ambitious intellectual systems created during the entire nineteenth century, a period notable for its system-building; Comte's theory aspired to encompass the totality of knowledge. It additionally claimed to provide access to the future, for if the 'laws of progress', as Comte called them, explained the condition of society now, they also permitted reliable prediction about society in the years ahead.[29]

Comtean philosophy, with its ostensibly scientific rigor, was attractive and had influence in a variety of fields. Military thought was no exception. One feature that accounted for its appeal was that it recognized, embraced, and explained change, while simultaneously holding that there was an underlying core of unalterable truth. One person who fell under the sway of positivism in the military, who in fact almost exemplifies it, was the French Colonel Ardant du Picq (1828–70).[30] The famous statement with which he began the second part of his book *Combat Studies* (*Études sur le Combat*) testified to the profound impression Comte had made on him: 'the art of war is subjected to numerous modifications by industrial and scientific progress, etc. But one thing does not change, the heart of man.'[31] Killed in the early stages of the Franco-Prussian war, du Picq did not live long enough to produce many published works. Virtually all his completed writings concern tactics, for he believed that effective tactics were the foundation of success in battle, and, by extension, in war. He was particularly interested in moral factors in war – the way in which such emotions as fear and the desire for self-preservation shaped the performance of troops in combat, which interest is epitomized in his famous aphorism that discipline was a matter of getting men to fight despite themselves.[32] Correct tactics, or 'a method of combat, sanely thought out in advance', could be developed not only by studying prior wars in books, but also, in true positivistic fashion, by administering exhaustive questionnaires to the eye-witnesses and survivors of the most recent wars.

Although few were as committed as du Picq to the value of accumulating a comprehensive database of modern combat experience, other later writers also betrayed the influence of positivism in various degrees. In his 1885 *Modern War*, General Victor Derrécagaix approved of tactical innovation, while insisting that 'the principles of the past preserve all of their importance'.[33] Even Ferdinand Foch, the future Marshal and Supreme Allied Commander in World War I, although an eclectic borrower from many military traditions, also owed his own debt to positivism, as was evidenced in his 1903 volume *Des Principes de la Guerre* (*The Principles of War*), which included what he described as a 'mathematical demonstration' that the latest innovations in the technology of rifles and artillery continued to favor the offense, not the defense.[34]

There is much of value in the works written from a positivist standpoint, particularly those of du Picq, whose perceptive insights about morale and military psychology still eminently repay the reading. Nevertheless, positivism comes freighted with its own dangers. Positivists or quasi-positivists are often prone to fall victim to what might be described as the fallacy of the linear projection – that is, the view that what has happened in the immediate past is going to happen again in the immediate future; that by means of a straight-line projection, one can deduce what will come next.[35] As an intellectual system positivism is utopian and presupposes a uniform continuity in history, from the past into the present and, by implication, into the future. Positivists are consequently interested in trends, and the quest for trends can blind them to aberration, accident, and chance, which of course are the engines of discontinuity. Moreover, whether conscious of it or not, those who make linear projections in military affairs are often basing them on unwarranted assumptions about the inevitability of prior military outcomes.

This fallacy is not solely the property of positivists, of course. All sorts of people have been seduced by the simplicity of the linear projection. It is, however, a fallacy against which adherents of the third approach take extreme precautions – perhaps too extreme. This third approach is that of pragmatic skepticism, which holds that general laws of war or eternal principles of war really cannot be said to exist. To the pragmatic skeptic, effectiveness in war is a function of the prevailing environment – of the time, of the place, of the level of technical development of armaments and so forth. To seek inner truths about war, or to speculate about the eternal essence or meaning of war, is therefore a futile waste of time.

Helmuth von Moltke was of this opinion. In an article of 1871, he observed that '[t]he doctrines of strategy hardly go beyond the first proposition of common sense; one can hardly call them a science; their value lies almost entirely in their concrete application'. 'Strategy', he insisted, 'is but a system of expedients.'[36]

Other theorists found pragmatic skepticism equally congenial. General Rudolf von Caemmerer, author of *The Development of Strategical Science during the Nineteenth Century*, shared Moltke's opinions and took great pains in his book to show how not only Napoleonic tactics, but Napoleonic operational principles had been rendered obsolete by technical progress and the industrialization of war. Caemmerer's debunking of Napoleon's methods did not mean that he thought there were no correct tactical or operational solutions to military problems; in his view, correct solutions did exist, but they were entirely situation-specific. It was the task of the gifted general armed with inspiration and willpower to choose judiciously from the options available to him. Were Napoleon to rise from the dead, insisted Caemmerer, he would be the first to repudiate those military techniques and procedures that he had employed with dazzling success against all of the powers of Europe in the early nineteenth century, techniques and procedures that were now completely passé, despite their servile emulation for generations.[37]

A skeptical posture can be quite healthy, for it can serve as a first line of defense against school solutions and the concept of 'war by algebra' against which Clausewitz warned us so eloquently. But, at the same time, skepticism can itself be a source of intellectual weakness, principally by leading people to succumb to what I call the fallacy of the significant exception. By accustoming the mind to look for differences, variations, and freak events, and suggesting that these severely limit the applicability of prior experience, skepticism can inhibit recognition of underlying patterns that can indeed provide food for thought as we contemplate the possible character of the wars to come. These three approaches to the reading of 'military lessons', particularly the last two, have significantly distorted the way in which future war has been conceptualized ever since the middle of the nineteenth century. To illustrate this point, I will take a closer look at the fallacies that stemmed from both positivism and skepticism, and at their implications for receptivity to 'military lessons'.

Fallacies and receptivity: linear projection

Let me begin with the fallacy of linear projection. A major consequence of the German wars of unification in the 1860s and 1870s was the creation of a paradigm for the future of European armed conflict that held sway for the ensuing 45 years.[38] It was assumed that to be victorious in a future war, a power would have to field an enormous army, composed both of regulars and reservists, who would be called to colors from civilian life on the eve of hostilities. The mobilization and concentration of such a force would have to be calculated with mathematical precision in accordance with a rigidly detailed plan for exploiting the national system of railroads. In such an environment, advantages would accrue to the power that struck earliest and with the most mass, which meant that increasing the speed and efficiency of one's own mobilization and one's own offensive became an obsession of European general staffs.

A parallel assumption was that the war would begin with a great battle, or set of great battles, that were likely to decide the entire conflict, just as Sadowa and Sedan were supposed to have done in 1866 and 1870 respectively. This misapprehension – the so-called 'short-war illusion' – led European military planners to conceive of wars that would last for weeks or a few months at most. It also led them to assume that wars would be fought with the munitions and equipment that had already been stockpiled in peacetime. There would be no need to put the economy on a war footing, for the conflict would be over before the stockpiles had been exhausted.

As a result of these premises, in August of 1914 the French, Germans, Austrians, and Russians all attempted to execute extraordinarily complicated plans for rapid offensives that were supposed to result in decision. None of the plans worked. In reality, as we all know, World War I did not feature early, decisive battles, was not short, and resulted in the virtually total militarization of the economies and societies of all the belligerents.

At first glance, the attachment of European elites to the 'short-war illusion' appears mystifying, for there were several conflicts at the turn of the century that one might think should have raised doubts about the Bismarckian paradigm, in general, and about the wisdom of offensives, in particular. The Russo-Japanese war of 1904–05 is a case in point. This conflict, a limited war fought in Korea and Manchuria, saw the use of such modern military technologies as machine-guns, magazine rifles, and QF artillery on a scale heretofore never seen. One thing that has impressed many historians (as well as Colonel Warden) is the degree to which certain episodes in the Russo-Japanese War seemed clearly to foreshadow events that would occur in the great European war that broke out just ten years later.

The Japanese siege of Russia's Pacific naval base at Port Arthur, for example, featured trench warfare, the stringing of miles of barbed (and electrified) wire, the employment of electric searchlights to foil night attacks, and the high-explosive shelling of field fortifications. It saw artillery preparation before attacks that in terms of intensity and duration seemed to presage the monster barrages of World War I. To cite just one instance, prior to an assault on a single Russian strongpoint on the outskirts of Port Arthur, the Japanese fired over a thousand artillery rounds in four hours.[39] Some of the land battles of this war, such as Mukden, involving as they did hundreds of thousands of troops, seemed to be eerie dress rehearsals for the Marne, the Somme, and Passchendaele. The combat in Manchuria also provided abundant evidence of the destructive power of modern ordnance, rifles, and machine-guns, particularly when used against infantry trying to take fortified positions by frontal assault.

Why, then, did not Europe's military planners foresee the deadlock and carnage of the

Western Front? Why did they not allow their knowledge of the Russo-Japanese War, and their knowledge of the devastating power of defensive military technologies, to temper their enthusiasm for the extraordinarily offensive plans they had all prepared? Why did they not allow this experience to inform their thinking?

One answer to these questions is that the dominant paradigm of warfare, derived by linear projection from the era of Bismarck and Moltke, was so strong that the Russo-Japanese War was interpreted as reinforcing, rather than undermining it. In the first place, no one failed to note the prodigality with which human life had been expended during the war. But many foreign military positivists were even more intrigued by the simple fact that the Japanese had after all won battles and indeed the entire war, despite the defensive firepower of modern military technologies. How had they managed to do this? On the tactical level, it seemed that they had done so through relentless offensive operations, high morale among the infantry, and a willingness to accept large numbers of casualties. The Japanese lost tens of thousands of lives in assault after assault on the famous 203 Meter Hill, which dominated Port Arthur, but in the end they took it – and it was this that impressed foreign observers.[40]

Study of the Russo-Japanese War consequently inspired two conclusions. The first was that the offense is always superior to the defense on the strategic level of war. The Russian Army had been on the strategic defensive for most of the war and had been defeated; initiative and surprise had been in the hands of the Japanese. Second, at the tactical level, the war was seen as proof that defensive positions, no matter how strongly fortified or held, can always be taken if the attacking force is motivated and willing to take casualties – even huge numbers of them. Major W.D. Bird of the British Army spoke for many when he condemned the Russians for adhering to 'the fallacy of the advantages inherent in the occupation of defensive positions'.[41] The important French theorist, General François de Négrier, shared this view, and wrote that 'the Russo-Japanese war had demonstrated yet again that by offensive tactics alone can victory be assured'. Négrier went on to argue that the war was an 'object-lesson in the overwhelming influence of moral forces'. Owing to their discipline, patriotism, and courage, the Japanese had seized positions despite the murderous fire the Russians trained on them. Ergo, reasoned Négrier, an army with superior moral force could fight and win, even if it was outnumbered and technologically outclassed.[42]

In other words, the Russo-Japanese War resulted in the adjustment of the Bismarckian paradigm of warfare, not its supersession. The linear projection involved here, of course, ignores the question of contingency entirely. Just because a war turned out one way does not mean that this was the only possible outcome. If, for example, Russia had not agreed to negotiations, but had instead managed to defeat Japan in the summer of 1905, as was by no means impossible, who then would have argued that ceaseless offensive operations were always the key to victory? But why, indeed, was the Bismarckian paradigm so strong? One reason is that the Prussian method had at one time been astonishingly successful and seemed to be a recipe for quick victory. Who would not prefer favorable outcomes that were rapid and cheap to those that were slow and expensive? Moreover, and this is very important, by 1904, military establishments had been operating in accord with the Bismarckian paradigm for over 30 years. Virtually all planning and training had been based on its assumptions.

This brings us to the first point about receptivity to military lessons. Military organizations are not loath to innovate, just as they are not averse to the study of the experience of recent wars. However, absent compelling reasons to the contrary (such as those supplied by catastrophic defeat), military institutions, like all complex organizations, prefer the stately pace of incremental change to the disquieting staccato of violent transformation. This resistance to radical innovation goes a long way towards explaining the popularity and longevity of the dominant paradigm. Of course, as it happened, World War I did not resemble the German Wars of Unification at all. But in exploding the old paradigm, the Great War gave birth to a new one: the view that future wars would be protracted conflicts fought largely from static positions. In other words, they would be repetitions of World War I, or at least key phases of World War I, with the defense superior to the offense, stalemate, and the problem of the break-through unresolved.

In the early 1920s, A. Kearsey, a retired lieutenant-colonel of Britain's Imperial General Staff, published a book on tactics and strategy that opined 'that a purely frontal attack against a well-entrenched position held by resolute troops must always involve prohibitive losses'.[43] He then proceeded to argue that if it could not be averted, the next general European war would be characterized by the employment of great fleets of tanks and immense clouds of poison gas. This prophecy was a direct linear projection into the future of the military experience of the Western Front in 1918. In other words, a second world war would be like the first, except more so.[44]

One practical result of the emergence of the new dominant paradigm was the construction of a series of defensive positions during the inter-war period, of which the most famous was, of course, the Maginot Line. An enormous band of fortifications that shielded the north-eastern borders of France, the Maginot Line was based on the insight that, in the words of Marshal Henri Pétain, 'assuring the inviolability of the national soil is . . . one of the major lessons of the [last] war'.[45] The French were not alone in their faith in fortifications, for almost everybody in Europe was building them: the Czechs constructed the Little Maginot Line; the Finns, the Mannerheim Line. Even countries with aggressive military intentions, such as National Socialist Germany and the Soviet Union, made investments in fortifications: the West Wall and Stalin Line were put up by the Nazis and the Communists, respectively, in the 1930s. The bitter irony is that in the end, of course, the defensive mindset of the World War I paradigm proved to be just as costly, deceptive, and perilous as the Bismarckian paradigm had been in 1914.

The temptation represented by linear projection, by the way, was not confined to theories of land warfare, for it had an impact on thinking about war at sea, as well. Consider Alfred Thayer Mahan and Sir Julian Corbett, two of the greatest of all naval theorists. When Mahan published *The Influence of Sea Power upon History* in 1890, the battle of Lissa in 1866 was the largest recent naval battle. Lissa (which had been decided by ramming) was nonetheless merely an episode in Austria's war with Italy and Prussia in that year, and of little significance to its outcome. Partly for this reason, Mahan insisted that, 'It is doubly necessary . . . to study critically the history and experience of naval warfare in the days of sailing ships, because while these will be found to afford lessons of present application and value, steam navies have as yet made no history . . .'.[46] Given this perspective, Mahan logically placed enormous stress on the lessons afforded by Britain's experience in the Napoleonic Wars. In particular, Horatio Nelson's defeat of the fleets of France and Spain off Trafalgar in 1805 shaped Mahan's views about naval strategy and the role of navies in war generally. To Mahan, it was the duty of navies to prepare to fight and win another Trafalgar against their chief competitors. Mahan, then, talked about the future of naval warfare by doing a linear projection that reached back to the Napoleonic Wars.

By contrast, Corbett, who published his *Principles of Maritime Strategy* in 1911, had a different vantage point. He was, after all, a British subject and thus belonged to a society that controlled the greatest maritime empire on earth, whereas Mahan was a representative of a country that was just beginning to move on to the world stage as a great power. But it must be noted as well that Corbett had a different set of historical examples before him in 1911 than Mahan had had in 1890. By that time, the Spanish–American War, the Boer War, and the Russo-Japanese War had all been fought, and it is to these wars that Corbett refers most often. All of these conflicts had been limited wars, had been fought on what we might describe as imperial peripheries, and had been won by countries that in the end successfully integrated land and sea power in relationships of mutual support. Although he admitted that there could be exceptions, Corbett tended to imagine future warfare as conforming to this pattern.[47] Thus, despite all of their theoretical sophistication, both Mahan and Corbett were by no means immune to the seduction of linear projection themselves.

Fallacies and receptivity: the significant exception

Positivists, of whatever stripe, were thus predisposed to linear projection, which could easily become a dangerous method for learning the lessons of war. Yet pragmatic skepticism could give rise to its own equally harmful fallacy – that of the 'significant exception'. As we have already seen, the Bismarckian paradigm's emphasis on the value of offensive action was not shaken by the Russo-Japanese War, which 'linear projectors' read as reinforcing that value. However, another characteristic of the Russo-Japanese War was that it was not short, but protracted. One might think that this would have raised the gravest doubts about the short-war illusion, but it really did not – especially among those who regarded the conflict in Manchuria as *sui generis*.

One person who perpetrated this fallacy was the great German theorist Friedrich von Bernhardi, a firm adherent of skeptical pragmatism. Bernhardi explicitly warned against using the Russo-Japanese War mechanically to forecast a future European war:

> The next war will not come off distinctly under the same conditions and circumstances as those of recent date. Experience of war can never be applied directly to the future. The creative mind must anticipate experience of the future. Not the lessons that the latest wars apparently or really have taught us must we adopt indiscriminately in the next war, but what appears to us to be the most suitable after close investigation of the likely conditions.[48]

On the face of it, this is a powerful and extremely intelligent statement. But this *aperçu* does not, however, provide us with much guidance. How precisely do we determine what the most 'suitable' lessons of any previous war are? Which lessons are we to accept and which are we to exclude? Obviously, the judgment will be subjective. Employing the familiar argument of pragmatic skepticism that wars were defined by the unique properties of time and place, Bernhardi insisted that key aspects of the Russo-Japanese War were highly unlikely to be replicated in a general European war, since, among other things, the scale and the geography of the theater would be so different.[49]

Thus, if the 'linear projectors' started with the presumption of continuity, Bernhardi began with a presumption of discontinuity; and this, of course, was the significant exception. Whereas in Manchuria the terrain had been rugged and the fronts extremely attenuated, in a general European war the terrain would be flat, and millions of men would be engaged, permitting operations and attacks in depth. He employed the same logic to explain why the European war would be short, rather than protracted, as the Russo-Japanese War had been. Then, too, he criticized the idea that numerical superiority had been a key to many of Japan's victories by observing that bold and decisive generalship could more than compensate for inferiority in numbers. In Bernhardi's view, the coming European war would be a short war of maneuver. Once again, this is exactly what World War I was not.

Why did someone as capable as Bernhardi start with the presumption of discontinuity? Why was he so obsessed with limning the differences between the war of 1904–05 and a general European war? Bernhardi gives the answer away in various places in his book: he needed to imagine a war that he thought that Germany could win.[50] If that war were a war of lengthy fronts and trenches, then it would by definition be a protracted war, a war of attrition. He believed that in such a conflict Germany and its allies would sooner or later *lose*, since they would be outnumbered by the powers arrayed against them – France, Russia, and perhaps Britain as well. To Bernhardi, this idea was impermissible and defeatist; accordingly, he censored his own thinking and rejected the possibility of protracted war a priori and out of hand. In other words, his own personal intellectual desires and needs decided for him what the useful lessons of the Russo-Japanese War would be, and what would be the significant exceptions.

This brings me to my second point about receptivity, which is that military establishments often prepare to fight the wars they would prefer to fight, rather than others that may actually be more likely. Lest anyone think that this failing is not to be met with in recent times, let me jump ahead to the US war in Vietnam. Some scholars maintain that William Westmoreland's relative neglect of counterinsurgency during his tenure at the head of Military Assistance Command Vietnam can be explained by his fear of the costs and risks to the US Army of a massive counterinsurgency campaign. He consequently decided that he did not want to wage one and instead planned for a large-unit war against the regular North Vietnam Army, a war with which the US Army would be more comfortable and for which it was better prepared.[51] This, of course, is not the only possible interpretation of his actions. However, arguably, even if the large-unit war had been a splendid success (which it was not), without a better program of counterinsurgency, US victory in Vietnam was simply not possible, given the constraints imposed on the use of force there and the value of the political object to the United States in general. In other words, what Westmoreland may actually have done was to fight the war he preferred rather than the one he had.

Ex post facto lessons

The search for 'military lessons' thus involves ransacking the past to acquire (putatively) valuable guidance for the future. There is nothing surprising about this enterprise. All military organizations would like to win wars quickly, decisively, and at the lowest possible cost in human lives. These are commendable aims, and no sane person can object to them. If the use of 'military lessons' assists in achieving these aims, so much the better. The problem is that 'military lessons' often do not facilitate such military effectiveness. This is so because the entire concept of the 'military lesson' may be dubious. That is not to say that we cannot learn valuable things by studying the wars of the past and reflecting upon them. There are all manner of things we can learn. We can, in fact, learn about the operation and maintenance of weapons and equipment. We can identify logistical and organizational failings and seek to rectify them. We can observe how certain tactics and approaches to operational problems worked in practice. The 'shelf-life' of such insights, however, may be short, and it may be a mistake to extrapolate from them. We can also use history to hone our ability to think creatively about strategy. But if we try to use a recent war, or even the most recent war, to deduce universal lessons about the nature of modern war, we will most assuredly fail.

The word 'lesson' connotes authority and permanence, for a lesson is freestanding. But war is not freestanding, for its nature is dependent, as Clausewitz shows us, on the interaction of the belligerents. Because the nature of war depends on interaction, it is therefore impermanent, in the same way that centers of gravity cannot exist outside particular political and military contexts. There are many reasons why this is so; let us adduce two.

First, say we presume that what succeeded against one adversary in the past will assuredly work against the next one in the future. But what if that new adversary acts unexpectedly, or merely differently, or figures out how to control the shape of the next conflict so as to maximize his strengths and exploit our weaknesses? A good illustration of this is the German Army during the Weimar period. After the humiliation of the Treaty of Versailles, Germany's military planners eventually reached consensus that insofar as was humanly possible, they had to try to prevent the next war from being fought as World War I had been: were a subsequent war to be another prolonged, attritional struggle, the probability was exceedingly high that Germany would once again suffer defeat. The upshot was the adoption of tactics, weapons, and doctrine that were all supposed to promote the staging of mobile and decisive offensives.[52] When London and Paris declared war on Hitler in 1939, the French were of the view that, despite its offensive doctrine, the German Army knew that it could not assault the Maginot Line defenses without incurring suicidal losses. Indeed, merely to attempt such an attack might provoke a domestic revolution against the Nazi regime. The war would therefore most likely be a long one, and Germany would be ground down by economic attrition, just as it had been in the conflict of 1914–18.[53] Their reading of the 'lessons' of the Great War, then, disadvantaged the French both intellectually and psychologically and helped prepare the way for the military collapse of their country in the spring of 1940.

Second, what happens if prospective belligerents learn exactly the same things from a recent war, or a recent trend, and this double knowledge cancels itself out? For example, by the end of the nineteenth century virtually everyone realized how devastating modern field artillery could be when fired from indirect positions against masses of infantry. As a result, all the major European powers increased the number of field guns and anti-personnel rounds in their arsenals prior to 1914. Indeed, artillery emerged as perhaps the dominant weapon of World War I; probably 60 per cent of all casualties in the war were the consequence of shelling.[54] Ironically, however, field artillery did not produce the rapid breakthroughs and victory that its advocates had expected. It was the abundance of field artillery firing shrapnel that as much as anything else forced armies into the trenches. The interactive collision of belligerents who had all learned the same 'lesson' helped produce the unintended consequence of dead-lock. In fact, the stalemate on the Western Front was the result of an entire series of unforeseen interactions among all the armies fighting there.[55]

At the strategic level of analysis, a 'military lesson' has two components: an interpretation of the nature and outcome of a previous war; and an explicit or implicit *prophecy* about the nature and outcome of the next one. An interpretation without the prophecy would merely be an exercise in historical reasoning and no contribution to military theory at all. In most so-called 'military lessons' the prophecy is as deeply embedded in the interpretation as a clove studded in an onion. In any 'military lesson' it is a discrete historical interpretation that both makes possible and validates the prediction. Yet both of the components of the 'military lesson' are often problematic. The hazards of prophecy are obvious and do not need to be belabored. Who can infallibly foresee everything that a future enemy might do? Still further, can one even confidently divine everything one's own side might do in a hypothetical prospective war? As Michael Handel wrote, frequently 'individuals and nations are unaware of their own limitations and weaknesses, let alone those of their adversaries'.[56] If it is difficult to know oneself, how can one be sure that one knows one's enemy? To prophesy about future war therefore involves lightly brushing aside all of these imponderables and dismissing the principle of interaction.

But the particular style of military-historical interpretation advanced by the 'military lesson' can have its analytic dangers, too, for it is usually anchored in retrospective determinism, of one kind or another. That is, it presupposes that the reasons one believes to have been most important in determining the outcome of a war equally ruled out any other dénouement. In other words, given a belligerent's superiority over his opponent in technology, generalship, doctrine, manpower, or any of a number of other factors either separately or in combination, the victory of the former and the defeat of the latter were inevitable. Whether acknowledged or not, it is the assumption of an inevitable outcome that permits the extraction of a 'lesson' from one war that can be applied to the next. However, the outcomes of previous wars frequently were not inevitable, but contingent. The way a war or a campaign turned out often depended on human choices and human interactions; had the choices or interactions been different, the outcomes might have been also. Therefore, to assume that success can be assured by emulating the performance of the winner and avoiding the mistakes of the loser in a previous conflict may well be to indulge in an impermissible exclusion of alternative possibilities. As we have already seen in the case of the Russo-Japanese War, if Japan had lost the war (and it could have, had the Russians made different decisions), then the 'lessons' of the war would have been different also. But an argument about a 'military lesson' denies the fact of contingency and ignores interaction, not only in the future but even in the past.

To put it another way, whether a lesson from a particular war is true or false can only be determined *ex post facto*, in an unpredictable future. And, in consequence, sometimes you can only learn what the 'true' lesson was when it is too late. It is because of this that the distinguished military historian Michael Howard insisted in an essay published a generation ago that in any war 'usually everybody starts even and everybody starts wrong'.[57] It is also because of this that Anthony Cordesman and Abraham Wagner ended an enormous three-volume work entitled *The Lessons of Modern Warfare* with the pessimistic observation that 'understanding the overall nature of modern conflict' is 'ultimately an impossible process'.[58]

Notes

1   In his *Life of Reason*, Santayana actually wrote: 'Those who cannot remember the past are condemned to fulfil it.' Georg Wilhelm Friedrich Hegel, *The Philosophy of History*, trans. J. Sibree (New York: Dover Publications, 1956), p. 6: 'peoples and governments have never learned anything from history, or acted on principles deduced from it'.

2   Bliokh was, of course, a pacifist who wanted to demonstrate that a future general war would be so murderous, costly, and indecisive that it could not be considered a rational instrument of policy. He wrote different sections of this massive work in Russian, Polish, and German. The first publication was in Russian. I. S. Bliokh, *Budushchaia voina v teknicheskom, ekonomicheskom i politicheskom otnosheniiakh*, 6 vols (St Petersburg: I. Efron, 1898). The complete French translation has been reprinted: Jean de Bloch [Ivan Bliokh], *La guerre future aux points de vue technique, économique et politique*, 6 vols (Paris: Guillaumin, 1898–1900; reprint: New York: Garland, 1973).

3   On the 'short-war illusion' see Archer Jones, *The Art of War in the Western World* (Urbana and Chicago, IL: University of Illinois Press, 1987), p. 423. See also Hew Strachan, *The First World War*, vol. I: *To Arms* (Oxford and New York: Oxford University Press, 2001), pp. 74, 173, 1010–13. Strachan presents a more nuanced interpretation of the 'short-war illusion' than has heretofore appeared in the historical literature. He identifies a number of European statesmen and military leaders who, prior to 1914, evidenced some awareness that a general war might become

protracted. Nonetheless, he also shows that European military establishments had generally planned for a short war.

4 I.A. Korotkov, *Istoriia sovetskoi voennoi mysli* (Moscow: Izdatel'stvo 'Nauka', 1980), pp. 143–4. Gabriel Gorodetsky, *Grand Delusion: Stalin and the German Invasion of Russia* (New Haven, CT: Yale University Press, 1999), p. 127.

5 Nobutaka Ike, ed. and trans., *Japan's Decision for War: Records of the 1941 Policy Conferences* (Stanford, CA: Stanford University Press, 1967), p. 153.

6 Lewis Sorley, *A Better War: The Unexamined Victories and Final Tragedy of America's Last Years in Vietnam* (New York: Harcourt Brace, 1999), pp. 4–5. See also Eric M. Bergerud, *The Dynamics of Defeat: The Vietnam War in Hau Nghia Province* (Boulder, CO: Westview Press, 1991), pp. 89–90.

7 (No name given) 'New Evidence on the Soviet Intervention in Afghanistan', *Cold War International History Project Bulletin*, 8–9 (winter 1996/97), pp. 128–84.

8 Carl von Clausewitz, *On War*, ed. and trans. Michael Howard and Peter Paret (Princeton, NJ: Princeton University Press, 1976), pp. 88–9.

9 Jay Luvaas, *The Military Legacy of the Civil War: The European Inheritance* (Lawrence, KS: University Press of Kansas, 1988), p. 126.

10 Col. John A. Warden III, USAF, 'Employing Air Power in the Twenty-First Century', in Richard H. Schultz, Jr and Robert L. Pfaltzgraff, Jr (eds), *The Future of Air Power in the Aftermath of the Gulf War* (Maxwell Air Force Base, AL: Air University Press, 1992), p. 80.

11 For example, the effects of the long bow became obvious to the French cavalry at the battle of Poitiers in 1356, that is, almost 60 years before Agincourt. The result, as one scholar has put it, was 'great changes in armor design intended in part to make men-at-arms less vulnerable to archery'. Clifford J. Rogers, 'The Efficacy of the English Long Bow: A Reply to Kelly DeVries', *War in History*, vol. 5, no. 2 (April 1998), p. 241. While it is true that at Cambrai in November 1917 the use of tanks allowed the British to make an advance of 6,000 yards, there was no break-through and the performance of the tanks was quite properly regarded as mixed. See Paddy Griffith, *Battle Tactics of the Western Front: The British Army's Art of Attack 1916–1918* (New Haven, CT: Yale University Press, 1994), pp. 164–5. As for the sinking of the *Ostfriesland*, Billy Mitchell's bombers did destroy it, but only by dropping 'bombs from an unrealistically low level to ensure fatal hits': I.B. Holley, Jr, 'Reflections on the Search for Airpower Theory,' in Col. Phillip S. Meilinger (ed.), *The Paths of Heaven: The Evolution of Airpower Theory* (Maxwell Air Force Base, AL: Air University Press, 1997), p. 582.

12 Brian Bond, *The Victorian Army and the Staff College, 1854–1914* (London: Eyre Methuen, 1972), p. 157. Brian Holden Reid, *Studies in British Military Thought* (Lincoln, NB: University of Nebraska Press, 1998), p. 136.

13 Luvaas, *Military Legacy*, pp. 128–42.

14 William C. Fuller, Jr, *Civil–Military Conflict in Imperial Russia, 1881–1914* (Princeton, NJ: Princeton University Press, 1985), p. 20.

15 Arvell T. Erickson, *Edward T. Cardwell, Peelite* (Philadelphia, PA: American Philosophical Society, 1959), pp. 80–5.

16 Quoted in M.V. Annenkov, *Voina 1870 goda. Zametki i vpetchatleniia russkogo ofitsera* (St Petersburg: Tipografiia tovarishchestva 'Obshchestvennaia pol'za', 1871), p. 9.

17 M. Zinov'ev, 'Zametki o Germanskoi armii', *Voennyi sbornik*, June (1873), part 1, p. 278.

18 G.F.R. Henderson, *The Science of War* (London: Longmans, Green, 1905), p. 184. See also Christopher Duffy, *The Military Life of Frederick the Great* (London: Routledge, 1986), p. 300.

19 B.H. Liddell Hart, *Strategy*, 2nd rev. edn (New York: New American Library, 1974), p. 3.

20 Azar Gat has developed the argument that virtually *all* military thought from 1780 to 1914 can be divided into 'Enlightenment' and 'Counter-Enlightenment' strands. By the early nineteenth century, the latter had become 'Romanticism'; by the mid-nineteenth century, the former, 'Positivism'. Although I find Gat's ideas stimulating, I do not think that his typology is ultimately successful. There are simply too many military intellectuals and theorists who have to be dragooned into their assigned categories under protest. Nonetheless, I do believe that there are typically 'positivist' and 'skeptical' approaches to the reading of military lessons. See Azar Gat, *The Origins of Military Thought: From the Enlightenment to Clausewitz* (Oxford: Oxford University Press, 1989), and *Military Thought: The Nineteenth Century* (Oxford: Oxford University Press, 1992).

21 *The Landmark Thucydides*, ed. Robert B. Strassler, trans. Richard Crawley (New York: The Free Press, 1996), p. 16.

22 Jay Luvaas (ed. and trans.), *Napoleon on the Art of War* (New York: Free Press, 1999), p. 24. Ironically enough, the argument has been made that this was not the way Napoleon himself acquired knowledge of the art of war. Jean Colin has maintained that the greatest intellectual influences on Napoleon's thinking about warfare were the works of such eighteenth-century French theorists as Guibert and Bourcet. See Jean Colin, *L'education militaire de Napoléon* (Paris: Chapleot, 1901), pp. 141–2.

23 Michael I. Handel, *Masters of War: Classical Strategic Thought*, 3rd ed (London: Frank Cass, 2001), p. xvii. See also Colin S. Gray, *Modern Strategy* (Oxford: Oxford University Press, 1999), a book-length defense of the proposition that: 'To understand modern strategy is to understand it in all ages' (p. 364).

24 Larry H. Addington, *The Patterns of War since the Eighteenth Century* (London: Croom Helm, 1984), pp. 44–5, 91–3, 106–8.

25 Baron de Jomini, *The Art of War*, trans. Capt. G.H. Mendel and Lieut. W.P. Craighill (1862; reprint, Westport, CT: Greenwood Press, 1992), p. 325.

26 Henderson, *Science of War*, pp. 340–1.

27 Quoted in Henderson, *Science of War*, p. 144.

28 In fairness, I must observe that Henderson died in 1903 and Dragomirov in 1905.

29 See, for example, Auguste Comte 'Fundamental Characteristics of the Positive Method in the Study of Social Phenomena', in Stanislav Andreski (ed.) and Margaret Clarke (trans.), *The Essential Comte* (New York: Barnes & Noble, 1974), pp. 144–50.

30 On du Picq, see Gat, *Military Thought*, pp. 28–39.

31 Ardant du Picq, *Études sur le combat* (Paris: Chapelot, 1914), p. 88.

32 Du Picq, *Études*, p. 94: 'Le but de la discipline est de faire combattre les gens souvent malgré eux.'

33 V. Derrécagaix, *Modern War*, trans. C.W. Foster, part 1 (Washington, DC: J.J. Chapman, 1888), pp. 1–2.

34 Marshal [Ferdinand] Foch, *The Principles of War*, trans. Hilaire Belloc (New York: Chapman & Hall, 1920), p. 32: 'Any improvement of firearms is ultimately bound to add strength to the offensive, to a cleverly conducted attack.' Foch assumes an attack of two battalions against one. If both sides are armed with rifles firing a round a minute, the attackers will discharge 2000 bullets to the defenders' 1000. Yet if each force is equipped with rifles capable of firing ten rounds a minute, the attackers will be capable of shooting 20,000 bullets to the attackers' 10,000 in the same sixty-second period. This argument is, of course, bizarre and completely overlooks such matters as the difficulty of aiming while on the run, the tactical advantages of firing from prone and/or fortified positions, not to mention the insalubrious effect of combat deaths on an attacker's rate of fire. An illustration of Foch's belief in the principle of continuity throughout all modern wars is the following observation, with which he concluded a brief account of the Russo-Japanese War: 'Once again, industrial improvements modified the forms of war and continued the evolution of the art, but without eliciting a revolution in it, without affecting in the slightest the fundamental principles of the conduct of war.' (Maréchal Ferdinand Foch), *Préceptes et Jugements du Maréchal Foch*, ed. A. Grasset (Paris: Berger-Levrault, 1919), pp. 227–8.

35 There are of course exceptions. The distinguished British theorist J.F.C. Fuller, for instance, can be assigned to the positivist camp. Not only did he believe that a 'science of war' was possible, he tried to develop one himself. See J.F.C. Fuller, *The Foundations of the Science of War* (London: Hutchinson, 1926), p. 43, for his debt to Comte. Yet Fuller, who had an original and powerful mind, most emphatically did not envision the next European war as aping the features of the war of 1914–18. See his *Machine Warfare: An Inquiry into the Influence of Mechanics on the Conduct of War* (Washington, DC: The Infantry Journal, 1943), pp. 44–5. See also Holden Reid, *British Military Thought*, pp. 66–7, 73–4, 82.

36 Daniel J. Hughes (ed.), *Moltke on the Art of War: Selected Writings*, trans. Daniel J. Hughes and Harry Bell (Novato, CA: Presidio, 1993), p. 124.

37 Lieut.-General [Rudolf] von Caemmerer, *The Development of Strategical Science During the Nineteenth Century*, trans. Karl von Donat (London: Hugh Rees, 1905), pp. xi–x, 212–13, 219, 276–7.

38 In an extremely interesting recent book, Antulio J. Echevarria II has argued that the application of the term 'paradigm' to changes in military theory is inappropriate. 'Thomas Kuhn's brilliant discussion of paradigm shifts relates better to the transposition of scientific models, where anomalies – the accretion of which indicates that the model is becoming obsolete – are the exception rather than the rule. In an environment characterized by friction, chance, fear, and uncertainty,

however, anomalies are more often the rule than the exception.' *After Clausewitz: German Military Thinkers before the Great War* (Lawrence, KS: University of Kansas Press, 2001), p. 226. However, as this passage makes clear, Echevarria (who incidentally uses the word 'paradigm' himself in other sections of his book) is confusing action with ratiocination. To make war is indeed to plunge into an environment of friction, chance, fear, and uncertainty; to *think* about making war is not.

39 This was the attack on the Waterworks redoubt prior to the second attempt to storm Port Arthur in September 1904.

40 Michael Howard, 'Men against Fire', in Peter Paret (ed.), *Makers of Modern Strategy from Machiavelli to the Nuclear Age* (Princeton, NJ: Princeton University Press, 1986), pp. 517–19. Also see Azar Gat, *Military Thought: The Nineteenth Century*, pp. 138–9.

41 W.D. Bird, *Lectures on the Strategy of the Russo-Japanese War* (London: Hugh Rees, 1909), p. 16.

42 General de Négrier, *Lessons of the Russo-Japanese War*, trans. E. Louis Spiers (London: Hugh Rees, 1906), pp. 54–5, 83.

43 Lt-Col. (Ret.) A. Kearsey, *A Study of the Strategy and Tactics of the Russo-Japanese War* (Aldershot: Gale & Polden, n.d.), p. 5.

44 The case of the USSR is a particularly interesting one, because Russia had suffered through *two* very different wars since 1913: the world war, and the Civil War that followed immediately on its heels. Throughout the 1920s and into the 1930s, Soviet military theorists debated whether the next war would bear a greater resemblance to the former or to the latter. M.V. Frunze, for instance, writing in 1921, clearly indicated his belief that the Russian Civil War would be the best model for thinking about a future conflict. See M.V. Frunze, 'Edinaia voennaia doktrina v Krasnoi Armii', in M.V. Frunze, *Izbrannye proizvedeniia* (Moscow: Voennoe izdatel'stvo, 1984), p. 46. See also V.A. Zolotarev (ed.), *Istoriia voennoi strategii Rossii* (Moscow: Izdatel'stvo 'Kuchkovo pole', 2000), pp. 196–7. In Germany, the new defensive paradigm was eventually rejected, but only after serious debate. General Walther Reinhardt, for example, made forceful arguments on behalf of a doctrine of defensive war. See James S. Corum, *The Roots of Blitzkrieg: Hans von Seeckt and German Military Reform* (Lawrence, KS: University of Kansas Press, 1992), pp. 55–7.

45 Eugenia C. Kiesling, *Arming against Hitler: France and the Limits of Military Planning* (Lawrence, KS: University of Kansas Press, 1996), p. 130.

46 Alfred Thayer Mahan, *The Influence of Sea Power upon History 1660–1783* (New York: Hill & Wang, 1957), p. 2.

47 Julian S. Corbett, *Some Principles of Maritime Strategy* (Annapolis, MD: Naval Institute Press, 1998).

48 Friedrich von Bernhardi, *On War of Today*, vol. II, trans. Karl von Donat (London: H. Rees, 1913), p. 98.

49 Friedrich von Bernhardi, On War of Today, vol. I, trans. Karl von Donat (London: H. Rees, 1912), pp. 77–8, 130; vol. II, pp. 10–11, 30–1.

50 The following passage is typical: 'If at some future time Germany is involved in the slowly threatening war, she need not recoil before the numerical superiority of her enemies. But . . . she can only rely on being successful if she is resolutely determined to break the superiority of her enemies by a victory over one or the other of them before their total strength can come into action, and if she prepares for war to that effect, and acts at the decisive moment . . .'. Bernhardi, *War of Today*, vol. I, pp. 100–1. See also Bernhardi, *War of Today*, vol. II, pp. 442–3.

51 For a sympathetic account that nonetheless makes this point, see Phillip B. Davidson, *Vietnam at War. The History 1946–1975* (New York: Oxford University Press, 1988), pp. 430–1. For a less sympathetic view, see Andrew F. Krepinevich, Jr, *The Army and Vietnam* (Baltimore, MD: Johns Hopkins University Press, 1986), pp. 165–7.

52 Corum, *Roots of Blitzkrieg*, pp. 66–7.

53 Ernest R. May, *Strange Defeat: Hitler's Conquest of France* (New York: Hill & Wang, 2000), pp. 285–8.

54 Griffith, *Battle Tactics of the Western Front*, p. 43.

55 For an elegant and persuasive argument about interaction and stalemate during World War, I, see Echevarria, *After Clausewitz*, pp. 224–5.

56 Handel, *Masters of War*, p. 238.

57 Michael Howard, 'Military Science in an Age of Peace', *RUSI Journal*, vol. 119, no. 1 (1974), p. 6.

58 Anthony H. Cordesman and Abraham R. Wagner, *The Lessons of Modern War*, vol. III: *The Afghan and Falklands Conflicts* (Boulder, CO: Westview Press, 1990), p. 436.

Part II

Interpretation of the classics

INTRODUCTION

The three essays in this section offer readers selections from some of the most significant works of classical strategic thought. They should be considered in relation to Carl von Clausewitz's *On War*, as the most important work of strategy and the starting point for any exploration of strategic theory.

The first selection is from Samuel B. Griffith's classic translation of Sun Tzu's *The Art of War*. The volume, written some 2,500 years ago, represents one of the oldest and most influential works of strategy. In contrast to Clausewitz, who views war as a violent clash of wills, Sun Tzu ("Master Sun") extols victory without bloodshed as the ideal, writing that "to subdue the enemy without fighting is the acme of skill."

Sun Tzu sees war as a search for comparative advantage. He believes that success in war is less a matter of destroying the adversary's army and more one of shattering his will to fight. In his view, the most successful strategies are those that emphasize psychology and deception.

To Sun Tzu, information represents a key to success in war. As he puts it in one of his most famous aphorisms, "Know the enemy and know yourself; in a hundred battles you will never be in peril." Typically, however, such pithy injunctions conceal the many challenges that make it difficult to understand one's self and one's adversary, including imperfect information, ethnocentrism, and mirror imaging.

Whereas Clausewitz writes that destroying the enemy's army is most often the key to victory in war, Sun Tzu recommends that the best alternative is to attack the enemy's strategy. The next best alternative is to attack the opponent's alliances. Destroying the enemy's army ranks third on his list of preferred strategies.

The second selection is from Basil H. Liddell Hart's book, *Strategy*. Liddell Hart (1895–1970), at times a British army officer, journalist, and analyst, echoes Sun Tzu in his argument that, "The perfection of strategy would be . . . to produce a decision without any serious fighting." He believes that the aim of strategy should be psychological dislocation—the act of creating in an adversary's mind the sense that he is trapped and defeat is imminent. This leads to what Liddell Hart termed the strategy of the indirect approach: in his view, in any contest of wills, the line of least expectation is the line of least resistance.

The final selection is from Thomas C. Schelling's *Arms and Influence*. Schelling, a Professor at the University of Maryland who won the 2005 Nobel Prize in Economics, can be credited with developing the theory of strategic coercion. He argues that "the power to hurt" gives an actor coercive leverage. Schelling notes that whereas brute force must be used to succeed, the power to coerce is most successful when threatened. To coerce successfully, one needs to know what an adversary values. One needs the adversary to understand what behaviour of his will cause violence to be inflicted and what will cause it to be withheld. Coercion also requires that the belligerents have at least some common interest. Although Schelling identifies instances of coercion throughout history, he argues that the advent of nuclear weapons has made coercion the only feasible strategy. As he puts it, "Not only *can* nuclear weapons hurt the enemy before the war has been won . . . but it is widely assumed that in a major war that is *all* they can do."

Although Schelling developed his theory of coercion with reference to nuclear weapons, it has been applied more broadly. Coercion was central to the US air campaign over North Vietnam during the Vietnam War, for example, as well as the NATO air campaign over Serbia during the 1999 Kosovo war.

Study questions

1. What are the main contributions of Sun Tzu to strategic theory?
2. What do political and military leaders need to do to ensure that battlefield victory translates into strategic success?
3. To what extent is Liddell Hart's "strategy of the indirect approach" valid today?
4. As Schelling puts it, "Violence is most purposive and most successful when it is threatened and not used." Do you agree or disagree, and why?

Further reading

Clausewitz, Carl von, *On War*, edited and translated by Michael Howard and Peter Paret (Princeton, NJ: Princeton University Press, 1989).

Corbett, Julian S., *Some Principles of Maritime Strategy* (London: Longmans Green and Co., 1911).

Danchev, Alex, "Liddell Hart and the Indirect Approach," *Journal of Military History* 63, no. 2 (1999), pp. 313–337.

Gray, Colin S., *Modern Strategy* (Oxford: Oxford University Press, 1999).

Handel, Michael I., *Masters of War*, third ed. (London: Frank Cass, 2001).

Luttwak, Edward N., *Strategy: The Logic of War and Peace*, revised and enlarged edition (Cambridge, MA: Belknap Press, 2001).

Paret, Peter, editor, *Makers of Modern Strategy: From Machiavelli to the Nuclear Age* (Princeton, NJ: Princeton University Press, 1986).

Wylie, J.C., *Military Strategy: A General Theory of Power Control* (Annapolis, MD: Naval Institute Press, 1989).

4 "The Art of War"

Sun Tzu

Estimates [1]

Sun Tzu said:

1. War is a matter of vital importance to the State; the province of life or death; the road to survival or ruin.[2] It is mandatory that it be thoroughly studied.

> *Li Ch'üan*: 'Weapons are tools of ill omen.' War is a grave matter; one is apprehensive lest men embark upon it without due reflection.

2. Therefore, appraise it in terms of the five fundamental factors and make comparisons of the seven elements later named.[3] So you may assess its essentials.

3. The first of these factors is moral influence; the second, weather; the third, terrain; the fourth, command; and the fifth, doctrine.[4]

> *Chang Yü*: The systematic order above is perfectly clear. When troops are raised to chastise transgressors, the temple council first considers the adequacy of the rulers' benevolence and the confidence of their peoples; next, the appropriateness of nature's seasons, and finally the difficulties of the topography. After thorough deliberation of these three matters a general is appointed to launch the attack.[5] After troops have crossed the borders, responsibility for laws and orders devolves upon the general.

4. By moral influence I mean that which causes the people to be in harmony with their leaders, so that they will accompany them in life and unto death without fear of mortal peril.[6]

> *Chang Yü*: When one treats people with benevolence, justice, and righteousness, and reposes confidence in them, the army will be united in mind and all will be happy to serve their leaders. The Book of Changes says: 'In happiness at overcoming difficulties, people forget the danger of death.'

5. By weather I mean the interaction of natural forces; the effects of winter's cold and summer's heat and the conduct of military operations in accordance with the seasons.[7]

6. By terrain I mean distances, whether the ground is traversed with ease or difficulty, whether it is open or constricted, and the chances of life or death.

> *Mei Yao-ch'en*: ... When employing troops it is essential to know beforehand the

conditions of the terrain. Knowing the distances, one can make use of an indirect or a direct plan. If he knows the degree of ease or difficulty of traversing the ground he can estimate the advantages of using infantry or cavalry. If he knows where the ground is constricted and where open he can calculate the size of force appropriate. If he knows where he will give battle he knows when to concentrate or divide his forces.[8]

7. By command I mean the general's qualities of wisdom, sincerity, humanity, courage, and strictness.

> *Li Ch'üan*: These five are the virtues of the general. Hence the army refers to him as 'The Respected One'.

> *Tu Mu*: . . . If wise, a commander is able to recognize changing circumstances and to act expediently. If sincere, his men will have no doubt of the certainty of rewards and punishments. If humane, he loves mankind, sympathizes with others, and appreciates their industry and toil. If courageous, he gains victory by seizing opportunity without hesitation. If strict, his troops are disciplined because they are in awe of him and are afraid of punishment.
>   Shen Pao-hsu . . . said: 'If a general is not courageous he will be unable to conquer doubts or to create great plans.'

8. By doctrine I mean organization, control, assignment of appropriate ranks to officers, regulation of supply routes, and the provision of principal items used by the army.

9. There is no general who has not heard of these five matters. Those who master them win; those who do not are defeated.

10. Therefore in laying plans compare the following elements, appraising them with the utmost care.

11. If you say which ruler possesses moral influence, which commander is the more able, which army obtains the advantages of nature and the terrain, in which regulations and instructions are better carried out, which troops are the stronger;[9]

> *Chang Yü*: Chariots strong, horses fast, troops valiant, weapons sharp—so that when they hear the drums beat the attack they are happy, and when they hear the gongs sound the retirement they are enraged. He who is like this is strong.

12. Which has the better trained officers and men;

> *Tu Yu*: . . . Therefore Master Wang said: 'If officers are unaccustomed to rigorous drilling they will be worried and hesitant in battle; if generals are not thoroughly trained they will inwardly quail when they face the enemy.'

13. And which administers rewards and punishments in a more enlightened manner;

> *Tu Mu*: Neither should be excessive.

14. I will be able to forecast which side will be victorious and which defeated.

15. If a general who heeds my strategy is employed he is certain to win. Retain him!

When one who refuses to listen to my strategy is employed, he is certain to be defeated. Dismiss him!

16. Having paid heed to the advantages of my plans, the general must create situations which will contribute to their accomplishment.[10] By 'situations' I mean that he should act expediently in accordance with what is advantageous and so control the balance.

17. All warfare is based on deception.

18. Therefore, when capable, feign incapacity; when active, inactivity.

19. When near, make it appear that you are far away; when far away, that you are near.

20. Offer the enemy a bait to lure him; feign disorder and strike him.

Tu Mu: The Chao general Li Mu released herds of cattle with their shepherds; when the Hsiung Nu had advanced a short distance he feigned a retirement, leaving behind several thousand men as if abandoning them. When the Khan heard this news he was delighted, and at the head of a strong force marched to the place. Li Mu put most of his troops into formations on the right and left wings, made a horning attack, crushed the Huns and slaughtered over one hundred thousand of their horsemen.[11]

21. When he concentrates, prepare against him; where he is strong, avoid him.

22. Anger his general and confuse him.

Li Ch'uan: If the general is choleric his authority can easily be upset. His character is not firm.

Chang Yü: If the enemy general is obstinate and prone to anger, insult and enrage him, so that he will be irritated and confused, and without a plan will recklessly advance against you.

23. Pretend inferiority and encourage his arrogance.

Tu Mu: Toward the end of the Ch'in dynasty, Mo Tun of the Hsiung Nu first established his power. The Eastern Hu were strong and sent ambassadors to parley. They said: 'We wish to obtain T'ou Ma's thousand-*li* horse.' Mo Tun consulted his advisers, who all exclaimed: 'The thousand-*li* horse! The most precious thing in this country! Do not give them that!' Mo Tun replied: 'Why begrudge a horse to a neighbour?' So he sent the horse.[12]

Shortly after, the Eastern Hu sent envoys who said: 'We wish one of the Khan's princesses.' Mo Tun asked advice of his ministers who all angrily said: 'The Eastern Hu are unrighteous! Now they even ask for a princess! We implore you to attack them!' Mo Tun said: 'How can one begrudge his neighbour a young woman?' So he gave the woman.

A short time later, the Eastern Hu returned and said: 'You have a thousand *li* of unused land which we want.' Mo Tun consulted his advisers. Some said it would be reasonable to cede the land, others that it would not. Mo Tun was enraged and said: 'Land is the foundation of the State. How could one give it away?' All those who had advised doing so were beheaded.

Mo Tun then sprang on his horse, ordered that all who remained behind were to be beheaded, and made a surprise attack on the Eastern Hu. The Eastern Hu were contemptuous of him and had made no preparations. When he attacked he annihilated

them. Mo Tun then turned westward and attacked the Yueh Ti. To the south he
annexed Lou Fan . . . and invaded Yen. He completely recovered the ancestral lands of
the Hsiung Nu previously conquered by the Ch'in general Meng T'ien.[13]

Ch'en Hao: Give the enemy young boys and women to infatuate him, and jades and silks
to excite his ambitions.

24. Keep him under a strain and wear him down.

Li Ch'üan: When the enemy is at ease, tire him.

Tu Mu: . . . Toward the end of the Later Han, after Ts'ao Ts'ao had defeated Liu Pei, Pei
fled to Yuan Shao, who then led out his troops intending to engage Ts'ao Ts'ao. T'ien
Fang, one of Yuan Shao's staff officers, said: 'Ts'ao Ts'ao is expert at employing troops;
one cannot go against him heedlessly. Nothing is better than to protract things and keep
him at a distance. You, General, should fortify along the mountains and rivers and hold
the four prefectures. Externally, make alliances with powerful leaders; internally, pursue
an agro-military policy. Later, select crack troops[14] and form them into extraordinary
units. Taking advantage of spots where he is unprepared, make repeated sorties and
disturb the country south of the river. When he comes to aid the right, attack his left;
when he goes to succour the left, attack the right; exhaust him by causing him continually to run about. . . . Now if you reject this victorious strategy and decide instead to risk
all on one battle, it will be too late for regrets.' Yuan Shao did not follow this advice and
therefore was defeated.[15]

25. When he is united, divide him.

Chang Yü: Sometimes drive a wedge between a sovereign and his ministers; on other
occasions separate his allies from him. Make them mutually suspicious so that they drift
apart. Then you can plot against them.

26. Attack where he is unprepared; sally out when he does not expect you.

Ho Yen-hsi: . . . Li Ching of the T'ang proposed ten plans to be used against Hsiao Hsieh,
and the entire responsibility of commanding the armies was entrusted to him. In the
eighth month he collected his forces at K'uei Chou.[16]
     As it was the season of the autumn floods the waters of the Yangtze were overflowing
and the roads by the three gorges were perilous, Hsiao Hsieh thought it certain that Li
Ching would not advance against him. Consequently he made no preparations.
     In the ninth month Li Ching took command of the troops and addressed them as
follows: 'What is of the greatest importance in war is extraordinary speed; one cannot
afford to neglect opportunity. Now we are concentrated and Hsiao Hsieh does not yet
know of it. Taking advantage of the fact that the river is in flood, we will appear
unexpectedly under the walls of his capital. As is said: 'When the thunder-clap comes,
there is no time to cover the ears.' Even if he should discover us, he cannot on the spur
of the moment devise a plan to counter us, and surely we can capture him.'
     He advanced to I Ling and Hsiao Hsieh began to be afraid and summoned
reinforcements from south of the river, but these were unable to arrive in time. Li Ching
laid siege to the city and Hsieh surrendered.

'To sally forth where he does not expect you' means as when, towards its close, the Wei dynasty sent Generals Chung Hui and Teng Ai to attack Shu.[17] . . . In winter, in the tenth month, Ai left Yin P'ing and marched through uninhabited country for over seven hundred *li*, chiselling roads through the mountains and building suspension bridges. The mountains were high, the valleys deep, and this task was extremely difficult and dangerous. Also, the army, about to run out of provisions, was on the verge of perishing. Teng Ai wrapped himself in felt carpets and rolled down the steep mountain slopes; generals and officers clambered up by grasping limbs of trees. Scaling the precipices like strings of fish, the army advanced.

Teng Ai appeared first at Chiang Yu in Shu, and Ma Mou, the general charged with its defence, surrendered. Teng Ai beheaded Chu-ko Chan, who resisted at Mien-chu, and marched on Ch'eng Tu. The King of Shu, Liu Shan, surrendered.

27. These are the strategist's keys to victory. It is not possible to discuss them beforehand.

Mei Yao-ch'en: When confronted by the enemy respond to changing circumstances and devise expedients. How can these be discussed beforehand?

28. Now if the estimates made in the temple before hostilities indicate victory it is because calculations show one's strength to be superior to that of his enemy; if they indicate defeat, it is because calculations show that one is inferior. With many calculations, one can win; with few one cannot. How much less chance of victory has one who makes none at all! By this means I examine the situation and the outcome will be clearly apparent.[18]

Waging war

Sun Tzu said:

1. Generally, operations of war require one thousand fast four-horse chariots, one thousand four-horse wagons covered in leather, and one hundred thousand mailed troops.

Tu Mu: . . . In ancient chariot fighting, 'leather-covered chariots' were both light and heavy. The latter were used for carrying halberds, weapons, military equipment, valuables, and uniforms. The *Ssu-ma Fa* said: 'One chariot carries three mailed officers; seventy-two foot troops accompany it. Additionally, there are ten cooks and servants, five men to take care of uniforms, five grooms in charge of fodder, and five men to collect firewood and draw water. Seventy-five men to one light chariot, twenty-five to one baggage wagon, so that taking the two together one hundred men compose a company.[19]

2. When provisions are transported for a thousand *li* expenditures at home and in the field, stipends for the entertainment of advisers and visitors, the cost of materials such as glue and lacquer, and of chariots and armour, will amount to one thousand pieces of gold a day. After this money is in hand, one hundred thousand troops may be raised.[20]

Li Ch'üan: Now when the army marches abroad, the treasury will be emptied at home.

Tu Mu: In the army there is a ritual of friendly visits from vassal lords. That is why Sun Tzu mentions 'advisers and visitors'.

3. Victory is the main object in war.[21] If this is long delayed, weapons are blunted and morale depressed. When troops attack cities, their strength will be exhausted.

4. When the army engages in protracted campaigns the resources of the state will not suffice.

> *Chang Yü*: . . . The campaigns of the Emperor Wu of the Han dragged on with no result and after the treasury was emptied he issued a mournful edict.

5. When your weapons are dulled and ardour damped, your strength exhausted and treasure spent, neighbouring rulers will take advantage of your distress to act. And even though you have wise counsellors, none will be able to lay good plans for the future.

6. Thus, while we have heard of blundering swiftness in war, we have not yet seen a clever operation that was prolonged.

> *Tu Yu*: An attack may lack ingenuity, but it must be delivered with supernatural speed.

7. For there has never been a protracted war from which a country has benefited.

> *Li Ch'üan*: The Spring and Autumn Annals says: 'War is like unto fire; those who will not put aside weapons are themselves consumed by them.'

8. Thus those unable to understand the dangers inherent in employing troops are equally unable to understand the advantageous ways of doing so.

9. Those adept in waging war do not require a second levy of conscripts nor more than one provisioning.[22]

10. They carry equipment from the homeland; they rely for provisions on the enemy. Thus the army is plentifully provided with food.

11. When a country is impoverished by military operations it is due to distant transportation; carriage of supplies for great distances renders the people destitute.

> *Chang Yü*: . . . If the army had to be supplied with grain over a distance of one thousand *li*, the troops would have a hungry look.[23]

12. Where the army is, prices are high; when prices rise the wealth of the people is exhausted. When wealth is exhausted the peasantry will be afflicted with urgent exactions.[24]

> *Chia Lin*: . . . Where troops are gathered the price of every commodity goes up because everyone covets the extraordinary profits to be made.[25]

13. With strength thus depleted and wealth consumed the households in the central plains will be utterly impoverished and seven-tenths of their wealth dissipated.

> *Li Ch'üan*: If war drags on without cessation men and women will resent not being able to marry, and will be distressed by the burdens of transportation.

14. As to government expenditures, those due to broken-down chariots, worn-out horses, armour and helmets, arrows and crossbows, lances, hand and body shields, draft animals and supply wagons will amount to sixty per cent of the total.[26]

15. Hence the wise general sees to it that his troops feed on the enemy, for one bushel of the enemy's provisions is equivalent to twenty of his; one hundredweight of enemy fodder to twenty hundredweight of his.

> *Chang Yü*: . . . In transporting provisions for a distance of one thousand *li*, twenty bushels will be consumed in delivering one to the army. . . . If difficult terrain must be crossed even more is required.

16. The reason troops slay the enemy is because they are enraged.[27]

> *Ho Yen-hsi*: When the Yen army surrounded Chi Mo in Ch'i, they cut off the noses of all the Ch'i prisoners.[28] The men of Ch'i were enraged and conducted a desperate defence. T'ien Tan sent a secret agent to say: 'We are terrified that you people of Yen will exhume the bodies of our ancestors from their graves. How this will freeze our hearts!'
>
> The Yen army immediately began despoiling the tombs and burning the corpses. The defenders of Chi Mo witnessed this from the city walls and with tears flowing wished to go forth to give battle, for rage had multiplied their strength by ten. T'ien Tan knew then that his troops were ready, and inflicted a ruinous defeat on Yen.

17. They take booty from the enemy because they desire wealth.

> *Tu Mu*: . . . In the Later Han, Tu Hsiang, Prefect of Chin Chou, attacked the Kuei Chou rebels Pu Yang, P'an Hung, and others. He entered Nan Hai, destroyed three of their camps, and captured much treasure. However, P'an Hung and his followers were still strong and numerous, while Tu Hsiang's troops, now rich and arrogant, no longer had the slightest desire to fight.
>
> Hsiang said: 'Pu Yang and P'an Hung have been rebels for ten years. Both are well-versed in attack and defence. What we should really do is unite the strength of all the prefectures and then attack them. For the present the troops shall be encouraged to go hunting.' Whereupon the troops both high and low went together to snare game.
>
> As soon as they had left, Tu Hsiang secretly sent people to burn down their barracks. The treasures they had accumulated were completely destroyed. When the hunters returned there was not one who did not weep.
>
> Tu Hsiang said: 'The wealth and goods of Pu Yang and those with him are sufficient to enrich several generations. You gentlemen did not do your best. What you have lost is but a small bit of what is there. Why worry about it?'
>
> When the troops heard this, they were all enraged and wished to fight. Tu Hsiang ordered the horses fed and everyone to eat in his bed, and early in the morning they marched on the rebels' camp.[29] Yang and Hung had not made preparations, and Tu Hsiang's troops made a spirited attack and destroyed them.

> *Chang Yü*: . . . In this Imperial Dynasty, when the Eminent Founder ordered his generals to attack Shu, he decreed: 'In all the cities and prefectures taken, you should, in my name, empty the treasuries and public storehouses to entertain the officers and troops. What the State wants is only the land.'

18. Therefore, when in chariot fighting more than ten chariots are captured, reward

those who take the first. Replace the enemy's flags and banners with your own, mix the captured chariots with yours, and mount them.

19. Treat the captives well, and care for them.

> *Chang Yü*: All the soldiers taken must be cared for with magnanimity and sincerity so that they may be used by us.

20. This is called 'winning a battle and becoming stronger'.

21. Hence what is essential in war is victory, not prolonged operations. And therefore the general who understands war is the Minister of the people's fate and arbiter of the nation's destiny.

> *Ho Yen-hsi*: The difficulties in the appointment of a commander are the same today as they were in ancient times.[30]

Offensive strategy

Sun Tzu said:

1. Generally in war the best policy is to take a state intact; to ruin it is inferior to this.

> *Li Ch'üan*: Do not put a premium on killing.

2. To capture the enemy's army is better than to destroy it; to take intact a battalion, a company or a five-man squad is better than to destroy them.

3. For to win one hundred victories in one hundred battles is not the acme of skill. To subdue the enemy without fighting is the acme of skill.

4. Thus, what is of supreme importance in war is to attack the enemy's strategy;[31]

> *Tu Mu*: . . . The Grand Duke said: 'He who excels at resolving difficulties does so before they arise. He who excels in conquering his enemies triumphs before threats materialize.'
>
> *Li Ch'üan*: Attack plans at their inception. In the Later Han, K'ou Hsün surrounded Kao Chun.[32] Chun sent his Planning Officer, Huang-fu Wen, to parley. Huang-fu Wen was stubborn and rude and K'ou Hsün beheaded him, and informed Kao Chun: 'Your staff officer was without propriety. I have beheaded him. If you wish to submit, do so immediately. Otherwise defend yourself.' On the same day, Chun threw open his fortifications and surrendered.
>
> All K'ou Hsün's generals said: 'May we ask, you killed his envoy, but yet forced him to surrender his city. How is this?'
>
> K'ou Hsün said: 'Huang-fu Wen was Kao Chun's heart and guts, his intimate counsellor. If I had spared Huang-fu Wen's life, he would have accomplished his schemes, but when I killed him, Kao Chun lost his guts. It is said: "The supreme excellence in war is to attack the enemy's plans." '
>
> All the generals said: 'This is beyond our comprehension.'

5. Next best is to disrupt his alliances:[33]

> *Tu Yu*: Do not allow your enemies to get together.

Wang Hsi: . . . Look into the matter of his alliances and cause them to be severed and dissolved. If an enemy has alliances, the problem is grave and the enemy's position strong; if he has no alliances the problem is minor and the enemy's position weak.

6. The next best is to attack his army.

Chia Lin: . . . The Grand Duke said: 'He who struggles for victory with naked blades is not a good general.'

Wang Hsi: Battles are dangerous affairs.

Chang Yü: If you cannot nip his plans in the bud, or disrupt his alliances when they are about to be consummated, sharpen your weapons to gain the victory.

7. The worst policy is to attack cities. Attack cities only when there is no alternative.[34]

8. To prepare the shielded wagons and make ready the necessary arms and equipment requires at least three months; to pile up earthen ramps against the walls an additional three months will be needed.

9. If the general is unable to control his impatience and orders his troops to swarm up the wall like ants, one-third of them will be killed without taking the city. Such is the calamity of these attacks.

Tu Mu: . . . In the later Wei, the Emperor T'ai Wu led one hundred thousand troops to attack the Sung general Tsang Chih at Yu T'ai. The Emperor first asked Tsang Chih for some wine.[35] Tsang Chih sealed up a pot full of urine and sent it to him. T'ai Wu was transported with rage and immediately attacked the city, ordering his troops to scale the walls and engage in close combat. Corpses piled up to the top of the walls and after thirty days of this the dead exceeded half his force.

10. Thus, those skilled in war subdue the enemy's army without battle. They capture his cities without assaulting them and overthrow his state without protracted operations.

Li Ch'üan: They conquer by strategy. In the Later Han the Marquis of Tsan, Tsang Kung, surrounded the 'Yao' rebels at Yüan Wu, but during a succession of months was unable to take the city.[36] His officers and men were ill and covered with ulcers. The King of Tung Hai spoke to Tsang Kung, saying: 'Now you have massed troops and encircled the enemy, who is determined to fight to the death. This is no strategy! You should lift the siege. Let them know that an escape route is open and they will flee and disperse. Then any village constable will be able to capture them!' Tsang Kung followed this advice and took Yüan Wu.

11. Your aim must be to take All-under-Heaven intact. Thus your troops are not worn out and your gains will be complete. This is the art of offensive strategy.

12. Consequently, the art of using troops is this: When ten to the enemy's one, surround him;

13. When five times his strength, attack him;

Chang Yü: If my force is five times that of the enemy I alarm him to the front, surprise him to the rear, create an uproar in the east and strike in the west.

14. If double his strength, divide him.[37]

> *Tu Yu*: . . . If a two-to-one superiority is insufficient to manipulate the situation, we use a distracting force to divide his army. Therefore the Grand Duke said: 'If one is unable to influence the enemy to divide his forces, he cannot discuss unusual tactics.'

15. If equally matched you may engage him.

> *Ho Yen-hsi*: . . . In these circumstances only the able general can win.

16. If weaker numerically, be capable of withdrawing;

> *Tu Mu*: If your troops do not equal his, temporarily avoid his initial onrush. Probably later you can take advantage of a soft spot. Then rouse yourself and seek victory with determined spirit.

> *Chang Yü*: If the enemy is strong and I am weak, I temporarily withdraw and do not engage.[38] This is the case when the abilities and courage of the generals and the efficiency of troops are equal.
>
> If I am in good order and the enemy in disarray, if I am energetic and he careless, then, even if he be numerically stronger, I can give battle.

17. And if in all respects unequal, be capable of eluding him, for a small force is but booty for one more powerful.[39]

> *Chang Yü*: . . . Mencius said: 'The small certainly cannot equal the large, nor can the weak match the strong, nor the few the many.'[40]

18. Now the general is the protector of the state. If this protection is all-embracing, the state will surely be strong; if defective, the state will certainly be weak.

> *Chang Yü*: . . . The Grand Duke said: 'A sovereign who obtains the right person prospers. One who fails to do so will be ruined.'

19. Now there are three ways in which a ruler can bring misfortune upon his army:[41]

20. When ignorant that the army should not advance, to order an advance or ignorant that it should not retire, to order a retirement. This is described as 'hobbling the army'.

> *Chia Lin*: The advance and retirement of the army can be controlled by the general in accordance with prevailing circumstances. No evil is greater than commands of the sovereign from the court.

21. When ignorant of military affairs, to participate in their administration. This causes the officers to be perplexed.

> *Ts'ao Ts'ao*: . . . An army cannot be run according to rules of etiquette.

> *Tu Mu*: As far as propriety, laws, and decrees are concerned, the army has its own code,

which it ordinarily follows. If these are made identical with those used in governing a state the officers will be bewildered.

Chang Yü: Benevolence and righteousness may be used to govern a state but cannot be used to administer an army. Expediency and flexibility are used in administering an army, but cannot be used in governing a state.

22. When ignorant of command problems to share in the exercise of responsibilities. This engenders doubts in the minds of the officers.[42]

Wang Hsi: . . . If one ignorant of military matters is sent to participate in the administration of the army, then in every movement there will be disagreement and mutual frustration and the entire army will be hamstrung. That is why Pei Tu memorialized the throne to withdraw the Army Supervisor; only then was he able to pacify Ts'ao Chou.[43]

Chang Yü: In recent times court officials have been used as Supervisors of the Army and this is precisely what is wrong.

23. If the army is confused and suspicious, neighbouring rulers will cause trouble. This is what is meant by the saying: 'A confused army leads to another's victory.'[44]

Meng: . . . The Grand Duke said: 'One who is confused in purpose cannot respond to his enemy.'

Li Ch'üan: . . . The wrong person cannot be appointed to command. . . . Lin Hsiang-ju, the Prime Minister of Chao, said: 'Chao Kua is merely able to read his father's books, and is as yet ignorant of correlating changing circumstances. Now Your Majesty, on account of his name, makes him the commander-in-chief. This is like glueing the pegs of a lute and then trying to tune it.'

24. Now there are five circumstances in which victory may be predicted:
25. He who knows when he can fight and when he cannot will be victorious.
26. He who understands how to use both large and small forces will be victorious.

Tu Yu: There are circumstances in war when many cannot attack few, and others when the weak can master the strong. One able to manipulate such circumstances will be victorious.

27. He whose ranks are united in purpose will be victorious.

Tu Yu: Therefore Mencius said: 'The appropriate season is not as important as the advantages of the ground; these are not as important as harmonious human relations.'[45]

28. He who is prudent and lies in wait for an enemy who is not, will be victorious.

Ch'en Hao: Create an invincible army and await the enemy's moment of vulnerability.

Ho Yen-hsi: . . . A gentleman said: 'To rely on rustics and not prepare is the greatest of crimes; to be prepared beforehand for any contingency is the greatest of virtues.'

29. He whose generals are able and not interfered with by the sovereign will be victorious.

> *Tu Yu*: . . . Therefore Master Wang said: 'To make appointments is the province of the sovereign; to decide on battle, that of the general.'
>
> *Wang Hsi*: . . . A sovereign of high character and intelligence must be able to know the right man, should place the responsibility on him, and expect results.
>
> *Ho Yen-hsi*: . . . Now in war there may be one hundred changes in each step. When one sees he can, he advances; when he sees that things are difficult, he retires. To say that a general must await commands of the sovereign in such circumstances is like informing a superior that you wish to put out a fire. Before the order to do so arrives the ashes are cold. And it is said one must consult the Army Supervisor in these matters! This is as if in building a house beside the road one took advice from those who pass by. Of course the work would never be completed!⁴⁶
>
> To put a rein on an able general while at the same time asking him to suppress a cunning enemy is like tying up the Black Hound of Han and then ordering him to catch elusive hares. What is the difference?

30. It is in these five matters that the way to victory is known.

31. Therefore I say: 'Know the enemy and know yourself; in a hundred battles you will never be in peril.

32. When you are ignorant of the enemy but know yourself, your chances of winning or losing are equal.

33. If ignorant both of your enemy and of yourself, you are certain in every battle to be in peril.'

> *Li Ch'üan*: Such people are called 'mad bandits'. What can they expect if not defeat?

Dispositions⁴⁷

Sun Tzu said:

1. Anciently the skilful warriors first made themselves invincible and awaited the enemy's moment of vulnerability.

2. Invincibility depends on one's self; the enemy's vulnerability on him.

3. It follows that those skilled in war can make themselves invincible but cannot cause an enemy to be certainly vulnerable.

> *Mei Yao-ch'en*: That which depends on me, I can do; that which depends on the enemy cannot be certain.

4. Therefore it is said that one may know how to win, but cannot necessarily do so.

5. Invincibility lies in the defence; the possibility of victory in the attack.⁴⁸

6. One defends when his strength is inadequate; he attacks when it is abundant.

7. The experts in defence conceal themselves as under the ninefold earth; those skilled in attack move as from above the ninefold heavens. Thus they are capable both of protecting themselves and of gaining a complete victory.⁴⁹

Tu Yu: Those expert at preparing defences consider it fundamental to rely on the strength of such obstacles as mountains, rivers and foothills. They make it impossible for the enemy to know where to attack. They secretly conceal themselves as under the nine-layered ground.

Those expert in attack consider it fundamental to rely on the seasons and the advantages of the ground; they use inundations and fire according to the situation. They make it impossible for an enemy to know where to prepare. They release the attack like a lightning bolt from above the nine-layered heavens.

8. To foresee a victory which the ordinary man can foresee is not the acme of skill;

Li Ch'üan: . . . When Han Hsin destroyed Chao State he marched out of the Well Gorge before breakfast. He said: 'We will destroy the Chao army and then meet for a meal.' The generals were despondent and pretended to agree. Han Hsin drew up his army with the river to its rear. The Chao troops climbed upon their breastworks and, observing this, roared with laughter and taunted him: 'The General of Han does not know how to use troops!' Han Hsin then proceeded to defeat the Chao army and after breakfasting beheaded Lord Ch'eng An.

This is an example of what the multitude does not comprehend.[50]

9. To triumph in battle and be universally acclaimed 'Expert' is not the acme of skill, for to lift an autumn down requires no great strength; to distinguish between the sun and moon is no test of vision; to hear the thunderclap is no indication of acute hearing.[51]

Chang Yü: By 'autumn down' Sun Tzu means rabbits' down, which on the coming of autumn is extremely light.

10. Anciently those called skilled in war conquered an enemy easily conquered.[52]
11. And therefore the victories won by a master of war gain him neither reputation for wisdom nor merit for valour.

Tu Mu: A victory gained before the situation has crystallized is one the common man does not comprehend. Thus its author gains no reputation for sagacity. Before he has bloodied his blade the enemy state has already submitted.

Ho Yen-hsi: . . . When you subdue your enemy without fighting who will pronounce you valorous?

12. For he wins his victories without erring. 'Without erring' means that whatever he does insures his victory; he conquers an enemy already defeated.

Chen Hao: In planning, never a useless move; in strategy, no step taken in vain.

13. Therefore the skilful commander takes up a position in which he cannot be defeated and misses no opportunity to master his enemy.
14. Thus a victorious army wins its victories before seeking battle; an army destined to defeat fights in the hope of winning.

Tu Mu: . . . Duke Li Ching of Wei said: 'Now, the supreme requirements of generalship are a clear perception, the harmony of his host, a profound strategy coupled with far-reaching plans, an understanding of the seasons and an ability to examine the human factors. For a general unable to estimate his capabilities or comprehend the arts of expediency and flexibility when faced with the opportunity to engage the enemy will advance in a stumbling and hesitant manner, looking anxiously first to his right and then to his left, and be unable to produce a plan. Credulous, he will place confidence in unreliable reports, believing at one moment this and at another that. As timorous as a fox in advancing or retiring, his groups will be scattered about. What is the difference between this and driving innocent people into boiling water or fire? Is this not exactly like driving cows and sheep to feed wolves or tigers?'

15. Those skilled in war cultivate the *Tao* and preserve the laws and are therefore able to formulate victorious policies.

Tu Mu: The *Tao* is the way of humanity and justice; 'laws' are regulations and institutions. Those who excel in war first cultivate their own humanity and justice and maintain their laws and institutions. By these means they make their governments invincible.

16. Now the elements of the art of war are first, measurement of space; second, estimation of quantities; third, calculations; fourth, comparisons; and fifth, chances of victory.
17. Measurements of space are derived from the ground.
18. Quantities derive from measurement, figures from quantities, comparisons from figures, and victory from comparisons.

Ho Yen-hsi:[53] 'Ground' includes both distances and type of terrain; 'measurement' is calculation. Before the army is dispatched, calculations are made respecting the degree of difficulty of the enemy's land; the directness and deviousness of its roads; the number of his troops; the quantity of his war equipment and the state of his morale. Calculations are made to see if the enemy can be attacked and only after this is the population mobilized and troops raised.

19. Thus a victorious army is as a hundredweight balanced against a grain; a defeated army as a grain balanced against a hundredweight.
20. It is because of disposition that a victorious general is able to make his people fight with the effect of pent-up waters which, suddenly released, plunge into a bottomless abyss.

Chang Yü: The nature of water is that it avoids heights and hastens to the lowlands. When a dam is broken, the water cascades with irresistible force. Now the shape of an army resembles water. Take advantage of the enemy's unpreparedness; attack him when he does not expect it; avoid his strength and strike his emptiness, and like water, none can oppose you.

Energy [54]

Sun Tzu said:
1. Generally, management of many is the same as management of few. It is a matter of organization.[55]

Chang Yü: To manage a host one must first assign responsibilities to the generals and their assistants, and establish the strengths of ranks and files. . . .

One man is a single; two, a pair; three, a trio. A pair and a trio make a five,[56] which is a squad; two squads make a section; five sections, a platoon; two platoons, a company; two companies, a battalion; two battalions, a regiment; two regiments, a group; two groups, a brigade; two brigades, an army.[57] Each is subordinate to the superior and controls the inferior. Each is properly trained. Thus one may manage a host of a million men just as he would a few.

2. And to control many is the same as to control few. This is a matter of formations and signals.

Chang Yü: . . . Now when masses of troops are employed, certainly they are widely separated, and ears are not able to hear acutely nor eyes to see clearly. Therefore officers and men are ordered to advance or retreat by observing the flags and banners and to move or stop by signals of bells and drums. Thus the valiant shall not advance alone, nor shall the coward flee.

3. That the army is certain to sustain the enemy's attack without suffering defeat is due to operations of the extraordinary and the normal forces.[58]

Li Ch'üan: The force which confronts the enemy is the normal; that which goes to his flanks the extraordinary. No commander of an army can wrest the advantage from the enemy without extraordinary forces.

Ho Yen-hsi: I make the enemy conceive my normal force to be the extraordinary and my extraordinary to be the normal. Moreover, the normal may become the extraordinary and vice versa.

4. Troops thrown against the enemy as a grindstone against eggs is an example of a solid acting upon a void.

Ts'ao Ts'ao: Use the most solid to attack the most empty.

5. Generally, in battle, use the normal force to engage; use the extraordinary to win.

6. Now the resources of those skilled in the use of extraordinary forces are as infinite as the heavens and earth; as inexhaustible as the flow of the great rivers.[59]

7. For they end and recommence; cyclical, as are the movements of the sun and moon. They die away and are reborn; recurrent, as are the passing seasons.

8. The musical notes are only five in number but their melodies are so numerous that one cannot hear them all.

9. The primary colours are only five in number but their combinations are so infinite that one cannot visualize them all.

10. The flavours are only five in number but their blends are so various that one cannot taste them all.

11. In battle there are only the normal and extrordinary forces, but their combinations are limitless; none can comprehend them all.

12. For these two forces are mutually reproductive; their interaction as endless as that of interlocked rings. Who can determine where one ends and the other begins?

13. When torrential water tosses boulders, it is because of its momentum;

14. When the strike of a hawk breaks the body of its prey, it is because of timing.[60]

> *Tu Yu*: Strike the enemy as swiftly as a falcon strikes its target. It surely breaks the back of its prey for the reason that it awaits the right moment to strike. Its movement is regulated.

15. Thus the momentum of one skilled in war is overwhelming, and his attack precisely regulated.[61]

16. His potential is that of a fully drawn crossbow; his timing, the release of the trigger.[62]

17. In the tumult and uproar the battle seems chaotic, but there is no disorder; the troops appear to be milling about in circles but cannot be defeated.[63]

> *Li Ch'üan*: In battle all appears to be turmoil and confusion. But the flags and banners have prescribed arrangements; the sounds of the cymbals, fixed rules.

18. Apparent confusion is a product of good order; apparent cowardice, of courage; apparent weakness, of strength.[64]

> *Tu Mu*: The verse means that if one wishes to feign disorder to entice an enemy he must himself be well-disciplined. Only then can he feign confusion. One who wishes to simulate cowardice and lie in wait for his enemy must be courageous, for only then is he able to simulate fear. One who wishes to appear to be weak in order to make his enemy arrogant must be extremely strong. Only then can he feign weakness.

19. Order or disorder depends on organization; courage or cowardice on circumstances; strength or weakness on dispositions.

> *Li Ch'üan*: Now when troops gain a favourable situation the coward is brave; if it be lost, the brave become cowards. In the art of war there are no fixed rules. These can only be worked out according to circumstances.

20. Thus, those skilled at making the enemy move do so by creating a situation to which he must conform; they entice him with something he is certain to take, and with lures of ostensible profit they await him in strength.

21. Therefore a skilled commander seeks victory from the situation and does not demand it of his subordinates.

> *Ch'en Hao*: Experts in war depend especially on opportunity and expediency. They do not place the burden of accomplishment on their men alone.

22. He selects his men and they exploit the situation.[65]

> *Li Ch'üan*: . . . Now, the valiant can fight; the cautious defend, and the wise counsel. Thus there is none whose talent is wasted.

> *Tu Mu*: . . . Do not demand accomplishment of those who have no talent.

When Ts'ao Ts'ao attacked Chang Lu in Han Chung, he left Generals Chang Liao, Li Tien, and Lo Chin in command of over one thousand men to defend Ho Fei. Ts'ao Ts'ao sent instructions to the Army Commissioner, Hsieh Ti, and wrote on the edge of the envelope: 'Open this only when the rebels arrive.' Soon after, Sun Ch'üan of Wu with one hundred thousand men besieged Ho Fei. The generals opened the instructions and read: 'If Sun Ch'üan arrives, Generals Chang and Li will go out to fight. General Lo will defend the city. The Army Commissioner shall not participate in the battle.[66] All the other generals should engage the enemy.'

Chang Liao said: 'Our Lord is campaigning far away, and if we wait for the arrival of reinforcements the rebels will certainly destroy us. Therefore the instructions say that before the enemy is assembled we should immediately attack him in order to blunt his keen edge and to stabilize the morale of our own troops. Then we can defend the city. The opportunity for victory or defeat lies in this one action.'

Li Tien and Chang Liao went out to attack and actually defeated Sun Ch'üan, and the morale of the Wu army was rubbed out. They returned and put their defences in order and the troops felt secure. Sun Ch'üan assaulted the city for ten days but could not take it and withdrew.

The historian Sun Sheng in discussing this observed: 'Now war is a matter of deception. As to the defence of Ho Fei, it was hanging in the air, weak and without reinforcements. If one trusts solely to brave generals who love fighting, this will cause trouble. If one relies solely on those who are cautious, their frightened hearts will find it difficult to control the situation.'

Chang Yü: Now the method of employing men is to use the avaricious and the stupid, the wise and the brave, and to give responsibility to each in situations that suit him. Do not charge people to do what they cannot do. Select them and give them responsibilities commensurate with their abilities.

24. He who relies on the situation uses his men in fighting as one rolls logs or stones. Now the nature of logs and stones is that on stable ground they are static; on unstable ground, they move. If square, they stop; if round, they roll.

25. Thus, the potential of troops skilfully commanded in battle may be compared to that of round boulders which roll down from mountain heights.

Tu Mu: . . . Thus one need use but little strength to achieve much.

Chang Yü: . . . Li Ching said: 'In war there are three kinds of situation:

'When the general is contemptuous of his enemy and his officers love to fight, their ambitions soaring as high as the azure clouds and their spirits as fierce as hurricanes, this is situation in respect to morale.

'When one man defends a narrow mountain defile which is like sheep's intestines or the door of a dog-house, he can withstand one thousand. This is situation in respect to terrain.

'When one takes advantage of the enemy's laxity, his weariness, his hunger and thirst, or strikes when his advanced camps are not settled, or his army is only half-way across a river, this is situation in respect to the enemy.'

Therefore when using troops, one must take advantage of the situation exactly as if he were setting a ball in motion on a steep slope. The force applied is minute but the results are enormous.

Weaknesses and strengths

Sun Tzu said:

1. Generally, he who occupies the field of battle first and awaits his enemy is at ease; he who comes later to the scene and rushes into the fight is weary.

2. And therefore those skilled in war bring the enemy to the field of battle and are not brought there by him.

3. One able to make the enemy come of his own accord does so by offering him some advantage. And one able to prevent him from coming does so by hurting him.

> *Tu Yu*: . . . If you are able to hold critical points on his strategic roads the enemy cannot come. Therefore Master Wang said: 'When a cat is at the rat hole, ten thousand rats dare not come out; when a tiger guards the ford, ten thousand deer cannot cross.'

4. When the enemy is at ease, be able to weary him; when well fed, to starve him; when at rest, to make him move.

5. Appear at places to which he must hasten; move swiftly where he does not expect you.

6. That you may march a thousand *li* without wearying yourself is because you travel where there is no enemy.

> *Ts'ao Ts'ao*: Go into emptiness, strike voids, bypass what he defends, hit him where he does not expect you.

7. To be certain to take what you attack is to attack a place the enemy does not protect. To be certain to hold what you defend is to defend a place the enemy does not attack.

8. Therefore, against those skilled in attack, an enemy does not know where to defend; against the experts in defence, the enemy does not know where to attack.

9. Subtle and insubstantial, the expert leaves no trace; divinely mysterious, he is inaudible. Thus he is master of his enemy's fate.

> *Ho Yen-hsi*: . . . I make the enemy see my strengths as weaknesses and my weaknesses as strengths while I cause his strengths to become weaknesses and discover where he is not strong. . . . I conceal my tracks so that none can discern them; I keep silence so that none can hear me.

10. He whose advance is irresistible plunges into his enemy's weak positions; he who in withdrawal cannot be pursued moves so swiftly that he cannot be overtaken.

> *Chang Yü*: . . . Come like the wind, go like the lightning.

11. When I wish to give battle, my enemy, even though protected by high walls and deep moats, cannot help but engage me, for I attack a position he must succour.

12. When I wish to avoid battle I may defend myself simply by drawing a line on the ground; the enemy will be unable to attack me because I divert him from going where he wishes.

> *Tu Mu*: Chu-ko Liang camped at Yang P'ing and ordered Wei Yen and various generals to combine forces and go down to the east. Chu-ko Liang left only ten thousand men to

defend the city while he waited for reports. Ssŭ-ma I said: 'Chu-ko Liang is in the city; his troops are few; he is not strong. His generals and officers have lost heart.' At this time Chu-ko Liang's spirits were high as usual. He ordered his troops to lay down their banners and silence their drums, and did not allow his men to go out. He opened the four gates and swept and sprinkled the streets.

Ssŭ-ma I suspected an ambush, and led his army in haste to the Northern Mountains.

Chu-ko Liang remarked to his Chief of Staff: 'Ssŭ-ma I thought I had prepared an ambush and fled along the mountain ranges.' Ssŭ-ma I later learned of this and was overcome with regrets.[67]

13. If I am able to determine the enemy's dispositions while at the same time I conceal my own then I can concentrate and he must divide. And if I concentrate while he divides, I can use my entire strength to attack a fraction of his.[68] There, I will be numerically superior. Then, if I am able to use many to strike few at the selected point, those I deal with will be in dire straits.[69]

> *Tu Mu*: . . . Sometimes I use light troops and vigorous horsemen to attack where he is unprepared, sometimes strong crossbowomen and bow-stretching archers to snatch key positions, to stir up his left, overrun his right, alarm him to the front, and strike suddenly into his rear.
>
> In broad daylight I deceive him by the use of flags and banners and at night confuse him by beating drums. Then in fear and trembling he will divide his forces to take precautionary measures.

14. The enemy must not know where I intend to give battle. For if he does not know where I intend to give battle he must prepare in a great many places. And when he prepares in a great many places, those I have to fight in any one place will be few.

15. For if he prepares to the front his rear will be weak, and if to the rear, his front will be fragile. If he prepares to the left, his right will be vulnerable and if to the right, there will be few on his left. And when he prepares everywhere he will be weak everywhere.[70]

> *Chang Yü*: He will be unable to fathom where my chariots will actually go out, or where my cavalry will actually come from, or where my infantry will actually follow up, and therefore he will disperse and divide and will have to guard against me everywhere. Consequently his force will be scattered and weakened and his strength divided and dissipated, and at the place I engage him I can use a large host against his isolated units.

16. One who has few must prepare against the enemy; one who has many makes the enemy prepare against him.

17. If one knows where and when a battle will be fought his troops can march a thousand *li* and meet on the field. But if one knows neither the battleground nor the day of battle, the left will be unable to aid the right, or the right, the left; the van to support the rear, or the rear, the van. How much more is this so when separated by several tens of *li*, or, indeed, by even a few!

> *Tu Yü*: Now those skilled in war must know where and when a battle will be fought. They measure the roads and fix the date. They divide the army and march in separate columns. Those who are distant start first, those who are nearby, later. Thus the

meeting of troops from distances of a thousand *li* takes place at the same time. It is like people coming to a city market.[71]

18. Although I estimate the troops of Yüeh as many, of what benefit is this superiority in respect to the outcome?[72]

19. Thus I say that victory can be created. For even if the enemy is numerous, I can prevent him from engaging.

> *Chia Lin*: Although the enemy be numerous, if he does not know my military situation, I can always make him urgently attend to his own preparations so that he has no leisure to plan to fight me.

20. Therefore, determine the enemy's plans and you will know which strategy will be successful and which will not;

21. Agitate him and ascertain the pattern of his movement.

22. Determine his dispositions and so ascertain the field of battle.[73]

23. Probe him and learn where his strength is abundant and where deficient.

24. The ultimate in disposing one's troops is to be without ascertainable shape. Then the most penetrating spies cannot pry in nor can the wise lay plans against you.

25. It is according to the shapes that I lay the plans for victory, but the multitude does not comprehend this. Although everyone can see the outward aspects, none understands the way in which I have created victory.

26. Therefore, when I have won a victory I do not repeat my tactics but respond to circumstances in an infinite variety of ways.

27. Now an army may be likened to water, for just as flowing water avoids the heights and hastens to the lowlands, so an army avoids strength and strikes weakness.

28. And as water shapes its flow in accordance with the ground, so an army manages its victory in accordance with the situation of the enemy.

29. And as water has no constant form, there are in war no constant conditions.

30. Thus, one able to gain the victory by modifying his tactics in accordance with the enemy situation may be said to be divine.

31. Of the five elements, none is always predominant; of the four seasons, none lasts forever; of the days, some are long and some short, and the moon waxes and wanes.

Manœuvre [74]

Sun Tzu said:

1. Normally, when the army is employed, the general first receives his commands from the sovereign. He assembles the troops and mobilizes the people. He blends the army into a harmonious entity and encamps it.[75]

> *Li Ch'üan*: He receives the sovereign's mandate and in compliance with the victorious deliberations of the temple councils reverently executes the punishments ordained by Heaven.

2. Nothing is more difficult than the art of manœuvre. What is difficult about manœuvre is to make the devious route the most direct and to turn misfortune to advantage.

3. Thus, march by an indirect route and divert the enemy by enticing him with a bait. So

doing, you may set out after he does and arrive before him. One able to do this understands the strategy of the direct and the indirect.

> *Ts'ao Ts'ao:* . . . Make it appear that you are far off. You may start after the enemy and arrive before him because you know how to estimate and calculate distances.

> *Tu Mu:*[76] He who wishes to snatch an advantage takes a devious and distant route and makes of it the short way. He turns misfortune to his advantage. He deceives and fools the enemy to make him dilatory and lax, and then marches on speedily.

4. Now both advantage and danger are inherent in manœuvre.[77]

> *Ts' ao Ts'ao:* One skilled will profit by it; if he is not, it is dangerous.

5. One who sets the entire army in motion to chase an advantage will not attain it.
6. If he abandons the camp to contend for advantage the stores will be lost.

> *Tu Mu:* If one moves with everything the stores will travel slowly and he will not gain the advantage. If he leaves the heavy baggage behind and presses on with the light troops, it is to be feared the baggage would be lost.

7. It follows that when one rolls up the armour and sets out speedily, stopping neither day nor night and marching at double time for a hundred *li*, the three commanders will be captured. For the vigorous troops will arrive first and the feeble straggle along behind, so that if this method is used only one-tenth of the army will arrive.[78]

> *Tu Mu:* . . . Normally, an army marches thirty *li* in a day, which is one stage. In a forced march of double distance it covers two stages. You can cover one hundred *li* only if you rest neither day nor night. If the march is conducted in this manner the troops will be taken prisoners. . . . When Sun Tzu says that if this method is used only one out of ten will arrive he means that when there is no alternative and you must contend for an advantageous position, you select the most robust man of ten to go first while you order the remainder to follow in the rear. So of ten thousand men you select one thousand who will arrive at dawn. The remainder will arrive continuously, some in late morning and some in mid-afternoon, so that none is exhausted and all arrive in succession to join those who preceded them. The sound of their marching is uninterrupted. In contending for advantage, it must be for a strategically critical point. Then, even one thousand will be sufficient to defend it until those who follow arrive.

8. In a forced march of fifty *li* the commander of the van will fall, and using this method but half the army will arrive. In a forced march of thirty *li*, but two-thirds will arrive.[79]
9. It follows that an army which lacks heavy equipment, fodder, food and stores will be lost.[80]

> *Li Ch'üan:* . . . The protection of metal walls is not as important as grain and food.

10. Those who do not know the conditions of mountains and forests, hazardous defiles, marshes and swamps, cannot conduct the march of an army;

11. Those who do not use local guides are unable to obtain the advantages of the ground.

> *Tu Mu*: The *Kuan Tzu* says: 'Generally, the commander must thoroughly acquaint himself beforehand with the maps so that he knows dangerous places for chariots and carts, where the water is too deep for wagons; passes in famous mountains,[81] the principal rivers, the locations of highlands and hills; where rushes, forests, and reeds are luxuriant; the road distances; the size of cities and towns; well-known cities and abandoned ones, and where there are flourishing orchards. All this must be known, as well as the way boundaries run in and out. All these facts the general must store in his mind; only then will he not lose the advantage of the ground.'
>
> Li Ching said: '. . . We should select the bravest officers and those who are most intelligent and keen, and using local guides, secretly traverse mountain and forest noiselessly and concealing our traces. Sometimes we make artificial animals' feet to put on our feet; at others we put artificial birds on our hats and quietly conceal ourselves in luxuriant undergrowth. After this, we listen carefully for distant sounds and screw up our eyes to see clearly. We concentrate our wits so that we may snatch an opportunity. We observe the indications of the atmosphere; look for traces in the water to know if the enemy has waded a stream, and watch for movement of the trees which indicates his approach.'
>
> *Ho Yen-hsi*: . . . Now, if having received instructions to launch a campaign, we hasten to unfamiliar land where cultural influence has not penetrated and communications are cut, and rush into its defiles, is it not difficult? If I go with a solitary army the enemy awaits me vigilantly. For the situations of an attacker and a defender are vastly different. How much more so when the enemy concentrates on deception and uses many misleading devices! If we have made no plans we plunge in headlong. By braving the dangers and entering perilous places we face the calamity of being trapped or inundated. Marching as if drunk, we may run into an unexpected fight. When we stop at night we are worried by false alarms; if we hasten along unprepared we fall into ambushes. This is to plunge an army of bears and tigers into the land of death. How can we cope with the rebels' fortifications, or sweep him out of his deceptive dens?
>
> Therefore in the enemy's country, the mountains, rivers, highlands, lowlands and hills which he can defend as strategic points; the forests, reeds, rushes and luxuriant grasses in which he can conceal himself; the distances over the roads and paths, the size of cities and towns, the extent of the villages, the fertility or barrenness of the fields, the depth of irrigation works, the amounts of stores, the size of the opposing army, the keenness of weapons—all must be fully known. Then we have the enemy in our sights and he can be easily taken.

12. Now war is based on deception. Move when it is advantageous and create changes in the situation by dispersal and concentration of forces.[82]

13. When campaigning, be swift as the wind; in leisurely march, majestic as the forest; in raiding and plundering, like fire; in standing, firm as the mountains.[83] As unfathomable as the clouds, move like a thunderbolt.

14. When you plunder the countryside, divide your forces.[84] When you conquer territory, divide the profits.[85]

15. Weigh the situation, then move.

16. He who knows the art of the direct and the indirect approach will be victorious. Such is the art of manœuvring.

17. The Book of Military Administration says: 'As the voice cannot be heard in battle, drums and bells are used. As troops cannot see each other clearly in battle, flags and banners are used.'[86]

18. Now gongs and drums, banners and flags are used to focus the attention of the troops. When the troops can be thus united, the brave cannot advance alone, nor can the cowardly withdraw. This is the art of employing a host.

> *Tu Mu*: . . . The Military Law states: 'Those who when they should advance do not do so and those who when they should retire do not do so are beheaded.'
>
> When Wu Ch'i fought against Ch'in, there was an officer who before battle was joined was unable to control his ardour. He advanced and took a pair of heads and returned. Wu Ch'i ordered him beheaded.
>
> The Army Commissioner admonished him, saying: 'This is a talented officer; you should not behead him.' Wu Ch'i replied: 'I am confident he is an officer of talent, but he is disobedient.'
>
> Thereupon he beheaded him.

19. In night fighting use many torches and drums, in day fighting many banners and flags in order to influence the sight and hearing of our troops.[87]

> *Tu Mu*: . . . Just as large formations include smaller ones, so large camps include smaller ones. The army of the van, rear, right and left has each its own camp. These form a circle round the headquarters of the commander-in-chief in the centre. All the camps encompass the headquarters. The several corners are hooked together so that the camp appears like the *Pi Lei* constellation.[88]
>
> The distance between camps is not greater than one hundred paces or less than fifty. The roads and paths join to enable troops to parade. The fortifications face each other so that each can assist the others with bows and crossbows.
>
> At every crossroad a small fort is built; on top firewood is piled; inside there are concealed tunnels. One climbs up to these by ladders; sentries are stationed there. After darkness, if a sentry hears drumbeats on the four sides of the camp he sets off the beacon fire. Therefore if the enemy attacks at night he may get in at the gates, but everywhere there are small camps, each firmly defended, and to the east, west, north or south he does not know which to attack.
>
> In the camp of the commander-in-chief or in the smaller camps, those who first know the enemy has come allow them all to enter; they then beat the drums and all the camps respond. At all the small forts beacon fires are lit, making it as light as day. Whereupon the officers and troops close the gates of the camps and man the fortifications and look down upon the enemy. Strong crossbows and powerful bows shoot in all directions . . .
>
> Our only worry is that the enemy will not attack at night, for if he does he is certain to be defeated.

20. Now an army may be robbed of its spirit and its commander deprived of his courage.[89]

> *Ho Yen-hsi*: . . . Wu Ch'i said: 'The responsibility for a martial host of a million lies in one man. He is the trigger of its spirit.'

Mei Yao-ch'en: . . . If an army has been deprived of its morale, its general will also lose his heart.

Chang Yü: Heart is that by which the general masters. Now order and confusion, bravery and cowardice, are qualities dominated by the heart. Therefore the expert at controlling his enemy frustrates him and then moves against him. He aggravates him to confuse him and harasses him to make him fearful. Thus he robs his enemy of his heart and of his ability to plan.

21. During the early morning spirits are keen, during the day they flag, and in the evening thoughts turn toward home.[90]

22. And therefore those skilled in war avoid the enemy when his spirit is keen and attack him when it is sluggish and his soldiers homesick. This is control of the moral factor.

23. In good order they await a disorderly enemy; in serenity, a clamorous one. This is control of the mental factor.

Tu Mu: In serenity and firmness they are not destroyed by events.

Ho Yen-hsi: For the lone general who with subtlety must control a host of a million against an enemy as fierce as tigers, advantages and disadvantages are intermixed. In the face of countless changes he must be wise and flexible; he must bear in mind all possibilities. Unless he is stout of heart and his judgement not confused, how would he be able to respond to circumstances without coming to his wits' end? And how settle affairs without being bewildered? When unexpectedly confronted with grave difficulties, how could he not be alarmed? How could he control the myriad matters without being confused?

24. Close to the field of battle, they await an enemy coming from afar; at rest, an exhausted enemy; with well-fed troops, hungry ones. This is control of the physical factor.

25. They do not engage an enemy advancing with well-ordered banners nor one whose formations are in impressive array. This is control of the factor of changing circumstances.[91]

26. Therefore, the art of employing troops is that when the enemy occupies high ground, do not confront him; with his back resting on hills, do no oppose him.

27. When he pretends to flee, do not pursue.

28. Do not attack his *élite* troops.

29. Do not gobble proferred baits.

Mei Yao-ch'en: The fish which covets bait is caught; troops who covet bait are defeated.

Chang Yü: The 'Three Strategies' says: 'Under fragrant bait there is certain to be a hooked fish.'

30. Do not thwart an enemy returning homewards.

31. To a surrounded enemy you must leave a way of escape.

Tu Mu: Show him there is a road to safety, and so create in his mind the idea that there is an alternative to death. Then strike.

Ho Yen-hsi: When Ts'ao Ts'ao surrounded Hu Kuan he issued an order: 'When the city is taken, the defenders will be buried.' For month after month it did not fall. Ts'ao Jen said:

'When a city is surrounded it is essential to show the besieged that there is a way to survival. Now, Sir, as you have told them they must fight to the death everyone will fight to save his own skin. The city is strong and has a plentiful supply of food. If we attack them many officers and men will be wounded. If we persevere in this it will take many days. To encamp under the walls of a strong city and attack rebels determined to fight to the death is not a good plan!' Ts'ao Ts'ao followed this advice, and the city submitted.

32. Do not press an enemy at bay.

Tu Yu: Prince Fu Ch'ai said: 'Wild beasts, when at bay, fight desperately. How much more is this true of men! If they know there is no alternative they will fight to the death.'

During the reign of Emperor Hsüan of the Han, Chao Ch'ung-kuo was suppressing a revolt of the Ch'iang tribe. The Ch'iang tribesmen saw his large army, discarded their heavy baggage, and set out to ford the Yellow River. The road was through narrow defiles, and Ch'ung Kuo drove them along in a leisurely manner.

Someone said: 'We are in pursuit of great advantage but proceed slowly.'

Ch'ung-kuo replied: 'They are desperate. I cannot press them. If I do this easily they will go without even looking around. If I press them they will turn on us and fight to the death.'

All the generals said: 'Wonderful!'

33. This is the method of employing troops.

Notes

1 The title means 'reckoning', 'plans', or 'calculations'. In the Seven Military Classics edition the title is 'Preliminary Calculations'. The subject first discussed is the process we define as an Estimate (or Appreciation) of the Situation.
2 Or 'for [the field of battle] is the place of life and death [and war] the road to survival or ruin'.
3 Sun Hsing-yen follows the *Tung T'ien* here and drops the character *shih* (事): 'matters', 'factors', or 'affairs'. Without it the verse does not make much sense.
4 Here *Tao* (道) is translated 'moral influence'. It is usually rendered as 'The Way', or 'The Right Way'. Here it refers to the morality of government; specifically to that of the sovereign. If the sovereign governs justly, benevolently, and righteously, he follows the Right Path or the Right Way, and thus exerts a superior degree of moral influence. The character *fa* (法), here rendered 'doctrine', has as a primary meaning 'law' or 'method'. In the title of the work it is translated 'Art'. But in v. 8 Sun Tzu makes it clear that here he is talking about what we call doctrine.
5 There are precise terms in Chinese which cannot be uniformly rendered by our word 'attack'. Chang Yü here uses a phrase which literally means 'to chastise criminals', an expression applied to attack of rebels. Other characters have such precise meanings as 'to attack by stealth', 'to attack suddenly', 'to suppress the rebellious', 'to reduce to submission', &c.
6 Or 'Moral influence is that which causes the people to be in accord with their superiors. . . .' Ts'ao Ts'ao says the people are guided in the right way (of conduct) by 'instructing' them.
7 It is clear that the character *t'ien* (天) (Heaven) is used in this verse in the sense of 'weather', as it is today.
8 'Knowing the ground of life and death . . .' is here rendered 'If he knows where he will give battle'.
9 In this and the following two verses the seven elements referred to in v. 2 are named.
10 Emending *i* (以) to *i* (巳). The commentators do not agree on an interpretation of this verse.
11 The Hsiung Nu were nomads who caused the Chinese trouble for centuries. The Great Wall was constructed to protect China from their incursions.
12 Mo Tun, or T'ou Ma or T'ouman, was the first leader to unite the Hsiung Nu. The thousand-*li*

horse was a stallion reputedly able to travel a thousand *li* (about three hundred miles) without grass or water. The term indicates a horse of exceptional quality, undoubtedly reserved for breeding.

13 Meng T'ien subdued the border nomads during the Ch'in, and began the construction of the Great Wall. It is said that he invented the writing-brush. This is probably not correct, but he may have improved the existing brush in some way.

14 This refers to agricultural military colonies in remote areas in which soldiers and their families were settled. A portion of the time was spent cultivating the land, the remainder in drilling, training, and fighting when necessary. The Russians used this policy in colonizing Siberia. And it is in effect now in Chinese borderlands.

15 During the period known as 'The Three Kingdoms', Wei in the north and west, Shu in the south-west, and Wu in the Yangtze valley contested for empire.

16 K'uei Chou is in Ssu Ch'uan.

17 This campaign was conducted *c.* A.D. 255.

18 A confusing verse difficult to render into English. In the preliminary calculations some sort of counting devices were used. The operative character represents such a device, possibly a primitive abacus. We do not know how the various 'factors' and 'elements' named were weighted, but obviously the process of comparison of relative strengths was a rational one. It appears also that two separate calculations were made, the first on a national level, the second on a strategic level. In the former the five basic elements named in v. 3 were compared; we may suppose that if the results of this were favourable the military experts compared strengths, training, equity in administering rewards and punishments, and so on (the seven factors).

19 The ratio of combat to administrative troops was thus 3:1.

20 Gold money was coined in Ch'u as early as 400 B.C., but actually Sun Tzu does not use the term 'gold'. He uses a term which meant 'metallic currency'.

21 I insert the character *kuei* (貴) following the 'Seven Martial Classics'. In the context the character has the sense of 'what is valued' or 'what is prized'.

22 The commentators indulge in lengthy discussions as to the number of provisionings. This version reads 'they do not require three'. That is, they require only two, i.e. one when they depart and the second when they return. In the meanwhile they live on the enemy. The TPYL version (following Ts'ao Ts'ao) reads: 'they do not require to be *again* provisioned', that is during a campaign. I adopt this.

23 This comment appears under V. 10 but seems more appropriate here.

24 Or, 'close to [where] the army [is]', (i.e. in the zone of operations) 'buying is expensive; when buying is expensive . . .'. The 'urgent [or 'heavy'] exactions' refers to special taxes, forced contributions of animals and grain, and porterage.

25 This comment, which appears under the previous verse, has been transposed.

26 Here Sun Tzu uses the specific character for 'crossbow'.

27 This seems out of place.

28 This siege took place in 279 B.C.

29 They ate a pre-cooked meal in order to avoid building fires to prepare breakfast?

30 Ho Yen-hsi probably wrote this about A.D. 1050.

31 Not, as Giles translates, 'to balk the enemy's plans'.

32 This took place during the first century A.D.

33 Not, as Giles translates, 'to prevent the junction of the enemy's forces'.

34 In this series of verses Sun Tzu is not discussing the art of generalship as Giles apparently thought. These are objectives or policies—*cheng* (政)—in order of relative merit.

35 Exchange of gifts and compliments was a normal preliminary to battle.

36 *Yao* (妖) connotes the supernatural. The Boxers, who believed themselves impervious to foreign lead, could be so described.

37 Some commentators think this verse 'means to divide one's own force', but that seems a less satisfactory interpretation, as the character *chih* (之) used in the two previous verses refers to the enemy.

38 Tu Mu and Chang Yü both counsel 'temporary' withdrawl, thus emphasizing the point that offensive action is to be resumed when circumstances are propitious.

39 Lit. 'the strength of a small force is . . .'. This apparently refers to its weapons and equipment.

40 CC II (Mencius), i, ch. 7.

41 Here I have transposed the characters meaning 'ruler' and 'army', otherwise the verse would read that there are three ways in which an army can bring misfortune upon the sovereign.

42 Lit. 'Not knowing [or 'not understanding' or 'ignorant of'] [where] authority [lies] in the army'; or 'ignorant of [matters relating to exercise of] military authority . . .'. The operative character is 'authority' or 'power'.

43 The 'Army Supervisors' of the T'ang were in fact political commissars. Pei Tu became Prime Minister in A.D. 815 and in 817 requested the throne to recall the supervisor assigned him, who must have been interfering in army operations.

44 'Feudal Lords' is rendered 'neighbouring rulers'. The commentators agree that a confused army robs itself of victory.

45 CC II (Mencius), ii, ch. I, p. 85.

46 A paraphrase of an ode which Legge renders:

> They are like one taking counsel with wayfarers
>   about building a house
> Which consequently will never come to completion.
>   (CC IV, ii, p. 332, Ode I.)

47 The character *hsing* (形) means 'shape', 'form', or 'appearance' or in a more restricted sense, 'disposition' or 'formation'. The Martial Classics edition apparently followed Ts'ao Ts'ao and titled the chapter *Chun Hsing* (軍 形;). 'Shape [or 'Dispositions'] of the Army'. As will appear, the character connotes more than mere physical dispositions.

48 'Invincibility is [means] defence; the ability to conquer is [means] attack.'

49 The concept that Heaven and Earth each consist of 'layers' or 'stages' is an ancient one.

50 Han Hsin placed his army in 'death ground'. He burned his boats and smashed his cooking pots. The river was at the rear, the Chao army to the front. Han Hsin had to conquer or drown.

51 To win a hard-fought battle or to win one by luck is no mark of skill.

52 The enemy was conquered easily because the experts previously had created appropriate conditions.

53 This comment appears in the text after V. 18. The factors enumerated are qualities of 'shape'.

54 *Shih* (執), the title of this chapter, means 'force', influence', 'authority', 'energy'. The commentators take it to mean 'energy' or 'potential' in some contexts and 'situation' in others.

55 *Fen Shu* (分 數) is literally 'division of [or by] numbers' (or 'division and numbering'). Here translated 'organization'.

56 Suggestive that the 'pair' and the 'trio' carried different weapons.

57 A ten-man section; one hundred to the company; two hundred to the battalion; four hundred to the regiment; eight hundred to the group; sixteen hundred to the brigade; thirty-two hundred to the army. This apparently reflects organization at the time Chang Yü was writing. The English terms for the units are arbitrary.

58 The concept expressed by *cheng* (正), 'normal' (or 'direct') and *ch'i* (奇), 'extraordinary' (or 'indirect') is of basic importance. The normal (*cheng*) force fixes or distracts the enemy; the extraordinary (*ch'i*) forces act when and where their blows are not anticipated. Should the enemy perceive and respond to a *ch'i* manœuvre in such a manner as to neutralize it, the manœuvre would automatically become *cheng*.

59 Sun Tzu uses the characters *chiang* (江) and *ho* (河), which I have rendered 'the great rivers'.

60 Or regulation of its distance from the prey.

61 Following Tu Mu.

62 Here again the specific character meaning 'crossbow' is used.

63 Sun Tzu's onomatopoetic terms suggest the noise and confusion of battle.

64 Following Tu Mu.

65 The text reads: 'Thus he is able to select men . . .'. That is, men capable of exploiting any situation. A system of selection not based on nepotism or favouritism is the inference.

66 Ts'ao Ts'ao took care to keep the political officer out of the picture!

67 This story provides the plot for a popular Chinese opera. Chu-ko Liang sat in a gate tower and played his lute while the porters swept and sprinkled the streets and Ssu-ma I's host hovered on the outskirts. Ssu-ma I had been fooled before by Chu-ko Liang and would be fooled again.

68 Lit. 'one part of his'.

69 Karlgren GS 1120m for 'dire straits'.

70 Lit. 'if there is no place he does not make preparations there is no place he is not vulnerable'. The double negative makes the meaning emphatically positive.

71 Tu Mu tells the following interesting story to illustrate the point:

Emperor Wu of the Sung sent Chu Ling-shih to attack Ch'iao Tsung in Shu. The Emperor Wu said: 'Last year Liu Ching-hsuan went out of the territory inside the river heading for Huang Wu. He achieved nothing and returned. The rebels now think that I should come from outside the river but surmise that I will take them unaware by coming from inside the river. If this is the case they are certain to defend Fu Ch'eng with heavy troops and guard the interior roads. If I go to Huang Wu, I will fall directly into their trap. Now, I will move the main body outside the river and take Ch'eng Tu, and use distracting troops towards the inside of the river. This is a wonderful plan for controlling the enemy.'

Yet he was worried that his plan would be known and that the rebels would learn where he was weak and where strong. So he handed a completely sealed letter to Ling Shih. On the envelope he wrote 'Open when you reach Pai Ti'. At this time the army did not know how it was to be divided or from where it would march.

When Ling Shih reached Pai Ti, he opened the letter which read: 'The main body of the army will march together from outside the river to take Ch'eng Tu. Tsang Hsi and Chu Lin from the central river road will take Kuang Han. Send the weak troops embarked in more than ten high boats from within the river toward Huang Wu.'

Chiao Tsung actually used heavy troops to defend within the river and Ling Shih exterminated him.

72 These references to Wu and Yüeh are held by some critics to indicate the date of composition of the text. This point is discussed in the Introduction.

73 Lit. 'the field of life and death'.

74 Lit. 'struggle' or 'contest of the armies' as each strives to gain an advantageous position.

75 This verse can be translated as I have, following Li Ch'uan and Chia Lin, or 'He encamps the army so that the Gates of Harmony confront one another' following Ts'ao Ts'ao and Tu Mu. After assembling the army the first task of a commander would be to organize it, or to 'harmonize' its diverse elements.

76 This comment appears under v. 2 in the text.

77 Giles based his reading on the TT and translated: 'Manœuvring with an army is advantageous; with an undisciplined multitude most dangerous.' Sun Hsing-yen also thought this was the meaning of the verse. This too literal translation completely misses the point. Ts'ao Ts'ao's interpretation is surely more satisfactory. The verse is a generalization which introduces what follows. A course of action which may appear advantageous usually contains within itself the seeds of disadvantage. The converse is also true.

78 By 'rolling up armour' Sun Tzu undoubtedly meant that heavy individual equipment would be bundled together and left at base.

79 This may also be rendered as 'The general of the Upper Army [as distinguished from the generals commanding the Central and Lower Armies] will be defeated' or 'will be checked'. Here the Upper Army would refer to the advance guard when the three divisions of the army marched in column. In other words; the advantages and disadvantages of forced marches must be carefully weighed, and the problem of what should be carried and what left in a secure base considered.

80 The verse which follows this one repeats a previous verse and is a *non sequitur* here. It has been dropped.

81 'Famous' because of their strategic significance.

82 Mao Tse Tung paraphrases this verse several times.

83 Adopted as his slogan by the Japanese warrior Takeda Shingen.

84 Yang P'ing-an emends and reads: 'Thus wherever your banners point, the enemy is divided.' There does not seem to be any justification for this change.

85 Rather than 'divide the profits' Yang P'ing-an reads: 'defend it to the best advantage'. The text does not substantiate this rendering.

86 This verse is interesting because in it Sun Tzu names a work which antedates his own.

87 Or 'the enemy', it is not clear which. Possibly both. Tu Mu's comment is not particularly relevant to the verse but is included because it indicates a remarkably high degree of skill in the science of castramentation.

88 Markal? *Pi* is Alpharatz.
89 Or 'of his wits', I am not sure which.
90 Mei Yao-ch'en says that 'morning', 'day', and 'evening' represent the phases of a long campaign.
91 Or the 'circumstantial factor'. 'They' in these verses refers to those skilled in war.

5   Strategy

The indirect approach

Basil Liddell Hart

Strategy has for its purpose the reduction of fighting to the slenderest possible proportions.

Aim of strategy

This statement may be disputed by those who conceive the destruction of the enemy's armed force as the only sound aim in war, who hold that the only goal of strategy is battle, and who are obsessed with the Clausewitzian saying that 'blood is the price of victory'. Yet if one should concede this point and meet its advocates on their own ground, the statement would remain unshaken. For even if a decisive battle be the goal, the aim of strategy must be to bring about this battle under the most advantageous circumstances. And the more advantageous the circumstances, the less, proportionately, will be the fighting.

The perfection of strategy would be, therefore, to produce a decision without any serious fighting. History, as we have seen, provides examples where strategy, helped by favourable conditions, has virtually produced such a result—among the examples being Caesar's Ilerda campaign, Cromwell's Preston campaign, Napoleon's Ulm campaign, Moltke's encirclement of MacMahon's army at Sedan in 1870, and Allenby's 1918 encirclement of the Turks in the hills of Samaria. The most striking and catastrophic of recent examples was the way that, in 1940, the Germans cut off and trapped the Allies' left wing in Belgium, following Guderian's surprise break-through in the centre at Sedan, and thereby ensured the general collapse of the Allied armies on the Continent.

While these were cases where the destruction of the enemy's armed forces was economically achieved through their disarming by surrender, such 'destruction' may not be essential for a decision, and for the fulfilment of the war-aim. In the case of a state that is seeking, not conquest, but the maintenance of its security, the aim is fulfilled if the threat be removed—if the enemy is led to abandon his purpose.

The defeat which Belisarius incurred at Sura through giving rein to his troops' desire for a 'decisive victory'—after the Persians had already given up their attempted invasion of Syria—was a clear example of unnecessary effort and risk. By contrast, the way that he defeated their more dangerous later invasion and cleared them out of Syria, is perhaps the most striking example on record of achieving a decision—in the real sense, of fulfilling the national object—by pure strategy. For in this case, the psychological action was so effective that the enemy surrendered his purpose without any physical action at all being required.

While such bloodless victories have been exceptional, their rarity enhances rather than detracts from their value—as an indication of latent potentialities, in strategy and grand strategy. Despite many centuries' experience of war, we have hardly begun to explore the field of psychological warfare.

From deep study of war, Clausewitz was led to the conclusion that—'All military action is permeated by intelligent forces and their effects.' Nevertheless, nations at war have always striven, or been driven by their passions, to disregard the implications of such a conclusion. Instead of applying intelligence, they have chosen to batter their heads against the nearest wall.

It rests normally with the government, responsible for the grand strategy of a war, to decide whether strategy should make its contribution by achieving a military decision or otherwise. Just as the military means is only one of the means to the end of grand strategy—one of the instruments in the surgeon's case—so battle is only one of the means to the end of strategy. If the conditions are suitable, it is usually the quickest in effect, but if the conditions are unfavourable it is folly to use it.

Let us assume that a strategist is empowered to seek a military decision. His responsibility is to seek it under the most advantageous circumstances in order to produce the most profitable result. Hence *his true aim is not so much to seek battle as to seek a strategic situation so advantageous that if it does not of itself produce the decision, its continuation by a battle is sure to achieve this.* In other words, dislocation is the aim of strategy; its sequel may be either the enemy's dissolution or his easier disruption in battle. Dissolution may involve some partial measure of fighting, but this has not the character of a battle.

Action of strategy

How is the strategic dislocation produced? In the physical, or 'logistical', sphere it is the result of a move which (*a*) upsets the enemy's dispositions and, by compelling a sudden 'change of front', dislocates the distribution and organization of his forces; (*b*) separates his forces; (*c*) endangers his supplies; (*d*) menaces the route or routes by which he could retreat in case of need and re-establish himself in his base or homeland.

A dislocation may be produced by one of these effects, but is more often the consequence of several. Differentiation, indeed, is difficult because a move directed towards the enemy's rear tends to combine these effects. Their respective influence, however, varies and has varied throughout history according to the size of armies and the complexity of their organization. With armies which 'live on the country', drawing their supplies locally by plunder or requisition, the line of communication has negligible importance. Even in a higher stage of military development, the smaller a force the less dependent it is on the line of communication for supplies. The larger an army, and the more complex its organization, the more prompt and serious in effect is a menace to its line of communication.

Where armies have not been so dependent, strategy has been correspondingly handicapped, and the tactical issue of battle has played a greater part. Nevertheless, even thus handicapped, able strategists have frequently gained a decisive advantage previous to battle by menacing the enemy's line of retreat, the equilibrium of his dispositions, or his local supplies.

To be effective, such a menace must usually be applied at a point closer, in time and space, to the enemy's army than a menace to his communications; and thus in early warfare it is often difficult to distinguish between the strategical and tactical manœuvre.

In the psychological sphere, dislocation is the result of the impression on the commander's mind of the physical effects which we have listed. The impression is strongly accentuated if his realization of his being at a disadvantage is *sudden*, and if he feels that he is unable to counter the enemy's move. *Psychological dislocation fundamentally springs from this sense of being trapped.*

This is the reason why it has most frequently followed a physical move on to the enemy's rear. An army, like a man, cannot properly defend its back from a blow without turning round to use its arms in the new direction. 'Turning' temporarily unbalances an army as it does a man, and with the former the period of instability is inevitably much longer. In consequence, the brain is much more sensitive to any menace to its back.

In contrast, to move directly on an opponent consolidates his balance, physical and psychological, and by consolidating it increases his resisting power. For in the case of an army it rolls the enemy back towards their reserves, supplies, and reinforcements, so that as the original front is driven back and worn thin, new layers are added to the back. At the most, it imposes a strain rather than producing a shock.

Thus a move round the enemy's front against his rear has the aim not only of avoiding resistance on its way but in its issue. In the profoundest sense, it takes the *line of least resistance*. The equivalent in the psychological sphere is the *line of least expectation*. They are the two faces of the same coin, and to appreciate this is to widen our understanding of strategy. For if we merely take what obviously appears the line of least resistance, its obviousness will appeal to the opponent also; and this line may no longer be that of least resistance.

In studying the physical aspect we must never lose sight of the psychological, and only when both are combined is the strategy truly an indirect approach, calculated to dislocate the opponent's balance.

The mere action of marching indirectly towards the enemy and on to the rear of his dispositions does not constitute a strategic indirect approach. Strategic art is not so simple. Such an approach may start by being indirect in relation to the enemy's front, but by the very directness of its progress towards his rear may allow him to change his dispositions, so that it soon becomes a direct approach to his new front.

Because of the risk that the enemy may achieve such a change of front, it is usually necessary for the dislocating move to be preceded by a move, or moves, which can best be defined by the term 'distract' in its literal sense of 'to draw asunder'. The purpose of this 'distraction' is to *deprive the enemy of his freedom of action*, and it should operate in both the physical and psychological spheres. In the physical, it should cause a distension of his forces or their diversion to unprofitable ends, so that they are too widely distributed, and too committed elsewhere, to have the power of interfering with one's own decisively intended move. In the psychological sphere, the same effect is sought by playing upon the fears of, and by deceiving, the opposing command. 'Stonewall' Jackson aptly expressed this in his stra-tegical motto—'Mystify, mislead, and surprise'. For to mystify and to mislead constitutes 'distraction', while surprise is the essential cause of 'dislocation'. It is through the 'distrac-tion' of the commander's mind that the distraction of his forces follows. The loss of his freedom of action is the sequel to the loss of his freedom of conception.

A more profound appreciation of how the psychological permeates and dominates the physical sphere has an indirect value. For it warns us of the fallacy and shallowness of attempting to analyse and theorize about strategy in terms of mathematics. To treat it quantitatively, as if the issue turned merely on a superior concentration of force at a selected place, is as faulty as to treat it geometrically: as a matter of lines and angles.

Even more remote from truth—because in practice it usually leads to a dead end—is the tendency of text-books to treat war as mainly a matter of concentrating superior force. In his celebrated definition of economy of force Foch termed this—'The art of pouring out *all* one's resources at a given moment on one spot; of making use there of *all* troops, and, to make such a thing possible, of making those troops permanently communicate with each other, instead of dividing them and attaching to each fraction some fixed and invariable function; its second part, a result having been attained, is the art of again so disposing the troops as to converge upon, and act against, a new single objective.'

It would have been more exact, and more lucid, to say that an army should always be so distributed that its parts can aid each other and combine to produce the maximum *possible* concentration of force at one place, while the minimum force *necessary* is used elsewhere to prepare the success of the concentration.

To concentrate *all* is an unrealizable ideal, and dangerous even as a hyperbole. Moreover, in practice the 'minimum necessary' may form a far larger proportion of the total than the 'maximum possible'. It would even be true to say that the larger the force that is effectively used for *distraction* of the enemy, the greater is the chance of the concentration succeeding in its aim. For otherwise it may strike an object too solid to be shattered.

Superior weight at the intended decisive point does not suffice unless that point cannot be reinforced *in time* by the opponent. It rarely suffices unless that point is not merely weaker numerically but has been weakened morally. Napoleon suffered some of his worst checks because he neglected this guarantee—and the need for distraction has grown with the delaying power of weapons.

6   Arms and influence

Thomas C. Schelling

The diplomacy of violence

The usual distinction between diplomacy and force is not merely in the instruments, words or bullets, but in the relation between adversaries—in the interplay of motives and the role of communication, understandings, compromise, and restraint. Diplomacy is bargaining; it seeks outcomes that, though not ideal for either party, are better for both than some of the alternatives. In diplomacy each party somewhat controls what the other wants, and can get more by compromise, exchange, or collaboration than by taking things in his own hands and ignoring the other's wishes. The bargaining can be polite or rude, entail threats as well as offers, assume a status quo or ignore all rights and privileges, and assume mistrust rather than trust. But whether polite or impolite, constructive or aggressive, respectful or vicious, whether it occurs among friends or antagonists and whether or not there is a basis for trust and goodwill, there must be some common interest, if only in the avoidance of mutual damage, and an awareness of the need to make the other party prefer an outcome acceptable to oneself.

With enough military force a country may not need to bargain. Some things a country wants it can take, and some things it has it can keep, by sheer strength, skill and ingenuity. It can do this *forcibly*, accommodating only to opposing strength, skill, and ingenuity and without trying to appeal to an enemy's wishes. Forcibly a country can repel and expel, penetrate and occupy, seize, exterminate, disarm and disable, confine, deny access, and directly frustrate intrusion or attack. It can, that is, if it has enough strength. "Enough" depends on how much an opponents has.

There is something else, though, that force can do. It is less military, less heroic, less impersonal, and less unilateral; it is uglier, and has received less attention in Western military strategy. In addition to seizing and holding, disarming and confining, penetrating and obstructing, and all that, military force can be used *to hurt*. In addition to taking and protecting things of value it can *destroy* value. In addition to weakening an enemy militarily it can cause an enemy plain suffering.

Pain and shock, loss and grief, privation and horror are always in some degree, sometimes in terrible degree, among the results of warfare; but in traditional military science they are incidental, they are not the object. If violence can be done incidentally, though, it can also be done purposely. The power to hurt can be counted among the most impressive attributes of military force.

Hurting, unlike forcible seizure or self-defense, is not unconcerned with the interest of others. It is measured in the suffering it can cause and the victims' motivation to avoid it. Forcible action will work against weeds or floods as well as against armies, but suffering requires a victim that can feel pain or has something to lose. To inflict suffering gains nothing and saves nothing directly; it can only make people behave to avoid it. The only purpose, unless sport or revenge, must be to influence somebody's behavior, to coerce his decision or choice. To be coercive, violence has to be anticipated. And it has to be avoidable by accommodation. The power to hurt is bargaining power. To exploit it is diplomacy—vicious diplomacy, but diplomacy.

The contrast of brute force with coercion

There is a difference between taking what you want and making someone give it to you, between fending off assault and making someone afraid to assault you, between holding what people are trying to take and making them afraid to take it, between losing what someone can forcibly take and giving it up to avoid risk or damage. It is the difference between defense and deterrence, between brute force and intimidation, between conquest and blackmail, between action and threats. It is the difference between the unilateral, "undiplomatic" recourse to strength, and coercive diplomacy based on the power to hurt.

The contrasts are several. The purely "military" or "undiplomatic" recourse to forcible action is concerned with enemy strength, not enemy interests; the coercive use of the power to hurt, though, is the very exploitation of enemy wants and fears. And brute strength is usually measured relative to enemy strength, the one directly opposing the other, while the power to hurt is typically not reduced by the enemy's power to hurt in return. Opposing strengths may cancel each other, pain and grief do not. The willingness to hurt, the credibility of a threat, and the ability to exploit the power to hurt will indeed depend on how much the adversary can hurt in return; but there is little or nothing about an adversary's pain or grief that directly reduces one's own. Two sides cannot both overcome each other with superior strength; they may both be able to hurt each other. With strength they can dispute objects of value; with sheer violence they can destroy them.

And brute force succeeds when it is used, whereas the power to hurt is most successful when held in reserve. It is the *threat* of damage, or of more damage to come, that can make someone yield or comply. It is *latent* violence that can influence someone's choice—violence that can still be withheld or inflicted, or that a victim believes can be withheld or inflicted. The threat of pain tries to structure someone's motives, while brute force tries to overcome his strength. Unhappily, the power to hurt is often communicated by some performance of it. Whether it is sheer terroristic violence to induce an irrational response, or cool premeditated violence to persuade somebody that you mean it and may do it again, it is not the pain and damage itself but its influence on somebody's behavior that matters. It is the expectation of *more* violence that gets the wanted behavior, if the power to hurt can get it at all.

To exploit a capacity for hurting and inflicting damage one needs to know what an adversary treasures and what scares him and one needs the adversary to understand what behavior of his will cause the violence to be inflicted and what will cause it to be withheld. The victim has to know what is wanted, and he may have to be assured of what is not wanted. The pain and suffering have to appear *contingent* on his behavior; it is not alone the threat that is effective—the threat of pain or loss if he fails to comply—but the corresponding assurance, possibly an implicit one, that he can avoid the pain or loss if he does comply. The prospect of certain death may stun him, but it gives him no choice.

Coercion by threat of damage also requires that our interests and our opponent's not be absolutely opposed. If his pain were our greatest delight and our satisfaction his greatest woe, we would just proceed to hurt and to frustrate each other. It is when his pain gives us little or no satisfaction compared with what he can do for us, and the action or inaction that satisfies us costs him less than the pain we can cause, that there is room for coercion. Coercion requires finding a bargain, arranging for him to be better off doing what we want—worse off not doing what we want—when he takes the threatened penalty into account.

It is this capacity for pure damage, pure violence, that is usually associated with the most vicious labor disputes, with racial disorders, with civil uprisings and their suppression, with racketeering. It is also the power to hurt rather than brute force that we use in dealing with criminals; we hurt them afterward, or threaten to, for their misdeeds rather than protect ourselves with cordons of electric wires, masonry walls, and armed guards. Jail, of course, can be either forcible restraint or threatened privation; if the object is to keep criminals out of mischief by confinement, success is measured by how many of them are gotten behind bars, but if the object is to *threaten* privation, success will be measured by how few have to be put behind bars and success then depends on the subject's understanding of the consequences. Pure damage is what a car threatens when it tries to hog the road or to keep its rightful share, or to go first through an intersection. A tank or a bulldozer can force its way regardless of others' wishes; the rest of us have to threaten damage, usually mutual damage, hoping the other driver values his car or his limbs enough to give way, hoping he sees us, and hoping he is in control of his own car. The threat of pure damage will not work against an unmanned vehicle.

This difference between coercion and brute force is as often in the intent as in the instrument. To hunt down Comanches and to exterminate them was brute force; to raid their villages to make them behave was coercive diplomacy, based on the power to hurt. The pain and loss to the Indians might have looked much the same one way as the other; the difference was one of purpose and effect. If Indians were killed because they were in the way, or somebody wanted their land, or the authorities despaired of making them behave and could not confine them and decided to exterminate them, that was pure unilateral force. If *some* Indians were killed to make *other* Indians behave, that was coercive violence—or intended to be, whether or not it was effective. The Germans at Verdun perceived themselves to be chewing up hundreds of thousands of French soldiers in a gruesome "meat-grinder." If the purpose was to eliminate a military obstacle—the French infantryman, viewed as a military "asset" rather than as a warm human being—the offensive at Verdun was a unilateral exercise of military force. If instead the object was to make the loss of young men—not of impersonal "effectives," but of sons, husbands, fathers, and the pride of French manhood—so anguishing as to be unendurable, to make surrender a welcome relief and to spoil the foretaste of an Allied victory, then it was an exercise in coercion, in applied violence, intended to offer relief upon accommodation. And of course, since any use of force tends to be brutal, thoughtless, vengeful, or plain obstinate, the motives themselves can be mixed and confused. The fact that heroism and brutality can be either coercive diplomacy or a contest in pure strength does not promise that the distinction will be made, and the strategies enlightened by the distinction, every time some vicious enterprise gets launched.

The contrast between brute force and coercion is illustrated by two alternative strategies attributed to Genghis Khan. Early in his career he pursued the war creed of the Mongols: the vanquished can never be the friends of the victors, their death is necessary for the victor's safety. This was the unilateral extermination of a menace or a liability. The turning point of his career, according to Lynn Montross, came later when he discovered how to use his power to hurt for diplomatic ends. "The great Khan, who was not inhibited by the usual mercies, conceived the plan of forcing captives—women, children, aged fathers, favorite sons—to march ahead of his army as the first potential victims of resistance."[1] Live captives have often proved more valuable than enemy dead; and the technique discovered by the Khan in his maturity remains contemporary. North Koreans and Chinese were reported to have quartered prisoners of war near strategic targets to inhibit bombing attacks by United Nations aircraft. Hostages represent the power to hurt in its purest form.

Coercive violence in warfare

This distinction between the power to hurt and the power to seize or hold forcibly is important in modern war, both big war and little war, hypothetical war and real war. For many years the Greeks and the Turks on Cyprus could hurt each other indefinitely but neither could quite take or hold forcibly what they wanted or protect themselves from violence by physical means. The Jews in Palestine could not expel the British in the late 1940s but they could cause pain and fear and frustration through terrorism, and eventually influence somebody's decision. The brutal war in Algeria was more a contest in pure violence than in military strength; the question was who would first find the pain and degradation unendurable. The French troops preferred—indeed they continually tried—to make it a contest of strength, to pit military force against the nationalists' capacity for terror, to exterminate or disable the nationalists and to screen off the nationalists from the victims of their violence. But because in civil war terrorists commonly have access to victims by sheer physical propinquity, the victims and their properties could not be forcibly defended and in the end the French troops themselves resorted, unsuccessfully, to a war of pain.

Nobody believes that the Russians can take Hawaii from us, or New York, or Chicago, but nobody doubts that they might destroy people and buildings in Hawaii, Chicago, or New York. Whether the Russians can conquer West Germany in any meaningful sense is questionable; whether they can hurt it terribly is not doubted. That the United States can destroy a large part of Russia is universally taken for granted; that the United States can keep from being badly hurt, even devastated, in return, or can keep Western Europe from being devastated while itself destroying Russia, is at best arguable; and it is virtually out of the question that we could conquer Russia territorially and use its economic assets unless it were by threatening disaster and inducing compliance. It is the power to hurt, not military strength in the traditional sense, that inheres in our most impressive military capabilities at the present time. We have a Department of *Defense* but emphasize *retaliation*—"to return evil for evil" (synonyms: requital, reprisal, revenge, vengeance, retribution). And it is pain and violence, not force in the traditional sense, that inheres also in some of the least impressive military capabilities of the present time—the plastic bomb, the terrorist's bullet, the burnt crops, and the tortured farmer.

War appears to be, or threatens to be, not so much a contest of strength as one of endurance, nerve, obstinacy, and pain. It appears to be, and threatens to be, not so much a contest of military strength as a bargaining process—dirty, extortionate, and often quite reluctant bargaining on one side or both—nevertheless a bargaining process.

The difference cannot quite be expressed as one between the *use* of force and the *threat* of force. The actions involved in forcible accomplishment, on the one hand, and in fulfilling a threat, on the other, can be quite different. Sometimes the most effective direct action inflicts enough cost or pain on the enemy to serve as a threat, sometimes not. The United States threatens the Soviet Union with virtual destruction of its society in the event of a surprise attack on the United States; a hundred million deaths are awesome as pure damage, but they are useless in stopping the Soviet attack—especially if the threat is to do it all afterward anyway. So it is worth while to keep the concepts distinct—to distinguish forcible action from the threat of pain—recognizing that some actions serve as both a means of forcible accomplishment and a means of inflicting pure damage, some do not. Hostages tend to entail almost pure pain and damage, as do all forms of reprisal after the fact. Some modes of self-defense may exact so little in blood or treasure as to entail negligible violence; and some forcible actions entail so much violence that their threat can be effective by itself.

The power to hurt, though it can usually accomplish nothing directly, is potentially more versatile than a straightforward capacity for forcible accomplishment. By force alone we cannot even lead a horse to water—we have to drag him—much less make him drink. Any affirmative action, any collaboration, almost anything but physical exclusion, expulsion, or extermination, requires that an opponent or a victim *do* something, even if only to stop or get out. The threat of pain and damage may make him want to do it, and anything he can do is potentially susceptible to inducement. Brute force can only accomplish what requires no collaboration. The principle is illustrated by a technique of unarmed combat: one can disable a man by various stunning, fracturing, or killing blows, but to take him to jail one has to exploit the man's own efforts. "Come-along" holds are those that threaten pain or disablement, giving relief as long as the victim complies, giving him the option of using his own legs to get to jail.

We have to keep in mind, though, that what is pure pain, or the threat of it, at one level of decision can be equivalent to brute force at another level. Churchill was worried, during the early bombing raids on London in 1940, that Londoners might panic. Against people the bombs were pure violence, to induce their undisciplined evasion; to Churchill and the government, the bombs were a cause of inefficiency, whether they spoiled transport and made people late to work or scared people and made them afraid to work. Churchill's decisions were not going to be coerced by the fear of a few casualties. Similarly on the battlefield: tactics that frighten soldiers so that they run, duck their heads, or lay down their arms and surrender represent coercion based on the power to hurt; to the top command, which is frustrated but not coerced, such tactics are part of the contest in military discipline and strength.

The fact that violence—pure pain and damage—can be used or threatened to coerce and to deter, to intimidate and to blackmail, to demoralize and to paralyze, in a conscious process of dirty bargaining, does not by any means imply that violence is not often wanton and meaningless or, even when purposive, in danger of getting out of hand. Ancient wars were often quite "total" for the loser, the men being put to death, the women sold as slaves, the boys castrated, the cattle slaughtered, and the buildings leveled, for the sake of revenge, justice, personal gain, or merely custom. If an enemy bombs a city, by design or by carelessness, we usually bomb his if we can. In the excitement and fatigue of warfare, revenge is one of the few satisfactions that can be savored; and justice can often be construed to demand the enemy's punishment, even if it is delivered with more enthusiasm than justice requires. When Jerusalem fell to the Crusaders in 1099 the ensuing slaughter was one of the bloodiest in military chronicles. "The men of the West literally waded in gore, their march to the church of the Holy Sepulcher being gruesomely likened to 'treading out the wine press' . . .," reports Montross (p. 138), who observes that these excesses usually came at the climax of the capture of a fortified post or city. "For long the assailants have endured more punishment than they were able to inflict; then once the walls are breached, pent-up emotions find an outlet in murder, rape and plunder, which discipline is powerless to prevent." The same occurred when Tyre fell to Alexander after a painful siege, and the phenomenon was not unknown on Pacific islands in the Second World War. Pure violence, like fire, can be harnessed to a purpose; that does not mean that behind every holocaust is a shrewd intention successfully fulfilled.

But if the occurrence of violence does not always bespeak a shrewd purpose, the absence of pain and destruction is no sign that violence was idle. Violence is most purposive and most successful when it is threatened and not used. Successful threats are those that do not have to be carried out. By European standards, Denmark was virtually unharmed in the Second World War; it was violence that made the Danes submit. Withheld violence—successfully threatened violence—can look clean, even merciful. The fact that a kidnap victim is returned unharmed, against receipt of ample ransom, does not make kidnapping a nonviolent enterprise. The American victory at Mexico City in 1847 was a great success; with a minimum of brutality we traded a capital city for everything we wanted from the war. We did not even have to say what we could do to Mexico City to make the Mexican government understand what they had at stake. (They had undoubtedly got the message a month earlier, when Vera Cruz was being pounded into submission. After forty-eight hours of shellfire, the foreign consuls in that city approached General Scott's headquarters to ask for a truce so that women, children, and neutrals could evacuate the city. General Scott, "counting on such internal pressure to help bring about the city's surrender," refused their request and added that anyone, soldier or noncombatant, who attempted to leave the city would be fired upon.)[2]

Whether spoken or not, the threat is usually there. In earlier eras the etiquette was more permissive. When the Persians wanted to induce some Ionian cities to surrender and join them, without having to fight them, they instructed their ambassadors to

> make your proposals to them and promise that, if they abandon their allies, there will be no disagreeable consequences for them; we will not set fire to their houses or temples, or threaten them with any greater harshness than before this trouble occurred. If, however, they refuse, and insist upon fighting, then you must resort to threats, and say exactly what we will do to them; tell them, that is, that when they are beaten they will be sold as slaves, their boys will be made cunuchs, their girls carried off to Bactria, and their land confiscated.[3]

It sounds like Hitler talking to Schuschnigg. "I only need to give an order, and overnight all the ridiculous scarecrows on the frontier will vanish . . . Then you will really experience something. . . . After the troops will follow the S.A. and the Legion. No one will be able to hinder the vengeance, not even myself."

Or Henry V before the gates of Harfleur:

> We may as bootless spend our vain command
> Upon the enraged soldiers in their spoil
> As send precepts to the leviathan
> To come ashore. Therefore, you men of Harfleur,
> Take pity of your town and of your people,
> Whiles yet my soldiers are in my command;
> Whiles yet the cool and temperate wind of grace
> O'erblows the filthy and contagious clouds
> Of heady murder, spoil and villainy.
> If not, why, in a moment look to see
> The blind and bloody soldier with foul hand

Defile the locks of your shrill-shrieking daughters;
Your fathers taken by the silver beard,
And their most reverent heads dash'd to the walls,
Your naked infants spitted upon pikes,
Whiles the mad mothers with their howls confused
Do break the clouds . . .
What say you? will you yield, and this avoid,
Or, guilty in defence, be thus destroy'd?

(Act III, Scene iii)

Pure violence, nonmilitary violence, appears most conspicuously in relations between unequal countries, where there is no substantial military challenge and the outcome of military engagement is not in question. Hitler could make his threats contemptuously and brutally against Austria; he could make them, if he wished, in a more refined way against Denmark. It is noteworthy that it was Hitler, not his generals, who used this kind of language; proud military establishments do not like to think of themselves as extortionists. Their favorite job is to deliver victory, to dispose of opposing military force and to leave most of the civilian violence to politics and diplomacy. But if there is no room for doubt how a contest in strength will come out, it may be possible to bypass the military stage altogether and to proceed at once to the coercive bargaining.

A typical confrontation of unequal forces occurs at the *end* of a war, between victor and vanquished. Where Austria was vulnerable before a shot was fired, France was vulnerable after its military shield had collapsed in 1940. Surrender negotiations are the place where the threat of civil violence can come to the fore. Surrender negotiations are often so one-sided, or the potential violence so unmistakable, that bargaining succeeds and the violence remains in reserve. But the fact that most of the actual damage was done during the military stage of the war, prior to victory and defeat, does not mean that violence was idle in the aftermath, only that it was latent and the threat of it successful.

Indeed, victory is often but a prerequisite to the exploitation of the power to hurt. When Xenophon was fighting in Asia Minor under Persian leadership, it took military strength to disperse enemy soldiers and occupy their lands; but land was not what the victor wanted, nor was victory for its own sake.

Next day the Persian leader burned the villages to the ground, not leaving a single house standing, so as to strike terror into the other tribes to show them what would happen if they did not give in. . . . He sent some of the prisoners into the hills and told them to say that if the inhabitants did not come down and settle in their houses to submit to him, he would burn up their villages too and destroy their crops, and they would die of hunger.[4]

Military victory was but the *price of admission*. The payoff depended upon the successful threat of violence.

Like the Persian leader, the Russians crushed Budapest in 1956 and cowed Poland and other neighboring countries. There was a lag of ten years between military victory and this show of violence, but the principle was the one explained by Xenophon. Military victory is often the prelude to violence, not the end of it, and the fact that successful violence is usually held in reserve should not deceive us about the role it plays.

What about pure violence during war itself, the infliction of pain and suffering as a military technique? Is the threat of pain involved only in the political use of victory, or is it a decisive technique of war itself?

Evidently between unequal powers it has been part of warfare. Colonial conquest has often been a matter of "punitive expeditions" rather than genuine military engagements. If the tribesmen escape into the bush you can burn their villages without them until they assent to receive what, in strikingly modern language, used to be known as the Queen's "protection." British air power was used punitively against Arabian tribesmen in the 1920s and 30s to coerce them into submission.[5]

If enemy forces are not strong enough to oppose, or are unwilling to engage, there is no need to achieve victory as a prerequisite to getting on with a display of coercive violence. When Caesar was pacifying the tribes of Gaul he sometimes had to fight his way through their armed men in order to subdue them with a display of punitive violence, but sometimes he was virtually unopposed and could proceed straight to the punitive display. To his legions there was more valor in fighting their way to the seat of power; but, as governor of Gaul, Caesar could view enemy troops only as an obstacle to his political control, and that control was usually based on the power to inflict pain, grief, and privation. In fact, he preferred to keep several hundred hostages from the unreliable tribes, so that his threat of violence did not even depend on an expedition into the countryside.

Pure hurting, as a military tactic, appeared in some of the military actions against the plains Indians. In 1868, during the war with the Cheyennes, General Sheridan decided that his best hope was to attack the Indians in their winter camps. His reasoning was that the Indians could maraud as they pleased during the seasons when their ponies could subsist on grass, and in winter hide away in remote places. "To disabuse their minds from the idea that they were secure from punishment, and to strike at a period when they were helpless to move their stock and villages, a winter campaign was projected against the large bands hiding away in the Indian territory."[6]

These were not military engagements; they were punitive attacks on people. They were an effort to subdue by the use of violence, without a futile attempt to draw the enemy's military forces into decisive battle. They were "massive retaliation" on a diminutive scale, with local effects not unlike those of Hiroshima. The Indians themselves totally lacked organization and discipline, and typically could not afford enough ammunition for target practice and were no military match for the cavalry; their own rudimentary strategy was at best one of harassment and reprisal. Half a century of Indian fighting in the West left us a legacy of cavalry tactics; but it is hard to find a serious treatise on American strategy against the Indians or Indian strategy against the whites. The twentieth is not the first century in which "retaliation" has been part of our strategy, but it is the first in which we have systematically recognized it.

Hurting, as a strategy, showed up in the American Civil War, but as an episode, not as the central strategy. For the most part, the Civil War was a military engagement with each side's military force pitted against the other's. The Confederate forces hoped to lay waste enough Union territory to negotiate their independence, but hadn't enough capacity for such violence to make it work. The Union forces were intent on military victory, and it was mainly General Sherman's march through Georgia that showed a conscious and articulate use of violence. "If the people raise a howl against my barbarity and cruelty, I will answer that war is war . . . If they want peace, they and their relatives must stop the war," Sherman wrote. And one of his associates said, "Sherman is perfectly right . . . The only possible way to end this unhappy and dreadful conflict . . . is to make it terrible beyond endurance."[7]

Making it "terrible beyond endurance" is what we associate with Algeria and Palestine, the crushing of Budapest and the tribal warfare in Central Africa. But in the great wars of the last hundred years it was usually military victory, not the hurting of the people, that was decisive; General Sherman's attempt to make war hell for the Southern people did not come to epitomize military strategy for the century to follow. To seek out and to destroy the enemy's military force, to achieve a crushing victory over enemy armies, was still the avowed purpose and the central aim of American strategy in both world wars. Military action was seen as an *alternative* to bargaining, not a *process* of bargaining.

The reason is not that civilized countries are so averse to hurting people that they prefer "purely military" wars. (Nor were all of the participants in these wars entirely civilized.) The reason is apparently that the technology and geography of warfare, at least for a war between anything like equal powers during the century ending in World War II, kept coercive violence from being decisive before military victory was achieved. Blockade indeed was aimed at the whole enemy nation, not concentrated on its military forces; the German civilians who died of influenza in the First World War were victims of violence directed at the whole country. It has never been quite clear whether blockade—of the South in the Civil War or of the Central Powers in both world wars, or submarine warfare against Britain— was expected to make war unendurable for the people or just to weaken the enemy forces by denying economic support. Both arguments were made, but there was no need to be clear about the purpose as long as either purpose was regarded as legitimate and either might be served. "Strategic bombing" of enemy homelands was also occasionally rationalized in terms of the pain and privation it could inflict on people and the civil damage it could do to the nation, as an effort to display either to the population or to the enemy leadership that surrender was better than persistence in view of the damage that could be done. It was also rationalized in more "military" terms, as a way of selectively denying war material to the troops or as a way of generally weakening the economy on which the military effort rested.[8]

But as terrorism—as violence intended to coerce the enemy rather than to weaken him militarily—blockade and strategic bombing by themselves were not quite up to the job in either world war in Europe. (They might have been sufficient in the war with Japan after straightforward military action had brought American aircraft into range.) Airplanes could not quite make punitive, coercive violence decisive in Europe, at least on a tolerable time schedule, and preclude the need to defeat or to destroy enemy forces as long as they had nothing but conventional explosives and incendiaries to carry. Hitler's V-1 buzz bomb and his V-2 rocket are fairly pure cases of weapons whose purpose was to intimidate, to hurt Britain itself rather than Allied military forces. What the V-2 needed was a punitive payload worth carrying, and the Germans did not have it. Some of the expectations in the 1920s and the 1930s that another major war would be one of pure civilian violence, of shock and terror from the skies, were not borne out by the available technology. The threat of punitive violence kept occupied countries quiescent; but the wars were won in Europe on the basis of brute strength and skill and not by intimidation, not by the threat of civilian violence but by the application of military force. Military victory was still the price of admission. Latent violence against people was reserved for the politics of surrender and occupation.

The great exception was the two atomic bombs on Japanese cities. These were weapons of terror and shock. They hurt, and promised more hurt, and that was their purpose. The few "small" weapons we had were undoubtedly of some direct military value, but their enormous advantage was in pure violence. In a military sense the United States could gain a little by destruction of two Japanese industrial cities; in a civilian sense, the Japanese could lose much. The bomb that hit Hiroshima was a threat aimed at all of Japan. The political target of the bomb was not the dead of Hiroshima or the factories they worked in, but the survivors in Tokyo. The two bombs were in the tradition of Sheridan against the Comanches and Sherman in Georgia. Whether in the end those two bombs saved lives or wasted them, Japanese lives or American lives; whether punitive coercive violence is uglier than straight-forward military force or more civilized; whether terror is more or less humane than military destruction; we can at least perceive that the bombs on Hiroshima and Nagasaki represented violence against the country itself and not mainly an attack on Japan's material strength. The effect of the bombs, and their purpose, were not mainly the military destruction they accomplished but the pain and the shock and the promise of more.

The nuclear contribution to terror and violence

Man has, it is said, for the first time in history enough military power to eliminate his species from the earth, weapons against which there is no conceivable defense. War has become, it is said, so destructive and terrible that it ceases to be an instrument of national power. "For the first time in human history," says Max Lerner in a book whose title, *The Age of Overkill*, conveys the point, "men have bottled up a power . . . which they have thus far not dared to use."[9] And Soviet military authorities, whose party dislikes having to accommodate an entire theory of history to a single technological event, have had to reexamine a set of principles that had been given the embarrassing name of "permanently operating factors" in warfare. Indeed, our era is epitomized by words like "the first time in human history," and by the abdication of what was "permanent."

For dramatic impact these statements are splendid. Some of them display a tendency, not at all necessary, to belittle the catastrophe of earlier wars. They may exaggerate the historical novelty of deterrence and the balance of terror.[10] More important, they do not help to identify just what is new about war when so much destructive energy can be packed in warheads at a price that permits advanced countries to have them in large numbers. Nuclear warheads are incomparably more devastating than anything packaged before. What does that imply about war?

It is not true that for the first time in history man has the capability to destroy a large fraction, even the major part, of the human race. Japan was defenseless by August 1945. With a combination of bombing and blockade, eventually invasion, and if necessary the deliberate spread of disease, the United States could probably have exterminated the population of the Japanese islands without nuclear weapons. It would have been a gruesome, expensive, and mortifying campaign; it would have taken time and demanded persistence. But we had the economic and technical capacity to do it; and, together with the Russians or without them, we could have done the same in many populous parts of the world. Against defenseless people there is not much that nuclear weapons can do that cannot be done with an ice pick. And it would not have strained our Gross National Product to do it with ice picks.

It is a grisly thing to talk about. We did not do it and it is not imaginable that we would have done it. We had no reason; if we had had a reason, we would not have the persistence of purpose, once the fury of war had been dissipated in victory and we had taken on the task of executioner. If we and our enemies might do such a thing to each other now, and to others as well, it is not because nuclear weapons have for the first time made it feasible.

Nuclear weapons can do it quickly. That makes a difference. When the Crusaders breached the walls of Jerusalem they sacked the city while the mood was on them. They burned things that they might, with time to reflect, have carried away instead and raped women that, with time to think about it, they might have married instead. To compress a catastrophic war within the span of time that a man can stay awake drastically changes the politics of war, the process of decision, the possibility of central control and restraint, the motivations of people in charge, and the capacity to think and reflect while war is in progress. It *is* imaginable that we might destroy 200,000,000 Russians in a war of the present, though not 80,000,000 Japanese in a war of the past. It is not only imaginable, it is imagined. It is imaginable because it could be done "in a moment, in the twinkling of an eye, at the last trumpet."

This may be why there is so little discussion of how an all-out war might be brought to a close. People do not expect it to be "brought" to a close, but just to come to an end when everything has been spent. It is also why the idea of "limited war" has become so explicit in recent years. Earlier wars, like World Wars I and II or the Franco-Prussian War, were limited by *termination*, by an ending that occurred before the period of greatest potential violence, by negotiation that brought the *threat* of pain and privation to bear but often precluded the massive *exercise* of civilian violence. With nuclear weapons available, the restraint of violence cannot await the outcome of a contest of military strength; restraint, to occur at all, must occur during war itself.

This is a difference between nuclear weapons and bayonets. It is not in the number of people they can eventually kill but in the speed with which it can be done, in the centralization of decision, in the divorce of the war from political processes, and in computerized programs that threaten to take the war out of human hands once it begins.

That nuclear weapons make it *possible* to compress the fury of global war into a few hours does not mean that they make it *inevitable*. We have still to ask whether that is the way a major nuclear war would be fought, or ought to be fought. Nevertheless, that the whole war might go off like one big string of fire-crackers makes a critical difference between our conception of nuclear war and the world wars we have experienced.

There is no guarantee, of course, that a slower war would not persist. The First World War could have stopped at any time after the Battle of the Marne. There was plenty of time to think about war aims, to consult the long-range national interest, to reflect on costs and casualties already incurred and the prospect of more to come, and to discuss terms of cessation with the enemy. The gruesome business continued as mechanically as if it had been in the hands of computers (or worse: computers might have been programmed to learn more quickly from experience). One may even suppose it would have been a blessing had all the pain and shock of the four years been compressed within four days. Still, it was terminated. And the victors had no stomach for doing then with bayonets what nuclear weapons could do to the German people today.

There is another difference. In the past it has usually been the victors who could do what they pleased to the enemy. War has often been "total war" for the loser. With deadly monotony the Persians, Greeks, or Romans "put to death all men of military age, and sold the women and children into slavery," leaving the defeated territory nothing but its name until new settlers arrived sometime later. But the defeated could not do the same to their victors. The boys could be castrated and sold only after the war had been won, and only on the side that lost it. The power to hurt could be brought to bear only after military strength had achieved victory. The same sequence characterized the great wars of this century; for reasons of technology and geography, military force has usually had to penetrate, to exhaust, or to collapse opposing military force—to achieve military victory—before it could be brought to bear on the enemy nation itself. The Allies in World War I could not inflict coercive pain and suffering directly on the Germans in a decisive way until they could defeat the German army; and the Germans could not coerce the French people with bayonets unless they first beat the Allied troops that stood in their way. With two-dimensional warfare, there is a tendency for troops to confront each other, shielding their own lands while attempting to press into each other's. Small penetrations could not do major damage to the people; large penetrations were so destructive of military organization that they usually ended the military phase of the war.

Nuclear weapons make it possible to do monstrous violence to the enemy without first achieving victory. With nuclear weapons and today's means of delivery, one expects to penetrate an enemy homeland without first collapsing his military force. What nuclear weapons have done, or appear to do, is to promote this kind of warfare to first place. Nuclear weapons threaten to make war less military, and are responsible for the lowered status of "military victory" at the present time. *Victory is no longer a prerequisite for hurting the enemy.* And it is no assurance against being terribly hurt. One need not wait until he has won the war before inflicting "unendurable" damages on his enemy. One need not wait until he has lost the war. There was a time when the assurance of victory—false or genuine assurance—could make national leaders not just willing but sometimes enthusiastic about war. Not now.

Not only *can* nuclear weapons hurt the enemy before the war has been won, and perhaps hurt decisively enough to make the military engagement academic, but it is widely assumed that in a major war that is *all* they can do. Major war is often discussed as though it would be only a contest in national destruction. If this is indeed the case—if the destruction of cities and their populations has become, with nuclear weapons, the primary object in an all-out war—the sequence of war has been reversed. Instead of destroying enemy forces as a prelude to imposing one's will on the enemy nation, one would have to destroy the nation as a means or a prelude to destroying the enemy forces. If one cannot disable enemy forces without virtually destroying the country, the victor does not even have the option of sparing the conquered nation. He has already destroyed it. Even with blockade and strategic bombing it could be supposed that a country would be defeated before it was destroyed, or would elect surrender before annihilation had gone far. In the Civil War it could be hoped that the South would become too weak to fight before it became too weak to survive. For "all-out" war, nuclear weapons threaten to reverse this sequence.

So nuclear weapons do make a difference, marking an epoch in warfare. The difference is not just in the amount of destruction that can be accomplished but in the role of destruction and in the decision process. Nuclear weapons can change the speed of events, the control of events, the sequence of events, the relation of victor to vanquished, and the relation of homeland to fighting front. Deterrence rests today on the threat of pain and extinction, not just on the threat of military defeat. We may argue about the wisdom of announcing "unconditional surrender" as an aim in the last major war, but seem to expect "unconditional destruction" as a matter of course in another one.

Something like the same destruction always *could* be done. With nuclear weapons there is an expectation that it *would* be done. It is not "overkill" that is new; the American army surely had enough 30 caliber bullets to kill everybody in the world in 1945, or if it did not it could have bought them without any strain. What is new is plain "kill"—the idea that major war might be just a contest in the killing of countries, or not even a contest but just two parallel exercises in devastation.

That is the difference nuclear weapons make. At least they *may* make that difference. They also may not. If the weapons themselves are vulnerable to attack, or the machines that carry them, a successful surprise might eliminate the opponent's means of retribution. That an enormous explosion can be packaged in a single bomb does not by itself guarantee that the victor will receive deadly punishment. Two gunfighters facing each other in a Western town had an unquestioned capacity to kill one another; that did not guarantee that both would die in a gunfight—only the slower of the two. Less deadly weapons, permitting an injured one to shoot back before he died, might have been more conducive to a restraining balance of terror, or of caution. The very efficiency of nuclear weapons could make them ideal for starting war, if they can suddenly eliminate the enemy's capability to shoot back.

And there is a contrary possibility: that nuclear weapons are not vulnerable to attack and prove not to be terribly effective against each other, posing no need to shoot them quickly for fear they will be destroyed before they are launched, and with no task available but the systematic destruction of the enemy country and no necessary reason to do it fast rather than slowly. Imagine that nuclear destruction *had* to go slowly—that the bombs could be dropped only one per day. The prospect would look very different, something like the most terroristic guerilla warfare on a massive scale. It happens that nuclear war does not have to go slowly; but it may also not have to go speedily. The mere existence of nuclear weapons does not itself determine that everything must go off in a blinding flash, any more than that it must go slowly. Nuclear weapons do not simplify things quite that much.

In recent years there has been a new emphasis on distinguishing what nuclear weapons make possible and what they make inevitable in case of war. The American government began in 1961 to emphasize that even a major nuclear war might not, and need not, be a simple contest in destructive fury. Secretary McNamara gave a controversial speech in June 1962 on the idea that "deterrence" might operate even in war itself, that belligerents might, out of self-interest, attempt to limit the war's destructiveness. Each might feel the sheer destruction of enemy people and cities would serve no decisive military purpose but that a continued *threat* to destroy them might serve a purpose. The continued threat would depend on their not being destroyed yet. Each might reciprocate the other's restraint, as in limited wars of lesser scope. Even the worst of enemies, in the interest of reciprocity, have often not mutilated prisoners of war; and citizens might deserve comparable treatment. The fury of nuclear attacks might fall mainly on each other's weapons and military forces.

"The United States has come to the conclusion," said Secretary McNamara,

> that to the extent feasible, basic military strategy in a possible general war should be approached in much the same way that more conventional military operations have been regarded in the past. That is to say, principal military objectives . . . should be the destruction of the enemy's military forces, not of his civilian population . . . giving the possible opponent the strongest imaginable incentive to refrain from striking our own cities.[11]

This is a sensible way to think about war, if one has to think about it and of course one does. But whether the Secretary's "new strategy" was sensible or not, whether enemy populations should be held hostage or instantly destroyed, whether the primary targets should be military forces or just people and their source of livelihood, this is not "much the same way that more conventional military operations have been regarded in the past." This is utterly different, and the difference deserves emphasis.

In World Wars I and II one went to work on enemy military forces, not his people, because until the enemy's military forces had been taken care of there was typically not anything decisive that one could do to the enemy nation itself. The Germans did not, in World War I, refrain from bayoneting French citizens by the millions in the hope that the Allies would abstain from shooting up the German population. They could not get at the French citizens until they had breached the Allied lines. Hitler tried to terrorize London and did not make it. The Allied air forces took the war straight to Hitler's territory, with at least some thought of doing in Germany what Sherman recognized he was doing in Georgia; but with the bombing technology of World War II one could not afford to bypass the troops and go exclusively for enemy populations—not, anyway, in Germany. With nuclear weapons one has that alternative.

To concentrate on the enemy's military installations while deliberately holding in reserve a massive capacity for destroying his cities, for exterminating his people and eliminating his society, on condition that the enemy observe similar restraint with respect to one's own society, is not the "conventional approach." In World Wars I and II the first order of business was to destroy enemy armed forces because that was the only promising way to make him surrender. To fight a purely military engagement "all-out" while holding in reserve a decisive capacity for violence, on condition the enemy do likewise, is not the way military operations have traditionally been approached. Secretary McNamara was proposing a new approach to warfare in a new era, an era in which the power to hurt is more impressive than the power to oppose.

From battlefield warfare to the diplomacy of violence

Almost one hundred years before Secretary McNamara's speech, the Declaration of St. Petersburg (the first of the great modern conferences to cope with the evils of warfare) in 1868 asserted, "The only legitimate object which states should endeavor to accomplish during war is to weaken the military forces of the enemy." And in a letter to the League of Nations in 1920, the President of the International Committee of the Red Cross wrote; "The Committee considers it very desirable that war should resume its former character, that is to say, that it should be a struggle between armies and not between populations. The civilian population must, as far as possible, remain outside the struggle and its consequences."[12] His language is remarkably similar to Secretary McNamara's.

The International Committee was fated for disappointment, like everyone who labored in the late nineteenth century to devise rules that would make war more humane. When the Red Cross was founded in 1863, it was concerned about the disregard for noncombatants by those who made war; but in the Second World War noncombatants were deliberately chosen as targets by both Axis and Allied forces, not decisively but nevertheless deliberately. The trend has been the reverse of what the International Committee hoped for.

In the present era noncombatants appear to be not only deliberate targets but primary targets, or at least were so taken for granted until about the time of Secretary McNamara's speech. In fact, noncombatants appeared to be primary targets at both ends of the scale of warfare; thermonuclear war threatened to be a contest in the destruction of cities and populations; and, at the other end of the scale, insurgency is almost entirely terroristic. We live in an era of dirty war.

Why is this so? Is war properly a military affair among combatants, and is it a depravity peculiar to the twentieth century that we cannot keep it within decent bounds? Or is war inherently dirty, and was the Red Cross nostalgic for an artificial civilization in which war had become encrusted with etiquette—a situation to be welcomed but not expected?

To answer this question it is useful to distinguish three stages in the involvement of noncombatants—of plain people and their possessions—in the fury of war. These stages are worth distinguishing; but their sequence is merely descriptive of Western Europe during the past three hundred years, not a historical generalization. The first stage is that in which the people may get hurt by inconsiderate combatants. This is the status that people had during the period of "civilized warfare" that the International Committee had in mind.

From about 1648 to the Napoleonic era, war in much of Western Europe was something superimposed on society. It was a contest engaged in by monarchies for stakes that were measured in territories and, occasionally, money or dynastic claims. The troops were mostly mercenaries and the motivation for war was confined to the aristocratic elite. Monarchs fought for bits of territory, but the residents of disputed terrain were more concerned with protecting their crops and their daughters from marauding troops than with whom they owed allegiance to. They were, as Quincy Wright remarked in his classic *Study of War*, little concerned that the territory in which they lived had a new sovereign.[13] Furthermore, as far as the King of Prussia and the Emperor of Austria were concerned, the loyalty and enthusiasm of the Bohemian farmer were not decisive considerations. It is an exaggeration to refer to European war during this period as a sport of kings, but not a gross exaggeration. And the military logistics of those days confined military operations to a scale that did not require the enthusiasm of a multitude.

Hurting people was not a decisive instrument of warfare. Hurting people or destroying property only reduced the value of the things that were being fought over, to the disadvantage of both sides. Furthermore, the monarchs who conducted wars often did not want to discredit the social institutions they shared with their enemies. Bypassing an enemy monarch and taking the war straight to his people would have had revolutionary implications. Destroying the opposing monarchy was often not in the interest of either side; opposing sovereigns had much more in common with each other than with their own subjects, and to discredit the claims of a monarchy might have produced a disastrous backlash. It is not surprising—or, if it is surprising, not altogether astonishing—that on the European continent in that particular era war was fairly well confined to military activity.

One could still, in those days and in that part of the world, be concerned for the rights of noncombatants and hope to devise rules that both sides in the war might observe. The rules might well be observed because both sides had something to gain from preserving social order and not destroying the enemy. Rules might be a nuisance, but if they restricted both sides the disadvantages might cancel out.

This was changed during the Napoleonic wars. In Napoleon's France, people cared about the outcome. The nation was mobilized. The war was a national effort, not just an activity of the elite. It was both political and military genius on the part of Napoleon and his ministers that an entire nation could be mobilized for war. Propaganda became a tool of warfare, and war became vulgarized.

Many writers deplored this popularization of war, this involvement of the democratic masses. In fact, the horrors we attribute to thermonuclear war were already foreseen by many commentators, some before the First World War and more after it; but the new "weapon" to which these terrors were ascribed was people, millions of people, passionately engaged in national wars, spending themselves in a quest for total victory and desperate to avoid total defeat. Today we are impressed that a small number of highly trained pilots can carry enough energy to blast and burn tens of millions of people and the buildings they live in; two or three generations ago there was concern that tens of millions of people using bayonets and barbed wire, machine guns and shrapnel, could create the same kind of destruction and disorder.

That was the second stage in the relation of people to war, the second in Europe since the middle of the seventeenth century. In the first stage people had been neutral but their welfare might be disregarded; in the second stage people were involved because it was *their* war. Some fought, some produced materials of war, some produced food, and some took care of children; but they were all part of a war-making nation. When Hitler attacked Poland in 1939, the Poles had reason to care about the outcome. When Churchill said the British would fight on the beaches, he spoke for the British and not for a mercenary army. The war was about something that mattered. If people would rather fight a dirty war than lose a clean one, the war will be between nations and not just between governments. If people have an influence on whether the war is continued or on the terms of a truce, making the war hurt people serves a purpose. It is a dirty purpose, but war itself is often about something dirty. The Poles and the Norwegians, the Russians and the British, had reason to believe that if they lost the war the consequences would be dirty. This is so evident in modern civil wars—civil wars that involve popular feelings—that we expect them to be bloody and violent. To hope that they would be fought cleanly with no violence to people would be a little like hoping for a clean race riot.

There is another way to put it that helps to bring out the sequence of events. If a modern war were a clean one, the violence would not be ruled out but merely saved for the postwar period. Once the army has been defeated in the clean war, the victorious enemy can be as brutally coercive as he wishes. A clean war would determine which side gets to use its power to hurt coercively after victory, and it is likely to be worth some violence to avoid being the loser.

"Surrender" is the process following military hostilities in which the power to hurt is brought to bear. If surrender negotiations are successful and not followed by overt violence, it is because the capacity to inflict pain and damage was successfully used in the bargaining process. On the losing side, prospective pain and damage were averted by concessions; on the winning side, the capacity for inflicting further harm was traded for concessions. The same is true in a successful kidnapping. It only reminds us that the purpose of pure pain and damage is extortion; it is *latent* violence that can be used to advantage. A well-behaved occupied country is not one in which violence plays no part; it may be one in which latent violence is used so skillfully that it need not be spent in punishment.

This brings us to the third stage in the relation of civilian violence to warfare. If the pain and damage can be inflicted during war itself, they need not wait for the surrender negotiation that succeeds a military decision. If one can coerce people and their governments while war is going on, one does not need to wait until he has achieved victory or risk losing that coercive power by spending it all in a losing war. General Sherman's march through Georgia might have made as much sense, possibly more, had the North been losing the war, just as the German buzz bombs and V-2 rockets can be thought of as coercive instruments to get the war stopped before suffering military defeat.

In the present era, since at least the major East–West powers are capable of massive civilian violence during war itself beyond anything available during the Second World War, the occasion for restraint does not await the achievement of military victory or truce. The principal restraint during the Second World War was a temporal boundary, the date of surrender. In the present era we find the violence dramatically restrained during war itself. The Korean War was furiously "all-out" in the fighting, not only on the peninsular battlefield but in the resources used by both sides. It was "all-out," though, only within some dramatic restraints: no nuclear weapons, no Russians, no Chinese territory, no Japanese territory, no bombing of ships at sea or even airfields on the United Nations side of the line. It was a contest in military strength circumscribed by the threat of unprecedented civilian violence. Korea may or may not be a good model for speculation on limited war in the age of nuclear violence, but it was dramatic evidence that the capacity for violence can be consciously restrained even under the provocation of a war that measures its military dead in tens of thousands and that fully preoccupies two of the largest countries in the world.

A consequence of this third stage is that "victory" inadequately expresses what a nation wants from its military forces. Mostly it wants, in these times, the influence that resides in latent force. It wants the bargaining power that comes from its capacity to hurt, not just the direct consequence of successful military action. Even total victory over an enemy provides at best an opportunity for unopposed violence against the enemy population. How to use that opportunity in the national interest, or in some wider interest, can be just as important as the achievement of victory itself; but traditional military science does not tell us how to use that capacity for inflicting pain. And if a nation, victor or potential loser, is going to use its capacity for pure violence to influence the enemy, there may be no need to await the achievement of total victory.

Actually, this third stage can be analyzed into two quite different variants. In one, sheer pain and damage are primary instruments of coercive warfare and may actually be applied, to intimidate or to deter. In the other, pain and destruction *in* war are expected to serve little or no purpose but *prior threats* of sheer violence, even of automatic and uncontrolled violence, are coupled to military force. The difference is in the all-or-none character of deterrence and intimidation. Two acute dilemmas arise. One is the choice of making prospective violence as frightening as possible or hedging with some capacity for reciprocated restraint. The other is the choice of making retaliation as automatic as possible or keeping deliberate control over the fateful decisions. The choices are determined partly by governments, partly by technology. Both variants are characterized by the coercive role of pain and destruction—of threatened (not inflicted) pain and destruction. But in one the threat either succeeds or fails altogether, and any ensuing violence is gratuitous; in the other, progressive pain and damage may actually be used to threaten more. The present era, for countries possessing nuclear weapons, is a complex and uncertain blend of the two.

Coercive diplomacy, based on the power to hurt, was important even in those periods of history when military force was essentially the power to take and to hold, to fend off attack and to expel invaders, and to possess territory against opposition—that is, in the era in which military force tended to pit itself against opposing force. Even then, a critical question was how much cost and pain the other side would incur for the disputed territory. The judgment that the Mexicans would concede Texas, New Mexico, and California once Mexico City was a hostage in our hands was a diplomatic judgment, not a military one. If one could not readily take the particular territory he wanted or hold it against attack, he could take something else and trade it.[14] Judging what the enemy leaders would trade—be it a capital city or national survival—was a critical part of strategy even in the past. Now we are in an era in which the power to hurt—to inflict pain and shock and privation on a country itself, not just on its military forces—is commensurate with the power to take and to hold, perhaps more than commensurate, perhaps decisive, and it is even more necessary to think of warfare as a process of violent bargaining. This is not the first era in which live captives have been worth more than dead enemies, and the power to hurt has been a bargaining advantage; but it is the first in American experience when that kind of power has been a dominant part of military relations.

The power to hurt is nothing new in warfare, but for the United States modern technology has drastically enhanced the strategic importance of pure, unconstructive, unacquisitive pain and damage, whether used against us or in our own defense. This in turn enhances the importance of war and threats of war as techniques of influence, not of destruction; of coercion and deterrence, not of conquest and defense; of bargaining and intimidation.

Quincy Wright, in his *Study of War*, devoted a few pages (319–20) to the "nuisance value" of war, using the analogy of a bank robber with a bomb in his hand that would destroy bank and robber. Nuisance value made the threat of war, according to Wright, "an aid to the diplomacy of unscrupulous governments." Now we need a stronger term, and more pages, to do the subject justice, and need to recognize that even scrupulous governments often have little else to rely on militarily. It is extraordinary how many treatises on war and strategy have declined to recognize that the power to hurt has been, throughout history, a fundamental character of military force and fundamental to the diplomacy based on it.

War no longer looks like just a contest of strength. War and the brink of war are more a contest of nerve and risk-taking, of pain and endurance. Small wars embody the threat of a larger war; they are not just military engagements but "crisis diplomacy." The threat of war has always been somewhere underneath international diplomacy, but for Americans it is now much nearer the surface. Like the threat of a strike in industrial relations, the threat of divorce in a family dispute, or the threat of bolting the party at a political convention, the threat of violence continuously circumscribes international politics. Neither strength nor goodwill procures immunity.

Military strategy can no longer be thought of, as it could for some countries in some eras, as the science of military victory. It is now equally, if not more, the art of coercion, of intimidation and deterrence. The instruments of war are more punitive than acquisitive. Military strategy, whether we like it or not, has become the diplomacy of violence.

Notes

1   Lynn Montross, *War Through the Ages* (3d ed. New York, Harper. and Brothers, 1960), p. 146.
2   Otis A. Singletary, *The Mexican War* (Chicago, University of Chicago Press, 1960), pp. 75–76. In a similar episode the Gauls, defending the town of Alesia in 52 B.C., "decided to send out of the town those whom age or infirmity incapacitated for fighting. . . . They came up to the Roman fortifications and with tears besought the soldiers to take them as slaves and relieve their hunger. But Caesar posted guards on the ramparts with orders to refuse them admission." Caesar, *The Conquest of Gaul*, S. A. Handford, transl. (Baltimore, Penguin Books, 1951), p. 227.
3   Herodotus, *The Histories*, Aubrey de Selincourt, transl. (Baltimore, Penguin Books, 1954), p. 362.
4   Xenophon, *The Persian Expedition*, Rex Warner, transl. (Baltimore, Penguin Books, 1949), p. 272. "The 'rational' goal of the threat of violence," says H. L. Nieburg, "is an accommodation of interests, not the provocation of actual violence. Similarly the 'rational' goal of actual violence is demonstration of the will and capability of action, establishing a measure of the credibility of future threats, not the exhaustion of that capability in unlimited conflict." "Uses of Violence," *Journal of Conflict Resolution*, 7 (1963), 44.
5   A perceptive, thoughtful account of this tactic, and one that emphasizes its "diplomatic" character, is in the lecture of Air Chief Marshal Lord Portal, "Air Force Cooperation in Policing the Empire." "The law-breaking tribe must be given an alternative to being bombed and . . . be told in the clearest possible terms what that alternative is." And, "It would be the greatest mistake to believe that a victory which spares the lives and feelings of the losers need be any less permanent or salutary than one which inflicts heavy losses on the fighting men and results in a 'peace' dictated on a stricken field." *Journal of the Royal United Services Institution* (London, May 1937), pp. 343–58.
6   Paul I. Wellman, *Death on the Prairie* (New York, Macmillan, 1934), p. 82.
7   J.F.C. Fuller reproduces some of this correspondence and remarks, "For the nineteenth century this was a new conception, because it meant that the deciding factor in the war—the power to sue for peace—was transferred from government to people, and that peace-making was a product of revolution. This was to carry the principle of democracy to its ultimate stage. . . ." *The Conduct of War: 1789–1961* (New Brunswick, Rutgers University Press, 1961), pp. 107–12.
8   For a reexamination of strategic-bombing theory before and during World War II, in the light of nuclear-age concepts, see George H. Quester, *Deterrence before Hiroshima* (New York, John Wiley and

Sons, 1966). See also the first four chapters of Bernard Brodie, *Strategy in the Missile Age* (Princeton, Princeton University Press, 1959), pp. 3–146.
 9 New York, Simon and Schuster, 1962, p. 47.
10 Winston Churchill is often credited with the term, "balance of terror," and the following quotation succinctly expresses the familiar notion of nuclear mutual deterrence. This, though, is from a speech in Commons in November 1934. "The fact remains that when all is said and done as regards defensive methods, pending some new discovery the only direct measure of defense upon a great scale is the certainty of being able to inflict simultaneously upon the enemy as great damage as he can inflict upon ourselves. Do not let us undervalue the efficacy of this procedure. It may well prove in practice—I admit I cannot prove it in theory—capable of giving complete immunity. If two Powers show themselves equally capable of inflicting damage upon each other by some particular process of war, so that neither gains an advantage from its adoption and both suffer the most hideous reciprocal injuries, it is not only possible but it seems probable that neither will employ that means." A fascinating reexamination of concepts like deterrence, preemptive attack, counterforce and countercity warfare, retaliation, reprisal, and limited war, in the strategic literature of the air age from the turn of the century to the close of World War II, is in Quester's book, cited above.
11 Commencement Address, University of Michigan, June 16, 1962.
12 International Committee of the Red Cross, *Draft Rules for the Limitation of the Dangers Incurred by the Civilian Population in Time of War* (2nd ed. Geneva, 1958), pp. 144, 151.
13 Chicago, University of Chicago Press, 1942, p. 296.
14 Children, for example. The Athenian tyrant, Hippias, was besieged in the Acropolis by an army of Athenian exiles aided by Spartans; his position was strong and he had ample supplies of food and drink, and "but for an unexpected accident" says Herodotus, the besiegers would have persevered a while and then retired. But the children of the besieged were caught as they were being taken out of the country for their safety. "This disaster upset all their plans; in order to recover the children, they were forced to accept . . . terms, and agreed to leave Attica within five days." Herodotus, *The Histories*, p. 334. If children can be killed at long distance, by German buzz bombs or nuclear weapons, they do not need to be caught first. And if both can hurt each other's children the bargaining is more complex.

Part III

Instruments of war: land, sea, and air power

INTRODUCTION

The essays in Parts I and II discussed the nature and foundations of strategic thought; the essays in this section examine the problem of theorising about war in specific operational environments, on land, on the sea, and in the air.

In the first essay, Brian Holden-Reid of King's College London assesses the ideas of the British army officer J.F.C. Fuller (1878–1966). Fuller, an eccentric military thinker with an affinity for Social Darwinism and fascist politics, argued that mechanization had transformed warfare. In Fuller's vision, elaborated in a series of essays and lectures written in the 1920s and 1930s, massed formations of machines would roam the battlefield with great velocity and force, spreading panic and terror among opposing troops. No longer would commanders seek the destruction of the opponent's formations, Fuller predicted, but instead their demoralization and disintegration through the paralyzing effects generated by tanks. Holden-Reid's essay demonstrates the difficulty of predicting the course of future wars: as he points out, many of Fuller's predictions exaggerated the impact of mechanisation. Oddly for someone with a fascination for Darwin's theory of human evolution, Fuller failed to fully account for interactive responses to mechanization.

Fuller was of course not the first or the last theorist to fully understand the impact of a technological development on the battlefield. Before World War II, the works of Fuller and other tank pioneers were widely read and reproduced. Proponents of mechanization everywhere predicted that the next war would bear out the operational supremacy of armour. When the German army defeated France in six weeks in the summer of 1940, the optimistic predictions of the mechanization enthusiasts appeared to have been confirmed.

Next are chapters from *Some Principles of Maritime Strategy* (1911), the seminal work of the celebrated British naval historian and thinker Julian S. Corbett (1854–1922). Corbett rejected the idea that naval strategy was ultimately about fighting one big battle to destroy the opponent's fleet. According to Corbett, history had shown that it was not always possible or necessary to win a fleet action to achieve one's objectives at sea. The whole point of attaining "command of the sea," he argued, was to employ maritime strength in all its forms to influence outcomes on land. In the chapter reproduced here, Corbett, drawing primarily on Clausewitz, analyses the distinctions between offensive and defensive war, and limited and unlimited war. He argues that continental thinking about "limited war" is especially appropriate to maritime warfare, where large distances and great waters separate the combatants, so providing an effective check on the strength that each could mobilize against the other. By commanding the sea, Corbett maintained, the British could make as much or as little war as they liked, bringing to bear a decisive amount of strength at the decisive point; this was the island nation's great advantage over its continental rivals.

The next two selections are about air power. In the first, R.J. Overy of Exeter University traces the origins of nuclear age deterrence theory in pre-1939 thinking. Before World War II, it was widely assumed that the bomber was a war-winning weapon. Air enthusiasts such as the Italian theorist General Giulo Douhet argued that mass fleets of bombers could swiftly pound an enemy population into surrender, topple governments, and paralyze armies and sink fleets. Despite the limitations of 1930s aviation technology, fear of a "knock-out blow" from the air was a driving force behind the air arms races of that decade, as well as the development of early counter force and air defense strategies in Europe. Fear that Germany might open a war with a deadly bombing campaign against London or Paris in part drove the diplomacy of appeasement. It also shaped British and American rearmament strategies. The threat from Germany and Japan, Overy writes, "locked the Western states into an upward spiral of military commitment until a weapon so devastating and unthinkable could be found which would stop all aggressors, rational or irrational, opportunistic or ideologically motivated, from risking all-out war."

Although the massed bomber offensives of World War II certainly contributed to the Allied victory, only die-hard air power radicals argued that air power alone had been decisive, or could be decisive, short of all-out nuclear war. In the same way Corbett thought about the proper role of sea power in a general theory of war and strategy, air power had to be coordinated with other means to produce maximum strategic effects against the foe.

The capitulation of Serbian President Slobodan Milosevic on June 9, 1999 after a 78-day NATO bombing campaign, however, rekindled the debate about whether wars could be won from the air alone. In an essay that examines the realities of coercion in international politics, Daniel L. Byman and Matthew C. Waxman, both employees of RAND at the time of publication, argue that the idea that air power alone won the Kosovo war is fundamentally flawed. Those who have argued otherwise skew the debate to overstate the effects of bombing. The NATO bombing campaign was one important coercive tool in a dynamic competition between the alliance and the Serbian leadership. To the extent that we can know, Milosevic's concerns over the stability of his regime, the threat of a ground invasion, and his inability to hit back played the "largest" roles in his capitulation. "Air power played a critical role in all three of these," Byman and Waxman argue, "but in none of them did air power truly operate in isolation from other coercive instruments or pressures."

Study questions

1. Was Fuller's enthusiasm about mechanization an overreaction to the experience of World War I?
2. What does Corbett mean by "command of the sea"?
3. What does the 1999 NATO bombing campaign tell us about the role of air power in contemporary war?
4. What unique attributes do land, sea, and air forces possess?

Further reading

Biddle, Stephen, *Military Power: Explaining Victory and Defeat in Modern Battle* (Princetown, NJ: Princeton University Press, 2004).

Biddle, Tami Davis, "British and American Approaches to Strategic Bombing: Their Origins and Implementation in the World War II Combined Bomber Offensive," *The Journal of Strategic Studies* 18, 1, (1994), pp. 91–144.

Frieser, Karl-Heinz, *The Blitzkrieg Legend: The 1940 Campaign in the West* (Maryland: Naval Institute Press, 2005).

Harris, J.P., "The Myth of Blitzkrieg," *War in History* 2, 3 (1995), pp. 335–352.

May, Ernest R., *Strange Victory: Hitler's Conquest of France* (London: I. B. Tauris, 2000).

Mombauer, Annika, "War Plans and War Guilt: The Debate Surrounding the Schlieffen Plan," *The Journal of Strategic Studies* 28, 5 (2005), pp. 857–885.

Philpott, William, "The Strategic Ideas of Sir John French," *The Journal of Strategic Studies* (1989), pp. 458–478.

Sumida, Jon, "Alfred Thayer Mahan, Geopolitician," *The Journal of Strategic Studies* 22, 2/3, (1999), pp. 39–62.

Till, Geoffrey, "Julian Corbett: Ten Maritime Commandments," in A. Dorman *et al.* (eds), *The Changing Face of Maritime Power* (London: Macmillan, 1999), pp. 19–33.

Till, Geoffrey, *Seapower: A Guide for the Twenty-First Century* (London: Routledge, 2005).

Warden III, John A., *The Air Campaign* (Washington: Brassey's, 1991).

7   J.F.C. Fuller's theory of mechanized warfare

Brian Holden Reid

Although a steady stream of articles and lectures had flowed from J.F.C. Fuller's pen on the subject of mechanization after 1918, it was not until the late twenties that he began to organize his arguments in much more precise and satisfying terms.[1] His proposals were controversial, as much for the tactless and dogmatic manner of their presentation as for their content. This essay will not attempt to gauge either the extent or nature of Fuller's influence in the British or foreign armies, but will confine itself to a dissection of the ideas underpinning Fuller's vision of future warfare. It will focus on three questions. Firstly, the importance of discussing Fuller's theory within the context of his military philosophy. Secondly, the extent to which Fuller's thinking on mechanization differed from Liddell Hart's. This problem has been clouded by Liddell Hart's own contribution to the history of mechanization which has done so much to influence the judgment of other writers, usually to Fuller's detriment. Thirdly, how do Fuller's predictions stand up to evaluation in the light of the campaigns of the Second World War?

The increased attention that Fuller gave to the problem of mechanization was mainly due to the leisure afforded by a series of untaxing commands he held following his resignation from command of the Experimental Brigade at Tidworth in 1927, the first major attempt to work out the tactics of mechanized warfare in the field. Fuller was not given another opportunity to practice what he preached; he had to content himself with the theory. In 1928 he was GSO 1 to 2nd Division at Catterick; in 1929 he commanded a brigade at Wiesbaden, and in 1930 he was placed on half-pay with the rank of Major-General.[2] Fuller's reputation at this stage in his career was a mixed one. Many soldiers acknowledged his brilliance. Many also thought him an unreliable crank. Fuller 'is damned silly', declared Major-General Sir Ernest Swinton in 1929, 'and has a sort of buffoon reputation'.[3] Conservative officers were only irritated by Fuller's arrogance and his extravagant language. General Montgomery-Massingberd felt that Fuller had 'an inordinate opinion of himself and his knowledge of war . . .'[4] Fuller's growing estrangement from the high command led him to concentrate in his writings on shaping the attitudes of junior officers. It was with this in mind that he published in 1928 a volume of essays entitled *On Future Warfare*. Two years later he gave his officers at Wiesbaden a series of lectures on the *Field Service Regulations*, explaining how changes in weapon technology would influence tactics. These were published in 1931 as *Lectures on FSR II*. Fuller also believed that there was room for a similar volume 'dealing with the speculative tactics of all new arms in all the circumstances in which we are likely to use them . . . Hitherto weapons have always been ahead of tactics and the result has been a gross lack of economy of force.'[5] This study developed into Fuller's seminal contribution to military thought, *Lectures on FSR III*. Like the earlier volume it began life as a series of lectures; undelivered, they were published in 1933.

The theory of mechanized warfare expounded in these books can be seen as the logical culmination of Fuller's sophisticated military philosophy, of which there is space here for only a cursory sketch. The foundation stone for all Fuller's thinking was what he termed the law of military development. An extension in part of Darwin's theory of evolution, it asserted that armies must adapt themselves to changes in their environment to remain fit for war. Weapons change because civilization changes. Thus, 'As the present age is largely a mechanical one, so will the armies of this age take on a similar complexion because military organization follows civil organization'. With this law as his basis, Fuller deduced that the impact of weapons on war was twofold as fighting was the product of will and instinct: 'the one urges man to close with his enemy and to destroy him, the other urges man to keep away so that he himself will not be destroyed'.[6] The basis of all weapon development, then, was a simple one, the sword and the shield, the offensive and the defensive. The basis of all generalship was audacity tempered by caution. Defence, therefore, 'is as closely related to offence as is the left arm to the right arm of a boxer'.[7] Fuller judged this intimate relationship between the offensive and the defensive to be the constant tactical factor.

> Every improvement in weapon-power (unconscious though it may be) has aimed at lessening the terror and danger on one side by increasing them on the other; consequently every improvement in weapons has eventually been met by a counter-improvement which has rendered the improvement obsolete; the evolutionary pendulum of weapon-power, slowly or rapidly, swinging from the offensive to the protective and back again in harmony with the speed of civil progress; each swing in a measurable degree eliminating danger.[8]

Within the context of these theories it is important to define closely Fuller's approach to war. Here his position has been distorted by the tendency of writers to link him closely with Liddell Hart—often rightly. However, because of the greater familiarity of most writers with Liddell Hart's work, it is assumed—often wrongly—that they shared the same assumptions and interests. In one important regard this was not so. What is so little appreciated is that it was the fighting and winning of battles and the means of achieving decisive victory that dominated Fuller's approach to war; Liddell Hart sought in his writings to find all possible means of avoiding battles.[9] Hence it was grand tactics, battlefield planning, and not field strategy, the manoeuvres that preface battle, that formed in Fuller's opinion, the truly vital sector of military activity. Fuller had comparatively little to say on field strategy, not because he lacked breadth of vision, far from it, but because he considered strategy to be a pragmatic science based on a number of immutable principles. Once these had been defined there was little more to add.[10]

Fuller believed that the decisive battle along Napoleonic lines would return as the supreme military act because of profound changes he detected in the nature and scope of war. Amid the muddle and slaughter of the First World War he detected that demoralization rather than destruction was gradually becoming the most important form of war. This would reinstate *quality*, and not quantity, as the norm in future warfare. Speed and decisiveness would return and the mass armies of the First World War would be banished from the battlefield.

> Hordes of infantry cannot face tanks and gas attacks; hordes of infantry are dependent on railways and immense supply depots; these are very vulnerable to air attack; consequently we may conclude that cavalry, infantry and artillery, as we know them today, have entered the stage of obsolescence.[11]

Consequently, generals would attempt to paralyse their opponents chiefly by manoeuvring against one another's supply lines; once an opponent was completely confused a crippling *coup de grâce* could be delivered. Fuller defined grand tactics 'as the organization and distribution of the fighting forces themselves in order to accomplish the grand strategical plan, or idea. The grand strategical object is the destruction of the enemy's policy, and whilst politically the decisive point is the will of the hostile nation, grand tactically it is the will of the enemy's commander'. He concluded, 'grand tactics is concerned more with disorganization and demoralization than with actual destruction which is the object of minor tactics'.[12] The tank was only one weapon whose effect was morally rather than physically destructive.

> It clearly showed that terror and demoralization and not destruction as the true aim of armed forces . . . [Because of] the power of aircraft to strike at the civil will, the power of mechanized forces to strike at the military will, and the power of motorized guerillas to spread dismay and confusion—we may predict that the power to effect physical destruction . . . will gradually and increasingly be replaced by attempts to demoralize the will of the enemy in its several forms . . .[13]

This new kind of warfare would be 'refined'—in the long run less brutal and far less destructive. Although Fuller's theory had tactical as well as strategical implications, in this essay it will be referred to as the doctrine of Strategic Paralysis.

Thus mechanization would usher in the 'greatest revolution that has ever taken place in the history of land warfare, a revolution as astounding in its effects as the introduction of firearms.'[14] Because tanks, like ships, enabled a gun to be fired from a moving platform, mechanized warfare would adapt naval to land tactics. Velocity was Fuller's watchword. 'The offensive cannot be too strong in reserves,' he insisted, 'therefore the defensive should not employ a weapon beyond the minimum necessary to establish security.'[15] As campaigns would be conducted at lightning speed and conclude with a dramatic clash of arms, more emphasis, in Fuller's opinion, should be placed on the pursuit. In 1922 Fuller told Liddell Hart that it was the pursuit, and not the attack, which gave decisive victory. He used the examples of the battles of Ligny and Jena to prove his point. 'The Prussians were dislodged at the first but were not destroyed, at the second they were dislodged, destruction being effected by cavalry.'[16] Fuller clearly realized that decisive pursuits had been the exception rather than the rule in the past, but he was also convinced that the tank, because it was so much more efficient than the horse, would be able to deliver crushing strokes. However, 'If tanks were allotted to infantry they will never be in hand for the pursuit.' In 1928 Fuller emphasised again that in battle it was vital to

> strike a crushing blow first . . . [because] we not only gain a physical victory but a moral victory over every man behind this force . . . Pursuit does not necessarily mean waiting until an infantry battle has been fought. If we are mobile soldiers let us get the infantryman out of our heads and pursue whenever we can.[17]

A close study of Fuller's writings on mechanization reveals, with some reservations, that he drew a remarkably accurate picture of the nature of future warfare, as it developed until 1941. Thereafter his predictions are less reliable. Several qualifications must be made to this statement, however. Firstly, Fuller believed that mechanized operations would occur 'in highly populated and developed areas'.[18] Yet it was in areas that were not industrialized—the Western Desert and the rolling plains of Soviet Russia—where the naval idea found some expression. Secondly, in the campaigns in Western Europe where armoured forces achieved spectacular successes, these were gained between forces that were indifferently mechanized. As Liddell Hart put it, the Wehrmacht in May 1940 'was only a few degrees more advanced than its opponents'.[19] Fuller had assumed that decisive success could be secured over opponents equally matched in mechanized sophistication. Fuller also believed, because of the expense involved in equipping mechanized armies, that they would remain small—a great mistake. He underestimated the capacity of major industrialized powers like the United States and the Soviet Union to equip mechanized armies on a massive scale. He therefore sanguinely supposed that speed would remain a constant protective factor. But defensive weapons developed on a par with offensive weapons. In 1943 Fuller conceded, 'I overestimated the protective power of speed and underestimated the likelihood of a general thickening of armour to neutralize a rise in the calibre of tank and anti-tank guns.'[20] The enormous size of future mechanized armies and the growing power of the defensive cancelled out the initial advantages held by the tank.

Nevertheless in the first two years of the Second World War Fuller was correct in emphasising that speed and demoralization was the key to victory. He rightly suggested that armoured formations would advance 'immediately before the declaration of war, or simultaneously with it'.[21] They would rush forward to seize the most favourable ground for battle and establish 'a protective fulcrum upon which to move an offensive lever'; this lever would strike a paralysing blow, whereupon the enemy would be boxed up and forced to surrender. On the battlefield, Fuller contended that the decisive point was the enemy's rear. In order to strike at this

> it is necessary not only to circumvent the enemy's front but to fix it, that is to immobilize it. Once this operation is accomplished and the enemy's army is pinned to his position, the next step is to circumvent this fixed front and by a rapid movement strike at the enemy's vitals in rear of it. Should this be accomplished, then this front will crumble to pieces.[22]

Discounting Fuller's overestimation of the power of speed, this is a remarkably clairvoyant sketch of German *blitzkrieg* methods. He was wrong, however, in exaggerating the extent of the thrust and parry that might take place before the decisive encounter.[23] The German victories were achieved rapidly because their opponents were in no position to manoeuvre—even against the relatively small German armoured forces.

Fuller was also correct in thinking that the speed of mechanized warfare would make arduous demands on commanders in the field. He argued that future warfare 'will require a general of high initiative . . . [who] will be with his fighting troops, he will be *in* the battle and not outside of it'.[24] This portends the day of what may be described as 'tank buccaneers' like Guderian and Rommel. The latter agreed with Fuller that mechanized warfare was akin to naval, and declared: 'no admiral ever won a battle from a shore base'.[25] Fuller stressed that 'to economize time in action will become the soul of every plan'. All schemes would have to be flexible to take advantage of the unexpected, striving to develop the 'highest possible initiative without loss of control . . .' The commanding general should place himself at the point of greatest importance. Fuller perhaps exorcised the ghost of Hugh Elles at the Battle of Cambrai when he declared that a commander should lead his troops into action, for such a drastic measure is unnecessary.[26] Nevertheless the qualities most needed by a general were quick intelligence, balance and decisiveness, particularly the latter because the 'fog of war' would remain just as dense in mechanized warfare.[27]

Tinged with exaggeration perhaps, yet these comments are a correct prediction of the influence of mechanization on generalship. Fuller's ideal of a commander, Rommel, in the opinion of Ronald Lewin, 'gives the impression of a commander whose mind is fresh and uninhibited, experimental and untrammelled by precedent'. He worked closely with his troops and was perhaps too fond of involving himself in minor tactical operations. He 'saw everything' in the words of von Mellenthin.[28] Sir Richard O'Connor, victor of Beda Fomm, was a general of a similar bent.[29] There can be little doubt that Rommel's closely knit command system conveyed great advantages when improvising sudden and unexpected attacks. A comparison of the relative closeness to the front lines of British HQs during Operations 'Battleaxe', 'Crusader' and the Battle of Gazala is instructive. General Beresford-Peirse was 60 miles, Cunningham 80 miles, and Ritchie 60 miles behind the line respectively.[30] Montgomery learnt from the failure of his predecessors in this regard and pushed his HQ further up to the front and insisted that subordinate officers be well forward; he also formed a group of liaison officers who ensured that his subordinates were acquainted with his wishes. General Patton later used a similar system, sending forward special patrols equipped with radios who reported directly to him.[31]

The least realistic part of Fuller's doctrine of strategic paralysis was that dealing with motorized guerillas. He defined them closely, explaining, 'I do not mean a partisan, but a uniformed soldier in a motor-car; he may or may not be a regular, but he is a soldier of some sort . . .'[32] Motorized guerillas would 'search the area of advance, picket bridges and tactical points, block roads, etc . . . fight off the enemy's swarm of motorized guerillas and so clear the area of advance'.[33] No such force appeared during the Second World War.[34] It was true, as Fuller was quick to point out in 1942, that the German advance through France and the Low Countries had been preceded by swarms of motorcyclists. This is straining the analogy. These troops certainly created panic and uncertainty, but they did not use civilian motor-cars, nor were they employed in an irregular way—crucial differences.[35] As Fuller admitted, motorized guerillas were restricted to road movement, thus 'swarming' would be impossible and they would be vulnerable not only to air attack but to small arms fire, because unarmoured vehicles can just as easily be incapacitated by rifle fire as horses.[36] If used by either side in the French campaign of 1940, motorized guerillas would only have succeeded in clogging already congested roads.

Furthermore, the continuing resistance of Britain in 1940 against the German onslaught must surely call into question the validity of strategic paralysis when employed against a determined opponent. When considering Fuller's doctrine in 1928, a reviewer thought that while 'it may have had an excellent chance when it was first thought out (for the campaign of 1919), it is not equally convincing today.'[37] There is some merit in this criticism, and Fuller was himself to realize this in 1943 when he admitted that his belief that demoralization rather than destruction would become the aim of warfare was an 'overstatement'.[38] Although the Germans waged a successful 'war of nerves' during the period 1939–41, it proved effective mainly against ill-organized countries whose morale was vulnerable before the crushing *coup de grâce* was delivered. Even so, Fuller's predictions concerning the beginnings of strategic bombing were correct. He cautioned his readers not to expect decisive air operations at the beginning of the next war, at least between the great powers, because of the importance they will attach in any 'war of nerves' to gaining the support of neutral opinion. Fuller doubted whether a belligerent 'will risk bombing its enemy's industrial cities for fear of being branded an international criminal'. Strategic bombing attacks, therefore, would not begin 'until excuses can be found to justify them'. Such was indeed the case during the Battle of Britain when both sides were convinced that the other had begun the bombing.

Fuller concluded that the strength of the civil will was intimately linked with the progress of its armies in the field; thus it could be more effectively attacked by defeating them decisively in the field and not by the indirect methods of aerial attack.[39]

On the battlefield Fuller had an acute grasp of the potential of strategic paralysis, but he exaggerated the moral effect an attack on the opposing commander's mind would have. Moreover he underestimated the steadiness of infantry. The limitations of strategic paralysis are evident during Operation 'Crusader', Auchinleck's reconquest of Cyrenaica 1941–2. This example is an important one as conditions in the Western Desert most closely accord with those set out in *Lectures on FSR III*. The most important lesson of this campaign was that, even in battles between small armies, speed alone was insufficient to achieve victory. Fuller was prone to assume that the tank would be a deadly weapon because infantry would instantly panic on its appearance. Here he was relying too heavily upon his experience in the First World War. The vision of another break-through like that secured at the Battle of Cambrai in 1917 never quite left him. Infantry were much steadier than he imagined. During Rommel's counter-attack in Cyrenaica, at the Battle of Tottensonntag, 23 November 1941, General Cruwell launched the 15th Panzer Division in 'cavalry' style waves against the unsupported infantry of the 5th South African Brigade. He drove the South Africans back inflicting 3,400 casualties; but they had resisted stubbornly and Cruwell lost 72 of his 162 tanks. The next day Rommel tried to unhinge the mind of the commander of the 8th Army, General Cunningham, by an advance into the British rear areas, the famous 'dash to the wire'. Rommel succeeded in causing chaos and Cunningham was almost killed as his aircraft took off. But after the initial shock had worn off, as General Jackson comments, 'it was found that remarkably little damage had been done. The fighting units had not panicked and were hanging on the flanks of the Afrika Korps as it plunged east-wards'. While Rommel's thrust degenerated into a series of uncoordinated actions, the British took the opportunity to restore morale and recover *at the very point when Fuller had predicted maximum panic*. Auchinleck remained unflinching in his determination to defeat Rommel, and it was the Afrika Korps that was forced to retreat.[40]

How does Fuller's doctrine of strategic paralysis compare with Liddel Hart's strategy of the indirect approach? On strategical matters the two thinkers are usually linked together. One writer refers to a 'British school' of classical military thinkers; 'everything they [Fuller and Liddell Hart] wrote,' he continues, 'revealed that they were obsessed by strategy . . .'.[41] The foregoing has already suggested the limitations of Fuller's interest in field strategy. He was at best sceptical of the value of the indirect approach. He warned Liddell Hart in 1929 that:

> It is wrong to look upon the indirect approach as a cure-all. The object is to defeat the enemy and if this can be done by direct approach so much the better. The indirect approach is a necessary evil. Which should be followed depends entirely on weapon-power. If I met a ruffian and I am armed with a pistol and he is not, my approach is direct; should however both of us be armed with knives my approach will probably be indirect.[42]

Liddell Hart judged this adherence to what he called 'conventional strategy' limiting. He maintained that Fuller expounded

> *deep tactical penetration* he did not advocate *deep strategical penetration* as I did. He favoured the armoured forces being used for a manoeuvre against the opposing army's immediate

rear, rather than against its communications far in the rear. Thus he preferred an advance by fairly long bounds instead of driving on as far as possible . . .[43]

This assessment is less than just, for it depends on the assumption that 'deep strategical penetration' can be successfully effected without battle. Fuller thought that it could not. Hence the importance he attached to fixing the enemy. 'Liddell Hart looks upon fixing,' he once explained, 'as a purely tactical operation—it is really a strategical one'.[44] Thus it is quite legitimate *strategically* to evolve plans whose execution depends on tactical means—the direct approach. The variation in emphasis renders the approach no less strategical. 'In war,' Fuller concluded, 'a general should aim at a decisive spot, if this point is also a soft spot so much the better, but if it is only a soft spot he is not a great general.'[45] Thus even though both thinkers agreed over the need to paralyse rather than physically destroy an enemy, Fuller thought that armies should seek battle to achieve this, Liddell Hart argued that they should avoid it by manoeuvring, a fundamental difference.

Fuller and Liddell Hart's discussion of the German invasion of Russia well illustrates these important strategical differences. Both men agreed that the major German effort should have been directed towards demoralizing the Red Army and forcing it to surrender. They differed in their estimation of the most effective means to achieve this. Fuller argued that 'objectives should not be far distant from each other, so that the forces may frequently reorganize'. Fuller thought that the German objectives were too distant; for Liddell Hart they were not distant enough. Moreover, whilst the latter thought it better to unleash the armour, seize Moscow and let confusion do the infantry's work, Fuller judged such thrusts 'mere raids'.[46] To securely box in the Red Army, Fuller advocated utilizing a defended base and an efficient anti-tank wing. He was, however, quite mistaken in assuming that once the Red Army was broken and boxed in, resistance within isolated pockets would be rare. On the contrary, resistance, like for example in the Minsk-Bialystok pocket, was stubborn and 'bloody and desperate' attempts were made to break out.[47] In 1942 he repeated his arguments, adding:

> as the Russians within these [pockets] were highly mechanized, unless the attackers could . . . refit and refuel, or when met by superior numbers fall back on a defended base, they had no choice but to withdraw . . . Had anti-tank wings existed, then for days on end the sally parties—the tank wings—could have held the field and continued to operate against the rear of the islands until the motorized troops came up to invest their rear and flanks.[48]

Fuller's stress on the need for anti-tank wings and co-operation with motorized infantry is all the more ironical when it is recalled that Liddell Hart is usually credited with calling for a 'balanced' force of all arms. There can be little doubt that in this regard Liddell Hart has been highly successful in influencing historians to write his version of history. Liddell Hart's viewpoint is summarized in his *Memoirs*:

> Fuller had come by now [c1927] to think that the tank alone would dominate future battlefields, and that the infantry would not be needed except to garrison the country that the tanks had conquered. On the other hand, I argued that there was both need and scope for a more mobile kind of infantry to co-operate with the tanks . . . for prompt aid in overcoming defended obstacles. I visualized them as what I called 'tank marines' . . . In short Fuller concentrated on the development of an all-tank army, while

I favoured an all-mobile army—in which all the tank-aiding arms would be mounted in armoured vehicles, and thus be able to accompany the tanks closely.[49]

This interpretation has been accepted by historians hitherto, and has become a commonplace of military criticism.[50] In this period Liddell Hart claimed that he had made numerous suggestions for the efficient co-operation of tanks and infantry which 'made little impression in British quarters, but caught the attention of fresh-minded soldiers in the German Army'. These were poured into a book called *The Future of Infantry* (1933). Liddell Hart also claimed that it had been used as a textbook in the training of the German Panzer divisions.[51] Liddell Hart's wisdom—and the folly of those who spurned his suggestions—was proved with deadly effect in 1940 when the 'balanced' Panzer divisions swept all before them.[52] There is a great deal of distortion in these comments, two sides of the same coin. Fuller's adherence to the 'all-tank' concept is exaggerated and so is Liddell Hart's preference for 'balanced' forces along the lines of the German Panzer Division.

All commentators would agree that Fuller's general framework was grounded on an overstatement, namely, that in mechanized warfare mobile armour would replace static earth as the main determining grand tactical factor. This he termed the primary tactical function, which aimed at maximising protected offensive power.[53] Thus the bullet would be eliminated as offensive power became increasingly based on shells and armour-piercing projectiles and protective power was based on bullet-proof armour. Fuller's view of mechanized battles was therefore to some degree a distorted one. He suggested wrongly that there would be no room for the infantry assault. The decisive act of battle would be the tank versus tank encounter. Tanks should be armed, then, with small calibre armour-piercing guns which could destroy their own kind. Fuller envisaged the tank battle as developing in four stages:

(1)   Movement from the anti-tank base.
(2)   Manoeuvre for position; feinting, forcing the enemy to draw upon his reserves.
(3)   Drive him into a corner; make him fight under a disadvanatge or starve him of petrol.
(4)   Move anti-tank base forward and hand occupied areas over to the army of occupation.[54]

The naval aspects of this scheme—which render it somewhat mechanical and artificial—are quite unrealistic. The emphasis which Fuller placed on 'digging in' an anti-tank base or 'laager' completely ignored the danger represented by tactical air power, and so does the sketch Fuller drew of the naval formation that he expected armoured forces to adopt. He greatly underestimated the future potential of aircraft, rigidly adhering to the belief that they could not hit small targets and that armour would be an ample deterrent; further, he illogically concluded that should one machine in a mechanized column be hit, the others would not suffer. His observations on airpower in *Lectures on FSR III* only amounted to the need to gain 'local command of the air'. Elsewhere he does remark on the need to bomb communications, but this is only vaguely, almost incidentally stated, and needs further amplification. Fuller could not perhaps have forseen the advent of the 'tankbuster' aircraft like the Hawker 'Typhoon', but his excuse that *Lectures on FSR III* was not primarily concerned with airpower was undercut by the fact that Fuller never grasped the significance of the Ju 87 'Stuka' dive bomber.[55]

It would, however, be mistaken to assume that Fuller was obsessed by the 'all-tank' notion. He did believe in the co-operation of arms as expressed in the defensive-offensive. Fuller argued that anti-tank guns should 'take up a position which the enemy will have to attack in order to carry out his plan, that it will generally be to the advantage of his opponents to let him attack, and directly his attack succeeds or fails, to launch a counter-offensive in full force against him'.[56] Thus tank and anti-tank forces were complementary instruments, facilitating mobile defence, the key to Rommel's tactics in Cyrenaica. Rommel pushed up anti-tank guns under cover around the 8th Army's flanks—a deadly supplement to tank fire. 'Their fire,' Fuller predicted, 'can drive tanks into areas where counter-attacks can defeat them.' Likewise in the retreat, Fuller suggested using a 'funnel' formation. During Operation 'Crusader', Rommel employed this effectively; British attempts to pursue and destroy his armour were frustrated by the protective screen of 88mm anti-aircraft guns used in an anti-tank role he posted on his flanks.[57]

Fuller also saw a role for infantry-tank co-operation. No other aspect of his military thought is so misunderstood as his attitude to infantry. True, Fuller saw no future for infantry acting independently, and told Liddell Hart that 'mixing up steel and muscle is no good and frontal attacks are absurd unless purely fixing operations'.[58] Yet this is far from suggesting that infantry would be completely absent from future battlefields. Fuller wanted to see infantry mechanized; to link marching infantry with mobile forces was 'tantamount to yoking a tractor to a carthorse.'[59] Fuller wanted infantry to be mechanized, carried in cross-country buses with their own close-support vehicles. What is more important, though he divided the battlefield into 'tank' and 'anti-tank' areas, he clearly recognized that

> frequently the ground will be of half and half description in which close co-operation between tanks and infantry becomes necessary. Normally infantry should not immediately follow tanks; . . . the infantry line of advance should be sufficiently close to the tanks to enable the infantry to rush forward under cover of the confusion caused by these weapons.[60]

Light infantry tactics should be employed, infiltration and rapid movement. In wooded areas, 'riflemen should precede the machines under cover of the wood on each flank, ready to open fire on any anti-tank weapon which may block the way'. Three types of infantry were therefore needed:

(1) Field pioneers with anti-tank guns.
(2) Field police to hold and occupy.
(3) Light infantry to co-operate with tanks.[61]

Fuller's view of infantry was undeniably a restricted one—though not so restricted as some writers believe—but it differed little from Liddell Hart's.

In *Great Captains Unveiled*, Liddell Hart analysed the military methods of the Mongols with an eye on future needs, pointing out that, 'Another canon they tore up was that mobile troops such as cavalry must rest on a stable infantry base.'[62] Such a comment bodes ill coming from the self-appointed champion of the infantry. Turning to *The Remaking of Modern Armies* we find his opinion of future infantry summarized thus:

> The effective role of infantry is now limited to 'mopping up' the ground that the tanks have conquered and holding it, if possible before the machine guns can be brought up. And with development of the six-wheeled carrier even this transitory role disappears, for the machine gun can be rushed forward more quickly than the infantry.[63]

Certainly, Liddell Hart indicated the need for infantry to fix the enemy, but in essence this idea hardly differed from Fuller's concept of 'anti-tank' which utilized infantry in this way. Moreover, Liddell Hart judged that 'in the light of their present uses, we see that the proper role of infantry is that of land marines; for the duties of "mopping up" and for hill and wood fighting . . . we could convey a proportion of land marines as part of the mechanized force'.[64] This quotation reveals that Liddell Hart's view of 'land marines' was a good deal narrower than he later claimed. It makes no mention of large-scale co-operation between tanks and infantry, and stressed that:

> A tank force may sometimes need men on foot to force river crossings for it, and also when halted, to enable the crews to rest undisturbed by snipers . . . But to attach a whole embussed brigade to it seems a mistake; it cramps its freedom of manoeuvre, and doubles the target. To carry a small number of 'tank marines', as one suggested years ago, still seemed the best solution.[65]

In *The Future of Infantry*, Liddell Hart followed Fuller's lead in stressing the need for light infantry, particularly in hilly and wooded country; under other conditions, 'Infantry . . . cannot replace the need for modernized cavalry because they cannot strike quickly enough or follow through soon enough for decisiveness in battle.' He also believed that the next war would see the appearance of motorized guerillas.[66] To sum up, despite the disclaimers of Liddell Hart to the contrary, his outlook was very similar to Fuller's over the composition of a future mechanized army. Because of this, and their important strategical differences, this paper argues that the usual comparison made between these two thinkers should be reversed.

Fuller's predictions stand up remarkably well to scrutiny. He sketched an accurate guide to the trends of future warfare until 1941. The armoured component of the Wehrmacht was small and highly professional. The German victories had been remarkably swift: Poland conquered in three weeks, Norway in two months, France and the Low Countries in six weeks. Furthermore, as Fuller predicted, casualties were low. In Scandinavia, the Germans lost 5,926 and the British 1,869. In the Balkans the Germans lost 5,000 casualties, but captured 90,000 Yugoslav, 270,000 Greek and 13,000 British prisoners. In the hardest fighting of this period, three weeks before Dunkirk, the Germans only sustained 5,700 casualties. It could be argued, then, that *blitzkrieg* had certainly refined war. The '*blitzkrieg* operations,' writes John Lukacs, 'hurt the conquered less than many wars of the past. What hurt them were the deprivations and tyranny of the occupation that followed.'[67] This period of 'limited war' came to an end with the German invasion of Russia. The onset of 'total war' and the limitations of Fuller's faith in decisive battles to bring wars quickly to an end revealed several flaws in his vision of future war.

Firstly, this war was quite unlimited in scope. Fuller had placed far too much emphasis on reason. He had contended that war was an outgrowth of peace, but he had calculated that wars could be limited by statesmen once their armies had been reduced in size and a new instrument that could terminate wars decisively had been put in their hands; and also, to limit wars was the reasonable, sensible thing to do. When states fight for their lives, reason alone does not prevail. Also the peace factor—industrial development which in turn influenced weapon development—gave determined states the ability to wage war on a scale hardly conceived in *Lectures on FRS III*. From 1942 onwards it was numbers and productive capacity, 180 million Russians and 150 million Americans and 'their willingness to fight even more than the quality of their equipment, [that] decided the war'. The fighting was bitter and bloody; units did not surrender because that was the sensible thing to do. In the battles before Moscow, as John Erickson notes, 'there was a compelling reason why units should stand and be pounded to pieces: Zhukov had no option but to fight for a breathing space'. Such factors were totally neglected in Fuller's exposition of the conduct of war.[68]

Secondly, the defensive returned to dominate battlefields. The culminating clinch on both the Western and Eastern fronts led to a reduction in the velocity of operations, and not to an increase as predicted by Fuller. Yet at the same time it is quite mistaken to assume that Fuller failed to forsee this. According to one writer, Fuller failed to realize that, 'given the resources of modern technology, a successful weapon rapidly generated its antidote'.[69] This argument fails to consider that Fuller's theory of the constant tactical factor led him to confidently expect a return to the defensive. Fuller can perhaps be more justifiably criticized on the score that he underestimated the speed with which the defensive reinstated itself. However, in *Lectures on FSR III* he stressed that 'field warfare always begets siege warfare; it did so in the last war and will do so in the next, but with this difference: where in the World War fronts will be fortified, in a war of armoured forces areas will be so instead'. Minefields would replace barbed wire, and networks of strong points would replace linear entrenchments. Defences would centre upon a series of fortresses and shielded anti-tank guns.[70] Rommel's defences at El Alamein consisted of three belts of minefields which, as Montgomery observed, were well 'sighted to canalize any penetration we may make'.[71] At Kursk the Russians were capable of laying 30,000 mines a day, and the defences bear out Fuller's predictions. They were based on the Pak anti-tank gun, carefully hidden, ten guns commanded by one officer so that enfilading fire could be brought to bear on threatened points.[72]

Thirdly, Fuller had not thought out the implications that fighting in urbanized areas would have for mechanized operations. He had pointed out that towns and villages were highly unsuitable for mechanized warfare but had complacently concluded that speed alone would be sufficient to neutralize them, leaving the infantry to mop up behind. This was a prime miscalculation. Faced by a determined opponent, urban areas proved a deadly brake on an army's freedom of manoeuvre. Fighting in these areas forced the tank to return to the role of an infantry support weapon. At Stalingrad the most effective weapon in street fighting was the machine gun and the hand grenade. Similarly, in Italy, street fighting revealed the tank's limitations. Colonel Sheppard notes how in fighting for Cassino in February 1943:

> One column of tanks was halted at a huge crater, too wide to span with their bridging tank. The other column only reached the outskirts of the town with superhuman efforts, with the crews working with pick and shovel and often under heavy fire . . . Each position had to be taken with the bomb and bayonet. Still no tanks could be got across the rubble and artillery support was impossible as only a few yards separated each side in the fight for a mound of rubble, a corner of a demolished building, or a cellar held by men who fought back for every yard of ground.[73]

Such conditions were quite alien to those outlined in *Lectures on FSR III*.

Fourthly, whereas Fuller had calculated that small armies of equal strength would move into open country to fight battles of manoeuvre accomplishing decisive results quickly, this proved to be an unduly optimistic expectation. Decisive victory can only be achieved by bringing overwhelming strength to bear on a weak or broken enemy. For example, in Normandy in 1944 Montgomery had to fight a set-piece infantry battle before breaking out. On the first day of Operation 'Goodwood' he lost 126 tanks. It was only after the German Army Group 'B' had been virtually annihilated at Falaise that Montgomery could declare that, 'The proper tactics are for strong armoured columns to bypass enemy centres of resistance and to push boldly ahead creating alarm and despondency in the enemy rear areas.'[74] The summer of 1944 saw advances of up to 230 miles in seven days. Likewise, on the Eastern Front, it was not until the German offensive at Kursk had been smashed that the Red Army made immense advances that in two great leaps took it to the frontiers of Romania. These great advances in their turn focused attention on the difficulties of supplying mechanized forces. Fuller believed in 1932 that the 'grip of supply on strategy is now far less tenacious'.[75] As Michael Howard observes, mechanization

> demanded hundreds of vehicles whose requirements in terms of supplies, petrol and ammunition made necessary the co-operation of thousands more. The inter-war dream of swift, skilful units operating against each other's supply lines, securing maximum decisions with minimum cost, turned into the reality of large armies with massive 'tails', highly vulnerable to enemy air attack and demanding considerable logistical ingenuity to keep them moving at all.[76]

Fuller failed to see that infantry would also be influenced by mechanization. In the Second World War more men would actually service the arms than fight with them—an important development, wholly in accordance with Fuller's law of military development and the impact of technology on war.[77]

General reflection on Fuller's theory of mechanized warfare suggests that in his expectation of a revolution in warfare he was mistaken. The introduction of the tank produced only (to employ the title of one of Fuller's earlier books) the reformation of war. Mechanized warfare led to a reassessment of the older arms (and with the exception of cavalry) not to their abolition. Because Fuller's theory was based on an overstatement he was able to indulge in some romantic wishful thinking about the capacity of mechanization to reduce the size of armies and their potential for destruction which flew in the face of reality. This notwithstanding, it is clear in retrospect that Fuller's contribution to the debate over mechanization was his most mature—and enduring—contribution to military thought.

Notes

All books and articles are by Fuller unless otherwise stated.
1 Jay Luvaas, *The Education of an Army: British Military Thought 1815–1940* (London 1965), 359.
2 For details of the Tidworth Affair see A.J. Trythall, *'Boney' Fuller: the Intellectual General 1878–1966* (London 1977), chapt 6. K.J. Macksey, *Armoured Crusader: a biography of Major-General Sir Percy Hobert* (London 1967), 81, considers that Fuller's tactless manner 'did more to create opposition to the tank idea than help its progress.'
3 Sir Ernest Swinton to Liddell Hart, 9 December 1929. Liddell Hart Papers 1/670/31.
4 General A.A. Montgomery-Massingberd to Liddell Hart, April 1926. Ibid., 1/520.
5 Fuller to Liddell Hart, 13 December 1928. Ibid., 1/302/155.
6 *The Dragon's Teeth: a study of war and peace* (London 1932), 204–5. The edition of *Lectures on FSR III* used throughout this essay unless otherwise stated is *Armoured Warfare: an annotated edition of Fifteen Lectures on Operations Between Mechanized Forces* (London 1943), 9.
7 *Lectures on FSR II* (London 1931), 112.
8 *Dragon's Teeth*, 212–3.
9 B.H. Liddell Hart, *The Remaking of Modern Armies* (London 1927), 92, declared that battle was 'clearly not, as is so often claimed, the main object or objective in war.' Fuller on the other hand, *Lectures on FSR II*, 2, 10, 34, though not approving of battle for its own sake, claimed that 'the object of tactics is to fulfill strategy, the accomplishment of a plan by upsetting the enemy's plan'—that is, bring him to battle.
10 This was the object of *The Foundations of the Science of War* (London 1926). In *On Future Warfare*

(London 1928), 105, Fuller defined strategy as 'the science of making the most of time for warlike ends, that is opportunity . . .'

11 'The Progress of War', *The Nineteenth Century and After*, XIX–XX, Oct. 1926, 492.
12 This definition is taken from *Grant and Lee: a study in personality and generalship* (London 1933), 258–9.
13 *Armoured Warfare*, 13.
14 Ibid., 7, 15; *On Future Warfare*, 228; *Lectures on FSR II*, 20.
15 *On Future Warfare*, 1.
16 Fuller to Liddell Hart, 19 January, 8 February 1922. Liddell Hart Papers 1/302/12/14.
17 Fuller to Liddell Hart, 25 August 1922, Ibid., 1/302/18; *On Future Warfare*, 295.
18 'The Mechanisation of War', *What Would Be the Character of a New War?* (London 1933), 66.
19 B.H. Liddell Hart, *History of the Second World War* (London 1970), 22.
20 *Armoured Warfare*, 6.
21 Ibid., 45, 101. See also John Lukacs, *The Last European War* (London 1977), 297; John Erickson, *The Road to Stalingrad* (London 1975), 120.
22 'The Mechanisation of War', 52.
23 *Armoured Warfare*, 80–81.
24 Ibid., 14.
25 Quoted in Ronald Lewin, *Rommell as Military Commander* (London 1968), 243.
26 *Armoured Warfare*, 53. For Wavell's opinion that leading troops into battle was not the function of a general, see A.P. Wavell, *Generals and Generalship* (London 1941), 15.
27 *Armoured Warfare*, 55; *Lectures on FSR II*, 6.
28 Quoted in Lewin, *Rommel*, 243.
29 John Connell, *Wavell: soldier and scholar* (London 1964), 325, says that O'Connor was always 'where he was needed.'
30 Figures taken from Lewin, *Rommel*, 243.
31 Charles Messenger, *The Art of Blitzkrieg* (London 1976), 201–2.
32 *Lectures on FSR II*, viii.
33 *Armoured Warfare*, 56.
34 Arguably, the 'Jock Columns' introduced in the Western Desert after Operation 'Battleaxe' can be considered motorized guerillas of some sort, but these included batteries of field and anti-tank guns and certainly did not use civilian motor-cars. See W.G.F. Jackson, *The North African Campaign 1940–43* (London 1975), 130.
35 *Machine Warfare* (London 1942), 57; in *Armoured Warfare*, 10, Fuller went as far as to declare: 'today every chauffeur is a potential motorized guerilla'.
36 Trythall, *Fuller*, 166.
37 Review of *On Future Warfare* by 'Ponocrates' in *Journal of the Royal United Services Institution*, 73, 1928, 784.
38 *Armoured Warfare*, 13n4.
39 Ibid., 58; 'Mechanisation of War', 70, 71. These predictions are far from being the lapse into 'pure Douhetism' remarked on by Messenger, *Art of Blitzkrieg*, 71.
40 A paragraph based on Lewin, *Rommel*, 69–74; Jackson, *North African Campaign*, 172–4; Liddell Hart, *Second World War*, 192–3.
41 Shelford Bidwell, *Modern Warfare: a study of men, weapons and theories* (London 1973), 51, 186–7.
42 Fuller to Liddell Hart, 19 June 1929. Liddell Hart Papers 1/302/158.
43 Liddell Hart, *Memoirs* (London 1965), 1, 91 See also Douglas Orgill, *The Tank: studies in the development and use of a weapon* (London 1970), 90–93.
44 Fuller to Skery, 2 March 1923. Liddell Hart Papers 1/302/36a.
45 *War and Western Civilization 1832–1932* (London 1932), 220.
46 *Armoured Warfare*, 88–9; Liddell Hart, *Second World War*, 160; *Armoured Warfare*, 86n3.
47 *Armoured Warfare*, 47.
48 *Machine Warfare*, 174.
49 Liddell Hart, *Memoirs*, 1, 90.
50 See Richard M. Ogorkiewicz, *Armour* (London 1960), 57, 385; Luvaas, *Education of an Army*, 404; Sir Frederick Pile, 'Liddell Hart and the British Army', Michael Howard (ed.), *The Theory and Practice of War* (London 1965), 173–5; Robin Higham, *Military Intellectuals in Britain* (London 1966), 85–6; John Wheldon, *Machine Age Armies* (London 1968), 37–8; Messenger, *Art of Blitzkrieg*, 42–4; Brian Bond, *Liddell Hart: a study of his military thought*, 29.

51 Liddell Hart, *Memoirs*, 1, 35.
52 Higham, *Military Intellectuals*, 70.
53 *On Future Warfare*, 224.
54 *Armoured Warfare*, 43, 64, 65, 20, 94; *On Future Warfare*, 340.
55 'One Hundred Problems on Mechanisation Part 2', *Army Quarterly*, XIV, 1930, 258; *Armoured Warfare*, 29; *Lectures on FSR III*, viii. Fuller's writing in the late thirties (eg. *Towards Armageddon* (London 1937), showed no appreciation of tactical air power. Whilst in Spain during the Civil War he was not allowed to visit the German air fields. See *Machine Warfare*, 57.
56 *Armoured Warfare*, 128.
57 Jackson, *North African Campaign*, 157–60; Liddell Hart, *Second World War*, 65, 68.
58 Fuller to Liddell Hart, 8 September 1928. Liddell Hart Papers 1/302/153.
59 *Armoured Warfare*, 19. Fuller meant by this infantry 1914 style, of course. The difficulties of combining infantry with little transport and a mechanized force is clearly shown in North Africa, where Rommel's Italian infantry were fearful of being abandoned during his retreats. See Lewin, *Rommel*, 91.
60 'One Hundred Problems on Mechanisation Part 1,' *Army Quarterly*, XIX, 1929, 18; See also *On Future Warfare*, 148, 151.
61 *Armoured Warfare*, 93–4.
62 Liddell Hart, *Great Captains Unveiled* (London 1927, 1971), 32.
63 Liddell Hart, *The Remaking of Modern Armies*, 8–9, 50–1.
64 Ibid., 15.
65 Liddell Hart, *When Britain Goes to War* (London 1932), 192, 261.
66 Liddell Hart, *The Future of Infantry* (London 1933), 35–7, 45–6.
67 Lukacs, *The Last European War*, 239–45.
68 Erickson, *Road to Stalingrad*, 249–251; Lukacs, *The Last European War*, 239–40.
69 Bidwell, *Modern Warfare*, 193. Liddell Hart is included in this context. Similar comments can be found in Orgill, *The Tank*, 219–20.
70 *Armoured Warfare*, 34, 78–9; Fuller also predicted, 131, that warfare may return to conditions 'as static as those experienced during 1914–17 . . .'.
71 Montgomery of Alamein, *El Alamein to the Sangro* (London 1946), 12.
72 Orgill, *The Tank*, 219.
73 On the need to hold and fight in cities, and the consequent difficulties for the tank, see Erickson, *Road to Stalingrad*, 214, 257, 382, 391–2, 404–5.
74 Liddell Hart, *The Tanks* (London 1959), II, 365, 377, 404.
75 *Armoured Warfare*, 37.
76 Michael Howard, *War in European History* (London 1976), 132–3.
77 Ibid. In a British infantry division of 18,000 men only 5,000 were riflemen on the ground. Liddell Hart criticized this development in *The Defence of the West* (London 1950), 290–2.

8 Some principles of maritime strategy

Julian Corbett

Natures of wars—offensive and defensive

Having determined that wars must vary in character according to the nature and importance of their object, we are faced with the difficulty that the variations will be of infinite
number and of all degrees of distinction. So complex indeed is the graduation presented
that at first sight it appears scarcely possible to make it the basis of practical study. But
on further examination it will be seen that by applying the usual analytical method the whole
subject is susceptible of much simplification. We must in short attempt to reach some system
of classification; that is, we must see if it is not possible to group the variations into some
well-founded categories. With a subject so complex and intangible the grouping must of
course be to some extent arbitrary, and in some places the lines of demarcation will be
shadowy; but if classification has been found possible and helpful in Zoology or Botany, with
the infinite and minute individual variations with which they have to deal, it should be no less
possible and helpful in the study of war.

The political theory of war will at any rate give us two broad and well-marked classifica-
tions. The first is simple and well known, depending on whether the political object of the
war is positive or negative. If it be positive—that is, if our aim is to wrest something from
the enemy—then our war in its main lines will be offensive. If, on the other hand, our aim
be negative, and we simply seek to prevent the enemy wresting some advantage to our
detriment, then the war in its general direction will be defensive.

It is only as a broad conception that this classification has value. Though it fixes the
general trend of our operations, it will not in itself affect their character. For a maritime
Power at least it is obvious that this must be so. For in any circumstances it is impossible for
such a Power either to establish its defence or develop fully its offence without securing a
working control of the sea by aggressive action against the enemy's fleets. Furthermore, we
have always found that however strictly our aim may be defensive, the most effective means
of securing it has been by counter-attack over-sea, either to support an ally directly or to
deprive our enemy of his colonial possessions. Neither category, then, excludes the use of
offensive operations nor the idea of overthrowing our enemy so far as is necessary to gain
our end. In neither case does the conception lead us eventually to any other objective than
the enemy's armed forces, and particularly his naval forces. The only real difference is this—
that if our object be positive our general plan must be offensive, and we should at least
open with a true offensive movement; whereas if our object be negative our general plan
will be preventive, and we may bide our time for our counter-attack. To this extent our
action must always tend to the offensive. For counter-attack is the soul of defence. Defence is
not a passive attitude, for that is the negation of war. Rightly conceived, it is an attitude of

alert expectation. We wait for the moment when the enemy shall expose himself to a counter-stroke, the success of which will so far cripple him as to render us relatively strong enough to pass to the offensive ourselves.

From these considerations it will appear that, real and logical as the classification is, to give it the designation "offensive and defensive" is objectionable from every point of view. To begin with, it does not emphasise what the real and logical distinction is. It suggests that the basis of the classification is not so much a difference of object as a difference in the means employed to achieve the object. Consequently we find ourselves continually struggling with the false assumption that positive war means using attack, and negative war being content with defence.

That is confusing enough, but a second objection to the designation is far more serious and more fertile of error. For the classification "offensive and defensive" implies that offensive and defensive are mutually exclusive ideas, whereas the truth is, and it is a fundamental truth of war, that they are mutually complementary. All war and every form of it must be both offensive and defensive. No matter how clear our positive aim nor how high our offensive spirit, we cannot develop an aggressive line of strategy to the full without the support of the defensive on all but the main lines of operation. In tactics it is the same. The most convinced devotee of attack admits the spade as well as the rifle. And even when it comes to men and material, we know that without a certain amount of protection neither ships, guns, nor men can develop their utmost energy and endurance in striking power. There is never, in fact, a clean choice between attack and defence. In aggressive operations the question always is, how far must defence enter into the methods we employ in order to enable us to do the utmost within our resources to break or paralyse the strength of the enemy. So also with defence. Even in its most legitimate use, it must always be supplemented by attack. Even behind the walls of a fortress men know that sooner or later the place must fall unless by counter-attack on the enemy's siege works or communications they can cripple his power of attack.

It would seem, therefore, that it were better to lay aside the designation "offensive and defensive" altogether and substitute the terms "positive and negative." But here again we are confronted with a difficulty. There have been many wars in which positive methods have been used all through to secure a negative end, and such wars will not sit easily in either class. For instance, in the War of Spanish Succession our object was mainly to prevent the Mediterranean becoming a French lake by the union of the French and Spanish crowns, but the method by which we succeeded in achieving our end was to seize the naval positions of Gibraltar and Minorca, and so in practice our method was positive. Again, in the late Russo-Japanese War the main object of Japan was to prevent Korea being absorbed by Russia. That aim was preventive and negative. But the only effective way of securing her aim was to take Korea herself, and so for her the war was in practice positive.

On the other hand, we cannot shut our eyes to the fact that in the majority of wars the side with the positive object has acted generally on the offensive and the other generally on the defensive. Unpractical therefore as the distinction seems to be, it is impossible to dismiss it without inquiring why this was so, and it is in this inquiry that the practical results of the classification will be found to lie—that is, it forces us to analyse the comparative advantages of offence and defence. A clear apprehension of their relative possibilities is the corner stone of strategical study.

Now the advantages of the offensive are patent and admitted. It is only the offensive that can produce positive results, while the strength and energy which are born of the moral stimulation of attack are of a practical value that outweighs almost every other consideration.

Every man of spirit would desire to use the offensive whether his object were positive or negative, and yet there are a number of cases in which some of the most energetic masters of war have chosen the defensive, and chosen with success. They have chosen it when they have found themselves inferior in physical force to their enemy, and when they believed that no amount of aggressive spirit could redress that inferiority.

Obviously, then, for all the inferiority of the defensive as a drastic form of war it must have some inherent advantage which the offensive does not enjoy. In war we adopt every method for which we have sufficient strength. If, then, we adopt the less desirable method of defence, it must be either that we have not sufficient strength for offence, or that the defence gives us some special strength for the attainment of our object.

What, then, are these elements of strength? It is very necessary to inquire, not only that we may know that if for a time we are forced back upon the defensive all is not lost, but also that we may judge with how much daring we should push our offensive to prevent the enemy securing the advantages of defence.

As a general principle we all know that possession is nine points of the law. It is easier to keep money in our pocket than to take it from another man's. If one man would rob another he must be the stronger or better armed unless he can do it by dexterity or stealth, and there lies one of the advantages of offence. The side which takes the initiative has usually the better chance of securing advantage by dexterity or stealth. But it is not always so. If either by land or sea we can take a defensive position so good that it cannot be turned and must be broken down before our enemy can reach his objective, then the advantage of dexterity and stealth passes to us. We choose our own ground for the trial of strength. We are hidden on familiar ground; he is exposed on ground that is less familiar. We can lay traps and prepare surprises by counter-attack, when he is most dangerously exposed. Hence the paradoxical doctrine that where defence is sound and well designed the advantage of surprise is against the attack.

It will be seen therefore that whatever advantages lie in defence they depend on the preservation of the offensive spirit. Its essence is the counter-attack—waiting deliberately for a chance to strike—not cowering in inactivity. Defence is a condition of restrained activity—not a mere condition of rest. Its real weakness is that if unduly prolonged it tends to deaden the spirit of offence. This is a truth so vital that some authorities in their eagerness to enforce it have travestied it into the misleading maxim, "That attack is the best defence." Hence again an amateurish notion that defence is always stupid or pusillanimous, leading always to defeat, and that what is called "the military spirit" means nothing but taking the offensive. Nothing is further from the teaching or the practice of the best masters. Like Wellington at Torres Vedras, they all at times used the defensive till the elements of strength inherent in that form of war, as opposed to the exhausting strain inherent in the form that they had fixed upon their opponents, lifted them to a position where they in their turn were relatively strong enough to use the more exhausting form.

The confusion of thought which has led to the misconceptions about defence as a method of war is due to several obvious causes. Counter-attacks from a general defensive attitude have been regarded as a true offensive, as, for instance, in Frederick the Great's best-known operations, or in Admiral Tegethoff's brilliant counterstroke at Lissa, or our own operations against the Spanish Armada. Again, the defensive has acquired an ill name by its being confused with a wrongly arrested offensive, where the superior Power with the positive object lacked the spirit to use his material superiority with sufficient activity and perseverance. Against such a Power an inferior enemy can always redress his inferiority by passing to a bold and quick offensive, thus acquiring a momentum both moral and physical which more than compensates his lack of weight. The defensive has also failed by the choice of a bad position which the enemy was able to turn or avoid. A defensive attitude is nothing at all, its elements of strength entirely disappear, unless it is such that the enemy must break it down by force before he can reach his ultimate objective. Even more often has it failed when the belligerent adopting it, finding he has no available defensive position which will bar the enemy's progress, attempts to guard every possible line of attack. The result is of course that by attenuating his force he only accentuates his inferiority.

Clear and well proven as these considerations are for land warfare, their application to the sea is not so obvious. It will be objected that at sea there is no defensive. This is generally true for tactics, but even so not universally true. Defensive tactical positions are possible at sea, as in defended anchorages. These were always a reality, and the mine has increased their possibilities. In the latest developments of naval warfare we have seen the Japanese at the Elliot Islands preparing a real defensive position to cover the landing of their Second Army in the Liaotung Peninsula. Strategically the proposition is not true at all. A strategical defensive has been quite as common at sea as on land, and our own gravest problems have often been how to break down such an attitude when our enemy assumed it. It usually meant that the enemy remained in his own waters and near his own bases, where it was almost impossible for us to attack him with decisive result, and whence he always threatened us with counter-attack at moments of exhaustion, as the Dutch did at Sole Bay and in the Medway. The difficulty of dealing decisively with an enemy who adopted this course was realised by our service very early, and from first to last one of our chief preoccupations was to prevent the enemy availing himself of this device and to force him to fight in the open, or at least to get between him and his base and force an action there.

Probably the most remarkable manifestation of the advantages that may be derived in suitable conditions from a strategical defensive is also to be found in the late Russo-Japanese War. In the final crisis of the naval struggle the Japanese fleet was able to take advantage of a defensive attitude in its own waters which the Russian Baltic fleet would have to break down to attain its end, and the result was the most decisive naval victory ever recorded.

The deterrent power of active and dexterous operations from such a position was well known to our old tradition. The device was used several times, particularly in our home waters, to prevent a fleet, which for the time we were locally too weak to destroy, from carrying out the work assigned to it. A typical position of the kind was off Scilly, and it was proved again and again that even a superior fleet could not hope to effect anything in the Channel till the fleet off Scilly had been brought to decisive action. But the essence of the device was the preservation of the aggressive spirit in its most daring form. For success it depended on at least the will to seize every occasion for bold and harassing counter-attacks such as Drake and his colleagues struck at the Armada.

To submit to blockade in order to engage the attention of a superior enemy's fleet is another form of defensive, but one that is almost wholly evil. For a short time it may do good by permitting offensive operations elsewhere which otherwise would be impossible. But if prolonged, it will sooner or later destroy the spirit of your force and render it incapable of effective aggression.

The conclusion then is that although for the practical purpose of framing or appreciating plans of war the classification of wars into offensive and defensive is of little use, a clear apprehension of the inherent relative advantages of offence and defence is essential. We must realise that in certain cases, provided always we preserve the aggressive spirit, the defensive will enable an inferior force to achieve points when the offensive would probably lead to its destruction. But the elements of strength depend entirely on the will and insight to deal rapid blows in the enemy's unguarded moments. So soon as the defensive ceases to be regarded as a means of fostering power to strike and of reducing the enemy's power of attack, it loses all its strength. It ceases to be even a suspended activity, and anything that is not activity is not war.

With these general indications of the relative advantages of offence and defence we may leave the subject for the present. It is possible of course to catalogue the advantages and disadvantages of each form, but any such bald statement—without concrete examples to explain the meaning—must always appear controversial and is apt to mislead. It is better to reserve their fuller consideration till we come to deal with strategical operations and are able to note their actual effect upon the conduct of war in its various forms. Leaving therefore our first classification of wars into offensive and defensive we will pass on to the second, which is the only one of real practical importance.

Natures of wars—limited and unlimited

The second classification to which we are led by the political theory of war, is one which Clausewitz was the first to formulate and one to which he came to attach the highest importance. It becomes necessary therefore to examine his views in some detail—not because there is any need to regard a continental soldier, however distinguished, as an indispensable authority for a maritime nation. The reason is quite the reverse. It is because a careful examination of his doctrine on this point will lay open what are the radical and essential differences between the German or Continental School of Strategy and the British or Maritime School—that is, our own traditional School, which too many writers both at home and abroad quietly assume to have no existence. The evil tendency of that assumption cannot be too strongly emphasised, and the main purpose of this and the following chapters will be to show how and why even the greatest of the continental strategists fell short of realising fully the characteristic conception of the British tradition.

By the classification in question Clausewitz distinguished wars into those with a "Limited" object and those whose object was "Unlimited." Such a classification was entirely characteristic of him, for it rested not alone upon the material nature of the object, but on certain moral considerations to which he was the first to attach their real value in war. Other writers such as Jomini had attempted to classify wars by the special purpose for which they were fought, but Clausewitz's long course of study convinced him that such a distinction was unphilosophical and bore no just relation to any tenable theory of war. Whether, that is, a war was positive or negative mattered much, but its special purpose, whether, for instance, according to Jomini's system, it was a war "to assert rights" or "to assist an ally" or "to acquire territory," mattered not at all.

Whatever the object, the vital and paramount question was the intensity with which the spirit of the nation was absorbed in its attainment. The real point to determine in approaching any war plan was what did the object mean to the two belligerents, what sacrifices would they make for it, what risks were they prepared to run? It was thus he stated his view. "The smaller the sacrifice we demand from our opponent, the smaller presumably will be the means of resistance he will employ, and the smaller his means, the smaller will ours be required to be. Similarly the smaller our political object, the less value shall we set upon it and the more easily we shall be induced to abandon it." Thus the political object of the war, its original motive, will not only determine for both belligerents reciprocally the aim of the force they use, but it will also be the standard of the intensity of the efforts they will make. So he concludes there may be wars of all degrees of importance and energy from a war of extermination down to the use of an army of observation. So also in the naval sphere there may be a life and death struggle for maritime supremacy or hostilities which never rise beyond a blockade.

Such a view of the subject was of course a wide departure from the theory of "Absolute War" on which Clausewitz had started working. Under that theory "Absolute War" was the ideal form to which all war ought to attain, and those which fell short of it were imperfect wars cramped by a lack of true military spirit. But so soon as he had seized the fact that in actual life the moral factor always must override the purely military factor, he saw that he had been working on too narrow a basis—a basis that was purely theoretical in that it ignored the human factor. He began to perceive that it was logically unsound to assume as the foundation of a strategical system that there was one pattern to which all wars ought to conform. In the light of his full and final apprehension of the value of the human factor he saw wars falling into two well-marked categories, each of which would legitimately be approached in a radically different manner, and not necessarily on the lines of "Absolute War."

He saw that there was one class of war where the political object was of so vital an importance to both belligerents that they would tend to fight to the utmost limit of their endurance to secure it. But there was another class where the object was of less importance, that is to say, where its value to one or both the belligerents was not so great as to be worth unlimited sacrifices of blood and treasure. It was these two kinds of war he designated provisionally "Unlimited" and "Limited," by which he meant not that you were not to exert the force employed with all the vigour you could develop, but that there might be a limit beyond which it would be bad policy to spend that vigour, a point at which, long before your force was exhausted or even fully developed, it would be wiser to abandon your object rather than to spend more upon it.

This distinction it is very necessary to grasp quite clearly, for it is often superficially confused with the distinction already referred to, which Clausewitz drew in the earlier part of his work—that is, the distinction between what he called the character of modern war and the character of the wars which preceded the Napoleonic era. It will be remembered he insisted that the wars of his own time had been wars between armed nations with a tendency to throw the whole weight of the nation into the fighting line, whereas in the seventeenth and eighteenth centuries wars were waged by standing armies and not by the whole nation in arms. The distinction of course is real and of far-reaching consequences, but it has no relation to the distinction between "Limited" and "Unlimited" war. War may be waged on the Napoleonic system either for a limited or an unlimited object.

A modern instance will serve to clear the field. The recent Russo-Japanese War was fought for a limited object—the assertion of certain claims over territory which formed no part of the possessions of either belligerent. Hostilities were conducted on entirely modern lines by two armed nations and not by standing armies alone. But in the case of one belligerent her interest in the object was so limited as to cause her to abandon it long before her whole force as an armed nation was exhausted or even put forth. The expense of life and treasure which the struggle was involving was beyond what the object was worth.

This second distinction—that is, between Limited and Unlimited wars—Clausewitz regarded as of greater importance than his previous one founded on the negative or positive nature of the object. He was long in reaching it. His great work *On War* as he left it proceeds almost entirely on the conception of offensive or defensive as applied to the Napoleonic ideal of absolute war. The new idea came to him towards the end in the full maturity of his prolonged study, and it came to him in endeavouring to apply his strategical speculations to the practical process of framing a war plan in anticipation of a threatened breach with France. It was only in his final section *On War Plans* that he began to deal with it. By that time he had grasped the first practical result to which his theory led. He saw that the distinction between Limited and Unlimited war connoted a cardinal distinction in the methods of waging it. When the object was unlimited, and would consequently call forth your enemy's whole war power, it was evident that no firm decision of the struggle could be reached till his war power was entirely crushed. Unless you had a reasonable hope of being able to do this it was bad policy to seek your end by force—that is, you ought not to go to war. In the case of a limited object, however, the complete destruction of the enemy's armed force was beyond what was necessary. Clearly you could achieve your end if you could seize the object, and by availing yourself of the elements of strength inherent in the defensive could set up such a situation that it would cost the enemy more to turn you out than the object was worth to him.

Here then was a wide difference in the fundamental postulate of your war plan. In the case of an unlimited war your main strategical offensive must be directed against the armed forces of the enemy; in the case of a limited war, even where its object was positive, it need not be. If conditions were favourable, it would suffice to make the object itself the objective of your main strategical offensive. Clearly, then, he had reached a theoretical distinction which modified his whole conception of strategy. No longer is there logically but one kind of war, the Absolute, and no longer is there but one legitimate objective, the enemy's armed forces. Being sound theory, it of course had an immediate practical value, for obviously it was a distinction from which the actual work of framing a war plan must take its departure.

A curious corroboration of the soundness of these views is that Jomini reached an almost identical standpoint independently and by an entirely different road. His method was severely concrete, based on the comparison of observed facts, but it brought him as surely as the abstract method of his rival to the conclusion that there were two distinct classes of object. "They are of two different kinds," he says, "one which may be called territorial or geographical . . . the other on the contrary consists exclusively in the destruction or disorganisation of the enemy's forces without concerning yourself with geographical points of any kind." It is under the first category of his first main classification "Of offensive wars to assert rights," that he deals with what Clausewitz would call "Limited Wars." Citing as an example Frederick the Great's war for the conquest of Silesia, he says, "In such a war . . . the offensive operations ought to be proportional to the end in view. The first move is naturally to occupy the provinces claimed" (not, be it noted, to direct your blow at the enemy's main force). "Afterwards," he proceeds, "you can push the offensive according to circumstances and your relative strength in order to obtain the desired cession by menacing the enemy at home." Here we have Clausewitz's whole doctrine of "Limited War"; firstly, the primary or territorial stage, in which you endeavour to occupy the geographical object, and then the secondary or coercive stage, in which you seek by exerting general pressure upon your enemy to force him to accept the adverse situation you have set up.

Such a method of making war obviously differs in a fundamental manner from that which Napoleon habitually adopted, and yet we have it presented by Jomini and Clausewitz, the two apostles of the Napoleonic method. The explanation is, of course, that both of them had seen too much not to know that Napoleon's method was only applicable when you could command a real physical or moral preponderance. Given such a preponderance, both were staunch for the use of extreme means in Napoleon's manner. It is not as something better than the higher road that they commend the lower one, but being veteran staff-officers and not mere theorists, they knew well that a belligerent must sometimes find the higher road beyond his strength, or beyond the effort which the spirit of the nation is prepared to make for the end in view, and like the practical men they were, they set themselves to study the potentialities of the lower road should hard necessity force them to travel it. They found that these potentialities in certain circumstances were great. As an example of a case where the lower form was more appropriate Jomini cites Napoleon's campaign against Russia in 1812. In his opinion it would have been better if Napoleon had been satisfied to begin on the lower method with a limited territorial object, and he attributes his failure to the abuse of a method which, however well suited to his wars in Germany, was incapable of achieving success in the conditions presented by a war with Russia.

Seeing how high was Napoleon's opinion of Jomini as a master of the science of war, it is curious how his views on the two natures of wars have been ignored in the present day. It is even more curious in the case of Clausewitz, since we know that in the plenitude of his powers he came to regard this classification as the master-key of the subject. The explanation is that the distinction is not very clearly formulated is his first seven books, which alone he left in anything like a finished condition. It was not till he came to write his eighth book *On War Plans* that he saw the vital importance of the distinction round which he had been hovering. In that book the distinction is clearly laid down, but the book unhappily was never completed. With his manuscript, however, he left a "Note" warning us against regarding his earlier books as a full presentation of his developed ideas. From the note it is also evident that he thought the classification on which he had lighted was of the utmost importance, that he believed it would clear up all the difficulties which he had encountered in his earlier books—difficulties which he had come to see arose from a too exclusive consideration of the Napoleonic method of conducting war. "I look upon the first six books," he wrote in 1827, "as only a mass of material which is still in a manner without form and which has still to be revised again. In this revision the two kinds of wars will be kept more distinctly in view all through, and thereby all ideas will gain in clearness, in precision, and in exactness of application." Evidently he had grown dissatisfied with the theory of Absolute War on which he had started. His new discovery had convinced him that that theory would not serve as a standard for all natures of wars. "Shall we," he asks in his final book, "shall we now rest satisfied with this idea and by it judge of all wars, however much they may differ?"[1] He answers his question in the negative. "You cannot determine the requirements of all wars from the Napoleonic type. Keep that type and its absolute method before you to use *when you can* or *when you must*, but keep equally before you that there are two main natures of war."

In his note written at this time, when the distinction first came to him, he defines these two natures of war as follows: "First, those in which the object is the *overthrow of the enemy*, whether it be we aim at his political destruction or merely at disarming him and forcing him to conclude peace on our terms; and secondly, those in which our object is *merely to make some conquests on the frontiers of his country*, either for the purpose of retaining them permanently or of turning them to account as a matter of exchange in settling terms of peace."[2] It was in his eighth book that he intended, had he lived, to have worked out the comprehensive idea he had conceived. Of that book he says, "The chief object will be to make good the two points of view above mentioned, by which everything will be simplified and at the same time be given the breath of life. I hope in this book to iron out many creases in the heads of strategists and statesmen, and at least to show the object of action and the real point to be considered in war."[3]

That hope was never realised, and that perhaps is why his penetrating analysis has been so much ignored. The eighth book as we have it is only a fragment. In the spring of 1830—an anxious moment, when it seemed that Prussia would require all her best for another struggle single-handed with France—he was called away to an active command. What he left of the book on "War Plans" he describes as "merely a track roughly cleared, as it were, through the mass, in order to ascertain the points of greatest moment." It was his intention, he says, to "carry the spirit of these ideas into his first six books"—to put the crown on his work, in fact, by elaborating and insisting upon his two great propositions, viz. that war was a form of policy, and that being so it might be Limited or Unlimited.

The extent to which he would have infused his new idea into the whole every one is at liberty to judge for himself; but this indisputable fact remains. In the winter in view of the threatening attitude of France in regard to Belgium he drew up a war plan, and it was designed not on the Napoleonic method of making the enemy's armed force the main strategical objective, but on seizing a limited territorial object and forcing a disadvantageous counter-offensive upon the French. The revolutionary movement throughout Europe had broken the Holy Alliance to pieces. Not only did Prussia find herself almost single-handed against France, but she herself was sapped by revolution. To adopt the higher form of war and seek to destroy the armed force of the enemy was beyond her power. But she could still use the lower form, and by seizing Belgium she could herself force so exhausting a task on France that success was well within her strength. It was exactly so we endeavoured to begin the Seven Years' War; and it was exactly so the Japanese successfully conducted their war with Russia; and what is more striking, it was on similar lines that in 1859 Moltke in similar circumstances drew up his first war plan against France. His idea at that time was on the lines which Jomini held should have been Napoleon's in 1812. It was not to strike directly at Paris or the French main army, but to occupy Alsace-Lorraine and hold that territory till altered conditions should give him the necessary preponderance for proceeding to the higher form or forcing a favourable peace.

In conclusion, then, we have to note that the matured fruit of the Napoleonic period was a theory of war based not on the single absolute idea, but on the dual distinction of Limited and Unlimited. Whatever practical importance we may attach to the distinction, so much must be admitted on the clear and emphatic pronouncements of Clausewitz and Jomini. The practical importance is another matter. It may fairly be argued that in continental warfare—in spite of the instances quoted by both the classical writers—it is not very great, for reasons that will appear directly. But it must be remembered that continental warfare is not the only form in which great international issues are decided. Standing at the final point which Clausewitz and Jomini reached, we are indeed only on the threshold of the subject. We have to begin where they left off and inquire what their ideas have to tell for the modern conditions of worldwide imperial States, where the sea becomes a direct and vital factor.

Limited war and maritime empires—development of Clausewitz's and Jomini's theory of a limited territorial object, and its application to modern imperial conditions

The German war plans already cited, which were based respectively on the occupation of Belgium and Alsace-Lorraine, and Jomini's remarks on Napoleon's disastrous Russian campaign serve well to show the point to which continental strategists have advanced along the road which Clausewitz was the first to indicate clearly. We have now to consider its application to modern imperial conditions, and above all where the maritime element forcibly asserts itself. We shall then see how small that advance has been compared with its far-reaching effects for a maritime and above all an insular Power.

It is clear that Clausewitz himself never apprehended the full significance of his brilliant theory. His outlook was still purely continental, and the limitations of continental warfare tend to veil the fuller meaning of the principle he had framed. Had he lived, there is little doubt he would have worked it out to its logical conclusion, but his death condemned his theory of limited war to remain in the inchoate condition in which he had left it.

It will be observed, as was natural enough, that all through his work Clausewitz had in his mind war between two contiguous or at least adjacent continental States, and a moment's consideration will show that in that type of war the principle of the limited object can rarely if ever assert itself in perfect precision. Clausewitz himself put it quite clearly. Assuming a case where "the overthrow of the enemy"—that is, unlimited war—is beyond our strength, he points out that we need not therefore necessarily act on the defensive. Our action may still be positive and offensive, but the object can be nothing more than "the conquest of part of the enemy's country." Such a conquest he knew might so far weaken your enemy or strengthen your own position as to enable you to secure a satisfactory peace. The path of history is indeed strewn with such cases. But he was careful to point out that such a form of war was open to the gravest objections. Once you had occupied the territory you aimed at, your offensive action was, as a rule, arrested. A defensive attitude had to be assumed, and such an arrest of offensive action he had previously shown was inherently vicious, if only for moral reasons. Added to this you might find that in your effort to occupy the territorial object, you had so irretrievably separated your striking force from your home-defence force as to be in no position to meet your enemy if he was able to retort by acting on unlimited lines with a stroke at your heart. A case in point was the Austerlitz campaign, where Austria's object was to wrest North Italy from Napoleon's empire. She sent her main army under the Archduke Charles to seize the territory she desired. Napoleon immediately struck at Vienna, destroyed her home army, and occupied the capital before the Archduke could turn to bar his way.

The argument is this: that, as all strategic attack tends to leave points of your own uncovered, it always involves greater or less provision for their defence. It is obvious, therefore, that if we are aiming at a limited territorial object the proportion of defence required will tend to be much greater than if we are directing our attack on the main forces of the enemy. In unlimited war our attack will itself tend to defend everything elsewhere, by forcing the enemy to concentrate against our attack. Whether the limited form is justifiable or not therefore depends, as Clausewitz points out, on the geographical position of the object.

So far British experience is with him, but he then goes on to say the more closely the territory in question is an annex of our own, the safer is this form of war, because then our offensive action will the more surely cover our home country. As a case in point he cites Frederick the Great's opening of the Seven Years' War with the occupation of Saxony—a piece of work which materially strengthened Prussian defence. Of the British opening in Canada he says nothing. His outlook was too exclusively continental for it to occur to him to test his doctrine with a conspicuously successful case in which the territory aimed at was distant from the home territory and in no way covered it. Had he done so he must have seen how much stronger an example of the strength of limited war was the case of Canada than the case of Saxony. Moreover, he would have seen that the difficulties, which in spite of his faith in his discovery accompanied his attempt to apply it, arose from the fact that the examples he selected were not really examples at all.

When he conceived the idea, the only kind of limited object he had in his mind was, to use his own words, "some conquests on the frontiers of the enemy's country," such as Silesia and

Saxony for Frederick the Great, Belgium in his own war plan, and Alsace-Lorraine in that of Moltke. Now it is obvious that such objects are not truly limited, for two reasons. In the first place, such territory is usually an organic part of your enemy's country, or otherwise of so much importance to him that he will be willing to use unlimited effort to retain it. In the second place, there will be no strategical obstacle to his being able to use his whole force to that end. To satisfy the full conception of a limited object, one of two conditions is essential. Firstly, it must be not merely limited in area, but of really limited political importance; and secondly, it must be so situated as to be strategically isolated or to be capable of being reduced to practical isolation by strategical operations. Unless this condition exists, it is in the power of either belligerent, as Clausewitz himself saw, to pass to unlimited war if he so desires, and, ignoring the territorial objective, to strike at the heart of his enemy and force him to desist.

If, then, we only regard war between contiguous continental States, in which the object is the conquest of territory on either of their frontiers, we get no real generic difference between limited and unlimited war. The line between them is in any case too shadowy or unstable to give a classification of any solidity. It is a difference of degree rather than of kind. If, on the other hand, we extend our view to wars between worldwide empires, the distinction at once becomes organic. Possessions which lie oversea or at the extremities of vast areas of imperfectly settled territory are in an entirely different category from those limited objects which Clausewitz contemplated. History shows that they can never have the political importance of objects which are organically part of the European system, and it shows further that they can be isolated by naval action sufficiently to set up the conditions of true limited war.

Jomini approaches the point, but without clearly detaching it. In his chapter "On Great Invasions and Distant Expeditions," he points out how unsafe it is to take the conditions of war between contiguous States and apply them crudely to cases where the belligerents are separated by large areas of land or sea. He hovers round the sea factor, feeling how great a difference it makes, but without getting close to the real distinction. His conception of the inter-action of fleets and armies never rises above their actual co-operation in touch one with the other in a distant theatre. He has in mind the assistance which the British fleet afforded Wellington in the Peninsula, and Napoleon's dreams of Asiatic conquest, pronouncing such distant invasions as impossible in modern times except perhaps in combination with a powerful fleet that could provide the army of invasion with successive advanced bases. Of the paramount value of the fleet's isolating and preventive functions he gives no hint.

Even when he deals with oversea expeditions, as he does at some length, his grip of the point is no closer. It is indeed significant of how entirely continental thought had failed to penetrate the subject that in devoting over thirty pages to an enumeration of the principles of oversea expeditions, he, like Clausewitz, does not so much as mention the conquest of Canada; and yet it is the leading case of a weak military Power succeeding by the use of the limited form of war in forcing its will upon a strong one, and succeeding because it was able by naval action to secure its home defence and isolate the territorial object.

For our ideas of true limited objects, therefore, we must leave the continental theatres and turn to mixed or maritime wars. We have to look to such cases as Canada and Havana in the Seven Years' War, and Cuba in the Spanish-American War, cases in which complete isolation of the object by naval action was possible, or to such examples as the Crimea and Korea, where sufficient isolation was attainable by naval action owing to the length and difficulty of the enemy's land communications and to the strategical situation of the territory at stake.

These examples will also serve to illustrate and enforce the second essential of this kind of war. As has been already said, for a true limited object we must have not only the power of isolation, but also the power by a secure home defence of barring an unlimited counterstroke. In all the above cases this condition existed. In all of them the belligerents had no contiguous frontiers, and this point is vital. For it is obvious that if two belligerents have a common frontier, it is open to the superior of them, no matter how distant or how easy to isolate the limited object may be, to pass at will to unlimited war by invasion. This process is even possible when the belligerents are separated by a neutral State, since the territory of a weak neutral will be violated if the object be of sufficient importance, or if the neutral be too strong to coerce, there still remains the possibility that his alliance may be secured.

We come, then, to this final proposition—that limited war is only permanently possible to island Powers or between Powers which are separated by sea, and then only when the Power desiring limited war is able to command the sea to such a degree as to be able not only to isolate the distant object, but also to render impossible the invasion of his home territory.

Here, then, we reach the true meaning and highest military value of what we call the command of the sea, and here we touch the secret of England's success against Powers so greatly superior to herself in military strength. It is only fitting that such a secret should have been first penetrated by an Englishman. For so it was, though it must be said that except in the light of Clausewitz's doctrine the full meaning of Bacon's famous aphorism is not revealed. "This much is certain," said the great Elizabethan on the experience of our first imperial war; "*he that commands the sea is at great liberty and may take as much or as little of the war as he will, whereas those that be strongest by land are many times nevertheless in great straits.*" It would be difficult to state more pithily the ultimate significance of Clausewitz's doctrine. Its cardinal truth is clearly indicated—that *limited wars do not turn upon the armed strength of the belligerents, but upon the amount of that strength which they are able or willing to bring to bear at the decisive point.*

It is much to be regretted that Clausewitz did not live to see with Bacon's eyes and to work out the full comprehensiveness of his doctrine. His ambition was to formulate a theory which would explain all wars. He believed he had done so, and yet it is clear he never knew how complete was his success, nor how wide was the field he had covered. To the end it would seem he was unaware that he had found an explanation of one of the most inscrutable problems in history—the expansion of England—at least so far as it has been due to success-ful war. That a small country with a weak army should have been able to gather to herself the most desirable regions of the earth, and to gather them at the expense of the greatest military Powers, is a paradox to which such Powers find it hard to be reconciled. The phenomenon seemed always a matter of chance—an accident without any foundation in the essential constants of war. It remained for Clausewitz, unknown to himself, to discover that explanation, and he reveals it to us in the inherent strength of limited war when means and conditions are favourable for its use.

We find, then, if we take a wider view than was open to Clausewitz and submit his latest ideas to the test of present imperial conditions, so far from failing to cover the ground they gain a fuller meaning and a firmer basis. Apply them to maritime warfare and it becomes clear that his distinction between limited and unlimited war does not rest alone on the moral factor. A war may be limited not only because the importance of the object is too limited to call forth the whole national force, but also because the sea may be made to present an insuperable physical obstacle to the whole national force being brought to bear. That is to say, a war may be limited physically by the strategical isolation of the object, as well as morally by its comparative unimportance.

Notes

1   Carl von Clausewitz, *On War*, edited and translated by Michael Howard and Peter Paret (Princeton, NJ: Princeton University Press, 1989), Book viii. chap. ii.
2   Ibid., Prefatory Notice, p. vii.
3   Ibid., p. viii.

9 Air power and the origins of deterrence theory before 1939

R.J. Overy

The roots of the modern theory of deterrence are to be found in the evolution of strategic air power before World War II. The word modern is used for a purpose. Deterrence is as old as fear itself; but as a formal description of a strategic aim it dates from the 1950s super-power confrontation. Though the concept is often used loosely, deterrence is generally taken to mean a strategic ambition in which a putative aggressor is deterred from military attack by fear of the consequences, not just for his own military forces, but for his society as a whole. Expressed in this way deterrence can only work if the threat of military retaliation is credible, and if there are no doubts about the political intention to use it.

In effect deterrence works in a relationship where both parties express a clear willingness and ability to resort to violence if deterrence breaks down, creating the central paradox of 'reducing the probability of war by increasing its apparent probability'.[1] Deterrence works only where the costs of attack vastly exceed the expected yield, as is manifestly the case with nuclear weapons. Of course, it is important to grasp that deterrence only describes the *effect* produced by nuclear confrontation. The primary military strategy pursued by the two superpowers since the 1950s has been nuclear air power, exercised first through bombers, then missiles. Deterrent effect is inseparable from the superpowers' war fighting capability, from the force preparation and military doctrine of their strategic forces. Deterrence is the effect, but it is credible and devastating war capability that produces it.

In this sense it is hardly an exaggeration to see the development of air power during the twentieth century as the central feature in the emergence of a strategy of deterrence. From its inception in World War I, air power was regarded as qualitatively different from conventional surface combat, for not only could aircraft attack the national fabric rather than the armed forces but they also did so in a rapid and annihilating way: 'The very heart of a country now lies open to a peculiarly horrible form of attack which neither science nor invention can prevent, and to which no human skill or courage can be successfully opposed.'[2] Long before aircraft or bombs really had the technical means to fulfil this nightmare, the Italian strategist, General Giulio Douhet (1869–1930), argued that 'the Independent Air Force is shown to be the best way to assure victory, regardless of any other circumstances whatever . . .'. The threat of the 'knock-out blow', a swift and decisive assault from the air on an enemy people, was identified with air warfare throughout the interwar period and has lived on into the nuclear age.[3]

While it is certainly true that nuclear weaponry has seen a radical qualitative jump in the air threat, there is a danger of exaggerating the change in 1945. Air power theory and force structure before 1939 show strong lines of continuity with the post-war world. Indeed many underlying assumptions, the categories and modes of thought which operate in deterrence theory, can be traced back to the pre-war era. Many central arguments in contemporary deterrence theory – defence/deterrence, first strike/retaliation, counter force/counter value targets – have their source in similar 1930s arguments about first strike capability, or targeting. In fact continuity of personnel made continuity in modes of expression and strategic outlook almost inevitable. This is not to argue that a fully-fledged deterrence theory already existed before the war. The development of deterrence theory has been a slow, incremental process, bound up closely with technological change, political receptivity and combat experience. Nor in practice did air power work as a deterrent between the major powers in 1939 or 1941. Experience in the 1930s showed that neither the weapon nor the delivery system was sophisticated enough to provide the 'knock-out blow'. The theory had run ahead of the technology. After 1945 the two reached a fresh alignment.

The framework for deterrence

Any understanding of the threat popularly represented by air power ever since the First World War rests on two fundamental assumptions produced by that conflict. The first was that any future war was likely to be a total war again, a war of whole nations pitted against each other rather than a war simply of armed forces. Total war eradicated the distinction between combatant and civilian which had emerged under the rules of war in the nineteenth century. The second was the realisation that science held the key to military security or military success, and that the remorseless progress of scientific discovery should not be reversed or halted in a world of competing powers.

Both these factors, totalisation of warfare and the direct harnessing of science for national security, made possible not only the 1930s development of modern bombing fleets and civilian targeting, but also the threat of effective city-busting in the thermo-nuclear age. Total war, what Raymond Aron called 'universalised violence', was regarded by the First World War generation as both inevitable and repugnant.[4] 'The very fact that this total war exists,' complained the British strategist, Cyril Falls, 'in itself threatens the destruction and implies the doom of civilization.'[5] Yet the emergence of the modern nation state, and the impact of popular mass politics on imperial rivalry destabilised the international structure and contributed to a widespread view that great states were engaged in a perennial struggle for survival. 'Modern war,' wrote the German Colonel Georg Thomas in 1926, 'is no longer a clash of armies, but a struggle for the existence of the peoples involved.'[6] The use of ideology as a political instrument made the conflict of whole societies more likely and widened the gulf between states even further. Ideological confrontation with its ingredients of irrationalism and narrow conviction increased the risks and threats of war and has continued to do so since.

The possibility of total war enormously raised the stakes in any future conflict, so much so that it was sometimes assumed after 1918 that its very prospect would deter any state contemplating it. But it also meant that in the war of the future the enemy's cities, industries, communications, even the civilian workforce were all targets for attack, a view which, despite its unhappy morality, became all too true between 1939 and 1945, and has remained enshrined in nuclear confrontation. The thresholds crossed in the First World War proved impossible to reverse. The view of civilian populations as in some sense hostage in great power confrontation, which has been a centrepiece of 1960s and 1970s deterrence theory, depended on the ability to take effective military action against them. Though seaborne blockade continued to be regarded as an indirect and traditional form of 'total warfare', most interwar military thinkers saw air power as the way in which war could be brought home to an enemy people rapidly and decisively.

Air power was in this sense the typical instrument of total war. Aircraft were capable of attacking the industrial and administrative system, the 'vital centres', without which the enemy state could not function effectively, either as a military force or in providing the infrastructure and resources to satisfy the needs of the population as a whole. Marshal of the RAF Sir Hugh Trenchard, the British Chief of Air Staff in 1928, argued that 'direct air attack on the centres of production, transportation and communications must succeed in paralysing the life and effort of the community and therefore in winning the war'.[7] The US Manual of Combined Air Tactics in 1926 was even more explicit about striking civilians: 'The objective is selected with a view to undermining the enemy's morale . . . Such employment of air forces is a method of imposing will by terrorizing the whole population of a belligerent country . . .'.[8] Though such views were hotly contested at the time, on grounds both of morality and of military efficiency, it was widely assumed that major war between the powers would not only be a war of nation against nation, but also a war in which air attack would so undermine and demoralise the war willingness of enemy populations that air strikes might procure surrender on their own.

In the context of the 1920s technology this was largely conjecture, even fantasy, the realms – as one German writer put it – of 'misty illusions'.[9] Yet at the time the perceived danger was taken very seriously. The threat of air attack lay in the eye of the beholder. In the 1920s, long before modern sensibilities were blunted by the World War II bombing offensives, the possibilities of air power seemed horrific. Moreover the potential of air power seemed inexhaustible and its technical transformation fast and prodigious. In 1932 the British Foreign Secretary told the Cabinet: 'If civil and military aviation were in a position to do what they could do after 15 years of evolution, what were the prospects by fifty years hence?'[10]

The second factor that has shaped the emergence of deterrence was the unwillingness to put any constraints on the development and harnessing of science for military purposes. Of course some constraints could have been imposed: the Great Powers made considerable efforts from the Washington Conference in 1922 to the Disarmament Conference in 1932–4 to find ways of outlawing bombardment and bomber aircraft. Agreement was reached to outlaw chemical and biological weapons, though not on the application of science to produce them. But a combination of fears that air disarmament would somehow cripple civil aviation (science, this time, in the service of mankind), and a deep mutual distrust that air disarmament would be taken seriously by all the states involved, or that effective verification procedures might be established, led to repeated failure. Moreover all the powers had to take military pressure and commercial good sense into account. The RAF campaigned vigorously against air disarmament: 'Surely,' asked a Chiefs of Staff memorandum in 1928, 'it is useless to suggest that we can put the clock back ten years and get the cat back into the bag?'[11]

The problem with aviation technology was the speed and unpredictability of change. The interwar transformation was radical: clumsy, short-range bi-planes at the beginning, experimental jet aircraft and trans-oceanic bombers at the end. No air force could afford to fall behind in the technological race. No government could risk unilateral restraint. Fear of obsolescence, and hence of increased vulnerability in the air, fuelled the scientific race. From World War I onwards, the search was essentially for air weapons of optimum military efficiency, aircraft with long ranges and great lifting power, payloads of greater destructive effect, a super-bomber and a super-bomb. The British late 1930s development of the heavy bomber was expressed entirely in these terms; the specification was even called 'the Ideal Bomber'. The development of larger bombs, or better incendiaries, even of gas and germ bombs, all served the same end, to maximise the destructive power of aerial warfare.

The subsequent development both of missiles and of atomic weapons (research which pre-dated war in 1939) was simply an extension of the search for better weapons.

If it was only after 1945 that the marriage was consummated between ideal weapon and 'universalised violence', the courtship can be traced back to the industrialisation of warfare after 1914. Without the interwar conviction that war was now a clash of national systems and ideologies, in which civilian and soldier alike stood in the front line, and without the limitless scientific pursuit of the weapons to fight total war, strategy might well have evolved along different paths. Both factors shaped the frame of mind that strategists brought to bear on questions of confrontation and deterrence after 1945.[12]

The evolution of deterrence theory

(a) The nature of the threat

To be plausible deterrence required a threat so substantial that the risks of going to war far outweighed possible gains. In the 1920s it was difficult to see such a threat from either sea or land power: not only was this familiar military terrain, and survivable, but the impact of either on a potential enemy was uncertain and slow, as the recent war had shown. On the other hand, the threat posed by air power was perceived in fundamentally different terms. The language used indicated this: the 'knock-out blow', air 'frightfulness', 'terror bombing'. By the 1930s apocalyptic science-fiction, which had foreseen devastation from the air for 40 years, seemed to be becoming grim reality. Some prognostications have a very contemporary ring about them: 'Both sides will be aware,' wrote Air Commodore L.E.O. Charlton in 1936, 'that at the pressing of a button, instead of by a slow method of mobilization . . . war can now ensue . . .'.[13] In 1921 Will Irwin predicted that in the next war Paris would find itself 'becoming a superheated furnace – the population struggling, piling up, shrivelling with the heat . . . the survivors ranging the open fields in the condition of starving animals'.[14]

Views such as these helped to popularise Douhet's concept of the knock-out blow. There was seldom agreement among air thinkers and air force officers about which targets were so vulnerable to attack as to produce an almost instantaneous end to hostilities. In the 1920s great emphasis was placed on the enemy will to resist and morale, on the assumption often loudly expressed in British air circles that the moral effect of bombing was 20 times greater than the material. In the 1930s the emphasis shifted to more mundane economic targets, though the purpose was the same, to render the enemy state powerless through a combination of demoralisation and crisis of supply. Throughout the interwar period populations lived with the terror that conventional bombing would be accompanied by gas attack, germ warfare and incendiary bombing. Terror is relative. Harold Macmillan later recalled that 'we thought of air warfare in 1938 rather as people think of nuclear warfare today'.[15] Despite efforts by more serious military analysts to undermine the alarmist views of air power, the belief that the 'bomber will always get through' and that the experience of mass bombing would be utterly debilitating and unendurable was accepted with the same disquiet with which modern populations contemplate nuclear winter.

The threat of air power, and hence its deterrent capability, embraced several different fears. For the decision-maker the central anxiety was that populations subjected to aerial attack would lose the will to resist and force a surrender on a more warlike government. Much interwar discussion of susceptibility to attack concentrated on the impact on cities. It was generally assumed that air attack would be directed at major urban centres, partly because they were the seat of government or the administrative nerve centres, partly because they were usually the site of industry, but largely because urban populations were regarded as more rootless and anxious, likely to crack under pressure.[16] In 1928 the Air Ministry presented the Chiefs of Staff with an analysis of city vulnerability:

> The psychology of the crowd differs enormously from that of a disciplined military force and civilians do differ essentially from soldiers in so far as the possession and maintenance of morale is concerned. Their morale is infinitely more susceptible to collapse than that of a disciplined army.[17]

Air Ministry surveys of World War I bombing made no attempt to hide the fact that widespread panic had occurred when London was attacked. German reports of Allied bombing of cities highlighted the 'general sense of nervousness' produced by the regular threat of bombing which, for a number of victims, 'ruined their nerves, in some cases for life'.[18]

The persistent interwar fear in Britain was of a knock-out blow directed against London, not only the Empire's heart but also the largest conurbation in Europe. Some of the more imaginative predictions – and even more sober assessments by the RAF or the British government – stressed how vulnerable London was to the kind of strategic blackmail which deterrence carries with it. In the 1920s the putative enemy was France ('we must face the fact that if we fight France, London is going to be bombed' wrote a senior RAF officer in 1928)[19], in the 1930s it was Germany. In another of Air Commodore Charlton's military fantasies, *War over England*, published in 1936, the country was brought to its knees in two days. First a small force of aircraft attacked the annual Hendon Air Show, killing two-fifths of all British pilots and all the air force leadership and 30,000 spectators; then further attacks on London disrupted electricity, water supply and the docks. The *coup de grâce* was delivered with a gas attack on London and Paris which brought immediate surrender.[20]

Charlton also expressed another powerful fear, widely shared in 1930s Europe; the belief that the experience of bombing would produce anarchy, and the menace of communism. He argued that Britain in 1936 had a fifth column of communists outside the threatened zone who would stab the government in the back once bombing started. Stanley Baldwin, when Prime Minister in 1936, conjured up a lurid vision of the consequences of air and gas attack: 'I have often uttered the truism that the next war will be the end of civilisation in Europe ... the raging peoples of every country, torn with passion, suffering and horror, would wipe out every Government in Europe and you would have a state of anarchy from end to end.'[21] At the time of Munich the former French prime minister, Étienne Flandin, warned the British that at the first sign of bombardment the French Communist Party would 'set up a Communist regime'.[22]

The threat of bombing, even on a relatively modest scale, compounded different anxieties, but they amounted together to a general apprehension that a surprise, annihilating air attack, without prior declaration of war, might achieve an internal social and political collapse and decisive victory. Even the Committee of Imperial Defence, not generally inclined to accept the more exaggerated claims for air power, admitted in 1936 that a well-aimed attack against 'our people' from the air 'might well succeed'.[23] The Air Staff told the Committee to expect 20,000 casualties in London on the first day, 150,000 in one week. These figures were on a scale that the government could not contemplate. Senior politicians and soldiers throughout Europe were haunted by the fear that air power might, in the end, produce the short, decisive conflict denied them in World War I. General Sir Edmund Ironside confided to his diary shortly before Munich: 'we cannot expose ourselves to a German air attack. We simply commit suicide if we do.'[24]

(b) The deterrent effect

There were two possible responses to the bombing threat and both were explored in the interwar years: first of all, the search for a satisfactory framework for mutual restraint, which was generally regarded as both more moral and less dangerous than the second, the search for a mutual deterrent. Mutual restraint implied a general willingness to accept that aerial bombardment was morally wrong, and that its prohibition was generally enforceable and verifiable. There was no shortage of goodwill, since all 1920s states found the threat of air attack a sufficient deterrent to search for agreement. But there proved to be numerous stumbling blocks. France refused to accept that Germany should be given parity of treatment; there were general fears that prohibition of bombing aircraft would somehow inhibit rapid expansion of civil aviation, which was generally approved; and Britain, though willing to disarm to an agreed level if everyone else would, refused to outlaw bombardment as such because of her commitment to empire 'air policing', which had proved a very cost-effective way of coping with imperial unrest throughout the 1920s.[25]

Nor, in the end, was there much confidence that all states would abide by the rules, particularly the Soviet Union, which then possessed the world's largest air force, and, after January 1933, Hitler's Germany. It was proposed as a compromise that the League of Nations should become the only organisation allowed to operate bombing aircraft, as the core of a genuine international deterrent to prevent aggression, but such a suggestion, with the problems it raised of sovereignty and unanimity, produced no more satisfactory outcome than 1940s American efforts to internationalise nuclear power. Not until the SALT discussions a generation later did mutual restraint once again become an option. Instead the final failure of disarmament in 1934 heralded the onset of an aerial arms race which was linked to a crude version of mutual deterrence.

It could well be argued that the Soviet Union had already based its rearmament drive since the late 1920s on the build-up of a deterrent threat directed at the capitalist world; Hitler was attracted to air power as a 'shop window' deterrent, keeping other states at bay while the broader rearmament programmes were completed. But from the point of view of the emergence of modern deterrence theory, the most significant change after 1934 was in the attitude of the two states, Britain and America, which had pressed most forcefully for air disarmament. This was a critical change, for it marked the point in the century when the democracies realised that their safety could be secured not through international co-operation alone, but by the possession of adequate military force. Without this shift in perception, which existed right through to the 1980s, the western world might not have survived either Hitler or Stalin.

From 1934 onwards in Britain, and from 1938 in the United States, the political leadership advanced the view that the only deterrent that would work against aggressor states was the threat of massive air power. Neville Chamberlain, first as Chancellor of the Exchequer with a keen interest in rearmament and then as Prime Minister, was personally convinced that Britain's security rested on the development of air power; 'The Air Arm has emerged in recent years as a factor of first-rate, if not decisive importance.'[26] President Franklin D. Roosevelt, after observing what he believed to be the deterrent effect of the *Luftwaffe* at Munich in 1938, urged on large-scale rearmament in the air: 'When I write to foreign countries I must have something to back up my words.' In 1939 he suggested to army leaders that 'the only check to a world war, which would be understood in Germany, would be the creation of a great French air force and a powerful force in this country'.[27] There was moreover a moral gloss that the democratic states could put on air rearmament. In Britain it was argued that a large air deterrent force was not necessarily an indication of aggressive intent but was designed to make war less likely. As one writer in the *RAF Quarterly* put it in 1938, air power 'is the one method in this mad world of ours of ensuring ourselves a reasonable chance of never having to use it . . . If it is the only way we can ensure peace, we must take it and pay the price.'[28]

(c) *The operation of deterrence*

Deterrence was not simply politically attractive. The air forces were quick to see all the ramifications of adopting a deterrence stance. The first issue, argued out at the highest level in Britain between 1934 and 1938, revolved around the question of whether deterrence required parity of air striking power or an overwhelming advantage in striking capability. At first the government accepted the thesis of parity, a force equivalent to that of any other major air force within striking distance of London. But by 1938, when the German threat was much greater, the RAF urged the view that to argue from strength it was necessary to build 'an immense bomber force'.[29] An Air Staff memorandum in July pointed out that neither the Navy nor the Army was likely to pose a serious threat to Germany, and that 'In the circumstances we must regard the Air Striking Force as constituting not only a strong deterrent and insurance in peace, but also as our only way of imposing our will on the enemy in war.'[30] Lord Weir, the man chosen to speed up air rearmament in 1936, very much favoured this view too. A keen champion of city bombing in World War I, Weir sought 'a striking and offensive air weapon . . . so powerful as to compel the most wholesome respect from friend or foe'.[31] The same ambition framed American air rearmament when the go-ahead was finally given in 1939. To make the deterrent effect possible at all overwhelming force advantage was preferred to parity.

Concern with numbers reflected deeper concerns about force credibility. This meant the development of an evident war-fighting capability if deterrence failed. As the US Assistant Secretary of War pointed out to Secretary of War Harry H. Woodring in 1938: 'We realise that airplanes alone do not make an air force. We must have skilled operators, trained maintenance and combat crews, efficient accessory equipment and ample bases.'[32] Though both air forces recognised the deterrent potential in large-scale air power, it had to be seen as a real deterrent, capable of bringing to the enemy high levels of damage if peaceful persuasion failed. Air power in this sense was regarded as primarily offensive, whether the intention was to deter, to defend or to act the aggressor. It was this emphasis on offensive capability that made it difficult for the US Air Corps to sell the idea of the four-engined bomber to the Army or to Congress in the mid-1930s. Moreover, the recognition of the offensive nature of modern air power raised just those questions of pre-emptive strike versus second strike capability that resurfaced again in the post-war debates on nuclear strategy.

For Britain and France the fear of a pre-emptive strike from the air hung on the belief that the potential enemy, Germany, would not hesitate to launch such an attack without even a declaration of war. The planning staff in the Air Ministry told Bomber Command in 1938:

> We have reason to believe that Germany will be ruthless and indiscriminate in her endeavour to paralyse and destroy our national effort and morale and unless immediate steps are taken to reduce the intensity of attack it is conceivable that the enemy may achieve her object.[33]

There were those in the Air Ministry who urged the need to plan for a first strike against

German targets, even where this would bring 'retaliation from the enemy', but the politicians were firmly against the idea of pre-emption for fear of losing the moral advantage of not striking first. 'It seems hardly possible,' wrote one official shortly before Munich, 'that in a war between major air Powers it can be very long before the gloves come off. But we certainly cannot be the first to take them off.'[34] The result was that the RAF was forced to think in terms of a second, retaliatory strike against Germany if, and when, the knockout blow was attempted. Much planning time was devoted to estimating what the potential German bomb tonnage was that could be delivered to British cities by an all-out effort, and what kind of force equation Bomber command should be working towards to give the retaliatory threat credibility.[35]

More important, the emphasis on second strike placed a considerable premium on select-ing the right targets. War-fighting capability was seen as a function of effective targeting, and this raised the issue that has still not been resolved in arguments about air strategy between counter-force and counter-value targets. This was peculiarly an issue for British and American forces. German air forces were directed by the German high command to concentrate on tactical air support, with medium-range bomb attacks against military targets in rear areas; French air forces, though they would have preferred a more independent role, were similarly directed to a mainly tactical objective in preventing an enemy military breakthrough on land, with bombardment aimed at the combat zone and its support organisation.[36] The RAF was much more sceptical of the value of attacking enemy armed forces. Once a strike force was officially sanctioned in Britain, the RAF set about deciding which targets should most profitably be attacked if deterrence failed and the 'gloves came off'.

The whole tenor of RAF 1920s thinking had been to emphasise attacks on the vital centres of the enemy with the object of paralysing his industry and demoralising his work-force. This view survived into the age of parity and deterrence. The RAF War Manual of 1935 spelt out that the air offensive should strike at the 'nerve centres, main arteries, heart and brain' of an enemy economic and administrative system, with the aim 'of weakening his resistance and his power to continue the war'.[37] But it also became clear that in any confron-tation with another power likely to possess a large air striking force that this kind of damage could be inflicted mutually. In the British War Office Manual of Combined Operations issued three years later the commitment to attacking counter-value targets was maintained, but it was recognised that counter-force strategy was also necessary in order to limit damage:

> we are also vulnerable to air attack, and a similar strategy is available to the enemy. Unless, therefore, we can be sure that our offensive will be successful before a counter-offensive can seriously affect us – and such a situation can but rarely exist – it will be necessary to employ a proportion of our air forces on operations aimed at destroying or diminishing the power of the enemy air force.[38]

The RAF nevertheless saw counter-force not in terms of attacking the enemy air force in being, which was popularly regarded as an unprofitable operational option, but of attacking the industries and supply systems that supported the enemy air force. 'Any industrial object-ive of major importance is a more vulnerable target than an aerodrome . . .', minuted one Air Ministry official the day before the Battle of France.[39]

Throughout the pre-war period senior airmen in Britain refused to accept that an enemy air force could be attacked decisively or effectively by bombing. Bombardment tests con-ducted in the late 1930s showed that airfield targets were difficult to destroy and that superficial damage could be repaired 'in hours'.[40] The chief argument, however, rested on the grounds that an air force would always be too well dispersed and camouflaged to present more than fleeting targets. To be effective air power had to be directed at targets which would hurt the enemy: 'It is of the utmost importance that, *when* we do initiate air action on a serious scale, we must be allowed to do so *in the most effective way and against those objectives which we consider will have the greatest effect in injuring Germany, unhampered by the inevitable fact that there is bound to be incidental loss, and possibly heavy loss of civilian life.*'[41]

When American airmen began to think seriously about what they would do with their striking force once they had it, they too favoured counter-value targets, and for largely the same reasons, that the enemy will-to-resist had to be broken by denying his society and economy access to vital resources. Colonel Frank M. Andrews, a 1930s champion of strategic bombardment, was even prepared to suggest that 'under certain conditions it may be necessary to carry on reprisal activities by attacking hostile population centres'.[42] Those conditions would be met when fighting an enemy who was also prepared to attack civilians. The framework for the more sophisticated 1960s counter-value threats can be traced back here to the recognition that the air threat had to be met not just by air defence, but by the promise of massive retaliation in kind, even against civilians.

These views still left the question of which targets really would have maximum damage effect on a potential enemy, and hence enhanced deterrence value. In December 1937 Bomber Command was directed to draw up detailed plans 'for attack of *all* profitable objectives in Germany'.[43] Over the following year Air Intelligence provided a series of air plans which highlighted in particular attack on communications, oil and electricity and the aviation industry. These remained priority targets until the end of the war, when precision attacks against them were at last technically feasible. But the Air Staff were particularly attracted to the Ruhr industrial area as a general target, not only because it was within range of western European bases, but because it was regarded as the only real equivalent to London as a major counter-value urban target. The so-called 'Ruhr Plan', sustained attack on the industries and workforce concentrated in the major steel cities, though grudgingly approved by the Chiefs of Staff, was enthusiastically endorsed by RAF planners and was finally introduced on a modest scale towards the end of the Battle of France.

American planners were much more concerned to pinpoint economic structures – 'national *organic* systems' [italics in original] – which were particularly susceptible to interruption from the air. When Lieutenant General Henry H. Arnold, the US air forces' Chief, ordered air intelligence surveys of the optimum targets in Germany in 1941, the planning unit came up with electric power, transportation and fuel oil, with the addition of attacks on the aviation industry and air force to reduce bomber losses. A whole range of other industries was selected by both the RAF and the Air Corps as second-rank targets, to be attacked after striking successfully against primary systems.[44] The object in striking non-military targets remained the central one of reducing enemy war capability and war willingness, and creating conditions where an enemy might surrender rather than face more serious devastation.

Overwhelming force, war-fighting preparation, counter-value targeting were all central features of the 1930s strategic arguments about air power. The object of force preparation was to make it clear that the threat of force was not mere bluff. 'Because the *riposte* is certain,' wrote the British air strategist J.M. Spaight in 1938, 'because it cannot be parried, a belligerent will think twice and again before he initiates a mode of warfare the final outcome of which is incalculable.'[45] Yet there remained one flaw in the strategy based on the build up of massive retaliatory threat: the growing awareness in the 1930s that despite the claims for air power's offensive capability there might be ways of defending a state against air attack once it had started, in other words that the knock-out blow might be survivable.

Such a view was widely held in German and French military circles. Military writers in both countries believed that a well-organised defence, using fighters and anti-aircraft fire, together with adequate passive precautions in evacuating populations and preparing for gas warfare, would blunt the impact of bombing.[46] The *Luftwaffe* was reasonably confident that the huge anti-aircraft preparations undertaken from 1937 onwards would deter an enemy even from attempting air attack. In Britain the RAF accepted the development of defensive capability with an ill grace. It was the government's realisation that defence preparations were a technical and organisational possibility, and that the dangers of popular revolt and demoralisation after air attacks might be mitigated by their active efforts, which prompted a switch of emphasis from 1937 to defensive rather than offensive aviation. Sir Thomas Inskip, Minister for the Co-ordination of Defence, claimed that 'The role of our Air Force is not an early knock-out blow . . . but to prevent the Germans from knocking us out.'[47] The chief of Fighter Command, Air Chief Marshal Hugh Dowding, was among those who took the view that the best form of counter-force activity was an active air defence. In February 1939 he wrote to the Chief of Air Staff: 'It is my considered opinion that a bomber attack from Germany on this country would be brought to a standstill in a month or less, owing to the moral effect of the terrific casualties which they would suffer whenever they are intercepted.'[48]

Though this largely undermined the strategic arguments for deterrent air power, the RAF was forced to accept the shift in priority. From 1938 onwards (and confirmed spectacularly in autumn 1940) British political and military leaders gambled on the ability to survive air attack, combined with a limited counter-strike against enemy targets to discourage further attacks. The evident contradiction this involved – the assumption that the enemy would not survive to the same extent – was glossed over by superficial arguments about the fragile nature of the 'German personality'. British air power rested on the apparent compatibility of enhanced defence capability and enhanced striking power. This was hardly an American problem, since no enemy state could yet reach the continental USA with any effective payload. The Air Corps was free to concentrate its efforts on developing a credible deterrent force, and massive air retaliation should deterrence fail, a strategic profile that emerged in an almost identical form after 1945.

For the air power deterrent to work at all it was necessary for the potential enemy to know what the threat was, and to be convinced that its possible use was seriously meant. It was recognised at the time that this placed the democracies at something of a disadvantage, since the high moral ground occupied by the western states confronting fascism would clearly be lost if they declared themselves openly prepared to inflict massive aerial destruction on an enemy. In an appeal for American air co-operation, Spaight argued that the democracies would have to adopt a new posture internationally: 'there is no security except armed strength. The golden rule has gone by the board. If the democracies are to survive they must be war-minded, almost bloody-minded – for the time being.'[49] This the British never succeeded in being until the war was under way. Though Chamberlain held out hopes for air power's deterrent effect and made public Britain's commitment to large-scale air rearmament, he eschewed the kind of declaratory policy which spelt out what the nature of the deterrent threat was. German leaders had no such qualms, even though the *Luftwaffe* had not been built up to deliver the knock-out blow.

Roosevelt was much more inclined to issue threats, and the contrast between his public statements and those of his predecessor, Herbert Hoover, who had called for abolition of bombing planes and bombardment altogether in 1932, make clear that the USA was drawing by the end of the 1930s towards a declaratory stance. Treasury Secretary, Henry Morgenthau, told Roosevelt in January 1939 that 'for your international speeches to be effective, you must be backed up with the best air fleet in the world'.[50] But Roosevelt, too, was not in a position, with a large isolationist component in public opinion, to make overt threats of aggression or retaliation, and attempts to make clear to Japan before Pearl Harbor through covert means that American air power was a real threat to further expansion proved woefully inadequate. Nevertheless the unhappy 1939–41 experience, when deterrent threats went unperceived or ignored, paved the way for a public posture much more declaratory in character. The United States emerged in 1945 much more willing to be 'bloody-minded'. The President's Air Policy Commission reporting in 1948 stressed the importance of making it clear that America was serious about war: 'the hope is that by serving notice that war with the United States would be a most unprofitable business we may persuade nations to work for peace instead of war'.[51]

Limitations on deterrence

(a) Technical credibility

The central weakness in any strategy that relies on deterrent effect is the need for credibility. This must be secured in two ways: a belief that the threat is capable of technical operation, and is sufficiently great to deter, must be present if the aggressor is to face unacceptable risk; second, the aggressor must be sure beyond all reasonable doubt that the potential enemy will actually use the forces he is threatening with. A failure to secure either belief will render deterrence inoperable.

Of the two aspects of credibility the technical one imposed severe limits on practical interwar deterrence. During the 1920s, on the basis of First World War experience, the air weapon's technical capabilities were greatly exaggerated. The numbers of aircraft and the weight of bombs which it was suggested would produce war-winning effects were tiny by Second World War standards. Charlton's picture of British defeat at the hand of German airmen began with a knock-out blow by only 18 aircraft. Even the RAF's more sober assessments tended to overstate the damage and injury expected from a conventional attack. In 1938 the head of Bomber Command asserted from operational research that 300 medium bombers needed only two weeks and 1,500 sorties to paralyse the Ruhr's heavy industry.[52] In truth no major state could undertake an effective bombing campaign in the 1930s. The aircraft lacked sufficient range – not until 1939 did the *Luftwaffe* have medium bombers capable of reaching northern England, and British bombers could penetrate little farther than north-west Germany from British bases. The bomb carrying capacity was small in proportion to the industrial and operational effort for each bombing sortie, and until the war's early stages navigation and bomb aiming were in their infancy.

Of course it is important to remember that the perceived threat was relative. Medical and psychological reports suggested that the damage inflicted by even a modest air attack, particularly if accompanied by gas or germ warfare, would have effects on urban populations more devastating than anything ever experienced. Though there were clear technical limitations to air attack which had not been transcended by 1939, politicians in the pre-Hiroshima years had no other benchmarks to measure atrocity and devastation than science fiction and gloomy military prognosis. Evidence from the wars in Spain, Ethiopia and China proved ambiguous; moreover British military chiefs regarded these as minor conflicts between unequal adversaries. In any future war they expected Germany to turn the full weight of her forbidding air effort on Britain.

In fact it was in Germany that air power's real limitations were most keenly felt. German military theorists saw what Britain was aiming for, but perceived a doctrine they regarded as muddled and incomplete.[53] The view that wars could be won by air power in its current technical state was considered simply illusory. The attack on cities for the purpose of demoralisation or terror was specifically forbidden in the *Luftwaffe* war manual.[54] The main emphasis was put on what aircraft could technically do to best effect: to combine their defensive capabilities and firepower with the surface forces in tactical support operations. This view made it highly unlikely that German forces, or politicians, would be susceptible to any deterrent threat. Even with the world's best quality bombers in 1939, operational surveys showed the *Luftwaffe* incapable of mounting a serious strategic campaign against Britain. German leaders could not bring themselves to believe that RAF capability was any better.

By contrast the RAF never ignored the threat posed by the *Luftwaffe* and assumed right up to the outbreak of war and beyond that the German air arm's central purpose was to mount massive strategic attacks from the outset of hostilities. Yet when the RAF was forced to think operationally about what it could do to strike back at Germany, a wide range of debilitating limitations was unearthed at once. There were too few bombers of any range or significant payload; there was a woeful lack of bombardment training and experience; navigation was rudimentary; and not until the end of 1938 was there any agreement on what targets such an exiguous force should attack. Measured by the technical capability of its 1939 force there simply was no serious deterrent threat that the RAF could offer.

Both sides were well aware that technical conditions changed rapidly and substantially. The late 1930s strategic weakness of both forces was not designed to last. In Germany scientists were working on missiles of great range and were beginning to think about atomic weapons. German engineers had produced the jet engine and were designing the first intercontinental bombers.[55] The rough technological balance restored by British and French rearmament would have been overturned, if war had not intervened, within two or three years. These were the weapons systems that later supported the 1950s confrontation. In Britain the technical gap was to be made good not with jets and missiles, but with a conventional bombing force of great size and lifting power. The RAF Expansion Scheme 'M' launched after Munich called for a large force of multi-engined bombers with a range that would reach right across Germany, or deep into the Soviet Union from Middle Eastern bases, and with the maximum bomb load possible.[56]

The technical standards set for the new generation of heavy bombers both in Britain and the United States represented a radical leap in strategic technology of a kind that would make strategic deterrence at least a technical possibility. In the USA the search for a new strategic weapon went back to 1934 when the Air Corps recognised that within the forseeable future aircraft would be able to attack the continental United States across the ocean. Though the Army obstructed research and development of very long-range aviation, the Air Force stuck to its guns and by 1930s' end the United States had in the pipeline the best range of heavy bombers then available, and were already looking at aircraft that would provide the core of the strategic air forces after 1945.[57]

(b) Political credibility

If Britain's deterrent lacked technical credibility, there was no real evidence for any potential enemy that Britain possessed the political will to use the weapons she was threatening with. For much of the interwar period Britain was at the forefront of those states arguing for disarmament. While permitting the build up of an air striking force, Chamberlain repeatedly called for policies of mutual restraint in use of the air weapon. Publicly he was committed to the April 1939 statement he made in the House of Commons that 'it is against international law to bomb civilians as such and to make deliberate attacks on civilian populations'.[58]

Bomber Command operated under this constraint until the German attack on Rotterdam in May 1940, even though the RAF had satisfied itself years before that there was no legal impediment to bombing non-military objectives as long as there existed some 'indirect' connection with the enemy war effort.[59] RAF planning throughout the 1930s was predicated on the assumption that civilian casualties were unavoidable even when attacking military targets, and that the incidental effect on morale would be a strategic bonus. But Chamberlain faced pressures that were political as much as ethical. During the 1930s pacifism and public dread of war were factors that had to be taken into account. It was thought unlikely in the 1935 General Election that the electorate would accept increases in rearmament, let alone a commitment to strategic bombing, even as a deterrent.[60] British spokesmen had the difficult task of appearing to be high-minded at home and threatening abroad. A major study of air strategy, published in 1936, illustrated the British dilemma: 'inhuman and brutal use of the air weapon does not appeal to the average Briton, whose moral and cultural level is considerably above Continental standards. Ideas of "wholesale destruction" strategy can be entertained in peacetime only by the less-civilized or morally inferior nations.'[61] The feeling that it was hypocritical for democratic nations to threaten large-scale damage in peacetime died hard. Even during the war Bomber Command was inhibited more than it would have liked by the exercise of public scruple.

The commitment to morally defensible positions internationally and domestically made the practice of deterrence almost impossible. Another imponderable made British strategy unstable. If the British government felt sure of its own moral credentials, this was far from the case when it came to potential enemies. The Foreign Office was never certain that the dictator states would not commit some 'mad dog act'. It was impossible to assume rationality in other leaders.[62] This problem of the perception of rationality was central to the deterrence argument both before and after the war. The central paradox – that you deter someone through rational pressure from behaving irrationally – was clear in British approaches to Hitler. The temptation to produce mirror image calculations was overwhelming in this case, as it was later with the Soviet Union. If Britain feared the impact of strategic air power, then Germany, it was argued, should fear it too, however irrational Hitler's ambitions might be. Chamberlain hoped up to the outbreak of war that Hitler would see sense, that he would recognise that he could not win a war against the West, even if he might not lose it either.

But British intelligence before 1939 was simply not up to the task of discovering whether or not Hitler was deterred, and instead produced what was regarded as powerful evidence of German economic and moral weaknesses to suggest that even mad dictators would see the futility of risking war.[63] In practice the failure to deter Hitler by the air threat, or for that matter by any other threat, rested not on his fundamental *irrationality*, but on a rational calculation of acceptable risks. Hitler knew that the British lacked an effective bombing capability, and was sceptical of all claims for independent air power, but he did think that the Western states had an exaggerated fear of the German air threat and that this, combined with his alliance with Soviet Russia, would be sufficient to deter them.

The simple truth was that in the absence of very top-level political intelligence it was impossible to tell whether the deterrent strategy would work, a problem that American strategists have faced throughout the post-war period. But so poor was western intelligence on the *Luftwaffe* that neither Britain nor France succeeded before the outbreak of war in realising that it was a tactical, not a strategic force. This misperception left the RAF overcommitted to a defence and counter-strike strategy for the German attack in 1939 which never came, and greatly inhibited what help it could give to French forces in 1940 when the German military finally did with its air force what it had intended. Failing better information on the enemy, all the British could do was build up a force which they hoped would be strong enough to act strategically if the deterrent effect proved ineffectual and an 'irrational' attack was launched against them. In practice very much the same position was taken by 1950s and 1960s American strategy. In both periods the margin between deterrence and willingness to fight rested not on any intrinsic virtues in the deterrent posture but on the potential enemy's self-restraint.

(c) Deterrence verses war-fighting

The final limitation lay in the hostility of much of the military establishment both to claims for independent or strategic air power and to the idea that war-fighting could in some sense be substituted by the strategic aim of deterrence. There were plenty of officers who would have echoed the sentiments expressed in 1939 by the French general, Maxime Weygand: 'There is something in these bombardments of defenceless people behind the front that smacks of cowardice which is repugnant to the soldier.'[64] American soldiers were strongly critical of 1930s claims for air power. Brigadier General Stanley D. Embick of the War Plans Division described military aviation in 1935 as essentially 'auxiliary in character'. Colonel Walter Krueger, in a memorandum penned the same year, agreed that 'Aircraft are admittedly powerful agents of destruction, but their power is curtailed by their inherent limitations.' He preferred a fleet of naval vessels to a 'decisively inferior air fleet'.[65] In Britain the Chiefs of Staff acted throughout the late 1930s to impose much more modest tasks on the bomber force than air theorists wanted, insisting on the tactical use of aviation and limited counter-force operations as the most effective use of aircraft under current technical conditions.

This was not mere conservatism for its own sake. There is no doubt that the claims for air power, and the nature of the air threat were greatly exaggerated and were increasingly seen to be so with the advent of more technically sophisticated defence systems based on radar and fast interceptor fighters. But such attitudes highlighted internal political conflict and professional jealousy between the three services over their future strategic role and allocation of military resources.[66] There was never any question that the German or French armies would abandon large-scale surface fighting in favour of massive aerial striking power, if only because even with a massive air deterrent the risk of being exposed to conventional army attack was still considerable. Britain was more geographically secure, but even here the Navy was able to win the lion's share of military spending for much of the interwar period because of British strategic obligations overseas. In the USA army hostility to air power claims might well have killed strategic aviation in its cradle had it not been for Roosevelt's personal enthusiasm for air power.

Most significant, however, was that up to the early 1940s no weapon or delivery system existed of sufficient and assured destructive power to pose as a plausible substitute for the other services. Hence the assumption accepted in all states that in any future war surface forces would not only take the bulk of the actual fighting, but could act as a deterrent threat every bit as effective as air power.[67] It is arguable whether the French were more afraid of the German Army or the German Air Force, or the British more afraid of Italian seapower than air power. Certainly Hitler, to the extent that he was affected by foreign military power at all, was more aware of Western naval strength and the French and Soviet armies than he was of air power. Though the British tried to develop a credible striking force once war had begun, following Churchill's view that 'our aim is to win the war by building up a crushing measure of air superiority . . .'[68], the key to deterrence credibility lay in German research into missile technology, and the Anglo-American decision to develop the atomic bomb.

The coming of deterrence

It would be wrong to argue that no deterrent effect could be found before 1939, but its application was limited, and it was difficult to separate air power from other military and political components which produced deterrence. It was certainly possible, as the RAF did, to deter colonial peoples from violent opposition by the threat of direct punishment, but this was a crude weapon, picking on tribal societies' vulnerability, their inability to oppose air power and deep awe for its technical novelty. Major states could certainly bring pressure to bear on minor powers by the threat of air attack, as Germany did with rump Czechoslovakia in March 1939. It was even possible to wield the air threat in relations between major states as Germany did, not entirely intentionally, during the Munich crisis. Fear of bomb attack did influence both Chamberlain and French Prime Minister Edouard Daladier in their approach to the Czech crisis, but it must be remembered that, despite this threat, on 28 September 1938 both powers would have gone to war with Germany if Czech territory were seized by force.[69]

The deterrent effect that developed after World War II with the rise of nuclear-armed superpowers was understood before the war but was still technically inoperable. The one area in which it was possible to see the effect actually working, the mutual restraint in using chemical and biological weapons, rested on just the criteria that would govern post-war deterrence – that the weapon would produce unacceptably high levels of damage, and that the damage could be mutually inflicted. By 1939 Germany had a substantial lead in chemical warfare, both in conventional chemicals used in World War I, and in pioneering new 'nerve' gases, but German intelligence was unaware of the lead, and assumed that the Western states had been stockpiling and experimenting to an extent greater than Germany, and had the capability to deliver gas bombs over Germany. Hitler accepted that these weapons should not be used after approaches from Britain at the beginning of the war, and although there were times when both sides contemplated using the materials (and every major state built up enormous stockpiles of chemical and biological weapons) the deterrent effect was sufficient to maintain restraint.[70] Of course the threat did not inhibit conventional warfare, nor did it avert atrocity in wartime. But the restraint shown by both sides was a classic result of deterrence, where both sides knew the other possessed the weapon, could deliver it and would, if attacked, retaliate.

It was some time after 1945 that anything like this situation was achieved with nuclear weapons. By 1948 America had only seven atomic bombs, each of which took a team of 24 men two days to assemble. It is all too often forgotten that for years after 1945 air power deterrence rested on the conventional as well as the nuclear bombing threat.[71] That is not to say that the threat of attack with even a handful of atomic bombs was ever taken lightly, though it was clearly survivable in the way that modern nuclear war is not, but the horrible damage inflicted by conventional strategic bombardment during the war was a constant reminder that the feeble 1930s air threat had become an operational reality at last. In that sense Dresden was as exemplary as Hiroshima.

There were thus some very obvious continuities between the pre- and post-war situations, not only in the lessons learned from the experience of pre-war diplomacy and wartime strategy, but also in the gradual adoption in the USA of a strategy whose shape and components were developed first in the interwar arguments about air power. Perhaps most important of all, wartime strategic bombing, and the fire-bombing of Japan in particular, pushed the Western states across psychological and ethical thresholds that made possible a strategy of mass destruction of civilians from the air, which would never have been countenanced in the 1930s.

For Americans the harshest lesson of all was that despite all their efforts for peace after 1918 war was still an ever-present threat in the international system. Moreover, Japanese aggression in 1941 showed that even rich, militarily powerful states were not immune to surprise attack. They blamed much of this situation on the Anglo-French failure to face up to Hitler in the 1930s with sufficient force to deter him. Ambassador William C. Bullitt remarked to Roosevelt after Munich: 'If you have enough airplanes you don't have to go to Berchtesgaden.'[72] The unpleasant consequence for Americans was that they would have to shoulder the responsibility after 1945 for defending the West by remaining a massively armed power, where all their traditions were of isolation and retrenchment. The report of the Air Policy Commission in 1948 took as its starting point that 'disarmament is out of the question'. It went on to ask: 'Where does relative security lie in a world in which all nations are free to arm and in which war is the final resort for the settlement of international disputes?' The Commission recommended that the USA should rely on air power as the basis of her military security. The strategy suggested formed the basis of American military policy in the nuclear age:[73]

> security is to be found only in a policy of arming the United States so strongly (1) that other nations will hesitate to attack us or our vital national interests because of the violence of the counter-attack they would have to face, and (2) that if we are attacked we will be able to smash the assault at the earliest possible moment.

Post-war strategy, like 1930s air power strategy, saw the deterrent effect as a desirable strategic consequence, but it was clear that the effect depended on willingness and ability to fight. In the charged atmosphere of early Cold War politics it did not seem out of the question that America might suffer what one commentator called an 'atomic Pearl Harbor'.[74] An earlier report highlighted the fact that with the atomic bomb had been created a 'weapon so ideally suited to sudden unannounced attack that a country's major cities might be destroyed overnight . . .'.[75] The nightmare of the knock-out blow spurred on American military preparations after 1945 as it had done British 1930s rearmament. The difference lay in the fact that atomic weapons raised the thresholds of damage and fear well beyond what they had been ten years before.

The US response was to continue nuclear research, to stockpile atomic weapons, and to think hard about how they might be used. The targeting debate about the relative merits of counter-force and counter-value objectives was revived. The American decision to opt for city attacks against the Soviet industrial heartlands not only reflected the fact that as yet US cities faced no comparable threat, but also the conviction that the surest way to convince an enemy to give way was to attack the vital centres and demoralise the population as the Army Air Forces had done in 1944–45. Nor was there much doubt in the early years of atomic weapons that America would use the weapons at her disposal if it became necessary. In 1947 the Joint Chiefs of Staff asked the Atomic Energy Corporation to supply 400 atomic bombs by 1953 capable of 'killing a nation'.[76] The deterrent effect rested entirely on the existence of a credible military strategy of conventional and atomic bombardment.

Until Mutual Assured Destruction it could even be argued that the deterrent effect was largely secondary to the active preparation for exercising strategic air power. Indeed there were writers who argued that atomic warfare could be fought against, using the same weapons produced to combat the 1930s bomber threat, fighter interception and well-organised passive defence.[77] The real breakthrough came later, with the hydrogen bomb, the growth of modern missile systems and weapons stockpiles, and the acquisition of nuclear weapons by other major states. The mid-1950s is a more critical turning point in many ways than 1945.

American strategy, with its support for Western Europe, rested on a determination not to return to the abortive aims of disarmament and world co-operation which internationalists had sought after 1918. The alternative, already adopted by all major states in 1935–41, was to build up massive armed force, to harness science and industry to refining the weapons systems, and to assume the posture of counter-threat. The outcome was not only the Second World War, but the structure and nature of great power strategy ever since. In their hostility to aggression and war-mongering, the two major Western states, Britain and America, opted for a strategy of deterring or containing the threat from Germany and Japan and, after 1945, the Soviet Union. This required the build up of large military forces and a specific threat, of air power retaliation, in order to keep the peace. It was a policy that locked the Western states into an upward spiral of military commitment until a weapon so devastating and unthinkable could be found which would stop all aggressors, rational or irrational, opportunistic or ideologically motivated, from risking all-out war.

This position was achieved not by 1939, nor by 1941, but was finally achieved after 1945 when the air threat had been fully revealed in war. Modern deterrence theory grew out of the strategic and moral dilemmas facing the Western states; its necessity first became apparent in response to the political and military revolution set in motion by Hitler and the Japanese armed forces. Deterrent credibility stemmed not from fear of the unknown, but from the evidence of what liberal democracies had done to Hamburg, Dresden and Hiroshima. This has been the central paradox in Western strategy, that in order to keep the peace Western states must be seen to be fully prepared to unleash the most unimaginably destructive of wars.

Writing of the Manhattan Project in 1945, the official report spoke of a new weapon available to the West 'that is potentially destructive beyond the wildest nightmares of the imagination'. Yet it was a weapon, the report went on, not produced by a warped genius inspired by the devil, 'but by the arduous labor of thousands of normal men and women working for the safety of their country'.[78] Just as the deterrent effect sought in the 1930s was based on the experience of bombing in World War I, in Spain and China and Ethiopia, so the deterrent effect after 1945 was rooted in the material catastrophe that overcame the Axis states, and the evident willingness of democracies to use any weapon in defence of their freedom.

Notes

1   R.B. Byers, 'Deterrence under attack: crisis and dilemma' in Byers (ed.), *Deterrence in the 1980s: Crisis and Dilemma* (London, 1985), p. 18; see too G. Quester, 'The Strategy of Deterrence: Is the concept credible?' in ibid. pp. 60–95; P. Morgan, *Deterrence: A Conceptual Analysis* (Beverly Hills, CA: London: Sage, 1977/83), esp. pp. 16–24, 205–15; G. Snyder, *Deterrence and Defense: Toward a Theory of National Security* (Princeton UP, 1961).
2   L.E.O. Charlton, *The Menace of the Clouds* (London, 1937), p. 25.
3   C. Messenger, *The Art of Blitzkrieg* (London, 1976) p. 31. On the origins of strategic air power, see

N. Jones, *The Beginnings of Strategic Air Power: A History of the British Bomber Force 1923–1939* (London: Frank Cass 1987); B. Brodie, *Strategy in the Missile Age* (Princeton UP, 1959) chs. 3–5; G. Quester, *Deterrence before Hiroshima* (NY, 1960).

4   R. Aron, *The Century of Total War* (London, 1954), p. 41.

5   C. Falls, *The Nature of Modern Warfare* (London, 1941) pp. 18–19. Falls regarded the bomber as the central weapon in total war: 'one might almost say that it is based upon indiscriminate attack, especially from the air, directed against the civilian population' (p. 6).

6   B.A. Carroll, *Design for Total War: Arms and Economics in the Third Reich* (The Hague, 1968) p. 40.

7   Public Record Office, London (PRO), AIR 9/8 COS 156, note by the First Sea Lord, 21 May 1928, p. 2.

8   PRO AIR 9/8, notes on a Memo, by the CIGS, 23 May 1928, p. 2. The author quotes similar views from French and German sources, including the following from one German writer: 'In wars of the future the initial hostile attack will be directed against the great nerve and communication centres of the enemy's territory . . . in fact against every life artery of the country . . . the war will frequently have the appearance of a destruction en masse of the entire civil population rather than a combat of armed men.'

9   H. Klotz, *Militärische Lehren des Bürgerkrieges in Spanien* (self-published, 1937), p. 53.

10 U. Bialer, *The Shadow of the Bomber: the Fear of Air Attack and British Bombing 1932–1939* (London: R. Hist. S. 1980) p. 21. See also Klotz, p. 50, who gives the following figures to indicate the development of air technology. The ratio of 1918 performance to that of 1937 was as follows: speed 1:3.8; rate of climb 1:5.8; bomb load 1:6.0; range 1:8.0.

11 PRO AIR 9/8, COS 76th Meeting, 'The War Object of an Air Force', May 1928, p. 1.

12 On the 'Ideal Bomber' see M. Smith, *British Air Strategy between the Wars* (Oxford: Clarendon Press, 1984) pp. 240–7. For a general discussion of the issues involved in mobilising science see S.J. Deitchman, *Military Power and the Advance of Technology* (Boulder, CO: Westview Press, 1983).

13 Charlton, *Menace*, p. 22.

14 M.S. Sherry, *The Rise of American Air Power: The Creation of Armageddon* (New Haven: Yale UP, 1987), p. 32.

15 H. Macmillan, *Winds of Change* (London: Macmillan 1960) p. 522.

16 J. Konvitz, 'Représentations urbaines et bombardements stratégiques 1914–1945' *Annales* No. 4 (1989), pp. 824–8.

17 PRO AIR 9/8, Air Ministry, note by planning dept., 17 May 1928, p. 3.

18 PRO AIR 9/39, 'Air Policy and Strategy', 23 Mar. 1936, Appendix L, pp. 3–6. See too AIR 9/8, Air Ministry note 26 May 1938, p. 6: 'There is ample evidence to prove that our industrial population is most susceptible to panic and loss of morale . . . German attacks on England greatly affected public opinion.'

19 PRO AIR 9/8, AVM P.B. Joubert de la Ferté to Air Ministry, 2 May 1929.

20 L.E.O. Charlton, *War over England* (London, 1936), pp. 158–81, 218–25.

21 New Fabian Research Bureau, *The Road to War, Being an Analysis of the National Government's Foreign Policy* (London, 1937), pp. 177–8.

22 Quester, *Deterrence*, p. 97.

23 Bialer, *Shadow of Bomber*, pp. 129–30.

24 R. Macleod (ed.), *The Ironside Diaries 1937–1940* (London: Cassell, 1962), p. 62, entry for 22 Sept. 1938.

25 R.A. Chaput, *Disarmament in British Foreign Policy* (London, 1935), pp. 335–59.

26 N. Gibbs, *Grand Strategy, Vol.I: Rearmament Policy* (London: HMSO, 1976), p. 534; see too U. Bialer, 'Elite Opinion and Defence Policy: Air Power Advocacy and British Rearmament during the 1930s', *British Journal of International Studies* 6/1 (1980), pp. 32–51.

27 Sherry, *American Air Power*, pp. 79–80; H. Ickes, *The Secret Diary of Harold L. Ickes* (London: 1955), Vol.II, pp. 468–9.

28 E.W. Sheppard, 'Hep! Hep!' *RAF Quarterly*, Vol.9 (1938), p. 40; see also Charlton, *Menace*, p. 13: '[Air power] can be treated as a threat, the mere hint of which may suffice to coerce a country which lies peculiarly open to attack . . . air forces may in course of time produce an equilibrium which could be the forerunner of universal peace . . .'; J.M. Spaight, *Can America Prevent Frightfulness from the Air?* (London, Sept. 1939), p. 42: 'in air power one finds the answer to those who believe that because war has become so terrible it will not be lightly engaged. What does prevent it from being lightly

engaged in the world as it is at present, is the possession by the intended victim, as well as the intending aggressor, of adequate force: that, and nothing else.'

29 PRO AIR 8/258, Bombing Policy file, 'Fighters or Bombers' n.d. [1938], p. 8.

30 PRO AIR 8/244, Air Staff, 'The Role of the Air Force in National Defence', 5 July 1938, p. 9.

31 W.J. Reader, *Architect of Air Power. The Life of the First Viscount Weir of Eastwood 1877–1959* (London: 1968), p. 231; see also M. Smith, 'Rearmament and Deterrence in Britain in the Thirties', *The Journal of Strategic Studies* (hereafter JSS) 1/3 (Dec. 1978) pp. 313–37.

32 National Archives, Washington DC, (NA), RG 94/508, Memo. for the Secretary of War, 16 Feb. 1938. 'Air Corps Program', p. 7.

33 PRO AIR 14/381, Plan W1 'Appreciation of the Employment of the British Air Striking Force against the German Air Striking Force', April 1938, p. 1.

34 PRO AIR 8/251, Air Ministry (Plans) to Chief of Air Staff (CAS hereafter), 9 Sept. 1938, p. 2; AIR 14/194, Bomber Command, 'Note on the question of relaxing the bombardment instructions and initiating extended air action', 7 Sept. 1939, p. 8.

35 PRO CAB 64/15, COS 603, 'Estimated Scale of air attack on England in the event of war with Germany', 20 July 1937. It was estimated that Germany could deliver 1,000 tons daily against Britain by April 1939, or 644 a day if France were also attacked. Even by 1940 Bomber Command could still only promise to deliver 100 tons a day in retaliation in the first week, dropping to 30 tons a day thereafter (AIR 14/194, record of a conference with CAS, 28 Apr. 1940). Scheme 'L' in spring 1939 planned a British bombing capacity of 3,795 tons by 1941 (total of all operational squadrons). See AIR 8/250, Cabinet Paper 218(38), 'Striking Power of the Metropolitan Bomber Force, 15 April 1939', p. 2.

36 R.J. Young, 'The Strategic Dream: French Air Doctrine in the Inter-war period 1919–39' *Journal of Contemporary History* 9/1 (1974), pp. 63–76; K-H. Völker, *Die deutsche Luftwaffe, 1933–1939: Aufbau, Führung und Rüstung der Luftwaffe sowie die Entwicklung der deutschen Luftkriegstheorie* (Stuttgart, 1967), pp. 86–9, 195–201.

37 NA RG18/223 Box 1, RAF War Manual, Part I, Operations (May 1935), p. 57.

38 PRO AIR 2/1830, Manual of Combined Operations, 1938, para. 22.

39 PRO AIR 9/99, Note, the attack of air forces on the ground, 9 May 1940, p. 2.

40 PRO AIR 9/8, CAS 'note upon the Memo. of the Chief of the Naval Staff', May 1928, p. 3: 'One Air Force cannot destroy the organisation of another Air Force by bombing': AIR 9/98, 'Reports on trials to determine the effect of air attack against aircraft dispersed about an aerodrome site', July 1938. See also M. Smith, 'The RAF and Counter-force Strategy before World War II', *RUSI Journal* 121/1 (Spring 1976), pp. 68–72.

41 PRO AIR 14/194, Bomber Command, Note, 7 Sept. 1939, (italics in original).

42 NA RG 18/231, Andrews Paper, 'The Airplane in National Defense' n.d. [1932]. See too Library of Congress, Washington D.C., Andrews Papers, Box 11, Lecture by Maj. Harold George, 'An Inquiry into the Subject War', 1936, for a clear summary of counter-value strategy: 'the very make-up of modern industrial nations are much more vulnerable because of the existence of the economic structure, which our present civilisation has created than were the nations of a century ago ... It appears that nations are susceptible to defeat by interruption of this economic web. It is possible that the moral collapse brought by the breaking of this closely knit web will be sufficient, but, closely connected therewith, is the industrial fabric which is absolutely essential for modern war.'

43 PRO AIR 14/225, Air Ministry Directive to Bomber Command, 13 Dec. 1937, p. 2 (italics in original).

44 H.S. Hansell, *The Strategic Air War against Germany and Japan* (Washington D.C., Office of AF Hist., 1986), pp. 10–19; idem, *The Air Plan that Defeated Hitler* (Atlanta, GA: Higgins-McArthur/Longino & Porter, 1972), pp. 50–63; R. Futrell, *Ideas, Concepts, Doctrine: A History of Basic Thinking in the United States Air Force 1907–1964* (Maxwell AFB, AL: Air University, Aerospace Studies Inst., 1972) pp. 59–62.

45 Quester, *Deterrence*, p. 102 (italics in original). See also Spaight, *Frightfulness*, p. 43; 'Make air attack less possible by making the defence stronger and readier, make the riposte to it certain to be more prompt and powerful if it does occur, and you go far to make war unlikely.'

46 On France, P. Le Goyet, 'Evolution de la doctrine d'emploi de l'aviation française entre 1919 et 1939'. *Revue d'histoire de la Deuxième Guerre Mondiale*, Vol.19 (1969).

47 C. Messenger, *'Bomber' Harris and the Strategic Bombing Offensive 1939–1945* (London, 1984), p. 23.

48 PRO AIR 16/261, ACM Dowding to ACM Newall, 24 Feb. 1939, pp. 1–2; see also AIR 9/99, HQ Bomber Command to Air Ministry, Dec. 1937, in which it was argued that the best counter-force strategy lay with fighter aircraft 'destroying enemy bombers in flight'.

49 Spaight, *Frightfulness*, p. 43.

50 Sherry, *American Air Power*, p. 82.

51 *Survival in the Air Age: A Report of the President's Air Policy Commission* (Washington, DC: US GPO, 1 Jan. 1948), p. 12.

52 PRO AIR 14/225, Draft of letter from ACM Sir Edgar Ludlow-Hewitt to Air Ministry, n.d. [early 1938]. These figures were rightly regarded as an exaggeration by the Air Staff.

53 O.E. Schüddekopf, *Britische Gedanken über den Einsatz des Luftheeres* (Berlin, 1939) pp. 42–55.

54 K-H. Völker (ed.), *Dokumente und Dokumentarfotos zur Geschichte der deutschen Luftwaffe* (Stuttgart, 1968), doc. 200, 'Luftkriegführung', 1936, p. 82: 'Attack on cities for the purpose of terrorisation of the population is fundamentally rejected'. See too K.A. Maier, 'Total War and German Air Doctrine before the Second World War' in W. Deist (ed.) *The German Military in the Age of Total War* (Leamington Spa: Berg 1985), pp. 213–18.

55 M. Walker, *German National Socialism and the Quest for Nuclear Power 1933–1949* (Cambridge, 1989), pp. 13–41: W. Dornberger, *V2* (London, 1954); R.J. Overy, 'From "Uralbomber" to "Amerikabomber": the *Luftwaffe* and Strategic Bombing', *JSS* 1/2 (Sept. 1978), pp. 154–75.

56 PRO AIR 8/250, RAF Expansion Scheme 'M', Memo. by the Secretary of State for Air, 'Relative Air Strength and Proposals for the Improvement of the Country's Position', 25 Oct. 1938.

57 R.W. Krauskopf, 'The Army and the Strategic Bomber 1930–1939', Part I, *Military Affairs*, Vol.22 (1958/9).

58 PRO AIR 9/105, Anglo-French Staff Conversations, 'Preparation of Joint Plans of Action for Franco-British Air Force', 19 Apr. 1939, pp. 2–3.

59 PRO AIR 9/8, 69th COS, 'The War Object of an Air Force', 22 May 1928, pp. 1–3: 'It is clear, therefore, that in the late war, military works, military establishments, workshops or plant, and also transportation systems and centres of communications which could be used directly or indirectly for the needs of the enemy army, navy or air force, were regarded as legitimate objectives of air bombardment, whether situated within or without the actual zone of military land operations.'

60 For a general discussion of British pacifism and public opinion see M. Ceadel, *Pacifism in Britain 1914–1945* (Oxford, 1981).

61 Gen. N.N. Golovine, 'Air Strategy', Part III, *RAF Quarterly* Vol.7, (1936) p. 429.

62 It is interesting to look at 1930s Air Ministry planning with this perception. There was much discussion of totalitarian states, of dictatorship, of populations whose leaders 'enslaved' them and disregarded their fate. See especially PRO AIR 9/8, Air Staff Memorandum. 'The Potential Dangers to the Security of the British Empire and our Consequent Defence Requirements', 15 Jan. 1936: 'In Russia,' ran the report, 'the Soviet system provides an inexhaustible mass of slave labour and permits a disregard of the interests and welfare of the individual which would not be tolerated in the British Empire . . . We are therefore faced not only with the necessity of providing the forces essential for our security, but of providing them in competition with systems which tend to simplify the tasks of our potential enemies . . .'.

63 R.J. Overy, 'Germany, "Domestic Crisis" and War in 1939' *Past & Present*, No. 116 (1987), pp. 141–7; W. Wark, *The Ultimate Enemy: British Intelligence and Nazi Germany* (OUP, 1986), Ch. 7.

64 Gen. M. Weygand, 'How France is Defended', *International Affairs*, Vol.18 (1939) pp. 471–1.

65 NA RG 165/888.96, Memo. by Brig. Gen. Embick, 'Aviation versus Coastal Fortifications', p. 2; Memo. by Col. W. Krueger, 'Air Defense as a Factor in National Defense', Dec. 1935, p. 2, 4.

66 This point has been made convincingly by H. Strachan. 'Deterrence Theory: The Problem of Continuity', *JSS* 7/4 (Dec. 1984) pp. 395–401.

67 See J. Mearsheimer, *Conventional Deterrence* (Ithaca, NY: Cornell UP, 1983), esp. Chs. 2–3. This is one of the few studies of deterrence before 1945. The argument developed here that deterrence is a direct function of military strategies rather than a function of existing weapons systems suffers from the almost complete absence of any discussion on air power and air forces before 1940.

68 PRO AIR 8/258, 'Draft Air Programme' n.d. [1941], p. 1.

69 On 'political' deterrence see H.S. Dinerstein, 'The Impact of Air Power on the International Scene 1930–1939', *Military Affairs*, Vol.19 (1955) pp. 65–70; E.M. Emme, 'Emergence of Nazi Luftpolitik as a Weapon in International Affairs', *Aerospace Historian* Vol. 7 (1960); M.S. Smith, 'The RAF, Air Power and British Foreign Policy', *Journal of Contemporary History* Vol. 12 (1977).

70 E.M. Spiers, *Chemical Warfare* (Urbana: Univ. of Illinois P. London: Macmillan 1986), esp. pp.58–64; R. Harris and J. Paxman, *A Higher Form of Killing: the Secret Story of Gas and Germ Warfare* (London: Paladin, 1982) pp. 53–67, 107–36.

71 N. Polmar, *Strategic Weapons: An Introduction* (NY: 1982), pp. 3–4; Quester, 'Strategy of Deterrence', pp. 71–3; Strachan, 'Deterrence', pp. 396–7; A.L. Friedberg, 'A History of US Strategic "Doctrine" 1945 to 1980', in A. Perlmutter and J. Gooch (ed.), *Strategy and the Social Sciences: Issues in defense policy* (London: Frank Cass, 1981), pp. 40–1, 45–7; D.A. Rosenberg, 'American Atomic Strategy and the Hydrogen Bomb Decision', *Journal of American History* 66/1 (1979), pp. 62–76. A strong sense of the continuities in air power from the 1930s to the 1950s can be found be reading the collected speeches and articles of Marshal of the RAF John Slessor, which he published in 1957 under the title *The Great Deterrent* (London, 1957).

72 Sherry, *American Air Force*, p. 76.

73 *Survival in the Air Age*, pp. 6–7.

74 D.O. Smith, 'The Role of Airpower since World War II', *Military Affairs* Vol.19 (1955), p. 72.

75 H.D. Smyth, *A General Account of the Development of Methods of Using Atomic Energy for Military Purposes under the Auspices of the United States Government 1940–1945* (London: HMSO, 1945) p. 134.

76 Rosenberg 'Atomic Strategy', p. 68. By 1950 the USA still lacked this atomic capability. The Harmon Committee set up in 1949 to evaluate impact of atomic attack on the Soviet Union estimated that the attack would produce 2.7 million dead, 4 million casualties, and would reduce Soviet industrial output by 30–40 per cent. This was substantially lower than Soviet losses in World War II. See Friedberg, 'Strategic Doctrine', p. 46.

77 See, e.g., Gen. L.M. Chassin, *Stratégie et bombe atomique* (Paris, 1948), p. 260 ff.

78 Smyth, *General Account*, p. 134.

10 Kosovo and the great air power debate

Daniel L. Byman and Matthew C. Waxman

The capitulation of Serbian President Slobodan Milosevic on June 9, 1999, after seventy-eight days of bombing by the North Atlantic Treaty Organization (NATO), is being portrayed by many as a watershed in the history of air power. For the first time, the use of air strikes alone brought a foe to its knees—and at the cost of no NATO lives. The prophecies of Giulio Douhet and other air power visionaries appear realized.[1] Lieut. Gen. Michael Short, who ran the bombing campaign, has argued that "NATO got every one of the terms it had stipulated in Rambouillet and beyond Rambouillet, and I credit this as a victory for air power."[2] This view is not confined to the air force. Historian John Keegan conceded, "I didn't want to change my beliefs, but there was too much evidence accumulating to stick to the article of faith. It now does look as if air power has prevailed in the Balkans, and that the time has come to redefine how victory in war may be won."[3] Dissenters, of course, raise their voices. Noting the failure of air power to fulfill its promise in the past, they are skeptical of its efficacy in Kosovo. Instead, they point to factors such as the threat of a ground invasion; the lack of Russian support for Serbia, or the resurgence of the Kosovo Liberation Army (KLA) as key to Milosevic's capitulation. Without these factors, dissenters argue, air strikes alone would not have forced Milosevic's hand. They also point out that air power failed to prevent the very ethnic cleansing that prompted Western leaders to act in the first place.[4]

The importance of this debate goes beyond bragging rights. Already, some military planners are using their interpretations of the air war in Kosovo, Operation Allied Force, to design future campaigns. All the services are drawing on Kosovo's supposed lessons in their procurement requests.[5]

Unfortunately, the current debate over air power's effectiveness confuses more than it enlightens. The Kosovo experience does little to vindicate the general argument that air attacks alone can compel enemy states to yield on key interests. But this caution to air power's champions should be tempered by an equally firm rejection of its critics: air power's past failures to coerce on its own do not discredit its role in successful coercive diplomacy. Air power is like any other instrument of statecraft. Instead of asking if air power alone can coerce, the important questions are: how can it contribute to successful coercion, and under what circumstances are its contributions most effective?

The academic contribution to this debate increases rather than untangles the confusion.[6] The U.S. military has spent more than a decade trying to learn to think in terms of joint operations—the synergistic integration of air, land, space, and sea forces—and move away from service-specific perspectives.[7] Despite a partial shift in the air force's own thinking, the most prominent work on air power theory remains focused on air power-centric or air power-only strategies.[8] At the same time, most academic examinations of *coercion* focus on a single coercive instrument at a time—does air power alone, for instance, cause adversaries to capitulate?—while in reality adversaries consider the damage wrought by air power only in the context of overall military balance, internal stability, diplomatic support, and a host of other factors.[9]

This article argues that the current air power debate is fundamentally flawed. The classic question—can air power alone coerce?—caricatures air power's true contributions and limits, leading to confusion over its effectiveness. In Kosovo the use of air power was a key factor in Belgrade's decision to surrender, but even here it was only one of many. U.S. and coalition experience in Kosovo and in other conflicts suggests that air power can make a range of contributions to the success of coercion, including: raising concern within an adversary regime over internal stability by striking strategic targets, including infrastructure; neutralizing an adversary's strategy for victory by attacking its fielded forces and the logistics upon which they depend; bolstering the credibility of other threats, such as a ground invasion; magnifying third-party threats from regional foes or local insurgents; and preventing an adversary from inflicting costs back on the coercing power by undermining domestic support or by shattering the coercing coalition.

In the Kosovo crisis, Serbian concerns over regime instability, NATO's threat of a ground invasion, and an inability to inflict costs on NATO (particularly an inability to gain Moscow's backing) probably played the largest role in motivating Milosevic's concessions. Air power played a critical role in all three of these, but in none of them did air power truly operate in isolation from other coercive instruments or pressures.

This article uses the Kosovo crisis to illustrate many of its arguments on the effectiveness of air power. It does not, however, pretend to offer a definitive case study. The motivations of Milosevic and other Serbian leaders—the key data for understanding coercion—remain opaque at this time.[10] We draw inferences about Serbian decisionmaking based on available evidence, and point out where more information is needed to assess popular hypotheses on why Belgrade capitulated. When possible, we try to indicate how new evidence from the Kosovo experience would affect our conclusions. Rather than settling the many controversies over air power's effectiveness and the broader Kosovo conflict, our primary intention is to reshape the air power debate.

The following section provides an overview of how to think about air power and coercion, addressing several key limits of the current literature. We next examine NATO goals in Kosovo and the mixed success eventually achieved. Using that baseline, we explore various explanations for Belgrade's eventual capitulation and clarify how air power's role in each of them should be understood; we leave aside the issue of whether coercion was a proper strategy for addressing the Balkan crisis and focus instead on how to assess air power as a tool of that strategy. We conclude with recommendations for recasting the air power debate to better reflect air power's true contributions and limits.

Air power and coercion: clarifying the debate

As NATO Commander Gen. Wesley Clark explained, the air war "was an effort to coerce, not to seize."[11] Discerning air power's contribution in Kosovo and elsewhere therefore requires first understanding the nature of "coercion."[12] This section defines this confusing term and then elaborates three general propositions critical to the air power debate: coercion should be understood dynamically; air power's impact is both additive and synergistic with other types of pressure; and the "successful" use of force must be assessed as a spectrum of possible outcomes, not as a binary variable. These points provide a foundation upon which to build hypotheses about how air power contributed to the outcome of the Kosovo crisis and, more broadly, when coercive diplomacy is likely to accomplish desired goals.

Defining coercion

Coercion is the use of threatened force, including the limited use of actual force to back up the threat, to induce an adversary to behave differently than it otherwise would.[13] Coercion is not destruction. Although partially destroying an adversary's means of resistance may be necessary to increase the effect and credibility of coercive threats, coercion succeeds when the adversary gives in while it still has the power to resist. Coercion can be understood in opposition to what Thomas Schelling termed "brute force": "Brute force succeeds when it is used, whereas the power to hurt is most successful when held in reserve. It is the threat of damage, or of more damage to come, that can make someone yield or comply."[14] Coercion may be thought of, then, as getting the adversary to act a certain way via anything short of brute force; the adversary must still have the capacity for organized violence but *choose* not to exercise it.[15]

Coercion as a dynamic process

There is a strong temptation to treat coercive threats as single, discrete events, failing to capture the dynamic nature of coercion. Analysts instead should view coercive contests as series of moves and countermoves, where each side acts not only based on and in anticipation of the other side's moves, but also based on other changes in the security environment.

Most standard explorations of coercion rely on an expected utility model to explain whether coercion succeeds or fails.[16] These models predict outcomes by comparing the expected costs and benefits of a particular action. In his study of strategic bombing as an instrument of coercion, for example, Robert Pape uses such a model: "Success or failure is decided by the target state's decision calculus with regard to costs and benefits. . . . When the benefits that would be lost by concessions and the probability of attaining these benefits by continued resistance are exceeded by the costs of resistance and the probability of suffering these costs, the target concedes."[17] Coercion should work when the anticipated suffering associated with a threat exceeds the anticipated gains of defiance.

This "equation" is useful for understanding coercion in the abstract, but it often confuses the study of coercion when taken as a true depiction of state behavior. One problem is that this equation fosters static, one-sided thinking about coercive contests. It encourages analysts to think about costs and benefits as independent variables that can be manipulated by the coercer, while the adversary stands idle and recalculates its perceived interests as various threats are made and implemented.

A more accurate picture requires viewing coercion as a dynamic, two-player (or more) contest. The adversary, too, can move so as to alter the perceived costs and benefits associated with certain actions.[18] It can divert resources from civilian to military functions, for example, to offset a coercer's attempts to undermine the adversary's defensive capacities. It can engage in internal repression to neutralize a coercer's efforts to foment instability. Rather than simply minimizing the effect of coercive threats, an adversary may try to impose costs on the coercing power; it can escalate militarily or attempt to drive a diplomatic wedge between states aligned against it, perhaps convincing the coercer to back down and withdraw its own threat to impose costs.[19]

Coercive pressure does not exist only at particular moments. Military capabilities and other forms of pressure, and the threat of their use, exert constant influence on allies and adversaries alike, though in varying degrees. When we think about a "case" of coercion, then, we are really not talking about a sudden appearance of the threat of force. Instead, we are talking about relative changes in the threat of force—usually denoted by demonstrative uses of force, explicit threats and demands, and other overt signs. In other words, there is an ever-present baseline, or level of background threat, and we seek to examine deviations from, or spikes in, that level of threat.[20] Using the 1972 Christmas bombings as an example, a standard question is: did the Christmas bombings coerce North Vietnam to negotiate terms more favorable to the United States? This is a poor and misleading proxy for the more useful question to understanding air power's contribution: did the marginal increase in force represented by the Christmas bombings increase the probability that North Vietnam would engage in behavior it would not otherwise choose?

Of course, the latter question is extremely difficult to answer because it requires inquiry into adversary decisionmaking, which in turn requires picking apart the many different coercive pressures bearing on an adversary at any given time and assessing their individual contribution. Did strategic air attacks cause Japan to surrender in World War II? Yes, Japan surrendered. And, yes, air attacks undoubtedly were a key element in its decisionmaking. But these attacks took place in the context of a crippling blockade, Soviet attacks in Manchuria, and so on.

Any assessment of air power's effectiveness should focus on the perceived costs it creates in an adversary's mind. But, viewing coercion dynamically, that assessment should incorporate the adversary's ability to neutralize those costs (or its belief that it can) as well as the set of other threats bearing down on the adversary at any given time.

Thinking synergistically

Not only are coercive pressures sometimes additive, but they may combine synergistically. A major limit of the air power debate is its focus on one instrument in isolation. Assessments of air power, or any other coercive instrument, should focus instead on its effect in combination with other instruments.

Pape's critical assessment of why the bombing of adversary populations does not lead to adversary capitulation is often wrongly used as evidence for the ineffectiveness of air power as a coercive instrument at all. This has contributed to an underestimation of air power's importance. As R.J. Overy pointed out about the bombing campaign against Germany and Japan: "There has always seemed something fundamentally implausible about the contention of bombing's critics that dropping almost 2.5 million tons of bombs on tautly-stretched industrial systems and war-weary urban populations would not seriously weaken them. . . . The air offensive was one of the decisive elements in Allied victory."[21] Overy's point is not that air power won the war single-handedly, but that air power contributed significantly to Allied success, as did victories at sea and on land. Air power and other instruments must be understood in context, not in isolation.

The bombing of North Korea during the Korean War highlights some synergistic effects of coercive air attacks. Pape argues that the risk posed by the U.S. atomic arsenal, not strategic bombing, pushed Pyongyang to the bargaining table.[22] But by separating these instruments for analytic purposes, we lose track of how they, in tandem, reinforce each other. Air power destroyed North Korean and Chinese fielded forces and logistics and demolished North Korean industrial complexes. Although North Korea and China retained the ability to continue military operations, U.S. air attacks made doing so more costly. When combined with the threat of atomic strikes, the costs of continuing fruitless conventional operations increased further. The combination of these instruments, however, may have been greater than the sum of their parts: escalating conventional air attacks may have bolstered the credibility of U.S. atomic threats by showcasing Washington's willingness to devastate North Korea's population and industrial base.[23]

The difficulties of dissecting adversary decisionmaking to assess the impact of particular coercive pressures are considerable. Hence analysts typically are tempted to focus on adversary states' observed behavioral response—did it *do* what the coercer wanted?—and correlate that response to particular events. But this is a misleading substitute for the more fundamental issue of whether specific threats, in the context of other pressures, significantly affected opponents' decisionmaking. A narrow focus on whether a coercive instrument either achieved objectives or failed outright leads to arbitrary and misleading coding of coercive strategies. Even limited, contributory effects, when combined with other coercive instruments, may be enough to force a policy change even though the use of an instrument in isolation may have failed.[24]

The uncertain meaning of "success"

Even if air power is evaluated in combination with other instruments rather than in isolation, assessing its contribution to successful coercion requires picking a baseline: what is success? Studies of coercion often pay inadequate attention to the range of goals pursued by a coercer. Moreover, they typically employ absolute, binary metrics of success, in which a coercive strategy either worked or it failed.[25] Assessments of coercive strategies must shed these tendencies and consider a spectrum of possible outcomes.

Classifying a case as "success" or "failure" depends on the particular definition of the behavior sought in that case, leading to confusion when comparing different analyses of the same event. For example, in Operation Desert Storm the behavior sought from Saddam Hussein might have been Iraq peacefully retreating from Kuwait. Or, it might have instead simply been Iraq not being in Kuwait, one way or another. One might conclude that the air campaign successfully coerced Iraq because Iraq was willing to withdraw by the end of the air campaign under conditions relatively favorable to the United States.[26] Classifying the air campaign as successful coercion, however, assumes that the coalition's objective was simply an Iraqi expulsion. But was that the objective? Janice Gross Stein concludes that the air campaign represented a failure of coercion because she interpreted differently what behavior the coalition sought.[27] To Stein, the air campaign represented a failure of coercion the moment the ground war began, because coalition objectives were to induce Iraq to withdraw *without having to forcefully expel it* through the use of ground troops.

The way in which the very issue of "success" is framed exacerbates this confusion. The use of absolute, binary measures—did air power coerce, yes or no?—does not capture the complex and often subtle effects of coercive threats. Iraq both conceded and defied the United States during Desert Storm: it offered a partial withdrawal from Kuwait while it refused to accept all U.S. demands. The straitjacket of binary metrics distorts the lessons we may draw from aggregated empirical data when cases in which air power helped move an adversary in favorable ways but short of the coercer's maximal objectives are coded as either absolute failures or absolute successes.[28]

At the same time as binary metrics may bias studies of coercion one way or the other, they may also overlook the detrimental effects of coercive strategies. Coercion carries the potential for backfire; threatening an adversary may provoke an increase in unwanted behavior rather than the desired course. The 1967 Arab-Israeli War and the 1969–70 Israeli-Egyptian War of Attrition are frequently cited examples of inadvertent escalation resulting from coercive threats.[29] In other words, coercive strategies can leave the coercer worse off than before. Yet within the binary framework, the worst outcome recognized is the null result: backfires and hardening of adversary resistance are coded just as if coercive threats caused no effect.

Conceptually, the dependent variable should be understood as a marginal change in probability of behavior. Against a fluctuating background level of threat (and blandishments, for that matter), the probability of the adversary altering its behavior is never zero. Viewing success in absolute terms, based on observed behavior, ignores this positive probability and classifies all desired behavior as "successful" coercion, regardless of how likely that behavior was prior to the additional coercive threat. Data limits may require a focus on observable behavior, but analysts should not forget that the true effects of coercive strategies lie in the altered—or, in some cases, hardened—policy preferences or decisionmaking calculi of the actors involved.

Conclusions for the study of air power

This critique of the air power debate and previous attempts to resolve it yields several implications for assessing the coercive use of air power in Kosovo or elsewhere. First, the dependent variable must be understood conceptually as a change in probability even though for measurement reasons we must largely focus on changes in observed behavior. That is, the effect of a coercive instrument such as air power should be thought of as the increased (or decreased) likelihood of an adversary's capitulation. Ultimately, such an assessment can be achieved only through an in-depth analysis of the Milosevic regime's decisionmaking process. Second, the independent variable must be thought of as a marginal increase in threatened costs that air power created, not the absolute level of force. In assessing NATO air attacks on Serbia, analysts should focus not on the role air power played *instead of* a ground invasion, for example, but on the role it played in combination with the possibility of one. Third, the likelihood of successful coercion depends on the expected impact of the coercer's threat as well as the available responses of the adversary. Analysts must therefore evaluate coercive strategies and the tools used to implement them not only by judging the perceived costs of resistance that threats create. They must also focus on the ability of these strategies to block possible counter-moves that would otherwise neutralize the threats.

NATO goals and Kosovo outcomes

A first step in determining the success or failure of air power in Kosovo is understanding the goals set by the NATO coalition. At the outset of the crisis, the Clinton administration articulated three goals of the bombing campaign: to "demonstrate the seriousness of NATO's opposition to aggression," to deter Milosevic's "continuing and escalating" attacks in Kosovo, and "to damage Serbia's capacity to wage war in the future."[30] These goals were reflected in official NATO statements, which required that Milosevic end repression in Kosovo, withdraw his forces from the province, agree to an international military presence there as well as to the safe return of refugees and displaced persons, and provide assurances of his willingness to work toward a political framework agreement along the lines of the Rambouillet accords.[31]

In practice these policy statements boiled down to several complementary objectives: to compel a cessation to the Milosevic regime's policy of ethnic terror; to force a withdrawal of Serbian troops to ensure the return of Albanian refugees; to compel Belgrade to accept a political settlement that promised a high degree of autonomy to Kosovo; and to demonstrate the viability of NATO to the post-Cold War world.[32]

In a defeat for overall strategy, NATO threats and bombing did not halt the ethnic terror for seventy-eight days, more than enough time for Serbia to displace almost a million Kosovar ethnic Albanians and kill thousands within Kosovo. But, in the end, Belgrade yielded. Most of the refugee and displaced Albanians have returned home, and Serbian troops are no longer in the Kosovo province. Milosevic accepted a deal that effectively ended Serbian control over the Kosovo province. "Success" for the objective of the cessation of ethnic terror becomes a definitional question: is stopping the terror and expulsion after two-and-a-half months too little too late or the best of a bad situation?

The answer is both. NATO forced Serbia to capitulate along lines similar to Rambouillet and remained relatively cohesive in the process. But NATO failed to prevent a massive ethnic cleansing campaign, and strains in alliance unity exposed limits to future operations.[33] When analyzing the Kosovo operations and air power's role, it is this decidedly limited victory that must be used as the benchmark.

Coercive air power and Kosovo

Commentators and analysts have advanced different explanations for why Milosevic eventually capitulated to NATO demands, with varying implications for the broader air power debate. None of these is mutually exclusive, and our analysis indicates that several of these factors indeed played a role in Milosevic's decision to surrender. These explanations include (1) NATO had destroyed a wide range of strategic targets in Serbia and threatened to continue destroying others, thus posing the specter of popular and elite dissatisfaction with the regime and increased internal unrest; (2) NATO had destroyed Serbia's fielded forces, making it impossible for Milosevic to hold Kosovo; (3) the prospect of a ground compaign intimidated Milosevic; (4) Milosevic and his forces perceived a growing military threat from the KLA; and (5) Serbia lacked any means of imposing costs on NATO countries, either militarily or diplomatically, or by shattering the coalition; most important, Serbia proved incapable of enlisting the support of Russia to offset NATO pressure.

These explanations are complementary rather than competing. All could have affected Milosevic's willingness to concede. For each of the first four arguments, this section first outlines the suggested hypothesis, offering theoretical or historical evidence that supports it. Next, it describes the NATO activities that would have contributed to this factor and any observed impact on Serbia's behavior or decisionmaking. Finally, it assesses the contribution of air power and proposes how this assessment, and future reassessments based on new evidence, should be interpreted within the broader air power debate. The analysis of the last hypothesis—the failure of Serbian counter-coercion—has a different structure given its counterfactual nature.

Our reading of available evidence indicates that the bombing of strategic targets inside Serbia, the threat of a ground invasion, and the failure of Serb counter-coercive strategies against NATO countries (particularly Belgrade's inability to gain Moscow's support) contributed greatly to the success of coercion. The KLA attacks probably counted for less, while the destruction of Serbian fielded forces played only a marginal role. Air power facilitated several of these factors, leading to the limited success of coercion, as qualified earlier.

Fostering discontent by striking strategic targets

Some analysts attribute NATO's success to air strikes that destroyed a wide range of "strategic" targets such as command bunkers, power stations, and infrastructure. As one NATO official proclaimed, hitting valuable targets in Belgrade is "what really counted."[34] The theory behind this explanation is that NATO was able to ratchet up pain on a recalcitrant Serbia until the attacks (and prospects of more to come) proved too costly. The weight of these attacks, it is argued, brought home the war to the people of Serbia and its leaders, demonstrating to them the price of continued resistance to NATO.

Beginning on March 29, 1999, after several days of tightly circumscribed targeting, NATO broadened and intensified the air campaign. Allied air attacks destroyed key roads and bridges in Yugoslavia, as well as oil refineries, military fuel installations, and other fixed targets, including army bases. NATO also attacked targets in Belgrade, such as the headquarters of Milosevic's Socialist Party and radio and television broadcasting facilities. On May 24, NATO aircraft disabled the national power grid.[35] Yugoslav government reporting indicates that NATO damaged or destroyed twelve railway stations, thirty-six factories, twenty-four bridges, seven airports, seventeen television transmitters, along with other infrastructure and communications targets.[36]

Air war planners hoped that NATO strikes would foster elite and popular discontent with the Milosevic regime. Gen. Klaus Naumann, who chaired the NATO alliance's military committee, declared NATO's intention "to loosen his grip on power and break his will to continue."[37] By striking military barracks and other military targets, NATO also sought to increase military dissatisfaction: through propaganda leaflets, air planners tried to create a direct link between the cutoff of gasoline, electricity, and other resources and the Milosevic regime's policies.[38]

Historical evidence suggests that threats to internal stability created through strategic attacks can contribute to coercion, though this contribution is seldom decisive by itself, and attempts often backfire in practice. Internal security is of overriding concern to developing states.[39] Even in cases where outside attacks failed to produce unrest—the norm, not the exception, despite the hopes of strategists in the coercing state—the *fear* of unrest has often prompted adversary leaderships to respond. In both World War II Japan and Germany, leaders spent vast sums of money on air defense and conducted otherwise senseless military operations to demonstrate that they were responding to the Allies' bombing attacks.[40] During the War of Attrition, Israeli strikes against a range of targets in Egypt generated intense leadership concern about unrest in Cairo, even though the Egyptian people remained behind their government.[41] Israeli air attacks on strategic targets in Syria during the 1973 Arab-Israeli war shook Hafez al-Asad's regime. More recently in Iraq, Saddam Hussein has demonstrated a penchant for backing down in the face of U.S. and other countries' threats when defiance risked eroding support for Saddam within his power base.[42] Popular or elite unrest is a sensitive point for many regimes but, as discussed later in this subsection, it is often one that adversary regimes are well equipped to counter.

Some evidence suggests that Milosevic capitulated in part because of concerns about internal unrest. Milosevic, like many demagogues, shows concern with his popularity, or at least the effects that unpopularity may have on his standing with elements of his power base.[43] Initially the air strikes bolstered the Yugoslav president's stature. Belgrade hosted large rallies in support of Milosevic after the NATO air strikes began.[44] Over time, however, NATO air strikes appear to have contributed to discontent in the federation. Rallies in support of the president receded, and Milosevic may have feared that continued conflict would lead to further losses in popularity.

The NATO bombing also fed dissatisfaction within the military.[45] The number of Serbian desertions increased during the campaign, and morale problems were considerable. Several of Milosevic's top generals had to be placed under house arrest, testifying to his sensitivity about possible loss of political control.[46]

The threat of unrest elsewhere in the federation may also have unnerved Milosevic. Before the conflict began, Montenegro had elected an anti-Milosevic leader and had relatively independent television and newspapers. In the months preceding Operation Allied Force, friction grew between Montenegrin leaders and the government in Belgrade. Montenegrin officials sought greater autonomy and opposed the war in Kosovo. The war heightened this tension, as Montenegro kept out of the war and stepped up efforts to develop its internal security forces.[47]

Air power played a major role in raising these various threats to regime stability. Although neither the Serbian population nor the military appeared ready to rebel and overthrow Milosevic, discontent from the air strikes was clearly growing by the end of the campaign. As in previous conflicts, the psychological impact of air strikes was probably magnified because Serbia could do little in retaliation or response.[48]

Although the Kosovo experience offers evidence that strategic attacks aimed at undermining regime support can, under some circumstances, contribute to coercive success, popular or elite unrest in response to coercion often does not occur or takes time to develop. Indeed, a recurring historical lesson is that attempts to force an adversary's hand by targeting its populace's will to resist may backfire.[49] Coercion often stiffens an adversary's determination, as the leadership and the country as a whole unite against the coercer. A coercive threat itself may raise the cost of compliance for an adversary's leadership by provoking a nationalist backlash. In Somalia, U.S. army helicopter strikes on Mohammed Farah Aideed's subordinates not only failed to intimidate the warlord but may have provoked anti-U.S. sentiment, contributing to the demise of the U.S.-led operation. Although many clan leaders had been critical of Aideed's confrontational stance toward the United States, they united behind him when faced with an outside threat. Russian attempts to bomb the Chechens into submission during the 1994–96 fighting produced unified defiance, as even residents who formerly favored peaceful solutions—or favored fighting each other—banded to expel the invader.[50] In Kosovo spontaneous pro-Milosevic rallies occurred in response to the initial bombing. Over time, support fell, but only after a sustained and lengthy campaign.[51]

Part of the difficulty of manipulating adversary regime support with military attacks stems from the ability of dictatorial regimes to maintain order through extensive and well-oiled propaganda machines, in addition to repressive police and security forces.[52] During Operation Allied Force, Milosevic shut down independent newspapers and radio stations inside Serbia, used state-run television to stoke nationalist reactions, electronically jammed some U.S. and NATO broadcasts intended for the Serbian populace, and prohibited the Western press from entering much of Kosovo (while granting it permission to film bombed sites).

To the extent that NATO air attacks fostered internal dissent and therefore moved Serbian leadership decisionmaking, the Kosovo experience confirms past lessons. Air power can contribute to coercion by striking targets whose destruction helps foment dissent and by raising fears among an adversary's leadership. However, while air power and other military instruments that can strike valuable targets may be extremely precise in a technological sense, fine-tuning their political effects on an adversary population remains largely beyond the capability of planners and political leaders.

It is in assessing this relationship between targeting and desired political effects—the heart of coercive strategy-making—that shedding the binary analytical framework is critical. On the one hand, NATO attacks eventually appeared to erode support among some segments of the Serbian population, thereby intensifying pressure on Milosevic to capitulate. On the other hand, these attacks also inflamed nationalist passions among other segments (especially in the short term), and Milosevic proved skilled at exploiting these passions with his propaganda machinery. Analyzing possible outcomes of coercive strategies and the impact of certain types of threats as either a "yes" or a "no" obscures the potential for strikes or any other use of force to backfire, hardening adversary resistance and alleviating coercive pressure. From a policy standpoint, the message should be one of caution: the threat of internal instability is often a critical element of adversary decisionmaking, but it is one that remains difficult to shape with coercive instruments.

The destruction of Serbian armed forces

One of air power's most important functions—one increasingly practical given continuing advances in intelligence and precision-strike capabilities—is threatening an adversary with defeat or otherwise preventing it from achieving its military objectives. Such a "denial" strategy focuses on the benefits side of the coercion equation, reducing the incentives for an adversary to engage in the unwanted behavior.[53] According to Pape, "Denial strategies seek to thwart the enemy's military strategy for taking or holding its territorial objectives, compelling concessions to avoid futile expenditures of further resources."[54]

The NATO air campaign made a priority of attacking Serbian armed forces. General Clark stated that "what we are trying to do is interdict and cut off Kosovo and make it much more difficult for [Milosevic] to sustain military operations there."[55] General Short described targeting fielded forces as Clark's "No. 1 priority."[56] NATO dedicated approximately 30 percent of its sorties to striking Serbian forces in addition to attacking air defenses, striking command-and-control assets, interdicting military supplies, and otherwise trying to damage Serbia's war machine.[57] NATO focused particular attention on striking Serbian heavy military equipment, both because NATO was better able to hit these targets than lighter Serbian forces and paramilitary units and because this entailed a relatively low risk of hitting civilian targets by mistake.[58] By degrading Serbian military capabilities in Kosovo, NATO planners sought to pry off Milosevic's grip on the province one finger at a time until he conceded in the face of potentially losing Kosovo without even nominal control—the ultimate threat to a man who rose in part by exploiting Serb nationalism over Kosovo.[59] Even if Milosevic refused to back down, it was hoped that degrading his forces would reduce his capacity for ethnic repression.

The historical record offers strong support for Pape's theses that neutralizing an adversary's ability to achieve its desired ends through force is critical to coercion, and that such denial is a key contribution that air power can make to coercion—an argument that we do not repeat here. Successful denial, however, requires defeating the enemy's particular *strategy*, not simply stopping its conventional military operations.[60]

The precision, flexibility, and versatility of the air arm suits it well for denying an adversary the perceived fruits of military operations—as long as the adversary's strategy relies on the employment of heavy forces or requires extensive resupply efforts. Air power can be extremely effective against fielded forces in certain environments. Desert Storm demonstrated this capability vividly, when U.S. air power disabled parts of two Iraqi corps before they even engaged U.S. ground forces near al-Khafji. The small Iraqi force that did capture the empty town was then easily isolated and destroyed by coalition ground and air forces.[61] Air power has also proven a powerful interdiction tool, as shown in Operation Desert Storm, the Linebacker operations in Vietnam, and Israel's experience in the 1967 war, where Israeli attacks on Egyptian supplies and reinforcements greatly contributed to Israel's success.[62]

But contrary to much of this historical experience, the air attacks directed at fielded Serbian forces in Kosovo appeared to play little role in Belgrade's concessions. The NATO campaign did not defeat Serbia's strategy for controlling Kosovo because Milosevic was able to induce the ethnic Albanian exodus he desired before NATO air attacks had significant effects on his fielded forces; even after Operation Allied Force reached its full intensity, these forces could continue to terrorize local populations without exposing themselves by massing. NATO's reporting of Serbian ground activity indicated that the air campaign had not halted Serbia's infantry and artillery attacks nor prevented Milosevic from increasing the size of his forces in Kosovo. Despite the massive air strikes, Milosevic could have maintained de facto control of Kosovo for many months and completed his ethnic cleansing.[63]

Although air strikes diminished the Serbs' offensive power, the degree of damage to Serbian armed forces is not known at this time. Using a range of deception techniques, the Serbian army limited damage done to its key assets, particularly tanks and artillery pieces. Even assuming considerable devastation to Serbian forces, however, they remained more than a match for KLA irregulars.[64] In operations during the last days of the war, KLA offensives pulled Serbian forces out into the open where they were substantially more vulnerable to NATO air attack. But even then the KLA failed to open a corridor to resupply its forces, nor did it demonstrate that it was capable of holding territory against the Serbian army for long.[65] It could be argued that the prospect of greater and greater losses created fear in Milosevic's mind that his forces might eventually be overrun. At this time, though, there is little evidence linking NATO's tactical success scored late in the conflict to the Serbian decision to surrender. Moreover, it is now clear that Milosevic retained considerable heavy forces and that his troops probably could have defeated the KLA with superior Serbian numbers and organization even had the bombing continued through the summer.

Operation Allied Force exposed several limits to air power's ability to coerce through denial. Most notably, air power's effectiveness is limited against particular types of targets and in particular environments. Adversaries fighting in mountainous, urban, or jungle terrain can often camouflage their movements, making them harder to attack. The effectiveness of air power against light infantry targets is limited in almost any environment.[66] Technological advances in surveillance, all-weather operations, and precision-guided munitions make air power more effective against these difficult-to-target foes, but such forces remain elusive. In Kosovo, air power faced an adversary skilled at deception and able to hide its forces. Perhaps more important, Pape's argument regarding the need to counter a foe's particular strategy is borne out in Kosovo: because only lightly armed forces were needed to purge village populations and defeat KLA insurgents, attacks on supply or on mechanized forces would not foil Milosevic's strategy.

The key lesson, however, for the broader coercive air power debate is not to cast general doubt on air power capabilities or their potential contribution to coercion. Rather, the Kosovo experience points to the need to assess coercive instruments and their effectiveness within the context of each crisis, including the strategic goals of the adversary and the extent to which its pursuit of those goals is vulnerable to military force.

The prospect of a ground campaign

NATO considered, and took several steps to prepare for, a ground campaign against Serbia, consideration of which featured heavily in the decisionmaking of both NATO and Serbia. General Clark argues that NATO ground troops posed an implicit threat that contributed to Milosevic's decision to capitulate, even though NATO leaders refused to issue any explicit threats of ground assault.[67] Indeed, Milosevic came to terms on the day that President Bill Clinton planned to discuss ground options with his U.S. generals. British Prime Minister Tony Blair pressed openly for a ground war, and many U.S. leaders, including General Clark, called for greater consideration of the option.[68] Several ground options were publicly debated, ranging from a limited push to secure a small enclave for fleeing ethnic Albanians to a large-scale invasion aimed at occupying Serbia and removing the Milosevic regime. Most options involved the risk to Milosevic that NATO would wrest at least a portion of the disputed territory from Serbia with significant numbers of troops.

To some degree, U.S. deployments corroborated the growing rhetoric surrounding possible ground action. The United States moved elements of the 82d Airborne Division and a limited number of ground combat forces to the region; NATO in total deployed some 25,000 troops to Albania and Macedonia and planned to deploy thousands more as part of an ostensible peacekeeping force that could be used for a ground invasion.[69] The United States also shored up roads to support heavy assets and took other limited steps to prepare for ground attacks.[70]

NATO's wielding of the ground threat, however, was uneven and unclear. Many NATO members, including Germany and France, openly opposed any ground deployment. President Clinton and various senior U.S. officials stated repeatedly that they had no plans to use ground forces.[71] At times, Clinton and his advisers took the wind out of their own sails by hinting publicly that the presence of Apache helicopters and other ground assets was meant only as a threat and would never be used.

A decision to use ground forces had not been reached by the end of the air campaign, though by then momentum toward a ground intervention was growing.[72] But its possibility was sufficiently plausible to influence Milosevic's calculus. A ground invasion, even if the preponderance of the evidence available to Milosevic suggested that it was unlikely, threatened to take away the very objective—Serbian control of the Kosovo province—that his policy aimed to hold. Still more frightening to Milosevic, a ground war might have led to the occupation of other parts of Serbia. Serbia's stationing of forces along likely attack routes and efforts to fortify against a ground attack evinced sufficient concern among its leaders that ground threats affected resource allocation decisions.[73]

When more evidence of Serbian decisionmaking emerges, what might it tell us about the broader air power debate? One view would hold that the more influence ground threats had on Serbian decisionmaking, the weaker the claim of air power advocates that air strikes alone can compel territorial concessions. Air advocates might retort that even if the ground threat mattered, it was still subordinate to coercive air power.

Both of these perspectives fail to understand the synergistic contribution of air power to the threat of ground invasion. In probabilistic terms, the threat of ground war at the outset of the Kosovo crisis carried immense potential costs for Serbia, but its likelihood was small. As the intensity of NATO air attacks increased, however, they enabled NATO potentially to launch a ground campaign at less cost to itself and at more cost to Serbia by softening up Serbian forces before the ground push. In the Gulf War, air attacks did not prompt Saddam Hussein's quick surrender, but they facilitated a coalition rout once the ground assault was launched. Viewing the crisis dynamically, Milosevic's most obvious counter to a NATO ground campaign and the biggest deterrent to its launch—heavy casualties on NATO forces—was far less viable in the face of the air supremacy that NATO would have enjoyed. The previous section emphasized the need to avoid viewing the effects of coercive strategies in absolute, binary terms. The analysis of this section, in turn, demands that independent variables such as "threat of ground invasion" be viewed not in terms of whether the threat existed—even in the face of ardent denials by administration officials, it remained a possibility—but in terms of whether a surge in its probability, made possible by air attacks, contributed to the Serbian decision to capitulate.

Even the Kosovo experience, where air operations were conducted in isolation more than has been typical of modern military campaigns, suggests that air power can be made far more effective when combined with ground forces.[74] Although NATO ground forces did not directly engage Serbian troops, air power's effectiveness increased when combined with ground assets and movements. Army radars from bases in Albania helped pinpoint Serbian artillery, enabling more accurate air strikes.[75] Reports circulated that British Special Forces may have helped direct NATO aircraft when poor weather hindered target identification.[76] Even the KLA's meager force augmented the devastation that air power could inflict. Air forces' effectiveness might have been enhanced still more through ground forces that could effectively reconnoiter, designate targets, assure safe air space for low-flying aircraft, and maneuver Serbian forces into vulnerable terrain. As the U.S. military services continue to progress in thinking jointly, it is critical that the broader air power debate progresses, too, and captures combined effects.

The threat from the KLA

Although Serbian forces' early thrust into Kosovo devastated the KLA, over time the guerrillas grew stronger, portending Milosevic's possible failure to secure Serbian hegemony over Kosovo. Had a potent KLA threat materialized, his terror campaign would have backfired. A popular explanation for Milosevic's eventual willingness to compromise posits that this scenario heavily influenced his calculus.[77] To those seeking to rebut the claims of air power advocates, this explanation has particular appeal because it emphasizes the importance of a ground presence, even if not a NATO one.

After the collapse of the Rambouillet talks, the lightly armed, poorly organized KLA cadres proved no match for the better-armed and -trained Serbian forces that poured into Kosovo. Ethnic cleansing, however, generated support for the KLA, swelling its ranks with refugee recruits. Albanians from abroad increased their financial support. The KLA began working with U.S. intelligence to locate Serbian forces and, toward the end of the campaign, the KLA began operations against Serbian forces, though with only limited success. Fighting from bases near the Albanian border, the KLA attacked Serbian troops and tried to conduct guerrilla operations throughout Kosovo. In the last weeks of the fighting, the KLA increasingly appeared to coordinate its actions with NATO.

Inside Kosovo itself, NATO air strikes and KLA attacks had synergistic effects. KLA ground offensives drew Serbian forces out of hiding, greatly increasing the lethality of air strikes. NATO aircraft were better able to strike tanks, armored personnel carriers, and artillery pieces as a result of KLA efforts. As one U.S. Army general claimed, "What you had, in effect, was the KLA acting as a surrogate ground force."[78]

The potential for an insurgency or other third-party force to act as a multiplier for coercive threats can be seen in many historical cases, the most recent demonstration being

Operation Deliberate Force, the NATO campaign against Bosnian Serb forces in 1995 that contributed to the Serb leadership's decision to enter negotiations at Dayton. For several years, the Bosnian Serbs had ignored United Nations and NATO ultimatums. NATO's September 1995 air strikes on Bosnian Serb forces occurred in conjunction with Croat and Muslim successes on the battlefield, particularly the Croat offensives against the Serbs in western Slavonia and in the Krajina. The strikes not only hurt the Bosnian Serbs directly, but they also posed the risk that Bosnian Muslim and Croat forces would make further advances at the Serbs' expense.[79] U.S. strikes that by themselves imposed only limited damage proved tremendously potent because they complemented the local military balance and exposed vulnerabilities in Serb defensive capabilities.[80]

The relative success of Operation Deliberate Force may have inflated the expectations of policymakers who assumed Milosevic would back down quickly in the face of air attacks over the Kosovo issue. This time, however, available evidence suggests that KLA successes had only marginal effects on the Serbian decision to negotiate. The KLA, despite having gained strength by the end of Operation Allied Force, still had not defeated the Serbian army in battle and had at best limited control over territory inside Kosovo. (Note that in Bosnia in 1995, the Serbs faced not an insurgency but, for the most part, regular forces; in Croatia, too, it was regular army units that launched offensives in the Krajina and western Slavonia.) Although information is scarce as to whether the growing strength of the KLA played into Milosevic's decision to capitulate, at the time he gave in the KLA posed no immediate threat to Serbian control over the province. Moreover, Belgrade had sounded out Russian and other mediators on the possibility of a settlement before the latest round of targeting successes in June, implying that Milosevic was already seriously considering capitulation.[81] Finally, the concessions Milosevic accepted—in essence the complete removal of his forces from Kosovo—were far more than what the KLA could have accomplished anytime soon, even with NATO air support.

The Kosovo experience illustrates some of the difficulties of exploiting insurgent threats facing an adversary. Operationally, coordination with the KLA proved difficult. Although KLA operations forced Serbian troops out of hiding, the KLA could not sustain anything near the intensity that even a relatively small NATO ground force would have. The KLA could not integrate air operations into its ground attacks or otherwise help coordinate air strikes in more than an ad hoc manner. On a political level, the KLA was an unattractive ally, with many of its leaders linked to undemocratic ideologies and the drug trade.[82] NATO's goal of creating regional stability also required that the KLA's strength not swell so much that it undermined post-operation political settlement efforts.

As is true with respect to the threat of ground invasion, the important insight for the broader air power debate is not whether the insurgents' ground presence was a decisive factor in this particular crisis, but under what conditions such a presence can contribute to coercion. Despite its limited impact on Milosevic in 1999, air power can be particularly effective in shifting the local balance of forces, leaving an adversary vulnerable to another external adversary. By interdicting the flow of men and arms to the front, air power can greatly enhance rivals' offensive power. Strikes on command-and-control facilities, as in Operation Deliberate Force, can hinder a foe's efforts to coordinate defenses against a rival. And the establishment and maintenance of "no-fly zones" can deprive one side of command of the air, oftentimes removing a critical element of its military prowess. In ways such as these, the use of air power, coordinated to exploit third-party threats, can not only threaten to impose immediate costs on an adversary, but can threaten to deny it benefits from resistance.

The experience of Bosnia revealed, and that of Kosovo corroborated in its converse, that magnifying a ground threat, even one not part of the coercing power's forces, is a potent source of coercive leverage. Such a strategy, however, requires a rare, preceding condition: the existence of a *viable* indigenous or allied force that the coercing power can support.

Serbia's inability to inflict costs on NATO

By viewing coercion dynamically, as chess-like contests of move and counter-move, it becomes clear that successful coercion requires not only effective threats, but also the neutralization of adversary responses.[83] By threatening to impose costs on a coercer, an adversary may be able to turn the tables and force the coercing power to back down. Inflicting costs back on the coercer is also important for psychological reasons, allowing the adversary leadership to demonstrate to its followers that they are not alone in suffering. Like past opponents, Serbia tried at least three strategies for imposing costs on NATO: creating casualties; fostering sympathy through its own suffering; and disrupting NATO cohesion. Serbia's inability to inflict costs—particularly its failure to gain Russian support—prevented it from defeating the NATO coercion effort and decreased its ability to shore up popular morale.

To varying degrees, the use of air power helped prevent Serbia from successfully propagating these counter-strategies, a major factor in the overall qualified success of coercion. This "explanation" would not account for Milosevic's capitulation on its own because neutralizing the counter-strategies imposed no direct costs by itself. But it is as important an explanation as the others considered above because negating counter-coercive strategies fortified the credibility of NATO threats: Milosevic realized that he could not escape the other costs being imposed upon his regime without conceding.[84]

Imposing casualties

A potentially fruitful means of countering U.S. coercion appears to be by killing or credibly threatening U.S. soldiers. Although a number of empirical studies have shown that the effects of U.S. casualties on public support depend heavily on other variables and contextual factors—for example, support is likely to erode with casualties when the public views victory as unlikely or when vital U.S. interests are not at stake—this sensitivity affects policy and planning decisions both prior to and during operations, when concern for potentially adverse public reactions weighs strongly.[85]

Adversaries often view casualty sensitivity as the United States' "center of gravity" and adopt their strategies accordingly. Ho Chi Minh famously warned the United States: "You can kill ten of my men for every one I kill of yours. But even at those odds, you will lose and I will win."[86] Somali militia leader Mohammed Farah Aideed echoed this view to U.S. Ambassador Robert Oakley: "We have studied Vietnam and Lebanon and know how to get rid of Americans, by killing them so that public opinion will put an end to things."[87] Even if these perceptions misunderstand U.S. politics, coupling them with a belief that U.S. forces are vulnerable may be enough to cause an adversary to hold out.

Milosevic appears to have shared previous estimations that American political will would erode as U.S. casualties mounted. As he noted in an interview, NATO is "not willing to sacrifice lives to achieve our surrender. But we are willing to die to defend our rights as an independent sovereign nation."[88] Rhetorically embellished as this statement may be, Milosevic probably perceived NATO's will to sustain operations in the face of casualties to be weak.[89]

Propagandizing collateral damage

Recent conflicts have highlighted U.S. decisionmakers' concern not only with potential U.S. casualties but with the deaths or suffering of enemy civilians, which policymakers worry can contribute to the breakdown of domestic or allied support for an operation. Toward the end of Operation Desert Storm, Saddam dramatized before the media Iraqi civilian deaths resulting from a U.S. intelligence failure—U.S. aircraft had struck the al-Firdos bunker, which was thought to house command-and-control facilities but was instead used at the time as a bomb shelter—hoping to play on the West's humanitarian sentiments and create a backlash in the United States and among its allies. Although this effort failed to disrupt the entire campaign or even to generate sympathy among the American people, it did lead U.S. commanders to curtail the air strikes on Baghdad.[90]

Some coalition partners may be more sensitive than the United States to civilian injuries resulting from military operations, and planners must at times design operations to fall within the political constraints of the most sensitive members. During the early phases of Operation Allied Force, most major targets were scrutinized by representatives of a number of allied capitals. To strike politically sensitive targets, General Clark required authorization from the Joint Staff in the Pentagon, which in turn passed decisions on major targets up to the defense secretary and ultimately the president.[91] Some European allies resisted escalated air attacks that would endanger civilians, and NATO officials also scrutinized the target list to comply with international legal proscriptions.[92]

Serbia tried to undermine allied support for the air war by propagandizing collateral damage. Belgrade publicized the deaths of Serb and Albanian civilians resulting from tragic target misidentifications or errant bombs, trying to capitalize on NATO's humanitarian conscience.[93] Milosevic's efforts to exploit collateral damage failed to erode significantly U.S. or allied support for the operation. It did, however, result in the short-term tightening of targeting restrictions on NATO bombers: in April, for instance, NATO modified its procedures to require that U.S. pilots receive authorization before striking military convoys, after a U.S. warplane mistakenly hit a refugee convoy.[94]

Disrupting NATO unity

Coalition members often have diverse goals or different preferences, leading the coalition as a whole to adopt positions that may reflect the "lowest common denominator" rather than more assertive positions. Coalitions sometimes have difficulty escalating their threats because diplomats must accede to restrictive operation mandates or rules of engagement as the price of allied cohesion.[95]

Exploiting coalition fissures offers adversaries an enticing counter-coercive strategy, as an alternative or adjunct to combating threats of force directly. Saddam Hussein attempted to widen coalition splits at several key junctures in the Gulf crisis and its aftermath, in an effort to undermine the threat of escalation against Iraq. Prior to the coalition ground assault, his attempted negotiations with the Soviet Union not only nearly averted war but also caused some coalition members to question the need for military action. Iraq simultaneously tried to dislodge Arab support for coalition operations by linking resolution of the Kuwaiti crisis to the Arab-Israeli dispute, thereby driving a wedge between the Arab states and the U.S.-Israeli axis.

Like Saddam, Milosevic appears to have believed that he could outlast the coalition arrayed against him. Diplomatic rifts among NATO partners and public disagreement over strategy likely contributed to his defiance by fostering his beliefs that NATO unity would collapse. Greece and Italy opposed an extended bombing campaign and pushed for limits on the damage inflicted, France resisted plans for a naval blockade, and Germany opposed any consideration of ground options.[96] But toward the end of the campaign, Milosevic's hopes of disrupting NATO unity seem to have evaporated, as the allies' momentum shift toward possible ground assault signaled greater cohesion than expected. In addition, the air campaign actually intensified as time went on, further diminishing hopes that NATO's own disagreements would collapse the coercion effort.[97]

Air power and counter-counter-coercion

Several of air power's attributes allow coercers to defend against common counter-coercive strategies, such as those just outlined. An understanding of these contributions, and their limits, is critical to assessing air power as a coercive instrument. These issues, however, are frequently put aside in air power debates because participants focus on actual damage inflicted and observed behavior, ignoring what an adversary is *unable* to do in response.

The most publicized advantage of air power in restricting adversary countermoves is the relative invulnerability of U.S. aircrews compared with that of engaged ground forces. By reducing force vulnerability, reliance on air power can help sustain robust domestic support by lowering the likelihood of U.S. casualties. At the same time, air power's ability to conduct precision operations can reduce concerns about adversary civilian suffering (though efforts to keep air forces relatively safe may create moral and legal concerns if doing so places civilians at much greater risk).[98] Both of these attributes of air power—relatively low force vulnerability and high precision—can also fortify coalition unity, which is itself susceptible to disruptions as friendly casualties and collateral damage mount.

These potential advantages of air power over other instruments were largely borne out in the Kosovo experience. Serbia inflicted zero NATO casualties, an amazing figure given the length and extent of the air campaign. Although NATO air strikes did lead to the deaths of innocents, collateral damage was sufficiently contained that domestic and international support remained steady.[99]

The advantages that air power offers in negating adversary counter-strategies are not cost-free, and there are typically trade-offs among them. To evade Serbian air defenses, NATO aircraft flew at medium or high altitudes (often 15,000 feet), therefore increasing the risk of collateral damage. Maintaining necessary levels of precision and force protection comes at the price of military effectiveness and overall cost, as alternatives that entail greater risk or fewer forces are shelved.[100] Appreciation of these trade-offs is critical; analysts must resist the temptation to compare coercive instruments only in terms of manifest effects, because the manifest destructive impact of coercive strikes is but one side of the equation.

While air power is well suited against some counter-strategies, those outlined in this section are only three of many. Adversaries also, for instance, try to impose costs and counter-coerce through nonmilitary means. If an adversary can forge a new alliance with a foe of the coercing power or otherwise raise the stakes, it can often succeed in halting a coercion campaign.

Serbia failed to gain Russian support for its cause, which likely played a key role in Milosevic's decision to concede. Had Serbia won strong Russian support, it would have gained a means of resistance and diplomatic escalation. The price to NATO of continued war in Kosovo would have meant alienating a great power on the edge of Europe. Initially, Russia pressed NATO to end the bombing as a prelude to a diplomatic settlement, and, even in late May, Russia publicly touted its opposition to NATO.[101] Although evidence is not available, Milosevic probably looked at Russia's rhetorical support and condemnation of the NATO campaign as an indication that Moscow would champion Belgrade's cause in the international arena. But while Russia opposed NATO's air war and complicated the subsequent occupation of Kosovo, it never sided firmly with Serbia. Russian envoy Viktor Chernomyrdin even acted as NATO's de facto envoy, pressing Milosevic to yield to NATO.[102] The timing of Milosevic's capitulation suggests the importance of this factor: NATO had long offered similar conditions to those ultimately accepted by Milosevic, but Russia's lack of support had not been clear until this point. Lieut. Gen. Michael Jackson, NATO's commander in Kosovo, concluded that Russia's decision to back NATO's position on June 3 "was the single event that appeared to me to have the greatest significance in ending the war."[103]

We emphasize Milosevic's failed efforts to exploit Russian sympathy because, unlike other counter-coercive strategies such as imposing U.S. casualties, there is little that air power or any other military instrument can do to neutralize such efforts.[104] Russia's unwillingness (or inability) to help Belgrade was a product of Moscow's own limits and Serbia's unattractiveness as an ally, not factors shaped by air power. The diplomatic importance of Russia in ending the conflict, of course, must also be seen in context. Without the constant battering of the air campaign, Russia's pressure on Belgrade probably would have accomplished little.

Kosovo and the future use of air power

As frequently happens in the aftermath of U.S. air operations, participants at both poles of the air power debate claimed vindication from Kosovo. But the key lesson of the Kosovo crisis is that neither side of this debate is, or can be, correct. This conclusion will strike many readers as unsatisfying because it urges participants to take several steps backward and reassess the terms of the debate rather than move forward and resolve it based on new data. The methodological propositions advanced in this article, however, should guide analysis of any instrument of coercion, whether military, economic, or diplomatic.

When weighing the balance of ground and air forces (as well as the type of air forces needed), policymakers must consider not only what they seek to accomplish through coercion, but also what they seek to prevent. As the Kosovo contest attests, air power's and other instruments' greatest accomplishments are often what they preclude an adversary from doing. The role air power can play, for example, in stopping an adversary from shattering a coalition or generating domestic opposition in the United States has value beyond the damage if inflicts. In the future, adversaries will develop new counters, both political and military, and air power may be of only limited value in stymieing these. Anticipating counter-strategies, and planning accordingly, is essential.

Finally, policymakers and military officials must recognize when reliance on air power may undermine U.S. and allied credibility. Use of air power can help sustain domestic support or coalition unity, but it cannot eliminate underlying political constraints. In Eliot Cohen's words, "Air power is an unusually seductive form of military strength, in part because, like modern courtship, it appears to offer gratification without commitment."[105] This view poses a challenge for air power. Because policymakers often see air strikes as a low-risk, low-commitment measure, air power will be called on when U.S. public or allied commitment is weak—a situation that will make successful coercion far harder when casualties do occur or when air strikes fail to break adversary resistance. Air power, like other military instruments, cannot overcome a complete lack of political will. Policymakers' use of coercive air power under inauspicious conditions and in inappropriate ways diminishes the chances of using it elsewhere when the prospects of success would be greater.

Notes

1 See Giulio Douhet, *The Command of the Air* (Washington, D.C.: Office of Air Force History, 1942). Works by other visionaries include H.H. Arnold and Ira C. Eaker, *Winged Warfare* (New York: Harper, 1941); and William M. Mitchell, *Winged Defense* (New York: G.P. Putnam's Sons, 1925). Much of the early debate over how best to use air power took place inside various air forces. For useful overviews of this history, see Robert Futrell, *Ideas, Concepts, Doctrine: Basic Thinking in the United States Air Force* (Maxwell Air Force Base, Ala.: Air University Press, 1989); and Phillip S. Meilinger, ed., *The Paths to Heaven: The Evolution of Airpower Theory* (Maxwell Air Force Base, Ala.: Air University Press, 1997).

2 Quoted in Craig R. Whitney, "Air Wars Won't Stay Risk Free, General Says," *New York Times*, June 18, 1999, p. A8. Gen. Michael J. Dugan, a former U.S. Air Force chief of staff, declared: "For the first time in history—5,000 years of history of man taking organized forces into combat—we saw an independent air operation produce a political result." Quoted in James A. Kitfield, "Another Look at the Air War That Was," *Air Force Magazine* (October 1999), p. 40.

3 Quoted in John Diamond, "Air Force Strategists Fight Overconfidence Built by Air Victory," *European Stars and Stripes*, July 4, 1999, p. 1.

4 The lessons drawn by both sides of this debate are outlined in Nick Cook, "War of Extremes," *Jane's Defence Weekly*, July 7, 1999, pp. 20–23. See also John D. Morrocco, "Kosovo Conflict Highlights Limits of Airpower and Capability Gaps," *Aviation Week & Space Technology*, May 17, 1999, pp. 31–33.

5 Clifford Beal, "Lessons from Kosovo," *Jane's Defence Weekly*, July 7, 1999, p. 20. One retired U.S. Army general fears that "the strategic relevancy and future of our Army have suffered a grave blow from the Kosovo experience." See Robert F. Wagner, "In Kosovo, the Army's Guns Were Silent and Forgotten," *Army Times*, July 12, 1999, p. 46. Various assessments of the bombing campaign, including its successes and limits, are summarized in Bradley Graham, "Air vs. Ground: The Fight Is On," *Washington Post*, June 22, 1999, p. A1; and Tim Butcher and Patrick Bishop, "Nato Admits Air Campaign Failed," *London Daily Telegraph*, July 22, 1999, p. 1.

6 The leading academic work on the use of air power as a coercive instrument is Robert A. Pape, *Bombing to Win* (Ithaca, N.Y.: Cornell University Press, 1996). See also Pape's works "The Air Force Strikes Back: A Reply to Barry Watts and John Warden," *Security Studies*, Vol. 7, No. 2 (Winter 1997/98), pp. 200–214; and "The Limits of Precision-Guided Air Power," *Security Studies*, Vol. 7, No. 2 (Winter 1997/98), pp. 93–114. For the best critique of Pape, see Karl Mueller, "Denial, Punishment, and the Future of Air Power," *Security Studies*, Vol. 7, No. 3 (Spring 1998), pp. 182–228. Other valuable works on the use of air power include Eliot A. Cohen, "The Mystique of U.S. Air Power," *Foreign Affairs*, Vol. 73, No. 1 (January/February 1994), pp. 109–124; Stuart Peach, ed., *Perspectives on Air Power* (London: Her Majesty's Stationery Office, 1998); Meilinger, *Paths to Heaven*; and Phillip S. Meilinger, *Ten Propositions Regarding Air Power* (Washington, D.C.: Air Force History and Museums Program, 1995).

7 A collection of military publications on joint operations can be found at http://www.dtic.mil/jcs.

8 In this respect, contemporary theory resembles that of air power pioneers, such as Giulio Douhet, Hugh Trenchard, and William (Billy) Mitchell. Their modern-day heirs, such as John Warden, Harian Ullman, and James Wade, also focus on air power's exclusive contributions, and have been properly criticized for making excessive claims. See John Warden, "Employing Air Power in the Twenty-first Century," in Richard Shultz, Jr., and Robert L. Pfaltzgraff, Jr., eds., *The Future of Air Power in the Aftermath of the Gulf War* (Maxwell Air Force Base, Ala.: Air University Press, 1992), pp. 57–82; John Warden, "Success in Modern War," *Security Studies*, Vol. 7, No. 2 (Winter 1997/98), pp. 172–190; and Harlan K. Ullman and James P. Wade, *Shock and Awe: Achieving Rapid Dominance* (Washington, D.C.: National Defense University, 1996). This focus of these scholars, however, largely ignores far more important developments such as the air-land battle and joint doctrine, which dictate how air power is most likely to be used in actual war.

9 These issues are elaborated in Daniel L. Byman, Matthew C. Waxman, and Eric Larson, *Air Power as a Coercive Instrument* (Santa Monica, Calif.: RAND, 1999).

10 As Gen. Wesley Clark noted when asked why Serbian forces withdrew, "You'll have to ask Milosevic, and he'll never tell you." Quoted in Michael Ignatieff, "The Virtual Commander," *New Yorker*, August 2, 1999, p. 31.

11 Quoted in Dana Priest, "The Commanders' War: The Battle inside Headquarters," *Washington Post*, September 21, 1999, p. A1.

12 Among the most widely cited works on coercion are those of Thomas C. Schelling and Alexander L. George and William E. Simons. See especially Schelling, *Arms and Influence* (New Haven, Conn.: Yale University Press, 1966); and George and Simons, eds., *The Limits of Coercive Diplomacy* (Boulder, Colo.: Westview, 1994). Other valuable works include Patrick M. Morgan, "Saving Face for the Sake of Deterrence," in Robert Jervis, Richard Ned Lebow, and Janice Gross Stein, eds., *Psychology and Deterrence* (Baltimore, Md.: Johns Hopkins University Press, 1985), pp. 125–152; John J. Mearsheimer, *Conventional Deterrence* (Ithaca, N.Y.: Cornell University Press, 1983); Jonathan Shimshoni, *Israel and Conventional Deterrence: Border Warfare from 1953 to 1970* (Ithaca, N.Y.: Cornell University Press, 1988); Uri Bar-Joseph, "Variations on a Theme: The Conceptualization of Deterrence in Israeli Strategic Thinking," *Security Studies*, Vol. 7, No. 3 (Spring 1998), pp. 145–181; Elli Lieberman, "What Makes Deterrence Work?: Lessons from the Egyptian-Israeli Enduring Rivalry," *Security Studies*, Vol. 4, No. 4 (Summer 1995), pp. 833–892; and Daniel Ellsberg, "Theory and Practice of Blackmail," P-3883 (Santa Monica, Calif.: RAND, 1968).

13 We use this particular definition to emphasize that coercion relies on the threat of future military force to influence adversary decisionmaking, but that limited uses of actual force may form key components of coercion. Limited uses of force sway adversaries not only because of their direct destructive impact but because of their effects on an adversary's perceptions of future force and the adversary's vulnerability to it. There are, to be sure, many types of coercive pressure (sanctions, diplomatic isolation, etc.); unless specified otherwise, we use the term "coercion" to mean *military* coercion.

14 Schelling, *Arms and Influence*, p. 3.

15 Pape, *Bombing to Win*, p. 13 (emphasis added).

16 In addition to Schelling's work, a rationalist, cost-benefit approach is employed in many other major works on coercion, including Bruce Bueno de Mesquita, *The War Trap* (New Haven, Conn.: Yale University Press, 1981); and Christopher H. Achen and Duncan Snidal, "Rational Deterrence Theory and Comparative Case Studies," *World Politics*, Vol. 41, No. 2 (January 1989), pp. 143–169.

17 Pape, *Bombing to Win*, pp. 15–16.

18 Pape examines this issue briefly in his discussion of why Germany did not surrender before May 1945. See ibid., p. 256, especially n. 4. This point is also implicit in Pape's discussion of how adversaries offset coercive pressure. For a summary, see ibid., p. 24.

19 For an assessment of such strategies, see Daniel L. Byman and Matthew Waxman, "Defeating U.S. Coercion," *Survival*, Vol. 41, No. 2 (Summer 1999), pp. 107–120.

20 These points are discussed in Karl Mueller, "Strategy, Asymmetric Deterrence, and Accommodation," Ph.D. dissertation, Princeton University, 1991, chap. 1; and John Mueller, *Quiet Cataclysm: Reflections on the Recent Transformation of World Politics* (New York: HarperCollins, 1995), chap. 4.

21 R.J. Overy, *Why the Allies Won* (New York: W.W. Norton, 1995), p. 133.

22 Pape, *Bombing to Win*, pp. 141–142.

23 See Robert F. Futrell, *The United States Air Force in Korea, 1950–1953*, rev. ed. (Washington, D.C.: Office of Air Force History, 1983), for a detailed account of the air campaign in Korea. A superb account of Chinese decisionmaking is Bin Yu, "What China Learned from Its 'Forgotten War' in Korea," *Strategic Review*, Vol. 26, No. 3 (Summer 1998), pp. 4–16.

24 As Barry Watts argues, mapping coercion to binary rankings is highly reductionist and wrongly assumes that complex campaigns can be reduced to zero or one. Watts, "Theory and Evidence in Security Studies," *Security Studies*, Vol. 7, No. 2 (Winter 1997/98), p. 136.

25 The use of these binary metrics of success stems largely from measurement concerns. If we wish to test certain hypotheses about coercion by correlating success with independent variables (such as type of force used or type of adversary assets threatened), then we would like to code as many cases as possible. A binary coding of success avoids the messy gray area into which many cases might fall if a nonabsolute measure were used.

26 Lawrence Freedman and Efraim Karsh, *The Gulf Conflict, 1990–1991* (Princeton, N.J.: Princeton University Press, 1993), pp. 380–385.

27 Janice Gross Stein, "Deterrence and Compellence in the Gulf, 1990–91: A Failed or Impossible Task?" *International Security*, Vol. 17, No. 2 (Fall 1992), pp. 147–179.

28 For an example of the binary coding of success or failure, see Walter J. Peterson, "Deterrence and Compellence: A Critical Assessment of Conventional Wisdom," *International Studies Quarterly*, Vol. 30, No. 3 (September 1986), pp. 269–294.

29 See Janice Gross Stein, "The Arab-Israeli War of 1967: Inadvertent War through Miscalculated Escalation," and Yaacov Bar-Siman-Tov, "The War of Attrition, 1969–1970," in Alexander L. George, ed., *Avoiding War: Problems of Crisis Management* (Boulder, Colo.: Westview, 1991), pp. 126–159 and pp. 320–341, respectively.

30 R.W. Apple, Jr., "A Fresh Set of U.S. Goals," *New York Times*, March 25, 1999, p. A1. See also Barton Gellman, "Allies Facing the Limits of Air Power," *Washington Post*, March 28, 1999, p. A1. General Clark described NATO goals as "the Serbs out; NATO in; the refugees home; a ceasefire in place; and a commitment to work for a peace settlement." See "Interview: General Wesley Clark," *Jane's Defence Weekly*, July 7, 1999, p. 40.

31 Statement Issued at the Extraordinary Ministerial Meeting of the North Atlantic Council, NATO Headquarters, Brussels, April 12, 1999, http://www.nato.int/docu/pr/1999/p99–051e.htm (visited August 8, 1999); and Statement on Kosovo Issued by the Heads of State and Government Participating in the Meeting of the North Atlantic Council in Washington, D.C., April 23–24, 1999, http://www.nato.int/docu/pr/1999/p99–062e.htm (visited August 8, 1999).

32 Another goal—deterring future Serbian aggression—cannot be judged as of this writing.

33 Joseph S. Nye, Jr., "Redefining the National Interest," *Foreign Affairs*, Vol. 78, No. 4 (July/August 1999), p. 34; and Peter W. Rodman, "The Fallout from Kosovo," ibid., pp. 45–51.

34 Matthew Kaminski and John Reed, "KLA Played Key Role in Allied Air War," *Wall Street Journal*, July 6, 1999, p. A11. A Joint Chiefs of Staff spokesman declared, "We're satisfied we destroyed enough stuff to get him to say uncle." Quoted in Steven Lee Meyers, "Damage to Serb Military Less than Expected," *New York Times*, June 28, 1999, p. A1. Some of the arguments for and against this view are summarized in Butcher and Bishop, "Nato Admits Air Campaign Failed," p. 1.

35 The June 10, 1999, Department of Defense briefing indicated that NATO had destroyed all of Yugoslavia's petroleum refining capability; most of its ammunition production capacity; 40 percent of its armored vehicle production; 100 percent of the rail bridges into Kosovo; and 45 percent of its TV broadcast capability. See Anthony Cordesman, "The Lessons and Non-Lessons of the Air and Missile War in Kosovo," July 27, 1999, http://www.csis.org (visited on August 3, 1999), p. 79; Meyers, "Damage to Serb Military Less than Expected," p. A1; and Eric Schmitt and Michael R. Gordon, "Shift in Targets Lets NATO Jets Tip the Balance," *New York Times*, June 5, 1999, p. 1. General Clark received authorization to go after a wider range of targets at the end of March, after several weeks of limited strikes. Ignatieff, "The Virtual Commander," p. 32.

36 Priest, "The Commanders' War: The Battle inside Headquarters."

37 Michael R. Gordon, "NATO Plans Weeks of Bombing to Break Grip of Serb Leader," *New York Times*, April 1, 1999, p. A1.

38 Steven Erlanger, "NATO Attack Darkens City and Areas of Serbia," *New York Times*, May 3, 1999, p. A13. John Warden has postulated: "Unless the stakes in the war are very high, most states will make desired concessions when their power-generation system is put under sufficient pressure or actually destroyed." Warden, "The Enemy as a System," *Air Power Journal*, Vol. 9, No. 1 (Spring 1995), p. 49.

39 See Mohammed Ayoob, "The Security Problematic of the Third World," *World Politics*, Vol. 43, No. 2 (January 1991), pp. 257–283; and Stephen David, *Choosing Sides: Alignment and Realignment in the Third World* (Baltimore, Md.: Johns Hopkins University Press, 1991).

40 Japan, for example, needlessly deployed air assets for homeland defense in December 1942 and overextended its naval forces to demonstrate that it was acting forcefully after the first U.S. bombing of Japan. For two superb analyses of World War II and the importance of adversary reactions (and overreactions) to Allied bombing, see James G. Roche and Barry D. Watts, "Choosing Analytic Measures," *The Journal of Strategic Studies*, Vol. 14, No. 2 (June 1991), pp. 165–209; and Overy, *Why the Allies Won*, pp. 101–133.

41 Trevor N. Dupuy, *Elusive Victory* (Dubuque, Iowa: Kendall Hunt, 1992), p. 372; and Shimshoni, *Israel and Conventional Deterrence*, p. 16.

42 See Daniel L. Byman, Kenneth Pollack, and Matthew Waxman, "Coercing Saddam Hussein: Lessons from the Past," *Survival*, Vol. 40, No. 3 (Autumn 1998), pp. 127–151.

43 In early 1997, Milosevic reinstated opposition municipal election victories after massive protest rallies threatened to expose weaknesses in his regime. See Dean E. Murphy, "Yugoslav Protesters Walk Fine Line," *Los Angeles Times*, February 8, 1997, p. A5; and Rod Nordland, "End of the Road," *Newsweek*, February 17, 1997, p. 26. For general accounts of Milosevic's concern with political support, see Franklin Foer, "Slobodan Milosevic: How a Genocidal Dictator Keeps Getting Away with It," *Slate*, June 20, 1998, http://www.slate.com; and Misha Glenny, *The Fall of Yugoslavia* (New York: Penguin, 1993), pp. 32–33, 60–70. An account of Milosevic as a diplomatic tactician can be found in Richard Holbrooke, *To End a War* (New York: Random House, 1998).

44 Gordon, "NATO Plans Weeks of Bombing."

45 Press reporting that NATO strikes increased Milosevic's popularity with the army in Serbia appear in retrospect to have been erroneous. See Steven Brill, "War Gets the Monica Treatment," *Brill's Content* (July / August 1999), pp. 103–104.

46 Ibid., pp. 104–105.

47 James M. Dorsey, "Montenegro Girds against Attempt by Milosevic to Topple Government," *Wall Street Journal*, April 5, 1999, p. 1; and Michael Dobbs, "Montenegro Easing Away from Serb Ally," *Washington Post*, June 25, 1999, p. A1.

48 Roche and Watts, "Choosing Analytic Measures," p. 182; and Stephen T. Hosmer, *Psychological Effects of U.S. Air Operations in Four Wars* (Santa Monica, Calif.: RAND, 1996), p. 196.

49 For various works on the psychological impact of bombing, see Hosmer, *Psychological Effects of U.S. Air Operations in Four Wars*; Mark Clodfelter, *The Limits of Air Power: The American Bombing of North Vietnam* (New York: Free Press, 1989); and Futrell, *The United States Air Force in Korea*. See also *U.S. Strategic Bombing Survey: The Effects of Strategic Bombing on German Morale* (Washington, D.C.: U.S. Government Printing Office, December 1946), in David MacIsaac, ed., *The United States Strategic Bombing Survey*, Vol. 4 (New York: Garland, 1976).

50 An excellent account of the air campaign in Chechnya and the Chechen response is Benjamin S. Lambeth, "Russia's Air War in Chechnya," *Studies in Conflict and Terrorism*, Vol. 19, No.4 (October 1996), pp. 365–388. On Somalia, see John Drysdale, "Foreign Military Intervention in Somalia," in Walter Clarke and Jeffrey Herbst, eds., *Learning from Somalia* (Boulder, Colo.: Westview, 1997), p. 118.

51 The resilience of police states in the face of wartime hardships was a key finding of the U.S. Strategic Bombing Survey of World War II air operations against Germany. See Clodfelter, *The Limits of Air Power*, p. 9.

52 When coercive operations threaten to foster instability, whether wittingly or unwittingly, target regimes often are well prepared to respond. If widespread domestic unrest appears likely, regimes will increase the police presence, use mass arrests, and even slaughter potential opposition members to preserve their power. Milosevic, for example, has constructed an extensive police state to resist both internal and external pressure. Susan L. Woodward, *Balkan Tragedy* (Washington, D.C.: Brookings, 1995), p. 293.

53 A denial strategy at times blurs with "brute force," as both usually seek to defeat an adversary's military, but coercive "denial" focuses on convincing an adversary that future benefits will not be gained, while more conventional war fighting focuses on physically stopping an adversary regardless of whether its leadership believes it can fight on.

54 Pape, "The Limits of Precision-Guided Air Power," p. 97.

55 Quoted in Cordesman, "The Lessons and Non-Lessons of the Air and Missile Campaign in Kosovo," p. 94.

56 Quoted in John A. Tirpak, "Short's View of the Air Campaign," *Air Force Magazine* (September 1999), p. 43. General Short believed that the focus of the air campaign should be strategic targets in Serbia proper.

57 Cordesman, "The Lessons and Non-Lessons of the Air and Missile Campaign in Kosovo," figs. 18, 19, 20.

58 Ibid., p. 118.

59 Glenny, *The Fall of Yugoslavia*, pp. 32–33; and Woodward, *Balkan Tragedy*, pp. 7, 133.

60 Pape, *Bombing to Win*, p. 30.

61 Thomas A. Keaney and Eliot A. Cohen, *Gulf War Air Power Survey Summary Report* (Washington, D.C.: Government Printing Office, 1993), p. 109.

62 Mark Clodfelter argues that air power was ineffective when North Vietnam employed a guerrilla strategy, but was effective when North Vietnam used conventional military operations: "Because of revamped American political objectives and the North's decision to wage conventional war,

Linebacker proved more effective than Rolling Thunder in furthering U.S. goals in Vietnam."
Clodfelter, *The Limits of Air Power*, p. 148. See also Pape, *Bombing to Win*, pp. 193–194. Analyses of
the Israeli experience can be found in Martin van Creveld with Steven L. Canby and Kenneth S.
Brower, *Air Power and Maneuver Warfare* (Maxwell Air Force Base, Ala.: Air University Press, 1994),
pp. 153–192; Dupuy, *Elusive Victory*; and Edgar O'Balance, *No Victor, No Vanquished: The Yom Kippur
War* (London: Barrier and Jenkins, 1979).

63 Cordesman, "The Lessons and Non-Lessons of the Air and Missile Campaign in Kosovo," p. 95.
After the war, many NATO commanders concluded that the Yugoslav 3d Army could have
held out for a considerable length of time despite NATO air attacks. See Dana Priest, "The
Commanders' War: The Plan to Invade Kosovo," *Washington Post*, September 19, 1999.

64 As of this writing, data on actual Serbian losses are limited. Press reports suggest that NATO may
have overestimated the initial damage it inflicted. Figures released by General Clark in September
1999 indicate that allied strikes destroyed or damaged roughly one-third of the Serbian army's
weaponry and vehicles in Kosovo. Priest, "The Commanders' War: The Battle inside Headquarters." The initial baseline of Serbian forces in Kosovo is not known at this time, however,
making actual losses very difficult to discern.

65 Kaminski and Reed, "NATO Link to KLA Rebels."

66 For ways to improve this capability, see Alan Vick, David T. Orletsky, John Bordeaux, and David A.
Shlapak, *Enhancing Airpower's Contribution against Light Infantry Targets* (Santa Monica, Calif.: RAND,
1996).

67 "Interview: General Wesley Clark."

68 National Security Advisor Samuel Berger also authorized General Clark to examine various
ground options. Priest, "The Commanders' War: The Plan to Invade Kosovo."

69 Carla Anne Robins and Thomas E. Ricks, "NATO Weighs Plan for Bigger Kosovo Force," *Wall
Street Journal*, May 19, 1999; and Schmitt and Gordon, "Shift in Targets." The deployment of
Apache helicopters may have been in part intended to convince Milosevic of the plausibility of a
ground invasion. Ignatieff, "The Virtual Commander," p. 33.

70 Priest, "The Commanders' War: The Plan to Invade Kosovo."

71 Apple, "A Fresh Set of U.S. Goals."

72 Robbins and Ricks, "NATO Weighs Plan for Bigger Kosovo Force"; Thomas E. Ricks, David
Rogers, and Carla Anne Robbins, "NATO to Reconsider the Issue of Ground Troops in Kosovo,"
Wall Street Journal, April 21, 1999; and Rowan Scarborough, "Apaches Were Sent to Scare Serbs,"
Washington Times, May 21, 1999, p. 1.

73 Michael R. Gordon, "NATO Says Serbs, Fearing Land War, Dig In on Border," *New York Times*,
May 19, 1999, p. 1.

74 See Thomas A. Keaney, "The Linkage of Air and Ground Power in the Future of Conflict,"
International Security, Vol. 22, No. 2 (Fall 1997), pp. 147–150.

75 Joseph Fitschett, "NATO Misjudged Bombing Damage," *International Herald Tribune*, June 23, 1999,
p. A1.

76 Michael Evans, "SAS 'On the Ground in Kosovo,' " *London Times*, April 13, 1999.

77 See Cordesman, "The Lessons and Non-Lessons of the Air and Missile War in Kosovo," p. 6.

78 Quoted in Graham, "Air vs. Ground," p. A1. See also Fitschett, "NATO Misjudged Bombing
Damage," p. A1. One of NATO's most effective strikes occurred on June 7, shortly before Milosevic
capitulated, when B-52 bombers caught Serbian soldiers exposed on an open plain and may have
killed several hundred—strikes that owed their success in part to KLA operations and intelligence.
Kaminski and Reed, "NATO Link to KLA Rebels." NATO, however, sought to avoid serving as
the KLA's air force and denied it communication equipment to serve as forward air controllers to
call in strikes.

79 One post-Operation Deliberate Force analysis concluded: "Hitting communication nodes,
weapons and ammunition storage areas, and lines of communication took away Serb mobility and
did not allow them to respond to . . . offensives elsewhere in Bosnia." Michael O. Beale, "Bombs
over Bosnia: The Role of Airpower in Bosnia-Herzegovina," master's thesis presented to the
School of Advanced Airpower Studies, Maxwell Air Force Base, Air University Press, August
1997, p. 37.

80 For a more complete description of Operation Deliberate Force, see Robert Owen, ed., *The
Air University Bosnian Air Campaign Study* (Maxwell Air Force Base, Ala.: Air University Press,
forthcoming).

81 Serbia's efforts to work with Russia for a diplomatic solution apparently began in earnest in mid-May, well before the early June strikes against Serbian forces that proved more effective because of the KLA's presence. See BBC News, "Belgrade Diplomacy Leaves NATO Unmoved," August 1, 1999, http://bbc.co.uk/hi/english/world/europe; and Steven Erlanger, "With Milosevic Unyielding on Kosovo, NATO Moved toward Invasion," *New York Times*, November 7, 1999, p. 1.

82 Chris Hedges, "Kosovo's Next Masters?" *Foreign Affairs*, Vol. 79, No. 3 (May/June 1999), pp. 24–42.

83 Byman and Waxman, "Defeating U.S. Coercion."

84 Note that a counter-coercive strategy such as inflicting casualties need not succeed for coercion to fail. Coercion relies on manipulating an adversary's perceptions of future costs, so even if an adversary is badly mistaken in its beliefs about a coercer's willingness and ability to incur costs, it may nevertheless hold out.

85 For such conclusions and evidence drawn from other studies, see Eric Larson, *Casualties and Consensus: The Historical Role of Casualties in Domestic Support for U.S. Military Operations* (Santa Monica, Calif.: RAND, 1996). See also John E. Mueller, *Policy and Opinion in the Gulf War* (Chicago: University of Chicago Press, 1994), pp. 76–77, who reports empirical findings from previous conflicts to support the theory that U.S. casualties, especially under certain circumstances, erode public support for continued operations. Harvey M. Sapolsky and Jeremy Shapiro present a strong argument that many empirical works underestimate casualty sensitivity among politicians. See Sapolsky and Shapiro, "Casualties, Technology, and America's Future Wars," *Parameters*, Vol. 26, No. 2 (Summer 1996), pp. 119–127.

86 Quoted in Stanley Karnow, *Vietnam: A History* (New York: Penguin, 1997), p. 184. Saddam Hussein shared this belief prior to the Gulf War, reportedly having told the U.S. ambassador to Baghdad shortly before the invasion of Kuwait, "Yours is a society which cannot accept 10,000 dead in one battle." Quoted in Freedman and Karsh, *The Gulf Conflict*, p. 276.

87 Quoted in Barry M. Blechman and Tamara Cofman Wittes, "Defining Moment: The Threat and Use of Force in American Foreign Policy," *Political Science Quarterly*, Vol. 114, No. 1 (Spring 1999), p. 5.

88 United Press International, text of Milosevic interview, April 30, 1999.

89 The head of Serbian forces in Kosovo also publicized the threat of heavy casualties to deter a NATO ground attack. BBC News, "NATO Promised 'Hell' in Kosovo," May 30, 1999, http://news.co./uk/hi/english/world/monitoring (visited on August 1, 1999).

90 William M. Arkin, "Baghdad: The Urban Sanctuary in Desert Storm?" *Air Power Journal*, Vol. 10, No. 1 (Spring 1997), pp. 4–20; and Michael R. Gordon and Bernard E. Trainor, *The Generals' War: The Inside Story of the Conflict in the Gulf* (Boston: Little, Brown, 1994), p. 326.

91 Steven Lee Myers, "All in Favor of This Target, Say Yes, Si, Oui, Ja," *New York Times*, April 25, 1999, sec. 4, p. 4.

92 Ignatieff, "The Virtual Commander," p. 33. For a sample of common arguments against the legality of some NATO targeting practices, see Michael Dobbs, "A War-Torn Reporter Reflects," *Washington Post*, July 11, 1999, p. B1.

93 Cordesman, "The Lessons and Non-Lessons of the Air and Missile War in Kosovo," pp. 45–46.

94 Elaine Harden and John M. Broder, "Clinton's War Aims: Win the War, Keep the U.S. Voters Content," *New York Times*, May 22, 1999, p. A1.

95 Matthew C. Waxman, "Coalitions and Limits on Coercive Diplomacy," *Strategic Review*, Vol. 25, No. 1 (Winter 1997), pp. 38–47.

96 Michael R. Gordon and Eric Schmitt, "Thwarted, NATO Agrees to Bomb Belgrade Sites," *New York Times*, March 31, 1999, p. A1.

97 The total number of strike aircraft tripled after the first month, and the overall sortie rate increased dramatically as well. Cordesman, "The Lessons and Non-Lessons of the Air and Missile War in Kosovo," pp. 11–14.

98 Interpretations of legal obligations and factual circumstances vary. Moreover, some political pressures push against rather than with the humanitarian goals of the legal regime; while concern with collateral damage may caution tremendous restraint in conducting air operations, concern with force protection, military effectiveness, and even financial cost may cause planners to undervalue civilian costs to operations, arguably beyond legal bounds. For critical appraisals of NATO's practices, see Fintan O'Toole, "Nato's Actions, Not Just Its Cause, Must Be Moral," *Irish Times*, April 24, 1999, p. 11; and Julian Manyon, "Robinson Criticizes Nato's Bombing," *Independent* (London), May 14, 1999, p. 4. It must be noted that such critiques often failed to address the immense risks that civilians would face in the event of a ground war.

99 Thomas E. Ricks, "NATO Commander's Job Is Maintaining Support from Members for Airstrikes," *Wall Street Journal*, April 13, 1999, p. 10.

100 Critics who complained that bombing from high altitudes undermined the sheer military effectiveness of air strikes generally miss the point that although such practices do carry disadvantages such as reduced accuracy or ability to hit key targets under certain weather conditions, they removed Milosevic's only practicable opportunity to inflict casualties.

101 See Viktor Chernomyrdin "Impossible to Talk Peace with Bombs Falling," *Washington Post*, May 27, 1999, p. A39.

102 David R. Sands, "U.S. and Russia Patch Up Relations," *Washington Times*, June 25, 1999, p. A1.

103 Quoted in Andrew Gilligan, "Russia, Not Bombs, Brought End to War in Kosovo Says Jackson," *London Sunday Telegraph*, August 1, 1999, p. 1. General Clark also refers to Serbia's "isolation" as a major factor in Milosevic's ultimate decisionmaking. See "Interview: General Wesley Clark."

104 Ironically, the most significant diplomatic windfall for Serbia occurred when a U.S. warplane hit—very precisely—the Chinese embassy based on faulty intelligence.

105 Cohen, "The Mystique of U.S. Air Power," p. 109.

Part IV

Nuclear strategy

INTRODUCTION

The two essays in this section explore the extent to which the advent of nuclear weapons changed the theory and practice of strategy.

The first selection is taken from Bernard Brodie's (1909–1978) *The Absolute Weapon*, published in 1946 at the dawn of the nuclear age. In it, Brodie attempts to answer some fundamental questions about the nuclear age, such as: Would war be more or less likely in a world with atomic weapons? What would a future war look like?

Brodie argues that the atomic age represents a major discontinuity in the history of warfare that necessitates a break from classical strategic theory. He notes, for example, that it was possible (even in 1946) for existing forces, armed with atomic weapons, "to wipe out all the cities of a great nation in a single day." Moreover, because no adequate defense against atomic attack was likely, geographic distance no longer offered immunity from atomic attack. Moreover, the likelihood of nuclear retaliation meant that military superiority no longer guaranteed a nation security.

In short, Brodie saw the advent of nuclear weapons leading to a condition of mutual deterrence. As he wrote, "if the aggressor state must fear retaliation, it will know that even if it is the victor, it will suffer a degree of physical destruction incomparably greater than that suffered by any defeated nation in history ... Under those circumstances, no victory ... would be worth the price." In his view, this should have a profound impact on strategy. As he put it, "Thus far the chief purpose of our military establishment has been to win wars. From now on its chief purpose must be to avert them."

The second selection is Albert Wohlstetter's essay, "The Delicate Balance of Terror." Wohlstetter worked with Brodie at the RAND Corporation and later taught at the University of Chicago. Wohlstetter took aim at those, like Brodie, who believed that nuclear deterrence was robust. Wohlstetter argued, by contrast that "deterrence ... is neither assured nor impossible but will be the product of sustained intelligent effort and hard choices, responsibly made." Whereas others emphasized the destructive power of nuclear weapons as the most important feature of the nuclear age, Wohlstetter emphasized "the uncertainties and interactions between our own wide range of choices and the moves open to the Soviets." He believed, in other words, that strategic choice had an important role to play in nuclear calculations.

Wohlstetter argued that maintaining a stable deterrent required not only the acquisition of sufficient numbers of nuclear weapons, but also their deployment in modes that would promote stability. Moreover, to be effective deterrents, they needed to pose a credible threat of retaliation. In the case of the United States, for example, they needed to survive a Soviet attack, receive permission to launch, reach enemy territory, avoid air defenses, and destroy their targets. In Wohlstetter's view, uncertainties with each of these tasks complicated deterrence. As he put it, "The notion that a carefully planned surprise attack can be checkmated almost effortlessly . . . is wrong and its nearly universal acceptance is terribly dangerous."

Study questions

1. To what extent is classical strategic thought, as embodied in the writings of Clausewitz and Sun Tzu, still relevant in the nuclear age?
2. Is there a universal logic of nuclear strategy?
3. Is victory possible in nuclear war?

Further reading

Ayson, Robert, "Bargaining with Nuclear Weapons: Thomas Schelling's 'General' Concept of Stability," *The Journal of Strategic Studies* 23, 2 (2000), pp. 48–71.

Freedman, Lawrence, *The Evolution of Nuclear Strategy* (New York: St. Martin's Press, 1981).

Heuser, Beatrice: "Victory in a Nuclear War? A Comparison of NATO and WTO War Aims and Strategies," *Contemporary European History* 7, Pt 3 (November 1998), pp. 311–328.

Kissinger, Henry A., *Nuclear Weapons and Foreign Policy* (New York: W.W. Norton, 1969).

Steiner, Barry, "Using the Absolute Weapon: Early Ideas of Bernard Brodie on Atomic Strategy," *The Journal of Strategic Studies* 7, 4 (1984), pp. 365–393.

Trachtenberg, Marc, *History and Strategy* (Princeton, NJ: Princeton University Press, 1991).

11 The absolute weapon

Bernard Brodie

War in the atomic age

Most of those who have held the public ear on the subject of the atomic bomb have been content to assume that war and obliteration are now completely synonymous, and that modern man must therefore be either obsolete or fully ripe for the millennium. No doubt the state of obliteration—if that should indeed be the future fate of nations which cannot resolve their disputes—provides little scope for analysis. A few degrees difference in nearness to totality is of relatively small account. But in view of man's historically-tested resistance to drastic changes in behavior, especially in a benign direction, one may be pardoned for wishing to examine the various possibilities inherent in the situation before taking any one of them for granted.

It is already known to us all that a war with atomic bombs would be immeasurably more destructive and horrible than any the world has yet known. That fact is indeed portentous, and to many it is overwhelming. But as a datum for the formulation of policy it is in itself of strictly limited utility. It underlines the urgency of our reaching correct decisions, but it does not help us to discover which decisions are in fact correct.

Men have in fact been converted to religion at the point of the sword, but the process generally required actual use of the sword against recalcitrant individuals. The atomic bomb does not lend itself to that kind of discriminate use. The wholesale conversion of mankind away from those parochial attitudes bound up in nationalism is a consummation devoutly to be wished and, where possible, to be actively promoted. But the mere existence of the bomb does not promise to accomplish it at an early enough time to be of any use. The careful handling required to assure long and fruitful life to the Age of Atomic Energy will in the first instance be a function of distinct national governments, not all of which, incidentally, reflect in their behavior the will of the popular majority.

Governments are of course ruled by considerations not wholly different from those which affect even enlightened individuals. That the atomic bomb is a weapon of incalculable horror will no doubt impress most of them deeply. But they have never yet responded to the horrific implications of war in a uniform way. Even those governments which feel impelled to the most drastic self-denying proposals will have to grapple not merely with the suspicions of other governments but with the indisputable fact that great nations have very recently been ruled by men who were supremely indifferent to horror, especially horror inflicted by them on people other than their own.

Statesmen have hitherto felt themselves obliged to base their policies on the assumption that the situation might again arise where to one or more great powers war looked less dangerous or less undesirable than the prevailing conditions of peace. They will want to know how the atomic bomb affects that assumption. They must realize at the outset that a weapon so terrible cannot but influence the degree of probability of war for any given period in the future. But the degree of that influence or the direction in which it operates is by no means obvious. It has, for example, been stated over and over again that the atomic bomb is *par excellence* the weapon of aggression, that it weights the scales overwhelmingly in favor of surprise attack. That, if true, would indicate that world peace is even more precarious than it was before, despite the greater horrors of war. But is it inevitably true? If not, then the effort to make the reverse true would deserve a high priority among the measures to be pursued.

Thus, a series of questions present themselves. Is war more or less likely in a world which contains atomic bombs? If the latter, is it *sufficiently* unlikely—sufficiently, that is, to give society the opportunity it desperately needs to adjust its politics to its physics? What are the procedures for effecting that adjustment within the limits of our opportunities? And how can we enlarge our opportunities? Can we transmute what appears to be an immediate crisis into a long-term problem, which presumably would permit the application of more varied and better considered correctives than the pitifully few and inadequate measures which seem available at the moment?

It is precisely in order to answer such questions that we turn our attention to the effect of the bomb on the character of war. We know in advance that war, if it occurs, will be very different from what it was in the past, but what we want to know is: How different, and in what ways? A study of those questions should help us to discover the conditions which will govern the pursuit of security in the future and the feasibility of proposed measures for furthering that pursuit. At any rate, we know that it is not the mere existence of the weapon but rather its effects on the traditional pattern of war which will govern the adjustments which states will make in their relations with each other.

The Truman-Attlee-King statement of November 15, 1945, epitomized in its first paragraph a few specific conclusions concerning the bomb which had evolved as of that date: "We recognize that the application of recent scientific discoveries to the methods and practice of war has placed at the disposal of mankind means of destruction hitherto unknown against which there can be no adequate military defense and in the employment of which no single nation can in fact have a monopoly."

This observation, it would seem, is one upon which all reasonable people would now be agreed. But it should be noted that of the three propositions presented in it the first is either a gross understatement or meaningless, the second has in fact been challenged by persons in high military authority, and the third, while generally admitted to be true, has nevertheless been the subject of violently clashing interpretations. In any case, the statement does not furnish a sufficient array of postulates for the kind of analysis we wish to pursue.

It is therefore necessary to start out afresh and examine the various features of the bomb, its production, and its use which are of military importance. Presented below are a number of conclusions concerning the character of the bomb which seem to this writer to be inescapable. Some of the eight points listed already enjoy fairly universal acceptance; most do not. After offering with each one an explanation of why he believes it to be true, the writer will attempt to deduce from these several conclusions or postulates the effect of the bomb on the character of war.

I. *The power of the present bomb is such that any city in the world can be effectively destroyed by one to ten bombs*

While this proposition is not likely to evoke much dissent,[1] its immediate implications have been resisted or ignored by important public officials. These implications are twofold. First, it is now physically possible for air forces no greater than those existing in the recent war to wipe out all the cities of a great nation in a single day—and it will be shown subsequently that what is physically possible must be regarded as tactically feasible. Secondly, with our present industrial organization the elimination of our cities would mean the elimination for military purposes of practically the whole of our industrial structure. But before testing these extraordinary implications, let us examine and verify the original proposition.

The bomb dropped on Hiroshima completely pulverized an area of which the radius from the point of detonation was about one and one-quarter miles. However, everything to a radius of two miles was blasted with some burning and between two and three miles the buildings were about half destroyed. Thus the area of total destruction covered about four square miles, and the area of destruction and substantial damage extended over some twenty-seven square miles. The bomb dropped on Nagasaki, while causing less damage than the Hiroshima bomb because of the physical characteristics of the city, was nevertheless considerably more powerful. We have it on Dr. J. Robert Oppenheimer's authority that the Nagasaki bomb "would have taken out ten square miles, or a bit more, if there had been ten square miles to take out."[2] From the context in which that statement appears it is apparent that Dr. Oppenheimer is speaking of an area of total destruction.

The city of New York is listed in the *World Almanac* as having an area of 365 square miles. But it obviously would not require the pulverization of every block of it to make the whole area one of complete chaos and horror. Ten well-placed bombs of the Nagasaki type would eliminate that city as a contributor to the national economy, whether for peace or war, and convert it instead into a catastrophe area in dire need of relief from outside. If the figure of ten bombs be challenged, it need only be said that it would make very little difference militarily if twice that number of bombs were required. Similarly, it would be a matter of relative indifference if the power of the bomb were so increased as to require only five to do the job. Increase of power in the individual bomb is of especially little moment to cities of small or medium size, which would be wiped out by one bomb each whether that bomb were of the Nagasaki type or of fifty times as much power. No conceivable variation in the power of the atomic bomb could compare in importance with the disparity in power between atomic and previous types of explosives.

The condition at this writing of numerous cities in Europe and Japan sufficiently under-lines the fact that it does not require atomic bombs to enable man to destroy great cities. TNT and incendiary bombs when dropped in sufficient quantities are able to do a quite thorough job of it. For that matter, it should be pointed out that a single bomb which contains in itself the concentrated energy of 20,000 tons of TNT is by no means equal in destructive effect to that number of tons of TNT distributed among bombs of one or two tons each. The destructive radius of individual bombs of any one type increases only with the cube root of the explosive energy released, and thus the very concentration of power in the atomic bomb prevents the full utilization of its tremendous energy. The bomb must be detonated from an altitude of at least 1,000 feet if the full spread of its destructive radius is to be realized, and much of the blast energy is absorbed by the air above the target. But the sum of initial energy is quite enough to afford such losses.

It should be obvious that there is much more than a logistic difference involved between a situation where a single plane sortie can cause the destruction of a city like Hiroshima and one in which at least 500 bomber sorties are required to do the same job. Nevertheless, certain officers of the United States Army Air Forces, in an effort to "deflate" the atomic bomb, have observed publicly enough to have their comments reported in the press that the destruction wrought at Hiroshima could have been effected by two days of routine bombing with ordinary bombs. Undoubtedly so, but the 500 or more bombers needed to do the job under those circumstances would, if they were loaded with atomic bombs, be physically capable of destroying 500 or more Hiroshimas in the same interval of time. That observation discounts certain tactical considerations. These will be taken up in due course, but for the moment it is sufficient to point out that circumstances do arise in war when it is the physical carrying capacity of the bombing vehicles rather than tactical considerations which will determine the amount of damage done.

II.   *No adequate defense against the bomb exists, and the possibilities of its existence in the future are exceedingly remote*

This proposition requires little supporting argument in so far as it is a statement of existing fact. But that part of it which involves a prediction for the future conflicts with the views of most of the high-ranking military officers who have ventured opinions on the implications of the atomic bomb. No layman can with equanimity differ from the military in their own field, and the present writer has never entertained the once-fashionable view that the military do not know their business. But, apart from the question of objectivity concerning professional interests—in which respect the record of the military profession is neither worse nor better than that of other professions—the fact is that the military experts have based their arguments mainly on presumptions gleaned from a field in which they are generally not expert, namely, military *history*. History is at best an imperfect guide to the future, but when imperfectly understood and interpreted it is a menace to sound judgment.

   The defense against hostile missiles in all forms of warfare, whether on land, sea, or in the air, has thus far depended basically on a combination of, first, measures to reduce the number of missiles thrown or to interfere with their aim (i.e., defense by offensive measures) and, secondly, ability to absorb those which strike. To take an obvious example, the large warship contains in itself and in its escorting air or surface craft a volume of fire power which usually reduces and may even eliminate the blows of the adversary. Unlike most targets ashore, it also enjoys a mobility which enables it to maneuver evasively under attack (which will be of little value under atomic bombs). But unless the enemy is grotesquely inferior in strength, the ship's ability to survive must ultimately depend upon its compartmentation and armor, that is, on its ability to absorb punishment.

   The same is true of a large city. London was defended against the German V-1, or "buzz-bomb," first by concerted bombing attacks upon the German experimental stations, industrial plants, and launching sites, all of which delayed the V-1 attack and undoubtedly greatly reduced the number of missiles ultimately launched. Those which were nevertheless launched were met by a combination of fighter planes, anti-aircraft guns, and barrage balloons. Towards the end of the eighty-day period which covered the main brunt of the attack, some 75 per cent of the bombs launched were being brought down, and, since many of the remainder were inaccurate in their flight, only 9 per cent were reaching London.[3] These London was able to "absorb"; that is, there were casualties and damage but no serious impairment of the vital services on which depended the city's life and its ability to serve the war effort.

It is precisely this ability to absorb punishment, whether one is speaking of a warship or a city, which seems to vanish in the face of atomic attack. For almost any kind of target selected, the so-called "static defenses" are defenses no longer. For the same reason too, mere reduction in the number of missiles which strike home is not sufficient to save the target, though it may have some effect on the enemy's selection of targets. The defense of London against V-1 was considered effective, and yet in eighty days some 2,300 of those missiles hit the city. The record bag was that of August 28, 1944, when out of 101 bombs which approached England 97 were shot down and only four reached London. But if those four had been atomic bombs, London survivors would not have considered the record good. Before we can speak of a defense against atomic bombs being effective, *the frustration of the attack for any given target area must be complete.* Neither military history nor an analysis of present trends in military technology leaves appreciable room for hope that means of completely frustrating attack by aerial missiles will be developed.

In his speech before the Washington Monument on October 5, 1945, Fleet Admiral Chester W. Nimitz correctly cautioned the American people against leaping to the conclusion that the atomic bomb had made armies and navies obsolete. But he could have based his cautionary note on better grounds than he in fact adopted. "Before risking our future by accepting these ideas at face value," he said, "let us examine the historical truth that, at least up to this time, there has never yet been a weapon against which man has been unable to devise a counterweapon or a defense."[4]

Apart from the possible irrelevancy for the future of this observation—against which the phrase "at least up to this time" provides only formal protection—the fact is that it is not historically accurate. A casual reading of the history of military technology does, to be sure, encourage such a doctrine. The naval shell gun of 1837, for example, was eventually met with iron armor, and the iron armor in turn provoked the development of the "built-up" gun with greater penetrating power; the submarine was countered with the hydrophone and supersonic detector and with depth charges of various types; the bombing airplane accounted for the development of the specialized fighter aircraft, the highly perfected anti-aircraft gun, and numerous ancillary devices. So it has always been, and the tendency is to argue that so it always will be.

In so far as this doctrine becomes dogma and is applied to the atomic bomb, it becomes the most dangerous kind of illusion. We have already seen that the defense against the V-1 was only *relatively* effective, and something approaching much closer to perfect effectiveness would have been necessary for V-1 missiles carrying atomic bombs. As a matter of fact, the defenses against the V-2 rocket were of practically zero effectiveness, and those who know most about it admit that thus far there has been no noteworthy progress in defenses against the V-2.[5]

These, to be sure, were new weapons. But what is the story of the older weapons? After five centuries of the use of hand arms with fire-propelled missiles, the large numbers of men killed by comparable arms in the recent war indicates that no adequate answer has yet been found for the bullet.[6] Ordinary TNT, whether in shell, bomb, or torpedo, can be "countered" to a degree by the dispersion of targets or by various kinds of armor, but the enormous destruction wrought by this and comparable explosives on land, sea, and in the air in World War II is an eloquent commentary on the limitations of the defenses. The British following the first World War thought they had in their "Asdic" and depth charges the complete answer to the U-boat, but an only slightly improved U-boat succeeded in the recent war in sinking over 23 million gross tons of shipping. So the story might go on endlessly. It has simply become customary to consider an "answer" satisfactory when it merely diminishes or qualifies the effectiveness of the weapon against which it is devised, and that kind of custom will not do for the atomic bomb.

Despite such statements as that of Canadian General A.G.L. McNaughton that means with which to counter the atomic bomb are already "clearly in sight,"[7] it seems pretty well established that there is no *specific* reply to the bomb. The physicists and chemists who produced the atomic bomb are apparently unanimous on this point: that while there was a scientific consensus long before the atomic bomb existed that it could be produced, no comparable opinion is entertained among scientists concerning their chances of devising effective countermeasures. The bomb itself is as free from direct interference of any kind as is the ordinary bomb. When the House Naval Affairs Committee circulated a statement that electronic means were already available for exploding atomic bombs "far short of their objective without the necessity of locating their position,"[8] scientists qualified to speak denied the truth of the assertion,[9] and it was indeed subsequently disowned by its originators.

Any active defense at all must be along the lines of affecting the carrier, and we have already noted that even when used with the relatively vulnerable airplane or V-1 the atomic bomb poses wholly new problems for the defense. A nation which had developed strong defenses against invading aircraft, which had found reliable means of interfering with radio-controlled rockets, which had developed highly efficient countersmuggling and counter-sabotage agencies, and which had dispersed through the surrounding countryside substantial portions of the industries and populations normally gathered in urban communities would obviously be better prepared to resist atomic attack than a nation which had either neglected or found itself unable to do these things. But it would have only a relative advantage over the latter; it would still be exposed to fearful destruction.

In any case, technological progress is not likely to be confined to measures of defense. The use of more perfect vehicles and of more destructive bombs in greater quantity might very well offset any gains in defense. And the bomb already has a fearful lead in the race.

Random and romantic reflections on the miracles which science has already wrought are of small assistance in our speculations on future trends. World War II saw the evolution of numerous instruments of war of truly startling ingenuity. But with the qualified exception of the atomic bomb itself (the basic principle of which was discovered prior to but in the same year as the outbreak of war in Europe), all were simply mechanical adaptations of scientific principles which were well known long before the war. It was no doubt a long step from the discovery in 1922 of the phenomenon upon which radar is based to the use of the principle in an antiaircraft projectile fuse, but here too realization that it might be so used considerably antedated the fuse itself.

The advent of a "means of destruction hitherto unknown"—to quote the Truman-Attlee-King statement—is certainly not new. The steady improvement of weapons of war is an old story, and the trend in that direction has in recent years been accelerated. But thus far each new implement has, at least initially, been limited enough in the scope of its use or in its strategic consequences to permit some timely measure of adaptation both on the battlefield and in the minds of strategists and statesmen. Even the most "revolutionary" developments of the past seem by contrast with the atomic bomb to have been minor steps in many-sided evolutionary process. This process never permitted any one invention in itself to subvert or even to threaten for long the previously existing equilibrium of military force. Any startling innovation either of offense or defense provoked some kind of answer in good time, but the answer was rarely more than a qualified one and the end result was usually a profound and sometimes a politically significant change in the methods of waging war.[10]

With the introduction, however, of an explosive agent which is several million times more potent on a pound-for-pound basis than the most powerful explosives previously known, we have a change of quite another character. The factor of increase of destructive efficiency is so great that there arises at once the strong presumption that the experience of the past concerning eventual adjustment might just as well be thrown out the window. Far from being something which merely "adds to the complexities of field commanders," as one American military authority put it, the atomic bomb seems so far to overshadow any military invention of the past as to render comparisons ridiculous.

III. *The atomic bomb not only places an extraordinary military premium upon the development of new types of carriers but also greatly extends the destructive range of existing carriers*

World War II saw the development and use by the Germans of rockets capable of 220 miles' range and carrying approximately one ton each of TNT. Used against London, these rockets completely baffled the defense. But for single-blow weapons which were generally inaccurate at long distances even with radio control,[11] they were extremely expensive. It is doubtful whether the sum of economic damage done by these missiles equaled the expenditure which the Germans put into their development, production, and use. At any rate, the side enjoying command of the air had in the airplane a much more economical and longer-range instrument for inflicting damage on enemy industry than was available in the rocket. The capacity of the rocket-type projectile to strike without warning in all kinds of weather with complete immunity from all known types of defenses guaranteed to it a supplementary though subordinate role to bomber-type aircraft. But its inherent limitations, so long as it carried only chemical explosives, were sufficient to warrant considerable reserve in predictions of its future development.

However, the power of the new bomb completely alters the considerations which previously governed the choice of vehicles and the manner of using them. A rocket far more elaborate and expensive than the V-2 used by the Germans is still an exceptionally cheap means of bombarding a country if it can carry in its nose an atomic bomb. The relative inaccuracy of aim—which continued research will no doubt reduce—is of much diminished consequence when the radius of destruction is measured in miles rather than yards. And even with existing fuels such as were used in the German V-2, it is theoretically feasible to produce rockets capable of several thousands of miles of range, though the problem of controlling the flight of rockets over such distances is greater than is generally assumed.

Of more immediate concern than the possibilities of rocket development, however, is the enormous increase in effective bombing range which the atomic bomb gives to *existing types of aircraft*. That it has this effect becomes evident when one examines the various factors which determine under ordinary—that is, non-atomic bomb—conditions whether a bombing campaign is returning military dividends. First, the campaign shows profit only if a large proportion of the planes, roughly 90 per cent or more, are returning from individual strikes.[12] Otherwise one's air force may diminish in magnitude more rapidly than the enemy's capacity to fight. Each plane load of fuel must therefore cover a two-way trip, allowing also a fuel reserve for such contingencies as adverse winds and combat action, thereby diminishing range by at least one-half from the theoretical maximum, except in the case of shuttle bombing, which in World War II was relatively rare.

But the plane cannot be entirely loaded with fuel. It must also carry besides its crew a heavy load of defensive armor and armament. Above all, it must carry a sufficient load of bombs to make the entire sortie worthwhile—a sufficient load, that is, to warrant attendant expenditures in fuel, engine maintenance, and crew fatigue. The longer the distance covered, the smaller the bomb load per sortie and the longer the interval between sorties. To load a plane with thirty tons of fuel and only two tons of bombs, as we did in our first B-29 raid on Japan, will not do for a systematic campaign of strategic bombing. One must get closer to the target and thus transfer a greater proportion of the carrying capacity from fuel to bombs.[13] What we then come out with is an effective bombing range less than one-fourth the straight-line cruising radius of the plane under optimum conditions. In other words a plane capable, without too much stripping of its equipment, of a 6,000-mile non-stop flight would probably have an effective bombing range of substantially less than 1,500 miles.

With atomic bombs, however, the considerations described above which so severely limit bombing range tend to vanish. There is no question of increasing the number of bombs in order to make the sortie profitable. One per plane is quite enough. The gross weight of the atomic bomb is secret, but even if it weighed four to six tons it would still be a light load for a B-29. It would certainly be a sufficient pay load to warrant any conceivable military expenditure on a single sortie. The next step then becomes apparent. Under the callously utilitarian standards of military bookkeeping, a plane and its crew can very well be sacrificed in order to deliver an atomic bomb to an extreme distance. We have, after all, the recent and unforgettable experience of the Japanese *Kamikaze*.[14] Thus, the plane can make its entire flight in one direction, and, depending on the weight of the bomb and the ultimate carrying capacity of the plane, its range might be almost as great with a single atomic bomb as it would be with no bomb load whatever. The non-stop flight during November, 1945, of a B-29 from Guam to Washington, D. C., almost 8,200 statute miles, was in this respect more than a stunt.[15]

If it be true, as has been hinted,[16] that the B-29 is the only existing bomber which can carry the atomic bomb, the fact might argue an even greater gross weight for the bomb than that surmised above. It might of course be that a bomb having a lighter container would still be highly effective though less efficient, but in any case we know that there is no need for the bomb to be *heavier* than either the Hiroshima or the Nagasaki bomb. The plane which carried the Hiroshima bomb apparently flew a distance of 3,000 miles, and bombers of considerably greater carrying capacity are definitely beyond the blueprint stage. With the bomb weight remaining fixed, the greater capacity can be given over entirely to fuel load and thus to added range. The great-circle-route distance between New York and Moscow is only 4,800 miles. With planes following the great-circle routes even across the Arctic wastes, as will undoubtedly prove feasible, it appears that no major city in either the Soviet Union or the United States is much beyond 6,000 miles from the territories of the other. And if American forces are able to utilize bases in northern Canada, the cities of the Soviet Union are brought considerably closer.

Under the conditions just described, any world power is able from bases within its own territories to destroy most of the cities of any other power. It is not *necessary*, despite the assertions to the contrary of various naval and political leaders including President Truman, to seize advanced bases close to enemy territory as a prerequisite to effective use of the bomb.[17] The lessons of the recent Pacific war in that respect are not merely irrelevant but misleading, and the effort to inflate their significance for the future is only one example of the pre-atomic thinking prevalent today even among people who understand fully the power of the bomb. To recognize that power is one thing; to draw out its full strategic implications is quite another.

The facts just presented do not mean that distance loses all its importance as a barrier to conflict between the major power centers of the world. It would still loom large in any plans to consolidate an atomic bomb attack by rapid invasion and occupation. It would no doubt also influence the success of the bomb attack itself. Rockets are likely to remain of lesser range than aircraft and less accurate near the limits of their range, and the weather hazards which still affect aircraft multiply with distance. Advanced bases will certainly not be value-less. But it is nevertheless a fact that under existing technology the distance separating, for example, the Soviet Union from the United States offers no direct immunity to either with respect to atomic bomb attack, though it does so for all practical purposes with respect to ordinary bombs.[18]

IV. Superiority in air forces, though a more effective safeguard in itself than superiority in naval or land forces, nevertheless fails to guarantee security

This proposition is obviously true in the case of very long range rockets, but let us continue to limit our discussion to existing carriers. In his *Third Report to the Secretary of War*, dated November 12, 1945, General H.H. Arnold, commanding the Army Air Forces, made the following statement: "Meanwhile [i.e., until very long range rockets are developed], the only known effective means of delivering atomic bombs in their present stage of development is the very heavy bomber, and that is certain of success only when the user has air superiority."[19]

This writer feels no inclination to question General Arnold's authority on matters pertaining to air combat tactics. However, it is pertinent to ask just what the phrase "certain of success" means in the sentence just quoted, or rather, how much certainty of success is necessary for each individual bomb before an atomic bomb attack is considered feasible. In this respect one gains some insight into what is in General Arnold's mind from a sentence which occurs somewhat earlier on the same page in the *Report:* "Further, the great unit cost of the atomic bomb means that as nearly as possible every one must be delivered to its intended target." Here is obviously the major premise upon which the conclusion above quoted is based, and one is not disputing General Arnold's judgment in the field of his specialization by examining a premise which lies wholly outside of it.

When the bombs were dropped on Hiroshima and Nagasaki in August, 1945, there were undoubtedly very few such bombs in existence—which would be reason enough for con-sidering each one precious regardless of cost. But the cost of their development and produc-tion then amounted to some two billions of dollars, and that figure would have to be divided by the number made to give the cost of each. If, for example, there were twenty in existence, the unit cost would have to be reckoned at $100,000,000. That, indeed, is a staggering sum for one missile, being approximately equivalent to the cost of one *Iowa* class battleship. It is quite possible that there were fewer than twenty at that time, and that the unit cost was proportionately higher. For these and other reasons, including the desirability for psycho-logical effect of making certain that the initial demonstration should be a complete success, one can understand why it was then considered necessary, as General Arnold feels it will remain necessary, to "run a large air operation for the sole purpose of delivering one or two atomic bombs."[20]

But it is of course clear that as our existing plant is used for the production of more bombs—and it has already been revealed that over three-fourths of the two billion dollars went into capital investment for plants and facilities[21]—the unit cost will decline. Professor Oppenheimer has estimated that even with existing techniques and facilities, that is, allowing for no improvements whatever in the production processes, the unit cost of the bomb should easily descend to something in the neighborhood of $1,000,000.[22]

Now a million dollars is a large sum of money for any purpose other than war. Just what it means in war may be gauged by the fact that it amounts to substantially less than the cost of two fully equipped Flying Fortresses (B.17s, not B-29s), a considerable number of which were expended in the recent war without waiting upon situations in which each sortie would be certain of success. The money cost of the war to the United States was sufficient to have paid for two or three hundred thousand of such million-dollar bombs. It is evident, therefore, that in the future it will not be the unit cost of the bomb but the number of bombs actually available which will determine the acceptable wastage in any atomic bomb attack.[23]

Thus, if Country A should have available 5,000 atomic bombs, and if it should estimate that 500 bombs dropped on the cities of Country B would practically eliminate the industrial plant of the latter nation, it could afford a wastage of bombs of roughly 9 to 1 to accomplish that result. If its estimate should prove correct and if it launched an attack on that basis, an expenditure of only five billions of dollars in bombs would give it an advantage so inconceivably overwhelming as to make easy and quick victory absolutely assured—provided it was able somehow to prevent retaliation in kind. The importance of the latter proviso will be elaborated in the whole of the following chapter. Meanwhile it should be noted that the figure of 5,000 bombs cited above is, as will shortly be demonstrated, by no means an impossible or extreme figure for any great power which has been producing atomic bombs over a period of ten or fifteen years.

To approach the same point from another angle, one might take an example from naval warfare. The commander of a battleship will not consider the money cost of his 16-inch shells (perhaps $3,000 each at the gun's breech) when engaging an enemy battleship. He will not hesitate, at least not for financial reasons, to open fire at extreme range, even if he can count on only one hit in thirty rounds. The only consideration which could give him pause would be the fear of exhausting his armor-piercing ammunition before he has sunk or disabled the enemy ship. The cost of each shell, to be sure, is much smaller than the cost of one atomic bomb, but the amount of damage each hit accomplishes is also smaller—disproportionately smaller by a wide margin.

In calculations of acceptable wastage, the money cost of a weapon is usually far overshadowed by considerations of availability; but in so far as it does enter into those calculations, it must be weighed against the amount of damage done to the enemy with each hit. A million dollar bomb which can do a billion dollars worth of damage—and that is a conservative figure—is a very cheap missile indeed. In fact, one of the most frightening things about the bomb is that it makes the destruction of enemy cities an immeasurably cheaper process than it was before, cheaper not alone in terms of missiles but also in terms of the air forces necessary to do the job. Provided the nation using them has enough such bombs available, it can afford a large number of misses for each hit obtained.

To return to General Arnold's observation, we know from the experience of the recent war that very inferior air forces can penetrate to enemy targets if they are willing to make the necessary sacrifices. The Japanese aircraft which raided Pearl Harbor were considerably fewer in number than the American planes available at Pearl Harbor. That, to be sure, was a surprise attack preceding declaration of hostilities, but such possibilities must be taken into account for the future. At any rate, the Japanese air attacks upon our ships off Okinawa occurred more than three years after the opening of hostilities, and there the Japanese, who were not superior in numbers on any one day and who did indeed lose over 4,000 planes in two months of battle, nevertheless succeeded in sinking or damaging no fewer than 253 American warships. For that matter, the British were effectively raiding targets deep in

Germany, and doing so without suffering great casualties, long before they had overtaken the German lead in numbers of aircraft. The war has demonstrated beyond the shadow of a doubt that the sky is much too big to permit one side, however superior, to shut out enemy aircraft completely from the air over its territories.

The concept of "command of the air," which has been used altogether too loosely, has never been strictly analogous to that of "command of the sea." The latter connotes something approaching absolute exclusion of enemy surface craft from the area in question. The former suggests only that the enemy is suffering losses greater than he can afford, whereas one's own side is not. But the appraisal of tolerable losses is in part subjective, and is also affected by several variables which may have little to do with the number of planes downed. Certainly the most important of those variables is the amount of damage being inflicted on the bombing raids. An air force which can destroy the cities in a given territory has for all practical purposes the fruits of command of the air, regardless of its losses.

Suppose, then, one put to the Army Air Forces the following question: If 3,000 enemy bombers flying simultaneously but individually (i.e., completely scattered)[24] invaded our skies with the intention of dividing between them as targets most of the 92 American cities which contain a population of 100,000 or over (embracing together approximately 29 per cent of our total population), if each of those planes carried an atomic bomb, and if we had 9,000 alerted fighters to oppose them, how much guarantee of protection could be accorded those cities? The answer would undoubtedly depend on a number of technical and geographic variables, but under present conditions it seems to this writer all too easy to envisage situations in which few of the cities selected as targets would be spared overwhelming destruction.

That superiority which results in the so-called "command of the air" is undoubtedly necessary for successful strategic bombing with ordinary bombs, where the weight of bombs required is so great that the same planes must be used over and over again. In a sense also (though one must register some reservations about the exclusion of other arms) General Arnold is right when he says of atomic bomb attack: "For the moment at least, absolute air superiority in being at all times, combined with the best antiaircraft ground devices, is the only form of defense that offers any security whatever, and it must continue to be an essential part of our security program for a long time to come."[25] But it must be added that the "only form of defense that offers any security whatever" falls far short, even without any consideration of rockets, of offering the already qualified kind of security it formerly offered.

V. *Superiority in numbers of bombs is not in itself a guarantee of strategic superiority in atomic bomb warfare*

Under the technical conditions apparently prevailing today, and presumably likely to continue for some time to come, the primary targets for the atomic bomb will be cities. One does not shoot rabbits with elephant guns, especially if there are elephants available. The critical mass conditions to which the bomb is inherently subject place the minimum of destructive energy of the individual unit at far too high a level to warrant its use against any target where enemy strength is not already densely concentrated. Indeed, there is little inducement to the attacker to seek any other kind of target. If one side can eliminate the cities of the other, it enjoys an advantage which is practically tantamount to final victory, provided always its own cities are not similarly eliminated.

The fact that the bomb is inevitably a weapon of indiscriminate destruction may carry no weight in any war in which it is used. Even in World War II, in which the bombs used could to a large extent isolate industrial targets from residential districts within an urban area, the distinctions imposed by international law between "military" and "non-military" targets disintegrated entirely.[26]

How large a city has to be to provide a suitable target for the atomic bomb will depend on a number of variables—the ratio of the number of bombs available to the number of cities which might be hit, the wastage of bombs in respect to each target, the number of bombs which the larger cities can absorb before ceasing to be profitable targets, and, of course, the precise characteristics and relative accessibility of the individual city. Most important of all is the place of the particular city in the nation's economy. We can see at once that it does not require the obliteration of all its towns to make a nation wholly incapable of defending itself in the traditional fashion. Thus, the number of *critical* targets is quite limited, and the number of hits necessary to win a strategic decision—always excepting the matter of retaliation—is correspondingly limited. That does not mean that additional hits would be useless but simply that diminishing returns would set in early; and after the cities of, say, 100,000 population were eliminated the returns from additional bombs expended would decline drastically.

We have seen that one has to allow for wastage of missiles in warfare, and the more missiles one has the larger the degree of wastage which is acceptable. Moreover, the number of bombs available to a victim of attack will always bear to an important degree on his ability to retaliate, though it will not itself determine that ability. But, making due allowance for these considerations, it appears that for any conflict a specific number of bombs will be useful to the side using it, and anything beyond that will be luxury. What that specific number would be for any given situation it is now wholly impossible to determine. But we can say that if 2,000 bombs in the hands of either party is enough to destroy entirely the economy of the other, the fact that one side has 6,000 and the other 2,000 will be of relatively small significance.

We cannot, of course, assume that if a race in atomic bombs develops each nation will be content to limit its production after it reaches what it assumes to be the critical level. That would in fact be poor strategy, because the actual critical level could never be precisely determined in advance and all sorts of contingencies would have to be provided for. Moreover, nations will be eager to make whatever political capital (in the narrowest sense of the term) can be made out of superiority in numbers. But it nevertheless remains true that superiority in numbers of bombs does not endow its possessor with the kind of military security which formerly resulted from superiority in armies, navies, and air forces.

VI.   *The new potentialities which the atomic bomb gives to sabotage must not be overrated*

With ordinary explosives it was hitherto physically impossible for agents to smuggle into another country, either prior to or during hostilities, a sufficient quantity of materials to blow up more than a very few specially chosen objectives. The possibility of really serious damage to a great power resulting from such enterprises was practically nil. A wholly new situation arises, however, where such materials as U-235 or Pu-239 are employed, for only a few pounds of either substance are sufficient, when used in appropriate engines, to blow up the major part of a large city. Should those possibilities be developed, an extraordinarily high premium will be attached to national competence in sabotage on the one hand and in countersabotage on the other. The F.B.I. or its counterpart would become the first line of national defense, and the encroachment on civil liberties which would necessarily follow would far exceed in magnitude and pervasiveness anything which democracies have thus far tolerated in peacetime.

However, it would be easy to exaggerate the threat inherent in that situation, at least for the present. From various hints contained in the *Smyth Report*[27] and elsewhere,[28] it is clear that the engine necessary for utilizing the explosive, that is, the bomb itself, is a highly intricate and fairly massive mechanism. The massiveness is not something which we can expect future research to diminish. It is inherent in the bomb. The mechanism and casing surrounding the explosive element must be heavy enough to act as a "tamper," that is, as a means of holding the explosive substance together until the reaction has made substantial progress. Otherwise the materials would fly apart before the reaction was fairly begun. And since the *Smyth Report* makes it clear that it is not the tensile strength of the tamper but the inertia due to mass which is important, we need expect no particular assistance from metallurgical advances.[29]

The designing of the bomb apparently involved some of the major problems of the whole "Manhattan District" project. The laboratory at Los Alamos was devoted almost exclusively to solving those problems, some of which for a time looked insuperable. The former director of that laboratory has stated that the results of the research undertaken there required for its recording a work of some fifteen volumes.[30] The detonation problem is not even remotely like that of any other explosive. It requires the bringing together instantaneously in perfect union of two or more subcritical masses of the explosive material (which up to that moment must be insulated from each other) and the holding together of the combined mass until a reasonable proportion of the uranium or plutonium atoms have undergone fission. A little reflection will indicate that the mechanism which can accomplish this must be ingenious and elaborate in the extreme, and certainly not one which can be slipped into a suitcase.

It is of course possible that a nation intent upon perfecting the atomic bomb as a sabotage instrument could work out a much simpler device. Perhaps the essential mechanism could be broken down into small component parts such as are easily smuggled across national frontiers, the essential mass being provided by crude materials available locally in the target area. Those familiar with the present mechanism do not consider such an eventuation likely. And if it required the smuggling of whole bombs, that too is perhaps possible. But the chances are that if two or three were successfully introduced into a country by stealth, the fourth or fifth would be discovered. Our federal police agencies have made an impressive demonstration in the past, with far less motivation, of their ability to deal with smugglers and saboteurs.

Those, at any rate, are some of the facts to consider when reading a statement such as Professor Harold Urey was reported to have made: "An enemy who put twenty bombs, each with a time fuse, into twenty trunks, and checked one in the baggage room of the main railroad station in each of twenty leading American cities, could wipe this country off the map so far as military defense is concerned."[31] Quite apart from the question of whether twenty bombs, even if they were considerably more powerful than those used at Hiroshima and Nagasaki, could produce the results which Professor Urey assumes they would, the mode of distribution postulated is not one which recommends itself for aggressive purposes. For the detection of one or more of the bombs would not merely compromise the success of the entire project but would give the intended victim the clearest and most blatant warning imaginable of what to expect and prepare for. Except for port cities, in which foreign ships are always gathered, a surprise attack by air is by every consideration a handier way of doing the job.

VII. *In relation to the destructive powers of the bomb, world resources in raw materials for its production must be considered abundant*

Everything about the atomic bomb is overshadowed by the twin facts that it exists and that its destructive power is fantastically great. Yet within this framework there are a large number of technical questions which must be answered if our policy decisions are to proceed in anything other than complete darkness. Of first importance are those relating to its availability.

The manner in which the bomb was first tested and used and various indications contained in the *Smyth Report* suggest that the atomic bomb cannot be "mass produced" in the usual sense of the term. It is certainly a scarce commodity in the sense in which the economist uses the term "scarcity," and it is bound to remain extremely scarce in relation to the number of TNT or torpex bombs of comparable size which can be produced. To be sure, the bomb is so destructive that even a relatively small number (as compared with other bombs) may prove sufficient to decide a war, especially since there will be no such thing as a "near miss"—anything near will have all the consequences of a direct hit. However, the scarcity is likely to be sufficiently important to dictate the selection of targets and the circumstances under which the missile is hurled.

A rare explosive will not normally be used against targets which are naturally dispersed or easily capable of dispersion, such as ships at sea or isolated industrial plants of no great magnitude. Nor will it be used in types of attack which show an unduly high rate of loss among the attacking instruments—unless, as we have seen, the target is so important as to warrant high ratios of loss provided one or a few missiles penetrate to it. In these respects the effects of scarcity in the explosive materials are intensified by the fact that it requires certain minimum amounts to produce an explosive reaction and that the minimum quantity is not likely to be reduced materially, if at all, by further research.[32]

The ultimate physical limitation on world atomic bomb production is of course the amount of ores available for the derivation of materials capable of spontaneous atomic fission. The only basic material thus far used to produce bombs is uranium, and for the moment only uranium need be considered.

Estimates of the amount of uranium available in the earth's crust vary between 4 and 7 parts per million—a very considerable quantity indeed. The element is very widely distributed, there being about a ton of it present in each cubic mile of sea water and about one-seventh of an ounce per ton (average) in all granite and basalt rocks, which together comprise about 95 per cent by weight of the earth's crust. There is more uranium present in the earth's crust than cadmium, bismuth, silver, mercury, or iodine, and it is about one thousand times as prevalent as gold. However, the number of places in which uranium is known to exist in concentrated form is relatively small, and of these places only four are known to have the concentrated deposits in substantial amounts. The latter deposits are found in the Great Bear Lake region of northern Canada, the Belgian Congo, Colorado, and Joachimsthal in Czechoslovakia. Lesser but nevertheless fairly extensive deposits are known to exist also in Madagascar, India, and Russian Turkestan, while small occurrences are fairly well scattered over the globe.[33]

The pre-war market was dominated by the Belgian Congo and Canada, who agreed in 1939 to share it in the ratio of 60 to 40,[34] a proportion which presumably reflected what was then thought to be their respective reserves and productive capacity. However, it now appears likely that the Canadian reserves are considerably greater than those of the Congo. In 1942 the Congo produced 1,021 tons of unusually rich ore containing 695.6 tons of

U_3O_8—or about 590 tons of uranium metal.[35] In general, however, the ores of Canada and the Congo are of a richness of about one ton of uranium in from fifty to one hundred tons of ore. The Czechoslovakian deposits yielded only fifteen to twenty tons of uranium oxide (U_3O_8) annually before the war.[36] This rate of extraction could not be very greatly expanded even under strained operations—since the total reserves of the Joachimsthal region are far smaller than those of the Congo or Canada or even Colorado.

The quantity of U-235 in metallic uranium is only about .7 per cent (or 1/140th) of the whole. To be sure, plutonium-239, which is equally as effective in a bomb as U-235, is derived from the more plentiful U-238 isotope, but only through a chain reaction that depends on the presence of U-235, which is broken down in the process. It is doubtful whether a given quantity of uranium can yield substantially more plutonium than U-235.[37] It appears also from the *Smyth Report* that the amount of U-235 which can profitably be extracted by separation of the isotopes is far below 100 per cent of the amount present, at least under present techniques.[38]

What all these facts add up to is perhaps summarized by the statement made by one scientist that there is a great deal more than enough fissionable material in known deposits to blow up all the cities in the world, though he added that there might not be enough to do so if the cities were divided and dispersed into ten times their present number (the size of cities included in that comment was not specified). Whatever solace that statement may bring is tempered by the understanding that it refers to *known* deposits of *uranium* ores only and assumes no great increase in the efficiency of the bombs. But how are these factors likely to change?

It is hardly to be questioned that the present extraordinary military premium on uranium will stimulate intensive prospecting and result in the discovery of many new deposits. It seems clear that some of the prospecting which went on during the war was not without result. The demand for uranium heretofore has been extremely limited and only the richer deposits were worth working—mainly for their vanadium or radium content—or for that matter worth keeping track of.[39] So far as uranium itself was concerned, no particular encouragement for prospecting existed.

It is true that the radioactivity of uranium affords a very sensitive test of its presence, and that the data accumulated over the last fifty years make it appear rather unlikely that wholly new deposits will be found comparable to those of Canada or the Congo. But it is not unlikely that in those regions known to contain uranium, further exploration will reveal much larger quantities than had previously been suspected. It seems hardly conceivable, for example, that in the great expanse of European and Asiatic Russia no additional workable deposits will be discovered.

In that connection it is worth noting that the cost of mining the ore and of extracting the uranium is so small a fraction of the cost of bomb production that (as is *not* true in the search for radium) even poorer deposits are decidedly usable. Within certain wide limits, in other words, the relative richness of the ore is not critical. In fact, as much uranium can be obtained as the nations of the world really desire. Gold is commonly mined from ores containing only one-fifth of an ounce per ton of rock, and there are vast quantities of granite which contain from one-fifth to one ounce of uranium per ton of rock.

Although the American experiment has thus far been confined to the use of uranium, it should be noted that the atoms of thorium and protoactinium also undergo fission when bombarded by neutrons. Protoactinium can be eliminated from consideration because of its scarcity in nature, but thorium is even more plentiful than uranium, its average distribution in the earth's crust being some twelve parts per million. Fairly high concentrations of thorium oxide are found in monazite sands, which exist to some extent in the United States, Ceylon, and the Netherlands East Indies, but to a much greater extent in Brazil and British India. The *Smyth Report* states merely that thorium has "no apparent advantage over uranium" (paragraph 2.21), but how important are its disadvantages is not stated. At any rate, it has been publicly announced that thorium is already being used in a pilot plant for the production of atomic energy set up in Canada.[40]

In considering the availability of ores to particular powers, it is always necessary to bear in mind that accessibility is not determined exclusively by national boundaries. Accessibility depends on a combination of geographic, political, and power conditions and on whether the situation is one of war or peace. During wartime a great nation will obviously enjoy the ore resources both of allied countries and of those territories which its armies have overrun, though in the future the ores made available only after the outbreak of hostilities may not be of much importance. Because of the political orientation of Czechoslovakia towards the Soviet Union, the latter will most likely gain in peacetime the use of the Joachimsthal ores,[41] just as the United States enjoys the use of the immensely richer deposits of Canada. The ores of the Belgian Congo will in peacetime be made available to those countries which can either have the confidence of or coerce the Belgian Government (unless the matter is decided by an international instrument to which Belgium is a party); in a time of general war the same ores would be controlled by the nation or nations whose sea and air power gave them access to the region.

Since the atoms of both U-235 and Pu-239 are normally extremely stable (in technical language: possess a long "half-life"), subcritical masses of either material may be stored practically indefinitely. Thus, even a relatively slow rate of production can result over a period of time in a substantial accumulation of bombs. But how slow need the rate of production be? The process of production itself is inevitably a slow one, and even with a huge plant it would require perhaps several months of operation to produce enough fissionable material for the first bomb. But the rate of output thereafter would depend entirely on the extent of the facilities devoted to production, which in turn could be geared to the amount of ores being made available for processing. The eminent Danish scientist, Niels Bohr, who was associated with the atomic bomb project, was reported as having stated publicly in October, 1945, that the United States was producing three kilograms (6.6 pounds) of U-235 daily.[42] The amount of plutonium being concurrently produced might well be considerably larger. Dr. Harold C. Urey, also a leading figure in the bomb development, considers it not unreasonable to assume that with sufficient effort 10,000 bombs could be produced,[43] and other distinguished scientists have not hesitated to put the figure considerably higher. Thus, while the bomb may remain, for the next fifteen or twenty years at least, scarce enough to dictate to its would-be users a fairly rigorous selection of targets and means of delivery, it will not be scarce enough to spare any nation against which it is used from a destruction immeasurably more devastating than that endured by Germany in World War II.

It is of course tempting to leave to the physicist familiar with the bomb all speculation concerning its future increase in power. However, the basic principles which must govern the developments of the future are not difficult to comprehend, and it is satisfying intellectually to have some basis for appraising in terms of probability the random estimates which have been presented to the public. Some of those estimates, it must be said, though emanating from distinguished scientists, are not marked by the scientific discipline which is so rigorously observed in the laboratory. Certainly they cannot be regarded as dispassionate. It might therefore be profitable for us to examine briefly (a) the relation of increase in power to increase of destructive capacity, and (b) the several factors which must determine the inherent power of the bomb.

As we have seen, the radius of destruction of a bomb increases only as the third root of the explosive energy released. Thus, if Bomb A has a radius of total destruction of one mile, it would take a bomb of 1,000 times the power (Bomb B) to have a radius of destruction of ten miles.[44] In terms of area destroyed the proportion does not look so bad; nevertheless the *area* destroyed by Bomb B would be only 100 times as great as that destroyed by Bomb A. In other words, the ratio of *destructive efficiency* to energy released would be only one-tenth as great in Bomb B as it is in Bomb A. But when we consider also the fact that the area covered by Bomb B is bound to include to a much greater degree than Bomb A sections of no appreciable military significance (assuming both bombs are perfectly aimed), the military efficiency of the bomb falls off even more rapidly with increasing power of the individual unit than is indicated above.[45] What this means is that even if it were technically feasible to accomplish it, an increase in the power of the bomb gained only by a proportionate increase in the mass of the scarce and expensive fissionable material within it would be very poor economy. It would be much better to use the extra quantities to make extra bombs.

It so happens, however, that in atomic bombs the total amount of energy released per kilogram of fissionable material (i.e., the efficiency of energy release) *increases* with the size of the bomb.[46] This factor, weighed against those mentioned in the previous paragraph, indicates that there is a theoretical optimum size for the bomb which has perhaps not yet been determined and which may very well be appreciably or even considerably larger than the Nagasaki bomb. But it should be observed that considerations of military economy are not the only factors which hold down the optimum size. One factor, already noted, is the steeply ascending difficulty, as the number of subcritical masses increases, of securing simultaneous and perfect union among them. Another is the problem of the envelope or tamper. If the increase of weight of the tamper is at all proportionate either to the increase in the amount of fissionable material used or to the amount of energy released, the gross weight of the bomb might quickly press against the tactically usable limits. In short, the fact that an enormous increase in the power of the bomb is theoretically conceivable does not mean that it is likely to occur, either soon or later. It has always been theoretically possible to pour 20,000 tons of TNT together in one case and detonate it as a single bomb; but after some forty years or more of its use, the largest amount of it poured into a single lump was about six tons.[47]

To be sure, greater power in the bomb will no doubt be attained by increasing the efficiency of the explosion without necessarily adding to the quantities of fissionable materials used. But the curve of progress in this direction is bound to flatten out and to remain far short of 100 per cent. The bomb is, to be sure, in its "infancy," but that statement is misleading if it implies that we may expect the kind of progress which we have witnessed over the past century in the steam engine. The bomb is new, but the people who developed it were able to avail themselves of the fabulously elaborate and advanced technology already existing. Any new device created today is already at birth a highly perfected instrument.

One cannot dismiss the matter of increasing efficiency of the bomb without noting that the military uses of radioactivity may not be confined to bombs. Even if the project to produce the bomb had ultimately failed, the by-products formed from some of the intermediate processes could have been used as an extremely vicious form of poison gas. It was estimated by two members of the "Manhattan District" project that the radioactive by-products formed in one day's run of a 100,000-kw. chain-reacting pile for the production of plutonium (the production rate at Hanford, Washington, was from five to fifteen times as great) might be sufficient to make a large area uninhabitable.[48] Fortunately, however, materials which are dangerously radioactive tend to lose their radioactivity rather quickly and therefore cannot be stored.

VIII. *Regardless of American decisions concerning retention of its present secrets, other powers besides Britain and Canada will possess the ability to produce the bombs in quantity within a period of five to ten years hence*

This proposition by-passes the possibility of effective international regulation of bomb production being adopted within that period. A discussion of that possibility is left to subsequent chapters. One may anticipate, however, to the extent of pointing out that it is difficult to induce nations like the Soviet Union to accept such regulation until they can start out in a position of parity with the United States in ability to produce the bomb. The State Department Board of Consultants' report of March 16, 1946, acknowledges as much when it states that "acceleration" of the disappearance of our monopoly must be "inherent in the adoption of any plan of international control."

Statements of public officials and of journalists indicate an enormous confusion concerning the extent and character of the secret now in the possession of the United States. Opinions vary from the observation that "there is no secret" to the blunt comment of Dr. Walter R.G. Baker, Vice-President of the General Electric Company, that no nation other than the United States has sufficient wealth, materials, and industrial resources to produce the bomb.[49]

Some clarification is discernible in President Truman's message to Congress of October 3, 1945, in which the President recommended the establishment of security regulations and the prescription of suitable penalties for their violation and went on to add the following: "Scientific opinion appears to be practically unanimous that the essential theoretical knowledge upon which the discovery is based is already widely known. There is also substantial agreement that foreign research can come abreast of our present theoretical knowledge in time." The emphasis, it should be noted, is on "theoretical knowledge." A good deal of basic scientific data are still bound by rigorous secrecy, but such data are apparently not considered to be crucial. While the retention of such secrets would impose upon the scientists of other nations the necessity of carrying through a good deal of time-consuming research which would merely duplicate that already done in this country, there seems to be little question that countries like the Soviet Union and France and probably several of the lesser nations of Europe have the resources in scientific talent to accomplish it. It is (a) the technical and engineering details of the manufacturing process for the fissionable materials and (b) the design of the bomb itself which are thought to be the critical hurdles.

At a public meeting in Washington on December 11, 1945, Major General Leslie R. Groves permitted himself the observation that the bomb was not a problem for us but for our grandchildren. What he obviously intended that statement to convey was the idea that it would take other nations, like Russia, many years to duplicate our feat. When it was submitted to him that the scientists who worked on the problem were practically unanimous in their disagreement, he responded that they did not understand the problem. The difficulties to be overcome, he insisted, are not primarily of a scientific but of an engineering character. And while the Soviet Union may have first-rate scientists, it clearly does not have the great resources in engineering talent or the industrial laboratories that we enjoy.

Perhaps so; but there are a few pertinent facts which bear on such a surmise. First of all, it has always been axiomatic in the armed services that the only way really to keep a device secret is to keep the fact of its existence secret. Thus, the essential basis of secrecy of the atomic bomb disappeared on August 6, 1945. But a few days later saw the release of the *Smyth Report*, which was subsequently published in book form and widely distributed. Members of the War Department who approved its publication, including General Groves himself, insist that it reveals nothing of importance. But scientists close to the project point out that the *Smyth Report* reveals substantially everything that the American and associated scientists themselves knew up to the close of 1942. It in fact tells much of the subsequent findings as well. In any case, from the end of 1942 it was only two and one-half years before we had the bomb.

The *Smyth Report* reveals among other things that five distinct and separate processes for producing fissionable materials were pursued, and that *all were successful*. These involved four processes for the separation of the U-235 isotope from the more common forms of uranium and one basic process for the production of plutonium. One of the isotope separation processes, the so-called "centrifuge process," was never pushed beyond the pilot plant stage, but it was successful as far as it was pursued. It was dropped when the gaseous diffusion and electromagnetic methods of isotope separation promised assured success.[50] The thermal diffusion process was restricted to a small plant. *But any of these processes would have sufficed to produce the fissionable materials for the bomb*. Each of these processes presented problems for which generally multiple rather than single solutions were discovered. Each of them, furthermore, is described in the report in fairly revealing though general terms. Finally, the report probably reveals enough to indicate to the careful reader which of the processes presents the fewest problems and offers the most profitable yield. Another nation wishing to produce the bomb can confine its efforts to that one process or to some modification of it.

Enough is said in the *Smyth Report* about the bomb itself to give one a good idea of its basic character. Superficially at least, the problem of bomb design seems a bottleneck, since the same bomb is required to handle the materials produced by any of the five processes mentioned above. But that is like saying that while gasoline can be produced in several different ways, only one kind of engine can utilize it effectively. The bomb is gadgetry, and it is a commonplace in the history of technology that mechanical devices of radically different design have been perfected to achieve a common end. The machine gun has several variants which operate on basically different principles, and the same is no doubt true of dishwashing machines.

Some of those who were associated with the bomb design project came away tremendously impressed with the seemingly insuperable difficulties which were overcome. Undoubtedly they were justified in their admiration for the ingenuity displayed. But they are not justified in assuming that aggregations of talented young men in other parts of the world could not display equally brilliant ingenuity.

We cannot assume that what took us two and one-half years to accomplish, without the certainty that success was possible, should take another great nation twenty to thirty years to duplicate with the full knowledge that the thing has been done. To do so would be to exhibit an extreme form of ethnocentric smugness. It is true that we mobilized a vast amount of talent, but American ways are frequently wasteful.

We were simultaneously pushing forward on a great many other scientific and engineering fronts having nothing to do with the atomic bomb. Another nation which has fewer engineers and scientists than we have could, nevertheless, by concentrating all its pertinent talent on this one job—and there is plenty of motivation—marshal as great a fund of scientific and engineering workers as it would need, perhaps as much as we did. The Japanese, for example, before the recent war, were intent on having a good torpedo, and by concentrating on that end produced a superb torpedo, though they had to accept inferiority to us in practically every other element of naval ordnance. One should expect a similar concentration in other countries on the atomic bomb, and one should expect also comparable results.

It is clear also that the money cost is no barrier to any nation of ordinary substance. The two billion dollars that the bomb development project cost the United States must be considered small for a weapon of such extraordinary military power. Moreover, that sum is by no means the measure of what a comparable development would cost other nations. The American program was pushed during wartime under extreme urgency and under war-inflated prices. Money costs were always considered secondary to the saving of time. The scientists and engineers who designed the plants and equipment were constantly pushing into the unknown. The huge plant at Hanford, Washington, for the production of plutonium, for example, was pushed forward on the basis of that amount of knowledge of the properties of the new element which could be gleaned from the study of half a milligram in the laboratories at Chicago.[51] Five separate processes for the production of fissionable materials were pushed concurrently, for the planners had to hedge against the possibility of failure in one or more. There was no room for weighing the relative economy of each. Minor failures and fruitless researches did in fact occur in each process.

It is fairly safe to say that another country, proceeding only on the information available in the *Smyth Report*, would be able to reach something comparable to the American production at less than half the cost—even if we adopt the American price level as a standard. Another country would certainly be able to economize by selecting one of the processes and ignoring the others—no doubt the plutonium production process, since various indices seem to point clearly to its being the least difficult and the most rewarding one—an impression which is confirmed by the public statements of some scientists.[52] General Groves has revealed that about one-fourth of the entire capital investment in the atomic bomb went into the plutonium production project at Hanford.[53] As fuller information seeps out even to the public, as it inevitably will despite security regulations, the signs pointing out to other nations the more fruitful avenues of endeavor will become more abundant. Scientists may be effectively silenced, but they cannot as a body be made to lie. And so long as they talk at all, the hiatuses in their speech may be as eloquent to the informed listener as the speech itself.

Implications for military policy

Under conditions existing before the atomic bomb, it was possible to contemplate methods of air defense keeping pace with and perhaps even outdistancing the means of offense. Long-range rockets baffled the defense, but they were extremely expensive per unit for inaccurate, single-blow weapons. Against bombing aircraft, on the other hand, fighter planes and antiaircraft guns could be extremely effective. Progress in speed and altitude performance of all types of aircraft, which on the whole tends to favor the attacker, was more or less offset by technological progress in other fields where the net result tends to favor the defender (e.g., radar search and tracking, proximity-fused projectiles, etc.).

At any rate, a future war between great powers could be visualized as one in which the decisive effects of strategic bombing would be contingent upon the *cumulative effect of prolonged bombardment efforts*, which would in turn be governed by aerial battles and even whole campaigns for mastery of the air. Meanwhile—if the recent war can serve as a pattern—the older forms of warfare on land and sea would exercise a telling effect not only on the ultimate decision but on the effectiveness of the strategic bombing itself. Conversely, the strategic bombing would, as was certainly true against Germany, influence or determine the decision mainly through its effects on the ground campaigns.

The atomic bomb seems, however, to erase the pattern described above, first of all because its enormous destructive potency is bound vastly to reduce the time necessary to achieve the results which accrue from strategic bombing—and there can no longer be any dispute about the decisiveness of strategic bombing. In fact, the essential change introduced by the atomic bomb is not primarily that it will make war more violent—a city can be as effectively destroyed with TNT and incendiaries—but that it will concentrate the violence in terms of time. A world accustomed to thinking it horrible that wars should last four or five years is now appalled at the prospect that future wars may last only a few days.

One of the results of such a change would be that a far greater proportion of human lives would be lost even in relation to the greater physical damage done. The problem of alerting the population of a great city and permitting resort to air raid shelters is one thing when the destruction of that city requires the concentrated efforts of a great enemy air force; it is quite another when the job can be done by a few aircraft flying at extreme altitudes. Moreover, the feasibility of building adequate air raid shelters against the atomic bomb is more than dubious when one considers that the New Mexico bomb, which was detonated over 100 feet above the ground, caused powerful earth tremors of an unprecedented type lasting over twenty seconds.[54] The problem merely of ventilating deep shelters, which would require the shutting out of dangerously radioactive gases, is considered by some scientists to be practically insuperable. It would appear that the only way of safeguarding the lives of city dwellers is to evacuate them from their cities entirely in periods of crisis. But such a project too entails some nearly insuperable problems.

What do the facts presented in the preceding pages add up to for our military policy? Is it worthwhile even to consider military policy as having any consequence at all in an age of atomic bombs? A good many intelligent people think not. The passionate and *exclusive* preoccupation of some scientists and laymen with proposals for "world government" and the like—in which the arguments are posed on an "or else" basis that permits no question of feasibility—argues a profound conviction that the safeguards to security formerly provided by military might are no longer of any use.

Indeed the postulates set forth and argued in the preceding chapter would seem to admit of no other conclusion. If our cities can be wiped out in a day, if there is no good reason to expect the development of specific defenses against the bomb, if all the great powers are already within striking range of each other, if even substantial superiority in numbers of aircraft and bombs offers no real security, of what possible avail can large armies and navies be? Unless we can strike first and eliminate a threat before it is realized in action—something which our national Constitution apparently forbids—we are bound to perish under attack without even an opportunity to mobilize resistance. Such at least seems to be the prevailing conception among those who, if they give any thought at all to the military implications of the bomb, content themselves with stressing its character as a weapon of aggression.

The conviction that the bomb represents the apotheosis of aggressive instruments is especially marked among the scientists who developed it. They know the bomb and its power. They also know their own limitations as producers of miracles. They are therefore much less sanguine than many laymen or military officers of their capacity to provide the instrument which will rob the bomb of its terrors. One of the most outstanding among them, Professor J. Robert Oppenheimer, has expressed himself quite forcibly on the subject:

"The pattern of the use of atomic weapons was set at Hiroshima. They are weapons of aggression, of surprise, and of terror. If they are ever used again it may well be by the thousands, or perhaps by the tens of thousands; their method of delivery may well be different, and may reflect new possibilities of interception, and the strategy of their use may well be different from what it was against an essentially defeated enemy. But it is a weapon for aggressors, and the elements of surprise and of terror are as intrinsic to it as are the fissionable nuclei."[55]

The truth of Professor Oppenheimer's statement depends on one vital but unexpressed assumption: that the nation which proposes to launch the attack will not need to fear retaliation. If it must fear retaliation, the fact that it destroys its opponent's cities some hours or even days before its own are destroyed may avail it little. It may indeed commence the evacuation of its own cities at the same moment it is hitting the enemy's cities (to do so earlier would provoke a like move on the opponent's part) and thus present to retaliation cities which are empty. But the success even of such a move would depend on the time interval between hitting and being hit. It certainly would not save the enormous physical plant which is contained in the cities and which over any length of time is indispensable to the life of the national community. Thus the element of surprise may be less important than is generally assumed.[56]

If the aggressor state must fear retaliation, it will know that even if it is the victor it will suffer a degree of physical destruction incomparably greater than that suffered by any defeated nation of history, incomparably greater, that is, than that suffered by Germany in the recent war. Under those circumstances no victory, even if guaranteed in advance—which it never is—would be worth the price. The threat of retaliation does not have to be 100 per cent certain; it is sufficient if there is a good chance of it, or if there is belief that there is a good chance of it. The prediction is more important than the fact.

The argument that the victim of an attack might not know where the bombs are coming from is almost too preposterous to be worth answering, but it has been made so often by otherwise responsible persons that it cannot be wholly ignored. That the geographical location of the launching sites of long-range rockets may remain for a time unknown is conceivable, though unlikely, but that the identity of the attacker should remain unknown is not in modern times conceivable. The fear that one's country might suddenly be attacked in the midst of apparently profound peace has often been voiced, but, at least in the last century and a half, it has never been realized. As advancing technology makes war more horrible, it also makes the decision to resort to it more dependent on an elaborate psychological preparation. In international politics today few things are more certain than that an attack must have an antecedent hostility of obviously grave character. Especially today, when there are only two or three powers of the first rank, the identity of the major rival would be unambiguous. In fact, as Professor Jacob Viner has pointed out, it is the lack of ambiguity concerning the major rival which makes the bipolar power system so dangerous.

There is happily little disposition to believe that the atomic bomb by its mere existence and by the horror implicit in it "makes war impossible." In the sense that war is something not to be endured if any reasonable alternative remains, it has long been "impossible." But for that very reason we cannot hope that the bomb makes war impossible in the narrower sense of the word. Even without it the conditions of modern war should have been a sufficient deterrent but proved not to be such. If the atomic bomb can be used without fear of substantial retaliation in kind, it will clearly encourage aggression. So much the more reason, therefore, to take all possible steps to assure that multilateral possession of the bomb, should that prove inevitable, be attended by arrangements to make as nearly certain as possible that the aggressor who uses the bomb will have it used against him.

If such arrangements are made, the bomb cannot but prove in the net a powerful inhibition to aggression. It would make relatively little difference if one power had more bombs and were better prepared to resist them than its opponent. It would in any case undergo incalculable destruction of life and property. It is clear that there existed in the thirties a deeper and probably more generalized revulsion against war than in any other era of history. Under those circumstances the breeding of a new war required a situation combining dictators of singular irresponsibility with a notion among them and their general staffs that aggression would be both successful and cheap. The possibility of irresponsible or desperate men again becoming rulers of powerful states cannot under the prevailing system of international politics be ruled out in the future. But it does seem possible to erase the idea—if not among madmen rulers then at least among their military supporters—that aggression will be cheap.

Thus, the first and most vital step in any American security program for the age of atomic bombs is to take measures to guarantee to ourselves in case of attack the possibility of retaliation in kind. The writer in making that statement is not for the moment concerned about who will *win* the next war in which atomic bombs are used. Thus far the chief purpose of our military establishment has been to win wars. From now on its chief purpose must be to avert them. It can have almost no other useful purpose.

Neither is the writer especially concerned with whether the guarantee of retaliation is based on national or international power. However, one cannot be unmindful of one obvious fact: for the period immediately ahead, we must evolve our plans with the knowledge that there is a vast difference between what a nation can do domestically of its own volition and on its own initiative and what it can do with respect to programs which depend on achieving agreement with other nations. Naturally, our domestic policies concerning the atomic bomb and the national defense generally should not be such as to prejudice real opportunities for achieving world security agreements of a worthwhile sort. That is an important proviso and may become a markedly restraining one.

Some means of international protection for those states which cannot protect themselves will remain as necessary in the future as it has been in the past.[57] Upon the security of such states our own security must ultimately depend. But only a great state which has taken the necessary steps to reduce its own direct vulnerability to atomic bomb attack is in a position to offer the necessary support. Reducing vulnerability is at least one way of reducing temptation to potential aggressors. And if the technological realities make reduction of vulnerability largely synonymous with preservation of striking power, that is a fact which must be faced. Under those circumstances any domestic measures which effectively guaranteed such preservation of striking power under attack would contribute to a more solid basis for the operation of an international security system.

It is necessary therefore to explore all conceivable situations where the aggressor's fear of retaliation will be at a minimum and to seek to eliminate them. The first and most obvious such situation is that in which the aggressor has a monopoly of the bombs. The United States has a monopoly today, but trusts to its reputation for benignity and—what is more impressive—its conspicuous weariness of war to still the perturbations of other powers. In any case, that special situation is bound to be short-lived. The possibility of a recurrence of monopoly in the future would seem to be restricted to a situation in which controls for the rigorous suppression of atomic bomb production had been imposed by international agreement but had been evaded or violated by one power without the knowledge of the others. Evasion or violation, to be sure, need not be due to aggressive designs. It might stem simply from a fear that other nations were doing likewise and a desire to be on the safe side.

Nevertheless, a situation of concealed monopoly would be one of the most disastrous imaginable from the point of view of world peace and security. It is therefore entirely reasonable to insist that any system for the international control or suppression of bomb production should include safeguards promising practically 100 per cent effectiveness.

The use of secret agents to plant bombs in all the major cities of an intended victim was discussed in the previous chapter, where it was concluded that except in port cities easily accessible to foreign ships such a mode of attack could hardly commend itself to an aggressor. Nevertheless, to the degree that such planting of bombs is reasonably possible, it suggests that one side might gain before the opening of hostilities an enormous advantage in the *deployment* of its bombs. Clearly such an ascendancy would contain no absolute guarantee against retaliation, unless the advantage in deployment were associated with a marked advantage in psychological preparation for resistance. But it is clear also that the relative position of two states concerning ability to use the atomic bomb depends not alone on the number of bombs in the possession of each but also on a host of other conditions, including respective positions concerning deployment of the bombs and psychological preparation against attack.

One of the most important of those conditions concerns the relative position of the rival powers in technological development, particularly as it affects the vehicle for carrying the bombs. At present the only instrument for bombardment at distances of over 200 miles is the airplane (with or without crew). The controlled rocket capable of thousands of miles of range is still very much in the future. The experience of the recent war was analyzed in the previous chapter as indicating that an inferior air force can usually penetrate the aerial defenses of its opponent so long as it is willing to accept a high loss ratio. Nevertheless, the same experience shows also that one side can be so superior quantitatively and qualitatively in both aerial offense and defense as to be able to range practically undisturbed over the enemy's territories while shutting him out largely, even if not completely, from incursions over its own. While such a disparity is likely to be of less importance in a war of atomic bombs than it has been in the past, its residual importance is by no means insignificant.[58] And in so far as the development of rockets nullifies that type of disparity in offensive power, it should be noted that the development of rockets is not likely to proceed at an equal pace among all the larger powers. One or several will far outstrip the others, depending not alone on the degree of scientific and engineering talent available to each country but also on the effort which its government causes to be channeled into such an enterprise. In any case, the possibilities of an enormous lead on the part of one power in effective use of the atomic bomb are inseparable from technological development in vehicles—at least up to a certain common level, beyond which additional development may matter little.

The consequences of a marked disparity between opponents in the spatial concentration of populations and industry are left to a separate discussion later in this chapter. But one of the aspects of the problem which might be mentioned here, particularly as it pertains to the United States, is that of having concentrated in a single city not only the main agencies of national government but also the whole of the executive branch, including the several successors to the presidency and the topmost military authorities. While an aggressor could hardly count upon destroying at one blow all the persons who might assume leadership in a crisis, he might, unless there were considerably greater geographic decentralization of national leadership than exists at present, do enough damage with one bomb to create complete confusion in the mobilization of resistance.

It goes without saying that the governments and populations of different countries will show different levels of apprehension concerning the effects of the bomb. It might be argued that a totalitarian state would be less unready than would a democracy to see the destruction of its cities rather than yield on a crucial political question. The real political effect of such a disparity, however—if it actually exists, which is doubtful—can easily be exaggerated. *For in no case is the fear of the consequences of atomic bomb attack likely to be low.* More important is the likelihood that totalitarian countries can impose more easily on their populations than can democracies those mass movements of peoples and industries necessary to disperse urban concentrations.

The most dangerous situation of all would arise from a failure not only of the political leaders but especially of the military authorities of a nation like our own to adjust to the atomic bomb in their thinking and planning. The possibility of such a situation developing in the United States is very real and very grave. We are familiar with the example of the French General Staff, which failed to adjust in advance to the kind of warfare obtaining in 1940. There are other examples, less well-known, which lie much closer home. In all the investigations and hearings on the Pearl Harbor disaster, there has at this writing not yet been mention of a fact which is as pertinent as any—that our ships were virtually naked in respect to antiaircraft defense. They were certainly naked in comparison to what was considered necessary a brief two years later, when the close-in antiaircraft effectiveness of our older battleships was estimated by the then Chief of the Bureau of Ordnance to have increased by no less than 100 times! That achievement was in great part the redemption of past errors of omission. The admirals who had spent so many of their waking hours denying that the airplane was a grave menace to the battleship had never taken the elementary steps necessary to validate their opinions, the steps, that is, of covering their ships with as many as they could carry of the best antiaircraft guns available.

Whatever may be the specific changes indicated, it is clear that our military authorities will have to bestir themselves to a wholly unprecedented degree in revising military concepts inherited from the past. That will not be easy. They must be prepared to dismiss, as possibly irrelevant, experience gained the hard way in the recent war, during which their performance was on the whole brilliant.

Thus far there has been no public evidence that American military authorities have begun really to think in terms of atomic warfare. The test announced with such fanfare for the summer of 1946, in which some ninety-seven naval vessels will be subjected to the blast effect of atomic bombs, to a degree confirms this impression. Presumably the test is intended mainly to gauge the defensive efficacy of tactical dispersion, since there can be little doubt of the consequences to any one ship of a near burst. While such tests are certainly useful it should be recognized at the outset that they can provide no answer to the basic question of the utility of sea power in the future.

Ships at sea are in any case not among the most attractive of military targets for atomic bomb attack. Their ability to disperse makes them comparatively wasteful targets for bombs of such concentrated power and relative scarcity; their mobility makes them practically impossible to hit with super-rockets of great range; and those of the United States Navy at least have shown themselves able, with the assistance of their own aircraft, to impose an impressively high ratio of casualties upon hostile planes endeavoring to approach them. But the question of how their own security is affected is not the essential point. *For it is still possible for navies to lose all reason for being even if they themselves remain completely immune.*

A nation which had lost most of its larger cities and thus the major part of its industrial plant might have small use for a fleet. One of the basic purposes for which a navy exists is to protect the sea-borne transportation by which the national industry imports its raw materials and exports its finished commodities to the battle lines. Moreover, without the national industrial plant to service it, the fleet would shortly find itself without the means to function. In a word, the strategic issues posed by the atomic bomb transcend all tactical issues, and the 1946 test and the controversy which will inevitably follow it will no doubt serve to becloud that basic point.

Outlines of a defense program in the atomic age

What are the criteria by which we can appraise realistic military thinking in the age of atomic bombs? The burden of the answer will depend primarily on whether one accepts as true the several postulates presented and argued in the previous chapter. One might go further and say that since none of them is obviously untrue, no program of military pre-paredness which fails to consider the likelihood of their being true can be regarded as comprehensive or even reasonably adequate.

It is of course always possible that the world may see another major war in which the atomic bomb is not used. The awful menace to both parties of a reciprocal use of the bomb may prevent the resort to that weapon by either side, even if it does not prevent the outbreak of hostilities. But even so, the shadow of the atomic bomb would so govern the strategic and tactical dispositions of either side as to create a wholly novel form of war. The kind of spatial concentrations of force by which in the past great decisions have been achieved would be considered too risky. The whole economy of war would be affected, for even if the govern-ments were willing to assume responsibility for keeping the urban populations in their homes, the spontaneous exodus of those populations from the cities might reach such pro-portions as to make it difficult to service the machines of war. The conclusion is inescapable that war will be vastly different because of the atomic bomb whether or not the bomb is actually used.

But let us now consider the degree of probability inherent in each of the three main situations which might follow from a failure to prevent a major war. These three situations may be listed as follows:

(a)   a war fought without atomic bombs or other forms of radioactive energy;
(b)   a war in which atomic bombs were introduced only considerably after the outbreak of hostilities;
(c)   a war in which atomic bombs were used at or near the very outset of hostilities.

We are assuming that this hypothetical conflict occurs at a time when each of the opposing sides possesses at least the "know-how" of bomb production, a situation which, as argued in the previous chapter, approximates the realities to be expected not more than five to ten years hence.

Under such conditions the situation described under (a) above could obtain only as a result of a mutual fear of retaliation, perhaps supported by international instruments outlawing the bomb as a weapon of war. It would *not* be likely to result from the operation of an international system for the suppression of bomb production, since such a system would almost certainly not survive the outbreak of a major war. If such a system were in fact effective at the opening of hostilities, the situation resulting would be far more likely to fall under (b) than under (a), unless the war were very short. For the race to get the bomb would not be an even one, and the side which got it first in quantity would be under enormous temptation to use it before the opponent had it. Of course, it is more reasonable to assume that an international situation which had so far deteriorated as to permit the outbreak of a major war would have long since seen the collapse of whatever arrangements for bomb production control had previously been imposed, unless the conflict were indeed precipitated by an exercise of sanctions for the violation of such a control system.

Thus we see that a war in which atomic bombs are not used is more likely to occur if both sides have the bombs in quantity from the beginning than if neither side has it at the outset or if only one side has it.[59] But how likely is it to occur? Since the prime motive in refraining from using it would be fear of retaliation, it is difficult to see why a fear of reciprocal use should be strong enough to prevent resort to the bomb without being strong enough to prevent the outbreak of war in the first place.

Of course, the bomb may act as a powerful deterrent to direct aggression against great powers without preventing the political crises out of which wars generally develop. In a world in which great wars become "inevitable" as a result of aggression by great powers upon weak neighbors, the bomb may easily have the contrary effect. Hitler made a good many bloodless gains by mere blackmail, in which he relied heavily on the too obvious horror of modern war among the great nations which might have opposed him earlier. A comparable kind of blackmail in the future may actually find its encouragement in the existence of the atomic bomb. Horror of its implications is not likely to be spread evenly, at least not in the form of overt expression. The result may be a series of *faits accomplis* eventuating in that final deterioration of international affairs in which war, however terrible, can no longer be avoided.

Nevertheless, once hostilities broke out, the pressures to use the bomb might swiftly reach unbearable proportions. One side or the other would feel that its relative position respecting ability to use the bomb might deteriorate as the war progressed, and that if it failed to use the bomb while it had the chance it might not have the chance later on. The side which was decidedly weaker in terms of industrial capacity for war would be inclined to use it in order to equalize the situation on a lower common level of capacity—for it is clear that the side with the more elaborate and intricate industrial system would, other things being equal, be more disadvantaged by mutual use of the bomb than its opponent. In so far as those "other things" were not equal, the disparities involved would also militate for the use of the bomb by one side or the other. And hovering over the situation from beginning to end would be the intolerable fear on each side that the enemy might at any moment resort to this dreaded weapon, a fear which might very well stimulate an anticipatory reaction.

Some observers in considering the chances of effectively outlawing the atomic bomb have taken a good deal of comfort from the fact that poison gases were not used, or at least not used on any considerable scale, during the recent war. There is little warrant, however, for assuming that the two problems are analogous. Apart from the fact that the recent war presents only a single case and argues little for the experience of another war even with respect to gas, it is clear that poison gas and atomic bombs represent two wholly different orders of magnitude in military utility. The existence of the treaty outlawing gas was important, but at least equally important was the conviction in the minds of the military policy-makers that TNT bombs and tanks of gelatinized gasoline—with which the gas bombs would have had to compete in airplane carrying capacity—were just as effective as gas if not more so. Both sides were prepared not only to retaliate with gas against gas attack but also to neutralize with gas masks and "decontamination units" the chemicals to which they might be exposed. There is visible today no comparable neutralization agent for atomic bombs.

Neither side in the recent war wished to bear the onus for violation of the obligation not to use gas when such violation promised no particular military advantage. But, unlike gas, the atomic bomb can scarcely fail to have fundamental or decisive effects if used at all. That is not to say that any effort to outlaw use of the bomb is arrant nonsense, since such outlawry might prove the indispensable crystallizer of a state of balance which operates against use of the bomb. But without the existence of the state of balance—in terms of reciprocal ability to retaliate in kind if the bomb is used—any treaty purposing to outlaw the bomb in war would have thrust upon it a burden far heavier than such a treaty can normally bear.

What do these conclusions mean concerning the defense preparations of a nation like the United States? In answering this question, it is necessary first to anticipate the argument that "the best defense is a strong offense," an argument which it is now fashionable to link with animadversions on the "Maginot complex." In so far as this doctrine becomes dogma, it may prejudice the security interests of the country and of the world. Although the doctrine is basically true as a general proposition, especially when applied to hostilities already under way, the political facts of life concerning the United States government under its present Constitution make it most probable that if war comes we will receive the first blow rather than deliver it. Thus, our most urgent military problem is to reorganize ourselves to survive a vastly more destructive "Pearl Harbor" than occurred in 1941. Otherwise we shall not be able to take the offensive at all.

The atomic bomb will be introduced into the conflict only on a gigantic scale. No belligerent would be stupid enough, in opening itself to reprisals in kind, to use only a few bombs. The initial stages of the attack will certainly involve hundreds of the bombs, more likely thousands of them. Unless the argument of Postulates II and IV in the previous chapter is wholly preposterous, the target state will have little chance of effectively halting or fending off the attack. If its defenses are highly efficient it may down nine planes out of every ten attacking, but it will suffer the destruction of its cities. That destruction may be accomplished in a day, or it may take a week or more. But there will be no opportunity to incorporate the strength residing in the cities, whether in the form of industry or personnel, into the forces of resistance or counterattack. *The ability to fight back after an atomic bomb attack will depend on the degree to which the armed forces have made themselves independent of the urban communities and their industries for supply and support.*

The proposition just made is the basic proposition of atomic bomb warfare, and it is the one which our military authorities continue consistently to overlook. They continue to speak in terms of peacetime military establishments which are simply cadres and which are expected to undergo an enormous but slow expansion *after* the outbreak of hostilities.[60] Therein lies the essence of what may be called "pre-atomic thinking." The idea which must be driven home above all else is that a military establishment which is expected to fight on after the nation has undergone atomic bomb attack must be prepared to fight with the men already mobilized and with the equipment already in the arsenals. And those arsenals must be in caves in the wilderness. The cities will be vast catastrophe areas, and the normal channels of transportation and communications will be in unutterable confusion. The rural areas and the smaller towns, though perhaps not struck directly, will be in varying degrees of disorganization as a result of the collapse of the metropolitan centers with which their economies are intertwined.

Naturally, the actual degree of disorganization in both the struck and non-struck areas will depend on the degree to which we provide beforehand against the event. A good deal can be done in the way of decentralization and reorganization of vital industries and services to avoid complete paralysis of the nation. More will be said on this subject later in the present chapter. But the idea that a nation which had undergone days or weeks of atomic bomb attack would be able to achieve a production for war purposes even remotely comparable in character and magnitude to American production in World War II simply does not make sense. The war of atomic bombs must be fought with stockpiles of arms in finished or semifinished state. A superiority in raw materials will be about as important as a superiority in gold resources was in World War II—though it was not so long ago that gold was the essential sinew of war.

All that is being presumed here is the kind of destruction which Germany actually underwent in the last year of the second World War, only telescoped in time and considerably multiplied in magnitude. If such a presumption is held to be unduly alarmist, the burden of proof must lie in the discovery of basic errors in the argument of the preceding chapter. The essence of that argument is simply that what Germany suffered because of her inferiority in the air may now well be suffered in greater degree and in far less time, so long as atomic bombs are used, even by the power which enjoys air superiority. And while the armed forces must still prepare against the possibility that atomic bombs will not be used in another war—a situation which might permit full mobilization of the national resources in the traditional manner—they must be at least equally ready to fight a war in which no such grand mobilization is permitted.

The forces which will carry on the war after a large-scale atomic bomb attack may be divided into three main categories according to their respective functions. The first category will comprise the force reserved for the retaliatory attacks with atomic bombs; the second will have the mission of invading and occupying enemy territory; and the third will have the purpose of resisting enemy invasion and of organizing relief for devastated areas. Professional military officers will perhaps be less disturbed at the absence of any distinction between land, sea, and air forces than they will be at the sharp distinction between offensive and defensive functions in the latter two categories. In the past it was more or less the same army which was either on the offensive or the defensive, depending on its strength and on the current fortunes of war, but, for reasons which will presently be made clear, a much sharper distinction between offensive and defensive forces seems to be in prospect for the future.

The force delegated to the retaliatory attack with atomic bombs will have to be maintained in rather sharp isolation from the national community. Its functions must not be compromised in the slightest by the demands for relief of struck areas. Whether its operations are with aircraft or rockets or both, it will have to be spread over a large number of widely dispersed reservations, each of considerable area, in which the bombs and their carriers are secreted and as far as possible protected by storage underground. These reservations should have a completely independent system of inter-communications, and the commander of the force should have a sufficient autonomy of authority to be able to act as soon as he has established with certainty the fact that the country is being hit with atomic bombs. The supreme command may by then have been eliminated, or its communications disrupted.

Before discussing the character of the force set apart for the job of invasion, it is necessary to consider whether invasion and occupation remain indispensable to victory in an era of atomic energy. Certain scientists have argued privately that they are not, that a nation committing aggression with atomic bombs would have so paralyzed its opponent as to make invasion wholly superfluous. It might be alleged that such an argument does not give due credit to the atomic bomb, since it neglects the necessity of preventing or minimizing retaliation in kind. If the experience with the V-1 and V-2 launching sites in World War II means anything at all, it indicates that only occupation of such sites will finally prevent their being used. Perhaps the greater destructiveness of the atomic bomb as compared with the bombs used against the V-1 and V-2 sites will make an essential difference in this respect, but it should be remembered that thousands of tons of bombs were dropped on those sites. At any rate, it is unlikely that any aggressor will be able to count upon eliminating with his initial blow the enemy's entire means of retaliation. If he knows the location of the crucial areas, he will seek to have his troops descend upon and seize them.

But even apart from the question of direct retaliation with atomic bombs, invasion to consolidate the effects of an atomic bomb attack will still be necessary. A nation which had inflicted enormous human and material damage upon another would find it intolerable to stop short of eliciting from the latter an acknowledgment of defeat implemented by a readiness to accept control. Wars, in other words, are fought to be terminated, and to be terminated definitely.

To be sure, a nation may admit defeat and agree to occupation before its homeland is actually invaded, as the Japanese did. But it by no means follows that such will be the rule. Japan was completely defeated strategically before the atomic bombs were used against her. She not only lacked means of retaliation with that particular weapon but was without hope of being able to take aggressive action of any kind or of ameliorating her desperate military position to the slightest degree. There is no reason to suppose that a nation which had made reasonable preparations for war with atomic bombs would inevitably be in a mood to surrender after suffering the first blow.

An invasion designed to prevent large-scale retaliation with atomic bombs to any considerable degree would have to be incredibly swift and sufficiently powerful to overwhelm instantly any opposition. Moreover, it would have to descend in one fell swoop upon points scattered throughout the length and breadth of the enemy territory. The question arises whether such an operation is possible, especially across broad water barriers, against any great power which is not completely asleep and which has sizable armed forces at its disposal. It is clear that existing types of forces can be much more easily reorganized to resist the kind of invasion here envisaged than to enable them to conduct so rapid an offensive.

Extreme swiftness of invasion would demand aircraft for transport and supply rather than surface vessels guarded by sea power. But the necessity of speed does not itself create the conditions under which an invasion solely by air can be successful, especially against large and well-organized forces deployed over considerable space. In the recent war the specialized air-borne infantry divisions comprised a very small proportion of the armies of each of the belligerents. The bases from which they were launched were in every case relatively close to the objective, and except at Crete their mission was always to co-operate with much larger forces approaching by land or sea. To be sure, if the air forces are relieved by the atomic bomb of the burden of devoting great numbers of aircraft to strategic bombing with ordinary bombs, they will be able to accept to a much greater extent than heretofore the task of serving as a medium of transport and supply for the infantry. But it should be noticed that the enormous extension of range for bombing purposes which the atomic bomb makes possible does not apply to the transport of troops and supplies.[61] For such operations distance remains a formidable barrier.

The invasion and occupation of a great country solely or even chiefly by air would be an incredibly difficult task even if one assumes a minimum of air opposition. The magnitude of the preparations necessary for such an operation might make very dubious the chance of achieving the required measure of surprise. It may well prove that the difficulty of consolidating by invasion the advantages gained through atomic bomb attack may act as an added and perhaps decisive deterrent to launching such an attack, especially since delay or failure would make retaliation all the more probable. But all hinges on the quality of preparation of the intended victim. If it has not prepared itself for atomic bomb warfare, the initial devastating attack will undoubtedly paralyze it and make its conquest easy even by a small invading force. And if it has not prepared itself for such warfare its helplessness will no doubt be sufficiently apparent before the event to invite aggression.

It is obvious that the force set apart for invasion or counter-invasion purposes will have to be relatively small, completely professional, and trained to the uttermost. But there must also be a very large force ready to resist and defeat invasion by the enemy. Here is the place for the citizen army, though it too must be comprised of trained men. There will be no time for training once the atomic bomb is used. Perhaps the old ideal of the "minute man" with his musket over his fireplace will be resurrected, in suitably modernized form. In any case, provision must be made for instant mobilization of trained reserves, for a maximum decentralization of arms and supply depots and of tactical authority, and for flexibility of operation. The trend towards greater mobility in land forces will have to be enormously accelerated, and strategic concentrations will have to be achieved in ways which avoid a high spatial density of military forces. And it must be again repeated, the arms, supplies, and vehicles of transportation to be depended upon are those which are *stockpiled* in as secure a manner as possible.

At this point it should be clear how drastic are the changes in character, equipment, and outlook which the traditional armed forces must undergo if they are to act as real deterrents to aggression in an age of atomic bombs. Whether or not the ideas presented above are entirely valid, they may perhaps stimulate those to whom our military security is entrusted to a more rigorous and better-informed kind of analysis which will reach sounder conclusions.

In the above discussion the reader will no doubt observe the absence of any considerable role for the Navy. And it is indisputable that the traditional concepts of military security which this country has developed over the last fifty years—in which the Navy was quite correctly avowed to be our "first line of defense"—seem due for revision, or at least for reconsideration.

For in the main sea power has throughout history proved decisive only when it was applied and exploited over a period of considerable time, and in atomic bomb warfare that time may well be lacking. Where wars are destined to be short, superior sea power may prove wholly useless. The French naval superiority over Prussia in 1870 did not prevent the collapse of the French armies in a few months, nor did Anglo-French naval superiority in 1940 prevent an even quicker conquest of France—one which might very well have ended the war.

World War II was in fact destined to prove the conflict in which sea power reached the culmination of its influence on history. The greatest of air wars and the one which saw the most titanic battles of all time on land was also the greatest of naval wars. It could hardly have been otherwise in a war which was truly global, where the pooling of resources of the great Allies depended upon their ability to traverse the highways of the seas and where American men and materials played a decisive part in remote theaters which could be reached with the requisite burdens only by ships. That period of greatest influence of sea power coincided with the emergence of the United States as the unrivaled first sea power of the world. But in many respects all this mighty power seems at the moment of its greatest glory to have become redundant.

Yet certain vital tasks may remain for fleets to perform even in a war of atomic bombs. One function which a superior fleet serves at every moment of its existence—and which therefore requires no time for its application—is the defense of coasts against sea-borne invasion. Only since the surrender of Germany, which made available to us the observations of members of the German High Command, has the public been made aware of something which had previously been obvious only to close students of the war—that it was the Royal

Navy even more than the R.A.F. which kept Hitler from leaping across the Channel in 1940. The R.A.F. was too inferior to the Luftwaffe to have stopped an invasion by itself, and was important largely as a means of protecting the ships which the British would have interposed against any invasion attempt.

We have noticed that if swiftness were essential to the execution of any invasion plan, the invader would be obliged to depend mainly, if not exclusively, on transport by air. But we also observed that the difficulties in the way of such an enterprise might be such as to make it quite impossible of achievement. For the overseas movement of armies of any size and especially of their larger arms and supplies, seaborne transportation proved quite indispensable even in an era when gigantic air forces had been built up by fully mobilized countries over four years of war. The difference in weight-carrying capacity between ships and planes is altogether too great to permit us to expect that it will become militarily unimportant in fifty years or more.[62] A force which is able to keep the enemy from using the seas is bound to remain for a long time an enormously important defense against overseas invasion.

However, the defense of coasts against sea-borne invasion is something which powerful and superior air forces are also able to carry out, though perhaps somewhat less reliably. If that were the sole function remaining to the Navy, the maintenance of huge fleets would hardly be justified. One must consider also the possible offensive value of a fleet which has atomic bombs at its disposal.

It was argued in the previous chapter that the atomic bomb enormously extends the effective range of bombing aircraft, and that even today the cities of every great power are inside effective bombing range of planes based on the territories of any other great power. The future development of aircraft will no doubt make bombing at six and seven thousand miles range even more feasible than it is today, and the tendency towards even higher cruising altitudes will ultimately bring planes above the levels where weather hazards are an important barrier to long flights. The ability to bring one's planes relatively close to the target before launching them, as naval carrier forces are able to do, must certainly diminish in military importance. But it will not wholly cease to be important, even for atomic bombs. Apparently today's carrier-borne aircraft cannot carry the atomic bomb, but no one would predict that they will remain unable to do so. And if the emphasis in vehicles is shifted from aircraft to long-range rockets, there will again be an enormous advantage in having one's missiles close to the target. It must be remembered that in so far as advanced bases remain useful for atomic bomb attack, navies are indispensable for their security and maintenance.

Even more important, perhaps, is the fact that a fleet at sea is not easily located and even less easily destroyed. The ability to retaliate if attacked is certainly enhanced by having a bomb-launching base which cannot be plotted on a map. A fleet armed with atomic bombs which had disappeared into the vastness of the seas during a crisis would be just one additional element to give pause to an aggressor. It must, however, be again repeated that the possession of such a fleet or of advanced bases will probably *not be essential* to the execution of bombing missions at extreme ranges.

If there should be a war in which atomic bombs were not used—a possibility which must always be taken into account—the fleet would retain all the functions it has ever exercised. We know also that there are certain policing obligations entailed in various American commitments, especially that of the United Nations Organization. The idea of using atomic bombs for such policing operations, as some have advocated, is not only callous in the extreme but stupid. Even general bombing with ordinary bombs is the worst possible way to coerce states of relatively low military power, for it combines the maximum of indiscriminate destruction with the minimum of direct control.[63]

At any rate, if the United States retains a strong navy, as it no doubt will, we should insist upon that navy retaining the maximum flexibility and adaptability to new conditions. The public can assist in this process by examining critically any effort of the service to freeze naval armaments at high quantitative levels, for there is nothing more deadening to techno-logical progress especially in the navy than the maintenance in active or reserve commission of a number of ships far exceeding any current needs. It is not primarily a question of how much money is spent or how much manpower is absorbed but rather of how efficiently money and manpower are being utilized. Money spent on keeping in commission ships built for the last war is money which might be devoted to additional research and experimen-tation, and existing ships discourage new construction. For that matter, money spent on maintaining a huge navy is perhaps money taken from other services and other instruments of defense which may be of far greater relative importance in the early stages of a future crisis than they have been in the past.

The dispersion of cities as a defense against the bomb

We have seen that the atomic bomb drastically alters the significance of distance *between* rival powers. It also raises to the first order of importance as a factor of power the precise spatial arrangement of industry and population *within* each country. The enormous concentration of power in the individual bomb, irreducible below a certain high limit except through deliberate and purposeless wastage of efficiency, is such as to demand for the full realization of that power targets in which the enemy's basic strength is comparably concentrated. Thus, the city is a made-to-order target, and the degree of urbanization of a country furnishes a rough index of its relative vulnerability to the atomic bomb.

And since a single properly aimed bomb can destroy a city of 100,000 about as effectively as it can one of 25,000, it is obviously an advantage to the attacker if the units of 25,000 are combined into units of 100,000. Moreover, a city is after all a fairly integrated community in terms of vital services and transportation. If half to two-thirds of its area is obliterated, one may count on it that the rest of the city will, under prevailing conditions, be effectively prostrated. Thus, the more the population and industry of a state are concentrated into urban areas and the larger individually those concentrations become, the fewer are the atomic bombs necessary to effect their destruction.[64]

In 1940 there were in the United States five cities with 1,000,000 or more inhabitants (one of which, Los Angeles, is spread out over more than 400 square miles), nine cities between 500,000 and 1,000,000, twenty-three cities between 250,000 and 500,000, fifty-five between 100,000 and 250,000, and one hundred and seven between 50,000 and 100,000 population. Thus, there were ninety-two cities with a population of 100,000 and over, and these con-tained approximately 29 per cent of our total population. Reaching down to the level of 50,000 or more, the number of cities is increased to 199 and the population contained in them is increased to some 34 per cent. Naturally, the proportion of the nation's factories contained in those 199 cities is far greater than the proportion of the population.

This is a considerably higher ratio of urban to non-urban population than is to be found in any other great power except Great Britain. Regardless of what international measures are undertaken to cope with the atomic bomb menace, the United States cannot afford to remain complacent about it. This measure of vulnerability, to be sure, must be qualified by a host of other considerations, such as the architectural character of the cities,[65] the manner in which they are individually laid out, and above all the degree of interdependence of industry and services between different parts of the individual city, between the city and its hinterland, and between the different urban areas. Each city is, together with its hinterland, an economic and social organism, with a character somewhat distinct from other comparable organisms.

A number of students have been busily at work evolving plans for the dispersal of our cities and the resettlement of our population and industries in a manner calculated to reduce the number of casualties and the amount of physical destruction that a given number of atomic bombs can cause. In their most drastic form these plans, many of which will shortly reach the public eye, involve the redistribution of our urban concentrations into "linear" or "cellular" cities.

The linear or "ribbon" city is one which is very much longer than it is wide, with its industries and services as well as population distributed along its entire length. Of two cities occupying nine square miles, the one which was one mile wide and nine long would clearly suffer less destruction from one atomic bomb, however perfectly aimed, than the one which was three miles square. The principle of the cellular city, on the other hand, would be realized if a city of the same nine-square-miles size were dispersed into nine units of about one square mile each and situated in such a pattern that each unit was three to five miles distant from another.

Such "planning" seems to this writer to show a singular lack of appreciation of the forces which have given birth to our cities and caused them to expand and multiply. There are always important geographic and economic reasons for the birth and growth of a city and profound political and social resistance to interference with the results of "natural" growth. Cities like New York and Chicago are not going to dissolve themselves by direction from the government, even if they could find areas to dissolve themselves into. As a linear city New York would be as long as the state of Pennsylvania, and would certainly have no organic meaning as a city. "Solutions" like these are not only politically and socially unrealistic but physically impossible.

Nor does it seem that the military benefits would be at all commensurate with the cost, even if the programs were physically possible and politically feasible. We have no way of estimating the absolute limit to the number of bombs which will be available to an attacker, but we know that unless production of atomic bombs is drastically limited or completely suppressed by international agreement, the number available in the world will progress far more rapidly and involve infinitely less cost of production and use than any concurrent dissolution or realignment of cities designed to offset that multiplication. If a city three miles square can be largely destroyed by one well aimed bomb, it will require only three well spaced bombs to destroy utterly a city nine miles long and one mile wide. And the effort required in producing and delivering the two extra bombs is infinitesimal compared to that involved in converting a square city into a linear one.

Unquestionably an invulnerable home front is beyond price, but there is no hope of gaining such a thing in any case. What the city-dispersion planners are advocating is a colossal effort and expenditure (estimated by some of them to amount to 300 billions of dollars) and a ruthless suppression of the inevitable resistance to such dispersion in order to achieve what is at best a marginal diminution of vulnerability. No such program has the slightest chance of being accepted.

However, it is clear that the United States can be made a good deal less vulnerable to atomic bomb attack than it is at present, that such reduction can be made great enough to count as a deterrent in the calculations of future aggressors, and that it can be done at immeasurably less economic and social cost and in a manner which will arouse far less resistance than any of the drastic solutions described above.

But first we must make clear in our minds what our ends are. Our first purpose, clearly, is to reduce the likelihood that a sudden attack upon us will be so paralyzing in its effects as to rob us of all chance of effective resistance. And we are interested in sustaining our power to retaliate primarily to make the prospect of aggression much less attractive to the aggressor. In other words, we wish to reduce our vulnerability in order to reduce the chances of our being hit at all. Secondly, we wish to reduce the number of casualties and of material damage which will result from an attack upon us of any given level of intensity.

These two ends are of course intimately interrelated, but they are also to a degree distinguishable. And it is necessary to pursue that distinction. We should notice also that while most industries are ultimately convertible or applicable to the prosecution of war, it is possible to distinguish between industries in the degree of their immediate indispensability for war purposes. Finally, while industries attract population and vice versa, modern means of transportation make possible a locational flexibility between an industry and those people who service it and whom it serves.

Thus it would seem that the first step in reducing our national vulnerability is to catalog the industries especially and immediately necessary to atomic bomb warfare—a relatively small proportion of the total—and to move them out of our cities entirely. Where those industries utilize massive plants, those plants should as far as possible be broken up into smaller units. Involved in such a movement would be the labor forces which directly service those industries. The great mass of remaining industries can be left where they are within the cities, but the population which remains with them can be encouraged, through the further development of suburban building, to spread over a greater amount of space. Whole areas deserving to be condemned in any case could be converted into public parks or even airfields. The important element in reducing casualties is after all not the shape of the individual city but the spatial density of population within it.

Furthermore, the systems providing essential services, such as those supplying or distributing food, fuel, water, communications, and medical care, could and should be rearranged geographically. Medical services, for example, tend to be concentrated not merely within cities but in particular sections of those cities. The conception which might govern the relocation of services within the cities is that which has long been familiar in warship design—*compartmentation*. And obviously where essential services for large rural areas are unnecessarily concentrated in cities, they should be moved out of them. That situation pertains especially to communications.

It would be desirable also to initiate a series of tests on the resistance of various kinds of structures to atomic bomb blast. It might be found that one type of structure has far greater resistance than another without being correspondingly more costly. If so, it would behoove the government to encourage that kind of construction in new building. Over a long period of years, the gain in resistance to attack of our urban areas might be considerable, and the costs involved would be marginal.

So far as safeguarding the lives of urban populations is concerned, the above suggestions are meaningful only for the initial stages of an attack. They would permit a larger number to survive the initial attacks and thereby to engage in that exodus from the cities by which alone their lives can be safeguarded. And the preparation for such an exodus would involve a vast program for the construction of temporary shelter in the countryside and the planting of emergency stores of food. What we would then have in effect is the dispersal not of cities but of air-raid shelters.

The writer is here presenting merely some general principles which might be considered in any plan for reducing our general vulnerability. Obviously, the actual content of such a plan would have to be derived from the findings of intensive study by experts in a rather large number of fields. It is imperative, however, that such a study be got under way at once. The country is about to launch into a great construction program, both for dwellings and for expanding industries. New sources of power are to be created by new dams. The opportunities thus afforded for "vulnerability control" are tremendous, and should not be permitted to slip away—at least not without intensive study of their feasibility.

Those who have been predicting attacks of 15,000 atomic bombs and upward will no doubt look with jaundiced eye upon these speculations. For they will say that a country so struck will not merely be overwhelmed but for all practical purposes will vanish. Those areas not directly struck will be covered with clouds of radioactive dust under which all living beings will perish.

No doubt there is a possibility that an initial attack can be so overwhelming as to void all opportunity of resistance or retaliation, regardless of the precautions taken in the target state. Not *all* eventualities can be provided against. But preparation to launch such an attack would have to be on so gigantic a scale as to eliminate all chances of surprise. Moreover, while there is perhaps little solace in the thought that the lethal effect of radioactivity is generally considerably delayed, the idea will not be lost on the aggressor. The more horrible the results of attack, the more he will be deterred by even a marginal chance of retaliation.

Finally, one can scarcely assume that the world will remain either long ignorant of or acquiescent in the accumulations of such vast stockpiles of atomic bombs. If existing international organization should prove inadequate to cope with the problem of controlling bomb production—and it would be premature to predict that it will prove inadequate, especially in view of the favorable official and public reception accorded the Board of Consultants' report of March 16, 1946—a runaway competition in such production would certainly bring new forces into the picture. In this chapter and in the preceding one, the writer has been under no illusions concerning the adequacy of a purely military solution.

Concern with the efficiency of the national defenses is obviously inadequate in itself as an approach to the problem of the atomic bomb. In so far as such concern prevails over the more fundamental consideration of eliminating war or at least of reducing the chance of its recurrence, it clearly defeats its purpose. That has perhaps always been true, but it is a truth which is less escapable today than ever before. Nations can still save themselves by their own armed strength from subjugation, but not from a destruction so colossal as to involve complete ruin. Nevertheless, it also remains true that a nation which is as well girded for its own defense as is reasonably possible is not a tempting target to an aggressor. Such a nation is therefore better able to pursue actively that progressive improvement in world affairs by which alone it finds its true security.

Notes

1 Always excepting Major Alexander P. de Seversky, who has reiterated in magazine articles and elsewhere the notion that the atomic bomb exploded over Hiroshima would not have damaged the New York financial district any more than a 10-ton bomb of TNT exploding on contact. Major de Seversky did in fact inspect the ruins of Hiroshima; but a great many others also did so, and those others seem well-nigh unanimous in regarding the Major's views as preposterous. Brig. Gen. Thomas F. Farrell rebutted Major de Seversky's testimony before the Senate Atomic Energy Committee by observing that it would have taken 730 B-29s to inflict the same damage on Hiroshima with TNT bombs that was done by the single Superfortress with the atomic bomb. He added that according to careful calculations, eight atomic bombs of the Nagasaki type would

suffice to destroy New York and that three of them could destroy Washington, D. C. New York *Times*, February 16, 1946, p. 17. See also below, p. 101.

2 "Atomic Weapons and the Crisis in Science," *Saturday Review of Literature*, November 24, 1945, p. 10.

3 Duncan Sandys, *Report on the Flying Bomb*, pamphlet issued by the British Information Services, September, 1944, p. 9.

4 For the text of the speech see the New York *Times*, October 6, 1945, p. 6. See also the speech of President Truman before Congress on October 23, 1945, in which he said: "Every new weapon will eventually bring some counterdefense against it."

5 See Ivan A. Getting, "Facts About Defense," *Nation*, Special Supplement, December 22, 1945, p. 704. Professor Getting played a key part in radar development for antiaircraft work and was especially active in measures taken to defend London against V-1 and V-2. See also General H.H. Arnold's *Third Report to the Secretary of War*, November 12, 1945, printed edition, p. 68.

6 The new glass-fiber body armor, "doron," the development of which was recently announced by the United States Navy, will no doubt prove useful but is not expected to be of more than marginal effectiveness.

7 New York *Herald Tribune*, October 6, 1945, p. 7.

8 New York *Times*, October 12, 1945, p. 1.

9 See New York *Times*, October 19, 1945, p. 2.

10 For a discussion of developing naval technology over the last hundred years and its political significance see Bernard Brodie, *Sea Power in the Machine Age*, 2nd ed., Princeton, Princeton University Press, 1943.

11 Accuracy is of course a matter of definition. Lieut. Col. John A. O'Mara of the United States Army considers the V-2 an accurate missile because at 200 miles' range some 1,230 out of the 4,300 launched against England were able to hit the target, "which was the London area." New York *Times*, March 8, 1946, p. 7. In the text above the writer is merely using a different base of comparison from the one Lieut. Col. O'Mara has in mind, namely, the capabilities of the bombing aircraft at any distance within its flying radius.

12 The actual figure of loss tolerance depends on a number of variables, including replacement rate of planes and crews, morale factors, the military value of the damage being inflicted on the enemy, and the general strategic position at the moment. The 10 per cent figure used for illustration in the text above was favored by the war correspondents and press analysts during the recent war, but it must not be taken too literally.

13 It should be noticed that in the example of the B-29 raid of June 15, 1944, cited above, a reduction of only one-fourth in the distance and therefore in the fuel load could make possible (unless the plane was originally overloaded) a tripling or quadrupling of the bomb load. Something on that order was accomplished by our seizure of bases in the Marianas, some 300 miles closer to the target than the original Chinese bases and of course much easier supplied. The utility of the Marianas bases was subsequently enhanced by our capture of Iwo Jima and Okinawa, which served as emergency landing fields for returning B-29s and also as bases for escorting fighters and rescue craft. Towards the end of the campaign we were dropping as much as 6,000 tons of bombs in a single 600-plane raid on Tokyo, thereby assuring ourselves high military dividends per sortie investment.

14 On several occasions the United States Army Air Forces also demonstrated a willingness to sacrifice availability of planes and crews—though not the lives of the latter—in order to carry out specific missions. Thus in the Doolittle raid against Japan of April, 1942, in which sixteen Mitchell bombers took off from the carrier *Hornet*, it was known beforehand that none of the planes would be recovered even if they succeeded in reaching China (which several failed to do for lack of fuel) and that the members of the crews were exposing themselves to uncommon hazard. And the cost of the entire expedition was accepted mainly for the sake of dropping sixteen tons of ordinary bombs! Similarly, several of the Liberators which bombed the Ploesti oil fields in August, 1943, had insufficient fuel to return to their bases in North Africa and, as was foreseen, had to land in neutral Turkey where planes and crews were interned.

15 See New York *Times*, November 21, 1945, p. 1. It should be noticed that the plane had left about 300 gallons, or more than one ton, of gasoline upon landing in Washington. It was of course stripped of all combat equipment (e.g., armor, guns, ammunition, gun-directors, and bombsights) in order to allow for a greater gasoline load. Planes bent on a bombing mission would probably have to carry some of this equipment, even if their own survival were not an issue, in order to give greater assurance of their reaching the target.

16 See below, p. 49.

17 See President Truman's speech before Congress on the subject of universal military training, reported in the New York *Times*, October 24, 1945, p. 3.

18 Colonel Clarence S. Irvine, who commanded the plane which flew non-stop from Guam to Washington, was reported by the press as declaring that one of the objects of the flight was "to show the vulnerability of our country to enemy air attack from vast distances." New York *Times*, November 21, 1945, p. 1.

19 See printed edition of the *Report*, p. 68. In the sentence following the one quoted, General Arnold adds that this statement is "perhaps true only temporarily," but it is apparent from the context that the factor he has in mind which might terminate its "truthfulness" is the development of rockets comparable to the V-2 but of much longer range. The present discussion is not concerned with rockets at all.

20 *Report*, p. 68.

21 According to the figures provided the McMahon Committee by Major General Leslie R. Groves, the total capital investment spent and committed for plants and facilities as of June 30, 1945, was $1,595,000,000. Total operating costs up to the time the bombs were dropped in August were $405,000,000. The larger sum is broken down as follows:

Manufacturing facilities alone	$1,242,000,000
Research	186,000,000
Housing for workers	162,500,000
Workmen's compensation and medical care	4,500,000
Total	$1,595,000,000

22 *Loc. cit.*

23 This discussion recalls the often repeated canard that admirals have been cautious of risking battleships in action because of their cost. The thirteen old battleships and two new ones available to us just after Pearl Harbor reflected no great money value, but they were considered precious because they were scarce and irreplaceable. Later in the war, when new battleships had joined the fleet, and when we had eliminated several belonging to the enemy, no battleships were withheld from any naval actions in which they could be of service. Certainly they were not kept out of the dangerous waters off Normandy, Leyte, Luzon, and Okinawa.

24 The purpose of the scattering would be simply to impose maximum confusion on the superior defenders. Some military airmen have seriously attempted to discount the atomic bomb with the argument that a hit upon a plane carrying one would cause the bomb to explode, blasting every other plane for at least a mile around out of the air. That is not why formation flying is rejected in the example above. Ordinary bombs are highly immune to such mishaps, and from all reports of the nature of the atomic bomb it would seem to be far less likely to undergo explosion as a result even of a direct hit.

25 *Loc. cit.*

26 This was due in part to deliberate intention, possibly legal on the Allied side under the principle of retaliation, and in part to a desire of the respective belligerents to maximize the effectiveness of the air forces available to them. "Precision bombing" was always a misnomer, though some selectivity of targets was possible in good weather. However, such weather occurred in Europe considerably less than half the time, and if the strategic air forces were not to be entirely grounded during the remaining time they were obliged to resort to "area bombing." Radar, when used, was far from being an approximate substitute for the human eye.

27 Henry D. Smyth, *Atomic Energy for Military Purposes, The Official Report on the Development of the Atomic Bomb under the Auspices of the United States Government, 1940–1945*, Princeton, Princeton University Press, 1945, paragraphs 12.9–12.22.

28 General Arnold, for example, in his *Third Report to the Secretary of War*, asserted that at present the only effective means of delivering the atomic bomb is the "very heavy bomber." See printed edition, p. 68.

29 One might venture to speculate whether the increase in power which the atomic bomb is reported to have undergone since it was first used is not due to the use of a more massive tamper to produce a more complete reaction. If so, the bomb has been increasing in weight rather than the reverse.

30 J. Robert Oppenheimer, *op. cit.*, p. 9.

31 The *New Republic*, December 31, 1945, p. 885. The statement quoted is that used by the *New Republic*, and is probably not identical in wording with Professor Urey's remark.

32 The figure for critical minimum mass is secret. According to the *Smyth Report*, it was predicted in May, 1941, that the critical mass would be found to lie between 2 kg and 100 kg (paragraph 4.49), and it was later found to be much nearer the minimum predicted than the maximum. It is worth noting, too, that not only does the critical mass present a lower limit in bomb size, but also that it is not feasible to use very much more than the critical mass. One reason is the detonating problem. Masses above the critical level cannot be kept from exploding, and detonation is therefore produced by the instantaneous assembly of subcritical masses. The necessity for *instant and simultaneous* assembly of the masses used must obviously limit their number. The scientific explanation of the critical mass condition is presented in the *Smyth Report* in paragraphs 2.3, 2.6, and 2.7. One must always distinguish, however, between the chain reaction which occurs in the plutonium-producing pile and that which occurs in the bomb. Although the general principles determining critical mass are similar for the two reactions, the actual mass needed and the character of the reaction are very different in the two cases. See also ibid., paragraphs 2.35, 4.15–17, and 12.13–15.

33 See "The Distribution of Uranium in Nature," an unsigned article published in the *Bulletin of the Atomic Scientists of Chicago*, Vol. 1, No. 4, February 1, 1946, p. 6. See also U.S. Bureau of Mines, *Minerals Year-book, 1940, Review of 1939*, p. 766; ibid., 1943, p. 828; H.V. Ellsworth, *Rare-Element Minerals of Canada*, Geological Survey (Canada), 1932, p.39.

34 *Minerals Yearbook, 1939*, p. 755.

35 *Op. cit., 1943*, p. 828. See also A.W. Postel, *The Mineral Resources of Africa*, University of Pennsylvania, 1943, p. 44.

36 *The Mineral Industry of the British Empire and Foreign Countries, Statistical Summary, 1935–37*, London, 1938, p. 419.

37 The *Smyth Report* is somewhat misleading on this score, in that it gives the impression that the use of plutonium rather than U-235 makes it possible to utilize 100 per cent of the U-238 for atomic fission energy. See paragraph 4.25. However, other portions of the same report give a more accurate picture, especially paragraphs 8.72–73.

38 Among numerous other hints is the statement that in September, 1942, the plants working on the atomic bomb were already receiving about one ton daily of uranium oxide of high purity (paragraph 6.11). Making the conservative assumption that this figure represented the minimum quantity of uranium oxide being processed daily during 1944–45, the U-235 content would be about 115 pounds. The actual figure of production is still secret, but from all available indices the daily production of U-235 and Pu-239 is even now very considerably below that amount.

39 "Material for U-235," *The Economist*, London, November 3, 1945, pp. 629–30.

40 New York *Herald Tribune*, December 18, 1945, p. 4. Incidentally, the Canadian pile is the first one to use the much-discussed "heavy water" (which contains the heavy hydrogen or deuterium atom) as a moderator in place of the graphite (carbon) used in the American piles.

41 However, Mr. Jan Masaryk, Czechoslovak Foreign Minister, asserted in a speech before the Assembly of the UNO on January 17, 1946, that "no Czechoslovak uranium will be used for destructive purposes." New York *Times*, January 18, 1946, p. 8.

42 *Time*, October 15, 1945, p. 22.

43 New York *Times*, October 22, 1945, p. 4.

44 Since the Hiroshima bomb had a radius of total destruction of something under 1¼ miles, its power would have to be increased by some 600 times to gain the hypothetical ten-mile radius.

45 The bomb of longer destructive radius would of course not have to be aimed as accurately for any given target; and this fact may prove of importance in very long range rocket fire, which can never be expected to be as accurate as bombing from airplanes. But here again, large numbers of missiles will also make up for the inaccuracy of the individual missile.

46 *Smyth Report*, paragraph 12.18. This phenomenon is no doubt due to the fact that the greater the margin above critical mass limits, the more atoms split per time unit and thus the larger the proportion of material which undergoes fission before the heat generated expands and disrupts the bomb. It might be noted also that even if there were no expansion or bursting to halt it, the reaction would cease at about the time the fissionable material remaining fell below critical mass conditions, which would also tend to put a premium on having a large margin above critical mass limits. At any rate, anything like 100 per cent detonation of the explosive contents of the atomic

bomb is totally out of the question. In this respect atomic explosives differ markedly from ordinary "high explosives" like TNT or torpex, where there is no difficulty in getting a 100 per cent reaction and where the energy released is therefore directly proportionate to the amount of explosive filler in the bomb.

47 In the 10-ton bomb, of which it is fair to estimate that at least 40 per cent of the weight must be attributed to the metal case. In armorpiercing shells and bombs the proportion of weight devoted to metal is very much higher, running above the 95 per cent mark in major-caliber naval shells.

48 *Smyth Report*, paragraphs 4.26–28.

49 New York *Times*, October 2, 1945, p. 6.

50 See *Smyth Report*, chaps. vii–xi, also paragraph 5.21.

51 *Smyth Report*, paragraph 7.3. A milligram is a thousandth of a gram (one United States dime weighs 2½ grams). See also ibid., paragraphs 5.21, 7.43, 8.1, 8.26, and 9.13.

52 Dr. J.R. Dunning, Director of Columbia University's Division of War Research and a leading figure in the research which led to the atomic bomb, declared before the American Institute of Electrical Engineers that improvements in the plutonium producing process "have already made the extensive plants at Oak Ridge technically obsolete." New York *Times*, January 24, 1946, p. 7. The large Oak Ridge plants are devoted almost exclusively to the isotope separation processes.

53 The Hanford, Washington, plutonium plant is listed as costing $350,000,000, and housing for workers at nearby Richland cost an additional $48,000,000. This out of a total country-wide capital investment, including housing, of $1,595,000,000. The monthly operating cost of the Hanford plant is estimated at $3,500,000, as compared with the $6,000,000 per month for the diffusion plant at Oak Ridge and $12,000,000 for the electro-magnetic plant, also at Oak Ridge. These figures have, of course, little meaning without some knowledge of the respective yields at the several plants, but it may be significant that in the projection of future operating costs, nothing is said about Hanford. According to General Groves the operating costs of the electro-magnetic plant will diminish, while those of the gaseous diffusion plant will increase only as a result of completion of plant enlargement. Of course, the degree to which less efficient processes were cut back and more efficient ones expanded would depend on considerations of existing capital investment and of the desired rate of current production.

54 *Time*, January 28, 1946, p. 75.

55 "Atomic Weapons and the Crisis in Science," *Saturday Review of Literature*, November 24, 1945, p. 10.

56 This idea was first suggested and elaborated by Professor Jacob Viner. See his paper: "The Implications of the Atomic Bomb for International Relations," *Proceedings of the American Philosophical Society*, Vol. 90, No. 1 (January 29, 1946), pp. 53ff. The present writer desires at this point to express his indebtedness to Professor Viner for numerous other suggestions and ideas gained during the course of several personal conversations.

57 The argument has been made that once the middle or small powers have atomic bombs they will have restored to them the ability to resist effectively the aggressions of their great-power neighbors—an ability which otherwise has well-nigh disappeared. This is of course an interesting speculation on which no final answer is forthcoming. It is true that a small power, while admitting that it could not win a war against a great neighbor, could nevertheless threaten to use the bomb as a penalizing instrument if it were invaded. But it is also true that the great-power aggressor could make counterthreats concerning its conduct while occupying the country which had used atomic bombs against it. It seems to this writer highly unlikely that a small power would dare threaten use of the bomb against a great neighbor which was sure to overrun it quickly once hostilities began. It seems, on the contrary, much more likely that Denmark's course in the second World War will be widely emulated if there is a third. The aggressor will not "atomize" a city occupied by its own troops, and the opposing belligerent will hesitate to destroy by such an unselective weapon the cities of an occupied friendly state.

58 It was stated in the previous chapter, p. 30, that before we can consider a defense against atomic bombs effective, "the frustration of the attack for any given target area must be complete." The emphasis in that statement is on a specific and limited target area such as a small or medium size city. For a whole nation containing many cities such absolute standards are obviously inapplicable. The requirements for a "reasonably effective" defense would still be far higher than would be the case with ordinary TNT bombs, but it would certainly not have to reach 100 per cent frustration of the attack. All of which says little more than that a nation can absorb more atomic bombs than can a single city.

59 One can almost rule out too the possibility that war would break out between two great powers where both knew that only one of them had the bombs in quantity. It is one of the old maxims of power politics that *c'est une crime de faire la guerre sans compter sur la supériorité*, and certainly a monopoly of atomic bombs would be a sufficiently clear definition of superiority to dissuade the other side from accepting the gage of war unless directly attacked.

60 General H.H. Arnold's *Third Report to the Secretary of War* is in general outstanding for the breadth of vision it displays. Yet one finds in it statements like the following: "An Air Force is always verging on obsolescence and, in time of peace, its size and replacement rate will always be inadequate to meet the full demands of war. Military Air Power should, therefore, be measured to a large extent by the ability of the existing Air Force to absorb in time of emergency the increase required by war together with new ideas and techniques" (page 62). Elsewhere in the *Report* (page 65) similar remarks are made about the expansion of personnel which, it is presumed, will always follow upon the outbreak of hostilities. But *nowhere* in the *Report* is the possibility envisaged that in a war which began with an atomic bomb attack there might be no opportunity for the expansion or even replacement either of planes or personnel. The same omission, needless to say, is discovered in practically all the pronouncements of top-ranking Army and Navy officers concerning their own plans for the future.

61 See above, pp. 36–40.

62 See Bernard Brodie, *A Guide to Naval Strategy*, 3rd ed., Princeton, Princeton University Press, 1944, p. 215.

63 There has been a good deal of confusion between automaticity and immediacy in the execution of sanctions. Those who stress the importance of bringing military pressure to bear *at once* in the case of aggression are as a rule really less concerned with having sanctions imposed quickly than they are with having them appear certain. To be sure, the atomic bomb gives the necessity for quickness of military response a wholly new meaning; but in the kinds of aggression with which the UNO is now set up to deal, atomic bombs are not likely to be important for a very long time.

64 In this respect the atomic bomb differs markedly from the TNT bomb, due to the much smaller radius of destruction of the latter. The amount of destruction the TNT bomb accomplishes depends not on what is in the general locality but on what is in the immediate proximity of the burst. A factory of given size requires a given number of bombs to destroy it regardless of the size of the city in which it is situated. To be sure, the "misses" count for more in a large city, but from the point of view of the defender there are certain compensating advantages in having the objects to be defended gathered in large concentrations. It makes a good deal easier the effective deployment of fighter patrols and antiaircraft guns. But the latter advantage does not count for much in the case of atomic bombs, since, as argued in the previous chapter, it is practically hopeless to expect fighter planes and antiaircraft guns to stop atomic attack so completely as to save the city.

65 The difference between American and Japanese cities in vulnerability to bombing attack has unquestionably been exaggerated. Most commentators who stress the difference forget the many square miles of predominantly wooden frame houses to be found in almost any American city. And those who were impressed with the pictures of ferro-concrete buildings standing relatively intact in the midst of otherwise total devastation at Hiroshima and Nagasaki will not be comforted by Dr. Philip Morrison's testimony before the McMahon Committee on December 6, 1945. Dr. Morrison, who inspected both cities, testified that the interiors of those buildings were completely destroyed and the people in them killed. Brick buildings, he pointed out, and even steel-frame buildings with brick walls proved extremely vulnerable. "Of those people within a thousand yards of the blast," he added, "about one in every house or two escaped death from blast or burn. But they died anyway from the effects of the rays emitted at the instant of explosion." He expressed himself as convinced that an American city similarly bombed "would be as badly damaged as a Japanese city, though it would look less wrecked from the air."

No doubt Dr. Morrison is exaggerating in the opposite direction. Obviously there must be a considerable difference among structures in their capacity to withstand blast from atomic bombs and to shelter the people within them. But that difference is likely to make itself felt mostly in the peripheral portions of a blasted area. Within a radius of one mile from the center of burst it is not likely to be of consequence.

12 The delicate balance of terror

Albert Wohlstetter

The first shock administered by the Soviet launching of sputnik has almost dissipated. The flurry of statements and investigations and improvised responses has died down, leaving a small residue: a slight increase in the schedule of bomber and ballistic missile production, with a resulting small increment in our defense expenditures for the current fiscal year; a considerable enthusiasm for space travel; and some stirrings of interest in the teaching of mathematics and physics in the secondary schools. Western defense policy has almost returned to the level of activity and the emphasis suited to the basic assumptions which were controlling before sputnik.

One of the most important of these assumptions—that a general thermonuclear war is extremely unlikely—is held in common by most of the critics of our defense policy as well as by its proponents. Because of its crucial rôle in the Western strategy of defense, I should like to examine the stability of the thermonuclear balance which, it is generally supposed, would make aggression irrational or even insane. The balance, I believe, is in fact precarious, and this fact has critical implications for policy. Deterrence in the 1960s is neither assured nor impossible but will be the product of sustained intelligent effort and hard choices, responsibly made. As a major illustration important both for defense and foreign policy, I shall treat the particularly stringent conditions for deterrence which affect forces based close to the enemy, whether they are U.S. forces or those of our allies, under single or joint control. I shall comment also on the inadequacy as well as the necessity of deterrence, on the problem of accidental outbreak of war, and on disarmament.[1]

The presumed automatic balance

I emphasize that requirements for deterrence are stringent. We have heard so much about the atomic stalemate and the receding probability of war which it has produced that this may strike the reader as something of an exaggeration. Is deterrence a necessary consequence of both sides having a nuclear delivery capability, and is all-out war nearly obsolete? Is mutual extinction the only outcome of a general war? This belief, frequently expressed by references to Mr. Oppenheimer's simile of the two scorpions in a bottle, is perhaps the prevalent one. It is held by a very eminent and diverse group of people—in England by Sir Winston Churchill, P.M.S. Blackett, Sir John Slessor, Admiral Buzzard and many others; in France by such figures as Raymond Aron, General Gallois and General Gazin; in this country by the titular heads of both parties as well as almost all writers on military and foreign affairs, by both Henry Kissinger and his critic, James E. King, Jr., and by George Kennan as well as Dean Acheson. Mr. Kennan refers to American concern about surprise attack as simply obsessive;[2] and many people have drawn the consequence of the stalemate as has Blackett, who states: "If it is in fact true, as most current opinion holds, that strategic air power has abolished global war, then an urgent problem for the West is to assess how little effort must be put into it to keep global war abolished."[3] If peace were founded firmly on mutual terror, and mutual terror on symmetrical nuclear capabilities, this would be, as Churchill has said, "a melancholy paradox;" none the less a most comforting one.

Deterrence, however, is not automatic. While feasible, it will be much harder to achieve in the 1960s than is generally believed. One of the most disturbing features of current opinion is the underestimation of this difficulty. This is due partly to a misconstruction of the technological race as a problem in matching striking forces, partly to a wishful analysis of the Soviet ability to strike first.

Since sputnik, the United States has made several moves to assure the world (that is, the enemy, but more especially our allies and ourselves) that we will match or overmatch Soviet technology and, specifically, Soviet offense technology. We have, for example, accelerated the bomber and ballistic missile programs, in particular the intermediate-range ballistic missiles. The problem has been conceived as more or better bombers—or rockets; or sputniks; or engineers. This has meant confusing deterrence with matching or exceeding the enemy's ability to strike first. Matching weapons, however, misconstrues the nature of the techno-logical race. Not, as is frequently said, because only a few bombs owned by the defender can make aggression fruitless, but because even many might not. One outmoded A-bomb dropped from an obsolete bomber might destroy a great many supersonic jets and ballistic missiles. To deter an attack means being able to strike back in spite of it. It means, in other words, a capability to strike second. In the last year or two there has been a growing awareness of the importance of the distinction between a "strike-first" and a "strike-second" capability, but little, if any, recognition of the implications of this distinction for the balance of terror theory.

Where the published writings have not simply underestimated Soviet capabilities and the advantages of a first strike, they have in general placed artificial constraints on the Soviet use of the capabilities attributed to them. They assume, for example, that the enemy will attack in mass over the Arctic through our Distant Early Warning line, with bombers refueled over Canada—all resulting in plenty of warning. Most hopefully, it is sometimes assumed that such attacks will be preceded by days of visible preparations for moving ground troops. Such assumptions suggest that the Soviet leaders will be rather bumbling or, better, cooperative. However attractive it may be for us to narrow Soviet alternatives to these, they would be low in the order of preference of any reasonable Russians planning war.

The quantitative nature of the problem and the uncertainties

In treating Soviet strategies it is important to consider Soviet rather than Western advantage and to consider the strategy of both sides quantitatively. The effectiveness of our own choices will depend on a most complex numerical interaction of Soviet and Western plans. Unfortunately, both the privileged and unprivileged information on these matters is pre-carious. As a result, competent people have been led into critical error in evaluating the prospects for deterrence. Western journalists have greatly overestimated the difficulties of a Soviet surprise attack with thermonuclear weapons and vastly underestimated the complexity of the Western problem of retaliation.

One intelligent commentator, Richard Rovere, recently expressed the common view: "If the Russians had ten thousand warheads and a missile for each, and we had ten hydrogen bombs and ten obsolete bombers, . . . aggression would still be a folly that would appeal only to an insane adventurer." Mr. Rovere's example is plausible because it assumes implicitly that the defender's hydrogen bombs will with certainty be visited on the aggressor; then the damage done by the ten bombs seems terrible enough for deterrence, and any more would be simply redundant. This is the basis for the common view. The example raises questions, even assuming the delivery of the ten weapons. For instance, the targets aimed at in retaliation might be sheltered and a quite modest civil defense could hold within tolerable limits the damage done to such city targets by ten delivered bombs. But the essential point is that the weapons would not be very likely to reach their targets. Even if the bombers were dispersed at ten different points, and protected by shelters so blast resistant as to stand up anywhere outside the lip of the bomb crater—even inside the fire ball itself—the chances of one of these bombers surviving the huge attack directed at it would be on the order of one in a million. (This calculation takes account of the unreliability and inaccuracy of the missile.) And the damage done by the small minority of these ten planes that might be in the air at the time of the attack, armed and ready to run the gauntlet of an alert air defense system, if not zero, would be very small indeed compared to damage that Russia has suffered in the past. For Mr. Rovere, like many other writers on this subject, numerical superiority is not important at all.

For Joseph Alsop, on the other hand, it is important, but the superiority is on our side. Mr. Alsop recently enunciated as one of the four rules of nuclear war: "The aggressor's problem is astronomically difficult; and the aggressor requires an overwhelming superiority of force."[4] There are, he believes, no fewer than 400 SAC bases in the NATO nations alone and many more elsewhere, all of which would have to be attacked in a very short space of time. The "thousands of coördinated air sorties and/or missile firings," he concludes, are not feasible. Mr. Alsop's argument is numerical and has the virtue of demonstrating that at least the relative numbers are important. But the numbers he uses are very wide of the mark. He overestimates the number of such bases by a factor of more than ten,[5] and in any case, missile firings on the scale of a thousand or more involve costs that are by no means out of proportion, given the strategic budgets of the great powers. Whether or not thousands are needed depends on the yield and the accuracy of the enemy missiles, something about which it would be a great mistake for us to display confidence.

Perhaps the first step in dispelling the nearly universal optimism about the stability of deterrence would be to recognize the difficulties in analyzing the uncertainties and interactions between our own range of choices and the moves open to the Soviets. On our side we must consider an enormous variety of strategic weapons which might compose our force, and for each of these several alternative methods of basing and operation. These are the choices that determine whether a weapons system will have any genuine capability in the realistic circumstances of a war. Besides the B-47E and the B-52 bombers which are in the United States strategic force now, alternatives will include the B-52G (a longer-range version of the B-52); the Mach 2 B-58A bomber and a "growth" version of it; the Mach 3 B-70 bomber; a nuclear-powered bomber possibly carrying long-range air-to-surface missiles; the Dynasoar, a manned glide-rocket; the Thor and the Jupiter, liquid-fueled intermediate-range ballistic missiles; the Snark intercontinental cruise missile; the Atlas and the Titan intercontinental ballistic missiles; the submarine-launched Polaris and Atlantis rockets; and Minuteman, one potential solid-fueled successor to the Thor and Titan; possibly unmanned bombardment satellites; and many others which are not yet gleams in anyone's eye and some that are just that.

The difficulty of describing in a brief article the best mixture of weapons for the long-term future beginning in 1960, their base requirements, their potentiality for stabilizing or upsetting the balance among the great powers, and their implications for the alliance, is not just a matter of space or the constraint of security. The difficulty in fact stems from some rather basic insecurities. These matters are wildly uncertain; we are talking about weapons and vehicles that are some time off and, even if the precise performances currently hoped for and claimed by contractors were in the public domain, it would be a good idea to doubt them.

Recently some of my colleagues picked their way through the graveyard of early claims about various missiles and aircraft: their dates of availability, costs and performance. These claims are seldom revisited or talked about: *de mortuis nil nisi bonum*. The errors were large and almost always in one direction. And the less we knew, the more hopeful we were. Accordingly the missiles benefited in particular. For example, the estimated cost of one missile increased by a factor of over 50—from about $35,000 in 1949 to some $2 million in 1957. This uncertainty is critical. Some but not all of the systems listed can be chosen and the problem of choice is essentially quantitative. The complexities of the problem, if they were more widely understood, would discourage the oracular confidence of writers on the subject of deterrence.

Some of the complexities can be suggested by referring to the successive obstacles to be hurdled by any system providing a capability to strike second, that is, to strike back. Such deterrent systems must have (a) a stable, "steady-state" peacetime operation within feasible budgets (besides the logistic and operational costs there are, for example, problems of false alarms and accidents). They must have also the ability (b) to survive enemy attacks, (c) to make and communicate the decision to retaliate, (d) to reach enemy territory with fuel enough to complete their mission, (e) to penetrate enemy active defenses, that is, fighters and surface-to-air missiles, and (f) to destroy the target in spite of any "passive" civil defense in the form of dispersal or protective construction or evacuation of the target itself.

Within limits the enemy is free to use his offensive and defensive forces so as to exploit the weaknesses of each of our systems. He will also be free, within limits, in the 1960s to choose that composition of forces which will make life as difficult as possible for the various systems we might select. It would be quite wrong to assume that we have the same degree of flexibility or that the uncertainties I have described affect a totalitarian aggressor and the party attacked equally. A totalitarian country can preserve secrecy about the capabilities and disposition of his forces very much better than a Western democracy. And the aggressor has, among other enormous advantages of the first strike, the ability to weigh continually our performance at each of the six barriers and to choose that precise time and circumstance for attack which will reduce uncertainty. It is important not to confuse our uncertainty with his. Strangely enough, some military commentators have not made this distinction and have founded their certainty of deterrence on the fact simply that there are uncertainties.

Unwarranted optimism is displayed not only in the writings of journalists but in the more analytic writings of professionals. The recent writings of General Gallois[6] parallel rather closely Mr. Alsop's faulty numerical proof that surprise attack is astronomically difficult—except that Gallois' "simple arithmetic," to borrow his own phrase, turns essentially on some assumptions which are at once inexplicit and extremely optimistic with respect to the blast resistance of dispersed missile sites subjected to attack from relatively close range.[7] Mr. Blackett's recent book, "Atomic Weapons and East-West Relations," illustrates the hazards confronting a most able analyst in dealing with the piecemeal information available to the general public. Mr. Blackett, a Nobel prize-winning physicist with wartime experience in military operations research, lucidly summarized the public information available when he was writing in 1956 on weapons for all-out war. But much of his analysis was based on the assumption that H-bombs could not be made small enough to be carried in an intercontinental missile. It is now widely known that intercontinental ballistic missiles will have hydrogen warheads, and this fact, a secret at the time, invalidates Mr. Blackett's calculations and, I might say, much of his optimism on the stability of the balance of terror. In sum, one of the serious obstacles to any widespread rational judgment on these matters of high policy is that critical elements of the problem *have* to be protected by secrecy. However, some of the principal conclusions about deterrence in the early 1960s can be fairly firmly based, and based on public information.

The delicacy of the balance of terror

The most important conclusion is that we must expect a vast increase in the weight of attack which the Soviets can deliver with little warning, and the growth of a significant Russian capability for an essentially warningless attack. As a result, strategic deterrence, while feasible, will be extremely difficult to achieve, and at critical junctures in the 1960s, we may not have the power to deter attack. Whether we have it or not will depend on some difficult strategic choices as to the future composition of the deterrent forces as well as hard choices on its basing, operations and defense.

Manned bombers will continue to make up the predominant part of our striking force in the early 1960s. None of the popular remedies for their defense will suffice—not, for example, mere increase of alertness (which will be offset by the Soviet's increasing capability for attack without significant warning), nor simple dispersal or sheltering alone or mobility taken by itself, nor a mere piling up of interceptors and defense missiles around SAC bases. Especially extravagant expectations have been placed on the airborne alert—an extreme form of defense by mobility. The impression is rather widespread that one-third of the SAC bombers are in the air and ready for combat at all times.[8] This belief is belied by the public record. According to the Symington Committee Hearings in 1956, our bombers averaged 31 hours of flying per month, which is about 4 percent of the average 732-hour month. An Air Force representative expressed the hope that within a couple of years, with an increase in the ratio of crews to aircraft, the bombers would reach 45 hours of flight per month—which is 6 percent. This 4 to 6 percent of the force includes bombers partially fueled and without bombs. It is, moreover, only an average, admitting variance down as well as up. Some increase in the number of armed bombers aloft is to be expected. However, for the current generation of bombers, which have been designed for speed and range rather than endurance, a continuous air patrol for one-third of the force would be extremely expensive.

On the other hand, it would be unwise to look for miracles in the new weapons systems, which by the mid-1960s may constitute a considerable portion of the United States force. After the Thor, Atlas and Titan there are a number of promising developments. The solid-fueled rockets, Minuteman and Polaris, promise in particular to be extremely significant components of the deterrent force. Today they are being touted as making the problem of deterrence easy to solve and, in fact, guaranteeing its solution. But none of the new developments in vehicles is likely to do that. For the complex job of deterrence, they all have limitations. The unvaryingly immoderate claims for each new weapons system should make us wary of the latest "technological breakthroughs." Only a very short time ago the ballistic missile itself was supposed to be intrinsically invulnerable on the ground. It is now more generally understood that its survival is likely to depend on a variety of choices in its defense.

It is hard to talk with confidence about the mid and late 1960s. A systematic study of an optimal or a good deterrent force which considered all the major factors affecting choice and dealt adequately with the uncertainties would be a formidable task. In lieu of this, I shall mention briefly why none of the many systems available or projected dominates the others in any obvious way. My comments will take the form of a swift run-through of the characteristic advantages and disadvantages of various strategic systems at each of the six successive hurdles mentioned earlier.

The first hurdle to be surmounted is the attainment of a stable, steady-state peacetime operation. Systems which depend for their survival on extreme decentralization of controls, as may be the case with large-scale dispersal and some of the mobile weapons, raise problems of accidents and over a long period of peacetime operation this leads in turn to serious political problems. Systems relying on extensive movement by land, perhaps by truck caravan, are an obvious example; the introduction of these on European roads, as is sometimes suggested, would raise grave questions for the governments of some of our allies. Any extensive increase in the armed air alert will increase the hazard of accident and intensify the concern already expressed among our allies. Some of the proposals for bombardment satellites may involve such hazards of unintended bomb release as to make them out of the question.

The cost to buy and operate various weapons systems must be seriously considered. Some systems buy their ability to negotiate a given hurdle—say, surviving the enemy attack—only at prohibitive cost. Then the number that can be bought out of a given budget will be small and this will affect the relative performance of competing systems at various other hurdles, for example penetrating enemy defenses. Some of the relevant cost comparisons, then, are between competing systems; others concern the extra costs to the enemy of canceling an additional expenditure of our own. For example, some dispersal is essential, though usually it is expensive; if the dispersed bases are within a warning net, dispersal can help to provide warning against some sorts of attack, since it forces the attacker to increase the size of his raid and so makes it more liable to detection as well as somewhat harder to coördinate. But as the sole or principal defense of our offensive force, dispersal has only a brief useful life and can be justified financially only up to a point. For against our costs of construction, maintenance and operation of an additional base must be set the enemy's much lower costs of delivering one extra weapon. And, in general, any feasible degree of dispersal leaves a considerable concentration of value at a single target point. For example, a squadron of heavy bombers costing, with their associated tankers and penetration aids, perhaps $500,000,000 over five years, might be eliminated, if it were otherwise unprotected, by an enemy intercontinental ballistic missile costing perhaps $16,000,000. After making allowance for the unreliability and inaccuracy of the missile, this means a ratio of some ten for one or better. To achieve safety by *brute* numbers in so unfavorable a competition is not likely to be viable economically or politically. However, a viable peacetime operation is only the first hurdle to be surmounted.

At the second hurdle—surviving the enemy offense—ground alert systems placed deep within a warning net look good against a manned bomber attack, much less good against intercontinental ballistic missiles, and not good at all against ballistic missiles launched from the sea. In the last case, systems such as the Minuteman, which may be sheltered and dispersed as well as alert, would do well. Systems involving launching platforms which are mobile and concealed, such as Polaris submarines, have particular advantage for surviving an enemy offense.

However, there is a third hurdle to be surmounted—namely that of making the decision to retaliate and communicating it. Here, Polaris, the combat air patrol of B-525, and in fact all of the mobile platforms—under water, on the surface, in the air and above the air—have severe problems. Long distance communication may be jammed and, most important, communication centers may be destroyed.

At the fourth hurdle—ability to reach enemy territory with fuel enough to complete the mission—several of our short-legged systems have operational problems such as coördination with tankers and using bases close to the enemy. For a good many years to come, up to the mid 1960s in fact, this will be a formidable hurdle for the greater part of our deterrent force. The next section of this article deals with this problem at some length.

The fifth hurdle is the aggressor's long-range interceptors and close-in missile defenses. To get past these might require large numbers of planes and missiles. (If the high cost of overcoming an earlier obstacle—using extreme dispersal or airborne alert or the like—limits the number of planes or missiles bought, our capability is likely to be penalized disproportionately here.) Or getting through may involve carrying heavy loads of radar decoys, electronic jammers and other aids to defense penetration. For example, vehicles like Minuteman and Polaris, which were made small to facilitate dispersal or mobility, may suffer here because they can carry fewer penetration aids.

At the final hurdle—destroying the target in spite of the passive defenses that may protect it—low-payload and low-accuracy systems, such as Minuteman and Polaris, may be frustrated by blast-resistant shelters. For example, five half-megaton weapons with an average inaccuracy of two miles might be expected to destroy half the population of a city of 900,000, spread over 40 square miles, provided the inhabitants are without shelters. But if they are provided with shelters capable of resisting over-pressures of 100 pounds per square inch, approximately 60 such weapons would be required; and deep rock shelters might force the total up to over a thousand.

Prizes for a retaliatory capability are not distributed for getting over one of these jumps. A system must get over all six. I hope these illustrations will suggest that assuring ourselves the power to strike back after a massive thermonuclear surprise attack is by no means as automatic as is widely believed.

In counteracting the general optimism as to the ease and, in fact, the inevitability of deterrence, I should like to avoid creating the extreme opposite impression. Deterrence demands hard, continuing, intelligent work, but it can be achieved. The job of deterring rational attack by guaranteeing great damage to an aggressor is, for example, very much less difficult than erecting a nearly airtight defense of cities in the face of full-scale thermonuclear surprise attack. Protecting manned bombers and missiles is much easier because they may be dispersed, sheltered or kept mobile, and they can respond to warning with greater speed. Mixtures of these and other defenses with complementary strengths can preserve a powerful remainder after attack. Obviously not all our bombers and missiles need to survive in order to fulfill their mission. To preserve the majority of our cities intact in the face of surprise attack is immensely more difficult, if not impossible. (This does not mean that the aggressor has the same problem in preserving his cities from retaliation by a poorly-protected, badly-damaged force. And it does not mean that *we* should not do more to limit the extent of the catastrophe to our cities in case deterrence fails. I believe we should.) Deterrence, however, provided we work at it, is feasible, and, what is more, it is a crucial objective of national policy.

What can be said, then, as to whether general war is unlikely? Would not a general thermonuclear war mean "extinction" for the aggressor as well as the defender? "Extinction" is a state that badly needs analysis. Russian casualties in World War II were more than

20,000,000. Yet Russia recovered extremely well from this catastrophe. There are several quite plausible circumstances in the future when the Russians might be quite confident of being able to limit damage to considerably less than this number—if they make sensible strategic choices and we do not. On the other hand, the risks of not striking might at some juncture appear very great to the Soviets, involving, for example, disastrous defeat in peripheral war, loss of key satellites with danger of revolt spreading—possibly to Russia itself—or fear of an attack by ourselves. Then, striking first, by surprise, would be the sensible choice for them, and from their point of view the smaller risk.

It should be clear that it is not fruitful to talk about the likelihood of general war without specifying the range of alternatives that are pressing on the aggressor and the strategic postures of both the Soviet bloc and the West. Deterrence is a matter of comparative risks. The balance is not automatic. First, since thermonuclear weapons give an enormous advantage to the aggressor, it takes great ingenuity and realism at any given level of nuclear technology to devise a stable equilibrium. And second, this technology itself is changing with fantastic speed. Deterrence will require an urgent and continuing effort.

The uses and risks of bases close to the Soviets

It may now be useful to focus attention on the special problems of deterrent forces close to the Soviet Union. First, overseas areas have played an important rôle in the past and have a continuing though less certain rôle today. Second, the recent acceleration of production of intermediate-range ballistic missiles and the negotiation of agreements with various NATO powers for their basing and operation have given our overseas bases a renewed importance in deterring attack on the United States—or so it would appear at first blush. Third, an analysis can throw some light on the problems faced by our allies in developing an independent ability to deter all-out attack on themselves, and in this way it can clarify the much agitated question of nuclear sharing. Finally, overseas bases affect in many critical ways, political and economic as well as military, the status of the alliance.

At the end of the last decade, overseas bases appeared to be an advantageous means of achieving the radius extension needed by our short-legged bombers, of permitting them to use several axes of attack, and of increasing the number of sorties possible in the course of an extended campaign. With the growth of our own thermonuclear stockpile, it became apparent that a long campaign involving many re-uses of a large proportion of our bombers was not likely to be necessary. With the growth of a Russian nuclear-delivery capability, it became clear that this was most unlikely to be feasible.

Our overseas bases now have the disadvantage of high vulnerability. Because they are closer than the United States to the Soviet Union, they are subject to a vastly greater attack by a larger variety as well as number of vehicles. With given resources, the Soviets might deliver on nearby bases a freight of bombs with something like 50 to 100 times the yield that they could muster at intercontinental range. Missile accuracy would more than double. Because there is not much space for obtaining warning—in any case, there are no deep-warning radar nets—and, since most of our overseas bases are close to deep water from which submarines might launch missiles, the warning problem is very much more severe than for bases in the interior of the United States.

As a result, early in the 1950s the U.S. Air Force decided to recall many of our bombers to the continental United States and to use the overseas bases chiefly for refueling, particularly poststrike ground refueling. This reduced drastically the vulnerability of U.S. bombers and at the same time retained many of the advantages of overseas operation. For some years now

SAC has been reducing the number of aircraft usually deployed overseas. The purpose is to reduce vulnerability and has little to do with any increasing radius of SAC aircraft. The early B-52 radius is roughly that of the B-36; the B-47, roughly that of the B-50 or B-29. In fact the radius limitation and therefore the basing requirements we have discussed will not change substantially for some time to come. We can talk with comparative confidence here, because the U.S. strategic force is itself largely determined for this period. Such a force changes more slowly than is generally realized. The vast majority of the force will consist of manned bombers, and most of these will be of medium range. *Some* U.S. bombers will be able to reach *some* targets from *some* U.S. bases within the 48 states without landing on the way back. On the other hand, some bomber-target combinations are not feasible without pre-target landing (and are therefore doubtful). The Atlas, Titan and Polaris rockets, when available, can of course do without overseas bases (though the proportion of Polaris submarines kept at sea can be made larger by the use of submarine tenders based overseas). But even with the projected force of aerial tankers, the greater part of our force, which will be manned bombers, cannot be used at all in attacks on the Soviet Union without at least some use of overseas areas.

What of the bases for Thor and Jupiter, our first intermediate-range ballistic missiles? These have to be close to the enemy, and they must of course be operating bases, not merely refueling stations. The Thors and Jupiters will be continuously in range of an enormous Soviet potential for surprise attack. These installations therefore re-open; in a most acute form, some of the serious questions of ground vulnerability that were raised about six years ago in connection with our overseas bomber bases. The decision to station the Thor and Jupiter missiles overseas has been our principal public response to the Russian advances in rocketry, and perhaps our most plausible response. Because it involves our ballistic missiles it appears directly to answer the Russian rockets. Because it involves using European bases, it appears to make up for the range superiority of the Russian intercontinental missile. And most important, it directly involves the NATO powers and gives them an element of control.

There is no question that it was genuinely urgent not only to meet the Russian threat but to do so visibly, in order to save the loosening NATO alliance. Our allies were fearful that the Soviet ballistic missiles might mean that we were no longer able or willing to retaliate against the Soviet Union in case of an attack on them. We hastened to make public a reaction which would restore their confidence. This move surely appears to increase our own power to strike back, and also to give our allies a deterrent of their own, independent of our decision. It has also been argued that in this respect it merely advances the inevitable date at which our allies will acquire "modern" weapons of their own, and that it widens the range of Soviet challenges which Europe can meet. But we must face seriously the question whether this move will in fact assure either the ability to retaliate or the decision to attempt it, on the part of our allies or ourselves. And we should ask at the very least whether further expansion of this policy will buy as much retaliatory power as other ways of spending the considerable sums involved. Finally, it is important to be clear whether the Thor and Jupiter actually increase the flexibility or range of response available to our allies.

One justification for this move is that it disperses retaliatory weapons and that this is the most effective sanction against the thermonuclear aggressor. The limitations of dispersal have already been discussed, but it remains to examine the argument that overseas bases provide *widespread* dispersal, which imposes on the aggressor insoluble problems of coördination.

There is of course something in the notion that forcing the enemy to attack many political entities increases the seriousness of his decision, but there is very little in the notion that dispersal in several countries makes the problem of destruction more difficult in the military sense. Dispersal does not require separation by the distance of oceans—just by the lethal diameters of enemy bombs. And the task of coördinating bomber attacks on Europe and the eastern coast of the United States, say, is not appreciably more difficult than coördinating attacks on our east and west coasts. In the case of ballistic missiles, the elapsed time from firing to impact on the target can be calculated with high accuracy. Although there will be some failures and delays, times of firing can be arranged so that impact on many dispersed points is almost simultaneous—on Okinawa and the United Kingdom, for instance, as well as on California and Ohio. Moreover, it is important to keep in mind that these far-flung bases, while distant from each other and from the United States, are on the whole close to the enemy. To eliminate them, therefore, requires a smaller expenditure of resources on his part than targets at intercontinental range. For close-in targets he can use a wider variety of weapons carrying larger payloads and with higher accuracy.

The seeming appositeness of an overseas-based Thor and Jupiter as an answer to a Russian intercontinental ballistic missile stems not so much from any careful analysis of their retaliatory power under attack as from the directness of the comparison they suggest: a rocket equals a rocket, an intercontinental missile equals an intermediate-range missile based at closer range to the target. But this again mistakes the nature of the technological race. It conceives the problem of deterrence as that of simply matching or exceeding the aggressor's capability to strike first. A surprising proportion of the debate on defense policy has betrayed this confusion. Matching technological developments are useful for prestige, and such demonstrations have a vital function in preserving the alliance and in reassuring the neutral powers. But propaganda is not enough. The only reasonably certain way of maintaining a reputation for strength is to display an actual power to our friends as well as our enemies. We should ask, then, whether further expansion of the current programs for basing Thor and Jupiter is an efficient way to increase American retaliatory power. If overseas bases are considered too vulnerable for manned bombers, will not the same be true for missiles?

The basis for the hopeful impression that they will not is rather vague, including a mixture of hypothetical properties of ballistic missiles in which perhaps the dominant element is their supposedly much more rapid, "push-button" response. What needs to be considered here are the response time of such missiles (including decision, preparation and launch times), and how they are to be defended.

The decision to fire a missile with a thermonuclear warhead is much harder to make than a decision simply to start a manned aircraft on its way, with orders to return to base unless instructed to continue to its assigned target. This is the "fail-safe" procedure practised by the U.S. Air Force. In contrast, once a missile is launched, there is no method of recall or deflection which is not subject to risks of electronic or mechanical failure. Therefore such a decision must wait for much more unambiguous evidence of enemy intentions. It must and will take a longer time to make and is less likely to be made at all. Where more than one country is involved, the joint decision is harder still, since there is opportunity to disagree about the ambiguity of the evidence, as well as to reach quite different interpretations of national interest. On much less momentous matters the process of making decisions in NATO is complicated, and it should be recognized that such complexity has much to do with the genuine concern of the various NATO powers about the danger of accidentally starting World War III. Such fears will not be diminished with the advent of I.R.B.M.s. In fact, widespread dispersion of nuclear armed missiles raises measurably the possibility of accidental war.

Second, it is quite erroneous to suppose that by contrast with manned bombers the first I.R.B.M.s can be launched almost as simply as pressing a button. Count-down procedures for early missiles are liable to interruption, and the characteristics of the liquid oxygen fuel limits the readiness of their response. Unlike JP-$_4$, the fuel used in jet bombers, liquid oxygen cannot be held for long periods of time in these vehicles. In this respect such missiles will be *less* ready than alert bombers. Third, the smaller warning time available overseas makes more difficult any response. This includes, in particular, any active defense, not only against ballistic missile attacks but, for example, against low altitude or various circuitous attacks by manned aircraft.

Finally, passive defense by means of shelter is more difficult, given the larger bomb yields, better accuracies and larger forces available to the Russians at such close range. And if the press reports are correct, the plans for I.R.B.M. installations do not call for bomb-resistant shelters. If this is so, it should be taken into account in measuring the actual contribution of these installations to the West's retaliatory power. Viewed as a contribution to deterring all-out attack on the United States, the Thor and Jupiter bases seem unlikely to compare favorably with other alternatives. If newspaper references to hard bargaining by some of our future hosts are to be believed, it would seem that such negotiations have been conducted under misapprehensions on both sides as to the benefits to the United States.

But many proponents of the distribution of Thor and Jupiter—and possibly some of our allies—have in mind not an increase in U.S. deterrence but the development of an independent capability in several of the NATO countries to deter all-out attack against themselves. This would be a useful thing if it can be managed at supportable cost and if it does not entail the sacrifice of even more critical measures of protection. But aside from the special problems of joint control, which would affect the certainty of response adversely, precisely who their legal owner is will not affect the retaliatory power of the Thors and Jupiters one way or the other. They would not be able to deter an attack which they could not survive. It is curious that many who question the utility of American overseas bases (for example, our bomber bases in the United Kingdom) simply assume that, for our allies, possession of strategic nuclear weapons is one with deterrence.

There remains the view that the provision of these weapons will broaden the range of response open to our allies. In so far as this view rests on the belief that the intermediate-range ballistic missile is adapted to limited war, it is wide of the mark. The inaccuracy of an I.R.B.M. requires high-yield warheads, and such a combination of inaccuracy and high yield, while quite appropriate and adequate against unprotected targets in a general war, would scarcely come within even the most lax, in fact reckless, definition of limited war. Such a weapon is inappropriate for even the nuclear variety of limited war, and it is totally useless for meeting the wide variety of provocation that is well below the threshold of nuclear response. In so far as these missiles will be costly for our allies to install, operate and support, they are likely to displace a conventional capability that might be genuinely useful in limited engagements. More important, they are likely to be used as an excuse for budget cutting. In this way they will accelerate the general trend toward dependence on all-out response and so will have the opposite effect to the one claimed.

Nevertheless, if the Thor and Jupiter have these defects, might not some future weapon be free of them? Some of these defects, of course, will be overcome in time. Solid fuels or storable liquids will eventually replace liquid oxygen, reliabilities will increase, various forms of mobility or portability will become feasible, accuracies may even be so improved that such weapons can be used in limited wars. But these developments are all years away. In consequence, the discussion will be advanced if a little more precision is given such terms as "missiles" or "modern" or "advanced weapons." We are not distributing a generic "modern" weapon with all the virtues of flexibility in varying circumstances and of invulnerability in all-out war. But even with advances in the state of the art on our side, it will remain difficult to maintain a deterrent, especially close in under the enemy's guns.

It follows that, though a wider distribution of nuclear weapons may be inevitable, or at any rate likely, and though some countries in addition to the Soviet Union and the United States may even develop an independent deterrent, it is by no means inevitable or even very likely that the power to deter all-out thermonuclear attack will be widespread. This is true even though a minor power would not need to guarantee as large a retaliation as we in order to deter attack on itself. Unfortunately, the minor powers have smaller resources as well as poorer strategic locations.[9] Mere membership in the nuclear club might carry with it prestige, as the applicants and nominees expect, but it will be rather expensive, and in time it will be clear that it does not necessarily confer any of the expected privileges enjoyed by the two charter members. The burden of deterring a general war as distinct from limited wars is still likely to be on the United States and therefore, so far as our allies are concerned, on the military alliance.

There is one final consideration. Missiles placed near the enemy, even if they could not retaliate, would have a potent capability for striking first by surprise. And it might not be easy for the enemy to discern their purpose. The existence of such a force might be a considerable provocation and in fact a dangerous one in the sense that it would place a great burden on our deterrent force which more than ever would have to guarantee extreme risks to the attacker—worse than the risks of waiting in the face of this danger. When not coupled with the ability to strike in retaliation, such a capability might suggest—erroneously, to be sure, in the case of the democracies—an intention to strike first. If so, it would tend to provoke rather than to deter general war.

I have dealt here with only one of the functions of overseas bases: their use as a support for the strategic deterrent force. They have a variety of important military, political and economic rôles which are beyond the scope of this paper. Expenditures in connection with the construction or operation of our bases, for example, are a form of economic aid and, moreover, a form that is rather palatable to the Congress. There are other functions in a central war where their importance may be very considerable and their usefulness in a limited war might be substantial.

Indeed nothing said here should suggest that deterrence is in itself an adequate strategy. The complementary requirements of a sufficient military policy cannot be discussed in detail here. Certainly they include a more serious development of power to meet limited aggression, especially with more advanced conventional weapons than those now available. They also include more energetic provision for active and passive defenses to limit the dimensions of the catastrophe in case deterrence should fail. For example, an economically feasible shelter program might make the difference between 50,000,000 survivors and 120,000,000 survivors.

But it would be a fatal mistake to suppose that because strategic deterrence is inadequate by itself it can be dispensed with. Deterrence is not dispensable. If the picture of the world I have drawn is rather bleak, it could none the less be cataclysmically worse. Suppose both the United States and the Soviet Union had the power to destroy each others' retaliatory forces and society, given the opportunity to administer the opening blow. The situation would then be something like the old-fashioned Western gun duel. It would be extraordinarily risky for one side *not* to attempt to destroy the other, or to delay doing so, since it not only can emerge unscathed by striking first but this is the sole way it can reasonably hope to emerge at all. Evidently such a situation is extremely unstable. On the other hand, if it is clear that the aggressor too will suffer catastrophic damage in the event of his aggression, he then has strong reason not to attack, even though he can administer great damage. A protected retaliatory capability has a stabilizing influence not only in deterring rational attack, but also in offering every inducement to both powers to reduce the chance of accidental war.

The critics who feel that deterrence is "bankrupt" sometimes say that we stress deterrence too much. I believe this is quite wrong if it means that we are devoting too much effort to protect our power to retaliate; but I think it is quite right if it means that we have talked too much of a strategic threat as a substitute for many things it cannot replace.

Deterrence, accidents and disarmament

Up to now I have talked mainly about the problem of deterring general war, of making it improbable that an act of war will be undertaken deliberately, with a clear understanding of the consequences, that is, rationally. That such deterrence will not be easy to maintain in the 1960s simply expresses the proposition that a surprise thermonuclear attack might *not* be an irrational or insane act on the part of the aggressor. A deterrent strategy is aimed at a rational enemy. Without a deterrent, general war is likely. With it, however, war might still occur.

In order to reduce the risk of a rational act of aggression, we are being forced to undertake measures (increased alertness, dispersal, mobility) which, to a significant extent, increase the risk of an irrational or unintentional act of war. The accident problem is serious, and it would be a great mistake to dismiss the recent Soviet charges on this subject as simply part of the war of nerves. In a clear sense the great multiplication and spread of nuclear arms throughout the world, the drastic increase in the degree of readiness of these weapons, and the decrease in the time available for the decision on their use must inevitably raise the risk of accident. The B-47 accidents this year at Sidi Slimane and at Florence, S. C., and the recent Nike explosion are just a beginning. Though incidents of this sort are not themselves likely to trigger misunderstanding, they suggest the nature of the problem.

There are many sorts of accidents that could happen. There can be electronic or mechanical failures of the sort illustrated by the B-47 and Nike mishaps; there can be aberrations of individuals, perhaps quite low in the echelon of command; there can be miscalculations on the part of governments as to enemy intent and the meaning of ambiguous signals. Not all deterrent strategies will involve the risk of accident equally. One of the principles of selecting a strategy should be to reduce the chance of accident, wherever we can, without a corresponding increase in vulnerability to a rational surprise attack. This is the purpose of the "fail-safe" procedures for launching SAC.

These problems are also relevant to the disarmament question. The Russians, exploiting an inaccurate United Press report which suggested that SAC started en masse toward Russia in response to frequent radar "ghosts," cried out against these supposed Arctic flights. The United States response, and its sequels, stated correctly that such flights had never been undertaken except in planned exercises and would not be undertaken in response to such unreliable warning. We pointed out the importance of quick response and a high degree of readiness in the protection of the deterrent force. The nature of the fail-safe precaution was also described.

We added, however, to cap the argument, that if the Russians were really worried about surprise attack they would accept the President's "open skies" proposal. This addition, however, conceals an absurdity. Aerial photography would have its uses in a disarmament plan—for example, to check an exchange of information on the location of ground bases. However, so far as surprise is concerned, an "open skies" plan would have direct use only to discover attacks requiring much more lengthy, visible and unambiguous preparations than are likely today.[10] The very readiness of our own strategic force suggests a state of technology which outmodes the "open skies" plan as a counter to surprise attack. Not even the most advanced reconnaissance equipment can disclose an intention from 40,000 feet. Who can say what the men in the blockhouse of an I.C.B.M. base have in mind? Or, for that matter, what is the final destination of training flights or fail-safe flights starting over the Pacific or North Atlantic from staging areas?

The actions that need to be taken on our own to deter attack might usefully be complemented by bilateral agreements for inspection and reporting and, possibly, limitation of arms and of methods of operating strategic and naval air forces. But the protection of our retaliatory power remains essential; and the better the protection, the smaller the burden placed on the agreement to limit arms and modes of operation and to make them subject to inspection. Reliance on "open skies" alone to prevent surprise would invite catastrophe and the loss of power to retaliate. Such a plan is worthless for discovering a well prepared attack with I.C.B.M.s or submarine-launched missiles or a routine mass training flight whose destination could be kept ambiguous. A tremendous weight of weapons could be delivered in spite of it.

Although it is quite hopeless to look for an inspection scheme which would permit abandonment of the deterrent, this does not mean that some partial agreement on inspection and limitation might not help to reduce the chance of any sizable surprise attack. We should explore the possibilities of agreements involving limitation and inspection. But how we go about this will be conditioned by our appreciation of the problem of deterrence itself.

The critics of current policy who perceive the inadequacy of the strategy of deterrence are prominent among those urging disarmament negotiations, an end to the arms race and a reduction of tension. This is a paramount interest of some of our allies. The balance of terror theory is the basis for some of the more light-hearted suggestions: if deterrence is automatic, strategic weapons on one side cancel those of the other, and it should be easy for both sides to give them up. So James E. King, Jr., one of the most sensible writers on the subject of limited war, suggests that weapons needed for "unlimited" war are those which both sides can most easily agree to abolish, simply because "neither side can anticipate anything but disaster" from their use. "Isn't there enough stability in the 'balance of terror,' " he asks, "to justify our believing that the Russians can be trusted—within acceptable limits—to abandon the weapons whose 'utility is confined to the threat or conduct of a war of annihilation'? "[11]

Indeed, if there were no real danger of a rational attack, then accidents and the "*n*th" country problem would be the only problems. As I have indicated, they are serious problems and some sorts of limitation and inspection agreement might diminish them. But if there is to be any prospect of realistic and useful agreement, we must reject the theory of automatic deterrence. And we must bear in mind that the more extensive a disarmament agreement is, the smaller the force that a violator would have to hide in order to achieve complete domination. Most obviously, "*the abolition* of the weapons necessary in a general or 'unlimited' war" would offer the most insuperable obstacles to an inspection plan, since the violator could gain an overwhelming advantage from the concealment of even a few weapons. The need for a deterrent, in this connection too, is ineradicable.

Summary

Almost everyone seems concerned with the need to relax tension. However, relaxation of tension, which everyone thinks is good, is not easily distinguished from relaxing one's guard, which almost everyone thinks is bad. Relaxation, like Miltown, is not an end in itself. Not all danger comes from tension. To be tense where there is danger is only rational.

What can we say then, in sum, on the balance of terror theory of automatic deterrence? It is a contribution to the rhetoric rather than the logic of war in the thermonuclear age. The notion that a carefully planned surprise attack can be checkmated almost effortlessly, that, in short, we may resume our deep pre-sputnik sleep, is wrong and its nearly universal accept-ance is terribly dangerous. Though deterrence is not enough in itself, it is vital. There are two principal points.

First, deterring general war in both the early and late 1960s will be hard at best, and hardest both for ourselves and our allies wherever we use forces based near the enemy.

Second, even if we can deter general war by a strenuous and continuing effort, this will by no means be the whole of a military, much less a foreign policy. Such a policy would not of itself remove the danger of accidental outbreak or limit the damage in case deterrence failed; nor would it be at all adequate for crises on the periphery.

A generally useful way of concluding a grim argument of this kind would be to affirm that we have the resources, intelligence and courage to make the correct decisions. That is, of course, the case. And there is a good chance that we will do so. But perhaps, as a small aid toward making such decisions more likely, we should contemplate the possibility that they may *not* be made. They *are* hard, *do* involve sacrifice, *are* affected by great uncertainties and concern matters in which much is altogether unknown and much else must be hedged by secrecy; and, above all, they entail a new image of ourselves in a world of persistent danger. It is by no means *certain* that we shall meet the test.

Notes

1   I want to thank C.J. Hitch, M.W. Hoag, W.W. Kaufman, A.W. Marshall, H.S. Rowen and W.W. Taylor for suggestions in preparation of this article.
2   George F. Kennan, "A Chance to Withdraw Our Troops in Europe," *Harper's Magazine*, February 1958, p. 41.
3   P.M.S. Blackett, "Atomic Weapons and East-West Relations" (New York: Cambridge University Press, 1956), p. 32.
4   Joseph Alsop, "The New Balance of Power," *Encounter*, May 1958, p. 4. It should be added that, since these lines were written, Mr. Alsop's views have altered.
5   *The New York Times*, September 6, 1958, p. 2.
6   General Pierre M. Gallois, "A French General Analyzes Nuclear-Age Strategy," *Réalités*, Nov. 1958, p. 19; "Nuclear Aggression and National Suicide," *The Reporter*, Sept. 18, 1958, p. 23.
7   See footnote, p. 228.
8   See, for example, "NATO, A Critical Appraisal," by Gardner Patterson and Edgar S. Furniss, Jr., Princeton University Conference on NATO, Princeton, June 1957, p. 32: "Although no one pre-tended to know, the hypothesis that one-third of the striking force of the United States Strategic Air Command was in the air at all times was regarded by most as reasonable."
9   General Gallois argues that, while alliances will offer no guarantee, "a small number of bombs and a small number of carriers suffice for a threatened power to protect itself against atomic destruc-tion." (*Réalités, op. cit.*, p. 71.) His numerical illustrations give the defender some 400 underground launching sites (ibid., p. 22, and *The Reporter, op. cit.*, p. 25) and suggest that their elimination would require between 5,000 and 25,000 missiles—which is "more or less impossible"—and that in any case the aggressor would not survive the fallout from his own weapons. Whether these are large numbers of targets from the standpoint of the aggressor will depend on the accuracy, yield and

reliability of offense weapons as well as the resistance of the defender's shelters and a number of other matters not specified in the argument. General Gallois is aware that the expectation of survival depends on distance even in the ballistic missile age and that our allies are not so fortunate in this respect. Close-in missiles have better bomb yields and accuracies. Moreover, manned aircraft—with still better yields and accuracies—can be used by an aggressor here since warning of their approach is very short. Suffice it to say that the numerical advantage General Gallois cites is greatly exaggerated. Furthermore, he exaggerates the destructiveness of the retaliatory blow against the aggressor's cities by the remnants of the defender's missile force—even assuming the aggressor would take no special measures to protect his cities. But particularly for the aggressor—who does not lack warning—a civil defense program can moderate the damage done by a poorly organized attack. Finally, the suggestion that the aggressor would not survive the fall-out from his own weapons is simply in error. The rapid-decay fission products which are the major lethal problem in the locality of a surface burst are not a serious difficulty for the aggressor. The amount of the slow-decay products, strontium-90 and cesium-137, in the atmosphere would rise considerably. If nothing were done to counter it, this might, for example, increase by many times the incidence of such relatively rare diseases as bone cancer and leukemia. However, such a calamity, implying an increase of, say, 20,000 deaths per year for a nation of 200,000,000, is of an entirely different order from the catastrophe involving tens of millions of deaths, which General Gallois contemplates elsewhere. And there are measures that might reduce even this effect drastically. (See the RAND Corporation Report R-322-RC, *Report on a Study of Non-Military Defense*, July 1, 1958.)

10 Aerial reconnaissance, of course, could have an *indirect* utility here for surveying large areas to determine the number and location of observation posts needed to provide more timely warning.

11 James E. King, Jr., "Arms and Man in the Nuclear-Rocket Era," *The New Republic*, September 1, 1958.

Part V

Irregular warfare and small wars

INTRODUCTION

The six essays in this section explore irregular warfare, asymmetric warfare, and terrorism. They include pieces by some of history's most significant theorists and practitioners of irregular warfare as well as by contemporary observers of military affairs.

The first selection is an essay by T.E. Lawrence ("Lawrence of Arabia," 1888–1935) on the "Science of Guerrilla Warfare." Drawing upon his experience in the Arab Revolt (1916–1918), Lawrence contrasts insurgents, whom he characterizes as "a thing invulnerable, intangible, without front or back, drifting about like a gas," with conventional units, which he likens to plants, "immobile as a whole, firm-rooted, nourished through long stems to the head." Whereas conventional forces seek to inflict casualties on their adversaries, insurgents attempt to avoid contact: "the contest was not physical, but moral, and so battles were a mistake." Overall, he argues that a successful rebellion requires a secure base of operations and a sympathetic population. As he puts it, "rebellions can be made by 2% active in a striking force, and 98% passively sympathetic."

The second selection is from Mao Tse Tung's "Strategy in China's Revolutionary War." As a leader of the Chinese Communist Party during the Chinese Civil War, Mao (1893–1976) was both a theorist and a practitioner. Whereas Sun Tzu (see Part II) argued that a protracted war was undesirable, Mao writes that it is only through protracted operations that an insurgency can overcome its material inferiority. In Mao's formulation, a revolutionary conflict takes the form of a strategic defensive followed by a strategic offensive. As he puts it, "Strategic retreat is aimed solely at switching over to the offensive and is merely the first stage of the strategic defensive. The decisive link in the entire strategy is whether victory can be won in the stage of the counter-offensive which follows."

Drawing upon both ancient Chinese history as well as the experience of the Chinese Civil War, Mao argues that a revolutionary war is mobile warfare characterized by a lack of front lines. Insurgents need to pick their battles, engaging when they can win but avoiding battle when they cannot.

The third selection is from David Galula's *Counterinsurgency Warfare: Theory and Practice*. Galula (1919–1967), a French officer with extensive experience in post-World War II irregular warfare, writes from the perspective of those who seek to defeat an insurgency. Galula notes that whereas conventional conflicts are aimed at the destruction of enemy forces and the conquest of territory, "an insurgency is a two-dimensional war fought for the control of the population."

Galula emphasizes the asymmetric nature of an irregular war: whereas the counterinsurgent possesses an overwhelming superiority in tangible assets, the insurgent often has an advantage in intangibles such as ideology. Whereas the counterinsurgent is charged with maintaining order, the insurgent must merely disrupt it—a much less expensive proposition. Whereas the counterinsurgent is bound by law, the insurgent is free to lie, cheat, and exaggerate.

Galula argues that a successful insurgency requires a cause—which may be political, social, economic, racial, or even artificial—to rally supporters and delegitimize the counter-insurgent. A number of considerations help determine a state's susceptibility to insurgency, including the level of popular support for the regime, the quality of political leadership, the effectiveness of mechanisms to control the population, and the state's geography. The nature and level of outside support for the insurgency is also an important consideration.

The fourth selection, by Andrew Mack, explores why powerful nations lose wars to much weaker insurgents. His frame of reference is cases where an outside power intervenes against a local insurgency, as occurred with the United States in Vietnam and France in Algeria. In Mack's view, such irregular wars of intervention are marked by a fundamental asymmetry: whereas it is a total war for the insurgents, it is a limited war for the external power. The limited stakes in the conflict constrain both the amount of force the intervening power is willing to use as well as the duration of the intervention. In these cases, he argues, "success for the insurgents arose not from a military victory on the ground . . . but rather from the progressive attrition of their opponents' *political* capability to wage war. In such asymmetric conflicts, insurgents may gain political victory from a situation of military stalemate *or even defeat*." If the external power's will to persevere is destroyed, its military capability becomes irrelevant. Specifically, by imposing steady incremental costs on their adversary, insurgents shift the balance of power in favour of the anti-war faction in the intervening state.

The fifth selection, by David J. Kilcullen of the Australian Land Warfare Studies Center, argues that the so-called Global War on Terrorism should be viewed as a campaign against an Islamic insurgency that operates globally, regionally, and locally. He argues that although counterinsurgency is a valuable lens through which to view the struggle, the global nature of the current insurgency calls for a new approach, which he terms "disaggregation." Such a strategy would seek to break the links that allow jihadists to operate worldwide.

The final piece, by Peter R. Neumann and M.L.R. Smith, both of King's College London, explores terrorism as a military strategy. They argue that strategic terrorism follows a distinctive modus operandi: alienating the authorities from their citizens, inducing the government to respond in a manner that favors the insurgents, and exploiting the emotional impact of the violence to establish legitimacy. Such a strategy is, however, based on assumptions about the behavior of the target population and government that are not always warranted. Strategic terrorism is therefore often an unreliable strategy.

Study questions

1. To what extent are Mao's theories of revolutionary warfare applicable in the early twenty-first century?
2. What are the similarities and differences between insurgency and terrorism?
3. What insights does strategic theory provide in thinking about irregular warfare?
4. In what ways does Kilcullen's "global Islamic jihad" resemble traditional insurgencies, and in what ways does it differ?

Further reading

Arreguin-Toft, Ivan, *How the Weak Win Wars: A Theory of Asymmetric Conflict* (Cambridge: Cambridge University Press, 2005).

Kitson, Frank, *Low-Intensity Operations: Subversion, Insurgency, and Peacekeeping.* (Mechanicsburg, PA: Stackpole Books, 1971).

Mahnken, Thomas G., "Why the Weak Win: Strong Powers, Weak Powers and the Logic of Strategy," in Bradford A. Lee and Karl F. Walling (eds), *Strategic Logic and Political Rationality* (London: Frank Cass, 2003).

Trinquier, Roger, *Modern Warfare: A French View of Counterinsurgency* (Fort Leavenworth, KS: US Army Command and General Staff College, 1985).

13 Science of guerrilla warfare

T.E. Lawrence

This study of the science of guerrilla, or irregular, warfare is based on the concrete experience of the Arab Revolt against the Turks 1916–1918. But the historical example in turn gains value from the fact that its course was guided by the practical application of the theories here set forth.

The Arab Revolt began in June, 1916, with an attack by the half-armed and inexperienced tribesmen upon the Turkish garrisons in Medina and about Mecca. They met with no success, and after a few days' effort withdrew out of range and began a blockade. This method forced the early surrender of Mecca, the more remote of the two centres. Medina, however, was linked by railway to the Turkish main army in Syria, and the Turks were able to reinforce the garrison there. The Arab forces which had attacked it then fell back gradually and took up a position across the main road to Mecca.

At this point the campaign stood still for many weeks. The Turks prepared to send an expeditionary force to Mecca, to crush the revolt at its source, and accordingly moved an army corps to Medina by rail. Thence they began to advance down the main western road from Medina to Mecca, a distance of about 250 miles. The first 50 miles were easy, then came a belt of hills 20 miles wide, in which were Feisal's Arab tribesmen standing on the defensive: next a level stretch, for 70 miles along the coastal plain to Rabegh, rather more than half-way. Rabegh is a little fort on the Red Sea, with good anchorage for ships, and because of its situation was regarded as the key to Mecca. Here lay Sherif Ali, Feisal's eldest brother, with more tribal forces, and the beginning of an Arab regular army, formed from officers and men of Arab blood who had served in the Turkish Army. As was almost inevitable in view of the general course of military thinking since Napoleon, the soldiers of all countries looked only to the regulars to win the war. Military opinion was obsessed by the dictum of Foch that the ethic of modern war is to seek for the enemy army, his centre of power, and destroy it in battle. Irregulars would not attack positions and so they were regarded as incapable of forcing a decision.

While these Arab regulars were still being trained, the Turks suddenly began their advance on Mecca. They broke through the hills in 24 hours, and so proved the second theorem of irregular war—namely, that irregular troops are as unable to defend a point or line as they are to attack it. This lesson was received without gratitude, for the Turkish success put the Rabegh force in a critical position, and it was not capable of repelling the attack of a single battalion, much less of a corps.

In the emergency it occurred to the author that perhaps the virtue of irregulars lay in depth, not in face, and that it had been the threat of attack by them upon the Turkish northern flank which had made the enemy hesitate for so long. The actual Turkish flank ran from their front line to Medina, a distance of some 50 miles: but, if the Arab force moved towards the Hejaz railway behind Medina, it might stretch its threat (and, accordingly, the enemy's flank) as far, potentially, as Damascus 800 miles away to the north. Such a move would force the Turks to the defensive, and the Arab force might regain the initiative. Anyhow, it seemed the only chance, and so, in January 1917, Feisal's tribesmen turned their backs on Mecca, Rabegh and the Turks, and marched away north 200 miles to Wejh.

This eccentric movement acted like a charm. The Arabs did nothing concrete, but their march recalled the Turks (who were almost into Rabegh) all the way back to Medina. There, one half of the Turkish force took up the entrenched position about the city, which it held until after the Armistice. The other half was distributed along the railway to defend it against the Arab threat. For the rest of the war the Turks stood on the defensive and the Arab tribesmen won advantage over advantage till, when peace came, they had taken 35,000 prisoners, killed and wounded and worn out about as many, and occupied 100,000 square miles of the enemy's territory, at little loss to themselves. However, although Wejh was the turning point its significance was not yet realized. For the moment the move thither was regarded merely as a preliminary to cutting the railway in order to take Medina, the Turkish headquarters and main garrison.

Strategy and tactics

However, the author was unfortunately as much in charge of the campaign as he pleased, and lacking a training in command sought to find an immediate equation between past study of military theory and the present movements—as a guide to, and an intellectual basis for, future action. The text books gave the aim in war as "the destruction of the organized forces of the enemy" by "the one process battle." Victory could only be purchased by blood. This was a hard saying, as the Arabs had no organized forces, and so a Turkish Foch would have no aim: and the Arabs would not endure casualties, so that an Arab Clausewitz could not buy his victory. These wise men must be talking metaphors, for the Arabs were indubitably winning their war . . . and further reflection pointed to the deduction that they had actually won it. They were in occupation of 99% of the Hejaz. The Turks were welcome to the other fraction till peace or doomsday showed them the futility of clinging to the window pane. This part of the war was over, so why bother about Medina? The Turks sat in it on the defensive, immobile, eating for food the transport animals which were to have moved them to Mecca, but for which there was no pasture in their now restricted lines. They were harmless sitting there; if taken prisoner, they would entail the cost of food and guards in Egypt, if driven out northward into Syria, they would join the main army blocking the British in Sinai. On all counts they were best where they were, and they valued Medina and wanted to keep it. Let them!

This seemed unlike the ritual of war of which Foch had been priest, and so it seemed that there was a difference of kind. Foch called his modern war "absolute." In it two nations professing incompatible philosophies set out to try them in the light of force. A struggle of two immaterial principles could only end when the supporters of one had no more means of resistance. An opinion can be argued with: a conviction is best shot. The logical end of a war of creeds is the final destruction of one, and Salammbo the classical textbook-instance. These were the lines of the struggle between France and Germany, but not, perhaps, between Germany and England, for all efforts to make the British soldier hate the enemy simply made him hate war. Thus the "absolute war" seemed only a variety of war; and beside it other sorts could be discerned, as Clausewitz had numbered them, personal wars for dynastic reasons, expulsive wars for party reasons, commercial wars for trading reasons.

Now the Arab aim was unmistakably geographical, to occupy all Arabic-speaking lands in Asia. In the doing of it Turks might be killed, yet "killing Turks" would never be an excuse or aim. If they would go quietly, the war would end. If not, they must be driven out: but at the cheapest possible price, since the Arabs were fighting for freedom, a pleasure only to be tasted by a man alive. The next task was to analyse the process, both from the point of view of strategy, the aim in war, the synoptic regard which sees everything by the standard of the whole, and from the point of view called tactics, the means towards the strategic end, the steps of its staircase. In each were found the same elements, one algebraical, one biological, a third psychological. The first seemed a pure science, subject to the laws of mathematics, without humanity. It dealt with known invariables, fixed conditions, space and time, inorganic things like hills and climates and railways, with mankind in type-masses too great for individual variety, with all artificial aids, and the extensions given our faculties by mechanical invention. It was essentially formulable.

In the Arab case the algebraic factor would take first account of the area to be conquered. A casual calculation indicated perhaps 140,000 square miles. How would the Turks defend all that—no doubt by a trench line across the bottom, if the Arabs were an army attacking with banners displayed ... but suppose they were an influence, a thing invulnerable, intangible, without front or back, drifting about like a gas? Armies were like plants, immobile as a whole, firm-rooted, nourished through long stems to the head. The Arabs might be a vapour, blowing where they listed. It seemed that a regular soldier might be helpless without a target. He would own the ground he sat on, and what he could poke his rifle at. The next step was to estimate how many posts they would need to contain this attack in depth, sedition putting up her head in every unoccupied one of these 100,000 square miles. They would have need of a fortified post every four square miles, and a post could not be less than 20 men. The Turks would need 600,000 men to meet the combined ill wills of all the local Arab people. They had 100,000 men available. It seemed that the assets in this sphere were with the Arabs, and climate, railways, deserts, technical weapons could also be attached to their interests. The Turk was stupid and would believe that rebellion was absolute, like war, and deal with it on the analogy of absolute warfare.

Humanity in battle

So much for the mathematical element; the second factor was biological, the breaking-point, life and death, or better, wear and tear. Bionomics seemed a good name for it. The war-philosophers had properly made it an art, and had elevated one item in it, "effusion of blood," to the height of a principle. It became humanity in battle, an art touching every side of our corporal being. There was a line of variability (man) running through all its estimates. Its components were sensitive and illogical, and generals guarded themselves by the device of a reserve, the significant medium of their art. Goltz had said that when you know the enemy's strength, and he is fully deployed, then you know enough to dispense with a reserve. But this is never. There is always the possibility of accident, of some flaw in materials, present in the general's mind: and the reserve is unconsciously held to meet it. There is a "felt" element in troops, not expressible in figures, and the greatest commander is he whose intuitions most nearly happen. Nine-tenths of tactics are certain, and taught in books: but the irrational tenth is like the kingfisher flashing across the pool and that is the test of generals. It can only be ensued by instinct, sharpened by thought practising the stroke so often that at the crisis it is as natural as a reflex.

Yet to limit the art to humanity seemed an undue narrowing down. It must apply to materials as much as to organisms. In the Turkish Army materials were scarce and precious, men more plentiful than equipment. Consequently the cue should be to destroy not the army but the materials. The death of a Turkish bridge or rail, machine or gun, or high explosive was more profitable than the death of a Turk. The Arab army just then was equally chary of men and materials: of men because they being irregulars were not units, but individuals, and an individual casualty is like a pebble dropped in water: each may make only a brief hole, but rings of sorrow widen out from them. The Arab army could not afford casualties. Materials were easier to deal with. Hence its obvious duty to make itself superior in some one branch, guncotton or machine guns, or whatever could be most decisive. Foch had laid down the maxim, applying it to men, of being superior at the critical point and moment of attack. The Arab army might apply it to materials, and be superior in equipment in one dominant moment or respect.

For both men and things it might try to give Foch's doctrine a negative twisted side, for cheapness' sake, and be weaker than the enemy everywhere except in one point or matter. Most wars are wars of contact, both forces striving to keep in touch to avoid tactical surprise. The Arab war should be a war of detachment: to contain the enemy by the silent threat of a vast unknown desert, not disclosing themselves till the moment of attack. This attack need be only nominal, directed not against his men, but against his materials: so it should not seek for his main strength or his weaknesses, but for his most accessible material. In railway cutting this would be usually an empty stretch of rail. This was a tactical success. From this theory came to be developed ultimately an unconscious habit of never engaging the enemy at all. This chimed with the numerical plea of never giving the enemy's soldier a target. Many Turks on the Arab front had no chance all the war to fire a shot, and correspondingly the Arabs were never on the defensive, except by rare accident. The corollary of such a rule was perfect "intelligence," so that plans could be made in complete certainty. The chief agent had to be the general's head (de Feuquière said this first), and his knowledge had to be faultless, leaving no room for chance. The headquarters of the Arab army probably took more pains in this service than any other staff.

The crowd in action

The third factor in command seemed to be the psychological, that science (Xenophon called it diathetic) of which our propaganda is a stained and ignoble part. It concerns the crowd, the adjustment of spirit to the point where it becomes fit to exploit in action. It considers the capacity for mood of the men, their complexities and mutability, and the cultivation of what in them profits the intention. The command of the Arab army had to arrange their men's minds in order of battle, just as carefully and as formally as other officers arranged their bodies: and not only their own men's minds, though them first; the minds of the enemy, so far as it could reach them; and thirdly, the mind of the nation supporting it behind the firing-line, and the mind of the hostile nation waiting the verdict, and the neutrals looking on.

It was the ethical in war, and the process on which the command mainly depended for victory on the Arab front. The printing press is the greatest weapon in the armoury of the modern commander, and the commanders of the Arab army being amateurs in the art, began their war in the atmosphere of the twentieth century, and thought of their weapons without prejudice, not distinguishing one from another socially. The regular officer has the tradition of 40 generations of serving soldiers behind him, and to him the old weapons are the most honoured. The Arab command had seldom to concern itself with what its men did, but much with what they thought, and to it the diathetic was more than half command. In

Europe it was set a little aside and entrusted to men outside the General Staff. But the Arab army was so weak physically that it could not let the metaphysical weapon rust unused. It had won a province when the civilians in it had been taught to die for the ideal of freedom: the presence or absence of the enemy was a secondary matter.

These reasonings showed that the idea of assaulting Medina, or even of starving it quickly into surrender, was not in accord with the best strategy. Rather, let the enemy stay in Medina, and in every other harmless place, in the largest numbers. If he showed a disposition to evacuate too soon, as a step to concentrating in the small area which his numbers could dominate effectively, then the Arab army would have to try and restore his confidence, not harshly, but by reducing its enterprises against him. The ideal was to keep his railway just working, but only just, with the maximum of loss and discomfort to him.

The Turkish army was an accident, not a target. Our true strategic aim was to seek its weakest link, and bear only on that till time made the mass of it fall. The Arab army must impose the longest possible passive defence on the Turks (this being the most materially expensive form of war) by extending its own front to the maximum. Tactically it must develop a highly mobile, highly equipped type of force, of the smallest size, and use it successively at distributed points of the Turkish line, to make the Turks reinforce their occupying posts beyond the economic minimum of 20 men. The power of this striking force would not be reckoned merely by its strength. The ratio between number and area determined the character of the war, and by having five times the mobility of the Turks the Arabs could be on terms with them with one-fifth their number.

Range over force

Success was certain, to be proved by paper and pencil as soon as the proportion of space and number had been learned. The contest was not physical, but moral, and so battles were a mistake. All that could be won in a battle was the ammunition the enemy fired off. Napoleon had said it was rare to find generals willing to fight battles. The curse of this war was that so few could do anything else. Napoleon had spoken in angry reaction against the excessive finesse of the eighteenth century, when men almost forgot that war gave licence to murder. Military thought had been swinging out on his dictum for 100 years, and it was time to go back a bit again. Battles are impositions on the side which believes itself weaker, made unavoidable either by lack of land-room, or by the need to defend a material property dearer than the lives of soldiers. The Arabs had nothing material to lose, so they were to defend nothing and to shoot nothing. Their cards were speed and time, not hitting power, and these gave them strategical rather than tactical strength. Range is more to strategy than force. The invention of bully-beef had modified land-war more profoundly than the invention of gunpowder.

The British military authorities did not follow all these arguments, but gave leave for their practical application to be tried. Accordingly the Arab forces went off first to Akaba and took it easily. Then they took Tafileh and the Dead Sea; then Azrak and Deraa, and finally Damascus, all in successive stages worked out consciously on these theories. The process was to set up ladders of tribes, which should provide a safe and comfortable route from the sea-bases (Yenbo, Wejh or Akaba) to the advanced bases of operation. These were sometimes 300 miles away, a long distance in lands without railways or roads, but made short for the Arab Army by an assiduous cultivation of desert-power, control by camel parties of the desolate and unmapped wilderness which fills up all the centre of Arabia, from Mecca to Aleppo and Baghdad.

The desert and the sea

In character these operations were like naval warfare, in their mobility, their ubiquity, their independence of bases and communications, in their ignoring of ground features, of strategic areas, of fixed directions, of fixed points. "He who commands the sea is at great liberty, and may take as much or as little of the war as he will": he who commands the desert is equally fortunate. Camel raiding-parties, self-contained like ships, could cruise securely along the enemy's land-frontier, just out of sight of his posts along the edge of cultivation, and tap or raid into his lines where it seemed fittest or easiest or most profitable, with a sure retreat always behind them into an element which the Turks could not enter.

Discrimination of what point of the enemy organism to disarrange came with practice. The tactics were always tip and run, not pushes, but strokes. The Arab army never tried to maintain or improve an advantage, but to move off and strike again somewhere else. It used the smallest force in the quickest time at the farthest place. To continue the action till the enemy had changed his dispositions to resist it would have been to break the spirit of the fundamental rule of denying him targets.

The necessary speed and range were attained by the frugality of the desert men, and their efficiency on camels. In the heat of summer Arabian camels will do about 250 miles comfortably between drinks: and this represented three days' vigorous marching. This radius was always more than was needed, for wells are seldom more than 100 miles apart. The equipment of the raiding parties aimed at simplicity, with nevertheless a technical superiority over the Turks in the critical department. Quantities of light machine guns were obtained from Egypt for use not as machine guns, but as automatic rifles, snipers' tools, by men kept deliberately in ignorance of their mechanism, so that the speed of action would not be hampered by attempts at repair. Another special feature was high explosives, and nearly everyone in the revolt was qualified by rule of thumb experience in demolition work.

Armoured cars

On some occasions tribal raids were strengthened by armoured cars, manned by Englishmen. Armoured cars, once they have found a possible track, can keep up with a camel party. On the march to Damascus, when nearly 400 miles off their base, they were first maintained by a baggage train of petrol-laden camels, and afterwards from the air. Cars are magnificent fighting machines, and decisive whenever they can come into action on their own conditions. But though each has for main principle that of "fire in movement," yet the tactical employments of cars and camel-corps are so different that their use in joint operations is difficult. It was found demoralizing to both to use armoured and unarmoured cavalry together.

The distribution of the raiding parties was unorthodox. It was impossible to mix or combine tribes, since they disliked or distrusted one another. Likewise the men of one tribe could not be used in the territory of another. In consequence, another canon of orthodox strategy was broken by following the principle of the widest distribution of force, in order to have the greatest number of raids on hand at once, and fluidity was added to speed by using one district on Monday, another on Tuesday, a third on Wednesday. This much reinforced the natural mobility of the Arab army, giving it priceless advantages in pursuit, for the force renewed itself with fresh men in every new tribal area, and so maintained its pristine energy. Maximum disorder was, in a real sense, its equilibrium.

An undisciplined army

The internal economy of the raiding parties was equally curious. Maximum irregularity and articulation were the aims. Diversity threw the enemy intelligence off the track. By the regular organization in identical battalions and divisions information builds itself up, until the presence of a corps can be inferred on corpses from three companies. The Arabs, again, were serving a common ideal, without tribal emulation, and so could not hope for any *esprit de corps*. Soldiers are made a caste either by being given great pay and rewards in money, uniform or political privileges; or, as in England, by being made outcasts, cut off from the mass of their fellow citizens. There have been many armies enlisted voluntarily: there have been few armies serving voluntarily under such trying conditions, for so long a war as the Arab revolt. Any of the Arabs could go home whenever the conviction failed him. Their only contract was honour.

Consequently the Arab army had no discipline, in the sense in which it is restrictive, submergent of individuality, the Lowest Common Denominator of men. In regular armies in peace it means the limit of energy attainable by everybody present: it is the hunt not of an average, but of an absolute, a 100-per-cent standard, in which the 99 stronger men are played down to the level of the worst. The aim is to render the unit a unit, and the man a type, in order that their effort shall be calculable, their collective output even in grain and in bulk. The deeper the discipline, the lower the individual efficiency, and the more sure the performance. It is a deliberate sacrifice of capacity in order to reduce the uncertain element, the bionomic factor, in enlisted humanity, and its accompaniment is *compound* or social war, that form in which the fighting man has to be the product of the multiplied exertions of long hierarchy, from workshop to supply unit, which maintains him in the field.

The Arab war, reacting against this, was *simple* and individual. Every enrolled man served in the line of battle, and was self-contained. There were no lines of communication or labour troops. It seemed that in this articulated warfare, the sum yielded by single men would be at least equal to the product of a compound system of the same strength, and it was certainly easier to adjust to tribal life and manners, given elasticity and understanding on the part of the commanding officers. Fortunately for its chances nearly every young Englishman has the roots of eccentricity in him. Only a sprinkling were employed, not more than one per 1,000 of the Arab troops. A larger proportion would have created friction, just because they were foreign bodies (pearls if you please) in the oyster: and those who were present controlled by influence and advice, by their superior knowledge, not by an extraneous authority.

The practice was, however, not to employ in the firing line the greater numbers which the adoption of a "simple" system made available theoretically. Instead, they were used in relay: otherwise the attack would have become too extended. Guerrillas must be allowed liberal work-room. In irregular war if two men are together one is being wasted. The moral strain of isolated action makes this simple form of war very hard on the individual soldier, and exacts from him special initiative, endurance and enthusiasm. Here the ideal was to make action a series of single combats to make the ranks a happy alliance of commanders-in-chief. The value of the Arab army depended entirely on quality, not on quantity. The members had to keep always cool, for the excitement of a blood-lust would impair their science, and their victory depended on a just use of speed, concealment, accuracy of fire. Guerrilla war is far more intellectual than a bayonet charge.

The exact science of guerrilla warfare

By careful persistence, kept strictly within its strength and following the spirit of these theories, the Arab army was able eventually to reduce the Turks to helplessness, and complete victory seemed to be almost within sight when General Allenby, by his immense stroke in Palestine, threw the enemy's main forces into hopeless confusion and put an immediate end to the Turkish war. His too-greatness deprived the Arab revolt of the opportunity of following to the end the dictum of Saxe that a war might be won without fighting battles. But it can at least be said that its leaders worked by his light for two years, and the work stood. This is a pragmatic argument that cannot be wholly derided. The experiment, although not complete, strengthened the belief that irregular war or rebellion could be proved to be an exact science, and an inevitable success, granted certain factors and if pursued along certain lines.

Here is the thesis: Rebellion must have an unassailable base, something guarded not merely from attack, but from the fear of it: such a base as the Arab revolt had in the Red Sea ports, the desert, or in the minds of men converted to its creed. It must have a sophisticated alien enemy, in the form of a disciplined army of occupation too small to fulfil the doctrine of acreage: too few to adjust number to space, in order to dominate the whole area effectively from fortified posts. It must have a friendly population, not actively friendly, but sympathetic to the point of not betraying rebel movements to the enemy. Rebellions can be made by 2% active in a striking force, and 98% passively sympathetic. The few active rebels must have the qualities of speed and endurance, ubiquity and independence of arteries of supply. They must have the technical equipment to destroy or paralyze the enemy's organized communications, for irregular war is fairly Willisen's definition of strategy, "the study of communication," in its extreme degree, of attack where the enemy is not. In 50 words: Granted mobility, security (in the form of denying targets to the enemy), time and doctrine (the idea to convert every subject to friendliness), victory will rest with the insurgents, for the algebraical factors are in the end decisive, and against them perfections of means and spirit struggle quite in vain.

14 Problems of strategy in China's civil war

Mao Tse Tung

The four principal characteristics of China's revolutionary war are: a vast semi-colonial country which is unevenly developed politically and economically and which has gone through a great revolution; a big and powerful enemy; a small and weak Red Army; and the agrarian revolution. These characteristics determine the line for guiding China's revolutionary war as well as many of its strategic and tactical principles. It follows from the first and fourth characteristics that it is possible for the Chinese Red Army to grow and defeat its enemy. It follows from the second and third characteristics that it is impossible for the Chinese Red Army to grow very rapidly or defeat its enemy quickly; in other words, the war will be protracted and may even be lost if it is mishandled.

These are the two aspects of China's revolutionary war. They exist simultaneously, that is, there are favourable factors and there are difficulties. This is the fundamental law of China's revolutionary war, from which many other laws ensue. The history of our ten years of war has proved the validity of this law. He who has eyes but fails to see this fundamental law cannot direct China's revolutionary war, cannot lead the Red Army to victories.

It is clear that we must correctly settle all the following matters of principle:

> Determine our strategic orientation correctly, oppose adventurism when on the offensive, oppose conservatism when on the defensive, and oppose flight-ism when shifting from one place to another.
>
> Oppose guerrilla-ism in the Red Army, while recognizing the guerrilla character of its operations.
>
> Oppose protracted campaigns and a strategy of quick decision, and uphold the strategy of protracted war and campaigns of quick decision.
>
> Oppose fixed battle lines and positional warfare, and favour fluid battle lines and mobile warfare.
>
> Oppose fighting merely to rout the enemy, and uphold fighting to annihilate the enemy.
>
> Oppose the strategy of striking with two "fists" in two directions at the same time, and uphold the strategy of striking with one "fist" in one direction at one time.[1]
>
> Oppose the principle of maintaining one large rear area, and uphold the principle of small rear areas.
>
> Oppose an absolutely centralized command, and favour a relatively centralized command.
>
> Oppose the purely military viewpoint and the ways of roving rebels,[2] and recognize that the Red Army is a propagandist and organizer of the Chinese revolution.
>
> Oppose bandit ways,[3] and uphold strict political discipline.

Oppose warlord ways, and favour both democracy within proper limits and an authoritative discipline in the army.

Oppose an incorrect, sectarian policy on cadres, and uphold the correct policy on cadres.

Oppose the policy of isolation, and affirm the policy of winning over all possible allies.

Oppose keeping the Red Army at its old stage, and strive to develop it to a new stage.

Our present discussion of the problems of strategy is intended to elucidate these matters carefully in the light of the historical experience gained in China's ten years of bloody revolutionary war.

"Encirclement and suppression" and counter-campaigns against it – the main pattern of China's civil war

In the ten years since our guerrilla war began, every independent Red guerrilla unit, every Red Army and every revolutionary base area has been regularly subjected by the enemy to "encirclement and suppression". The enemy looks upon the Red Army as a monster and seeks to capture it the moment it shows itself. He is forever pursuing the Red Army and forever trying to encircle it. For ten years this pattern of warfare has not changed, and unless the civil war gives place to a national war, the pattern will remain the same till the day the enemy becomes the weaker contestant and the Red Army the stronger.

The Red Army's operations take the form of counter-campaigns against "encirclement and suppression". For us victory means chiefly victory in combating "encirclement and suppression", that is, strategic victory and victories in campaigns. The fight against each "encirclement and suppression" campaign constitutes a counter-campaign, which usually comprises several or even scores of battles, big and small. Until an "encirclement and suppression" campaign has been basically smashed, one cannot speak of strategic victory or of victory in the counter-campaign as a whole, even though many battles may have been won. The history of the Red Army's decade of war is a history of counter-campaigns against "encirclement and suppression".

In the enemy's "encirclement and suppression" campaigns and the Red Army's counter-campaigns against them, the two forms of fighting, offensive and defensive, are both employed, and here there is no difference from any other war, ancient or modern, in China or elsewhere. The special characteristic of China's civil war, however, is the repeated alternation of the two forms over a long period of time. In each "encirclement and suppression" campaign, the enemy employs the offensive against the Red Army's defensive, and the Red Army employs the defensive against his offensive; this is the first stage of a counter-campaign against "encirclement and suppression". Then the enemy employs the defensive against the Red Army's offensive, and the Red Army employs the offensive against his defensive; this is the second stage of the counter-campaign. Every "encirclement and suppression" campaign has these two stages, and they alternate over a long period.

By repeated alternation over a long period we mean the repetition of this pattern of warfare and these forms of fighting. This is a fact obvious to everybody. An "encirclement and suppression" campaign and a counter-campaign against it – such is the repeated pattern of the war. In each campaign the alternation of the forms of fighting consists of the first stage in which the enemy employs the offensive against our defensive and we meet his offensive with our defensive, and of the second stage in which the enemy employs the defensive against our offensive and we meet his defensive with our offensive.

As for the content of a campaign or of a battle, it does not consist of mere repetition but is different each time. This, too, is a fact and obvious to everybody. In this connection it has become a rule that with each campaign and each counter-campaign, the scale becomes larger, the situation more complicated and the fighting more intense.

But this does not mean that there are no ups and downs. After the enemy's fifth "encirclement and suppression" campaign, the Red Army was greatly weakened, and all the base areas in the south were lost. Having shifted to the Northwest, the Red Army now no longer holds a vital position threatening the internal enemy as it did in the south, and as a result the scale of the "encirclement and suppression" campaigns has become smaller, the situation simpler and the fighting less intense.

What constitutes a defeat for the Red Army? Strategically speaking, there is a defeat only when a counter-campaign against "encirclement and suppression" fails completely, but even then the defeat is only partial and temporary. For only the total destruction of the Red Army would constitute complete defeat in the civil war; but this has never happened. The loss of extensive base areas and the shift of the Red Army constituted a temporary and partial defeat, not a final and complete one, even though this partial defeat entailed losing 90 per cent of the Party membership, of the armed forces and of the base areas. We call this shift the continuation of our defensive and the enemy's pursuit the continuation of his offensive. That is to say, in the course of the struggle between the enemy's "encirclement and suppression" and our counter-campaign we allowed our defensive to be broken by the enemy's offensive instead of turning from the defensive to the offensive; and so our defensive turned into a retreat and the enemy's offensive into a pursuit. But when the Red Army reached a new area, as for example when we shifted from Kiangsi Province and various other regions to Shensi Province, the repetition of "encirclement and suppression" campaigns began afresh. That is why we say that the Red Army's strategic retreat (the Long March) was a continuation of its strategic defensive and the enemy's strategic pursuit was a continuation of his strategic offensive.

In the Chinese civil war, as in all other wars, ancient or modern, in China or abroad, there are only two basic forms of fighting, attack and defence. The special characteristic of China's civil war consists in the long-term repetition of "encirclement and suppression" campaigns and of our counter-campaigns together with the long-term alternation of the two forms of fighting, attack and defence, with the inclusion of the phenomenon of the great strategic shift of more than ten thousand kilometres (the Long March).[4]

A defeat for the enemy is much the same. It is a strategic defeat for the enemy when his "encirclement and suppression" campaign is broken and our defensive becomes an offensive, when the enemy turns to the defensive and has to reorganize before launching another "encirclement and suppression" campaign. The enemy has not had to make a strategic shift of more than ten thousand kilometres such as we have, because he rules the whole country and is much stronger than we are. But there have been partial shifts of his forces. Sometimes, enemy forces in White strongholds encircled by the Red Army in some base areas have broken through our encirclement and withdrawn to the White areas to organize new offensives. If the civil war is prolonged and the Red Army's victories become more extensive, there will be more of this sort of thing. But the enemy cannot achieve the same results as the Red Army, because he does not have the help of the people and because his officers and men are not united. If he were to imitate the Red Army's long-distance shift, he would certainly be wiped out.

In the period of the Li Li-san line in 1930, Comrade Li Li-san failed to understand the protracted nature of China's civil war and for that reason did not perceive the law that in the course of this war there is repetition over a long period of "encirclement and suppression" campaigns and of their defeat (by that time there had already been three in the Hunan-Kiangsi border area and two in Fukien). Hence, in an attempt to achieve rapid victory for the revolution, he ordered the Red Army, which was then still in its infancy, to attack Wuhan, and also ordered a nation-wide armed uprising. Thus he committed the error of "Left" opportunism.

Likewise the "Left" opportunists of 1931–34 did not believe in the law of the repetition of "encirclement and suppression" campaigns. Some responsible comrades in our base area along the Hupeh-Honan-Anhwei border held an "auxiliary force" theory, maintaining that the Kuomintang army had become merely an auxiliary force after the defeat of its third "encirclement and suppression" campaign and that the imperialists themselves would have to take the field as the main force in further attacks on the Red Army. The strategy based on this estimate was that the Red Army should attack Wuhan. In principle, this fitted in with the views of those comrades in Kiangsi who called for a Red Army attack on Nanchang, were against the work of linking up the base areas and the tactics of luring the enemy in deep, regarded the seizure of the capital and other key cities of a province as the starting point for victory in that province, and held that "the fight against the fifth 'encirclement and suppression" campaign represents the decisive battle between the road of revolution and the road of colonialism". This "Left" opportunism was the source of the wrong line adopted in the struggles against the fourth "encirclement and suppression" campaign in the Hupeh-Honan-Anhwei border area and in those against the fifth in the Central Base Area in Kiangsi; and it rendered the Red Army helpless before these fierce enemy campaigns and brought enormous losses to the Chinese revolution.

The view that the Red Army should under no circumstances adopt defensive methods was directly related to this "Left" opportunism, which denied the repetition of "encirclement and suppression" campaigns, and it, too, was entirely erroneous.

The proposition that a revolution or a revolutionary war is an offensive is of course correct. A revolution or a revolutionary war in its emergence and growth from a small force to a big force, from lack of political power to the seizure of political power, from lack of a Red Army to the creation of a Red Army, and from lack of revolutionary base areas to their establish-ment, must be on the offensive and cannot be conservative; and tendencies to conservatism must be opposed.

The only entirely correct proposition is that a revolution or a revolutionary war is an offensive but also involves defence and retreat. To defend in order to attack, to retreat in order to advance, to move against the flanks in order to move against the front, and to take a roundabout route in order to get on to the direct route – this is inevitable in the process of development of many phenomena, especially military movements.

Of the two propositions stated above, the first may be correct in the political sphere, but it is incorrect when transposed to the military sphere. Moreover, it is correct politically only in one situation (when the revolution is advancing), but incorrect when transposed to another situation (when the revolution is in retreat, in general retreat as in Russia in 1906[5] and in China in 1927, or in partial retreat as in Russia at the time of the Treaty of Brest-Litovsk in 1918).[6] Only the second proposition is entirely correct and true. The "Left" opportunism of 1931–34, which mechanically opposed the employment of defensive military measures, was nothing but infantile thinking.

When will the pattern of repeated "encirclement and suppression" campaigns come to an end? In my opinion, if the civil war is prolonged, this repetition will cease when a funda-mental change takes place in the balance of forces. It will cease when the Red Army has become stronger than the enemy. Then we shall be encircling and suppressing the enemy and he will be resorting to counter-campaigns, but political and military conditions will not allow him to attain the same position as that of the Red Army in its counter-campaigns. It can be definitely asserted that by then the pattern of repeated "encirclement and suppression" campaigns will have largely, if not completely, come to an end.

The strategic defensive

Under this heading I would like to discuss the following problems: (1) active and passive defence; (2) preparations for combating "encirclement and suppression" campaigns; (3) strategic retreat; (4) strategic counter-offensive; (5) starting the counter-offensive; (6) concentration of troops; (7) mobile warfare; (8) war of quick decision; and (9) war of annihilation.

Active and passive defence

Why do we begin by discussing defence? After the failure of China's first national united front of 1924–27, the revolution became a most intense and ruthless class war. While the enemy ruled the whole country, we had only small armed forces; consequently, from the very beginning we have had to wage a bitter struggle against his "encirclement and suppression" campaigns. Our offensives have been closely linked with our efforts to break these "encirclement and suppression" campaigns, and our fate depends entirely on whether or not we are able to break them. The process of breaking an "encirclement and suppression" campaign is usually circuitous and not as direct as one would wish. The primary problem, and a serious one too, is how to conserve our strength and await an opportunity to defeat the enemy. Therefore, the strategic defensive is the most complicated and most important problem facing the Red Army in its operations.

In our ten years of war two deviations often arose with regard to the strategic defensive; one was to belittle the enemy, the other was to be terrified of the enemy.

As a result of belittling the enemy, many guerrilla units suffered defeat, and on several occasions the Red Army was unable to break the enemy's "encirclement and suppression".

When the revolutionary guerrilla units first came into existence, their leaders often failed to assess the enemy's situation and our own correctly. Because they had been successful in organizing sudden armed uprisings in certain places or mutinies among the White troops, they saw only the momentarily favourable circumstances, or failed to see the grave situation actually confronting them, and so usually understimated the enemy. Moreover, they had no understanding of their own weaknesses (*i.e.*, lack of experience and smallness of forces). It was an objective fact that the enemy was strong and we were weak, and yet some people refused to give it thought, talked only of attack but never of defence or retreat, thus mentally disarming themselves in the matter of defence, and hence misdirected their actions. Many guerrilla units were defeated on this account.

Examples in which the Red Army, for this reason, failed to break the enemy's "encirclement and suppression" campaigns were its defeat in 1928 in the Haifeng-Lufeng area of Kwangtung Province,[7] and its loss of freedom of action in 1932 in the fourth counter-campaign against the enemy's "encirclement and suppression" in the Hupeh-Honan-Anhwei border area, where the Red Army acted on the theory that the Kuomintang army was merely an auxiliary force.

There are many instances of setbacks which were due to being terrified of the enemy.

As against those who underestimated the enemy, some people greatly overestimated him and also greatly underestimated our own strength, as a result of which they adopted an unwarranted policy of retreat and likewise disarmed themselves mentally in the matter of defence. This resulted in the defeat of some guerrilla units, or the failure of certain Red Army campaigns, or the loss of base areas.

The most striking example of the loss of a base area was that of the Central Base Area in Kiangsi during the fifth counter-campaign against "encirclement and suppression". The mistake here arose from a Rightist viewpoint. The leaders feared the enemy as if he were a tiger, set up defences everywhere, fought defensive actions at every step and did not dare to advance to the enemy's rear and attack him there, which would have been to our advantage, or boldly to lure the enemy troops in deep so as to herd them together and annihilate them. As a result, the whole base area was lost and the Red Army had to undertake the Long March of over 12,000 kilometres. However, this kind of mistake was usually preceded by a "Left" error of underestimating the enemy. The military adventurism of attacking the key cities in 1932 was the root cause of the line of passive defence adopted subsequently in coping with the enemy's fifth "encirclement and suppression" campaign.

The most extreme example of being terrified of the enemy was the retreatism of the "Chang Kuo-tao line". The defeat of the Western Column of the Fourth Front Red Army west of the Yellow River[8] marked the final bankruptcy of this line.

Active defence is also known as offensive defence, or defence through decisive engagements. Passive defence is also known as purely defensive defence or pure defence. Passive defence is actually a spurious kind of defence, and the only real defence is active defence, defence for the purpose of counter-attacking and taking the offensive. As far as I know, there is no military manual of value nor any sensible military expert, ancient or modern, Chinese or foreign, that does not oppose passive defence, whether in strategy or tactics. Only a complete fool or a madman would cherish passive defence as a talisman. However, there are people in this world who do such things. That is an error in war, a manifestation of conservatism in military matters, which we must resolutely oppose.

The military experts of the newer and rapidly developing imperialist countries, namely, Germany and Japan, loudly trumpet the advantages of the strategic offensive and are opposed to the strategic defensive. Military thinking of this kind is absolutely unsuited to China's revolutionary war. These military experts assert that a serious weakness of the defensive is that it shakes popular morale, instead of inspiring it. This applies to countries where class contradictions are acute and the war benefits only the reactionary ruling strata or the reactionary political groups in power. But our situation is different. With the slogan of defending the revolutionary base areas and defending China, we can rally the overwhelming majority of the people to fight with one heart and one mind, because we are the oppressed and the victims of aggression. It was also by using the form of the defensive that the Red Army of the Soviet Union defeated its enemies during the civil war. When the imperialist countries organized the Whites for attack, the war was waged under the slogan of defending the Soviets, and even when the October Uprising was being prepared, the military mobilization was carried out under the slogan of defending the capital. In every just war the defensive not only has a lulling effect on politically alien elements, it also makes possible the rallying of the backward sections of the masses to join in the war.

When Marx said that once an armed uprising is started there must not be a moment's pause in the attack,[9] he meant that the masses, having taken the enemy unawares in an insurrection, must give the reactionary rulers no chance to retain or recover their political power, must seize this moment to beat the nation's reactionary ruling forces when they are unprepared, and must not rest content with the victories already won, underestimate the enemy, slacken their attacks or hesitate to press forward, and so let slip the opportunity of destroying the enemy, bringing failure to the revolution. This is correct. It does not mean, however, that when we are already locked in battle with an enemy who enjoys superiority, we revolutionaries should not adopt defensive measures even when we are hard pressed. Only a prize idiot would think in this way.

Taken as a whole, our war has been an offensive against the Kuomintang, but militarily it has assumed the form of breaking the enemy's "encirclement and suppression".

Militarily speaking, our warfare consists of the alternate use of the defensive and the offensive. In our case it makes no difference whether the offensive is said to follow or to precede the defensive, because the crux of the matter is to break the "encirclement and suppression". The defensive continues until an "encirclement and suppression" campaign is broken, whereupon the offensive begins, these being but two stages of the same thing; and one enemy "encirclement and suppression" campaign is closely followed by another. Of the two stages, the defensive is the more complicated and the more important. It involves numerous problems of how to break the "encirclement and suppression". The basic principle here is to stand for active defence and oppose passive defence.

In our civil war, when the strength of the Red Army surpasses that of the enemy, we shall, in general, no longer need the strategic defensive. Our policy then will be the strategic offensive alone. This change will depend on an over-all change in the balance of forces. By that time the only remaining defensive measures will be of a partial character.

Preparations for combating "encirclement and suppression" campaigns

Unless we have made necessary and sufficient preparations against a planned enemy "encirclement and suppression" campaign, we shall certainly be forced into a passive position. To accept battle in haste is to fight without being sure of victory. Therefore when the enemy is preparing an "encirclement and suppression" campaign, it is absolutely necessary for us to prepare our counter-campaign. To be opposed to such preparations, as some people in our ranks were at one time, is childish and ridiculous.

There is a difficult problem here on which controversy may easily arise. When should we conclude our offensive and switch to the phase of preparing our counter-campaign against "encirclement and suppression"? When we are victoriously on the offensive and the enemy is on the defensive, his preparations for the next "encirclement and suppression" campaign are conducted in secret, and therefore it is difficult for us to know when his offensive will begin. If our work of preparing the counter-campaign begins too early, it is bound to reduce the gains from our offensive and will sometimes even have certain harmful effects on the Red Army and the people. For the chief measures in the preparatory phase are the military preparations for withdrawal and the political mobilization for them. Sometimes, if we start preparing too early, this will turn into waiting for the enemy; after waiting a long time without the enemy appearing, we will have to renew our offensive. And sometimes, the enemy will start his offensive just as our new offensive is beginning, thus putting us in a difficult position. Hence the choice of the right moment to begin our preparations is an important problem. The right moment should be determined with due regard both to the enemy's situation and our own and to the relation between the two. In order to know the enemy's situation, we should collect information on his political, military and financial position and the state of public opinion in his territory. In analysing such information we must take the total strength of the enemy into full account and must not exaggerate the extent of his past defeats, but on the other hand we must not fail to take into account his internal contradictions, his financial difficulties, the effect of his past defeats, etc. As for our side, we must not exaggerate the extent of our past victories, but neither should we fail to take full account of their effect.

Generally speaking, however, on the question of timing the preparations, it is preferable to start them too early rather than too late. For the former involves smaller losses and has the advantage that preparedness averts peril and puts us in a fundamentally invincible position.

The essential problems during the preparatory phase are the preparations for the withdrawal of the Red Army, political mobilization, recruitment, arrangements for finance and provisions, and the handling of politically alien elements.

By preparations for the Red Army's withdrawal we mean taking care that it does not move in a direction jeopardizing the withdrawal or advance too far in its attacks or become too fatigued. These are the things the main forces of the Red Army must attend to on the eve of a large-scale enemy offensive. At such a time, the Red Army must devote its attention mainly to planning the selection and preparation of the battle areas, the acquisition of supplies, and the enlargement and training of its own forces.

Political mobilization is a problem of prime importance in the struggle against "encirclement and suppression". That is to say, we should tell the Red Army and the people in the base area clearly, resolutely and fully that the enemy's offensive is inevitable and imminent and will do serious harm to the people, but at the same time, we should tell them about his weaknesses, the factors favourable to the Red Army, our indomitable will to victory and our general plan of work. We should call upon the Red Army and the entire population to fight against the enemy's "encirclement and suppression" campaign and defend the base area. Except where military secrets are concerned, political mobilization must be carried out openly, and, what is more, every effort should be made to extend it to all who might possibly support the revolutionary cause. The key link here is to convince the cadres.

Recruitment of new soldiers should be based on two considerations, first, on the level of political consciousness of the people and the size of the population and, second, on the current state of the Red Army and the possible extent of its losses in the whole course of the counter-campaign.

Needless to say, the problems of finance and food are of great importance to the counter-campaign. We must take the possibility of a prolonged enemy campaign into account. It is necessary to make an estimate of the minimum material requirements—chiefly of the Red Army but also of the people in the revolutionary base area — for the entire struggle against the enemy's "encirclement and suppression" campaign.

With regard to politically alien elements we should not be off our guard, but neither should we be unduly apprehensive of treachery on their part and adopt excessive precautionary measures. Distinction should be made between the landlords, the merchants and the rich peasants, and the main point is to explain things to them politically and win their neutrality, while at the same time organizing the masses of the people to keep an eye on them. Only against the very few elements who are most dangerous should stern measures like arrest be taken.

The extent of success in a struggle against "encirclement and suppression" is closely related to the degree to which the tasks of the preparatory phase have been fulfilled. Relaxation of preparatory work due to underestimation of the enemy and panic due to being terrified of the enemy's attacks are harmful tendencies, and both should be resolutely opposed. What we need is an enthusiastic but calm state of mind and intense but orderly work.

Strategic retreat

A strategic retreat is a planned strategic step taken by an inferior force for the purpose of conserving its strength and biding its time to defeat the enemy, when it finds itself confronted with a superior force whose offensive it is unable to smash quickly. But military adventurists stubbornly oppose such a step and advocate "engaging the enemy outside the gates".

We all know that when two boxers fight, the clever boxer usually gives a little ground at first, while the foolish one rushes in furiously and uses up all his resources at the very start, and in the end he is often beaten by the man who has given ground.

In the novel *Shui Hu Chuan*,[10] the drill master Hung, challenging Lin Chung to a fight on Chai Chin's estate, shouts, "Come on! Come on! Come on!" In the end it is the retreating Lin Chung who spots Hung's weak point and floors him with one blow.

During the Spring and Autumn Era, when the states of Lu and Chi[11] were at war, Duke Chuang of Lu wanted to attack before the Chi troops had tired themselves out, but Tsao Kuei prevented him. When instead he adopted the tactic of "the enemy tires, we attack", he defeated the Chi army. This is a classic example from China's military history of a weak force defeating a strong force. Here is the account given by the historian Tsochiu Ming:[12]

> In the spring the Chi troops invaded us. The Duke was about to fight. Tsao Kuei requested an audience. His neighbours said, "This is the business of meat-eating officials, why meddle with it?" Tsao replied, "Meat-eaters are fools, they cannot plan ahead." So he saw the Duke. And he asked, "What will you rely on when you fight?" The Duke answered, "I never dare to keep all my food and clothing for my own enjoyment, but always share them with others." Tsao said, "Such paltry charity cannot reach all. The people will not follow you." The Duke said, "I never offer to the gods less sacrificial beasts, jade or silk than are due to them. I keep good faith." Tsao said, "Such paltry faith wins no trust. The gods will not bless you." The Duke said, "Though unable personally to attend to the details of all trials, big and small, I always demand the facts." Tsao said, "That shows your devotion to your people. You can give battle. When you do so, I beg to follow you." The Duke and he rode in the same chariot. The battle was joined at Changshuo. When the Duke was about to sound the drum for the attack, Tsao said, "Not yet." When the men of Chi had drummed thrice, Tsao said, "Now we can drum." The army of Chi was routed. The Duke wanted to pursue. Again Tsao said, "Not yet." He got down from the chariot to examine the enemy's wheel-tracks, then mounted the arm-rest of the chariot to look afar. He said, "Now we can pursue!" So began the pursuit of the Chi troops. After the victory the Duke asked Tsao why he had given such advice. Tsao replied, "A battle depends upon courage. At the first drum courage is aroused, at the second it flags, and with the third it runs out. When the enemy's courage ran out, ours was still high and so we won. It is difficult to fathom the moves of a great state, and I feared an ambush. But when I examined the enemy's wheel-tracks and found them criss-crossing and looked afar and saw his banners drooping, I advised pursuit."

That was a case of a weak state resisting a strong state. The story speaks of the political preparations before a battle — winning the confidence of the people; it speaks of a battle-field favourable for switching over to the counter-offensive — Changshuo; it indicates the favourable time for starting the counter-offensive — when the enemy's courage runs out and one's own is high; and it points to the moment for starting the pursuit — when the enemy's tracks are criss-crossed and his banners are drooping. Though the battle was not a big one, it illustrates the principles of the strategic defensive. China's military history contains numerous instances of victories won on these principles. In such famous battles as the Battle of Chengkao between the states of Chu and Han,[13] the Battle of Kunyang between the states of Hsin and Han,[14] the Battle of Kuantu between Yuan Shao and Tsao Tsao,[15] the Battle of Chihpi between the states of Wu and Wei,[16] the Battle of Yiling between the states of Wu and Shu,[17] and the Battle of Feishui between the states of Chin and Tsin,[18] in each case the contending sides were unequal, and the weaker side, yielding some ground at first, gained mastery by striking only after the enemy had struck and so defeated the stronger side.

Our war began in the autumn of 1927, and at that time we had no experience at all. The Nanchang Uprising[19] and the Canton Uprising[20] failed, and in the Autumn Harvest Uprising[21] the Red Army in the Hunan-Hupeh-Kiangsi border area also suffered several defeats and shifted to the Chingkang Mountains on the Hunan-Kiangsi border. In the following April the units which had survived the defeat of the Nanchang Uprising also moved to the Chingkang Mountains by way of southern Hunan. By May 1928, however, basic principles of guerrilla warfare, simple in nature and suited to the conditions of the time, had already been evolved, that is, the sixteen-character formula: "The enemy advances, we retreat; the enemy camps, we harass; the enemy tires, we attack; the enemy retreats, we pursue." This sixteen-character formulation of military principles was accepted by the Central Committee before the Li Li-san line. Later our operational principles were developed a step further. At the time of our first counter-campaign against "encirclement and suppression" in the Kiangsi base area, the principle of "luring the enemy in deep" was put forward and, moreover, successfully applied. By the time the enemy's third "encirclement and suppression" campaign was defeated, a complete set of operational principles for the Red Army had taken shape. This marked a new stage in the development of our military principles, which were greatly enriched in content and underwent many changes in form, mainly in the sense that although they basically remained the same as in the sixteen-character formula, they transcended their originally simple nature. The sixteen-character formula covered the basic principles for combating "encirclement and suppression"; it covered the two stages of the strategic defensive and the strategic offensive, and within the defensive, it covered the two stages of the strategic retreat and the strategic counter-offensive. What came later was only a development of this formula.

But beginning from January 1932, after the publication of the Party's resolution entitled "Struggle for Victory First in One or More Provinces After Smashing the Third 'Encirclement and Suppression' Campaign", which contained serious errors of principle, the "Left" opportunists attacked these correct principles, finally abrogated the whole set and instituted a complete set of contrary "new principles" or "regular principles". From then on, the old principles were no longer to be considered as regular but were to be rejected as "guerrilla-ism". The opposition to "guerrilla-ism" reigned for three whole years. Its first stage was military adventurism, in the second it turned into military conservatism and, finally, in the third stage it became flight-ism. It was not until the Central Committee held the enlarged meeting of the Political Bureau at Tsunyi, Kweichow Province, in January 1935 that this wrong line was declared bankrupt and the correctness of the old line reaffirmed. But at what a cost!

Those comrades who vigorously opposed "guerrilla-ism" argued along the following lines. It was wrong to lure the enemy in deep because we had to abandon so much territory. Although battles had been won in this way, was not the situation different now? Moreover, was it not better to defeat the enemy without abandoning territory? And was it not better still to defeat the enemy in his own areas, or on the borders between his areas and ours? The old practices had had nothing "regular" about them and were methods used only by guerrillas. Now our own state had been established and our Red Army had become a regular army. Our fight against Chiang Kai-shek had become a war between two states, between two great armies. History should not repeat itself, and everything pertaining to "guerrilla-ism" should be totally discarded. The new principles were "completely Marxist", while the old had been created by guerrilla units in the mountains, and there was no Marxism in the mountains. The new principles were the antithesis of the old. They were: "Pit one against ten, pit ten against a hundred, fight bravely and determinedly, and exploit victories by hot pursuit"; "Attack on all fronts"; "Seize key cities"; and "Strike with two 'fists' in two directions at the same time". When the enemy attacked, the methods of dealing with him were: "Engage the enemy outside the gates", "Gain mastery by striking first", "Don't let our pots and pans be smashed", "Don't give up an inch of territory" and "Divide the forces into six routes". The war was "the decisive battle between the road of revolution and the road of colonialism", a war of short swift thrusts, blockhouse warfare, war of attrition, "protracted war". There were, further, the policy of maintaining a great rear area and an absolutely centralized command. Finally there was a large-scale "house-moving". And anyone who did not accept these things was to be punished, labelled an opportunist, and so on and so forth.

Without a doubt these theories and practices were all wrong. They were nothing but subjectivism. Under favourable circumstances this subjectivism manifested itself in petty-bourgeois revolutionary fanaticism and impetuosity, but in times of adversity, as the situation worsened, it changed successively into desperate recklessness, conservatism and flight-ism. They were the theories and practices of hotheads and ignoramuses; they did not have the slightest flavour of Marxism about them; indeed they were anti-Marxist.

Here we shall discuss only strategic retreat, which in Kiangsi was called "luring the enemy in deep" and in Szechuan "contracting the front". No previous theorist or practitioner of war has ever denied that this is the policy a weak army fighting a strong army must adopt in the initial stage of a war. It has been said by a foreign military expert that in strategically defensive operations, decisive battles are usually avoided in the beginning, and are sought only when conditions have become favourable. That is entirely correct and we have nothing to add to it.

The object of strategic retreat is to conserve military strength and prepare for the counter-offensive. Retreat is necessary because not to retreat a step before the onset of a strong enemy inevitably means to jeopardize the preservation of one's own forces. In the past, however, many people were stubbornly opposed to retreat, considering it to be an "opportunist line of pure defence". Our history has proved that their opposition was entirely wrong.

To prepare for a counter-offensive, we must select or create conditions favourable to ourselves but unfavourable to the enemy, so as to bring about a change in the balance of forces, before we go on to the stage of the counter-offensive.

In the light of our past experience, during the stage of retreat we should in general secure at least two of the following conditions before we can consider the situation as being favourable to us and unfavourable to the enemy and before we can go over to the counter-offensive. These conditions are:

1   The population actively supports the Red Army.
2   The terrain is favourable for operations.
3   All the main forces of the Red Army are concentrated.

4   The enemy's weak spots have been discovered.
5   The enemy has been reduced to a tired and demoralized state.
6   The enemy has been induced to make mistakes.

The first condition, active support of the population, is the most important one for the Red Army. It means having a base area. Moreover, given this condition, it is easy to achieve conditions 4, 5 and 6. Therefore, when the enemy launches a full-scale offensive, the Red Army generally withdraws from the White area into the base area, because that is where the population is most active in supporting the Red Army against the White army. Also, there is a difference between the borders and the central district of a base area; in the latter the people are better at blocking the passage of information to the enemy, better at reconnaissance, transportation, joining in the fighting, and so on. Thus when we were combating the first, second and third "encirclement and suppression" campaigns in Kiangsi, all the places selected as "terminal points for the retreat" were situated where the first condition, popular support, was excellent, or rather good. This characteristic of our base areas made the Red Army's operations very different from ordinary operations and was the main reason why the enemy subsequently had to resort to the policy of blockhouse warfare.

One advantage of operating on interior lines is that it makes it possible for the retreating army to choose terrain favourable to itself and force the attacking army to fight on its terms. In order to defeat a strong army, a weak army must carefully choose favourable terrain as a battleground. But this condition alone is not enough and must be accompanied by other conditions. The first of these is popular support. The next is a vulnerable enemy, for instance, an enemy who is tired or has made mistakes, or an advancing enemy column that is comparatively poor in fighting capacity. In the absence of these conditions, even if we have found excellent terrain, we have to disregard it and continue to retreat in order to secure the desired conditions. In the White areas there is no lack of good terrain, but we do not have the favourable condition of active popular support. If other conditions are not yet fulfilled, the Red Army has no alternative but to retreat towards its base area. Distinctions such as those between the White areas and the Red areas also usually exist between the borders and the central district of a base area.

Except for local units and containing forces, all our assault troops should, on principle, be concentrated. When attacking an enemy who is on the defensive strategically, the Red Army usually disperses its own forces. Once the enemy launches a full-scale offensive, the Red Army effects a "retreat towards the centre". The terminal point chosen for the retreat is usually in the central section of the base area, but sometimes it is in the frontal or rear sections, as circumstances require. By such a retreat towards the centre all the main forces of the Red Army can be concentrated.

Another essential condition for a weak army fighting a strong one is to pick out the enemy's weaker units for attack. But at the beginning of the enemy's offensive we usually do not know which of his advancing columns is the strongest and which the second strongest, which is the weakest and which the second weakest, and so a process of reconnaissance is required. This often takes a considerable time. That is another reason why strategic retreat is necessary.

If the attacking enemy is far more numerous and much stronger than we are, we can accomplish a change in the balance of forces only when the enemy has penetrated deeply into our base area and tasted all the bitterness it holds for him. As the chief of staff of one of Chiang Kai-shek's brigades remarked during the third "encirclement and suppression" campaign, "Our stout men have worn themselves thin and our thin men have worn themselves to death." Or, in the words of Chen Ming-shu, Commander-in-Chief of the Western Route of the Kuomintang's "Encirclement and Suppression" Army, "Everywhere the National Army gropes in the dark, while the Red Army walks in broad daylight." By then the enemy army, although still strong, is much weakened, its soldiers are tired, its morale is sagging and many of its weak spots are revealed. But the Red Army, though weak, has conserved its strength and stored up its energy, and is waiting at its ease for the fatigued enemy. At such a time it is generally possible to attain a certain parity between the two sides, or to change the enemy's absolute superiority to relative superiority and our absolute inferiority to relative inferiority, and occasionally even to become superior to the enemy. When fighting against the third "encirclement and suppression" campaign in Kiangsi, the Red Army executed a retreat to the extreme limit (to concentrate in the rear section of the base area); if it had not done so, it could not have defeated the enemy because the enemy's "encirclement and suppression" forces were then over ten times the size of the Red Army. When Sun Wu Tzu said, "Avoid the enemy when he is full of vigour, strike when he is fatigued and withdraws", he was referring to tiring and demoralizing the enemy so as to reduce his superiority.

Finally, the object of retreat is to induce the enemy to make mistakes or to detect his mistakes. One must realize that an enemy commander, however wise, cannot avoid making some mistakes over a relatively long period of time, and hence it is always possible for us to exploit the openings he leaves us. The enemy is liable to make mistakes, just as we ourselves sometimes miscalculate and give him openings to exploit. In addition, we can induce the enemy to make mistakes by our own actions, for instance, by "counterfeiting an appearance", as Sun Wu Tzu called it, that is, by making a feint to the east but attacking in the west. If we are to do this, the terminal point for the retreat cannot be rigidly limited to a definite area. Sometimes when we have retreated to the predetermined area and not yet found openings to exploit, we have to retreat farther and wait for the enemy to give us an opening.

The favourable conditions which we seek by retreating are in general those stated above. But this does not mean that a counter-offensive cannot be launched until all these conditions are present. The presence of all these conditions at the same time is neither possible nor necessary. But a weak force operating on interior lines against a strong enemy should strive to secure such conditions as are necessary in the light of the enemy's actual situation. All views to the contrary are incorrect.

The decision on the terminal point for retreat should depend on the situation as a whole. It is wrong to decide on a place which, considered in relation to only part of the situation, appears to be favourable for our passing to the counter-offensive, if it is not also advantageous from the point of view of the situation as a whole. For at the start of our counter-offensive we must take subsequent developments into consideration, and our counter-offensives always begin on a partial scale. Sometimes the terminal point for retreat should be fixed in the frontal section of the base area, as it was during our second and fourth counter-campaigns against "encirclement and suppression" in Kiangsi and our third counter-campaign in the Shensi-Kansu area. At times it should be in the middle section of the base area, as in our first counter-campaign in Kiangsi. At other times, it should be fixed in the rear section of the base area, as in our third counter-campaign in Kiangsi. In all these cases the decision was taken by correlating the partial situation with the situation as a whole. But during the fifth counter-campaign in Kiangsi, our army gave no consideration whatsoever to retreat, because it did not take account of either the partial or the whole situation, and this was really a rash and foolhardy conduct. A situation is made up of a number of factors; in considering the relation between a part of the situation and the whole, we should base our judgements on whether the factors on the enemy's side and those on our side, as manifested in both the partial and the whole situation, are to a certain extent favourable for our starting a counter-offensive.

The terminal points for retreat in a base area can be generally divided into three types: those in the frontal section, those in the middle section, and those in the rear section of the base area. Does this, however, mean refusing to fight in the White areas altogether? No. It is only when we have to deal with a large-scale campaign of enemy "encirclement and suppression" that we refuse to fight in the White areas. It is only when there is a wide disparity between the enemy's strength and ours that, acting on the principle of conserving our strength and biding our time to defeat the enemy, we advocate retreating to the base area and luring the enemy in deep, for only by so doing can we create or find conditions favourable for our counter-offensive. If the situation is not so serious, or if it is so serious that the Red Army cannot begin its counter-offensive even in the base area, or if the counter-offensive is not going well and a further retreat is necessary to bring about a change in the situation, then we should recognize, theoretically at least, that the terminal point for the retreat may be fixed in a White area, though in the past we have had very little experience of this kind.

In general, the terminal points for retreat in a White area can also be divided into three types: (1) those in front of our base area, (2) those on the flanks of our base area, and (3) those behind our base area. Here is an example of the first type.

> During our first counter-campaign against "encirclement and suppression" in Kiangsi, had it not been for the disunity inside the Red Army and the split in the local Party organization (the two difficult problems created by the Li Li-san line and the A-B Group),[22] it is conceivable that we might have concentrated our forces within the triangle formed by Kian, Nanfeng and Changshu and launched a counter-offensive. For the enemy force advancing from the area between the Kan and Fu Rivers was not very greatly superior to the Red Army in strength (100,000 against 40,000). Though the popular support there was not as active as in the base area, the terrain was favourable; moreover, it would have been possible to smash, one by one, the enemy forces advancing along separate routes.

Now for an example of the second type.

> During our third counter-campaign in Kiangsi, if the enemy's offensive had not been on so large a scale, if one of the enemy's columns had advanced from Chienning, Lichuan and Taining on the Fukien-Kiangsi border, and if that column had not been too strong for us to attack, it is likewise conceivable that the Red Army might have massed its forces in the White area in western Fukien and crushed that column first, without having to make a thousand-*li* detour through Juichin to Hsingkuo.

Finally, an example of the third type.

> During that same third counter-campaign in Kiangsi, if the enemy's main force had headed south instead of west, we might have been compelled to withdraw to the Huichang-Hsunwu-Anyuan area (a White area), in order to induce the enemy to move further south; the Red Army could have then driven northward into the interior of the base area, by which time the enemy force in the north of the base area would not have been very large.

The above, however, are all hypothetical examples not based on actual experience; they should be regarded as exceptional and not treated as general principles. When the enemy launches a large-scale "encirclement and suppression" campaign, our general principle is to lure him in deep, withdraw into the base area and fight him there, because this is our surest method of smashing his offensive.

Those who advocate "engaging the enemy outside the gates" oppose strategic retreat, arguing that to retreat means to lose territory, to bring harm on the people ("to let our pots and pans be smashed", as they call it), and to give rise to unfavourable repercussions outside. During our fifth counter-campaign, they argued that every time we retreated a step the enemy would push his blockhouses forward a step, so that our base areas would continuously shrink and we would have no way of recovering lost ground. Even though luring the enemy deep into our territory might have been useful in the past, it would be useless against the enemy's fifth "encirclement and suppression" campaign in which he adopted the policy of blockhouse warfare. The only way to deal with the enemy's fifth campaign, they said, was to divide up our forces for resistance and make short, swift thrusts at the enemy.

It is easy to give an answer to such views, and our history has already done so. As for loss of territory, it often happens that only by loss can loss be avoided; this is the principle of "Give in order to take". If what we lose is territory and what we gain is victory over the enemy, plus recovery and also expansion of our territory, then it is a paying proposition. In a business transaction, if a buyer does not "lose" some money, he cannot obtain goods; if a seller does not "lose" some goods, he cannot obtain money. The losses incurred in a revolutionary movement involve destruction, and what is gained is construction of a progressive character. Sleep and rest involve loss of time, but energy is gained for tomorrow's work. If any fool does not understand this and refuses to sleep, he will have no energy the next day, and that is a losing proposition. We lost out in the fifth counter-campaign for precisely such reasons. Reluctance to give up part of our territory resulted in the loss of all our territory. Abyssinia, too, lost all her territory when she fought the enemy head-on, though that was not the sole cause of her defeat.

The same holds true on the question of bringing damage on the people. If you refuse to let the pots and pans of some households be smashed over a short period of time, you will cause the smashing of the pots and pans of all the people to go on over a long period of time. If you are afraid of unfavourable short-term political repercussions, you will have to pay the price in unfavourable long-term political repercussions. After the October Revolution, if the Russian Bolsheviks had acted on the opinions of the "Left Communists" and refused to sign the peace treaty with Germany, the new-born Soviets would have been in danger of early death.[23]

Such seemingly revolutionary "Left" opinions originate from the revolutionary impetuosity of the petty-bourgeois intellectuals as well as from the narrow conservatism of the peasant small producers. People holding such opinions look at problems only one-sidedly and are unable to take a comprehensive view of the situation as a whole; they are unwilling to link the interests of today with those of tomorrow or the interests of the part with those of the whole, but cling like grim death to the partial and the temporary. Certainly, we should cling tenaciously to the partial and the temporary when, in the concrete circumstances of the time, they are favourable – and especially when they are decisive – for the whole current situation and the whole period, or otherwise we shall become advocates of letting things slide and doing nothing about them. That is why a retreat must have a terminal point. We must not go by the short-sightedness of the small producer. We should learn the wisdom of the Bolsheviks. The naked eye is not enough, we must have the aid of the telescope and the microscope. The Marxist method is the telescope and the microscope in political and military matters.

Of course, strategic retreat has its difficulties. To pick the time for beginning the retreat, to select the terminal point, to convince the cadres and the people politically – these are difficult problems demanding solution.

The problem of timing the beginning of the retreat is very important. If in the course of our first counter-campaign against "encirclement and suppression" in Kiangsi Province our retreat had not been carried out just when it was, that is, if it had been delayed, then at the very least the extent of our victory would have been affected. Both a premature and a belated retreat, of course, bring losses. But generally speaking, a belated retreat brings more losses than a premature one. A well-timed retreat, which enables us to keep the initiative entirely, is of great assistance to us in switching to the counter-offensive when, having reached the terminal point for our retreat, we have regrouped our forces and are waiting at our ease for the fatigued enemy. When smashing the enemy's first, second and fourth campaigns of "encirclement and suppression" in Kiangsi, we were able to handle the enemy confidently and without haste. It was only during the third campaign that the Red Army was very fatigued by the detour it had had to make in order to reassemble, because we had not expected the enemy to launch a new offensive so quickly after suffering such a crushing defeat in the second campaign (we ended our second counter-campaign on May 29, 1931, and Chiang Kai-shek began his third "encirclement and suppression" campaign on July 1). The timing of the retreat is decided in the same way as the timing of the preparatory phase of a counter-campaign which we discussed earlier, that is, entirely on the basis of the requisite information we have collected and of the appraisal of the general situation on the enemy side and on our own.

It is extremely difficult to convince the cadres and the people of the necessity of strategic retreat when they have had no experience of it, and when the prestige of the army leadership is not yet such that it can concentrate the authority for deciding on strategic retreat in the hands of a few persons or of a single person and at the same time enjoy the confidence of the cadres. Because the cadres lacked experience and had no faith in strategic retreat, great difficulties were encountered at the beginning of our first and fourth counter-campaigns and during the whole of the fifth. During the first counter-campaign the cadres, under the influence of the Li Li-san line, were in favour of attack and not of retreat until they were convinced otherwise. In the fourth counter-campaign the cadres, under the influence of military adventurism, objected to making preparations for retreat. In the fifth counter-campaign, they at first persisted in the military adventurist view, which opposed luring the enemy in deep, but later turned to military conservatism. Another case is that of the adherents of the Chang Kuo-tao line, who did not admit the impossibility of establishing our bases in the regions of the Tibetan and the Hui peoples,[24] until they ran up against a brick wall. Experience is essential for the cadres, and failure is indeed the mother of success. But it is also necessary to learn with an open mind from other people's experience, and it is sheer "narrow empiricism" to insist on one's own personal experience in all matters and, in its absence, to adhere stubbornly to one's own opinions and reject other people's experience. Our war has suffered in no small measure on this account.

The people's lack of faith in the need for a strategic retreat, which was due to their inexperience, was never greater than in our first counter-campaign in Kiangsi. At that time the local Party organizations and the masses of the people in the counties of Kian, Hsingkuo and Yungfeng were all opposed to the Red Army's withdrawal. But after the experience of the first counter-campaign, no such problem occurred in the subsequent ones. Everyone was convinced that the loss of territory in the base area and the sufferings of the people were temporary and was confident that the Red Army could smash the enemy's "encirclement and suppression". However, whether or not the people have faith is closely tied up with whether or not the cadres have faith, and hence the first and foremost task is to convince the cadres.

Strategic retreat is aimed solely at switching over to the counter-offensive and is merely the first stage of the strategic defensive. The decisive link in the entire strategy is whether victory can be won in the stage of the counter-offensive which follows.

Strategic counter-offensive

To defeat the offensive of an enemy who enjoys absolute superiority we rely on the situation created during the stage of our strategic retreat, a situation which is favourable to ourselves, unfavourable to the enemy and different from that at the beginning of the enemy's offensive. It takes many elements to make up such a situation. All this has been dealt with above.

However, the presence of these conditions and of a situation favourable to ourselves and unfavourable to the enemy does not yet mean that we have defeated the enemy. Such conditions and such a situation provide the possibility for our victory and the enemy's defeat, but do not constitute the reality of victory or defeat; they have not yet brought actual victory or defeat to either army. To bring about victory or defeat a decisive battle between the two armies is necessary. Only a decisive battle can settle the question as to which army is the victory and which the vanquished. This is the sole task in the stage of strategic counter-offensive. The counter-offensive is a long process, the most fascinating, the most dynamic, and also the final stage of a defensive campaign. What is called active defence refers chiefly to this strategic counter-offensive which is in the nature of a decisive engagement.

Conditions and situation are created not only in the stage of the strategic retreat, but continue to be created in the stage of the counter-offensive. Whether in form or in nature, they are not exactly the same in the latter stage as in the former.

What could remain the same in form and in nature, for example, is the fact that the enemy troops will be even more fatigued and depleted, which is simply a continuation of their fatigue and depletion in the previous stage.

But wholly new conditions and a wholly new situation are bound to emerge. Thus, when the enemy has suffered one or more defeats, the conditions advantageous to us and disadvantageous to him will not be confined to his fatigue, etc., but a new factor will have been added, namely, that he has suffered defeats. New changes will take place in the situation, too. When the enemy begins to manoeuvre his troops in a disorderly way and to make false moves, the relative strengths of the two opposing armies will naturally no longer be the same as before.

But if it is not the enemy's forces but ours that have suffered one or more defeats, then both the conditions and the situation will change in the opposite direction. That is to say, the enemy's disadvantages will be reduced, while on our side disadvantages will make their appearance and even grow. That again will be something entirely new and different.

A defeat for either side will lead directly and speedily to a new effort by the defeated side to avert disaster, to extricate itself from the new conditions and situation unfavourable to it and favourable to the enemy and to re-create such conditions and such a situation as are favourable to it and unfavourable to its opponent, in order to bring pressure to bear on the latter.

The effort of the winning side will be exactly the opposite. It will strive to exploit its victory and inflict still greater damage on the enemy, add to the conditions that are in its favour and further improve its situation, and prevent the enemy from succeeding in extricating himself from his unfavourable conditions and situation and averting disaster.

Thus, for either side, the struggle at the stage of decisive battle is the most intense, the most complicated and the most changeful as well as the most difficult and trying in the whole war or the whole campaign; it is the most exacting time of all from the point of view of command.

In the stage of counter-offensive, there are many problems, the chief of which are the starting of the counter-offensive, the concentration of troops, mobile warfare, war of quick decision and war of annihilation.

Whether in a counter-offensive or in an offensive, the principles with regard to these problems do not differ in their basic character. In this sense we may say that a counter-offensive is an offensive.

Still, a counter-offensive is not exactly an offensive. The principles of the counter-offensive are applied when the enemy is on the offensive. The principles of the offensive are applied when the enemy is on the defensive. In this sense, there are certain differences between a counter-offensive and an offensive.

For this reason, although the various operational problems are all included in the discussion of the counter-offensive in the present chapter on the strategic defensive, and in order to avoid repetition the chapter on the strategic offensive will deal only with other problems, yet, when it comes to actual application, we should not overlook either the similarities or the differences between the counter-offensive and the offensive.

Starting the counter-offensive

The problem of starting a counter-offensive is the problem of the "initial battle" or "prelude".

Many bourgeois military experts advise caution in the initial battle, whether one is on the strategic defensive or on the strategic offensive, but more especially when on the defensive. In the past we, too, have stressed this as a serious point. Our operations against the five enemy campaigns of "encirclement and suppression" in Kiangsi Province have given us rich experience, a study of which will not be without benefit.

In his first campaign, the enemy employed about 100,000 men, divided into eight columns, to advance southward from the Kian-Chienning line against the Red Army's base area. The Red Army had about 40,000 men and was concentrated in the area of Huangpi and Hsiaopu in Ningtu County, Kiangsi Province.

The situation was as follows:

1   The "suppression" forces did not exceed 100,000 men, none of whom were Chiang Kai-shek's own troops, and the general situation was not very grave.
2   The enemy division under Lo Lin, defending Kian, was located across the Kan River to the west.
3   The three enemy divisions under Kung Ping-fan, Chang Hui-tsan and Tan Tao-yuan had advanced and occupied the Futien-Tungku-Lungkang-Yuantou sector southeast of Kian and northwest of Ningtu. The main body of Chang Hui-tsan's division was at Lungkang and that of Tan Tao-yuan's division at Yuantou. It was not advisable to select Futien and Tungku as the battleground, as the inhabitants, misled by the A-B Group, were for a time mistrustful of and opposed to the Red Army.
4   The enemy division under Liu Ho-ting was far away in Chienning in the White area of Fukien, and was unlikely to cross into Kiangsi.
5   The two enemy division under Mao Ping-wen and Hsu Ke-hsiang had entered the Toupi-Lokou-Tungshao sector lying between Kuangchang and Ningtu. Toupi was a White area, Lokou a guerrilla zone, and Tungshao, where there were A-B Group

elements, was a place from which information was liable to leak out. Furthermore, if we were to attack Mao Ping-wen and Hsu Ke-hsiang and then drive westward, the three enemy divisions in the west under Chang Hui-tsan, Tan Tao-yuan and Kung Ping-fan might join forces, thus making it difficult for us to win victory and impossible to bring the issue to a final solution.

6   The two divisions under Chang Hui-tsan and Tan Tao-yuan, which made up the enemy's main force, were troops belonging to Lu Ti-ping, who was commander-in-chief of this "encirclement and suppression" campaign and governor of Kiangsi Province, and Chang Hui-tsan was the field commander. To wipe out these two divisions would be practically to smash the campaign. Each of the two divisions had about fourteen thousand men and Chang's was divided between two places, so that if we attacked one division at a time we would enjoy absolute superiority.

7   The Lungkang-Yuantou sector, where the main forces of the Chang and Tan divisions were located, was close to our concentrations, and there was good popular support to cover our approach.

8   The terrain in Lungkang was good. Yuantou was not easy to attack. But were the enemy to advance to Hsiaopu to attack us, we would have good terrain there too.

9   We could mass the largest number of troops in the Lung-kang sector. In Hsingkuo, less than a hundred *li* to the southwest of Lungkang, we had an independent division of over one thousand men, which could manoeuvre in the enemy's rear.

10   If our troops made a breakthrough at the centre and breached the enemy's front, his columns to the east and west would be cut into two widely separated groups.

For the above reasons, we decided that our first battle should be against Chang Hui-tsan's main force, and we successfully hit two of his brigades and his divisional headquarters, capturing the entire force of nine thousand men and the divisional commander himself, without letting a single man or horse escape. This one victory scared Tan's division into fleeing towards Tungshao and Hsu's division into fleeing towards Toupi. Our troops then pursued Tan's division and wiped out half of it. We fought two battles in five days (December 27, 1930 to January 1, 1931), and, fearing defeat, the enemy forces in Futien, Tungku and Toupi retreated in disorder. So ended the first campaign of "encirclement and suppression".

The situation in the second "encirclement and suppression" campaign was as follows:

1   The "suppression" forces numbering 200,000 were under the command of Ho Ying-chin with headquarters at Nanchang.

2   As in the first enemy campaign, none of the forces were Chiang Kai-shek's own troops. Among them the 19th Route Army under Tsai Ting-kai, the Twenty-sixth under Sun Lien-chung and the Eighth under Chu Shao-liang were strong, or fairly strong, while all the rest were rather weak.

3   The A-B Group had been cleaned up, and the entire population of the base area supported the Red Army.

4   The Fifth Route Army under Wang Chin-yu, newly arrived from the north, was afraid of us, and, generally speaking, so were the two divisions on its left flank under Kuo Hua-tsung and Hao Meng-ling.

5   If our troops attacked Futien first and then swept across to the east, we could expand the base area to the Chienning-Lichuan-Taining sector on the Fukien-Kiangsi border and acquire supplies to help smash the next "encirclement and suppression" campaign. But if we were to thrust westward, we would come up against the Kan River and have no

room for expansion after the battle. To turn east again after the battle would tire our troops and waste time.

6   Though our army (numbering over thirty thousand men) was somewhat smaller than in the first campaign, it had had four months in which to recuperate and build up energy.

For these reasons, we decided, for our first battle, to engage the forces of Wang Chin-yu and of Kung Ping-fan (totalling eleven regiments) in the Futien sector. After winning that battle we attacked Kuo Hua-tsung, Sun Lien-chung, Chu Shao-liang and Liu Ho-ting in succession. In fifteen days (from May 16 to May 30, 1931) we marched seven hundred *li*, fought five battles, captured more than twenty thousand rifles and roundly smashed the enemy's "encirclement and suppression" campaign. When fighting Wang Chin-yu, we were between the two enemy forces under Tsai Ting-kai and Kuo Hua-tsung, some ten *li* from the latter and forty *li* from the former, and some people said we were "getting into a blind alley", but we got through all the same. This was mainly due to the popular support we enjoyed in the base area and to the lack of co-ordination among the enemy units. After Kuo Hua-tsung's division was defeated, Hao Meng-ling's division fled by night back to Yungfeng, and so avoided disaster.

The situation in the third "encirclement and suppression" campaign was as follows:

1   Chiang Kai-shek personally took the field as commander-in-chief. Under him there were three subordinate commanders, each in charge of a column – the left, the right and the centre. The central column was commanded by Ho Ying-chin, who, like Chiang Kai-shek, had his headquarters in Nanchang, the right was commanded by Chen Ming-shu with headquarters at Kian, and the left by Chu Shao-liang with headquarters at Nanfeng.

2   The "suppression" forces numbered 300,000. The main forces, totalling about 100,000 men, were Chiang Kai-shek's own troops and consisted of five divisions (of nine regiments each), commanded by Chen Cheng, Lo Cho-ying, Chao Kuan-tao, Wei Li-huang and Chiang Ting-wen respectively. Besides these, there were three divisions (totalling forty thousand men) under Chiang Kuang-nai, Tsai Ting-kai and Han Teh-chin. Then there was Sun Lien-chung's army of twenty thousand. In addition, there were other, weaker forces that were likewise not Chiang's own troops.

3   The enemy's strategy in this "suppression" campaign was to "drive straight in", which was vastly different from the strategy of "consolidating at every step" he used in the second campaign. The aim was to press the Red Army back against the Kan River and annihilate it there.

4   There was an interval of only one month between the end of the second enemy campaign and the beginning of the third. The Red Army (then about thirty thousand strong) had had neither rest nor replenishments after much hard fighting and had just made a detour of a thousand *li* to concentrate at Hsingkuo in the western part of the southern Kiangsi base area, when the enemy pressed it hard from several directions.

In this situation the plan we first decided on was to move from Hsingkuo by way of Wanan, make a breakthrough at Futien, and then sweep from west to east across the enemy's rear communication lines, thus letting the enemy's main forces make a deep but useless penetration into our base area in southern Kiangsi; this was to be the first phase of our operation. Then when the enemy turned back northward, inevitably very fatigued, we were to seize the opportunity to strike at his vulnerable units; that was to be the second phase of our operation.

The heart of this plan was to avoid the enemy's main forces and strike at his weak spots. But when our forces were advancing on Futien, we were detected by the enemy, who rushed the two divisions under Chen Cheng and Lo Cho-ying to the scene. We had to change our plan and fall back to Kaohsinghsu in the western part of Hsingkuo County, which, together with its environs of less than a hundred square *li*, was then the only place for our troops to concentrate in. The day after our concentration we decided to make a thrust eastward towards Lientang in eastern Hsingkuo County, Liangtsun in southern Yungfeng County and Huangpi in northern Ningtu County. That same night, under cover of darkness, we passed through the forty-*li* gap between Chiang Ting-wen's division and the forces of Chiang Kuang-nai, Tsai Ting-kai and Han Teh-chin, and swung to Lientang. On the second day we skirmished with the forward units under Shangkuan Yun-hsiang (who was in command of Hao Meng-ling's division as well as his own). The first battle was fought on the third day with Shangkuan Yun-hsiang's division and the second battle on the fourth day with Hao Meng-ling's division; after a three-day march we reached Huangpi and fought our third battle against Mao Ping-wen's division. We won all three battles and captured over ten thousand rifles. At this point all the main enemy forces, which had been advancing westward and southward, turned eastward. Focusing on Huangpi, they converged at furious speed to seek battle and closed in on us in a major compact encirclement. We slipped through in the high mountains that lay in the twenty-*li* gap between the forces of Chiang Kuang-nai, Tsai Ting-kai and Han Teh-chin on the one side and Chen Cheng and Lo Cho-ying on the other, and thus, returning from the east to the west, reassembled within the borders of Hsingkuo County. By the time the enemy discovered this fact and began advancing west again, our forces had already had a fortnight's rest, whereas the enemy forces, hungry, exhausted and demoralized, were no good for fighting and so decided to retreat. Taking advantage of their retreat, we attacked the forces of Chiang Kuang-nai, Tsai Ting-kai, Chiang Ting-wen and Han Teh-chin, wiping out one of Chiang Ting-wen's brigades and Han Teh-chin's entire division. As for the divisions under Chiang Kuang-nai and Tsai Ting-kai, the fight resulted in a stalemate and they got away.

The situation in the fourth "encirclement and suppression" campaign was as follows. The enemy was advancing on Kuangchang in three columns; the eastern one was his main force, while the two divisions forming his western column were exposed to us and were also very close to the area where our forces were concentrated. Thus we had the opportunity to attack his western column in southern Yihuang County first, and at one stroke we annihilated the two divisions under Li Ming and Chen Shih-chi. As the enemy then sent two divisions from the eastern column to give support to his central column and advanced further, we were again able to wipe out a division in southern Yihuang County. In these two battles we captured more than ten thousand rifles and, in the main, smashed this campaign of "encirclement and suppression".

In the fifth "encirclement and suppression" campaign the enemy advanced by means of his new strategy of building blockhouses and first occupied Lichuan. But, in attempting to recover Lichuan and engage the enemy outside the base area, we made an attack north of Lichuan at Hsiaoshih, which was an enemy strongpoint and was situated, moreover, in the White area. Failing to win the battle, we shifted our attack to Tsehsichiao, which was also an enemy strongpoint situated in the White area southeast of Hsiaoshih, and again we failed. Then in seeking battle we milled around between the enemy's main forces and his block-houses and were reduced to complete passivity. All through our fifth counter-campaign against "encirclement and suppression", which lasted a whole year, we showed not the slightest initiative or drive. In the end we had to withdraw from our Kiangsi base area.

Our army's experience in these five counter-campaigns against "encirclement and suppression" proves that the first battle in the counter-offensive is of the greatest importance for the Red Army, which is on the defensive, if it is to smash a large and powerful enemy "suppression" force. Victory or defeat in the first battle has a tremendous effect upon the entire situation, all the way to the final engagement. Hence we arrive at the following conclusions.

First, the first battle must be won. We should strike only when positively certain that the enemy's situation, the terrain and popular support are all in our favour and not in favour of the enemy. Otherwise we should rather fall back and carefully bide our time. There will always be opportunities; we should not rashly accept battle. In our first counter-campaign we originally planned to strike at Tan Tao-yuan's troops; we advanced twice but each time had to restrain ourselves and pull back, because they would not budge from their commanding position on the Yuantou heights. A few days later we sought out Chang Hui-tsan's troops, which were more vulnerable to our attack. In our second counter-campaign our army advanced to Tungku where, for the sole purpose of waiting for Wang Chin-yu's men to leave their strongpoint at Futien, we encamped close to the enemy for twenty-five days even at the risk of leakage of information; we rejected all impatient suggestions for a quick attack and finally attained our aim. In our third counter-campaign, although the storm was breaking all around us and we had made a detour of a thousand *li*, and although the enemy had discovered our plan to outflank him we nevertheless exercised patience, turned back, changed our tactics to a breakthrough in the centre, and finally fought the first battle successfully at Lientang. In our fourth counter-campaign, after our attack on Nanfeng had failed, we unhesitatingly withdrew, wheeled round to the enemy's right flank, and reassembled our forces in the area of Tungshao, whereupon we launched our great and victorious battle in southern Yihuang County. It was only in the fifth counter-campaign that the importance of the first battle was not recognized at all. Taking alarm at the loss of the single country town of Lichuan, our forces marched north to meet the enemy in an attempt to recover it. Then, the unexpected encounter at Hsunkou, which had resulted in a victory (in which an enemy division was annihilated), was not treated as the first battle, nor were the changes that were bound to ensue foreseen, but instead Hsiaoshih was rashly attacked with no assurance of success. Thus the initiative was lost at the very first move, and that is really the worst and most stupid way to fight.

Second, the plan for the first battle must be the prelude to, and an organic part of, the plan for the whole campaign. Without a good plan for the whole campaign it is absolutely impossible to fight a really good first battle. That is to say, even though victory is won in the first battle, if the battle harms rather than helps the campaign as a whole, such a victory can only be reckoned a defeat (as in the case of the battle of Hsunkou in the fifth campaign). Hence, before fighting the first battle one must have a general idea of how the second, third, fourth, and even the final battle will be fought, and consider what changes will ensue in the enemy's situation as a whole if we win, or lose, each of the succeeding battles. Although the result may not – and, in fact, definitely will not – turn out exactly as we expect, we must think everything out carefully and realistically in the light of the general situation on both sides. Without a grasp of the situation as a whole, it is impossible to make any really good move on the chessboard.

Third, one must also consider what will happen in the next strategic stage of the war. Whoever directs strategy will not be doing his duty if he occupies himself only with the counter-offensive and neglects the measures to be taken after it succeeds, or in case it fails. In a particular strategic stage, he should take into consideration the succeeding stages, or, at the very least, the following one. Even though future changes are difficult to foresee and the farther ahead one looks the more blurred things seem, a general calculation is possible and an appraisal of distant prospects is necessary. In war as well as in politics, planning only one step at a time as one goes along is a harmful way of directing matters. After each step, it is necessary to examine the ensuing concrete changes and to modify or develop one's strategic and operational plans accordingly, or otherwise one is liable to make the mistake of rushing straight ahead regardless of danger. However, it is absolutely essential to have a long-term plan which has been thought out in its general outline and which covers an entire strategic stage or even several strategic stages. Failure to make such a plan will lead to the mistake of hesitating and allowing oneself to be tied down, which in fact serves the enemy's strategic objects and reduces one to a passive position. It must be borne in mind that the enemy's supreme command has some strategic insight. Only when we have trained ourselves to be a head taller than the enemy will strategic victories be possible. During the enemy's fifth "encirclement and suppression" campaign, failure to do so was the main reason for the errors in strategic direction under the "Left" opportunist and the Chang Kuo-tao lines. In short, in the stage of retreat we must see ahead to the stage of the counter-offensive, in the stage of the counter-offensive we must see ahead to that of the offensive, and in the stage of the offensive we must again see ahead to a stage of retreat. Not to do so but to confine ourselves to considerations of the moment is to court defeat.

The first battle must be won. The plan for the whole campaign must be taken into account. And the strategic stage that comes next must be taken into account. These are the three principles we must never forget when we begin a counter-offensive, that is, when we fight the first battle.

Concentration of troops

The concentration of troops seems easy but is quite hard in practice. Everybody knows that the best way is to use a large force to defeat a small one, and yet many people fail to do so and on the contrary often divide their forces up. The reason is that such military leaders have no head for strategy and are confused by complicated circumstances; hence, they are at the mercy of these circumstances, lose their initiative and have recourse to passive response.

No matter how complicated, grave and harsh the circumstances, what a military leader needs most of all is the ability to function independently in organizing and employing the forces under his command. He may often be forced into a passive position by the enemy, but the important thing is to regain the initiative quickly. Failure to do so spells defeat.

The initiative is not something imaginary but is concrete and material. Here the most important thing is to conserve and mass an armed force that is as large as possible and full of fighting spirit.

It is easy to fall into a passive position in defensive warfare, which gives far less scope for the full exercise of initiative than does offensive warfare. However, defensive warfare, which is passive in form, can be active in content, and can be switched from the stage in which it is passive in form to the stage in which it is active both in form and in content. In appearance a fully planned strategic retreat is made under compulsion, but in reality it is effected in order to conserve our strength and bide our time to defeat the enemy, to lure him in deep and prepare for our counter-offensive. On the other hand, refusal to retreat and hasty acceptance of battle (as in the battle of Hsiaoshih) may appear a serious effort to gain the initiative, while in reality it is passive. Not only is a strategic counter-offensive active in content, but in form, too, it discards the passive posture of the period of retreat. In relation to the enemy, our counter-offensive represents our effort to make him relinquish the initiative and put him in a passive position.

Concentration of troops, mobile warfare, war of quick decision and war of annihilation are all necessary conditions for the full achievement of this aim. And of these, concentration of troops is the first and most essential.

Concentration of troops is necessary for the purpose of reversing the situation as between the enemy and ourselves. First, its purpose is to reverse the situation as regards advance and retreat. Previously it was the enemy who was advancing and we who were retreating; now we seek a situation in which we advance and he retreats. When we concentrate our troops and win a battle, then in that battle we gain the above purpose, and this influences the whole campaign.

Second, its purpose is to reverse the situation with regard to attack and defence. In defensive warfare the retreat to the prescribed terminal point belongs basically to the passive, or "defence", stage. The counter-offensive belongs to the active, or "attack", stage. Although the strategic defensive retains its defensive character throughout its duration, still as compared with the retreat the counter-offensive already represents a change not only in form but in content. The counter-offensive is transitional between the strategic defensive and the strategic offensive, and in the nature of a prelude to the strategic offensive; it is precisely for the purpose of the counter-offensive that troops are concentrated.

Third, its purpose is to reverse the situation with regard to interior and exterior lines. An army operating on strategically interior lines suffers from many disadvantages, and this is especially so in the case of the Red Army, confronted as it is with "encirclement and suppression". But in campaigns and battles we can and absolutely must change this situation. We can turn a big "encirclement and suppression" campaign waged by the enemy against us into a number of small, separate campaigns of encirclement and suppression waged by us against the enemy. We can change the converging attack directed by the enemy against us on the plane of strategy into converging attacks directed by us against the enemy on the plane of campaigns and battles. We can change the enemy's strategic superiority over us into our superiority over him in campaigns and battles. We can put the enemy who is in a strong position strategically into a weak position in campaigns and battles. At the same time we can change our own strategically weak position into a strong position in campaigns and battles. This is what we call exterior-line operations within interior-line operations, encirclement and suppression within "encirclement and suppression", blockade within blockade, the offensive within the defensive, superiority within inferiority, strength within weakness, advantage within disadvantage, and initiative within passivity. The winning of victory in the strategic defensive depends basically on this measure – concentration of troops.

In the war annals of the Chinese Red Army, this has often been an important controversial issue. In the battle of Kian on October 4, 1930, our advance and attack were begun before our forces were fully concentrated, but fortunately the enemy force (Teng Ying's division) fled of its own accord; by itself our attack was ineffective.

Beginning from 1932, there was the slogan "Attack on all fronts", which called for attacks from the base area in all directions – north, south, east and west. This is wrong not only for the strategic defensive but even for the strategic offensive. As long as there is no fundamental change in the over-all balance of forces, both strategy and tactics involve the defensive and the offensive, containing actions and assaults, and "attacks on all fronts" are in fact extremely rare. This slogan expresses the military equalitarianism which accompanies military adventurism.

In 1933 the exponents of military equalitarianism put forward the theory of "striking with two 'fists'" and splitting the main force of the Red Army in two, to seek victories simultaneously in two strategic directions. As a result, one fist remained idle while the other was tired out with fighting, and we failed to win the greatest victory possible at the time. In my opinion, when we face a powerful enemy, we should employ our army, whatever its size, in only one main direction at a time, not two. I am not objecting to operations in two or more directions, but at any given time there ought to be only one main direction. The Chinese Red Army, which entered the arena of the civil war as a small and weak force, has since repeatedly defeated its powerful antagonist and won victories that have astonished the world, and it has done so by relying largely on the employment of concentrated strength. Any one of its great victories can prove this point. When we say, "Pit one against ten, pit ten against a hundred", we are speaking of strategy, of the whole war and the over-all balance of forces, and in the strategic sense that is just what we have been doing. However, we are not speaking of campaigns and tactics, and in this sphere we must never do such a thing. Whether in counter-offensives or offensives, we should always concentrate a big force to strike at one part of the enemy forces. We suffered every time we did not concentrate our troops, as in the battles against Tan Tao-yuan in the Tungshao area of Ningtu Country in Kiangsi Province in January 1931, against the 19th Route Army in the Kaohsinghsu area of Hsingkuo County in Kiangsi in August 1931, against Chen Chi-tang in the Shuikouhsu area of Nanhsiung County in Kwangtung Province in July 1932, and against Chen Cheng in the Tuantsun area of Lichuan County in Kiangsi in March 1934. In the past, battles such as those of Shuikouhsu and Tuantsun were generally deemed victories or even big victories (in the former we routed twenty regiments under Chen Chi-tang, in the latter twelve regiments under Chen Cheng), but we never welcomed such victories and in a certain sense even regarded them as defeats. For, in our opinion, a battle has little significance when there are no prisoners or war booty, or when they do not outweigh the losses. Our strategy is "pit one against ten" and our tactics are "pit ten against one" – this is one of our fundamental principles for gaining mastery over the enemy.

Military equalitarianism reached its extreme point in our fifth counter-campaign against "encirclement and suppression" in 1934. It was thought that we could beat the enemy by "dividing the forces into six routes" and "resisting on all fronts", but instead we were beaten by the enemy, and the reason was fear of losing territory. Naturally one can scarcely avoid loss of territory when concentrating the main forces in one direction while leaving only containing forces in others. But this loss is temporary and partial and is compensated for by victory in the place where the assault is made. After such a victory is won, territory lost in the area of the containing forces can be recovered. The enemy's first, second, third and fourth campaigns of "encirclement and suppression" all entailed the loss of territory – particularly the third campaign, in which the Kiangsi base area of the Red Army was almost completely lost – but in the end we not only recovered but extended our territory.

Failure to appreciate the strength of the people in the base area has often given rise to unwarranted fear of moving the Red Army too far away from the base area. This happened when the Red Army in Kiangsi made a long drive to attack Changchow in Fukien Province in 1932, and also when it wheeled around to attack Fukien after the victory in our fourth counter-campaign in 1933. There was fear in the first case that the enemy would seize the entire base area, and in the second case that he would seize part of it; consequently there was opposition to concentrating the forces and advocacy of dividing them up for defence, but in the end all this proved to be wrong. As far as the enemy is concerned, he is afraid to advance into our base area, but the main danger in his eyes is a Red Army that has driven into the White area. His attention is always fixed on the whereabouts of the main force of the Red

Army, and he rarely takes his eyes off it to concentrate on the base area. Even when the Red Army is on the defensive, it is still the centre of the enemy's attention. Part of his over-all plan is to reduce the size of our base area, but if the Red Army concentrates its main force to annihilate one of his columns, the enemy's supreme command will be compelled to focus greater attention on the Red Army and concentrate larger forces against it. Hence it is possible to wreck an enemy plan for reducing the size of a base area.

Also, it was wrong to say, "In the fifth 'encirclement and suppression' campaign which is being carried on by means of blockhouse warfare, it is impossible for us to operate with concentrated forces, and all we can do is to divide them up for defence and for short, swift thrusts." The enemy's tactics of pushing forward 3, 5, 8, or 10 *li* at a time and building blockhouses at each halt were entirely the result of the Red Army's practice of fighting defensive actions at every successive point. The situation would certainly have been different if our army had abandoned the tactics of point-by-point defence on interior lines and, when possible and necessary, had turned and driven into the enemy's interior lines. The principle of concentration of forces is precisely the means for defeating the enemy's blockhouse warfare.

The kind of concentration of forces we advocate does not mean the abandonment of people's guerrilla warfare. To abandon small-scale guerrilla warfare and "concentrate every single rifle in the Red Army", as advocated by the Li Li-san line, has long since been proved wrong. Considering the revolutionary war as a whole, the operations of the people's guerrillas and those of the main forces of the Red Army complement each other like a man's right arm and left arm; and if we had only the main forces of the Red Army without the people's guerrillas, we would be like a warrior with only one arm. In concrete terms, and especially with regard to military operations, when we talk of the people in the base area as a factor, we mean that we have an armed people. That is the main reason why the enemy is afraid to approach our base area.

It is also necessary to employ Red Army detachments for operations in secondary directions; not all the forces of the Red Army should be concentrated. The kind of concentration we advocate is based on the principle of guaranteeing absolute or relative superiority on the battlefield. To cope with a strong enemy or to fight on a battlefield of vital importance, we must have an absolutely superior force; for instance, a force of forty thousand was concentrated to fight the nine thousand men under Chang Hui-tsan on December 30, 1930, in the first battle of our first counter-campaign. To cope with a weaker enemy or to fight on a battlefield of no great importance, a relatively superior force is sufficient; for instance, only some ten thousand Red Army men were employed to fight Liu Ho-ting's division of seven thousand men in Chienning on May 29, 1931, in the last battle of our second counter-campaign.

That is not to say we must have numerical superiority on every occasion. In certain circumstances, we may go into battle with a relatively or absolutely inferior force. Take the case of going into battle with a relatively inferior force when we have only a rather small Red Army force in a certain area (it is not that we have more troops and have not concentrated them). Then, in order to smash the attack of the stronger enemy in conditions where popular support, terrain and weather are greatly in our favour, it is of course necessary to concentrate the main part of our Red Army force for a surprise attack on a segment of one flank of the enemy while containing his centre and his other flank with guerrillas or small detachments, and in this way victory can be won. In our surprise attack on that segment of the enemy flank, the principle of using a superior force against an inferior force, of using the many to defeat the few, still applies. The same principle also applies when we go into battle with an absolutely inferior force, for example, when a guerrilla force makes a surprise attack on a large White army force, but is attacking only a small part of it.

As for the argument that the concentration of a large force for action in a single battle area is subject to the limitations of terrain, roads, supplies and billeting facilities, it should be evaluated according to the circumstances. There is a difference in the degree to which these limitations affect the Red Army and the White army, as the Red Army can stand greater hardships than the White army.

We use the few to defeat the many – this we say to the rulers of China as a whole. We use the many to defeat the few – this we say to each separate enemy force on the battlefield. That is no longer a secret, and in general the enemy is by now well acquainted with our way. However, he can neither prevent our victories nor avoid his own losses, because he does not know when and where we shall act. This we keep secret. The Red Army generally operates by surprise attacks.

Mobile warfare

Mobile warfare or positional warfare? Our answer is mobile warfare. So long as we lack a large army or reserves of ammunition, and so long as there is only a single Red Army force to do the fighting in each base area, positional warfare is generally useless to us. For us, positional warfare is generally inapplicable in attack as well as in defence.

One of the outstanding characteristics of the Red Army's operations, which follows from the fact that the enemy is powerful while the Red Army is deficient in technical equipment, is the absence of fixed battle lines.

The Red Army's battle lines are determined by the direction in which it is operating. As its operational direction often shifts, its battle lines are fluid. Though the main direction does not change in a given period of time, within its ambit the secondary directions may shift at any moment; when we find ourselves checked in one direction, we must turn to another. If, after a time, we find ourselves checked in the main direction too, then we must change even the main direction.

In a revolutionary civil war, there cannot be fixed battle lines, which was also the case in the Soviet Union. The difference between the Soviet Army and ours is that its battle lines were not so fluid as ours. There cannot be absolutely fixed battle lines in any war, because the vicissitudes of victory and defeat, advance and retreat, preclude it. But relatively fixed battle lines are often to be found in the general run of wars. Exceptions occur only where an army faces a much stronger enemy, as is the case with the Chinese Red Army in its present stage.

Fluidity of battle lines leads to fluidity in the size of our base areas. Our base areas are constantly expanding and contracting, and often as one base area falls another rises. This fluidity of territory is entirely a result of the fluidity of the war.

Fluidity in the war and in our territory produces fluidity in all fields of construction in our base areas. Construction plans covering several years are out of the question. Frequent changes of plan are all in the day's work.

It is to our advantage to recognize this characteristic. We must base our planning on this characteristic and must not have illusions about a war of advance without any retreats, take alarm at any temporary fluidity of our territory or of the rear areas of our army, or endeavour to draw up detailed long-term plans. We must adapt our thinking and our work to the circumstances, be ready to sit down as well as to march on, and always have our marching rations handy. It is only by exerting ourselves in today's fluid way of life that we can secure relative stability tomorrow, and then full stability.

The exponents of the strategy of "regular warfare" which dominated our fifth counter-campaign denied this fluidity and opposed what they called "guerrilla-ism". Those comrades, who opposed fluidity, managed affairs as though they were the rulers of a big state, and the result was an extraordinary and immense fluidity – the 25,000-*li* Long March.

Our workers' and peasants' democratic republic is a state, but today it is not yet a full-fledged one. Today we are still in the period of strategic defensive in the civil war, the form of our political power is still far from that of a full-fledged state, our army is still much inferior to the enemy both in numbers and technical equipment, our territory is still very small, and our enemy is constantly out to destroy us and will never rest content till he has done so. In defining our policy on the basis of these facts, we should not repudiate guerrilla-ism in general terms but should honestly admit the guerrilla character of the Red Army. It is no use being ashamed of this. On the contrary, this guerrilla character is precisely our distinguishing feature, our strong point, and our means of defeating the enemy. We should be prepared to discard it, but we cannot do so today. In the future this guerrilla character would definitely become something to be ashamed of and to be discarded, but today it is invaluable and we must stick to it.

"Fight when you can win, move away when you can't win" – this is the popular way of describing our mobile warfare today. There is no military expert anywhere in the world who approves only of fighting and never of moving, though few people do as much moving as we do. We generally spend more time in moving than in fighting and would be doing well if we fought an average of one sizable battle a month. All our "moving" is for the purpose of "fighting", and all our strategy and tactics are built on "fighting". Nevertheless, there are times when it is inadvisable for us to fight. In the first place, it is inadvisable to fight when the force confronting us is too large; second, it is sometimes inadvisable to fight when the force confronting us, though not so large, is very close to other enemy forces; third, it is generally inadvisable to fight an enemy force that is not isolated and is strongly entrenched; fourth, it is inadvisable to continue an engagement in which there is no prospect of victory. In any one of these situations we are prepared to move away. Such moving away is both permissible and necessary. For our recognition of the necessity of moving away is based on our recognition of the necessity of fighting. Herein lies the fundamental characteristic of the Red Army's mobile warfare.

Mobile warfare is primary, but we do not reject positional warfare where it is possible and necessary. It should be admitted that positional warfare should be employed for the tenacious defence of particular key points in a containing action during the strategic defensive, and when, during the strategic offensive, we encounter an enemy force that is isolated and cut off from help. We have had considerable experience in defeating the enemy by such positional warfare; we have cracked open many enemy cities, blockhouses and forts and broken through fairly well-fortified enemy field positions. In future we shall increase our efforts and remedy our inadequacies in this respect. We should by all means advocate positional attack or defence when circumstances require and permit it. At the present time, what we are opposed to is the general use of positional warfare or putting it on an equal footing with mobile warfare; that is impermissible.

During the ten years' civil war, have there been no changes whatsoever in the guerrilla character of the Red Army, its lack of fixed battle lines, the fluidity of its base areas, or the fluidity of construction work in its base areas? Yes, there have been changes. The period from the days in the Chingkang Mountains to our first counter-campaign against "encirclement and suppression" in Kiangsi was the first stage, the stage in which the guerrilla character and fluidity were very pronounced, the Red Army being in its infancy and the base areas still guerrilla zones. In the second stage, which comprised the period from the first to the third counter-campaign, both the guerrilla character and the fluidity were considerably reduced, front armies having been formed, and base areas with a population of several millions established. In the third stage, which comprised the period from the end of the third to the fifth counter-campaign, the guerrilla character and the fluidity were further reduced, and a central government and a revolutionary military commission had already been set up. The fourth stage was the Long March. The mistaken rejection of guerrilla warfare and fluidity on a small scale had led to guerrilla warfare and fluidity on a great scale. Now we are in the fifth stage. Because of our failure to smash the fifth "encirclement and suppression" campaign and because of this great fluidity, the Red Army and the base areas have been greatly reduced, but we have planted our feet in the Northwest and consolidated and developed our base area here, the Shensi-Kansu-Ningsia Border Region. The three front armies which form the main forces of the Red Army have been brought under a unified command, which is unprecedented.

Going by the nature of our strategy, we may also say the period from the days in the Chingkang Mountains to our fourth counter-campaign was one stage, the period of the fifth counter-campaign was another stage, and the period from the Long March to the present is the third. During the fifth counter-campaign the correct policy of the past was wrongly discarded; today we have correctly discarded the wrong policy adopted during the fifth counter-campaign and revived the earlier and correct policy. However, we have not thrown out everything in the fifth counter-campaign, nor revived everything that preceded it. We have revived only what was good in the past, and discarded only the mistakes of the period of the fifth counter-campaign.

Guerrilla-ism has two aspects. One is irregularity, that is, decentralization, lack of uniformity, absence of strict discipline, and simple methods of work. These features stemmed from the Red Army's infancy, and some of them were just what was needed at the time. As the Red Army reaches a higher stage, we must gradually and consciously eliminate them so as to make the Red Army more centralized, more unified, more disciplined and more thorough in its work — in short, more regular in character. In the directing of operations we should also gradually and consciously reduce such guerrilla characteristics as are no longer required at a higher stage. Refusal to make progress in this respect and obstinate adherence to the old stage are impermissible and harmful, and are detrimental to large-scale operations.

The other aspect of guerrilla-ism consists of the principle of mobile warfare, the guerrilla character of both strategic and tactical operations which is still necessary at present, the inevitable fluidity of our base areas, flexibility in planning the development of the base areas, and the rejection of premature regularization in building the Red Army. In this connection, it is equally impermissible, disadvantageous and harmful to our present operations to deny the facts of history, oppose the retention of what is useful, and rashly leave the present stage in order to rush blindly towards a "new stage", which is as yet beyond reach and has no real significance at the present time.

We are now on the eve of a new stage with respect to the Red Army's technical equipment and organization. We must be prepared to go over to the new stage. Not to prepare ourselves would be wrong and harmful to our future warfare. In the future, when the technical and organizational conditions in the Red Army have changed and the building of the Red Army has entered a new stage, its operational directions and battle lines will become more stable; there will be more positional warfare; the fluidity of the war, of our territory and of our construction work will be greatly reduced and finally disappear; and we will no longer be handicapped by present limitations, such as the enemy's superiority and his strongly entrenched positions.

At present we oppose the wrong measures of the period of the domination of "Left" opportunism and, at the same time, the revival of many of the irregular features which the Red Army had in its infancy but which are now unnecessary. But we should be resolute in restoring the many valuable principles of army building and of strategy and tactics by which the Red Army has consistently won its victories. We must sum up all that is good from the past in a systematic, more highly developed and richer military line, in order to win victories over the enemy today and prepare to go over to the new stage in the future.

The waging of mobile warfare involves many problems, such as reconnaissance, judgement, decision, combat disposition, command, concealment, concentration, advance, deployment, attack, pursuit, surprise attack, positional attack, positional defence, encounter action, retreat, night fighting, special operations, evading the strong and attacking the weak, besieging the enemy in order to strike at his reinforcements, feint attack, defence against aircraft, operating amongst several enemy forces, by-passing operations, consecutive operations, operating without a rear, the need for rest and building up energy. These problems exhibited many specific features in the history of the Red Army, features which should be methodically dealt with and summed up in the science of campaigns, and I shall not go into them here.

War of quick decision

A strategically protracted war and campaigns or battles of quick decision are two aspects of the same thing, two principles which should receive equal and simultaneous emphasis in civil wars and which are also applicable in anti-imperialist wars.

Revolutionary forces grow only gradually because the reactionary forces are very strong, and this fact determines the protracted nature of our war. Here impatience is harmful and advocacy of "quick decision" incorrect. To wage a revolutionary war for ten years, as we have done, might be surprising in other countries, but for us it is like the opening sections in an "eight-legged essay" – the "presentation, amplification and preliminary exposition of the theme"[25] – and many exciting parts are yet to follow. No doubt developments in the future will be greatly accelerated under the influence of domestic and international conditions. As changes have already taken place in the international and domestic situation and greater changes are coming, it can be said that we have outgrown the past state of slow development and fighting in isolation. But we should not expect successes overnight. The aspiration to "wipe out the enemy before breakfast" is admirable, but it is bad to make concrete plans to do so. As China's reactionary forces are backed by many imperialist powers, our revolutionary war will continue to be a protracted one until China's revolutionary forces have built up enough strength to breach the main positions of our internal and external enemies, and until the international revolutionary forces have crushed or contained most of the international reactionary forces. To proceed from this point in formulating our strategy of long-term warfare is one of the important principles guiding our strategy.

The reverse is true of campaigns and battles – here the principle is not protractedness but quick decision. Quick decision is sought in campaigns and battles, and this is true at all times and in all countries. In a war as a whole, too, quick decision is sought at all times and in all countries, and a long drawn-out war is considered harmful. China's war, however, must be handled with the greatest patience and treated as a protracted war. During the period of the Li Li-san line, some people ridiculed our way of doing things as "shadow-boxing tactics" (meaning our tactics of fighting many battles back and forth before going on to seize the big cities), and said that we would not see the victory of the revolution until our hair turned white. Such impatience was proved wrong long ago. But if their criticism had been applied not to strategy but to campaigns and battles, they would have been perfectly right, and for the following reasons. First, the Red Army has no sources from which to replenish its arms and especially its ammunition; second, the White forces consist of many armies while there is only one Red Army, which must be prepared to fight one operation after another in quick succession in order to smash each campaign of "encirclement and suppression"; and third, though the White armies advance separately, most of them keep fairly close to one another, and if we fail to gain a quick decision in attacking one of them, all the others will converge upon us. For these reasons we have to fight battles of quick decision. It is usual for us to conclude a battle in a few hours, or in a day or two. It is only when our plan is to "besiege the enemy in order to strike at his reinforcements" and our purpose is to strike not at the besieged enemy but at his reinforcements that we are prepared for a certain degree of protractedness in our besieging operations; but even then we seek a quick decision against the reinforcements. A plan of protracted operations is often applied in campaigns or battles when we are strategically on the defensive and are tenaciously defending positions on a holding front, or when, in a strategic offensive, we are attacking isolated enemy forces cut off from help, or are eliminating White strongholds within our base areas. But protracted operations of this kind help rather than hinder the main Red Army force in its battles of quick decision.

A quick decision cannot be achieved simply by wanting it, but requires many specific conditions. The main requirements are: adequate preparations, seizing the opportune moment, concentration of superior forces, encircling and outflanking tactics, favourable terrain, and striking at the enemy when he is on the move, or when he is stationary but has not yet consolidated his positions. Unless these requirements are satisfied, it is impossible to achieve quick decision in a campaign or battle.

The smashing of an enemy "encirclement and suppression" is a major campaign, but the principle of quick decision and not that of protractedness still applies. For the manpower, financial resources and military strength of a base area do not allow protractedness.

While quick decision is the general principle, we must oppose undue impatience. It is altogether necessary that the highest military and political leading body of a revolutionary base area, having taken into account the circumstances in its base area and the situation of the enemy, should not be overawed by the enemy's truculence, dispirited by hardships that can be endured, or dejected by setbacks, but should have the requisite patience and stamina. The smashing of the first enemy "encirclement and suppression" campaign in Kiangsi Province took only one week from the first battle to the last; the second was smashed in barely a fortnight; the third dragged on for three months before it was smashed; the fourth took three weeks; and the fifth taxed our endurance for a whole year. When we were compelled to break through the enemy's encirclement after the failure to smash his fifth campaign, we showed an unjustifiable haste. In the circumstances then obtaining, we could well have held out for another two or three months, giving the troops some time for rest and reorganization. If that had been done, and if the leadership had been a little wiser after our breakthrough, the outcome would have been very different.

For all that, the principle of shortening the duration of a campaign by every possible means remains valid. Campaign and battle plans should call for our maximum effort in concentration of troops, mobile warfare, and so on, so as to ensure the destruction of the enemy's effective strength on the interior lines (that is, in the base area) and the quick defeat of his "encirclement and suppression" campaign, but where it is evident that the campaign cannot be terminated on our interior lines, we should employ the main Red Army force to break through the enemy's encirclement and switch to our exterior lines (that is, the enemy's interior lines) in order to defeat him there. Now that the enemy has developed his blockhouse warfare to a high degree, this will become our usual method of operation. At the time of the Fukien Incident,[26] two months after the commencement of our fifth counter-campaign, the main forces of the Red Army should undoubtedly have thrust into the Kiangsu-Chekiang-Anhwei-Kiangsi region, with Chekiang as the centre, and swept over the length and breadth of the area between Hangchow, Soochow, Nanking, Wuhu, Nanchang and Foochow, turning our strategic defensive into a strategic offensive, menacing the enemy's vital centres and seeking battles in the vast areas where there were no blockhouses. By such means we could have compelled the enemy, who was attacking southern Kiangsi and western Fukien, to turn back to defend his vital centres, broken his attack on the base area in Kiangsi and rendered aid to the People's Government in Fukien – we certainly could have aided it by this means. As this plan was rejected, the enemy's fifth "encirclement and suppression" campaign could not be broken, and the People's Government in Fukien inevitably collapsed. Even after a year's fighting, though it had become inopportune for us to advance on Chekiang, we could still have turned to the strategic offensive in another direction by moving our main forces towards Hunan, that is, by driving into central Hunan instead of going through Hunan to Kweichow, and in this way we could have manoeuvred the enemy from Kiangsi into Hunan and destroyed him there. As this plan, too, was rejected, all hope of breaking the enemy's fifth campaign was finally dashed, and we had no alternative but to set out on the Long March.

War of annihilation

It is inappropriate to advocate a "contest of attrition" for the Chinese Red Army today. A "contest of treasures" not between Dragon Kings but between a Dragon King and a beggar would be rather ludicrous. For the Red Army which gets almost all its supplies from the enemy, war of annihilation is the basic policy. Only by annihilating the enemy's effective strength can we smash his "encirclement and suppression" campaigns and expand our revolutionary base areas. Inflicting casualties is a means of annihilating the enemy, or otherwise there would be no sense to it. We incur losses ourselves in inflicting casualties on the enemy but we replenish ourselves by annihilating his units, thereby not only making good our losses but adding to the strength of our army. A battle in which the enemy is routed is not basically decisive in a contest with an enemy of great strength. A battle of annihilation, on the other hand, produces a great and immediate impact on any enemy. Injuring all of a man's ten fingers is not as effective as chopping off one, and routing ten enemy divisions is not as effective as annihilating one of them.

Our policy for dealing with the enemy's first, second, third and fourth "encirclement and suppression" campaigns was war of annihilation. The forces annihilated in each campaign constituted only part of the enemy's total strength, and yet all these "encirclement and suppression" campaigns were smashed. In our fifth counter-campaign, however, the opposite policy was pursued, which in fact helped the enemy to attain his aims.

War of annihilation entails the concentration of superior forces and the adoption of encircling or outflanking tactics. We cannot have the former without the latter. Conditions such as popular support, favourable terrain, a vulnerable enemy force and the advantage of surprise are all indispensable for the purpose of annihilation.

Merely routing one enemy force or permitting it to escape has meaning only if, in the battle or campaign as a whole, our main force is concentrating its operations of annihilation against another enemy force, or otherwise it is meaningless. Here the losses are justified by the gains.

In establishing our own war industry we must not allow ourselves to become dependent on it. Our basic policy is to rely on the war industries of the imperialist countries and of our domestic enemy. We have a claim on the output of the arsenals of London as well as of Hanyang, and, what is more, it is delivered to us by the enemy's transport corps. This is the sober truth, it is not a jest.

Notes

1 For an explanation, see pp. 132–33 of this volume.
2 See "On Correcting Mistaken Ideas in the Party", Notes 4 and 5, pp. 61–62 of this volume.
3 "Bandit ways" refers to plundering and looting resulting from lack of discipline, organization and clear political direction.
4 The Long March of 25,000 *li* (12,500 kilometres) was made by the Red Army from Kiangsi Province to northern Shensi Province. In October 1934 the First Front Army, *i.e.*, the Central Red Army, comprising the First, the Third and the Fifth Army Groups of the Chinese Workers' and Peasants' Red Army, began its great strategic shift. Setting out from Changting and Ninghua in western Fukien and from Juichin and Yutu in southern Kiangsi, the Red Army traversed the eleven provinces of Fukien, Kiangsi, Kwangtung, Hunan, Kwangsi, Kweichow, Szechuan, Yunnan, Sikang, Kansu and Shensi. It climbed over high mountains perpetually covered with snow and marched across uninhabited wild marshes. Having undergone untold tribulations and repeatedly defeated the enemy in his attempts to encircle, pursue or intercept it, the Red Army ended its continuous march of 25,000 *li* by victoriously arriving in the revolutionary base area in northern Shensi in October 1935.
5 The period after the December uprising of 1905 was defeated, in which the revolutionary tide in Russia gradually receded. See *History of the Communist Party of the Soviet Union (Bolsheviks), Short Course,* Chapter 3, Sections 5 and 6.
6 The peace treaty of Brest-Litovsk was concluded between Soviet Russia and Germany in March 1918. Confronted with obviously superior enemy forces, the revolutionary forces had to make a temporary retreat in order to prevent the German imperialists from launching an attack on the new-born Soviet Republic which as yet had no army of its own. The conclusion of this treaty gained time for the Soviet Republic to consolidate the political power of the proletariat, reorganize its economy and build up the Red Army. It enabled the proletariat to maintain its leadership over the peasantry and build up sufficient strength to defeat the White Guards and the armed intervention of Britain, the United States, France, Japan, Poland and other countries in 1918–20.
7 On October 30, 1927 the peasants of Haifeng and Lufeng in Kwangtung Province launched their third insurrection under the leadership of the Communist Party of China. They occupied Haifeng and Lufeng and the surrounding area, organized a Red Army and established the democratic political power of the workers and peasants. They were later defeated because they made the mistake of underestimating the enemy.
8 The Fourth Front Army and the Second Front Army of the Red Army joined forces in the autumn of 1936 and shifted northward from the northeastern part of Sikang. Chang Kuo-tao was then still persisting in his anti-Party stand and in his policy of retreat and liquidation which he had hitherto pursued. In October of the same year, when the Second and Fourth Front Armies arrived in Kansu, Chang Kuo-tao ordered the advance units of the Fourth Front Army, numbering more than 20,000, to organize the Western Column for crossing the Yellow River and advancing westward to Chinghai. The Western Column was practically defeated after suffering blows in battles in December 1936 and was completely defeated in March 1937.
9 See letter from Marx to Kugelmann on the Paris Commune.
10 *Shui Hu Chuan* is a celebrated Chinese novel describing a peasant war. The novel is attributed to Shih Nai-an who lived around the end of the Yuan Dynasty and the beginning of the Ming Dynasty (fourteenth century A.D.). Lin Chung and Chai Chin are both heroes in this novel. Hung is the drill master on Chai Chin's estate.
11 Lu and Chi were two feudal states in the Spring and Autumn Era (722–481 B.C.). Chi was a big state in the central part of the present Shantung Province, and Lu was a smaller one in the southern part. Duke Chuang reigned over Lu from 693 to 662 B.C.

12 Tsochiu Ming was the author of *Tso Chuan*, a classical chronicle of the Chou Dynasty. For the passage quoted, see the section in *Tso Chuan* entitled "The 10th Year of Duke Chuang" (684 B.C.).

13 The ancient town of Chengkao, in the northwest of the present Chengkao County, Honan Province, was of great military importance. It was the scene of battles fought in 203 B.C. between Liu Pang, King of Han, and Hsiang Yu, King of Chu. At first Hsiang Yu captured Yunyang and Chengkao and Liu Pang's troops were almost routed. Liu Pang waited until the opportune moment when Hsiang Yu's troops were in midstream crossing the Chishui River, and then crushed them and recaptured Chengkao.

14 The ancient town of Kunyang, in the north of the present Yehhsien County, Honan Province, was the place where Liu Hsiu, founder of the Eastern Han Dynasty, defeated the troops of Wang Mang, Emperor of the Hsin Dynasty, in 23 B.C. There was a huge numerical disparity between the two sides, Liu Hsiu's forces totalling 8,000 to 9,000 men as against Wang Mang's 400,000. But taking advantage of the negligence of Wang Mang's generals, Wang Shun and Wang Yu, who underestimated the enemy, Liu Hsiu with only three thousand picked troops put Wang Mang's main forces to rout. He followed up this victory by crushing the rest of the enemy troops.

15 Kuantu was in the northeast of the present Chungmou County, Honan Province and the scene of the battle between the armies of Tsao Tsao and Yuan Shao in A.D. 200. Yuan Shao had an army of 100,000, while Tsao Tsao had only a meagre force and was short of supplies. Taking advantage of lack of vigilance on the part of Yuan Shao's troops, who belittled the enemy, Tsao Tsao dispatched his light-footed soldiers to spring a surprise attack on them and set their supplies on fire. Yuan Shao's army was thrown into confusion and its main force wiped out.

16 The state of Wu was ruled by Sun Chuan, and the state of Wei by Tsao Tsao. Chihpi is situated on the south bank of the Yangtse River, to the northeast of Chiayu, Hupeh Province. In A.D. 208 Tsao Tsao led an army of over 500,000 men, which he proclaimed to be 800,000 strong, to launch an attack on Sun Chuan. The latter, in alliance with Tsao Tsao's antagonist Liu Pei, mustered a force of 30,000. Knowing that Tsao Tsao's army was plagued by epidemics and was unaccustomed to action afloat, the allied forces of Sun Chuan and Liu Pei set fire to Tsao Tsao's fleet and crushed his army.

17 Yiling, to the east of the present Ichang, Hupeh Province, was the place where Lu Sun, a general of the state of Wu, defeated the army of Liu Pei, ruler of Shu, in A.D. 222. Liu Pei's troops scored successive victories at the beginning of the war and penetrated five or six hundred *li* into the territory of Wu as far as Yiling. Lu Sun, who was defending Yiling, avoided battle for over seven months until Liu Pei "was at his wits' end and his troops were exhausted and demoralized". Then he crushed Liu Pei's troops by taking advantage of a favourable wind to set fire to their tents.

18 Hsieh Hsuan, a general of Eastern Tsin Dynasty, defeated Fu Chien, ruler of the stage of Chin, in A.D. 383 at the Feishui River in Anhwei Province. Fu Chien had an infantry force of more than 600,000, a cavalry force of 270,000 and a guards corps of more than 30,000, while the land and river forces of Eastern Tsin numbered only 80,000. When the armies lined up on opposite banks of the Feishui River, Hsieh Hsuan, taking advantage of the overconfidence and conceit of the enemy troops, requested Fu Chien to move his troops back so as to leave room for the Eastern Tsin troops to cross the river and fight it out. Fu Chien complied, but when he ordered withdrawal, his troops got into a panic and could not be stopped. Seizing the opportunity, the Eastern Tsin troops crossed the river, launched an offensive and crushed the enemy.

19 Nanchang, capital of Kiangsi Province, was the scene of the famous uprising on August 1, 1927 led by the Communist Party of China in order to combat the counter-revolution of Chiang Kai-shek and Wang Ching-wei and to continue the revolution of 1924–27. More than thirty thousand troops took part in the uprising which was led by Comrades Chou En-lai, Chu Teh, Ho Lung and Yeh Ting. The insurrectionary army withdrew from Nanchang on August 5 as planned, but suffered a defeat when approaching Chaochow and Swatow in Kwangtung Province. Led by Comrades Chu Teh, Chen Yi and Lin Piao, part of the troops later fought their way to the Chingkang Mountains and joined forces with the First Division of the First Workers' and Peasants' Revolutionary Army under Comrade Mao Tse Tung.

20 See "Why Is It That Red Political Power Can Exist in China?", Note 8, pp. 17–18 of this volume.

21 The famous Autumn Harvest Uprising under the leadership of Comrade Mao Tse Tung was launched in September 1927 by the people's armed forces of Hsiushui, Pinghsiang, Pingkiang and Liuyang Counties on the Hunan-Kiangsi border, who formed the First Division of the

First Workers' and Peasants' Revolutionary Army. Comrade Mao Tse Tung led this force to the Chingkang Mountains where a revolutionary base was established.

22 The A–B (initials for "Anti-Bolshevik") Group was a counter-revolutionary organization of undercover Kuomintang agents in the Red areas.

23 See V.I. Lenin, *Selected Works* (two-volume English ed.), Vol. II. Moscow, 1947, "Theses on the Question of the Immediate Conclusion of a Separate and Annexationist Peace", "Strange and Monstrous", "A Serious Lesson and a Serious Responsibility", "Report on War and Peace" and also *History of the Communist Party of the Soviet Union (Bolsheviks), Short Course*, Chapter 7, Sector 7.

24 The regions referred to here are those inhabited by the Tibetans in Sikang and the Hui people in Kansu, Chinghai and Sinkiang Provinces.

25 The "eight-legged essay" was the prescribed form in the imperial competitive examinations in feudal China from the fifteenth to the nineteenth century. The main body of the essay was made up of the inceptive paragraph, the middle paragraph, the rear paragraph and the concluding paragraph, with each paragraph comprising two parts. Here, Comrade Mao Tse Tung is using the development of the theme in this kind of essay as a metaphor to illustrate the development of the revolution through its various stages. However. Comrade Mao Tse Tung generally uses the term "eight-legged essay!" to ridicule dogmatism.

26 In November 1933, under the influence of the anti-Japanese upsurge of the people throughout China, the leaders of the Kuomintang's 19th Route Army, in alliance with the Kuomintang forces under Li Chi-shen, publicly renounced Chiang Kai-shek and established the "People's Revolutionary Government of the Republic of China" in Fukien, concluding an agreement with the Red Army to attack Chiang Kai-shek and resist Japan. This episode was referred to as the Fukien Incident. The 19th Route Army and the People's Government of Fukien, however, collapsed under the attacks of Chiang Kai-shek's troops.

15 Counterinsurgency warfare
Theory and practice

David Galula

Revolutionary war: nature and characteristics

What is a revolutionary war?

A revolutionary war is primarily an internal conflict, although external influences seldom fail to bear upon it. Although in many cases, the insurgents have been easily identifiable national groups—Indonesians, Vietnamese, Tunisians, Algerians, Congolese, Angolans today—this does not alter the strategically important fact that they were challenging a *local* ruling power controlling the existing administration, police, and armed forces. In this respect, colonial revolutionary wars have not differed from the purely indigenous ones, such as those in Cuba and South Vietnam.

The conflict results from the action of the insurgent aiming to seize power—or to split off from the existing country, as the Kurds are attempting to do now—and from the reaction of the counterinsurgent aiming to keep his power. At this point, significant differences begin to emerge between the two camps. Whereas in conventional war either side can initiate the conflict, only one—the insurgent—can initiate a revolutionary war, for counterinsurgency is only an effect of insurgency. Furthermore, counterinsurgency cannot be defined except by reference to its cause.

Paraphrasing Clausewitz, we might say that "Insurgency is the pursuit of the policy of a party, inside a country, by every means." It is not like an ordinary war—a "continuation of the policy by other means"—because an insurgency can start long before the insurgent resorts to the use of force.

Revolution, plot, insurgency

Revolution, plot (or *coup d'état*), and insurgency are the three ways to take power by force. It will be useful to our analysis to try to distinguish among them.

A revolution usually is an explosive upheaval—sudden, brief, spontaneous, unplanned (France, 1789; China, 1911; Russia, 1917; Hungary, 1956). It is an *accident*, which can be explained afterward but not predicted other than to note the existence of a revolutionary situation. How and exactly when the explosion will occur cannot be forecast. A revolutionary situation exists today in Iran. Who can tell what will happen, whether there will be an explosion, and if so, how and when it will erupt?

In a revolution, masses move and then leaders appear. Sun Yat-sen was in England when the Manchu dynasty was overthrown, Lenin in Switzerland when the Romanovs fell.

A plot is the clandestine action of an insurgent group directed at the overthrow of the top leadership in its country. Because of its clandestine nature, a plot cannot and does not involve the masses. Although preparations for the plot may be long, the action itself is brief and sudden. A plot is always a *gamble* (the plot against Hitler in 1944; the plots in Iraq against King Faisal and Nuri al-Said in 1958, and against Kassem in 1963).

On the other hand, an insurgency is a *protracted struggle* conducted methodically, step by step, in order to attain specific intermediate objectives leading finally to the overthrow of the existing order (China, 1927–49; Greece, 1945–50; Indochina, 1945–54; Malaya, 1948–60; Algeria, 1954–62). To be sure, it can no more be predicted than a revolution; in fact, its beginnings are so vague that to determine exactly when an insurgency starts is a difficult legal, political, and historical problem. In China, for instance, should it be dated from 1927, when the Kuomintang-Communist alliance broke and force came into play, or from 1921, when the Chinese Communist Party was founded to establish a Communist regime in the country? But though it cannot be predicted, an insurgency is usually slow to develop and is not an accident, for in an insurgency leaders appear and then the masses are made to move. Although all recent insurgencies—with the exception of that in Greece— were clearly tied to a revolutionary situation, the cases of Malaya (1948–60), Tunisia (1952–55), Morocco (1952–56), Cyprus (1955–59), Cuba (1957–59), and others seem to show that the revolutionary situation did not have to be acute in order for the insurgency to be initiated.

Insurgency and civil war

An insurgency is a civil war. Yet there is a difference in the form the war takes in each case.

A civil war suddenly splits a nation into two or more groups which, after a brief period of initial confusion, find themselves in control of part of both the territory and the existing armed forces, which they proceed immediately to develop. The war between these groups soon resembles an ordinary international war except that the opponents are fellow citizens, such as in the American War Between the States and the Spanish Civil War.

Asymmetry between the insurgent and counterinsurgent

There is an asymmetry between the opposite camps of a revolutionary war. This phenomenon results from the very nature of the war, from the disproportion of strength between the opponents at the outset, and from the difference in essence between their assets and their liabilities.

Since the insurgent alone can initiate the conflict (which is not to say that he is necessarily the first to use force), strategic initiative is his by definition. He is free to choose his hour, to wait safely for a favorable situation, unless external factors force him to accelerate his moves. However, in the world of today, polarized as it is between East and West, no revolutionary war can remain a purely internal affair. It is probable that the Malayan and the Indonesian Communist Parties were ordered to start the violent phase of their insurgency at the 1948 Calcutta Communist-sponsored Conference of Youth and Students of Southeast Asia. Thus, the decision was not entirely left to the Malayan and Indonesian Parties.

Until the insurgent has clearly revealed his intentions by engaging in subversion or open violence, he represents nothing but an imprecise, potential menace to the counterinsurgent and does not offer a concrete target that would justify a large effort. Yet an insurgency can reach a high degree of development by legal and peaceful means, at least in countries where political opposition is tolerated. This greatly limits pre-emptive moves on the part of the counterinsurgent. Usually, the most he can do is to try to eliminate or alleviate the conditions propitious for an insurgency.

An appraisal of the contending forces at the start of a revolutionary war shows an overwhelming superiority in tangible assets in favor of the counterinsurgent. Endowed with the normal foreign and domestic perquisites of an established government, he has virtually everything—diplomatic recognition; legitimate power in the executive, legislative, and judicial branches; control of the administration and police; financial resources; industrial and agricultural resources at home or ready access to them abroad; transport and communications facilities; use and control of the information and propaganda media; command of the armed forces and the possibility of increasing their size. He is *in* while the insurgent, being *out*, has none or few of these assets.

The situation is reversed in the field of intangibles. The insurgent has a formidable asset— the ideological power of a cause on which to base his action. The counterinsurgent has a heavy liability—he is responsible for maintaining order throughout the country. The insurgent's strategy will naturally aim at converting his intangible assets into concrete ones, the counterinsurgent's strategy at preventing his intangible liability from dissipating his concrete assets.

The insurgent thus has to grow in the course of the war from small to large, from weakness to strength, or else he fails. The counterinsurgent will decline from large to small, from strength to weakness, in direct relation to the insurgent's success.

The peculiarities that mark the revolutionary war as so different from the conventional one derive from this initial asymmetry.

Objective: the population

Afflicted with his congenital weakness, the insurgent would be foolish if he mustered whatever forces were available to him and attacked his opponent in a conventional fashion, taking as his objective the destruction of the enemy's forces and the conquest of the territory. Logic forces him instead to carry the fight to a different ground where he has a better chance to balance the physical odds against him.

The population represents this new ground. If the insurgent manages to dissociate the population from the counterinsurgent, to control it physically, to get its active support, he will win the war because, in the final analysis, the exercise of political power depends on the tacit or explicit agreement of the population or, at worst, on its submissiveness.

Thus the battle for the population is a major characteristic of the revolutionary war.

Revolutionary war is a political war

All wars are theoretically fought for a political purpose, although in some cases the final political outcome differs greatly from the one intended initially.

In the conventional war, military action, seconded by diplomacy, propaganda, and economic pressure, is generally the principal way to achieve the goal. Politics *as an instrument of war* tends to take a back seat and emerges again—as an instrument—when the fighting ends. We are not implying that politics vanishes entirely as the main directing force but rather that, in the course of the conventional war, once political goals have been set (although the government may change them), once directives have been given to the armed forces (although the government may modify them), military action becomes foremost. "*La parole passe aux armes*"; the gun becomes the "*ultima ratio regum.*" With the advent of the nuclear age and its consequent risks of mutual destruction, politics, no doubt, will interfere more closely—as it did in the recent case of Korea—with the conduct of the war (limited objectives) and with the actual conduct of the operations (privileged sanctuaries, exclusion of nuclear weapons). Nevertheless, military action remains the principal instrument of the conventional war.

As a result, it is relatively easy to allocate tasks and responsibilities among the government, which directs operations, the population, which provides the tools, and the soldier, who utilizes them.

The picture is different in the revolutionary war. The objective being the population itself, the operations designed to win it over (for the insurgent) or to keep it at least submissive (for the counterinsurgent) are essentially of a political nature. In this case, consequently, political action remains foremost throughout the war. It is not enough for the government to set political goals, to determine how much military force is applicable, to enter into alliances or to break them; *politics becomes an active instrument of operation.* And so intricate is the interplay between the political and the military actions that they cannot be tidily separated; on the contrary, every military move has to be weighed with regard to its political effects, and vice versa.

The insurgent, whose political establishment is a party and whose armed forces are the party's forces, enjoys an obvious advantage over his opponent, whose political establishment is the country's government, which may or may not be supported by a party or by a coalition of parties with their centrifugal tendencies, and whose army is the nation's army, reflecting the consensus or the lack of consensus in the nation.

Gradual transition from peace to war

In the conventional war, the aggressor who has prepared for it within the confines of his national territory, channeling his resources into the preparation, has much to gain by attacking suddenly with all his forces. The transition from peace to war is as abrupt as the state of the art allows; the first shock may be decisive.

This is hardly possible in the revolutionary war because the aggressor—the insurgent—lacks sufficient strength at the outset. Indeed, years may sometimes pass before he has built up significant political, let alone military, power. So there is usually little or no first shock, little or no surprise, no possibility of an early decisive battle.

In fact, the insurgent has no interest in producing a shock until he feels fully able to withstand the enemy's expected reaction. By delaying the moment when the insurgency appears as a serious challenge to the counterinsurgent, the insurgent delays the reaction. The delay may be further prolonged by exploiting the fact that the population realizes the danger even later than the counterinsurgent leadership.

Revolutionary war is a protracted war

The protracted nature of a revolutionary war does not result from a design by either side; it is imposed on the insurgent by his initial weakness. It takes time for a small group of insurgent leaders to organize a revolutionary movement, to raise and to develop armed forces, to reach a balance with the opponent, and to overpower him. A revolutionary war is short only if the counterinsurgency collapses at an early stage, as in Cuba, where the Batista regime disintegrated suddenly, less under the blows from the insurgents than through its own weakness; or if, somehow, a political settlement is reached, as in Tunisia, Morocco, Cyprus. To date, there has never been an early collapse of an insurgency.

The revolutionary war in China lasted twenty-two years, if 1927 is taken as the starting year. The war lasted five years in Greece, nine in Indochina, nine in the Philippines, five in Indonesia, twelve in Malaya, three in Tunisia, four in Morocco, eight in Algeria. The war started in 1948 in Burma and still goes on, though in a feeble way.

Insurgency is cheap, counterinsurgency costly

Promoting disorder is a legitimate objective for the insurgent. It helps to disrupt the economy, hence to produce discontent; it serves to undermine the strength and the authority of the counterinsurgent. Moreover, disorder—the normal state of nature—is cheap to create and very costly to prevent. The insurgent blows up a bridge, so every bridge has to be guarded; he throws a grenade in a movie theater, so every person entering a public place has to be searched. When the insurgent burns a farm, all the farmers clamor for protection; if they do not receive it, they may be tempted to deal privately with the insurgent, as happened in Indochina and Algeria, to give just two examples. Merely by making anonymous phone calls warning of bombs planted in luggage, the insurgent can disrupt civilian airline schedules and scare away tourists.

Because the counterinsurgent cannot escape the responsibility for maintaining order, the ratio of expenses between him and the insurgent is high. It may be ten or twenty to one, or higher. The figure varies greatly, of course, from case to case, and in each situation during the course of the revolutionary war. It seems to apply particularly when the insurgent reaches the initial stages of violence and resorts to terrorism and guerrilla warfare. The British calculated the cost of every rebel in Malaya at more than $200,000. In Algeria, the FLN budget at its peak amounted to $30 or $40 million a year, less than the French forces had to spend in two weeks.

There is, it seems, an upper limit to this ratio. When the insurgent increases his terrorism or guerrilla activity by a factor of two, three, or five, he does not force the counterinsurgent to multiply his expenditures by the same factor. Sooner or later, a saturation point is reached, a point where the law of diminishing returns operates for both sides.

Once the insurgent has succeeded in acquiring stable geographical bases, as, for instance, the Chinese Communists did in northwest China, or the Vietminh in Tonkin, he becomes *ipso facto* a strong promoter of order within his own area, in order to show the difference between the effectiveness of his rule and the inadequacy of his opponent's.

Because of the disparity in cost and effort, the insurgent can thus accept a protracted war; the counterinsurgent should not.

Fluidity of the insurgent, rigidity of the counterinsurgent

The insurgent is fluid because he has neither responsibility nor concrete assets; the counterinsurgent is rigid because he has both, and no amount of wailing can alter this fact for either side. Each must accept the situation as it is and make the best of it.

If the counterinsurgent wanted to rid himself of his rigidity, he would have to renounce to some extent his claim to the effective rule of the country, or dispose of his concrete assets. One way of doing this, of course, would be to hand over everything to the insurgent, and then start an insurgency against him, but no counterinsurgent on record has dared apply this extreme solution.

On the other hand, the insurgent is obliged to remain fluid at least until he has reached a balance of forces with the counterinsurgent. However desirable for the insurgent to possess territory, large regular forces, and powerful weapons, to possess them and to rely on them prematurely could spell his doom. The failure of the Greek Communist insurgents may be attributed in part to the risk they took when they organized their forces into battalions, regiments, and divisions, and accepted battle. The Vietminh made the same mistake in 1951 in Tonkin, and suffered serious setbacks.

In the revolutionary war, therefore, and until the balance of forces has been reached, only the insurgent can consistently wage profitable hit-and-run operations because the counterinsurgent alone offers profitable and fixed targets; only the insurgent, as a rule, is free to accept or refuse battle, the counterinsurgent being bound by his responsibility. On the other hand, only the counterinsurgent can use substantial means because he alone possesses them.

Fluidity for one side and rigidity for the other are further determined by the nature of the operations. They are relatively simple for the insurgent—promoting disorder in every way until he assumes power; they are complicated for the counterinsurgent, who has to take into account conflicting demands (protection of the population and the economy, and offensive operations against the insurgent) and who has to coordinate all the components of his forces—the administrator, the policeman, the soldier, the social worker, etc. The insurgent can afford a loose, primitive organization; he can delegate a wide margin of initiative, but his opponent cannot.

The power of ideology

The insurgent cannot seriously embark on an insurgency unless he has a well-grounded cause with which to attract supporters among the population. A cause, as we have seen, is his sole asset at the beginning, and it must be a powerful one if the insurgent is to overcome his weakness.

Can two explosive but antagonistic causes exist simultaneously in a single country—one for the insurgent, the other for his opponent? Such a situation has happened occasionally, for example, in the United States, when the antislavery movement clashed with the doctrine of states' rights. The most likely result in this case is a civil war, not an insurgency.

The probability is that only one cause exists. If the insurgent has pre-empted it, then the force of ideology works for him and not for the counterinsurgent. However, this is true largely in the early parts of the conflict. Later on, as the war develops, war itself becomes the paramount issue, and the original cause consequently loses some of its importance.

It has been asserted that a counterinsurgent confronted by a dynamic insurgent ideology is bound to meet defeat, that no amount of tactics and technique can compensate for his ideological handicap. This is not necessarily so, because the population's attitude in the middle stage of the war is dictated not so much by the relative popularity and merits of the opponents as by the more primitive concern for safety. Which side gives the best protection, which one threatens the most, which one is likely to win, these are the criteria governing the population's stand. So much the better, of course, if popularity and effectiveness are combined.

Propaganda—A one-sided weapon

The asymmetrical situation has important effects on propaganda. The insurgent, having no responsibility, is free to use every trick; if necessary, he can lie, cheat, exaggerate. He is not obliged to prove; he is judged by what he promises, not by what he does. Consequently, propaganda is a powerful weapon for him. With no positive policy but with good propaganda, the insurgent may still win.

The counterinsurgent is tied to his responsibilities and to his past, and for him, facts speak louder than words. He is judged on what he does, not on what he says. If he lies, cheats, exaggerates, and does not prove, he may achieve some temporary successes, but at the price of being discredited for good. And he cannot cheat much unless his political structures are monolithic, for the legitimate opposition in his own camp would soon disclose his every psychological maneuver. For him, propaganda can be no more than a secondary weapon, valuable only if intended to inform and not to fool. A counterinsurgent can seldom cover bad or nonexistent policy with propaganda.

Revolutionary war remains unconventional until the end

Once the insurgent has acquired strength and possesses significant regular forces, it would seem that the war should become a conventional one, a sort of civil war in which each camp holds a portion of the national territory from which he directs blows at the other. But if the insurgent has understood his strategic problems well, revolutionary war never reverts to a conventional form.

For one reason, the creation of a regular army by the insurgent does not mean an end to subversion and guerrilla activity. On the contrary, they increase in scope and intensity in order to facilitate the operations of the regular army and to amplify their effects.

For another reason, the insurgent has involved the population in the conflict since its beginning; the active participation of the population was indeed a *sine qua non* for his success. Having acquired the decisive advantage of a population organized and mobilized on his side, why should he cease to make use of an asset that gives his regular forces the fluidity and the freedom of action that the counter-insurgent cannot achieve? As long as the population remains under his control, the insurgent retains his liberty to refuse battle except on his own terms.

In 1947, the Chinese Nationalists launched an offensive against Yenan, the Communist capital, in northern Shensi. They took it without difficulty; the Communist Government and regular forces evacuated the area without a fight. Soon after, however, the population, the local militias, and a small core of guerrilla and regional troops began harassing the Nationalists while regular Communist units attacked their long communication lines, which extended north from Sian. The Nationalists were finally obliged to withdraw, having gained nothing and lost much in the affair.

In 1953, the French forces in Indochina found a study made by the Vietminh command to determine whether in Vietminh territory there was any area, any fixed installation worth defending. The answer was no. Indeed, that same year, in Vietminh territory northwest of Hanoi, the French seized a huge depot of trucks and ammunitions left totally unguarded.

We have indicated above the general characteristics of revolutionary war. They are an ineluctable product of the nature of this war. An insurgent or a counterinsurgent who would conduct his war in opposition to any of these characteristics, going against the grain, so to speak, would certainly not increase his chances for success.

The prerequisites for a successful insurgency

The cause of most recent insurgencies can easily be attributed to revolutionary situations that might have exploded into spontaneous revolutions but bred instead a group of leaders who then proceeded to organize and conduct the insurgencies. In view of this fact, it would be wrong and unjust to conclude that insurgencies are merely the product of personal ambitions on the part of their leaders who developed the whole movement artificially.

For the sake of demonstration, let us suppose that in Country X a small group of discontented men—possessing the attributes of leadership, inspired by the success of so many insurgencies in the past twenty years, well aware of the strategic and tactical problems involved in such an enterprise—have met and decided to overthrow the existing order by the path of insurgency.

In light of the counterinsurgents' material superiority at the outset, their chances of victory will obviously depend on whether certain preliminary conditions are met. What conditions? Are these conditions a must? In other words, what are the prerequisites for a successful insurgency?

Knowing what they are would help in assessing, from a counterinsurgent's point of view, how vulnerable a country would be to an insurgency.

A cause

Necessity of a cause

How can the insurgent ever hope to pry the population away from the counterinsurgent, to control it, and to mobilize it? By finding supporters among the population, people whose support will range from active participation in the struggle to passive approval. The first basic need for an insurgent who aims at more than simply making trouble is an attractive cause, particularly in view of the risks involved and in view of the fact that the early supporters and the active supporters—not necessarily the same persons—have to be recruited by persuasion.

With a cause, the insurgent has a formidable, if intangible, asset that he can progressively transform into concrete strength. A small group of men *sans* cause can seize power by a lucky plot—this has happened in history—but then a plot is not an insurgency. The lack of an attractive cause is what restrains a priori apolitical crime syndicates from attempting to assume power, for they realize that only criminals will follow them.

The 1945–50 Communist insurgency in Greece, a text-book case of everything that can go wrong in an insurgency, is an example of failure due, among other less essential reasons, to the lack of a cause. The Communist Party, the EAM, and its army, the ELAS, grew during World War II, when the entire population was resisting the Germans. Once the country was liberated, the EAM could find no valid cause. Greece had little industry and consequently no proletariat except the dockers of Piraeus and tobacco factory workers; the merchant sailors, whose jobs kept them moving about, could provide no constant supply. There was no appalling agrarian problem to exploit. The wealthy Greek capitalists, whose fortunes had usually been made abroad, were an object of admiration rather than hostility in a trade-minded nation. No sharply fixed class existed; the Minister of the Navy might well be the cousin of a café waiter. To make matters worse, the Greek Communists were perforce allied to Bulgaria, Greece's traditional enemy; to Yugoslavia, which claims a part of Greece's Macedonia; to Albania, from which Greece claims part of Epirus. With national feelings running as high as they do in the Balkans, these associations did not increase the popularity of the Greek Communists.

Using what forces they had at the end of the war, taking advantage of the difficult terrain, withdrawing into safe asylum across the satellites' borders when necessary, the Communist insurgents were able to wage commando-type operations but not true guerrilla warfare; in fact, their infiltrating units had to hide from the population when they could not cow it, and their operations lasted generally as long as the supplies they carried with them. The ELAS was obliged to enlist partisans by force. Whenever the unwilling recruits found the political commissar behind their back less dangerous than the nationalist forces in front, they deserted.

The main reason the insurgency lasted so long was that, at the start, the regular government forces consisted of only a single brigade, which had fought with the Allies in the Mediterranean Theater and was greatly outnumbered by the insurgents. As soon as the army was reorganized and strengthened, first with British, then with U.S. aid, the nationalist command undertook to clean the country area by area, by purely military action. A cleaned area was kept clean by arming local militias; this presented little difficulty since the population was definitely anti-Communist and could be relied upon.

Strategic criteria of a cause

The best cause for the insurgent's purpose is one that, by definition, can attract the largest number of supporters and repel the minimum of opponents. Thus, a cause appealing to the proletariat in an industrialized country (or to the peasants in an underdeveloped one) is a good cause. A purely Negro movement trying to exploit the Negro problem as a basis for an insurgency in the United States (with a population of 20 million Negroes and 160 million whites) would be doomed from the start. In South Africa (with 11 million Negroes and 4 million whites), its chances would be good—other factors aside. Independence from colonial rule was automatically a good cause in Indonesia, Indochina, Tunisia, Morocco, Algeria, Cyprus, the Belgian Congo, and now Angola.

The insurgent must, of course, be able to identify himself totally with the cause or, more precisely, with the entire majority of the population theoretically attracted by it. In Malaya, independence from Great Britain was the cause chosen by the insurgents, the Malayan Communist Party. However, 90 per cent of the Party members were Chinese, not true Malays; the Malays consequently remained largely indifferent to the struggle. The same story occurred in Kenya (if one chooses to qualify what took place there as a revolutionary war; the insurgency was conducted in so crude a fashion as to make its inclusion in this category questionable). Independence was pursued by members of a single tribe, the Kikuyus; no other tribe moved in support.

To be perfectly sound, the cause must be such that the counterinsurgent cannot espouse it too or can do so only at the risk of losing his power, which is, after all, what he is fighting for. Land reform looked like a promising cause to the Hukbalahaps after the defeat of Japan and the accession of the Philippines to independence; but when the government offered land to the Huks' actual and potential supporters, the insurgents lost their cause and the game. The same disaster struck the Malayan Communist Party, once Britain promised independence to the country and set a date for it.

A cause, finally, must also be lasting, if not for the duration of the revolutionary war, at least until the insurgent movement is well on its feet. This differentiates a strategic cause from a tactical one, a deep-seated cause from a temporary one resulting from the exploitation of an ephemeral difficulty, such as, for instance, the high price and the scarcity of food after a year of natural calamities.

The nature of the cause

What is a political problem? It is "an unsolved contradiction," according to Mao Tse Tung. If one accepts this definition, then a political cause is the championing of one side of the contradiction. In other words, where there is no problem, there is no cause, but there are always problems in any country. What makes one country more vulnerable than another to insurgency is the depth and the acuity of its existing problems.

Problems of all natures are exploitable for an insurgency, provided the causes they lead to meet the above criteria. The problem may be essentially political, related to the national or international situation of the country. The dictatorship of Batista for the Cuban insurgents, the Japanese aggression for the Chinese are examples of political problems. It follows that any country where the power is invested in an oligarchy, whether indigenous or foreign, is potential ground for a revolutionary war.

The problem may be social, as when one class is exploited by another or denied any possibility of improving its lot. This has been exhaustively discussed since Karl Marx, and little need be added here. The problem becomes particularly dangerous when the society does not integrate those who, by the level of their education or by their achievements, have proved to belong to the true elite. For it is among this rejected elite that the insurgents can find the indispensable leaders.

The problem may be economic, such as the low price of agricultural products in relation to industrial goods, or the low price of raw material in relation to finished products, or the import of foreign goods rather than the development of a national industry. The issue of neocolonialism today is closely related to this problem.

The problem may be racial, as it would be in South Africa. Or religious, as it would be in Lebanon, although here the population is evenly divided between Christians and Moslems. Or cultural, as in India, where the multiplicity of languages has already produced considerable agitation.

The problem may even be artificial so long as it has a chance to be accepted as a fact. The lot of the Chinese farmers—victims of exactions by the authorities and of the rapacity of the local usurers—was no doubt a hard one. The Chinese Communists did exploit this problem. However, their chief cause, borrowed from Sun Yat-sen, was land reform. Its revolutionary value lies in the idea that land ownership was concentrated in a small minority; a class war on the issue would theoretically bring to their side the majority of the farmers. The sole comprehensive work on the subject of land tenure in China, by J. Lossing Buck, contradicted the Communist picture of the situation,[1] but this fact did not decrease in the slightest the psychological value of the slogan "Land to the Tiller." An efficient propaganda machine can turn an artificial problem into a real one.

It is not absolutely necessary that the problem be acute, although the insurgent's work is facilitated if such is the case. If the problem is merely latent, the first task of the insurgent is to make it acute by "raising the political consciousness of the masses." Terrorism may be a quick means of producing this effect. Batista's dictatorship did not by itself suddenly become unbearable to the Cuban people; they had lived under other dictatorships in the past, including a previous Batista regime. And the country was prosperous in 1958, although there was great disparity in the distribution of wealth. Batista might perhaps have lasted many more years had it not been for Castro and his followers, who spectacularly raised the issue and focused the latent opposition on their movement.

Tactical manipulation of the cause

The insurgent is not restricted to the choice of a single cause. Unless he has found an over-all cause, like anti-colonialism, which is sufficient in itself because it combines all the political, social, economic, racial, religious, and cultural causes described above, he has much to gain by selecting an assortment of causes especially tailored for the various groups in the society that he is seeking to attract.

Let us suppose that the revolutionary movement is tentatively made up, as it was in China, of the Communist Party ("vanguard of the revolution, party of the workers and the poor farmers") and its allies (medium and rich peasants, artisans, plus the "national bourgeoisie" and the capitalists who suffer from "bureaucratic capitalism" and from the economic encroachments of the imperialists). The insurgent has to appeal to the whole, and a cause is necessary for that. Since it is easier to unite "against" than "for," particularly when the components are so varied, the general cause will most probably be a negative one, something like "throw the rascals out" (the rascals in this case: Chiang Kai-shek and the Kuomintang reactionaries; the feudal warlords; "bureaucratic capitalism"; the compradores, "running dogs of imperialism"; and the landlords). In addition, the insurgent must appeal to each component of the movement, and in this aspect, the various causes will probably contain a constructive element: for the proletariat, a Marxist society; for the poor farmers, land; for the medium farmers, fair taxes; for the rich farmers, just, reasonable, and lasting settlement; for the national bourgeoisie, defense of the national interests, order, fair taxes, development of trade and industry, protection against imperialist competition.

Nothing obliges the insurgent to stick to the same cause if another one looks more profitable. Thus, in China, the Communists initially took the classic Marxist stand in favour of the workers (1921–25). Then they actively espoused the national cause of the Kuomintang, for the unification of China against the warlords (1925–27). After the Kuo-mintang-Communist split, they largely dropped the workers in favor of the poor peasants, advocating land reform by radical means (1928–34). Then Japanese aggression became the central issue in China, and the Communists advocated a patriotic united front against Japan (1927–45), adopting meanwhile a moderate agrarian policy: Land redistribution would be ended, but instead, the Communists would impose strict control of rents and interest rates. After the Japanese surrender, they finally reverted to land reform with the temperate proviso that landlords themselves would be entitled to a share of land (1945–49). What the Communists actually did after their victory, between 1950 and 1952, was to carry out their land reform "through violent struggles" in order to conduct a class war among the rural population and thereby definitely to commit the activists on their side, if only because these activists had shared in the crimes. Once this was achieved, the Party buried land reform for good and started collectivizing the land.

Thus, if idealism and a sense of ethics weigh in favor of a consistent stand, tactics pull toward opportunism.

Diminishing importance of the cause

The importance of a cause, an absolute essential at the outset of an insurgency, decreases progressively as the insurgent acquires strength. The war itself becomes the principal issue, forcing the population to take sides, preferably the winning one. This has already been explained in the previous chapter.

Weakness of the counterinsurgent

Let us assume now that our minute group of insurgent leaders in Country X has found several good causes, some acute, some latent, some even artificial, on which to base their insurgency. They all have agreed on a potent platform. Can they start operating? Not unless another preliminary condition has been met. The insurgent, starting from almost zero while his enemy still has every means at his disposal, is as vulnerable as a new-born baby. He cannot live and grow without some sort of protection, and who but the counterinsurgent himself can protect him? Therefore, we must analyze what makes a body politic resistant to infection.

Strengths and weaknesses of the political regime

1. *Absence of problems.* A country fortunate enough to know no problem is obviously immune from insurgency. But since we have assumed that our potential insurgent leaders have found a cause, let us eliminate these countries—if there are any—from our consideration.

2. *National consensus.* The solidity of a regime is primarily based upon this factor. Thailand may live under a dictatorship or a democratic system, but her national consensus—which is not apathy, for the Thais would react vigorously to any attempt against their King and their way of life—has so far always strengthened the regime in power. On the other hand, no national consensus backs up East Germany's government.

3. *Resoluteness of the counterinsurgent leadership.* Resoluteness is a major factor in any sort of conflict, but particularly so in a revolutionary war for the reasons that (a) the insurgent has the initial benefit of a dynamic cause; (b) an insurgency does not grow suddenly into a national danger and the people's reaction against it is slow. Consequently, the role of the counterinsurgent leaders is paramount.

4. *Counterinsurgent leaders' knowledge of counterinsurgency warfare.* It is not enough for the counterinsurgent leaders to be resolute; they must also be aware of the strategy and tactics required in fighting an insurgency. Generalissimo Chiang Kai-shek's determination cannot be questioned; he proved it against Japan and still shows it in Taiwan. But did he know how to cope with the Communists' methods?

5. *The machine for the control of the population.* Four instruments of control count in a revolutionary war situation: the political structure, the administrative bureaucracy, the police, the armed forces.

a. *The political structure.* If Country X is located behind the Iron Curtain, where political opposition is not tolerated and where the population is kept under a system of terror and mutual suspicion, the initial group of insurgents has no chance to develop; at best, the group will be able to survive in total secrecy—and hence be completely inactive—while waiting for better times.

Since there are people who dream of unleashing insurgencies in certain Communist countries—"Don't the people hate the regime there?"—it may be useful to give an idea of the extent of population control achieved by the Communist techniques of terror and mutual suspicion, of which the Red Chinese are past masters.

In Canton, in 1954, a neighbor saw an old Chinese lady giving some rice to her cat.

"I am sorry, but I will be obliged to report you at the next street meeting," said the neighbor to the owner of the cat.

"Why?" asked the old lady.

"Because rice is rationed and you have been wasting it on your cat."

"If you report me, they will cut off my rice ration. Why don't you just keep silent?"

"Suppose someone else saw you and reports you. What will happen to me, your neighbor, if I have not reported you first? I am your friend. If they suppress your ration I will give you half of mine."

This is exactly what happened, in a city where, according to some Western visitors, Chinese Communist control was less efficient than elsewhere in China.

At the end of 1952, a European was expelled from Hainan Island, where he had lived for many years. On reaching Hong Kong, he reported that the peasants "hated" the regime, and he gave much convincing evidence of it. He mentioned later that the Nationalists had twice attempted to drop agents in his area from Taiwan. In each case, the militia on duty at night heard the planes, saw the parachutes coming down, gave the alert, and the Nationalist agents were cornered and captured by several hundred armed villagers.

The European was challenged on this: "Isn't there a contradiction between your state-ment concerning the feelings of the peasants toward the regime and the attitude of the militiamen who, after all, are peasants too? Why didn't they keep silent?"

"Put yourself in the place of one of these militiamen," he explained. "How does he know whether the other members of the militia won't give the alert? If they do and he hasn't, he will be in great trouble when the Communist cadres make their usual post-mortem investigations."

In July, 1953, during the Korean War, the Nationalists decided to make a raid on the mainland of China. They selected as their objective the small peninsula of Tungshan, jutting out of the Fukien coast, which is transformed into an island at high tide. The Communist garrison was made up of a regular battalion plus a thousand-man militia. The latter, the Nationalists thought, would put up no real fight. Indeed, every piece of available intelligence indicated that the population was thoroughly fed up with the Communists. The plan was to drop a regiment of paratroopers to neutralize the Communist battalion and to control the isthmus in order to prevent reinforcement from the mainland; an amphibious landing would follow to wipe out the opposition.

Because of a miscalculation in computing the local tide, the amphibious landing was delayed, and the Nationalist paratroopers bore the brunt of the opposition alone. They were virtually annihilated. The militia fought like devils. How could they act otherwise when they knew that the Nationalist action was just a raid?

A control of this order rules out the possibility of launching an insurgency. As long as there is no privacy, as long as every unusual move or event is reported and checked, as long as parents are afraid to talk in front of their children, how can contacts be made, ideas spread, recruiting accomplished?

What is possible is terrorism in a limited way, because a single man, even though com-pletely isolated, can conduct a terrorist campaign; witness the case of the "mad bomber" in New York. But terrorism itself has far less value than the publicity that it is expected to produce, and it is rather doubtful that Communist authorities would complacently furnish publicity.

Another tactic that continues to be possible is one used in Greece by the Communists—unsustained commando-type operations where terrain conditions are favorable.

At the other extreme, if anarchy prevails in Country X, the insurgent will find all the facilities he needs in order to meet, to travel, to contact people, to make known his program, to find and organize the early supporters, to receive and to distribute funds, to agitate and to subvert, or to launch a widespread campaign of terrorism.

In between these extremes lies a wide range of political structures that in varying degrees facilitate or hinder the task of the insurgent: dictatorship with a one-party system, dictator-ship with no link to the grass roots, vigilant democracy, indolent democracy, etc.

b. *The administrative bureaucracy.* A country is run in its day-to-day life by its bureaucracy, which has a force of its own that has sometimes no relation to the strength or weakness of the top political leadership. France under the Third and Fourth Republics had a weak leadership but a strong administrative apparatus; the opposite appears to be the case in South Vietnam today. Since an insurgency is a bottom-to-top movement, an administrative vacuum at the bottom, an incompetent bureaucracy, plays into the hands of the insurgent.

The case of Algeria may be taken as an example. The territory was notoriously under-administered on the eve of the insurgency, not because the civil servants were incompetent but rather because the bureaucratic establishment had no relation to the size of the country and its population. Algeria (not counting the Sahara) extends more than 650 miles along the Mediterranean Sea and 350 miles inland, with an area of 115,000 square miles and a population of 10,500,000 of whom 1,200,000 are of European stock.

Under a governor general in Algiers, the territory was divided into three *départements* with seats in Oran, Algiers, and Constantine, each under a *préfet* assisted by a large staff. A *département* was in turn divided into *sous-préfectures;* for instance, in the *département* of Algiers, there was the *sous-préfecture* of Kabylia, with its seat in Tizi-Ouzou. Kabylia consisted of 5,000 square miles of rugged mountain terrain, with 1,200,000 inhabitants, of whom 90 per cent were Moslems.

The lower echelon in predominantly Moslem areas was the *commune-mixte* under a French administrator with 1 or 2 assistants and 5 gendarmes; the *commune-mixte* of Tigzirt, in Kabylia, measured 30 miles by 20 miles, with some 80,000 inhabitants.

At the lowest level was the *douar*, where the power of the state was embodied in a *garde-champêtre*, a native rural policeman armed with an old pistol in a holster on which shone a brass sign engraved with the awe-inspiring words: "*La Loi*." One such *douar* covered an area of 10 miles by 6 miles, with a population of 15,000 Kabyles.

With this setup, the insurgents had a field day.

c. *The police*. The eye and the arm of the government in all matters pertaining to internal order, the police are obviously a key factor in the early stages of an insurgency; they are the first counterinsurgent organization that has to be infiltrated and neutralized.

Their efficiency depends on their numerical strength, the competency of their members, their loyalty toward the government, and, last but not least, on the backing they get from the other branches of the government—particularly the judicial system. If insurgents, though identified and arrested by the police, take advantage of the many normal safeguards built into the judicial system and are released, the police can do little. Prompt adaptation of the judicial system to the extraordinary conditions of an insurgency, an agonizing problem at best, is a necessity. Algeria may again serve as an example. The total police force in 1954 was less than 50,000, barely larger than the police force for the city of Paris. When the insurgency was brewing, the Algerian police gave timely warnings, which were not heeded. A year after the insurgency broke out, the French National Assembly finally granted the government the "special powers" required to deal with the situation. By that time, the police—particularly its Moslem members—had been engulfed in the chaos.

d. *The armed forces*. Leaving aside the factors of strength applicable to the armed forces in all wars, those that are relevant in a revolutionary war are:

i. The numerical strength of the armed forces in relation to the size and the population of the country. An insurgency is a two-dimensional war fought for the control of the population. There is no front, no safe rear. No area, no significant segment of the population can be abandoned for long—unless the population can be trusted to defend itself. This is why a ratio of force of ten or twenty to one between the counterinsurgent and the insurgent is not uncommon when the insurgency develops into guerrilla warfare. The French forces in Indochina never approached this ratio, a fact that, more than any other, explains why the French could not have won there even if they had been led by Napoleon, regardless of the power of the nationalist cause initially.

ii. The composition of the armed forces. A conventional war today requires a modern, well-balanced force, with its air, sea, and ground components. But a revolutionary war is primarily a war of infantry. Paradoxically, the less sophisticated the counterinsurgent forces, the better they are. France's NATO divisions were useless in Algeria; their modern equipment had to be left behind, and highly specialized engineer or signal units had to be hurriedly converted into ordinary infantry. Naval operations by the insurgent being unlikely, all a navy needs is a sufficient force to blockade the coast line effectively. As for an air force, whose supremacy the insurgent cannot challenge, what it needs are slow assault fighters, short take-off transport planes, and helicopters.

iii. The feeling of the individual soldier toward the insurgent's cause and toward the counterinsurgent regime. Whereas the insurgent initially can use only a few combatants and can therefore select volunteers, the counterinsurgent's manpower demands are so high that he is compelled to draft soldiers, and he may well be plagued by the problem of loyalty. A few cases of collective desertions may cast so much suspicion on counterinsurgent units that their value may evaporate altogether. This happened with Algerian Rifle units in the early stage of the war in Algeria; although basically sound and trustworthy, these units had to be retired from direct contact with the population and used in a purely military capacity.

iv. The time lapse before intervention. Because of the gradual transition from peace to war in a revolutionary war, the armed forces are not ordered into action as fast as they would be in a conventional war. This delay is another characteristic of revolutionary wars. To reduce it is a political responsibility of the country's leaders.

6. *Geographic conditions.* Geography can weaken the strongest political regime or strengthen the weakest one. This question will subsequently be examined in more detail.

It is the combination of all these factors that determines whether an insurgency is possible or not once the potential insurgent has a cause.

Crisis and insurgency

The insurgent cannot, of course, choose his opponent; he must accept him as he is. If he is confronted by a powerful counterinsurgent, he has no recourse but to wait until his opponent is weakened by some internal or external crisis.

The recent series of colonial insurgencies is, no doubt, a consequence of World War II, which constituted a formidable crisis for the colonial powers. The record shows that no insurgency or revolt succeeded in colonial territories before 1938, although the situation then was no less revolutionary than after the war. Few were even attempted—a revolt in the Dutch East Indies in 1926–27 and the extraordinary passive-resistance movement headed by Gandhi in India virtually exhaust the list.

The history of the Chinese Communist insurgency offers another example of the exploitation of a crisis. After a slow climb from 50 members in 1921 to 1,000 in 1925, the Chinese Communist Party associated itself with the Kuomintang, and its membership rose suddenly to 59,000 in 1926. The expansion was facilitated by the state of anarchy prevailing in China and by the popularity of the struggle led by the Kuomintang against the warlords and the imperialists. The two parties split in 1927, and the CCP went into open rebellion. Immediately, the membership fell to 10,000. A Communist group with Mao Tse Tung took refuge in the Kiangsi-Hunan area, while other groups scattered in various places. They slowly initiated guerrilla warfare, and, although at first they committed the mistake of attacking well-defended towns, they managed to develop their military strength. Membership rose to

300,000 in 1934. The Kuomintang had succeeded by that time in establishing itself as the central government of China, and the Communists alone presented a challenge to its authority. The Kuomintang, by now a strong power, was energetically trying to stamp out the rebellion. After several unsuccessful offensives against the Communists, the Nationalist forces pressed them so hard that the CCP was really fighting for its survival. In order to escape annihilation, the Communists set off on their Long March, from Kiangsi to a remote area in the north of Shensi. In 1937, after the Long March, membership had fallen again to 40,000. Chiang Kai-shek was preparing another powerful offensive to finish off the Reds when they were saved by a crisis, the Japanese aggression against China. By V-J day, the Party had grown to 1,200,000, controlled an area of 350,000 square miles with a population of 95 million, and had a regular army of 900,000 men and a militia force of 2,400,000. It was no longer vulnerable.

The border doctrine

Every country is divided for administrative and military purposes into provinces, counties, districts, zones, etc. The border areas are a permanent source of weakness for the counter-insurgent whatever his administrative structures, and this advantage is usually exploited by the insurgent, especially in the initial violent stages of the insurgency. By moving from one side of the border to the other, the insurgent is often able to escape pressure or, at least, to complicate operations for his opponent.

It was no accident that the Chinese Communist-dominated areas included the Shensi-Kansu-Ningsia Border Area, the Shansi-Chahar-Hopei Military Region, the Hopei-Shantung-Honan Military Region. Operating astride borders had become a matter of doctrine for them.

Geographic conditions

The role of geography, a large one in an ordinary war, may be overriding in a revolutionary war. If the insurgent, with his initial weakness, cannot get any help from geography, he may well be condemned to failure before he starts. Let us examine briefly the effects of the various geographic factors.

1. *Location*. A country isolated by natural barriers (sea, desert, forbidding mountain ranges) or situated among countries that oppose the insurgency is favorable to the counterinsurgent.

2. *Size*. The larger the country, the more difficult for a government to control it. Size can weaken even the most totalitarian regime; witness China's present troubles in Tibet.

3. *Configuration*. A country easy to compartmentalize hinders the insurgent. Thus the Greek national forces had an easy task cleaning the Peloponnesus peninsula. If the country is an archipelago, the insurgency cannot easily spread, as was the case in the Philippines. The Indonesian Government, which is not remarkable for its strength, managed nevertheless to stamp out rebellions in the Moluccas, Amboina, and other islands.

4. *International borders*. The length of the borders, particularly if the neighboring countries are sympathetic to the insurgents, as was the case in Greece, Indochina, and Algeria, favors the insurgent. A high proportion of coast line to inland borders helps the counterinsurgent because maritime traffic can be controlled with a limited amount of technical means, which the counterinsurgent possesses or is usually able to acquire. It was cheaper in money and manpower to suppress smuggling along the coast of Algeria than along the Tunisian

and Moroccan borders, where the French Army had to build, maintain, and man an artificial fence.

5. *Terrain.* It helps the insurgent insofar as it is rugged and difficult, either because of mountains and swamps or because of the vegetation. The hills of Kiangsi, the mountains of Greece, the Sierra Maestra, the swamps of the Plain of Reeds in Cochinchina, the paddy fields of Tonkin, the jungle of Malaya gave a strong advantage to the insurgents. The Chinese Communists in Manchuria profitably used the time when the fields were covered with high kaoliang stalks.

On the other hand, the FLN was never able to operate for any sustained period in the vast expanses of the Sahara, with the French forces securing the oases and vital wells and air surveillance detecting every move and even traces of movement left on sand.

6. *Climate.* Contrary to the general belief, harsh climates favor the counterinsurgent forces, which have, as a rule, better logistical and operational facilities. This will be especially favorable if the counterinsurgent soldier is a native and, therefore, accustomed to the rigors of the climate. The rainy season in Indochina hampered the Vietminh more than it did the French. Winter in Algeria brought FLN activity almost to a standstill. Merely to keep scarce weapons and ammunition in good condition when one lives continuously in the open, as the guerrilla does, is a perpetual headache.

7. *Population.* The size of the population affects the revolutionary war in the same way as does the size of the country: the more inhabitants, the more difficult to control them. But this factor can be attenuated or enhanced by the density and the distribution of the population. The more scattered the population, the better for the insurgent; this is why counterinsurgents in Malaya, in Algeria, and in South Vietnam today have attempted to regroup the population (as in Cambodia in 1950–52). A high ratio of rural to urban population gives an advantage to the insurgent; the OAS in Algeria was doomed tactically because it could rely only on the European population, which was concentrated in cities, particularly Algiers and Oran. The control of a town, which is extremely dependent on outside supplies, requires smaller forces than the control of the same number of people spread over the countryside—except in the case of a mass uprising, which can never last long in any event.

8. *Economy.* The degree of development and sophistication of the economy can work both ways. A highly developed country is very vulnerable to a short and intense wave of terrorism. But if terrorism lasts, the disruption becomes such that the population may not be able to endure it and, consequently, may turn against the insurgent even when it was not initially hostile to him.

An underdeveloped country is less vulnerable to terrorism but much more open to guerrilla warfare, if only because the counterinsurgent cannot count on a good network of transport and communication facilities and because the population is more autarchic.

To sum up, the ideal situation for the insurgent would be a large land-locked country shaped like a blunt-tipped star, with jungle-covered mountains along the borders and scattered swamps in the plains, in a temperate zone with a large and dispersed rural population and a primitive economy. (See Figure 15.1.) The counterinsurgent would prefer a small island shaped like a pointed star, on which a cluster of evenly spaced towns are separated by desert, in a tropical or arctic climate, with an industrial economy. (See Figure 15.2.)

Figure 15.1

Figure 15.2

Outside support

Outside support to an insurgency can take the form of:

1. *Moral support*, from which the insurgent will benefit without any effort on his part, provided his cause goes along with "the wind of history." Thus, in the present struggle between Angolans and the Portuguese Government, the former benefit from considerable moral support, while the latter is isolated. Moral support is expressed by the weight of public opinion and through various communications media. Propaganda is the chief instrument of moral support, used to sway public opinion when it is adverse, or to reinforce existing public sympathy.

2. *Political support*, with pressure applied directly on the counterinsurgent, or indirectly by diplomatic action in the international forum. Taking the same case as an example, we see that many African states have broken off diplomatic relations with Lisbon and recognized a provisional government of Angola; they have also succeeded in expelling Portugal from various international organizations such as the International Labor Organization.

3. *Technical support*, in the form of advice to the insurgent for the organization of his movement and the conduct of his political and military operations. The similarity between the Vietminh and the Chinese Communists' methods was not accidental.

4. *Financial support*, overt or covert. A great part of the FLN budget came from grants by the Arab League. Red China shipped tea to the FLN in Morocco, where it was sold on the open market.

5. *Military support*, either through direct intervention on the insurgent's side or by giving him training facilities and equipment.

No outside support is absolutely necessary at the start of an insurgency, although it obviously helps when available.

Military support short of direct intervention, in particular, cannot be absorbed in a significant amount by the insurgent until his forces have reached a certain level of development. The initial military phase of an insurgency, whether terrorism or guerrilla warfare, requires little in the way of equipment, arms, ammunition, and explosives. These can usually be found locally or smuggled in.

When the time comes, however, for the insurgent to pass from guerrilla warfare to a higher form of operations, to create a regular army, the need for much larger and more varied supplies becomes acute. Either he is able to capture it from the counterinsurgent, or it must come from the outside. If not, the development of the insurgent military establishment is impossible.

The Communists in China received little or no support from abroad until Manchuria was occupied by the Soviet Army; the arms and equipment of the Japanese Kwantung Army were turned over to 100,000 soldiers from the People's Liberation Army who had crossed into Manchuria from Jehol and Shantung. The Communists in Manchuria were at once able to conduct large-scale sustained operations, and the nature of the fighting in this area was markedly different from the Communist operations south of the Great Wall. Access to the Japanese Army stores was not the decisive factor in the outcome of the war, since the Communist forces in China proper, who received few supplies from Manchuria, succeeded in arming themselves with captured Nationalist equipment; but it certainly hastened the defeat of the best Nationalist troops in Manchuria. The Communists boasted that their quartermaster and ordnance depots were conveniently located forward, in the hands of the Nationalists. Their slogan "Feed the War by War" was not an empty assertion.

In Indochina, the turning point occurred in 1950, when the Vietminh began receiving aid from Red China. Until then, they had been unable to develop their forces and to stage large-scale operations, not because they suffered from manpower problems—they had more potential soldiers than they could use—but because their primitive arsenals could not fill their needs, and they could not capture significant amounts of French weapons. Although the Vietminh could have fought a protracted guerrilla warfare, and thus could have denied the French any benefit from a prolonged occupation of the country, they would not have been able to raise a powerful regular army without Chinese aid. By September, 1950, 20,000 men in the Vietminh forces had been equipped with machine guns, heavy mortars, anti-aircraft weapons. The Vietminh command was able to organize a Heavy Division, the 351st. In 1951, according to French estimates, Chinese aid amounted to 18,000 rifles, 1,200 machine guns, 150–200 heavy mortars, and about 50 recoilless guns.[2]

In Malaya and the Philippines, the insurgents received no outside military support and did not develop.

In Greece, the Communist insurgents received support from and through the satellite countries, but the split between Tito and Stalin interrupted the flow just when the insurgents, having organized their forces into large—and vulnerable—units, needed it most.

In Algeria, the French naval blockade and the sealing of the borders prevented the flow of supplies to Algeria from Tunisia and Morocco, where large rebel stocks had been accumulated. No development was possible. The situation of the FLN forces after 1959 became so critical that most of their automatic weapons were buried for lack of ammunition.

The East-West conflict that today covers the entire world cannot fail to be affected by any insurgency occurring anywhere. Thus, a Communist insurgency is almost certain to receive automatic support from the Communist bloc. Chances for Communist support are good even for non-Communist insurgents, provided, of course, that their opponent is an "imperialist" or an ally of "imperialism."

Conversely, the East-West conflict sometimes accelerates the outbreak of insurgencies— and this is not always a blessing for the insurgents, as we have seen in the cases of the Communist movements in Asia after the 1948 Calcutta meeting—and sometimes slows them down or inhibits them entirely, when insurgencies do not fit in with the over-all policy of the Communist bloc. This last point cannot be documented, naturally, but there are strong presumptions that the surprisingly quiet attitude of the Indonesian Communist Party today, which seems powerful enough to go into violent action, may be attributed to some sort of veto from Moscow and/or Peking.

If outside support is too easily obtainable, it can destroy or harm self-reliance in the insurgent ranks. For this reason, partly, Communist insurgents in Asia have always emphasized the necessity of counting on their own efforts. The resolution of the First Session of the Vietnamese Central Committee of the Lao Dong (Communist) Party in 1951 reminded Party members that "our Resistance War is a long and hard struggle" and "we have mainly to rely on our own forces."

In conclusion, (1) a cause, (2) a police and administrative weakness in the counterinsurgent camp, (3) a not-too-hostile geographic environment, and (4) outside support in the middle and later stages of an insurgency—these are the conditions for a successful insurgency. The first two are musts. The last one is a help that may become a necessity.

Notes

1   Buck's *Land Utilization in China* (London: Oxford University Press, 1937) was based on investigations conducted in 1929–33 in 16,786 farms, 168 localities. 154 hsien (counties), 22 provinces.
Table 22 gives the percentages of farmers who were owners, part-owners, and tenants:

   Owners: 54.2%   Part-owners: 39.9%   Tenants: 5.9%

   In the wheat region of North China, where the Communists were strongly established, the percentages were:

   Owners: 76.1%   Part-owners: 21.8%   Tenants: 2.1%

   Table 23 gives the average sizes of farms (in hectares) by class of ownership. In the wheat region:

   Owners: 2.25   Part-owners: 2.25   Tenants: 2.05

   Another table gives the numbers and percentages of farms in each size class. For the wheat region:

   Very Small: 2   Small: 24   Medium: 34   Medium Large: 17   Large: 12
   Very Large: 9   Very, Very Large: 2   Very, Very, Very Large: 0

The Chinese Communist figures on land distribution, based on a report by Liu Shao-ch'i in June, 1950, were these: "Landlords and peasants, who account for less than 10 per cent of the rural population, own 70 to 80 per cent of all the land, while poor peasants, agricultural laborers and middle peasants, who account for about 90 per cent of the rural population, own only 20 to 30 per cent of the land. . . ." (Editorial in *Jen-min Jih-Pao*, as quoted in C.K. Yang, *A Chinese Village in Early Communist Transition* [Cambridge, Mass.: The Technology Press, Massachusetts Institute of Technology, 1959].)

2   Bernard Fall, *Le Viet-Minh* (Paris: Librairie Armand Colin, 1960), p. 195.

16 Why big nations lose small wars

The politics of asymmetric conflict

*Andrew Mack**

A cursory examination of the history of imperialist expansion in the late nineteenth and early twentieth century reveals one thing very clearly: Third-World resistance, where it existed, was crushed with speedy efficiency. In terms of conventional military thinking such successes were not unexpected. Indeed, together with the Allied experience in the first and second World Wars, they served to reinforce and to rigidify the pervasive notion that superiority in military capability (conventionally defined) will mean victory in war. However, the history of a number of conflicts in the period following World War II showed that military and technological superiority may be a highly unreliable guide to the outcome of wars. In Indochina (1946–54), Indonesia (1947–49), Algeria, Cyprus, Aden, Morocco, and Tunisia, local nationalist forces gained their objectives in armed confrontations with industrial powers which possessed an overwhelming superiority in conventional military capability. These wars were not exclusively a colonial phenomenon, as was demonstrated by the failure of the United States to defeat its opponents in Vietnam.

For some idea of the degree to which the outcome of these wars presents a radical break with the past, it is instructive to examine the case of Indochina. The French successfully subjugated the peoples of Indochina for more than sixty years with a locally based army only fifteen thousand strong. The situation changed dramatically after 1946, when the Vietnamese took up arms in guerrilla struggle. By 1954 the nationalist forces of the Vietminh had forced the French—who by this time had deployed an expeditionary force of nearly two hundred thousand men—to concede defeat and withdraw their forces in ignominy. Within twenty years, a vast U.S. military machine with an expeditionary force five hundred thousand strong had also been forced to withdraw.

The purpose of this paper is to attempt to provide a "pre-theoretical perspective" within which the *outcome* of such "asymmetric conflicts" may be explained. In the field of conflict research, the study of the outcome and the conduct of wars, as against that of their *etiology*, has received remarkably little attention.[1] The outcome of "asymmetric conflicts" as described in this paper has been almost totally neglected.[2]

Arguably, it is easier to explain why the insurgents were *not* defeated than it is to explain the related but more interesting question—namely, how and why the external power was forced to withdraw. Since the former problem has been the subject of intense investigation both by specialists in counter-insurgency and strategists of guerrilla warfare, the greater part of this paper will deal with the latter problem. However, a few fairly obvious points need to be made before going on.

In analyzing the successes of the British at Omdurman against the Sudanese and the Italians in their war against local insurgents in Abyssinia, Mao Tse Tung has noted that defeat is the invariable outcome where native forces fight with inferior weapons against modernized forces *on the latter's terms*. Katzenbach writes in this context: "By and large, it would seem that what made the machinery of European troops so successful was that native troops saw fit to die, with glory, with honor, en masse, and in vain."[3] Second, it should be noted that in general this type of war met with little domestic opposition; success only served to increase public support.[4] Two interesting exceptions were the Boer War and the Irish Rebellion (1916–22); it is significant that in these conflicts the resistance to the British was both protracted and bitter and, in the metropolis, generated domestic opposition to the war.[5] Thus, the first condition for avoiding defeat is to refuse to confront the enemy on his own terms. To avoid being crushed, the insurgent forces must retain a degree of invulnerability, but the defensive *means* to this end will depend on the conditions of the war. In guerrilla warfare in the classical sense, the "people sea" forms a sanctuary of popular support for the "guerrilla fish"; in urban guerrilla warfare the anonymity of the city provides protection. Operating in uninhabited areas and supplied from without (e.g., the post-1968 North Vietnamese operations along the Ho Chi Minh Trail in the Vietnam War), the insurgents may simply rely on the mountains and forests to conceal and protect them.

For students of strategy the importance of these wars lies in the fact that the simplistic but once prevalent assumption—that conventional military superiority necessarily prevails in war—has been destroyed. What is also interesting is that although the metropolitan powers did not *win* militarily, neither were they *defeated* militarily. Indeed the military defeat of the metropolis itself was impossible since the insurgents lacked an invasion capability. In every case, success for the insurgents arose not from a military victory on the ground—though military successes may have been a contributory cause—but rather from the progressive attrition of their opponents' *political* capability to wage war. In such asymmetric conflicts, insurgents may gain political victory from a situation of military stalemate *or even defeat*.

The most recent and obvious example of this type of conflict is the American war in Vietnam, which has brought home several important lessons. First, it has provided the most obvious demonstration of the falsity of the assumptions that underlie the "capability" conception of power.[6] Not only does superiority in military force (conventionally defined) not guarantee victory; it may, under certain circumstances, be positively counter-productive.[7] Second, the Vietnam conflict has demonstrated how, under certain conditions, the theatre of war extends well beyond the battlefield to encompass the polity and social institutions of the external power. The Vietnam war may be seen as having been fought on two fronts—one bloody and indecisive in the forests and mountains of Indochina, the other essentially nonviolent—but ultimately more decisive—within the polity and social institutions of the United States. The nature of the relationship between these two conflicts—which are in fact different facets of the same conflict—is critical to an understanding of the outcome of the war. However, the American experience was in no sense unique, except to Americans. In 1954 the Vietminh destroyed the French forces which were mustered at Dien Bien Phu in a classic set piece battle. The direct military costs to the French have been much exaggerated; only 3 per cent of the total French forces in Indochina were involved. The psychological effects—like those of the Tet offensive some fourteen years later—were shattering, however. The Vietminh did not of course defeat France militarily. They lacked not only the capability but also any interest in attempting such a move. Dien Bien Phu, however, had the effect of destroying the *political* capability ("will" in the language of classical strategy) of the French Government to mobilize further troops and to continue the struggle—this despite the fact that the greater part of the financial costs of the war were being borne by the United States. Third, the Vietnam war, which for the Vietnamese revolutionaries has now lasted over a quarter of a century, has emphasized the enormous importance which guerrilla strategists place on "protracted warfare." This is articulated most clearly in Mao Tse Tung's works, but it is also found in the military writings of General Giap and Truong Chinh and in the works of the leading African guerrilla strategists, Cabral and Mondlane. The certainty of eventual victory which is the result of intensive political mobilization by the guerrilla leadership is the key to what Rosen sees as a critical factor in such conflicts—namely, the willingness to absorb costs.[8] Katzenbach has noted of Mao's strategic theory that it is based on the premise that "if the totality of the population can be made to resist surrender, this resistance can be turned into a war of attrition which will eventually and inevitably be victorious."[9] Or, as Henry Kissinger more succinctly observed in 1969: "The guerrilla wins if he does not lose."[10]

Above all, Vietnam has been a reminder that in war the ultimate aim must be to affect the will of the enemy. Most strategic theorists would of course concur with this view. But in practice, and at the risk of oversimplification, it may be noted that it is a prevalent military belief that if an opponent's military capability to wage war can be destroyed, his "will" to continue the struggle is irrelevant since the means to that end are no longer available. It is not surprising that this should be a prevalent belief in modern industrial societies: strategic doctrine tends to mold itself to available technology, as critics of strategic weapons deployment have forcefully pointed out. Neither is it surprising that guerrilla strategists should see strategy in very different terms. Lacking the technological capability or the basic resources to destroy the external enemy's military capability, they must of necessity aim to destroy his political capability. If the external power's "will" to continue the struggle is destroyed, then its military capability—no matter how powerful—is totally irrelevant. One aim of this paper is to show how and why, in certain types of conflict, conventional military superiority is not merely useless, but may actually be counter-productive. The implications for those military systems which rely almost wholly on industrial power and advanced technology need hardly be spelled out.

As I have noted above, in none of the asymmetric conflicts did the local insurgents have the capability to invade their metropolitan opponents' homeland. It *necessarily* follows that insurgents can only achieve their ends if their opponents' *political* capability to wage war is destroyed. This is true whether the insurgents are revolutionaries or right-wing nationalists, whether they rely on guerrilla warfare, urban terrorism, or even nonviolence. The destruction of the external power's forces in the field places no *material* obstacle in its path which will prevent it from simply mobilizing more forces at home and dispatching them to the battlefront. The constraints on mobilization are political, not material. In none of the conflicts noted was more than a fraction of the total *potential* military resources of the metropolitan power in fact mobilized. The U.S. war in Vietnam has by any measure had the greatest impact on international and American domestic politics of any conflict since World War II, but the maximum number of U.S. troops in Vietnam at the peak of the ground war in 1968 amounted to less than one quarter of one per cent of the American population. The political constraints operating against full mobilization of the metropolitan forces arise as a consequence of the conflicts in the metropolis—both within the political elite and in the wider society—which the war, *by its very nature*, will inevitably tend to generate. To paraphrase Clausewitz, politics may become the continuation of war by other means. Therefore the military struggle on the ground must be evaluated not in terms of the narrow calculus of military tactics, but in terms of its political impact in the metropolis: "Battles and campaigns are amenable to analysis as rather self-contained contests of military power. . . . By contrast, the final outcome of wars depends on a much wider range of factors, many of them highly elusive—such as the war's impact on domestic politics. . . ."[11] The significance of particular battles does not lie in their outcome as "self-contained contests of military power." Thus, although the United States could contend that the 1968 Tet offensive marked a dramatic defeat for the revolutionary forces in terms of the macabre military calculus of "body counts," the offensive was in fact a major strategic defeat for the U.S., marking the turning point in the war. The impact of Tet on American domestic politics led directly to the incumbent President's decision not to stand for another term of office. And, for the first time, military requests for more resources (a further 200,000 men) were refused *despite the fact* that the military situation had worsened.

Even where military victory over the insurgents is unambiguous—as in General Massu's destruction of the FLN infrastructure in the notorious Battle of Algiers—this is still no sure guide to the outcome of the conflict. Despite the fact that the FLN never regained the military initiative, the French abandoned their struggle within four years. Indeed, the barbarous methods used by Massu to achieve that victory, including the widespread use of torture, were instrumental in catalyzing opposition to the war in metropolitan France.

The Algerian war is an instructive example of our thesis. Between 1954 and 1962 there was a radical shift in the balance of political forces in metropolitan France. The *colon* (white settler) class of Algeria was the chief political victim. A few days after fighting broke out, the leftist Minister of the Interior, François Mitterand, responded to a suggestion that Paris should negotiate with the rebels by stating flatly that in the Algerian *départements* "the only negotiation is war." Yet seven-and-a-half years later, De Gaulle had not only granted the rebels all their initial demands (including some they had not even considered when fighting broke out), but received overwhelming support from the majority of the French population in doing so. Significantly, the last task of the French Army (which had itself attempted a coup against the Gaullist government) was to hunt down the terrorists of the OAS—the diehard remnants of the *colon* class in whose interests the military had intervened in the first place.

French policy throughout this conflict—as metropolitan policy in other asymmetric conflicts—was beset by what Mao Tse Tung calls "contradictions." The initial military repression directed against the rebels achieved for the militants what they had been unable to achieve for themselves—namely, the political mobilization of the masses against the French.

As the rebellion became more broadly based, more numerous forces and ever more extreme methods were used to attempt to quell it. The French also tried to buy off nationalist aspirations by offering to grant some of the political demands which had initially been made by the insurgents—only to find that these had been radically escalated. Offers of concessions were—as is frequently the case in such conflicts—both too small and too late. The more forces the French deployed (ultimately four hundred thousand men), the greater was the impact which the war had in the metropolis. It was not so much the inhumanity of the war *per se* that generated opposition in France; the majority of French men and women were no more sympathetic to the FLN than were the majority of Americans to the NLF in Vietnam. The major cause of opposition lay not in the enormous costs of the war to the *Algerians* (though this was a factor), but in the costs of the war to the French themselves. The progressively greater human, economic, and political costs gave rise to the phenomenon of "*war weariness*" which many writers have described without analyzing, and to the "loss of political will" of the government to which the military invariably ascribed the defeat. Thus it can be seen that the shift in the balance of political forces in metropolitan France was of critical importance in determining the outcome of the war. Political leaders in such conflicts do not grant insurgent demands because they undergo a sudden change of heart. They concede because they have no choice.

Why are asymmetries in structure important, and what do we in fact mean by "asymmetry" in this context? We must first note that the *relationship* between the belligerents is *asymmetric*. The insurgents can pose no direct threat to the survival of the external power because, as already noted, they lack an invasion capability. On the other hand, the metropolitan power poses not simply the threat of invasion, but the reality of occupation. This fact is so obvious that its implications have been ignored. It means, crudely speaking, that for the insurgents the war is "total," while for the external power it is necessarily "limited." Full mobilization of the total military resources of the external power is simply not politically possible. (One might conceive of cases where this is not the case—as in a popularly backed "holy war" for example—but such possibilities are of no relevance to the present discussion.) Not only is full mobilization impossible politically, it is not thought to be in the least *necessary*. The asymmetry in conventional military capability is so great and the confidence that military might will prevail is so pervasive that expectation of victory is one of the hallmarks of the initial endeavor.

The fact that one belligerent possesses an invasion capability and the other does not is a function of the differences in level of industrial and technological capability of the two sides. The asymmetric *relationship* is thus a function of the asymmetry in "resource power."

Some strategic implications of symmetric and asymmetric conflict relations may now be spelled out. The insurgents, faced with occupation by a hostile external power, are able to capitalize on those powerful forces to which political scientists have given the label "nationalism." What this means essentially is that disparate and sometimes conflicting national groups may find a common unity—a national interest—in opposing a common enemy. In that case the cohesion generated is only *indirectly* a consequence of the asymmetry in resource power: its social and psychological bonds are to be found in the common hostility felt toward the external enemy.

Clausewitz noted that war only approximates to its "pure form" when a "grand and powerful purpose" is at stake.[12] Only then will the full mobilization of national resources become a possibility, and only then will the diverse and sometimes conflicting goals that various national groups pursue in time of peace be displaced by a single overriding strategic aim—"the overthrow of the enemy." In a *symmetric*, "total war" situation where the survival of *both sides* is at stake, both have a "grand and powerful purpose" to defend. Thus, other things being equal, the potential for internal divisions arising in either camp is small relative to the potential for domestic conflict in the homeland of the metropolitan power involved in an *asymmetric* conflict. In symmetric conflicts, *ceteris paribus*, the absence of constraints on the mobilization and the use of conventional military force maximize the strategic utility of conventional warfare. Examples of *symmetric* "total wars" are the first and second World Wars and civil wars in which the struggle can be seen in zero-sum terms—as one of survival. However, although the external-enemy/internal-cohesion thesis of sociologists like Simmel and Coser has been widely accepted, the relationship is not as simple as some writers appear to think. Coser follows Williams in agreeing that there has to be a minimal consensus that the group (or nation) is a "going concern," and that there must be recognition of an outside threat which is thought to menace the group *as a whole*, not just some part of it. Coser notes of the second World War that "attempts at centralization by the French Government were unavailing and could not mend the basic cleavages nor remedy the lack of social solidarity."[13] We may add to this two more conditions which will affect national unity in the face of external threat. First, resistance must be perceived as a viable alternative to surrender. It is noteworthy that after the collapse of the Nazi-Soviet Pact in the second World War, resistance to the Nazis in occupied Europe was very often led by Communists for whom surrender meant extermination. A majority of the population of the occupied countries perceived surrender as a more viable alternative than resistance—at least until it appeared that the tide of the war had turned against the Nazis. Resistance movements whose members share a revolutionary ideology which has as one of its basic tenets the belief that "protracted war" will ultimately be victorious, will, by definition, see resistance as an obvious alternative to surrender. Second, since occupation is likely to have adverse consequences for all groups, but much worse for some than for others, such national unity as does occur will not be unshakable. But it will be enormously reinforced by what may be called the "bandwagon effect."[14] Dissent will be heavily proscribed and sanctioned socially as well as by the leadership.

Even though it is not possible to be precise about the conditions which *necessarily* generate national solidarity in the face of an external threat, we may note the following two points with respect to asymmetric conflicts:

(a) An external threat is a necessary if not sufficient condition for the emergence of a popular front.
(b) Occupation and military repression by the metropolitan power has *in fact* produced the nationalist unity predicted by the Coser-Simmel thesis. (One interesting exception is the confrontation in Malaysia, where there was a deep cleavage dividing the Chinese insurgents from the Malays.) Indeed, it is possible to argue that in some cases the repression did not so much intensify a pre-existing basic consensus as create one.
(c) More importantly, there was no comparable unifying external force in the case of the metropolitan power. On the contrary, in every case where the insurgents won, the war was a profoundly divisive issue.

Those scholars who are expounding the "paradox" that external conflict will both increase and decrease domestic conflict (see below) are guilty of creating a false dichotomy. Contrast the situation in the United States, as the war escalated in Vietnam, with that of Britain facing the Nazis in the second World War. In the former case we see the progressive escalation of domestic opposition to the war creating deep divisions within U.S. society. In the latter, "The Nazi attack appreciably increased the internal cohesion of the British social system, temporarily narrowing the various political, social and economic fissures that existed in British society."[15] In Britain the electoral process was suspended for the duration of the conflict in order to form a coalition "national government." In the various "wars of national liberation" we see precisely the same process in the formation of "popular fronts." Indeed, the label "National Liberation Front" is found in some guise in nearly all these conflicts, though rarely in civil wars.[16]

It is my contention that the process of political attrition of the metropolitan power's capability to continue to wage war is *not* the consequence of errors of generalship, though these may well occur. Rather, it is a function of the *structure* of the conflict, of the nature of the conflictual relationship between the belligerents. Where the war is perceived as "limited"—because the opponent is "weak" and can pose no direct threat—the prosecution of the war does not take automatic primacy over other goals pursued by factions within the government, or bureaucracies or other groups pursuing interests which compete for state resources. In a situation of total war, the prosecution of the war *does* take automatic primacy above all other goals. Controversies over "guns or butter" are not only conceivable in a Vietnam-type conflict, but inevitable. In a total-war situation they would be inconceivable: guns would get *automatic* priority. In contrast to the total-war situation, the protagonists of a limited war have to compete for resources—human, economic, and political—with protagonists of other interest—governmental, bureaucratic, "interest groups," and so forth. Clearly, if the war is terminated quickly and certain benefits are believed to be accruing from victory (as in the case of the mini-wars of colonial expansion) the *potential* for divisive domestic conflict on the war issue will not be realized. But this is simply another way of stating that if the insurgents are to win, they must not lose.

In his highly prophetic paper published in 1969, Henry Kissinger observed of America's war in Vietnam: "We fought a military war; our opponents fought a political one. We sought physical attrition; our opponents aimed for our psychological exhaustion. In the process, we lost sight of one of the cardinal maxims of guerrilla warfare: the guerrilla wins if he does not lose. The conventional army loses if it does not win."[17]

In a similar vein, E.L. Katzenbach in 1962 described Mao Tse Tung's general strategic approach as follows: "Fundamental to all else, Mao says, is the belief that countries with legislative bodies simply cannot take a war of attrition, either financially or, in the long run, psychologically. Indeed, the very fact of a multi-party structure makes commitment to a long war so politically suicidal as to be quite impossible. . . . When the financial burden increases from month to month, the outcry against the war will itself weaken the ability of the troops to fight. The war that Mao's theory contemplates is the cheapest for him to fight and the most expensive for the enemy."[18]

In order to avoid defeat, the insurgents must retain a minimum degree of invulnerability. In order to *win*, they must be able to impose a steady accumulation of "costs" on their opponent. They must not only be undefeated; they must be *seen* to be undefeated. Strategically, the insurgents' aim must be to provoke the external power into escalating its forces on the ground. This *in itself* will incur economic and political costs in the metropolis. Such a process of escalation did in fact mark the history of the conflicts in Indochina, Algeria, Portuguese Africa, Vietnam, and the current conflict in Ulster. The *direct* costs the insurgents impose on the external power will be the normal costs of war-troops killed and matériel destroyed. But the aim of the insurgents is not the destruction of the military capability of their opponents as an *end in itself*. To attempt such a strategy would be lunatic for a small Third-World power facing a major industrial power. Direct costs become of strategic importance when, and only when, they are translated into indirect costs. These are psychological and political: their objective is to amplify the "contradictions in the enemy's camp."

In the metropolis, a war with no visible payoff against an opponent who poses no direct threat will come under increasing criticism as battle casualties rise and economic costs escalate. Obviously there will still be groups in the metropolis whose ideological commitments will lead them to continue to support the government's war policy; others (munitions manufacturers, for example) may support the war because they have more material interests at stake. But if the war escalates dramatically, as it did in Algeria and Vietnam, it makes a definite impact on the economic and political resources which might otherwise have been allocated to, say, public welfare projects. Tax increases may be necessary to cover the costs of the war, a draft system may have to be introduced, and inflation will be an almost certain by-product. Such costs are seen as part of the "necessary price" when the security of the nation is directly threatened. When this is not the case, the basis for consensus disappears. In a limited war, it is not at all clear to those groups whose interests are adversely affected why such sacrifices are necessary.[19]

But that is only part of the story. Just as important is the fact that the necessity for the sacrifices involved in fighting and risking death will appear less obvious to the conscripts and even the professional soldiers when the survival of the nation is not directly at stake. American soldiers fought well in the second World War, but the last years in Vietnam were marked by troop mutinies, widespread drug addiction, high levels of desertion, and even the murders of over-zealous officers intent on sending their men out on dangerous patrols. This in fact led to a strong feeling among some senior U.S. Army officers that it was necessary to get out of Vietnam before morale collapsed completely. It is impossible to explain such a dramatic deterioration of morale within the army and the massive opposition to the draft without reference to the *type* of war being fought.

There is also the question of the morality of the war. When the survival of the nation is not directly threatened, and when the obvious asymmetry in conventional military power bestows an underdog status on the insurgent side, the morality of the war is more easily questioned. It is instructive to note that during World War II the deliberate Allied attempt to terrorize the working-class populations of Dresden and other German cities generated no moral outrage in Britain. This despite the fact that the thousand-bomber raids were designed to create fire storms so devastating in effect that more people died in one night of bombing over Dresden than perished in the Hiroshima holocaust. On the other hand, the aerial bombardment of civilian localities in Vietnam, the use of herbicides and defoliants, napalm, and anti-personnel weapons have been all met with widespread controversy and protest. One should not deduce from this that the British public was more callous to the effects of human suffering than was the American. Moral outrage is in large part a function of the interests perceived to be at stake in the conflict. Where survival is the issue, the propensity to question and protest the morality of the means used to defeat the enemy is markedly attenuated.

As the war drags on and the costs steadily escalate without the "light at the end of the tunnel" becoming more visible, the divisions generated within the metropolis become *in themselves* one of the political costs of the war. The government—or, more precisely, that faction of the government which is committed to the war—will continue to argue that prosecuting the war *is* in the national interest, that vital security interests *are* at stake, that the international credibility and prestige of the nation is at issue, and so forth. Whether or not these claims bear any relationship to reality—whether they are wholly true or wholly false—is quite immaterial. What counts in the long run is what the opponents of the war believe to be at stake and how much political capital they can muster.

Finally, another word about "contradiction." Mao and Giap have repeatedly emphasized that the principal contradiction which the imperialist army must confront on the ground derives from the fact that forces dispersed to control territory become spread so thinly that they are vulnerable to attack. If forces are concentrated to overcome this weakness, other areas are left unguarded. For the external power to overcome this contradiction requires a massive increase in metropolitan forces; but this immediately increases the domestic costs of the war. On the other hand, if the imperialists wish to pacify the opposition at home by withdrawing some of their forces, the contradiction on the battlefronts is sharpened. Any attempt to resolve one contradiction will magnify the other. The guerrilla strategists understand perfectly that the war they fight takes place on two fronts and the conflict must be perceived as an integrated whole. From this perspective, those who oppose the war in the metropolis act *objectively*—regardless of their subjective political philosophies—as a strategic resource for the insurgents. Governments are well aware of this, since it is they who have to confront the political constraints. Yet government accusations that those opposed to the war are "aiding the enemy" are contemptuously rejected. They are nevertheless objectively correct. From this perspective we can also see why the slogan "imperialism is a paper tiger" is by no means inaccurate. It is not that the material resources of the metropolitan power are in themselves underestimated by the revolutionaries; rather, there is an acute awareness that the political constraints on their maximum deployment are as real as if those resources did not exist, and that these constraints become more rather than less powerful as the war escalates.

Few attempts have been made to analyze the outcome of asymmetric conflicts systematic-ally. Among those few, even fewer have seen the asymmetries which characterize the conflict as being critical to an understanding of the outcome. However, some aspects have been touched on. Rosen considers the asymmetry in power and "willingness to suffer costs"; Katzenbach examines the asymmetry in "tangible" and "intangible resources"; Galtung distinguishes between "social" and "territorial defense" (asymmetry in goals); Kissinger, as already noted, mentions asymmetry in overall strategy (physical versus psychological attri-tion); and Kraemer distinguishes "colonial" versus "non-colonial" guerrilla wars.[20] An exam-ination of the conflict in the light of any of *these* asymmetries provides certain insights into particular aspects of the war, but misses the overall picture. The asymmetries described in this paper—in the interests perceived to be at stake, in mobilization, in intervention capabil-ity, in "resource power," and so forth—are abstracted from their context for the sake of analytical clarity. But the whole remains greater than the sum of its parts, and it is the conflict *as a whole* which must be studied in order to understand its evolution and outcome.

Some writers interested in the *etiology* of conflict have argued that the nature of the state polity mediates the link between internal and external conflict.[21] The same question is of relevance with respect to the relatively neglected problem of understanding the *outcome* of international conflicts. *Is* the process of attrition of the political capability to wage war, which we observe so clearly in the Vietnam and Algerian conflicts, a function of the nature of the polity of the metropolitan powers involved? Some writers clearly believe that it is. With respect to Vietnam, Edmund Ions notes: "Whilst the freedom to demonstrate—even for defeatism in foreign policy—is clearly one of the strengths of a free society, *it is also one of its weaknesses so far as power politics is concerned.*"[22] The argument of Ions and other writers is roughly as follows. In contrast to "open" societies, where dissent is permitted, dissent is repressed in "closed" or "totalitarian" societies. Therefore totalitarian societies will not be troubled by the domestic constraints which have bedeviled U.S. policy-makers on Vietnam, for instance. In some of the best-known examples of asymmetric conflict in which the insurgents gained their objectives—Indochina, Algeria, Cyprus, Aden, Palestine, and Indonesia—the metropolitan power which conceded defeat was a "democracy." Asymmetric conflicts in which the external power successfully crushed the opposition (or has yet to be beaten) include Hungary (1956), Czechoslovakia (1968), and Portugal's ongoing war in Africa. In these cases, the metropolitan regime may be described as "closed," "centrist," "totalitarian," or whatever; in any case, popular domestic opposition is not tolerated. In addition to the government proscribing opposition, it may be withholding information. The brutalities inflicted on civilians may go unreported, the costs of the war to the economy concealed, and the number of troops killed minimized. Ions in the paper quoted, and other supporters of the U.S. war in Indochina, have come close to recommending censorship for precisely these reasons. The French military strategist Trinquier, with greater concern for logic than for political reality, argues that in order to prevent the rot of "defeatism" or "lack of political will" from betraying the troops in the field, the entire structure of the metro-politan society must be altered.[23] The general point has some validity. In Laos, a greater number of civilian refugees was created by U.S. bombing missions than in Vietnam, yet the "secret war" in Laos attracted far less attention and controversy because the press was specifically excluded from the battle zones. Despite these obvious points, my main contention—that limited wars by their very nature will generate domestic constraints if the war continues—is not disproved. In terms of the argument put forward here, "politics" under *any* political system involves conflict over the allocation of resources. In closed or centrist polities, these conflicts will by and large be confined to the ruling elite—but not

necessarily so. The argument may be exemplified by examining the case of Portugal.*
Clearly, popular opposition to the war in Angola, Mozambique, and Guinea Bissau could
not manifest itself in Portugal as did opposition to the Vietnam war in the United States. But
there were nevertheless major controversies within the ruling Portuguese elite concerning the
desirability—the costs and benefits—of continuing war in Africa: "[T]here seem to be three
main currents when it comes to the major direction of orientation for Portugal: the colonial-
ist tradition in various versions which still believe in 'Portuguese Africa,' the old 'Lucitanian
tradition' that would base Portuguese future on the Portugal/Brazil axis, and the 'Europeans' for whom the European Community must appear as a very attractive haven of escape."[24]
The younger generation of "modernizing technocrats" clearly see Portugal's future as allied
with the European Community and realize equally clearly that the price of a closer association with the EEC is the cessation of the war in Africa. Portugal is also an interesting case in
the sense that, in addition to domestic constraints, there are also powerful *international* constraints, Portugal being critically dependent on the NATO countries for the arms needed to
fight the war in Africa. This support is, needless to say, highly undependable, not only because
it has already come under sustained attack from some of the north-European NATO powers,
but more obviously because Portugal has a far greater dependence on NATO than NATO
has on Portugal. Finally, popular domestic opposition has in the past manifested itself *indirectly*,
as thousands of Portuguese "voted with the feet" by emigrating to the European Community.

It remains to be explained why Portugal, the oldest and weakest of imperial powers,
should have clung to her colonies long after her more powerful rivals surrendered by
granting independence to their colonial dependencies. The usual explanation is that it is
a matter of an ideological—and essentially irrational—obsession with "manifest destiny."
However, without denying that there may be a powerful contingent of genuine ideologues
within the Portuguese polity who support the war for these reasons, this does not provide
the whole answer. Those most loyal to the "Portuguese connection" are the Portuguese
settlers in the territories themselves—loyal in the sense of total opposition to black rule.
But this loyalty—like the loyalty of Ulster Protestants, white Rhodesians or white *colons* in
Algeria—is highly unreliable.[25] The settler class will bitterly resist any attempt to hand over
control to the indigenous population; it thereby provides a powerful brake on any move
towards independence.

For the settler class, *qua* settler class, the granting of independence to the indigenous
population poses a direct threat to local European hegemony in both the political and
economic spheres. If pressures in the metropolis are such that withdrawal from the colonies
appears likely—as seems highly possible following the Spinola coup of the spring of 1974—
there may well be moves by the settlers to attempt a type of go-it-alone, Unilateral Declaration
of Independence strategy along Rhodesian lines. The *colons* in Algeria tried this strategy
when it became obvious that De Gaulle was going to give in to Moslem demands for
independence. They failed, but the white Rhodesians succeeded. In the current Ulster crisis
there is little doubt that such a strategy would be attempted—and would most likely succeed
if it became clear to the Protestant majority that the British were going to withdraw—as
seems increasingly possible. The "settlers" exhibit "ultra-loyalism" towards the "mother
country" up to the moment at which they appear to have been deserted. If the break *does*
succeed, the structure of the conflict changes completely. If the metropolitan power does not
intervene against the settlers' rebellion (Algeria) but instead simply makes nonmilitary
protests (Britain against Rhodesia) then the conflict becomes symmetric: a zero-sum struggle
for ascendancy, essentially a civil war in which the settler class has a survival stake in the
outcome. The settlers will in many ways prove to be a more formidable enemy than was the

vastly more powerful metropolitan power, because the constraints against the use of force will be almost completely absent in their case. Thus the task of nationalist movements trying to bring down the settler regimes in Israel, Rhodesia, and South Africa is extremely onerous. The question for these regimes is not *whether* to fight the insurgents but *how*. In other words, despite superficial similarities in tactics and in descriptive language—"Palestinian guerrillas," "national liberation struggle,"—the "settler-regime" conflicts are fundamentally different from asymmetric conflicts.

There is another, perhaps equally powerful reason why the Portuguese resisted independence so bitterly. It is extremely difficult to calculate the economic costs and benefits which Portugal derives from her overseas territories, in part because exchange controls are artificially manipulated. However, even if it could be unequivocally demonstrated that the costs of the war exceed by a wide margin the *present* economic benefits which Portugal derives from her colonies—most particularly Angola—it would not invalidate the hypothesis that a major Portuguese interest in maintaining the colonial possessions is economic. Oil in large quantities has already been discovered in the overseas territories, and there are also extensive and as yet barely exploited mineral reserves. Portugal therefore has a considerable economic interest in trying to maintain control in these areas.[26] When France and Britain relinquished their African colonies, they relinquished also the economic costs of administration while retaining whatever benefits they derived from their investments and from special trade relationships. Portugal is in a very different position. Since Portugal is relatively underdeveloped economically, the benefits she derives from her overseas territories are based on political rather than economic control. The key economic enterprises in the overseas territories are increasingly dominated by non-Portuguese capital (in contrast to the situation in French and British African colonies before independence). If Portugal were to relinquish political control in Africa, she would lose not only the present economic benefits but also the more important future benefits. The so-called neo-colonial solution is not a possibility for the Portuguese.

In discussing Portugal by way of exemplification of my argument, I have raised three possible hypotheses, which might be formulated as follows:

(1)   The political attrition of the metropolitan power's war-making capability appears to be positively correlated with the degree of "openness" of the political system and negatively correlated with the degree of "closeness" of the political system. Democratic polyarchies are apparently most susceptible to internal opposition to external wars, while totalitarian "centrist" states are less susceptible to such opposition. This argument is subject to severe qualification (see below).

(2)   Where a metropolitan settler class exists in the insurgents' homeland, it will have a survival interest in the conflict and will thus act as a powerful countervailing "brake" to forces in the metropolis which favor a pull-out. If the latter forces prevail, there will be a strong push from the settler class for a U.D.I.-type break with the metropolis along Rhodesian lines. If this succeeds, the conflict ceases to be asymmetric as defined here.

(3)   In a limited war, despite the fact that there is no direct threat to physical survival of the metropolis, there may well be other powerful interests to be protected. The greater the salience of these interests, the greater the resistance to withdrawal will be in the metropolis.

The last point brings us to the two other examples noted above—the Russian interventions in Hungary (1956) and Czechoslovakia (1968). It is obvious that one of the necessary conditions noted earlier for the process of political attrition to manifest itself was absent. In both cases the local resistance was effectively and rapidly crushed.[27]

From the Soviet point of view, the security interest, while not one of a direct threat of invasion, was nevertheless highly salient. For example, Russian interests in maintaining Czechoslovakia under Soviet control were two-fold. As Zeman notes, Czechoslovakia had a key position in the Soviet system: "It is a workshop where a lot of Russian and East-European raw material is processed; the country's territory forms a tunnel leading from western Europe directly to the Soviet Union."[28] Second, for the U.S.S.R., twice invaded this century from the West at a cost of millions of lives, a certain fixation on security interests was understandable. But the strategic costs of relinquishing control over Czechoslovakia were not simply the direct costs of creating a *physical* gap in the chain of satellite buffer states. The real risk from the Soviet point of view was that the subversive ideology of national determination, of "socialism with a human—i.e., non-Russian—face" might spread first to the other satellite states of Eastern Europe and ultimately to the Soviet Union itself. The Soviet intervention in Hungary in 1956 is a similar case in point.

These examples show that it is virtually impossible to produce a model of asymmetric conflict which would be sufficiently flexible to account for the outcome of the cases of conflict that might be included under that rubric. Neither is it evident that this would be desirable. The problem with using models to explain conflicts is that there is a natural tendency to attempt to force the data to fit the requirements of the theory. The risks lie in ignoring other factors which might fall within the category sometimes labeled "accidents of history," but which may nevertheless be of critical importance in determining the outcome of a particular conflict.

Most of the discussion thus far has dealt with the *domestic* constraints which will be generated in the metropolis as a consequence of asymmetries in the structure of the conflict. We can quite easily point to the mechanisms that generate such constraints—though the *form* they will take in practice will vary according to the interests perceived to be at stake and according to the nature of the polity of the external power. But little or nothing can be said with respect to *external* constraints. For example, there were few external constraints bearing down on British policy in the Mau Mau rebellion in Kenya, yet in the case of the nationalist struggle in Indonesia against the Dutch the situation was very different. The critical factor here was the U.S. threat to cut off Marshall Plan aid to the Dutch if they failed to make a settlement with the Indonesian nationalists. A completely different set of potential external pressures could be brought to bear against Portugal vis-à-vis the Portuguese wars in Africa, and so on.

In an asymmetric conflict, the *potential* for the generation of internal divisions in the metropolitan power exists *regardless* of the historical epoch, the nature of the polity of the external power, the interests perceived to be at stake, and the international context in which the conflict takes place. Though these factors may influence the form and intensity taken by these internal divisions in any particular conflict, the *cause* of these divisions is independent from all of them. It arises from the nature of the asymmetric relationships which exist between the belligerents. On the other hand, nothing can be said in the abstract about any *external* constraints which may be brought to bear on the external power. These are dependent on the conditions of a particular historical epoch.

Summary

The initial problem was one of explaining how the militarily powerful could be defeated in armed confrontation with the militarily weak. This was not just idle speculation; in a number of critically important conflicts in the post-World War II epoch, industrial powers *have* failed to gain their objectives in wars fought on foreign soil against local nationalist forces. In all of these cases the superiority in conventional military capability of the external power was overwhelming. In a sense, these wars may be seen as a replay of the mini-wars of colonial conquest which took place in the late nineteenth and early twentieth centuries, but with a critical difference. In the earlier era, the industrial powers used minimal force to achieve rapid success, whereas in the post-World War II conflicts, the same industrial powers confronted the same Third-World countries with massive forces and lost.

In explaining the successes of the "weaker" party, I pointed out that an obvious minimal requirement for victory was that the insurgents should not lose. They achieved this by refusing to confront the industrial powers on their own terms and by resorting instead to "unconventional" forms of warfare—guerrilla war, urban terrorism, or even nonviolent action. However, I did not examine this aspect of the problem in any detail. I took the fact that the insurgents did not lose as a "given" when I inquired into the more interesting problem—namely, how did they *win?* I noted that one of the key asymmetries which charac- terized the relationships of the belligerents was that, as a consequence of the asymmetry in wealth and economic and technological development, the insurgents lacked the physical capability to attack the metropolitan power. It thus followed *logically* that the metropolitan power could not be defeated militarily. In turn, victory for the insurgents could only come about as a consequence of the destruction of the external power's *political* capability to wage war. The historical evidence of the outcome of the post-World War II conflicts confirms the logic of the argument.

As a next step, I examined the dynamics of the process of political attrition, arguing that the asymmetries which characterized the conflict provided the basis, not only for the initial restraints on mobilization of military forces, but also for the emergence of internal divisions as the war dragged on and costs accumulated. The fact that the war was by definition "limited" also provided the basis for a sustained moral critique of the military means employed—from torture to napalm—while reducing the willingness of troops to risk their lives in combat and of the domestic population to make economic sacrifices. However, the process of attrition was not seen as arising primarily from a steady across-the-board incre- ment of "war weariness," as some writers have suggested; still less was it seen as a process of conversion at the top whereby the political leadership was gradually persuaded of the immorality or undesirability of its policies. The controversies *themselves* became one of the costs of the war. Time is a resource in politics, and the bitter hostilities such wars generate may come to dominate political debate to the detriment of the pursuit of other objectives. Provided the insurgents can maintain a steady imposition of "costs" on their metropolitan opponent, the balance of political forces in the external power will *inevitably* shift in favor of the anti-war factions.

Although the main discussion dealt essentially with domestic constraints, I also recognized that *international* constraints were often of great importance in asymmetric conflicts. How- ever, whereas the mechanisms giving rise to internal constraints could be identified, it was impossible to say anything in the abstract about external constraints.

Having outlined in fairly general terms the conditions under which the process of political attrition might be expected to manifest itself in practice, I then briefly examined the countervailing forces. I noted that the nature of the polity of the external power might either inhibit or facilitate the generation of domestic conflict. But I also argued that internal divisions were primarily a function of the conflict *relationship* and not of differences in the political structure of the metropolis. Finally, I noted that the salience of the interest which the external power—or rather factions within it—had in pursuing the war would also affect the process of political attrition.

Note on methodology

Examples of the types of hypotheses which this analysis might suggest were given earlier in the paper. It would be easy to think of others, for instance:

> The greater the interest a particular metropolitan faction has in the prosecution of the war and the wider the basis of its domestic support, the greater will be the support for continuing the war.

Another example would be:

> The weaker and more dependent the external power is on external support in order to prosecute the war, the more important external constraints will be in determining the outcome.

The objections to these alternative approaches—other than for the purpose of illustrating points in the argument—are several. First, they would slice the conflict up into parts (either temporally or spatially) which are then examined in relative isolation. I have argued that a full understanding can only come from an analysis of the conflict as a whole. Second, there is the technical problem of operationalizing such vague concepts as "interest" or "faction." Third, even if operationalization were possible, the hypotheses would remain untestable by the traditional statistical significance tests. That is a problem which has been largely ignored in most of the quantitative studies in conflict research where conflicts tend to get lumped together—symmetric and asymmetric and across periods of up to a hundred years or more—in order to obtain a sufficiently large sample for statistical manipulation. Thus the quantitative studies undertaken by Rummel and Tanter with the object of testing the relationship between external and internal conflicts arrive at the conclusion that no such relationship exists.[29] However, the relationships may well exist but be hidden by precisely the methodological methods intended to reveal them. Contrary to writers like Stohl and Wilkenfeld, there is no "paradox" in the *apparently* contradictory assertions that, on the one hand, external conflicts cause internal conflict and, on the other, that they create internal solidarity.[30] Whether or not this *is* the case is a function of the nature of the conflict. But since the *type* of conflict is not identified, the relationships are lost in the aggregation of data. It is not possible to consider asymmetric conflicts (as defined here) on their own, since the size of the sample is far too small. The only way out of this dilemma is to attempt a "time series" analysis.[31] Here, instead of many conflicts being examined once, the data matrix is filled by examining one conflict (or a few) over many time intervals. The methodological and epistemological problems with this type of analysis are enormous, however, and the results produced thus far are extremely modest.

If we move away from the quantitative literature to examine other attempts at explaining the outcome of asymmetric conflicts, different problems arise. The literature on counterinsurgency, for example, concentrates almost exclusively on the development of the war on the ground and ignores its impact on the metropolis. Iklé notes: "When it comes to actual fighting, the scores that count are, for instance, the number of enemy units destroyed, square miles of territory gained, and other successes or failures in battle. Where such an attitude prevails, professional military men would consider it unusual, if not somewhat improper, to ask whether these 'mid-game' successes will improve the ending."[32] Counter-insurgency theorists can thus provide a partial explanation of why insurgents may *lose*, but they cannot, almost by definition, grasp how it is that they may *win*. Awareness that insurgent successes are a consequence of "lack of political will" or "defeatism" on the part of the metropolitan governments is of course there, but this is seen as a contingent phenomenon almost wholly unrelated to the conduct of the war. More sophisticated works in the counter-insurgency field *do* consider political factors in the *insurgents'* homeland—namely, the payoffs of social and economic reform as a means of reducing popular support for the insurgents. But only Trinquier provides a sustained analysis of the political and social changes necessary in the *metropolis* if such wars are to succeed—and in this case the demands of logic are followed with no regard for political reality.

Although much of the research literature on conflict deals with events leading up to the outbreak of war, there has been a recent renewal of interest in "war-termination studies."[33] However, these concentrate on the final phases of the war, in particular those leading to negotiations or offering possibilities for third-party mediation. The *evolution* of the war and its wider sociopolitical dimensions are largely ignored.

A number of excellent historical case studies of the various asymmetric conflicts have been mentioned in this paper. Many of them have a virtue manifestly lacking in other works, namely that of treating the conflict as a whole rather than examining particular "technical" dimensions or temporal slices. However, individual case studies can provide no conceptual basis for distinguishing between what might in this context be called "structural necessity" from historically unique factors. Since narrative history is unable to discriminate between the universal and the particular when analyzing conflicts, it is a most unreliable guide to the future. Military history is replete with "Maginot lines," illustrating the dangers of relying on historical precedents.

Specific problems raised by these different methodological approaches to asymmetric conflicts and the different foci of interest which have been employed will be dealt with in depth in a forthcoming study.[34] In particular, that study will examine the writings of the leading revolutionary strategists. In the present paper, I have dealt essentially with the *process* of attrition as a function of the asymmetries which characterize the conflict. An asymmetric *strategy* would be one which sought to amplify this process of attrition *indirectly*. An outline of the basic requirements of such an "asymmetric strategy" (derived from the strategic writings of Clausewitz, Glucksman, and Mao Tse Tung) is provided in the final chapter of *War Without Weapons*.[35]

Finally, it should be obvious that my aim in this paper has not been to provide a "model" which may then be "tested" by applying it mechanically and ahistorically to a wide range of conflicts. Rather, it has been to construct a conceptual framework which will provide a focus for empirical studies. Like the "paradigm" of the physical sciences which Thomas Kuhn has described, this conceptual framework functions essentially to direct the researcher's attention toward particular aspects of the real world—to distinctions and relationships which "common sense" often does not take into account. The framework defines the necessary questions which must be asked; it does not seek to provide automatic answers.

Conclusion

Recent developments in two ongoing asymmetric conflicts have tended to bear out the main thrust of my argument. The most dramatic development has been the Spinola coup in Portugal which clearly has far-reaching implications for the wars of national liberation in Angola, Mozambique, and Guinea Bissau.[36] The second is the conflict in Ulster. The spring of 1974 saw the emergence, in England, of significant domestic opposition to the war, with several campaigns for troop withdrawal attracting growing support from very different political constituencies. Since the British Government has exhausted all the obvious "initiatives" (juggling the local Ulster leadership, direct rule, the Northern Ireland Assembly, and the Council of Ireland) to no avail, and since the I.R.A. remains not only undefeated but capable of escalating its offensive where necessary, it seems certain that the campaign for withdrawal will gather strength. One of the most significant aspects of current I.R.A. activity is its role in maintaining and solidifying Protestant "extremism." The bombing functions essentially to prevent the "moderate" political solution, favored by the Westminster government and the Catholic and Protestant center groups which dominate the Assembly, from coming to fruition. The Spinola government in Portugal faces a similar problem. Having explicitly abandoned the belief that the war is winnable, the regime's current strategy is to seek a "political" solution. General Spinola advocates greatly increased autonomy, but "the overseas territories must be an integral part of the Portuguese nation." It is already obvious that such a solution is acceptable neither to the European settlers nor to the liberation movements. Withdrawal is now clearly a serious political option for both metropolitan powers. In admitting that the colonial wars are unwinnable, General Spinola has in fact admitted defeat: "the conventional army loses if it does not win." In both countries the key question is no longer whether to withdraw but rather when and how.

To conclude, it hardly needs pointing out that—if correct—the implications of the foregoing analysis for industrial powers which become embroiled in long drawn-out wars in the Third World are far-reaching. Governments which become committed to such wars for whatever reason should realize that, over time, the costs of the war will inevitably generate widespread opposition at home. The causes of dissent lie beyond the control of the political elite; they lie in the structure of the conflict itself—in the type of war being pursued and in the asymmetries which form its distinctive character. Anti-war movements, on the other hand, have tended to underestimate their political effectiveness. They have failed to realize that in every asymmetric conflict where the external power has been forced to withdraw, it has been as a consequence of internal dissent. Thus, any analysis of the outcome of asymmetric conflicts must of necessity take into account and explain not only the tenacity and endurance of the nationalist forces, but also the generation of internal divisions in the homeland of their metropolitan enemy. In this type of conflict, anti-war movements—and this includes all the social forces that oppose the war—have, despite their short-term failures and frustrations, proven to be remarkably successful in the long run.

Notes

* Research for this article was supported by the British Social Science Research Council. An ongoing project examining a number of case histories of "asymmetric conflicts" is currently being supported by the Rockefeller Foundation.
1 See Berenice A. Carroll, "War Termination and Conflict Theory," and William T.R. Fox, "The Causes of Peace and the Conditions of War," both in *How Wars End, Annals of the American Academy*

324   *Andrew Mack*

of Political and Social Science, Vol. 392 (November 1970); and Elizabeth Converse, "The War of All Against All: A Review of the Journal of Conflict Resolution, 1957–68," *Journal of Conflict Resolution*, xii (December 1968).

2 Exceptions are found in E.L. Katzenbach, "Time, Space and Will: The Politico-Military Strategy of Mao Tse Tung," in Lt. Col. T.N. Greene, ed., *The Guerrilla and How To Fight Him* (New York 1962); Robert Taber, *The War of the Flea* (New York 1965); and Joseph S. Kraemer, "Revolutionary Guerrilla Warfare and the Decolonization Movement," *Polity*, iv (Winter 1971).

3 Katzenbach (fn. 2), 15.

4 See, for example, H. Wehler, "Industrial Growth and Early German Imperialism" in Robert Owen and Robert Sutcliffe, eds., *Theories of Imperialism* (London 1972).

5 Two excellent recent studies dealing directly with domestic opposition to these wars are: Stephen Koss, *The Pro-Boers: The Anatomy of an Anti-War Movement* (Chicago 1973), and D. G. Boyce, *Englishmen and Irish Troubles: British Public Opinion and the Making of Irish Policy 1918–22* (London 1972).

6 Problems with different conceptions of power in this context are examined in Andrew Mack, "The Concept of Power and its Uses in Explaining Asymmetric Conflict," Richardson Institute for Conflict and Peace Research (London 1974).

7 The least ambiguous demonstrations of this apparently paradoxical assertion are to be found in the relatively rare cases of successful nonviolent resistance to armed aggression. See Anders Boserup and Andrew Mack, *War Without Weapons: Non-Violence in National Defence* (London 1974).

8 Steven Rosen, "War Power and the Willingness to Suffer," in Bruce M. Russett, ed., *Peace, War, and Numbers* (London 1972).

9 Katzenbach (fn. 2), 18.

10 Henry A. Kissinger, "The Vietnam Negotiations," *Foreign Affairs*, XLVII (January 1969), 214.

11 Fred Charles Iklé, *Every War Must End* (London 1971), 1–2.

12 The final chapter of Boserup and Mack (fn. 7) discusses Clausewitzian strategic theory and its application to "asymmetric conflicts."

13 Lewis A. Coser, *The Functions of Social Conflict* (New York 1956), 87–110.

14 Boserup and Mack (fn. 7), chap. 1.

15 Coser (fn. 13), 87–110; quotation from p. 95.

16 The obvious point here is that "nationalism" is normally a meaningless concept except in relation to an external environment. "Nationalism" may be significant in civil wars that are based on an ethnic conflict but not on class conflict.

17 Kissinger (fn. 10), 214.

18 Katzenbach (fn. 2), 18.

19 Some interesting and recent theoretical work in the "issue area" literature is relevant to this discussion; see in particular Theodore J. Lowi, "Making Dernocracy Safe for the World: National Politics," in Jarrics Rosenau, ed., *Domestic Sources of Foreign Policy* (New York 1967); and William Zimrnernsan, "Issue Area and Foreign Policy Process," *American Political Science Review*, LXVIt (December 1973). The literature on "bureaucratic politics" and "linkage politics" is also relevant.

20 Rosen (fn. 8); Katzenbach (fn. 2); Kissinger (fn. 10); Kraemer (fn. 2); see also Johan Galtung, "Mot et Nytt Forsvarsbegrep," *Pax*, No. 1 (Oslo 1965).

21 E.g., Jonathan Wilkenfeld, "Models for the Analysis of Foreign Conflict Behavior of States," in Russett (fn. 8).

22 Edmund Ions, "Dissent in America: The Constraints on Foreign Policy," *Conflict Studies*, No. 18 (London 1971); emphasis in original.

23 P. Trinquier, *Modern Warfare* (New York 1964).

* This article was completed before the Spinola coup in Portugal in the spring of 1974. A brief discussion of the implications of the coup, and those of the recent developments in the Ulster crisis, has been added to the conclusion.

24 Johan Galtung, *The European Community: A Superpower in the Making* (London 1973), 166.

25 As Emmanuel notes of the "settler class" in "colonial" situations: "They benefitted from colonialism and therefore promoted it, without reserve or contradiction—and for that very reason they were basically anti-imperialist, however paradoxical that may seem. From the very beginning they were in conflict with their parent countries ... objectively so at all times, subjectively so at times of crisis, going so far as to take up arms against it." Argirihi Emmanuel, "White Settler Colonialism and the Myth of Investment Imperialism," *New Left Review*, No. 73 (May/June 1972), 38–39.

26 For a detailed argument of this point see Eduardo de Sousa Ferreira, *Portuguese Colonialism from South Africa to Europe* (Freiburg 1972).

27 For an analysis of the breakdown of the resistance in the Czech case see Boserup and Mack (fn. 7), chap. VI.

28 Z.A.B. Zeman, *Prague Spring* (London 1969).

29 R.J. Rummel, "Dimensions of Conflict Behavior Within and Between Nations," *General Systems Yearbook*, VIII (1963), 1–50; and Raymond Tanter, "Dimensions of Conflict Behavior Within and Between Nations, 1958–60," *Journal of Conflict Resolution*, x (March 1966), 41–64.

30 Michael Stohl, "Linkages between War and Domestic Political Violence in the United States, 1890–1923" in J. Caporaso and L. Roos, eds., *Quasi-Experimental Approaches* (Evanston 1973); and Jonathan Wilkenfeld, "Introduction" to Wilkenfeld, ed., *Conflict Behavior and Linkage Politics* (New York 1973).

31 See Robert Burrowes and Bertram Spector, "The Strength and Direction of Relationships Between Domestic and External Conflict and Cooperation: Syria, 1961–67" in Wilkenfeld, ibid.; also Stohl (fn. 30).

32 Iklé (fn. 11).

33 Carroll (fn. 1); Fox (fn. 1); Iklé (fn. 11); and R.F. Randle, *The Origins of Peace* (New York 1973).

34 Andrew Mack, "Working Papers on Asymmetric Conflict," Nos. I–VI, Richardson Institute (London 1974).

35 Boserup and Mack (fn. 7).

36 Since this conclusion was written, the new Portuguese Government has abandoned the earlier insistence that the "overseas territories must be an integral part of the Portuguese nation." The threat of a possible settler bid for a unilateral declaration of independence was briefly raised in Mozambique, but evaporated with the considerable exodus of whites to Portugal and South Africa. In Angola, with a larger settler population, far greater mineral resources, and deep divisions between competing liberation movements, the situation remains unclear.

17 Countering global insurgency

David J. Kilcullen

Introduction

When the United States (US) declared a global War on Terrorism after the 9/11 attacks, some viewed the whole notion as logically flawed. Francis Fukuyama commented that 'terrorism is only a means to an end; in this regard, a war on terrorism makes no more sense than a war on submarines'. Such views are irrelevant in a policy sense: the term 'War on Terrorism' was chosen on political, not analytical grounds. Nevertheless, to win this war we must understand it—'neither mistaking it for, nor trying to turn it into, something that is alien to its nature'.[1] Those prosecuting the war must clearly distinguish Al Qaeda and the militant movements it symbolizes—entities that *use* terrorism—from the tactic of terrorism itself.

Anatomy of the global *jihad*

Osama bin Laden, leader of the World Islamic Front, *al Qa'ida* ('the base'), declared war on the West on 23 February 1998. After 9/11, the senior Al Qaeda ideologue, Ayman al Zawahiri, published a strategy for global *jihad*. Both statements illuminate a global pattern of Islamist militancy.

Bin Laden's declaration announced a global war against the US and the broader Western-dominated world order. It issued a *fatwa* calling for *jihad*, indicating that bin Laden claimed religious authority (necessary to issue a *fatwa*) and political authority as a Muslim ruler (needed to issue a call to *jihad*).[2] Subsequent Al Qaeda statements refer to bin Laden as the *Sheikh* or *Emir* (Prince or Commander) of the World Islamic Front, staking a claim to authority over a broad united front of Islamist militant fighters worldwide.[3]

Zawahiri's statement outlined a two-phase strategy. In the first phase, the *'jihad* would . . . turn things upside down in the region and force the US out of it. This would be followed by the earth-shattering event, which the West trembles at: the establishment of an Islamic caliphate in Egypt'. The second stage would use this Caliphate as a launch pad to 'lead the Islamic world in a *jihad* against the West. It could also rally the world [sic] Muslims around it. Then history would make a new turn, God willing, in the opposite direction against the empire of the United States and the world's Jewish government'.[4]

Al Qaeda has cells in at least 40 countries and, though disrupted by the loss of its Afghan base in 2001, is still functioning globally. A recent article in the Al Qaeda military journal *Al-Battar* asserted that:

> In the beginning of their war against Islam, [the Crusaders] had announced that one of their main goals was to destroy the Al-Qaeda organization in Afghanistan; and now,

look what happened? Thanks to God, instead of being limited to Afghanistan, Al-Qaeda broke out into the entire Islamic world and was able to establish an international expansion, in several countries, sending its brigades into every Islamic country, destroying the Blasphemers' fortresses, and purifying the Muslims' countries.[5]

Islamist movements appear to function through regional 'theaters of operation' where operatives cooperate, or conduct activities in neighboring countries. Evidence suggests that Islamist groups within theaters follow general ideological or strategic approaches aligned with Al Qaeda pronouncements, and share a common tactical style and operational lexicon. But there is no clear evidence that Al Qaeda directly controls *jihad* in each theater. Indeed, rather than a monolithic organization, the global *jihad* is a much more complex phenomenon. Nine principal Islamist theaters have been identified, including the Americas; Western Europe; Australasia; the Iberian Peninsula and *Maghreb* (Muslim Northwest Africa); the Greater Middle East; East Africa; South and Central Asia; the Caucasus and European Russia; and Southeast Asia.

All but the first three theaters include active insurgencies. Indeed, there is a greater than 85 per cent correlation between Islamist insurgency and terrorist activity or Al Qaeda presence in a given theater. Except for 9/11 itself, all Al Qaeda-linked terrorist activity has occurred in theaters with ongoing Islamist insurgencies. Not all Islamist insurgency is linked to Al Qaeda—but most Al Qaeda activity occurs in areas of Islamist insurgency.

There is also a correlation between the geographical area of the historical Caliphate, the broader pan-Islamic Caliphate sought by Al Qaeda (which never fully existed in a historical sense) and Islamist insurgency. A glance at a map of current Islamist insurgencies (Figure 17.1) shows that virtually all are on the fringes of the historical Caliphate or on the 'civilisational frontier' between the Caliphate and surrounding non-Islamic peoples.

This seems to indicate that Al Qaeda is executing the strategy outlined by Zawahiri, of re-establishing an Islamic Caliphate then using this as a springboard to extend jihadist control over the globe. The reality is much more complex. But there is clearly a global spread of Islamist movements seeking to overturn the existing Western-dominated world order and replace it with a jihadist vision, through subversion, terrorism and insurgency.

Links between theaters

These theaters, and groups within them, are connected through a nested series of links into an aggregated pattern of global *jihad*. Links include common ideologies, shared languages, cultures and a common Islamic faith.[6] Moreover, as these groups originate from specific subcultures within Islam, they share a common sense of alienation from mainstream traditions of political moderation.[7]

The personal histories of individuals across the *jihad* movements are also closely linked. Many fought the Soviets together in Afghanistan. Many studied under Wahhabi clerics in Saudi Arabia and maintain relationships with these mentors. Later generations of *mujahidin* fought together in Kosovo, Bosnia or Chechnya. Many went to school together, fought together in sectarian conflicts and trained together in terrorist camps. Webs of friendship and networks of mutual obligation stretch worldwide between and among groups.

Unsurprisingly, many members of the global *jihad* are related by birth or marriage. Alliances between groups are cemented by marriage, as in the marriage of Osama bin Laden to the daughter of Taliban leader Mullah Omar. Sons of jihadists often follow their fathers, and widows often avenge their husbands by becoming suicide bombers. This pattern

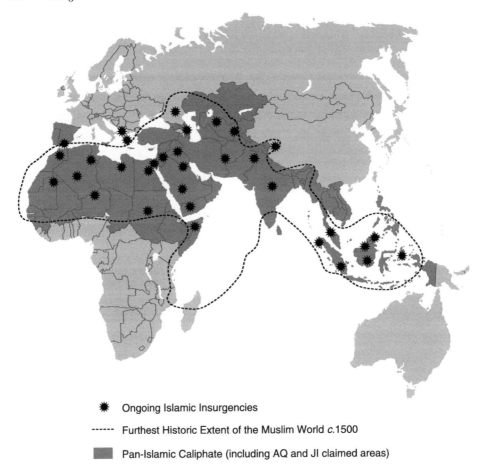

> ✳   Ongoing Islamic Insurgencies
>
> ------ Furthest Historic Extent of the Muslim World *c.*1500
>
> ▓   Pan-Islamic Caliphate (including AQ and JI claimed areas)

Figure 17.1 Insurgencies, Terrorism and the Caliphate.

Sources: Insurgency and terrorism data from *Patterns of Global Terrorism 2004*; boundary of the Islamic world from
http://ccat.sas.upenn.edu/~rs143/map6.jpg

has become so common in Chechnya that such women, known as 'Black Widows', have
gained independent status as a distinct sub-category of *jihad* terrorist.[8]

Financial links also abound. Groups in different theaters fund each other's activities.
Non-governmental organizations, including traditional *hawala* banking networks, charitable
organizations and religious orders become witting or unwitting conduits for funding. Many
of these organizations are based in the Arabian Peninsula. Middle East oil has provided
the bulk of terrorist and insurgent funding, making Arabia a hub in the web of financial
links joining dispersed movements. An intricate network of private patronage, financial
obligation and mutual commitment links groups and individuals in geographically dispersed
regions.

The evidence is that Al Qaeda is not a central headquarters or 'high command' for
the global *jihad*. Bin Laden does not issue directives for insurgent or terrorist action to
'subordinate' groups. Rather, planning and operational tasking seems to occur through a
sponsorship system, with Al Qaeda providing funding, advice and specialist expertise to

allied groups. Meanwhile, local groups gather intelligence and targeting data and share it across theaters in the *jihad*. For example, the planned attack on Singapore by Al Qaeda's regional affiliate Jema'ah Islamiyah (JI) in 2002 was foiled through the discovery of targeting data in an Al Qaeda safe house in Afghanistan. A recent terrorist alert was sparked by the discovery of targeting data on American schools and public buildings on a captured terrorist's computer in South Asia. So although there is no centralized command and control hierarchy, it appears that local groups plan and conduct their own operations, but cooperate within and between regions. Simultaneously, global players like Al Qaeda provide encouragement, tactical support, finance and intelligence for specific operations.[9]

Groups across the *jihad* contribute to a common flow of propaganda materials, supporting each other's local causes and sharing grievances. For example, the English-language website *Jihad Unspun* is managed by a Canadian convert to Islam, and provides reportage, analysis, comment and 'spin' on issues across all theaters of the *jihad*. Al Qaeda issues a fortnightly propaganda bulletin, *Sawt al-Jihad*, and publishes a jihadist women's magazine, *al-Khansa*. Similarly, a flow of cassette tapes, videos and CDs, many depicting so-called 'martyrdom operations', terrorist bombings or the execution of infidel prisoners, moves throughout *jihad* groups worldwide. For example, the *Russian Hell* series of videos, many depicting the torture and execution of Russian troops captured in Chechnya, is popular viewing across South Asia, the Middle East and Indonesia, and is current among certain militant extremist sub-cultures within the Australian Muslim community.[10] Imagery portraying oppression of Muslims worldwide is also used to stir up resentment and motivate *mujahidin*. The Internet has become a potent tool for groups to share propaganda and ideological material across international boundaries, contributing to a shared consciousness among dispersed groups within the *jihad*.[11]

Terrorist and insurgent groups worldwide have shared access to a body of techniques, doctrine and procedures that exists in hard copy, and on the Internet, primarily in Arabic. It includes political tracts, military manuals, and CD-ROM and videotaped materials. Al Qaeda also publishes a fortnightly online military training manual, *Al-Battar*. This creates a common tactical approach and operational lexicon across Islamist groups worldwide: tactics that first appear in one theater permeate across the global movement, via the Internet and doctrinal publications.[12]

Local, regional and global players

Within each theater there are local actors, issues and grievances. Many have little to do with pan-Islamic objectives, and often pre-date the global *jihad* by decades or centuries. For example, Russians have been fighting Muslim guerrillas in the Caucasus since the 1850s, while there has been a Moro separatist issue in the Philippines for more than a century. Local insurgent and terrorist groups – in some cases, little distinguishable from bandits – continue to operate in these areas.

But what is new about today's environment is that, because of the links provided by tools of globalization like the Internet, global media and satellite communications, a new class of regional or theater-level actors has emerged. These groups *do* have links to the global *jihad*, often act as regional allies or affiliates of Al Qaeda, and prey on local groups and issues to further the *jihad*. For example, in Indonesia the regional Al Qaeda affiliate, Jema'ah Islamiyah, has fuelled sectarian conflicts in Sulawesi in order to generate recruits, anti-Western propaganda, funding and grievances that can be exploited for *jihad* purposes. In general, Al Qaeda seems not to have direct dealings with local insurgent groups, but to deal primarily with its regional affiliates in each theater. This makes the regional-level players in the *jihad* a critical link.

Sitting above the regional actors are global players like Al Qaeda. But Al Qaeda is simply the best known of several worldwide actors. Al Qaeda has competitors, allies and clones at the global level who could step into the breach should Al Qaeda be destroyed. For example, Hizbullah has global reach, works closely with Sunni movements world-wide, sponsors approximately 80 per cent of Palestinian terrorism (including by Sunni groups such as Hamas) and has strong links to Iran.[13] Hizbullah is one of several groups that could replace Al Qaeda in its niche of 'top predator', as the *jihad* evolves. Similarly, financial, religious, educational and cultural networks (based largely on Saudi Arabia) function at the global level in unifying the effect of disparate actors across the *jihad*, and often have greater penetration and influence than Al Qaeda itself.

Clearly, therefore, there *is* a global jihadist movement, but it comprises a loosely aligned confederation of independent networks and movements, not a single unified organization. Global players link and exploit local players through regional affiliates – they rarely interact directly with local players, but sponsor and support them through intermediaries. Each theater has operational players who are able to tap into the global *jihad*, and these tend to be regional Al Qaeda affiliates. Saudi Arabia is a central factor, with greater 'reach' than Al Qaeda itself. As Al Qaeda is disrupted, its clones and competitors will probably tend to move into its niche and assume some of its role.

Understanding the *jihad*

Western analysts often struggle to characterize the *jihad*. Is it a formal organization, a mass movement or a loose confederation of allies? Is it a franchised business model with centralized corporate support and autonomous regional divisions? Is it merely a myth, a creation of Western intelligence services and authoritarian governments? On the contrary, the emerging picture of global *jihad* suggests that the network is all too real. But Western models may not be able to fully describe it. Rather, analysis suggests, social and ethnographic models may be more applicable.

Karl Jackson (during fieldwork in 1968) and this author (during fieldwork in 1995–97) independently demonstrated that a model of traditional patron–client authority relationships is applicable to Islamic insurgent movements.[14] Under this model, the *jihad* is a variant on a traditional Middle Eastern patronage network. It is an intricate, ramified web of dependency and, critically, the patterns of patronage and dependency are its central defining features, rather than the insurgent cells or their activities. Analysts have sometimes seen the marriage relationships, money flows, alumni relationships and sponsorship links in the *jihad* as secondary, subordinate to a military core of terrorist activity. But fieldwork analysis indicates that jihadist military activity may actually be merely one of the shared activities that the network engages in, while the core is the patronage network. In fact, the *jihad* appears to function more like a tribal group, organized crime syndicate or extended family, than like a military organization.[15] Many desert tribes traditionally raised camels: but the essence of the tribe was its web of traditional authority structures, family allegiances and tribal honor, not the essentially secondary activity of camel herding. Thus, the Islamist network appears to reside in the pattern of relationships itself – *jihad* is simply one activity the network *does*, it does not define the network itself.

Global Islamist insurgency

This globalized *jihad* network is best understood as an insurgency. Insurgency can be defined as 'a popular movement that seeks to overthrow the status quo through subversion, political activity, insurrection, armed conflict and terrorism'.[16] By definition, insurgent movements are grassroots uprisings that seek to overthrow established governments or societal orders. They are popular uprisings that employ subversion, guerrilla tactics and terrorism against the established power of states and conventional military forces. Many, including the Islamist *jihad*, draw their foot soldiers from deprived socio-economic groups and their leadership from alienated, radicalized elites.

Conversely, terrorism can be defined as 'politically motivated violence against non-combatants with the intention to coerce through fear', and is in the tactical repertoire of virtually every insurgency. Terrorism is a component in virtually all insurgencies, and insurgent objectives (that is, a desire to change the status quo through subversion and violence) lie behind almost all terrorism.[17]

By this definition, the global *jihad* is clearly an insurgency – a popular movement that seeks to change the status quo through violence and subversion. But whereas traditional insurgencies sought to overthrow established governments or social orders in one state or district, this insurgency seeks to transform the entire Islamic world and remake its relationship with the rest of the globe. It looks back to a golden age, seeking to re-establish a Caliphate throughout the Muslim world and, ultimately, expand the realm of Islam (*Dar al Islam*) to all human society.[18] The scale of the Islamists' agenda is new, but their grievances and methods would be familiar to any insurgent in history.

The *jihad* is, therefore, a global insurgency. Al Qaeda and similar groups feed on local grievances, integrate them into broader ideologies, and link disparate conflicts through globalized communications, finances and technology. In this, Al Qaeda resembles the Communist Internationale of the twentieth century – a holding company and clearing-house for world revolution. But whereas the Comintern was a state-sponsored support organization for local revolutions and insurgencies, the global *jihad* is itself an insurgent movement. Moreover, whereas the Comintern was sponsored by the Soviet Union, the Islamist *jihad* seeks to form the basis for a new supra-national state.

Thus the distinguishing feature of the jihadists is not their use of terrorism, a tactic they share with dozens of movements worldwide. Rather, it is that they represent a global insurgency, which – like other insurgent movements – uses terrorism, subversion, propaganda and open warfare.

Competing paradigms – terrorism and insurgency

The study of terrorism, as an academic discipline, emerged in the 1970s in response to the growing phenomenon of international terrorism.[19] Before then, terrorism was seen primarily as a component within localized insurgencies. Indeed, in Malaya in the 1950s the principal British counter-*insurgency* manual was entitled 'The Conduct of Anti-*Terrorist* Operations in Malaya', indicating that the two activities were seen as synonymous.[20] In this period, insurgency and terrorism were seen as practically the same phenomenon—the term 'terrorism' was primarily of political and propaganda value. The term was used to label an insurgent as illegitimate, or portray an insurgent's methods as 'beyond the pale'.

But the international terrorism that emerged in the 1970s included groups such as the Baader-Meinhof Group, the Italian Red Brigades and the Japanese Red Army with little apparent link to any mass movement or insurgency. These were 'disembodied' terrorist groups comprising cells of alienated individuals within Western society, rather than insurgent movements with definite achievable aims. In analyzing these groups, a new paradigm emerged in popular thinking about terrorism.

Under this paradigm, shared by many Western legislators and policy-makers although not by terrorism specialists, terrorists are seen as unrepresentative aberrant individuals, misfits within society. Partly because they are unrepresentative, partly to discourage emulation, 'we do not negotiate with terrorists'. Terrorists are criminals, whose methods and objectives are both unacceptable. They use violence partly to shock and influence populations and governments, but also because they are psychologically or morally flawed ('evil') individuals. In this paradigm, terrorism is primarily a law enforcement problem, and we therefore adopt a case-based approach where the key objective is to apprehend the perpetrators of terrorist attacks.

This paradigm has been highly influential in our approach to the War on Terrorism— largely because of the word 'terrorism' in the title. Thus the US seeks to apprehend Osama bin Laden, and some commentators regard the failure to do so as evidence of failure to prosecute the war effectively. Likewise, Australia's response to the Bali bombing of 2002 focused on 'bringing terrorists to justice' —hence the central role of police work in a law enforcement-style approach.

The insurgency paradigm is different. Under this approach, insurgents are regarded as representative of deeper issues or grievances within society. We seek to defeat insurgents through 'winning the hearts and minds' of the population, a process that involves compromise and negotiation. We regard insurgents' methods as unacceptable, but their grievances are often seen as legitimate, provided they are pursued peacefully. This may be why mainstream society often accepts insurgents—like Nelson Mandela and Xanana Gusmaō – who renounce violence but seek the same objectives through political means. We see insurgents as using violence within an integrated politico-military strategy, rather than as psychopaths. In this paradigm, insurgency is a whole-of-government problem rather than a military or law-enforcement issue. Based on this, we adopt a strategy-based approach to counterinsurgency, where the objective is to defeat the insurgent's strategy, rather than to 'apprehend the perpetrators' of specific acts.

Figure 17.2 provides a summary of the principal differences identified between the terrorism and insurgency paradigms. However, as noted, the terrorism paradigm largely represents a popular stereotype, not the views of most specialist analysts who tend to regard terrorism as a subset or sub-category of insurgency.

The insurgency paradigm supports a different interpretation of the current war than does the terrorism paradigm. Indeed, actions in the war appear disparate if viewed through a terrorism paradigm. Some (like international law-enforcement cooperation and actions to counter terrorist financing) fit the terrorism paradigm neatly, while others (the Iraq War, counter-proliferation initiatives, building influence in Central Asia, policies toward North Korea and Iran) appear unrelated to an anti-terrorism agenda. However, viewed through the lens of counterinsurgency, these actions fit neatly into three streams of classical counterinsurgency: pacification, winning hearts and minds, and the denial of sanctuary and external sponsorship.

If the War on Terrorism is a global insurgency, then the counterinsurgency paradigm (which includes action against terrorism as a subset of insurgency) is a better mental model for the war than is counterterrorism. Indeed, the key to defeating global *jihad* may not lie in traditional counterterrorism (police work, intelligence, special operations or security measures) at all. Instead, counterinsurgency theory may provide the most useful insights.

Terrorism	Insurgency
Terrorist is an unrepresentative aberration	*Insurgent represents deeper issues in society*
No negotiation with terrorists	*Winning hearts and minds is critical and often involves negotiation*
Methods and objectives are both unacceptable	*Methods are unacceptable; objectives are not necessarily so*
Terrorists are psychologically and morally flawed with personal (psychopathic) tendencies toward violence	*Insurgents use violence within an integrated politico-military strategy – violence is instrumental not central to their approach*
Terrorism is a law-enforcement problem	*Insurgency is a whole-of-government problem*
Counterterrorism adopts a case-based approach focused on catching the perpetrators of terrorist actions.	*Counterinsurgency uses a strategy-based approach focused on defeating insurgents' strategy – catching them is secondary.*

Figure 17.2 Terrorism and Insurgency as Competing Paradigms.

Counterinsurgency *redux*

Despite its relevance to this conflict, traditional counterinsurgency techniques from the era of the 'Wars of National Liberation' of the 1960s cannot merely be applied to today's problems in a simplistic fashion. This is because counterinsurgency, in its 'classical' form, is optimised to defeat insurgency in one country, not counter a global insurgency. For example, pacification programs in classic counter-insurgency demand the ability to coordinate information operations, development, governance, military and police security operations, and overt and covert counter-guerrilla operations across a geographical area – often a province or region. At the national level, control of all counterinsurgent actions in the hands of a single 'supremo' is recognized as a key element.[21]

This *can* be achieved in one country: Malaya, Northern Ireland and other campaigns demonstrated this. But to achieve this level of integration requires excellent governmental stability, unity and restraint. Moreover, it demands extremely close coordination and integration between and within police, intelligence, military, development, aid, information and administrative agencies. For example, the successful Malayan campaign rested on an overall supremo with combined military, political and administrative powers, supported by an intricate system of federal, state, district and sub-district executive inter-agency committees. Likewise, successful classic counterinsurgency in the Americas, Africa and Asia has been closely tied to improvements in governance, integrated administrative systems and joint inter-agency action.

At the global level, no world government exists with the power to integrate the actions of independent nations to the degree required by traditional counterinsurgency theory; nor can regional counterinsurgency programs be closely enough aligned to block all insurgent maneuver. This is particularly true when the enemy – as in this case – is not a Maoist-style mass rural movement, but an insurgency operating in small cells and teams with low 'tactical signature' in the urban clutter of globalized societies.

As Robert Kagan has argued, the current 'crisis of legitimacy' affecting US efforts to exercise global leadership in the War on Terrorism is a symptom, rather than a cause, of a deepening geo-strategic division between Europe and America.[22] While this division persists, under the international system as currently constituted, any nation powerful enough to act as a global counterinsurgency supremo would tend to lack legitimacy. Conversely, any collective or multinational grouping (such as the UN Security Council) that could muster unquestioned legitimacy would tend to lack sufficient power to act effectively. It would be fatally constrained by the very factors (sovereign equality of states, non-intervention in the internal affairs of states, multilateral consensus) that generated its legitimacy. Thus the entire concept of counterinsurgency is problematic when applied at the global level.

Similarly, classic counterinsurgency seeks to deny enemy sanctuaries, prevent infiltration into theater, and isolate insurgents from support. A global insurgency has limited vulnerability to many of these measures, because of the phenomenon of failed and failing states, and under-administered areas between states (such as the tribal areas on the Pakistan/Afghan border). This allows geographical sanctuary for insurgents, while international flows of information and finances provide 'cyber-sanctuaries' (like the Al Qaeda Internet presence described above) for insurgents.

So a globalized insurgency demands a rethink of traditional counterinsurgency. What is required is counterinsurgency *redux*, not the templated application of 1960s techniques. Both counterterrorism and counterinsurgency provide some answers, but an integrated approach is needed that draws on both disciplines, modifies them for current conditions, and develops new methods applicable to globalized insurgency. How might 'counterinsurgency *redux*' look?

The problem of strategy

US strategy for the overall War on Terrorism remains vaguely understood. Indeed, despite substantial policy work in the national security community, some have seriously questioned whether the US actually *has* a coherent overall strategy for the war and, if so, what it is.[23]

In fact, analysis of action in the war so far indicates a de facto strategy of 'aggregation' – lumping together all terrorism, all rogue or failed states and all strategic competitors. This de facto strategy creates several problems. It runs the risk of creating new enemies, and fighting simultaneously enemies that could have been fought sequentially. A strategy of aggregation tends to the logical outcome of a war against all terrorists or – far worse – all Muslims simultaneously. This creates enormous potential for overstretch, exhaustion of popular will, and ultimate failure.[24]

Moreover, such a strategy undermines US legitimacy (and thus effectiveness as global counterterrorism supremo), because it tends to link apparently disparate conflicts, giving the appearance that the war is an attempt to settle old scores. Similarly, it encourages support for morally dubious regimes and undermines opportunities for common cause with other democracies.

But if the global *jihad* is best understood as a globalized insurgency, this suggests an alternative – indeed, a diametrically opposed – strategy for the War on Terrorism, namely 'disaggregation'.

Disaggregation strategy

As described, dozens of local movements, grievances and issues have been aggregated (through regional and global players) into a global *jihad* against the West. These regional and global players prey upon, link and exploit local actors and issues that are pre-existing. What makes the *jihad* so dangerous is its global nature. Without the 'series of nested interactions' this article has described, or the ability to aggregate dozens of conflicts into a broad movement, the global *jihad* ceases to exist. It becomes simply a series of disparate local conflicts that can be addressed at the regional or national level without interference from global enemies such as Al Qaeda.

Indeed, it can be argued that the essence of jihadist 'operational art' is the ability to aggregate numerous tactical actions, dispersed across time and space, to achieve an overall strategic effect. This was the conception behind the 9/11 attacks, the Bali bombing, the 1998 African embassy bombings, the Christmas 2000 bombings in Indonesia, and various attempted or planned attacks including the so-called 'Operation Bojinka' – which sought to hijack simultaneously up to a dozen airliners over the Pacific Ocean.

A strategy of disaggregation would attack this operational method, by breaking the links that allow the *jihad* to function as a global entity. In this strategy, victory does not demand that we pacify every insurgent theater from the Philippines to Chechnya. It demands only that we identify, and neutralize, those elements in each theater that are linked to the global *jihad*. For example, Chechen separatism pre-dates the involvement of Islamists in the Caucasus. Disaggregation does not demand an immediate resolution to the Chechen insurgency, rather it demands that we deny the Chechen *jihad* its links to the global movement, then support Russia in addressing Chechen separatism. Similarly, disaggregation does not demand that we resolve the Moro separatist issue in the Philippines. It requires only that we isolate groups like Abu Sayyaf from the global *jihad*, and assist the Philippines to resolve its conflict with groups like the Moro National Liberation Front which, although composed of Islamic separatists, is seeking regional self-government not endless global *jihad*.

Thus, although dozens of local insurgencies contribute to the global *jihad*, victory under a disaggregation strategy does not demand the destruction of all local insurgents. Rather (systems analysis indicates) counterinsurgency at the systemic level is a matter of de-linking local issues from the global insurgent system, as much as it is about dealing with local insurgents themselves.

At the global level, disaggregation would interdict the Al Qaeda core leadership's ability to influence regional and local players – by cutting off their communications, discrediting their ideological authority, and global operations to keep them off balance. At the regional level, disaggregation would isolate theater-level actors from global sponsors, local populations and local insurgent groups they might seek to exploit in support of *jihad*. This would involve regional campaigns in locations such as Southeast Asia, the greater Middle East, North Africa and Central/South Asia. At the local level, disaggregation would involve creating a local security framework by training, equiping and enabling partner states, to prevent the overthrow of responsible governments by Al Qaeda-linked movements, influence oppressive or weak states to improve their governance, and ensure that local governments were strong enough to outlast the jihadist threat.

This would demand a re-conceptualization of the war as a three-tier campaign at the global, regional and local level. Importantly, it would also allow us to define the war in terms of what it *supports* rather than solely what it *opposes*. If the war is truly a global counterinsurgency against a movement that seeks to overthrow the existing world order in favour of a pre-modern Islamist super-state, then it is not just a negative campaign against non-state terrorist actors. Rather, it is a positive campaign in support of the modern world order of responsibly governed nation-states linked by an increasingly globalized world economy and robust international institutions. While many countries are suspicious of the US agenda for the war as currently presented, every democracy in the world has an interest in preserving effective governance against the threat of nihilist terrorism. Thus a disaggregation approach would create a substantially larger pool of potential allies – including the world's mainstream Muslim communities. A strategy of disaggregation would focus on:

- Attacking the 'intricate web of dependency' – the links that allow the *jihad* to function effectively.
- Interdicting links between Islamist theaters of operation within the global insurgency.
- Denying the ability of regional and global actors to link and exploit local actors.
- Interdicting flows of information, personnel, finance and technology (including WMD technology) between and within *jihad* theaters.
- Denying sanctuary areas (including failed and failing states, and states that support terrorism) within theaters.
- Isolating Islamists from local populations, through theater-specific measures to win hearts and minds, counter-Islamist propaganda, create alternative institutions and remove the drivers for popular support to insurgents.
- Disrupting inputs (personnel, money and information) from the sources of Islamism in the greater Middle East to dispersed *jihad* theaters worldwide.

In a global insurgency, this strategy requires that regional counterinsurgency campaigns be conducted so as to reduce the energy level in the global *jihad*. It also demands that legitimate Muslim aspirations are addressed through a constitutional path, and military forces adopt an enabling, rather than a dominant, role. Military force is still essential and will probably be applied in large-scale counterinsurgency-style tasks, not limited counterterrorist operations. Nonetheless military force can only create pre-conditions for non-military measures to succeed.

In practical terms, disaggregation does not provide a template of universally applicable counterinsurgency measures. Indeed, such a template probably does not exist and, if it did, the proven adaptiveness of our jihadist enemy would render it rapidly obsolete. Instead, much like containment during the Cold War, a strategy of disaggregation means different things at different times or in different theaters, but provides a unifying strategic conception for a protracted global confrontation. Nevertheless, several practical insights arise from this strategic conception.

A global 'CORDS program'

As explained, the enemy in this war comprises a multifarious, intricately ramified web of dependencies that – like a tribal group or crime family – behaves more like a traditional patronage network than a mass guerrilla movement. *Jihad* is what the network does, not the network itself.

Disrupting this network demands that we target the links (the web of dependencies itself) and the energy flows (inputs and outputs that pass between actors in the *jihad*) as the primary method of disrupting the network. An exclusive focus on attempting to stop terrorist attacks or catch terrorists themselves simply imposes an evolutionary pressure that makes insurgents adapt and improve.

The concept of 'de-linking' is central to disaggregation. It would target the insurgent infrastructure in a similar fashion to the maligned (but extremely effective) Vietnam-era Civil Operations and Rural Development Support (CORDS) program, headed by Ambassador Robert Komer. Contrary to popular mythology, CORDS was largely a civilian aid and development program, supported by targeted military pacification operations and intelligence activity to disrupt the Viet Cong Infrastructure. A global CORDS program is a useful model for understanding how disaggregation would develop in practice.[25]

A constitutional path

A key technique of classic counterinsurgency is to counter the grievances on which insurgencies feed, denying energy to their recruiting and propaganda subsystems, and ultimately marginalizing them. For example, in Malaya the British countered the Communist appeal to nationalism by setting a date for independence and commencing a transition to self-government. Over time, this marginalized the insurgents – people saw their grievances being peacefully addressed anyway, so why support the insurgency? Similarly, strong anti-Communist trade unions were a key development in the Cold War. These provided a 'constitutional path' for workers seeking a better life and legitimized their aspirations, while de-legitimizing the Communist revolutionary methods. Instead of a stark choice between revolution and poverty, trade unions gave workers a constitutional path – accessing justice through the labor movement, without recourse to (or need for) extra-legal means.

A constitutional path is needed, but lacking, to counter global *jihad:* most measures so far have been 'all stick and no carrot'. For Muslims in much of the world, there is no middle way: only a stark choice between *jihad* and acceptance of permanent second-class citizenship in a world order dominated by the West and apparently infused with anti-Islamic values. For many self-respecting Muslims, the choice of *jihad* rather than surrender is both logical and honorable. So a constitutional path is critical – one that addresses Muslim aspirations without recourse to *jihad*, thus marginalizing Islamists and robbing their movement of energy.

It would require a separate article to articulate such a path in detail. But key elements might include exporting elements of the Malaysian and Turkish approaches to representative government in Muslim societies; addressing the role of women, education and governance; and building effective representational bodies for the world's Muslims. Measures like the Middle East Free Trade Zone, the Broader Middle East and North Africa Initiative, and the proposals canvassed in the UNDP's Arab Human Development Report series would represent moves in the right direction, but 'these ideas have so far been ineffectual for a range of reasons. Their limited funding and haphazard administration suggests an uncertain commitment on the part of the US'[26]—implying the need for greater commitment to this aspect of the War on Terrorism.

Cultural capability

Cultures – organizational, ethnic, national, religious or tribal – provide key links in the global *jihad*. Cultures determine how each actor in an insurgency perceives the actions of the others, and generate unperceived cultural boundaries that limit their freedom of action. Culture imbues otherwise random or apparently senseless acts with meaning and subjective rationality. Hence, it may be impossible for counterinsurgent forces to perceive the true meaning of insurgent actions, or influence populations and their perceptions, without access to local culture. Many links in the *jihad* – and virtually all the grievances and energies that circulate within it – are culturally determined. Culture is intimately connected with language, since humans use language to make sense of reality and communicate meaning. Therefore, in counterinsurgency, linguistic and cultural competence is a critical combat capability. It generates a permissive operating environment and enables access to cultural centers of gravity, situational awareness and interaction with the population.

This is true of both traditional and globalized counterinsurgency. But in globalized counterinsurgency, security forces must work at several cultural levels simultaneously. For example, forces in Iraq must understand local Iraqi culture, jihadist organisational culture, cultural pressure points for tribal and sectarian groups in the population, cultural triggers for opinion in neighboring countries and the culture of foreign fighters in theater. They must also understand the implications of actions within Iraq upon events culturally different theaters elsewhere, and the overall systemic culture of the global *jihad*. Identifying cultural pressure points of this kind is critical in generating deterrence and influence against insurgents.[27]

Linguistic and cultural competence must exist at several levels within a counterinsurgent force. At the most basic level, everyone in the force – regardless of role – must have a basic degree of cultural awareness. This demands basic language training, understanding cultural norms and expectations, and – most importantly – understanding how local populations and insurgents think. At the intermediate level, planners, intelligence personnel, civil-military operations teams and advisers need higher levels of cultural understanding. This involves more advanced language capability, an ability to 'fit in' with local groups, and to perform effectively while immersed in local culture. At the highest level of cultural capability, key personnel need an ability to use culture to generate leverage within an insurgent system. Commanders working with local community and government leaders need such capability. It is also needed by personnel working in the intelligence and covert action fields, and in key nation-building programs. At this level, individuals are bilingual and bi-cultural, and can exploit cultural norms and expectations to generate operational effects.[28]

No nation's regular armed forces will ever be able to generate more than a small number of individuals with this capability, but only a small number are actually needed – provided they are developed and employed effectively. This is difficult within the organizational culture of regular armies, and such officers are likely to be mavericks: 'renaissance men' in the mould of T.E. Lawrence, Orde Wingate or Edward Lansdale. They often emerge from an 'inter-agency' background and have experience working in several related fields. For example, Orde Wingate was an Arabic linguist, desert explorer, member of the Sudan Civil Service and highly successful leader of irregular troops in Israel, Sudan and Ethiopia before embarking on his Burma campaign as leader of the Long-Range Penetration Group (the 'Chindits'). Similarly, Ambassador Robert Komer was a former US Army Lieutenant Colonel who subsequently served with the CIA, the Foreign Service, the US Agency for International Development and the RAND Corporation – combining a range of highly relevant skills for his task of leading the CORDS effort in Vietnam.

Whatever the cultural capability of a deployed force, it will never be able to dispense with extensive use of, and reliance on, local populations and security forces. Only locals have the access to the population, and deep understanding of a particular insurgency, necessary to combat it.[29] Conversely, those directing the war against Al Qaeda must understand issues across the three tiers (global, regional and local) of the *jihad* – so key personnel need cultural agility. As noted, there is a distinct jihadist culture. Jihadists do not operate in a completely savage and random fashion. Indeed, there are very specific self-imposed limitations on their operational and targeting methods. Understanding and exploiting these limitations is important in global counterinsurgency. It should go without saying, but unfortunately does not, that every key operator in the War on Terrorism needs a comprehensive understanding of Islam, *jihad*, Islamist ideology and Muslim culture. Achieving this would be an important step toward victory.

Conclusions

In summary, this article has proposed a new strategic concept for the Global War on Terrorism.

As explained, the war is best understood as a globalized insurgency, initiated by a diffuse confederation of Islamist movements seeking to re-make Islam's role in the world order. They use terrorism as their primary, but not their sole tactic. Therefore counterinsurgency rather than traditional counterterrorism may offer the best approach to defeating global *jihad*. But classic counterinsurgency, as developed in the 1960s, is designed to defeat insurgency in a single country. It demands measures – coordinated political-military responses, integrated regional and inter-agency measures, protracted commitment to a course of action – that cannot be achieved at the global level in today's international system. Therefore a traditional counterinsurgency paradigm will not work for the present war: instead, a fundamental reappraisal of counterinsurgency is needed, to develop methods effective against a globalized insurgency.

Applying the counterinsurgency model generates a new strategy for the War on Terrorism – disaggregation. Like containment in the Cold War, a disaggregation strategy means different things in different theaters or at different times. But it provides a unifying strategic conception for the war. Disaggregation focuses on interdicting links between theaters, denying the ability of regional and global actors to link and exploit local actors, disrupting flows between and within *jihad* theaters, denying sanctuary areas, isolating Islamists from local populations and disrupting inputs from the sources of Islamism in the greater Middle East. It approaches the war as a three-tier problem at the global, regional and local levels – seeking to interdict global links via a worldwide CORDS program, isolate regional players through a series of regional counterinsurgencies and strengthen local governance through a greatly enhanced security framework at the country level.

If one key message emerges from this study, it is that the moden world order of responsibly governed nation-states *can* defeat the threat from Islamist terrorism. The jihadist enemy is neither inscrutable nor invincible; Al Qaeda methods have flaws that can be exploited, and global *jihad* cannot ultimately offer the world's Muslim population the security, prosperity and social justice that can only come through good governance at the level of nation-states. Therefore victory, in the long-term, is both possible and likely. But there are enormous challenges on the way. Counterinsurgency practitioners – strategists, soldiers and intelligence operators – must re-build our mental model of this conflict, re-design our classical counterinsurgency and counterterrorism methods, and continually develop innovative and culturally effective approaches to meet the challenge of new conditions. This process must go well beyond addressing today's immediate problems, to ultimately transform our whole approach to countering global insurgency.

Notes

1 Carl von Clausewitz, *On War*, trans. Michael Howard and Peter Paret (Princetown, NJ: Princeton UP 1989) p.88.
2 Muslims disagree over precisely who can issue a *fatwa*. It is generally agreed, however, that only an Islamic cleric can issue such a religious ruling, and only the legitimate ruler of a Muslim state can

issue a call to *jihad*. In this sense, by issuing a call to *jihad* in the form of a *fatwa*, bin Laden was claiming both religious and temporal authority. For a detailed discussion of these issues, see Bernard Lewis, *The Crisis of Islam: Holy War and Unholy Terror* (London: Weidenfeld & Nicholson 2003). See also Peter L. Bergen, *Holy War, Inc: Inside the Secret World of Osama bin Laden* (London: Weidenfeld & Nicolson 2001).

3   See collected Al Qaeda statements available at <www.siteinstitute.org> for a variety of references to bin Laden as *emir* or *sheikh* in official Al Qaeda communiqués.

4   Ayman al-Zawahiri, 'Knights under the Prophet's Banner', in *Al-Sharq al-Awsat*, 2 Dec. 2001.

5   See <http://siteinstitute.org/bin/articles.cgi?ID=publications9504&Category=publications& Subcategory=0>.

6   The Qur'an is read and studied only in the original Arabic, and strict Islamic religious instruction worldwide is conducted in Arabic. Vernacular translations of the Qur'an are not considered to be genuine copies of the Book. Thus Arabic language is fundamental in the Muslim worldview.

7   Michael Vlahos, *Terror's Mask: Insurgency within Islam* (Laurel, MD: Occasional Paper, Johns Hopkins University Applied Physics Laboratory 2002).

8   See Overseas Security Advisory Council, *Chechen Female Suicide Bombers*, at <www.dsosac.org>.

9   For detailed open-source descriptions of Al Qaeda planning and operational methods see Bergen (note 1). See also Rohan Gunaratna, *Inside Al Qa'eda* (NY: Columbia UP 2002) and Jane Corbin, *The Base: Al-Qaeda and the Changing Face of Global Terror* (London: Pocket Books 2003).

10 *Pers. Comm.* confidential source, May 2004.

11 For a listing of Islamist propaganda websites and produces, see <www.internet-haganah.com>.

12 See <www.fas.org/irp/world/para/docs> for a series of extracts from Al Qaeda's operational manual. See <www.siteinstitute.org/terroristpublications.html> for a series of translated summaries of *al-Battar*.

13 For a detailed discussion of Hizbullah's global reach, see Ely Karmon, *Fight on All Fronts: Hizballah, the War on Terror, and the War in Iraq* (Washington, DC: Washington Institute for Near East Policy 2003).

14 See Karl Jackson, *Traditional Authority, Islam and Rebellion* (Berkeley, CA: University of California Press 1980).

15 Recent research on Al Qaeda operational patterns tends to support this view. See David Ronfeldt, 'Al Qaeda and its Affiliates: A Global Tribe Waging Segmental Warfare?', in *First Monday* 10/3 (March 2005), at <http://firstmonday.org/issues/issue101113/ronfeldt/index.html>.

16 This definition and that of terrorism, which follows, were developed specifically for this article. Both were derived through synthesising several definitions used in the Western intelligence and security communities.

17 See Thomas A. Marks, 'Ideology of Insurgency: New Ethnic Focus or Old Cold War Distortions?', in *Small Wars and Insurgencies* 15/1 (Spring 2004) p.107.

18 As expressed in statements by bin Laden, particularly the *World Islamic Front Declaration of War against Jews and Crusaders*. See also comments in Paul K. Davis and Brian Michael Jenkins, 'A System Approach to Deterring and Influencing Terrorists', in *Conflict Management and Peace Science*, 21 (2004) pp. 3–15, 2004.

19 Ajai Sahni, 'Social Science and Contemporary Conflicts: The Challenge of Research on Terrorism' at *South Asia Terrorism Portal* <www.satp.org> accessed 10 Nov. 2004. See also F. Schorkopf, 'Behavioural and Social Science Perspectives on Political Violence' in C. Walter, S. Vöneky, V. Röben and F. Schorkopf (eds), *Terrorism as a Challenge for National and International Law: Security versus Liberty?* (Berlin/Heidelberg: Springer Verlag 2003).

20 Federation of Malaya, *Conduct of Anti-Terrorist Operations in Malaya*, 3rd edn (Kuala Lumpur: Government Printer 1958).

21 See Bruce Hoffman, *Insurgency and Counterinsurgency in Iraq* (Santa Monica, CA: RAND 2004), for a discussion of this concept in relation to counterinsurgency in Malaya and Cyprus.

22 See Robert Kagan, *Of Paradise and Power: America and Europe in the New World Order* (NY: Knopf 2003). See also Robert Kagan, *America and the World: The Crisis of Legitimacy*, 21st Bonython Lecture, 9 Nov. 2004, at <www.cis.org.au>.

23 *Pers. Comm.*, senior US government official, Oct. 2004.

24 For a detailed discussion of these concerns see Jeffrey Record, *Bounding the Global War on Terrorism* (Carlisle, PA: Strategic Studies Institute 2003).

25 For detailed discussion on the Phoenix Program and the broader CORDS system, see Steven

Metz, *Counterinsurgency: Strategy and the Phoenix of American Capability* (Carlisle, PA: Strategic Studies Institute 1995). See also B.R. Brewington, 'Combined Action Platoons: A Strategy for Peace Enforcement' at <www.smallwars.quantico.usmc.mil/search/Papers/brewington.pdf>; and S. Metz and R. Millen, *Insurgency and Counterinsurgency in the Twenty-First Century – Reconceptualizing Threat and Response* (Carlisle, PA: Strategic Studies Institute 2004).

26 A. Billingsley, 'The Native Scene' in *The Diplomat*, Aug./Sept. 2004, p. 23.

27 Davis and Jenkins (note 20).

28 These insights are based on the author's experience as an advisor with Indonesian Special Forces in 1994–95 and as an instructor with East Timorese irregular troops in 2003. However, almost every military advisor, SF team leader and training team member whom the author has debriefed has raised the same points.

29 For example, in Sept. 2004 the author debriefed an intelligence officer serving in Baghdad, who indicated that local Iraqi security forces' insights into the origins of foreign fighters revolutionized that operator's approach to the problem. Local insights, combined with broader understanding of issues in the global *jihad*, create powerful synergies.

18 Strategic terrorism

The framework and its fallacies

Peter R. Neumann and M.L.R. Smith

Introduction

Since September 11, 2001, no issue has generated more public interest than terrorism. At the internet bookseller, Amazon, 20,000 books on the topic are currently available, ranging from survival guides to complex post-modernist analyses.[1] Among this flood of (often forgettable) books, what stands out is the absence of any meaningful examination of terrorism as a military strategy. This seems odd given that the restructuring of entire armies is based on the assumption that the 'new battles' of the twenty-first century are not going to be fought with tanks and missiles, but 'by customs officers stopping suspicious persons at our borders and diplomats securing cooperation against money laundering'.[2] Of course, there are many good reasons for this reluctance to engage with terrorism as a strategy. After all, we are constantly told that the so-called 'new terrorism' is nihilist and irrational, and that attempting to understand its logic would be futile.[3] Furthermore, there can be no doubt that many among the older generation of strategists feel more comfortable dealing with the supposedly purposeful behavior of states, and have therefore focused on the state's response rather than on the phenomenon itself.[4]

In our view, the gap in the scholarly literature must be addressed urgently because the lack of a theoretical framework in which to understand terrorism leads to questionable assertions about its practice.[5] There is a tendency to treat terrorism as an aberrant form of violent activity devoid of any meaning. For example, Bruce Cumings declared in the wake of September 11 that:

> ... in its utter recklessness and indifference to consequences, its craven anonymity, and its lack of any discernible 'program' save for inchoate revenge, this was an apolitical act. The 9/11 attack had no rational military purpose [because] they lacked the essential relationship between violent means and political ends that, as Clausewitz taught us, must govern any act of war.[6]

Elsewhere, terrorism is viewed through the prism of an ideological showdown between the forces of good and evil. This is most graphically embodied in the notion of the 'war against terrorism'. Other commentators, meanwhile, see terrorism as a matter that is essentially the product of relative deprivation. Stella Rimington, the former head of MI5, the British security service, stated that 'Terrorism is going to be there for a long time. It's going to be there as long as there are people with grievances that they feel terrorism will help solve.'[7]

It is our contention that terrorism – even that of the supposedly 'nihilist' variety – does not necessarily fall within the realm of the abnormal. Neither should terrorism be employed as an 'abstract noun'.[8] For, ultimately, a war against terrorism has no more meaning than a 'war against war' or a 'war against poverty' in that it defines no specific threat or realizable political ends. Nor is terrorism simply an outgrowth of grievance. Instead, terrorism should more appropriately be viewed as a military strategy. It is a method that has been employed by actors who believe, rightly or wrongly, that through such means they can advance their agenda. It is possible, therefore, to treat terrorism as a bona fide method for distributing military means to fulfill the ends of policy.[9] Indeed, the main purpose of this article is to describe the military dynamics of terrorism and evaluate their effectiveness, as well as to theorize upon – and clarify the correlation between – political ends and terrorist means.

Before doing so, it seems useful to clarify our methodological approach, especially in view of the numerous misconceptions that have been filtered through the popular – as well as some of the more serious – literature. The theoretical model used in this article is that of a non-state terrorist group competing for absolute power with a government against which its efforts are targeted. This is not to say that so-called single-issue terrorists (such as anti-abortionists, animal rights campaigners, etc.) and the issue of state terrorism are less important.[10] It just so happens that the ideas and concepts involved remain much the same in each case, and that to constantly separate out each type would make the analysis unnecessarily verbose.

Furthermore, we think that – for analytical as well as practical reasons – it makes sense to begin our evaluation of terrorism by looking at its military content. The starting point will therefore be the theoretical notion of a campaign of 'strategic terrorism', that is, one that is based on achieving political effects primarily through terrorist violence. While there is a very substantial number of contemporary terrorist campaigns to which our theoretical model of strategic terrorism can be applied (that of Al Qaeda, for example), we are conscious that there are many groups who combine terrorism with other methods of warfare as well as forms of non-violent social or political agitation. We are of the opinion that only by examining the dynamics of strategic terrorism is it possible to create the necessary conceptual basis from which to arrive at a fuller understanding of the role played by terrorist violence in the campaigns of some of the groups that have gone beyond the use of strategic terrorism in advancing their aims. In fact, we believe that outlining some of the flaws and limitations of strategic terrorism goes some way to explaining why some groups have chosen to broaden their strategy to include some of the elements mentioned above.

Finally, popular notions like terrorism as a strategy of the 'weak' and 'illegitimate' are often taken as matters of fact without further exploring them. We believe that legitimacy and relative military weakness are important variables in strategic terrorism, and they will play a central part in our analysis. However, instead of assuming these variables to be a conceptual given, we will demonstrate how they relate to, and originate from, the military dynamics of strategic terrorism, thus providing a sound theoretical rationale for their inclusion in a general strategy of terrorism rather than proceeding on the basis of supposedly objective *a priori* notions of important concepts, which frequently lead to conceptual confusion.

This methodological approach informs the way in which this article is organized. Following an attempt to provide a working definition of strategic terrorism, we will distil its unique modus operandi and then describe the different stages which are essential to its successful conclusion. In the second part, we will demonstrate that strategic terrorism is a potentially flawed strategy, which – except in the most favorable circumstances – is unlikely to achieve the ends for which it is used. Our argument is that actors which see fit to use strategic terrorism need to generate considerable strategic momentum in order to trigger the processes which they hope to exploit. The need to escalate, however, will expose them to a number of adverse responses, which will prevent these actors from acquiring legitimacy *in the eyes of their target audience* or even cause their own destruction.

Definition

The trouble with terrorism is that most people think they know what it is but few can adequately define it.[11] The confusion surrounding the issue stems from a number of sources. The distinctive methods that many of us associate with terrorism involves the willful taking of human life and the infliction of severe mental distress, sometimes entailing, whether randomized or calculated, attacks on the innocent. Naturally, for many this introduces an ethical dimension and raises all the questions relating to concepts like just war and non-combatant immunity.[12] Furthermore, because terrorism is not considered to be value neutral, the word itself becomes an object for contention among conflicting parties in a conflict. Political conflicts are struggles for power and influence, and part of that struggle is about who labels whom. Since power tends to be largely concentrated in the hands of states, it is normally they who are able to attach the meaning to certain forms of political behavior, which is why state terror is often ignored in studies of terrorism.[13] The result of this conceptual mess is that – in trying to tie terrorism down for academic analysis – the word has been all but defined out of existence. Certainly the writers of this article know of no meaningful conclusion reached using these approaches.[14]

We do not believe that the definitional problem, which has haunted (as well as hindered) research on the subject for many decades, can be resolved through our contribution. Nevertheless, we would contend that – strictly for the purposes of this analysis – it is possible to describe terrorism as *the deliberate creation of a sense of fear, usually by the use or threat of use of symbolic acts of physical violence, to influence the political behavior of a given target group.* This definition draws on the work by T.P. Thornton, whose main study – although 40 years old – still forms one of the most informative and insightful analyses of terrorism.[15] It highlights three facets of the phenomenon:

- The violent quality of most terrorist acts, which distinguishes a program of terror from other forms of non-violent propagation, such as mass demonstration, leafleting, etc. Indeed, although people will sometimes experience fear and anxiety without the threat of physical harm being present, it appears to be the case that the most common vehicle for the inducement of terror is forms of physical violence.
- The nature of the violence itself. Thornton calls it 'extra-normal', meaning that for a certain level of organized political violence to be called terrorism, it must go beyond the norms of violent political agitation accepted by a particular society.
- The symbolic character of the violent act. An act of terror will imply a broader meaning than the immediate effects of the act itself; that is to say, the damage, deaths and injuries caused by the act are of limited relevance to the political message which the terrorist hopes to communicate. For this reason, the terrorist act can only be understood by appreciating its symbolic content or 'message'.

A significant problem regarding this definition of terrorism concerns the subjective nature of the emotional phenomenon of terror itself. Almost all of us have different ideas of what constitutes fear. Our thresholds of terror are likely to differ. As we will see, a terrorist can quite easily create an atmosphere of defiance rather than fear and anxiety. Neither are our thresholds of terror absolute and unchanging. A feeling of terror may dissipate the longer a terrorist campaign goes on giving rise to an atmosphere of indifference. Likewise, the sensation of terror may be influenced by the perception of the justness of the cause accorded to the actions of the terrorist by the affected populace. In that sense, we may end up back in the old dilemma of having to describe terrorism by context and notions of morality. There is, it seems, no easy way out of the terrorist enigma.

The strategy of terrorism

While a definition may help us to identify some of the essential 'ingredients' of terrorism, it tells us little about its dynamics. In this section, we aim to establish the unique modus operandi of strategic terrorism. This will be done by detailing the process whereby terrorists seek to manipulate particular variables in order to satisfy their political demands. To show how this process is distinctive, we will begin by clarifying the location of strategic terrorism within the wider spectrum of military strategies.

As indicated above, terrorism – like most forms of organized political violence – is employed to produce certain effects on a specific set of people in order to attain an objective of policy. Unlike conventional warfare, however, the aim of a strategy of terrorism is not to kill or destroy but to break the spirit and create a sensation of fear within a target group, which will cause it to initiate political change. Terrorism, therefore, is a particular form of psychological warfare; a battle of wills played out in people's minds.[16] It can thus be regarded as a prime example of coercive diplomacy, where the terrorist group seeks to deprive the enemy of things which he holds dear, not necessarily in terms of material resources, but those more elusive aspects of life such as a relatively peaceful, stable and law abiding society.[17]

In this regard, terrorism bears many similarities to forms of guerrilla warfare. Terrorism and guerrilla warfare are both dedicated to triggering the asking of a question on the part of the target group: 'is it worth paying the price to maintain the present situation?' The aim will be to raise this 'price' to a level whereby the opponent returns to reexamine the notion of vital interest.[18] Historically, this process could be observed in many anti-colonial conflicts in which violence was used in order to trigger a reassessment of values in the colonial metropolis. As the cost of maintenance came to outweigh the benefits, the target's perception changed from a determination to preserve what was considered to be an asset to a willingness to give it up. This idea has been embodied in the concept of the 'asset to liability shift', whereby the 'asset' at the centre of a conflict does not inevitably relate to some territorial possession, but can also refer to something more intangible, such as a policy or ideology.[19]

Whereas terrorism and guerrilla warfare share the same objectives and while both are commonly seen as members of one strategic family loosely referred to as 'irregular' warfare,[20] the means to those ends differ radically, and it is here that we can discern a unique terrorist modus operandi. Much guerrilla warfare theorizing, particularly those ideas that have been filtered through Maoist and Leninist understandings, emphasizes the involvement of the masses through political organization which in many respects is considered even more important than the military struggle itself.[21] Moreover, Maoist theory postulates that the slow accumulation of military assets is necessary in order to meet enemy forces on equal terms in set-piece battles of a conventional nature in the final phase of the confrontation.[22] By contrast, those groups which employ terrorism as the main plank of their strategy – 'strategic terrorists' – seek to bypass both the mass agitation and conventional military elements of guerrilla warfare theory, believing that the use of symbolic violence alone will be sufficient to achieve the desired political ends. The process whereby they hope to achieve their aims can be thought of as involving three stages, which will be elaborated upon in the following.

Stage 1: Disorientation

While the first modern terrorists – the Russian anarchists of the late nineteenth century – believed that carrying out a few daring acts of violence would be sufficient to incite the masses to rise up and bring down the government,[23] most contemporary terrorists have come to recognize that the status quo usually tends to favor the government as it controls the organs of power, and because it will therefore be regarded as the primary provider of stability and security by the vast majority of the population. As long as this remains the case, it will be difficult for the terrorists to be seen as anything but an anti-social element, bringing death and destruction to a hitherto stable society. The strategic terrorists' initial task is therefore to change this perception by undermining the psychological bond which binds the population to the regime. To use Thornton's terminology, the terrorists must attempt to remove the 'structural supports' which give a society its strength and cohesion.[24]

In this respect, disorientation is the key objective. The terrorists hope that their actions will alienate the authorities by portraying them as impotent in the defense of their citizens. To achieve this, those who adopt a program of terrorism need to disrupt the normal patterns of social interaction by escalating the violence to a level where it appears that the authorities are unable to prevent the spread of chaos.[25] Further, by sowing division, destroying cooperation and interdependence, and replacing stability with suspicion and mistrust, the terrorists aim to isolate the individual from the regime and his environment. The victim becomes concerned merely with his own survival, unable to identify the source of his fears.[26] Having thus detached the individual from his social moorings, the terrorists hope that he will become susceptible to the alternative political program offered by the terrorists and that, at the very least, a sizeable proportion of the population will align itself with them, if only by remaining neutral in the struggle.

Something of a paradox emerges here. If we assume a degree of rationality on behalf of the terrorists, we might imagine that – being interested in winning the support of the masses – they would prefer not to carry out indiscriminate attacks because most societies put a premium on the sanctity of human life, especially those people who are deemed to be uninvolved in the conflict. And indeed, in most cases, terrorists will make an attempt to distinguish between legitimate and illegitimate targets. Legitimate targets, which typically include the institutions and the representatives of the state (politicians, officials, military personnel, policemen, judges, etc.) can be rationalized as agents of repression and, to that extent, attacks on them will represent a discriminate targeting policy. Still, continual attacks against specific targets will tend to make the threat predictable, diminishing the sense of fear as the bulk of the target group may come to feel sufficiently removed from the campaign of violence to experience a high degree of threat. It is precisely in order to create an atmosphere of terror and disorientation, to get an audience and to gain political leverage, that terrorists will feel the need to transcend established ethical barriers. Hence, a measure of indiscrimination, or at least the appearance of indiscrimination, is extremely important in order to shatter the psychological defenses of those who have escaped the immediate physical consequences of a terrorist attack – a breaking of the notion that 'it couldn't happen to me'.[27]

While this scenario sounds far-fetched, there are numerous examples – both historical and current – which illustrate the effectiveness of strategic terrorism in causing disorientation through more or less indiscriminate acts of violence. In 1957, the Algerian *Front de la Libération Nationale* (FLN) massacred a group of villagers at Melouza for supporting a rival nationalist group. The FLN denied responsibility for the atrocity and placed the blame on the French authorities. Since the French themselves were responsible for many atrocities against Algerians, most Algerians preferred to believe the FLN's version of events. Paradoxically, therefore, the legitimacy of French rule in Algeria was undermined by an atrocity that had been carried out by Paris' staunchest enemy.[28] Likewise, US forces were blamed for the terrorist bombing of a police station in Baghdad in July 2004, because American planes had been seen flying over the city at the time of the explosion. According to a news report, within minutes, crowds assembled, 'appearing angry and aggrieved, insisting that those killed were martyrs of American aggression'. Even once it had become clear that Iraqi terrorists, not American forces, had been responsible for the attack, Arabic television channels continued to blame the coalition forces, arguing that they were not doing enough to provide security. Again, the result was a loss of legitimacy and credibility for the authorities, not the terrorists who had actually committed the assault.[29]

These examples hint at one of the key variables which may determine how successful the terrorists will be at undermining the psychological bond between the population and the authorities. Clearly, when a government enjoys little popular legitimacy and is widely suspected to act contrary to the interests of the population, the terrorists will find it much easier to replace the idea of the government as a provider of security and stability. This explains why strategic terrorism has been particularly successful when the target government was a colonial or occupying power, such as in Algeria. Moreover, because the target group is different from the one whose allegiance the terrorists hope to gain, there will be little compunction about widening one's definition of legitimate targets, especially if the terrorist attacks occur in what is believed to be the colonial metropolis.[30] As a by-product, indiscriminate attacks against a foreign enemy may also have the effect of invigorating adherents to the terrorists' cause: sympathizers will see such attacks as a sign of strength and defiance, and this might compel them to take up arms themselves in order to become part of what seems like an inevitable victory. In this type of situation, therefore, acts of terrorist violence may not only cause disorientation and deepen the populace's alienation from the authorities but in fact inspire the uprising of the masses which the Russian anarchists had envisaged.

This, indeed, could be thought of as the rationale for Al Qaeda's current campaign. On the one hand, Osama bin Laden and his affiliates aim to trigger disorientation, chaos and civil strife in secular Arab countries like Egypt by launching more or less indiscriminate attacks against government targets, foreign commercial installations, etc. On the other hand, believing that Western – and especially American – military, political and financial support is the key element which sustains many of these regimes, they have set out to strike blows at the Western 'metropolis'. This, they think, will not only drive a wedge between the Arab governments and their Western sponsors, but also incite latent militants to follow their example and commit themselves to the *jihad*.[31]

In its first stage, therefore, the strategy of terrorism primarily aims at overturning the most basic expectations of order and societal interaction, leaving the individual confused, fearful and alienated. To complete this process, however, those who employ strategic terrorism crucially depend on the inadvertent help of the target government. This represents the second stage of a terrorist campaign, which will be examined in the following section.

Stage 2: Target response

As noted above, terrorism is frequently described as a strategy chosen by the 'weak', because its proponents are conscious that they lack the firepower necessary to stand a chance in a direct, conventional confrontation.[32] This often leads to the seemingly straightforward conclusion that the terrorists need to appeal to 'hearts and minds' and generate political strength in order to compensate for their military weakness. In our view, this way of looking at terrorism prevents a full understanding of the military dynamics of terrorist violence. It ignores an important element of any terrorist strategy, which is to set the target a series of (military) dilemmas and then challenge it to react. Indeed, it is our contention that – before setting out to win support for one's alternative political program – strategic terrorism relies on the target to respond in a way which unwittingly undermines its own authority.

N.O. Berry put forward a number of hypotheses that provide an idea as to what effects the terrorists hope to achieve to manipulate their enemy's response.[33] The first hypothesis is the concept of *target overreaction*, which constitutes an essential part of the process of disorientation (see above). The terrorists want to goad the government into operating beyond the legally constituted methods and into using extra-legal action. As a result, terrorist acts will often be committed with the express purpose of triggering reprisals of a heavy-handed and possibly illegal nature.[34] Yet, even if it does not get drawn into excessive force, the government may have to rely on special police and judicial measures which will impinge on everyday life and inconvenience the ordinary citizen. The arch exponent of this theory, Carlos Marighella, was forthright on this point: he believed that curfews, road blocks, house searches, internment without trial, state-sponsored death squads and the like would make life unbearable for the ordinary citizen and cause him to turn against the government *irrespective* of whether the terrorists had made any effort at mass agitation or introduced themselves and their political ideas to the population.[35]

Berry suggests that most governments will be tempted to overreact because they tend to have an acute self-image, believing that they possess overwhelming power as well as the legitimacy to crush any challenge to its authority, and viewing the terrorists as evil. Such perceptions were evident in the response of some Latin American governments towards terrorist challenges during the 1960s and 1970s. They could also be detected in the US and Soviet reactions to the insurgencies faced in Vietnam and Afghanistan respectively. The dehumanizing of the 'communists' and 'imperialists' justified free-fire zones and village-razing. Yet, despite the massive resources fielded against the insurgents, they were unable to bring the conflict to a satisfactory conclusion. Rather, the overreactive nature of their counter-insurgency campaigns had de-legitimized the cause for which they fought, thereby increasing support for the rebels.[36]

The second hypothesis – *power deflation* – represents the opposite of target overreaction. This is a scenario where a target loses public support because it appears incapable of dealing adequately with a terrorist threat. The target believes it lacks a public consensus for its policy in dealing with a terrorist opponent it sees as cunning, formidable and even possessing a degree of legitimacy. Although the target possesses greater power than the terrorists, it will therefore be wary of taking a hard line, as it believes the terrorists to be skilful and audacious enough to try to match any counter terrorist action with an even more spectacular reaction. In effect, the target is a prisoner of its own conscience. It wants to be seen to be acting correctly and not overreacting; yet by doing so, it prevents the implementation of an adequate anti-terrorist program which could deal effectively with the insurgent violence. This is the classic dilemma which many regimes, particularly those of a liberal democratic persuasion, are faced with in dealing with a terrorist challenge: how to balance civil liberties and accepted norms of legitimate conduct with adequate security measures to deal with a significant threat to its authority.

Another type of response is the so-called *failed repression of the moderates*. During a terrorist campaign, the target government may choose to suppress moderate, non-violent opposition.

Such repression could take the form of banning political parties, closing critical newspapers, or even the arrest, torture and killing of moderates. The problem is that if the repression is not efficient, ruthless and total,[37] there is a risk that the surviving moderates will become more extreme. Believing that there will be little value in seeking compromise within the present system, the moderates may then be driven into joining those members of the opposition who seek a violent solution. The most rational explanation for pursuing any such policy is that the target recognizes the potential of an emerging coalition between extremists and moderates, and that it wants to forestall this possibility while the relative capabilities are still in its favor.[38] In suppressing the moderates, however, it actually helps to make its 'nightmare scenario' a reality. The fall of the Shah of Iran provides a good example.

SAVAK, the Shah's secret police, was thoroughly inefficient in repressing the opponents of the regime which allowed opposition groups to coalesce against the regime. In mid-1978 the opposition was such that the Shah believed it necessary to attack a moderate protest rally in central Tehran with the result that up to 1,000 protesters were killed. This event crystallized all factions against him and he was overthrown shortly afterwards.[39]

The so-called *appeasement of the moderates* is the fourth hypothesis Berry suggests.[40] A political authority may come to believe that a terrorist insurgency is caused by legitimate grievances. The target attempts to introduce reforms to redress these grievances in the hope that doing so will undercut support for the terrorists and dissuade the moderates from being attracted to violent action. The underlying idea is that isolating the hard-liners from the moderates will make it easier for the target to crack down on the terrorists, as they will be deprived of the shelter they may have been afforded by the moderates. However, this policy entails a number of dangers.

First, the reforms will be interpreted by the terrorists as a sign of weakness, and they will therefore be encouraged to step up their campaign to force the target to capitulate to all of their political demands.[41]

Second, the target may isolate the traditional supporters of the regime who believe that the appeasement of moderates is tantamount to giving in to the terrorists. This may lead to the emergence of reactionary 'pro-state terrorists', who will complicate the target's overall position by creating yet another violent challenge to its authority.[42] Examples include the *Organisation Armée Secrete* (OAS) during the Algerian war of independence, the various Loyalist factions in Northern Ireland, as well as the United Self Defense Forces of Colombia (AUC).

Needless to say, in most situations, the government would be well-advised to avoid both over- and under-reaction, and practice a sensible policy mix of reforms and firmness. This, however, is easier said than done. Whenever governments are challenged by a terrorist campaign, the target needs to determine the relative strengths and weaknesses of the insurgent movement, and – because its authority is being challenged – it must also examine its own vulnerabilities and calculate the likely effects of the options open to it. Of course, this greater intellectual burden for the government means that the potential to make analytical and policy mistakes is greater too. Indeed, it is these opportunities that the terrorists will be waiting to exploit.

Stage 3: Gaining legitimacy

Having alienated the individual from the government, the terrorists need to hold out an attractive vision of a 'new' legitimacy. In many ways, this represents the most important, yet also most difficult, stage in a campaign of strategic terrorism. Most regimes will be able to withstand the attacks of a small band of conspirators – it is only when the majority of people transcends the state of disorientation and begins to lend support to the terrorists that terrorism becomes an existential threat.

One of the main obstacles to any terrorist in effecting the shift from 'old' to 'new' legitimacy is the transmission of their political message. Where a society does not permit free and uninhibited transmission of information, the insurgents will be unable to advertise their vision of a new society, as all the channels of mass communication are controlled by the authorities. In some cases, the terrorist acts themselves will go unreported, thus negating the psychological effect of terrorism beyond those directly affected. Even in democracies, it is not all plain sailing. The vast bulk of the media is likely to be concentrated in the hands of a few media entrepreneurs, who have – by and large – benefited from the status quo and are unlikely to desire any change. Also, with its accumulated expertise and free access to the media, the government will be able to put its 'spin' on events while the terrorists may be in no position to answer any of the charges thrown at them.[43]

There are, in principle, two ways in which this barrier can be overcome. The first is through the *skilful manipulation of the media*. Sophisticated terrorists will recognize that there is a potentially symbiotic relationship between themselves and the media. All they need to do is to satisfy the media's appetite for a 'good story', which means providing the 'mystery, quick action, tension [and] drama' for which the big television networks are longing.[44] Indeed, this may be one of the reasons why hostage-takings have proved such a popular tactic. While inducing a high and sustained level of terror, they rarely end up with large numbers of casualties. Most importantly, hijackings provide days – if not weeks – of prime time news coverage. During this period, the terrorists will be granted endless opportunities to explain the rationale of their campaign.[45]

However, even the most seamless dissemination of one's political vision will not guarantee success. After all, just because a terrorist group is successful in transmitting its political message to the general public through the media does not mean that anyone will be persuaded. It is at this stage of a terrorist campaign that ideology becomes a crucial factor. The ideology of an insurgent movement offers a critique of the existing order, and it articulates an alternative set of values and beliefs. It rationalizes grievances against the prevailing order and legitimizes violent action. Most importantly, though, it determines the potential level of popular support, and will therefore ultimately affect the ability of those who employ terrorism to gain sufficient legitimacy to be recognized as an alternative provider of authority. In this respect, the most advantageous scenario for the terrorists occurs when the revolutionary ideology is already widely disseminated amongst the population, so that – when the revolt breaks out – the terrorists are accorded an instant legitimacy. This tends to be the case when their ideology is based on strong pre-existing sources of identity, such as nationality, ethnicity or religion. It has proved to be more difficult when the terrorists have espoused purely political ideologies, such as Marxism or fascism.[46]

One of the best examples of successful media manipulation is that provided by the 1970 October crisis, when the Canadian *Front de Liberation du Quebec* (FLQ) kidnapped a British diplomat as well as the Deputy Prime Minister of Quebec.[47] By issuing a series of communiqués to the media, which (apparently) leapt at the chance to broadcast them, the terrorists were able to gain maximum publicity for their demands. The terrorists deliberately ignored the Canadian government's request to negotiate through an intermediary, preferring to communicate to the authorities via the media, thus ensuring the highest possible profile for the negotiations which in itself appeared to confer a degree of recognition and legitimacy on the FLQ. Moreover, the group's manifesto struck an emotional chord among many ordinary Quebecois. More than 50 per cent of callers on Radio Canada were sympathetic. Influential intellectuals issued a statement giving implicit support for the FLQ's aims. Thousands of students in the province staged rallies and demonstrations. The original issue – the kidnappings of the two men – had become secondary to a much wider debate concerning the limits of provincial government and the legitimacy of Quebec's nationalist aspirations.[48]

The second way in which legitimacy can be acquired is by disseminating one's message directly, that is, through *grassroots political agitation*. Although the Internet may offer a range of opportunities for doing so clandestinely, in most cases – and especially in countries where Internet access remains the privilege of the educated few – this still entails the need for a more or less open political organization, which works to broaden the support for the terrorist group through active involvement in the community. Apart from sustaining the existing political backing, political front groups may therefore mobilize sections of the population that had previously not been thought of as susceptible to the group's ideology. These people may be drawn into the movement by a charismatic local leader or the services provided by the political front organizations. As an added benefit, the grassroots organizations can be useful in providing quasi-military support to the military cells, such as intelligence, shelter and supplies. If the support is concentrated in particular regions or areas of a city, these locations may become 'no go' areas in which the terrorists can organize and recruit freely.

There are numerous examples of terrorist groups that have successfully established political front organizations in order to consolidate and broaden their support. In Western Europe, this has mostly been in the form of political parties, such as *Heri Batasuna* (the political wing of the Basque terrorist organization ETA) and *Sinn Fein* (the IRA's political front). In the Middle East, on the other hand, terrorist groups have set up extensive welfare networks, including hospitals, kindergartens and schools. Terrorist organizations like *Hamas* in the Palestinian territories and *Hezbollah* in Lebanon have thus been able to grow into genuine mass movements that command a large and relatively stable political constituency.[49]

Grassroots political agitation can undoubtedly be effective. However, it raises the question if – at this stage – the activity of a terrorist group can still be described as strategic terrorism. After all, one of the central tenets of this strategy is that calculated terrorist violence alone is sufficient to bring about political change. By engaging in long-term grassroots activism, the terrorists suggest that mass organization – as proposed by Mao and others – is a necessary requirement for political success, and that the utility of terrorism is limited in gaining legitimacy. Indeed, by shifting their focus from acts of terrorism to political agitation, they concede that all that strategic terrorism can ever hope for is to destroy the legitimacy of the existing regime and thus create an opening for new political actors, but that terrorist violence will at some point have to give way, allowing more conventional forms of struggle to emerge. The wider question, therefore, seems obvious: what are the limitations of strategic terrorism?

The limitations of strategic terrorism

As mentioned above, the central objective of most terrorist organizations is to drain the political authority of the target, undermine its ability to maintain the allegiance of its people and prevent it from responding adequately to the terrorist challenge. The eventual purpose of doing so is to erode the target's legitimacy and replace it with that of the insurgents. It is easy to reduce terrorist struggles to these few semantic equations, but they hide a myriad of practical and analytical problems.[50] The main problem with the strategy of terrorism concerns the very element which is meant to make terrorism such a potent weapon, the manipulation of the psychology of fear. In this respect, terrorism is based on a series of assumptions about individual, collective and institutional behavior under stress which are either false or wholly unproven. In the following, we will first address the assumptions we believe to be the most doubtful, and then show how, as a result, terrorist strategies are likely to end up in either defeat or irrelevance.

Assumptions

One of the key assumptions of strategic terrorism is that the target group's determination to hold on to a particular policy or possession will collapse once it has been exposed to terrorist violence. This assumption is based on the colonial experience, when terrorists demonstrated that the will of the target group can be undermined, government repression induced and support for the terrorist cause gained. As noted above, situations of foreign occupation are by far the most favorable from the terrorists' point of view, because the authorities' legitimacy can be assumed to be very low to begin with. In our view, it is highly questionable whether these conditions can easily be imitated in different contexts.

Furthermore, even during the period of de-colonization, contexts varied widely. Rather than merely relying on the correct application of certain military mechanics, the insurgents' success depended on a full appreciation of the specific political and even cultural circumstances within which the campaign was taking place. For instance, it would have been inadequate if the Algerian FLN had calculated that all they needed to do to get the French to leave Algeria would be to increase the violence to the level of that inflicted by Jewish terrorist groups on the British, which is regarded as a factor that induced Britain to evacuate Palestine.[51] Undoubtedly, this would have caused the French a large measure of inconvenience but it would have never forced them to leave Algeria. The nature of the relationship that France had with her colonies was altogether different from Britain's. For many, Algeria was an extension of metropolitan France and a strong emotional attachment had developed and ingrained itself into the French psyche in the form of *Algérie française*.[52] It was the prime task of the rebels to break this psychological bond, not just to escalate the violence to a particular level. In terms of military dynamics, this meant that the FLN strategy had to sustain a high and widespread level of violence for a considerable period of time while being prepared to endure enormous losses themselves.

Removing an independent, indigenous government is even less clearcut. On the one hand, the target is going to be more determined to resist, as its core interest – that is, its own survival – is threatened. More importantly, in contrast to an anti-colonial situation in which a wide cross-section of the community will be latently sympathetic to the terrorists' cause, the population is likely to be divided between backers and opponents of the terrorists' cause. As a consequence, those who utilize terrorist methods need to minimize civilian casualties in order not to alienate support, which in turn will make it more difficult to develop the dynamics of violence necessary to unleash the sense of fear and terror that will trigger the anticipated disorientation and eventual transfer of legitimacy. Indeed, while most societies – like most people – have some psychological breaking point, the abject failure of contemporary terrorists to achieve their political aims demonstrates that most terrorist groups grossly underestimate the scale of violence needed to reach this point.

The second assumption, which we consider overly optimistic, relates to the idea that a terrorist campaign will instill a degree of fear within the target population. In fact, even if the terrorists manage to generate an atmosphere of fear and apprehension, this will not necessarily be channeled in the direction the terrorists would hope. Instead of becoming disoriented, the public may blame the terrorists for the deteriorating situation; and rather than being alienated by the repressive reaction of the regime, the counter-terrorist measures may turn out to have the full support of the people. Therefore, far from estranging the people from state structures, it is the terrorists who become alienated and repudiated. In that sense, a terrorist campaign may reinforce people's faith in the government and increase their reliance on the state, which is exactly the reverse of what the terrorists want to happen.[53] A good example is the British public's response to the IRA's so-called England campaign, which aimed at weakening the resolve to uphold British sovereignty over Northern Ireland. As it turned out, whenever the IRA committed atrocities in England, there emerged a strong notion of defiance, that is, that one must not 'give in to terrorists'. When asked what effect IRA bombs had, only 28 per cent of the respondents to a 1984 MORI poll declared that they were more likely to support British withdrawal, while a majority (53 per cent) favored 'tougher action'.[54]

Another possible effect of a terrorist campaign – especially if it goes on for an extended period – is that, far from creating and sustaining an atmosphere of terror, a climate of indifference arises. Constant acts of terror may simply numb the public to a point where they are prepared to tolerate a degree of terrorism just as they may tolerate a degree of crime, deaths through road accidents and other abnormal events. In this context, terrorism becomes meaningless, as it loses its symbolism, its unpredictability and therefore its power to terrify. Grant Wardlaw investigated this aspect of the terrorist phenomenon by looking at some studies of individual reactions to stress cause by air raids in World War Two. These studies revealed that people who suffered personal loss, injury and narrow escape were caused considerable psychological stress. However, they also revealed that those who were not directly affected became anaesthetized to the bombing.[55] This tends to confirm that people can adjust to even high levels of violence and physical threat.

Furthermore, the longer a terrorist campaign goes on, not only will the power to terrify be diminished, but its propaganda will also become less effective. Of course, there is always the option of engaging in highly indiscriminate attacks, which will guarantee widespread and attentive media coverage regardless of how long a campaign had been going on. At the same time, when carried out in the 'gaining legitimacy' stage of a terrorist campaign, the large-scale killing of civilians will focus public attention on the purely negative aspects of a campaign to the exclusion of the presumably 'positive' political message that the terrorists will hope to project. Rather than helping to make the terrorists' cause more popular, one may speculate that such attacks would enable the target to 'turn the tables' and crush the conspirators. On the other hand, the propaganda yield of low-risk operations will dissipate over time with the eventual result that people may simply ignore the terrorists. As a result, the terrorists will face a difficult task convincing the public of the justice of their cause while maintaining the strategic momentum. Indeed, it is this latent contradiction between military needs, capabilities and desired impact that creates severe and continued dilemmas, which we will deal with next.

The escalation trap

In terms of military dynamics, for a group that practices strategic terrorism to achieve maximum effectiveness, its campaign must be sudden, brutal, unpredictable and indiscriminate. The aim must be to shock, disorientate and psychologically bludgeon a target group into submission in the shortest possible time. To allow a campaign to become extended or escalate incrementally may provide enough time for the target group to re-orientate itself and to adapt and accept a new level of violence. Therefore, if a campaign becomes prolonged, there is only one option open to the terrorists to maintain any sort of coherence to their strategy, and that is to escalate the campaign to a new, higher level of destruction sufficient to maintain a sense of terror. If they are to have any expectation of victory, they must be prepared to continually escalate the conflict at each stage in order to prevent re-orientation.

The need to escalate, however, raises a number of difficulties.

First, it is doubtful whether terrorist organizations possess the necessary capabilities to increase the scale of violence to unacceptable levels. Not only is it likely that organizations will lack the personnel, logistical and financial support to maintain the military momentum, but the probability of factional divisions is liable to limit any attempt at escalation.

Second, there is the constant danger that brutal and indiscriminate violence will lead to an erosion of public sympathy. If the various stages of a terrorist campaign are designed to overcome the latent contradiction between engaging in more or less indiscriminate violence and the attempt to gain legitimacy, the need for escalation is bound to intensify this paradox.

The third – and possibly most significant – danger is that any effort to escalate a terrorist campaign may provoke counter-escalation from the target government, which will result in the destruction of the insurgent movement. The dilemma here is that, while the terrorists need to elicit an inefficient act of repression that will highlight the 'unjust' nature of the regime, any belligerent that faces a militarily more potent adversary has to take extreme care not to push the enemy into a corner to a point where it feels sufficiently desperate to escalate the war to a level at which the repression becomes ruthless and total, thus threatening the terrorist group's very existence.

The terrorist experience in Latin America provides some poignant examples. Initially, the terrorist campaigns in Argentina and Uruguay provoked an incompetent as well as inefficient response on behalf of their respective governments. Yet, in both countries, there appeared to be a point when the inefficient repression stopped and the brutal repression began. Fearful of the deteriorating situation and of the revolutionary goals of the terrorists, important interest groups – normally the armed forces backed by large sections of the community – took over and carried out a more rigorous counter-terrorist policy. Even if some people disapproved of the methods, the terrorist movements in question were unable to survive the concerted onslaught which followed their decision to escalate.[56] A similar response pattern could be observed in Egypt. Following years of unrest and sporadic terrorist violence, including a near-successful attempt to assassinate President Hosni Mubarak, the terrorist campaign of various Islamist factions reached its height with the massacre of 60 people – most of them tourists – at Luxor in November 1997. This attack had resulted from a conscious decision to escalate the campaign. However, rather than forcing a political crisis that would lead to the downfall of the secular regime, the government embarked on a campaign of full-scale repression. Striking back at the various Islamist factions with brute force, the Egyptian security forces managed to destroy some of the smaller groups, and rendered the capabilities of the others ineffective.[57]

These examples lead us to an important insight, which helps to establish a key correlation between military and political dynamics in any campaign of strategic terrorism. Because the terrorists have to exercise caution for fear of inducing a response that will destroy them, they would have to empathize with their enemy in order to understand the sort of pressures which impinge upon their decision making. The terrorists would need to assess the limit to which a target might be able to concede without alienating important political constituencies, how favorably it would respond to compromise and what its reactions to increased military pressure are likely to be. In other words, they would have to engage in an ongoing analysis of their own strategic position, and be ready to adjust their means in the light of changing military and political conditions more appropriate to their ends. While some sub-revolutionary terrorists may be capable of forming such judgments (indeed, they may have adopted sub-revolutionary goals precisely because they realize that they are unlikely to win against a stronger opponent), most revolutionary terrorists – especially those of an absolutist variety, such as religiously-inspired insurgents – are not. For them, there can be no question of compromise within the prevailing order. The only satisfactory outcome is complete victory and the transformation of the political system.[58]

As a consequence, terrorist campaigns usually take one of two possible turns. The terrorists who are either incapable of increasing the violence or careful not to fall into the 'escalation trap' are likely to lose strategic momentum and get bogged down in drawn-out, low-level campaigns which never achieves the impetus necessary to bring about political change. Those, however, who manage to escalate their campaigns will face internal divisions, a hostile reaction from the population in whose name they claim to act, and may invite their own destruction by provoking a ruthless and effective campaign of repression from the target government.

Conclusion

Often the notion of terrorism is employed either as an empty rhetorical noun or dismissed as an aberrant form of behavior without any rational explanation. Yet the employment of organized armed force, no matter how deviant or apolitical it may appear, will invariably be undertaken to achieve a particular set of goals. This analysis has sought to lay out a strategic framework by which those who utilize a campaign of terrorism seek to attain their ends through military means. In doing so, this study has identified a distinctive modus operandi that points at the dynamics a strategy of terrorism will seek to unleash in order to further political and military objectives:

1   Disorientation: to alienate the authorities from their citizens, reducing the government to impotence in the eyes of the population, which will be perceived as unable to cope with a situation of evolving chaos.
2   Target response: to induce a government to respond in a manner that is favorable to the insurgent cause such as provoking it into actions that are illegal or regarded as repressive overreactions that destroy the political middle-ground.
3   Gaining legitimacy: to exploit the emotional impact of the violence to insert an alternative political message and seek to broaden support, often through the media or political front organizations.

In highlighting the military dynamics that arise during these phases, we were able to derive some of the key variables that interact with the terrorist application of military force, and shed some light on the relationship between ends and means in strategic terrorism. For example, rather than simply stating that terrorism is a strategy of the 'weak' and 'illegitimate' as a matter of fact, our analysis made it possible to explain how legitimacy and military weakness influence the military dynamics of a terrorist group at the different stages of its strategic evolution, and how they may condition its overall success. In this regard, we were also able to explain why terrorist groups may at some point have to resort to grassroots agitation in order to gain legitimacy, thus diluting the reliance on strategic terrorism as the main plank of their strategy.

Throughout this assessment we have endeavored to show that this framework does not exist purely as a theoretical hypothesis. We have sought to empirically validate this framework by demonstrating that groups have employed terrorist means in the manner described above to facilitate their goals through a rational calculation of the utility of their methods. At the same time, by elucidating the strategy of terrorism, the analysis reveals not only the instrumentality of terrorist methods but also their inherent limitations. The potential fallacies stem primarily from the fact that terrorism relies on inducing a reaction in the target that is favorable to the terrorists' goals. Strategic terrorism, therefore, rests on a series of assumptions about how a target audience will respond to a campaign of terrorist violence. The success of a terrorist strategy is thus crucially dependent on the wider context of a conflict. If the target population is prepared to endure a campaign of terror, then its potency will be eroded – terrorism will lose its power to terrify. Or, even worse for the terrorists, the lack of target reaction leads to an escalation in the terror campaign which provokes a backlash of such ferocity that the terrorists themselves are unable to survive the 'overreaction' that they wish to induce in their opponent.

In this respect, the main weakness in any terrorist campaign is that it seeks to overcome deficiencies in military power by the manipulation of the emotional impact of (usually) relatively small-scale attacks. The strategy rests on the premise that a militarily more powerful adversary will in some way feel restrained, either for political or moral reasons, from bringing the full force of its military superiority to bear on its inferior enemy. Herein lies the main flaw in the strategy of terrorism: it relies exclusively on the exploitation of the psychological rather than the destructive effects of armed action, thereby rendering it vulnerable to those who are willing to view the resolution of clashes of interest principally in terms of the tangibles of military power.

The philosopher of war, Carl von Clausewitz, whose writings are seen, wrongly, by many contemporary analysts as having little to say on the current condition of an international environment characterized by an increasing recourse to terrorist violence, presciently observed: 'If the political aims [in war] are small, the motives slight and tensions low, a prudent general may look for any way to avoid major crises and decisive actions, exploit any weaknesses in the opponent's military and political strategy, and reach a political settlement'.[59] This encapsulates the primary elements in a strategy of terrorism: namely, that if the goals of a combatant are relatively limited and do not affect issues of national survival then they may be able to attain their objectives through less direct means than destroying an opponent's means of resistance (that is, the adversary's armed forces). As Clausewitz noted, if the general's 'assumptions are sound and promise success we are not entitled to criticize him'. 'But,' as Clausewitz went on to caution, 'he must never forget he is moving on a devious path where the god of war may catch him unawares.'[60]

Notes

1   Bazzam Baz, *Terrorism Survival Handbook* (Los Angeles, CA: Costa Communications 2001); Giovanna Borradori, Juergen Habermas and Jacques Derrida, *Philosophy in a Time of Terror* (Chicago, IL: University of Chicago Press 2003).
2   Donald H. Rumsfeld, 'A New Kind of War', *New York Times*, 27 Sept. 2001.
3   See Walter Laqueur, 'Postmodern Terrorism: New Rules for an Old Game', *Foreign Affairs 75/5* (1996) pp.24–36.
4   See, for example, Barry R. Posen, 'The Struggle Against Terrorism: Grand Strategy, Strategy, and Tactics', *International Security 26/3* (2001) pp.39–55.
5   The only scholar to have explored terrorism as a strategy is Martha Crenshaw, whose work

continues to be essential in developing a comprehensive understanding of the phenomenon. See, for example, Martha Crenshaw, 'The Logic of Terrorism: Terrorist Behavior as a Product of Strategic Choice', in Walter Reich (ed.), *Origins of Terrorism*, 2nd edn (Washington, DC: Woodrow Wilson Center Press 1998) pp.7–24; and Martha Crenshaw, 'Theories of Terrorism: Instrumental and Organizational Approaches', in David C. Rapoport (ed.), *Inside Terrorist Organizations*, 2nd edn (London: Frank Cass 2001) pp.13–31.

6   Bruce Cumings, quoted in Craig Calhoun, Paul Price and Ashley Timmer (eds), *Understanding September 11* (New York: New Press/Social Science Research Council 2002) p.198.

7   Quoted in Alastair Sooke, 'Rimington Hits Out at US Over Detainees', *Daily Telegraph*, 18 Aug. 2004.

8   A phrase coined by Tom Utley. See 'The Moment I Saw Bush Had Grasped the Point of the War', *Daily Telegraph*, 28 Sept. 2001.

9   This, of course, reflects Clausewitz' classical understanding of strategy 'the use of engagements for the object of war'. See Carl von Clausewitz, *On War* (trans. and ed.) Michael Howard and Peter Paret (Princeton, NJ: Princeton UP 1984) p.128.

10   On the issue of state terrorism, see Alexander George (ed.), *Western State Terrorism* (Cambridge: Polity Press 1991). For single-issue terrorism, see G. Davidson Smith, 'Single Issue Terrorism', *Commentary* 74 (Winter 1998). The full text can be found at <www.csis-scrs.gc.ca/eng/comment/com74111e.html>; also Walter Laqueur, *New Terrorism* (London: Phoenix, 2001), esp. Chap. 8 ('Exotic Terrorism').

11   Ibid., pp.5–6.

12   For definitions based on terrorism as a form of violence against the 'innocent', see Christopher C. Harmon, *Terrorism Today* (London: Frank Cass 2000) p.21; Jessica Stern, *The Ultimate Terrorists* (Cambridge, MA: Harvard UP 1999) p.11.

13   See, for example, Eqbal Ahmad and David Barsmain, *Terrorism: Theirs and Ours* (New York: Seven Stories Press 2001).

14   For further definitions of terrorism, see Bruce Hoffman, *Inside Terrorism* (New York: Columbia UP 1998), esp. Chap. 1 ('Defining Terrorism'); Alex P. Schmid *et al.* (eds), *Political Terrorism: A Guide to Actors, Authors, Concepts, Data Bases, Theories, and Literature* (New Brunswick: Transaction Books 1988).

15   T.P. Thornton, 'Terror as a Weapon of Political Agitation' in Harry Eckstein (ed.), *Internal War: Problems and Approaches* (New York: Free Press 1964) pp.71–99.

16   Gerard Chaliand, *Terrorism: From Popular Struggle to Media Spectacle* (London: Saqi Books 1987) pp.107–12.

17   Ernest Evans, *Calling a Truce to Terror* (Westport, CO: Greenwood Press 1979) p.29.

18   J. Bowyer Bell, *The Myth of the Guerrilla* (New York: Knopf 1971) p.55.

19   For a concise explanation of the concept, see Maurice Tugwell, 'Politics and Propaganda of the Provisional IRA', in Paul Wilkinson (ed.), *British Perspectives on Terrorism* (London: George Allen and Unwin 1981) pp.14–16.

20   For an elaboration of the problems with terms like 'small wars', 'insurgency', 'irregular' or 'low-intensity' warfare, see M.L.R. Smith, 'Guerrillas in the Mist: Reassessing Strategy and Low Intensity Warfare', *Review of International Studies* 29/1 (2003) pp.20–23.

21   See Colin S. Gray, *Modern Strategy* (Oxford: Oxford UP 1999) pp.281–96.

22   Mao Tse Tung, *On Guerrilla Warfare* (New York: Anchor Press 1978) pp.25–9.

23   This idea became known as the 'propaganda of the deed'. See Peter Kropotkin, *Paroles d'un Revolte* (Paris: Ernest Flammarion 1885) p.286.

24   Thornton, 'Terror as a Weapon' (note 15) p.74.

25   Peter Knauss and D.A. Strickland, 'Political Disintegration and Latent Terror', in Michael Stohl (ed.), *The Politics of Terrorism* (New York: Marcel Dekker 1979) p.77.

26   Martha Crenshaw, 'The Concept of Revolutionary Terrorism', *Journal of Conflict Resolution* 6 (1973) p.388.

27   See Irving Janis, *Air War and Emotional Stress* (New York: McGraw Hill 1979) p.23.

28   See Grant Wardlaw, *Political Terrorism: Theory, Tactics and Counter-measures* (Cambridge: Cambridge UP 1982) p.7.

29   Doug Struck, 'One Bombing, Many Versions', *Washington Post*, 20 July 2004.

30   Lawrence Freedman, 'Terrorism and Strategy', in Lawrence Freedman *et al.* (eds.), *Terrorism and International Order* (London: Routledge 1986) p.61.

31   Jason Burke, 'Think Again: Al Qaeda', *Foreign Policy*, May/June 2004.

32 See, for example, Crenshaw, 'The Logic of Terrorism' (note 5) pp.13–15.

33 N.O. Berry, 'Theories on the Efficacy of Terrorism', in Paul Wilkinson and A.M. Stewart (eds), *Contemporary Research on Terrorism* (Aberdeen: Aberdeen UP 1987) pp.293–304.

34 Paul Wilkinson, *Terrorism and the Liberal State* (London: Macmillan 1986) pp.296–8.

35 Carlos Marighella, *Minimanual of the Urban Guerrilla* (Montreal: Abraham Guillen Press 2002). The full text can be found at <www.marxists.org/archive/marighella-carlos/1969/06/ minimanual-urban-guerrilla/>.

36 For an account of the Soviet experience in Afghanistan, see Scott R. McMichael, *Stumbling Bear* (London: Brassey's 1991). On the strategy and tactics of the US Army in Vietnam, see Andrew F. Krepinevich, *The Army in Vietnam* (Baltimore, MA: Johns Hopkins Press 1986) pp.194–214.

37 Leonard Weinberg found that terrorism is more likely to occur in democracies than in non-democracies, but also that it is 'weak repressive' regimes rather than those that are ruthless and total which provide a breeding ground for terrorists. See William Lee Eubank and Leonard Weinberg, 'Does Democracy Encourage Terrorism?', *Terrorism and Political Violence* 6/4 (1994) pp.417–43.

38 Berry, 'Theories' (note 33) pp.298–300.

39 See Amir Tahiri, *The Spirit of Allah: Khomeini and the Islamic Revolution* (London: Hutchinson 1985).

40 Berry, 'Theories' (note 33) pp.299–300.

41 Reforms carried out during an insurgency raise the question of what is known as relative success. Robert Taber, for example, believes that any government concessions which try to accommodate the insurgents can be regarded as surrender because the government is an agent and protector of the status quo and anything which forces an alteration is a defeat. On the other hand, it could be argued that the very essence of counter-insurgency is not to prevent change but to manage it to one's own advantage. See Robert Taber, *War of the Flea* (London: Paladin 1970) p.24.

42 Steve Bruce, 'The Problem of Pro-State Terrorism: Loyalist Paramilitaries in Northern Ireland', *Terrorism and Political Violence* 4/1 (1992) pp.67–88.

43 See Brigitte Nacos, *Mass-mediated Terrorism: the Central Role of the Media in Terrorism and Counterterrorism* (Oxford: Rowman and Littlefield 2002); David L. Paletz and Alex P. Schmid (eds), *Terrorism and the Media* (London: Sage 1992).

44 Walter Laqueur, 'Terrorism – a Balance Sheet', in Walter Laqueur (ed.), *The Terrorism Reader* (Philadelphia, PA: Temple UP 1978) p.261.

45 See, for example, the hijacking of TWA flight 847 by Lebanese Shiite terrorists in 1985: Hoffman, *Inside Terrorism* (note 14) pp.132–5.

46 See Laqueur, 'Terrorism – a Balance Sheet' (note 44) p.258.

47 Ronald D. Crelinsten, 'Power and Meaning: Terrorism as Struggle over Access to the Communication Structure', in Paul Wilkinson and A.M. Stewart (eds), *Contemporary Research on Terrorism* (Aberdeen: Aberdeen UP 1987) pp.419–50: see also Ronald D. Crelinsten, 'The Internal Dynamics of the FLQ During the October Crisis of 1970', in David C. Rapoport (ed.), *Inside Terrorist Organizations*, 2nd edn. (London: Frank Cass 2001) pp.59–89.

48 Crelinsten, 'Power and Meaning' (note 47) p.427.

49 See Cynthia L. Irvin, *Militant Nationalism: Between Movement and Party in Ireland and the Basque Country* (Minneapolis, MN: University of Minnesota Press 1999); Judith Palmer Harik, *Hezbollah: The Changing Face of Terrorism* (London: I.B. Tauris 2004), esp. Chap. 6 ('Serving the Umma – Hezbollah as Employer and Welfare Organization'); Shaul Mishal and Avraham Sela, *The Palestinian Hamas* (New York: Columbia UP 2000), esp. Chaps 1 and 6 ('Social Roots and Institutional Development' and 'Controlled Participation').

50 For example, there are numerous operational and tactical weaknesses resulting from the fact that all terrorist organizations begin as small conspiratorial groups, making them vulnerable to institutional dynamics, deficiencies in command and control, lack of logistical support, etc. Many of these problems are addressed in the writings of Abraham Guillen, who was close to the Uruguayan *Tupamaros*. See Abraham Guillen, *Philosophy of the Urban Guerrilla: The Revolutionary Writings of Abraham Guillen* (New York: William Morrow 1973). For a more contemporary, academic assessment of group dynamics within terrorist groups, see Jerrold M. Post, 'Terrorist Psycho-logic: Terrorist Behavior as a Product of Psychological Forces' in Walter Reich, *Origins of Terrorism* (note 5) pp.25–40.

51 See Hoffman, *Inside Terrorism* (note 14) pp.48–58.

52 See Alistair Horne, *A Savage War of Peace, Algeria, 1954–1962* (London: Penguin 1987) pp.183–207.

53 Knauss and Strickland, 'Political Disintegration' (note 5) pp.87–8.

54 'For Prior's Heir, An Even Harder Task', *The Times*, 23 Aug. 1984.

55 Wardlaw, *Political Terrorism* (note 28) pp.35–6. The sources cited by Wardlaw are P.E. Vernon, 'Psychological Effects of Air Raids', *Journal of Abnormal and Social Psychology* 36 (1941) pp.457–76 and Melitta Schmideberg, 'Some Observations on Individual Reactions to Air Raids', *International Journal of Psychoanalysis* 23 (1942) pp.146–76.

56 See Richard Gillespie, 'Political Violence in Argentina: Guerrillas, Terrorists, and *Carapintadas*', in Martha Crenshaw, *Terrorism in Context* (University Park, PA: University of Pennsylvania Press 1995) pp.211–48.

57 See Gilles Keppel, *Jihad: The Trail of Political Islam* (London: I.B. Tauris 2003), esp. Chap. 12 ('The Threat of Terrorism in Egypt').

58 See Mark Juergensmeyer, *Terror in the Name of God*, 2nd edn (Berkeley, CA: University of California Press 2000); Magnus Ranstorp, 'Terrorism in the Name of Religion', *Journal of International Affairs* 50 (Summer 1996) pp.41–62.

59 Clausewitz, *On War* (note 9) p.99.

60 Ibid.

Part VI

Future warfare, future strategy

Introduction

No strategy reader would be complete without a selection of essays about the problem of future warfare and the importance of strategic studies today.

In the first essay, Andrew F. Krepinevich, Director of the Center for Strategic and Budgetary Assessments, employs the concept of "military revolutions" to describe what shape coming developments in warfare may take. Writing just after the 1990–91 Gulf War, Krepinevich sets out four elements that interact to make a military revolution occur: technological change, systems development, operational innovation and organizational adaptation. He identifies ten such revolutions from the fourteenth century on. In each case, emerging technologies offered a competitive advantage to armed forces that adapted organizationally, doctrinally and operationally to exploit them. Military organizations that did so won a pronounced if short-lived operational advantage. The lesson of past revolutions, according to Krepinevich, is that armed forces that fail to adapt to emerging technologies will fall behind their competitors, or they will fail to anticipate how rivals will exploit new technologies in a nationally distinctive yet no less potent way. Even a huge technological and organizational lead, Krepinevich warns, is no guarantee of lasting military supremacy.

The second essay by Michael Evans of the Australian Land Warfare Studies Centre surveys the recent complex changes in world affairs and the military art to offer a tentative analysis of future trends. According to Evans, future war may be characterised by the almost simultaneous occurrence of conventional and unconventional and of symmetric and asymmetric modes of war, between states and/or between states and non-state actors, overlapping in time and space. Advanced warfare will largely be "joint service", in which domination of the "battle space" requires the concurrent and highly coordinated concentration of effort of each service. Battlefield maneuvre will probably look more like large-scale "ambushes" than more orthodox encounter operations. Advanced states will probably deploy fewer troops, but the individual soldier will be much more lethal owing to networked surveillance and long-range precision strike capabilities. Even so, the advent of precision-guided munitions will not replace the infantry in close battle, or artillery and amour to support them against scattered enemies. While the coming threats to Western societies are likely to be in the form of disruption rather than invasion, Evans advises, the vulnerability of advanced societies to such attacks "obliges defence experts and politicians to think rigorously about the kinds of war that might lie ahead."

While Krepinevich and Evans offer useful thoughts about the future, they are both right to be guarded in their analyses. As Colin S. Gray of the University of Reading argues in his essay, one reason "why strategy is difficult" is that the future is "unforeseeable". Nonetheless, the strategist can cope with the unforeseeable and the other bewildering complexities of war that all too often conspire to frustrate attempts to bridge policy and armed combat. Three sources of practical advice, Gray suggests, can guide the practitioners into an uncertain future: "historical experience, the golden rule of prudence (we do not allow hopes to govern plans), and common sense."

Gray's advice that strategists should read history is the theme of the next essay by Adam Roberts of Oxford University. Despite all the unprecedented aspects of the "war on terror", he argues, a study of the long history of terror and counter-terror campaigns can guide policy-makers to avoid the errors made in earlier eras. To make his case, he examines eight propositions to uncover the lessons of campaigns. He sets out four assets that are important to a patient and prudent approach to a "war on terrorism": public confidence in official decision-making; public confidence in intelligence on which that decision-making is based; operation with respect for a framework of law; and a willingness to address some of the problems that have contributed to the emergence of terrorism. An important aim of an international campaign against terrorism, Roberts concludes, must be "not the capture of every last terrorist leader, but their relegation to a status of near-irrelevance as life moves on, long-standing grievances are addressed, and peoples can see that a grim terrorist war of attrition is achieving little and damaging their own societies."

In the final essay in this volume, Hew Strachan of Oxford University argues that strategy has lost its meaning in contemporary usage. By tracing the changing definition of the word from its nineteenth-century origins to today, he illustrates how twentieth-century experiences of total war and cold war have eroded the distinction made by Clausewitz and other theorists between *policy* and *strategy*. This conceptual trend towards conflating policy and strategy has been driven forward since the end of the Cold War by a scholarly and professional preoccupation with the operational level of war, the notion that "war" is no more, and what Strachan describes as the "militarization" of foreign policy. This is not simply a scholarly concern about definitions, but a practical one about the respective roles of politicians and military professionals in an iterative process of dialogue in which military means are related to the policy ends. "Strategy is designed to make war useable by the state," Strachan argues, "so that it can, if need be, use force to fulfil its political objectives." The application of force requires concepts that are "robust because they are precise".

Study questions

1. Does the concept of "military revolutions" provide a useful guide to thinking about future warfare?
2. What impact has globalization had on contemporary warfare? Do you agree with Evans' future projections?
3. What can be learned from past campaigns against terrorism?
4. Has strategy lost its meaning?

Further reading

Betts, Richard K., "Is Strategy an Illusion?" *International Security* 25, no. 2 (2000), pp. 5–50.

Biddle, Stephen, "Assessing Theories of Future Warfare," *Security Studies* 8, no. 1 (1998), pp. 1–74.

Clarke, Ignatius Francis, *Voices Prophesying War: Future Wars 1763–3749* (Oxford: Oxford University Press, 1992).

Cohen, Eliot A., "A Revolution in Warfare," *Foreign Affairs*, vol. 75, no. 2 (March/April 1996).

Gray, Colin S., *Strategic Studies: A Critical Assessment* (London: Aldwych Press, 1982).

Imlay, Talbot C. and Toft, Monica Duffy, *The Fog of Peace and War Planning: Military and Strategic Planning under Uncertainty* (London: Routledge, 2006).

Lee, Bradford A., "Winning the War but Losing the Peace? The United States and the Strategic Logic of War Termination," in Bradford A. Lee and Karl F. Walling, eds. *Strategic Logic and Political Rationality: Essays in Honor of Michael I. Handel.* (London: Frank Cass, 2003), pp. 249–273.

Rosen, Stephen P., *Winning the Next War: Innovation and the Modern Military* (Ithaca, NY: Cornell University Press, 1991).

19 Cavalry to computer

The pattern of military revolutions

Andrew F. Krepinevich

Over the next several decades, the world is destined to experience a revolution in the character of warfare. Indeed, the way in which the United States and its allies won a quick and overwhelming victory in the Gulf War suggests to many that we are already in the early stages of such a military revolution. But if so, there is much more to come.

As it progresses, this revolution will have profound consequences for global and regional military balances, and thus for U.S. defense planning. In the past, military revolutions have induced major changes in both the nature of the peacetime competition between states and their military organizations, as well as in the ways wars are deterred, fought, and resolved. By changing radically the nature of the military competition in peace and war, military revolutions have changed the "rules of the game." In so doing, they have often dramatically devalued formerly dominant elements of military power, including weaponry, weapons platforms, and doctrines. Military organization that did not adapt in a rapidly changing, highly competitive environment have declined, often quite quickly.

What is a military revolution? It is what occurs when the application of new technologies into a significant number of military systems combines with innovative operational concepts and organizational adaptation in a way that fundamentally alters the character and conduct of conflict. It does so by producing a dramatic increase—often an order of magnitude or greater—in the combat potential and military effectiveness of armed forces.

Military revolutions comprise four elements: technological change, systems development, operational innovation, and organizational adaptation. Each of these elements is in itself a necessary, but not a sufficient, condition for realizing the large gains in military effectiveness that characterize military revolutions. In particular, while advances in technology typically underwrite a military revolution, they alone do not constitute the revolution. The phenomenon is much broader in scope and consequence than technological innovation, however dramatic.

The transition from the Cold War period of warfare to a new military era that is now anticipated may take several decades—or it may arrive within the next ten or fifteen years. There is no common transition period from one military regime to another: the naval transition from wood and sail to the all big-gun dreadnoughts with their steel hulls and turbine engines took roughly half a century; the emergence of nuclear weapons, ballistic missile delivery systems, and associated doctrine and organizational structures took roughly fifteen years. The rate of transition is typically a function not only of the four elements noted above, but of the level of competition among the international system's major players, and the strategies the competitors choose to pursue in exploiting the potential of the emerging military revolution.

It may be argued that with recent transition periods of ten to twenty years, we are discussing a continuous military evolution rather than a revolution. But what is revolutionary is not the speed with which the entire shift from one military regime to another occurs, but rather the recognition, over some relatively brief period, that the character of conflict has changed dramatically, requiring equally dramatic—if not radical—changes in military doctrine and organizations. Just as water changes to ice only when the falling temperature reaches 32 degrees Fahrenheit, at some critical point the cumulative effects of technological advances and military innovation will invalidate former conceptual frameworks and demand a fundamental change in the accepted definitions and measurement of military effectiveness. When this occurs, military organizations will either move to adapt rapidly or find themselves at a severe competitive disadvantage.

Ten revolutions

There appear to have been as many as ten military revolutions since the fourteenth century. The Hundred Years' War (1337–1453) spawned two of them. The first was the so-called Infantry Revolution, which saw infantry displacing the dominant role of heavy cavalry on the battlefield.[1] During the period leading up to this military revolution, infantry typically employed tight formations of pole-arms and crossbowmen to protect the cavalry while it formed up for a charge. During the first half of the fourteenth century, however, the infantry—in the form of Swiss pikemen and English archers—emerged as a combat arm fully capable of winning battles, as was demonstrated at the battles of Laupen (1339) and Crecy (1346).[2] Following these engagements, major cavalry actions on the field of battle became increasingly rare.

Clifford Rogers cites several factors as responsible for the Infantry Revolution. One key factor was the development of the six-foot yew longbow, which gave archers a much enhanced ability to penetrate the armor of cavalrymen. It also gave archers both missile and range superiority over their adversaries. England, which developed a pool of yeoman archers over decades of warfare against the Scots and Welsh, established a significant competitive advantage over the formerly dominant army, that of the French, which failed to exploit the revolution until late in the fifteenth century.

But it was not the longbow alone that fueled the revolution. Once the ability of infantrymen to win battles was clearly established, tactical innovations followed. The English developed a tactical system based on integrating archers with dismounted men-at-arms. Interestingly, the dominance of infantry was given an additional boost by the fact that archers were far less expensive to equip and train than men-at-arms. Thus, Rogers points out, the tiny kingdom of Flanders, which was relatively quick in exploiting the revolution, was able to muster a larger army at Courtrai (1302) than the entire kingdom of France. Finally, the Infantry Revolution marked a sharp increase in casualties on the battlefield. Whereas formerly it had been important to capture knights for the purpose of realizing a ransom, common infantrymen neither held that value, nor did they share knightly notions of chivalry. Battles thus became more sanguine affairs.

The Infantry Revolution was succeeded by the Artillery Revolution, which dramatically altered war in the latter period of the Hundred Years' War. Although Roger Bacon's recipe for gunpowder dates back to 1267, cannons only began to appear on the European battlefield in significant numbers some sixty years later. Even then, almost a full century passed before artillery began to effect a military revolution. During this period besieged cities typically surrendered due to a lack of supplies. In the 1420s, however, a major increase occurred in the number of besieged cities surrendering as a consequence of the besiegers' artillery fire fatally degrading the cities' defenses. In the span of a few decades, gunpowder artillery displaced the centuries-old dominance of the defense in siege warfare.

Several technological improvements underwrote the Artillery Revolution. One was the lengthening of gun barrels, which permitted substantial increases in accuracy and muzzle velocity, translating into an increase in range and destructive force (and also the rate of fire). Metallurgical breakthroughs reduced the cost of iron employed in fabricating gun barrels, reducing the overall cost of cannons by about a third. Finally, the "corning" of gunpowder made artillery more powerful and cheaper to use.[3] As one Italian observer noted, artillery could now "do in a few hours what . . . used to take days."[4] Unlike the Infantry Revolution, the Artillery Revolution was expensive to exploit. As early as 1442 the French government was spending over twice as much on its artillery arm as on more "traditional" military equipment.[5]

A kind of snowball effect developed. The richer states could exploit the Artillery Revolution to subdue their weaker neighbors (or internal powerful regional nobles), which in turn increased the resources available to exploit their advantage further. This phenomenon was a significant factor in the growth of centralized authority in France and Spain. Along with the changes in technologies that spawned the great improvements in artillery and changes in siege warfare, new military organizational elements, such as artillery siege trains, were formed to cement the revolution. Once this occurred, defenders could no longer rely on castles for protection. This led to further changes in military organizations and operations, as the defenders now had to abandon their fortified castles and garrison units and move the contest into the field. And, as Francesco Guicciardini wrote, "Whenever the open country was lost, the state was lost with it."

Military revolutions were not limited to land. The Revolution of Sail and Shot saw the character of conflict at sea change dramatically, as the great navies of the Western world moved from oar-driven galleys to sailing ships that could exploit the Artillery Revolution by mounting large guns. Galleys, being oar-driven, had to be relatively light, and, unlike ships propelled by sail, could not mount the heavy cannon that could shatter a ship's timbers, thus sinking enemy ships rather than merely discouraging boarding parties. Indeed, prior to the late fourteenth century, ship design had not improved significantly for two millennia, since the age of classical Greece. The French first mounted cannons on their sailing ships in 1494. But the death knell for the galley did not sound clearly until the Battle of Preveza, when Venetian galleasses won an overwhelming victory against Turkish galleys. The result was repeated at Lepanto in 1571.[6] By 1650 the warship had been transformed from a floating garrison of soldiers to an artillery platform.

The sixteenth century witnessed the onset of the Fortress Revolution, which involved the construction of a new style of defensive fortification employing lower, thicker walls featuring bastions, crownworks, ravelins, and horn-works, all of which were part of a defensive fortification system known as the trace italienne. As Geoffrey Parker observes, "normally the capture of a stronghold defended by the trace italienne required months, if not years." Static defenses thus effected a kind of "comeback" against the Artillery Revolution. However, as with artillery, the new fortification system was terribly expensive, a fact that limited its application and left considerable opportunity for operations in the field. This, in turn, shifted the focus back to infantry, where revolutionary developments permitted a new use of firepower; infantry moving beyond archers to the combination of artillery and musket fire on the battlefield in what might be termed the Gunpowder Revolution.

Muskets capable of piercing plate armor at a range of one hundred meters were introduced in the 1550s. The English abandoned longbows in the 1560s in favor of firearms.

Finally, in the 1590s the Dutch "solved" the problem of muskets' slow rate of fire through a tactical innovation that saw them abandon the tight squares of pikemen in favor of drawing up their forces in a series of long lines. These linear tactics allowed for a nearly continuous stream of fire as one rank fired while the others retired to reload. Muskets were also attractive because they required little training in comparison to the years necessary to develop a competent archer (although linear tactics did require considerable drill). The large, tight squares of pikemen, which had proved so effective against cavalry, now became attractive targets for musket and artillery fire.

This revolution reached full flower in the campaigns of Gustavus Adolphus during the Thirty Years' War, which saw the melding of technology, military systems, operational concept, and new military organizations: a combination of pike, musketeers, cavalry and a large rapid-firing artillery component utilizing linear tactics—what has been described as the Swedish military system—yielded stunning success at Brietenfeld, Lutzen, Wittstock, Brietenfeld II, and Jankov.[7]

Linear tactics were perfected under the Prussian military system of Frederick the Great, who achieved significant improvements in the rate of fire, as well as major improvements in supply. But this refined system would be overturned by the Napoleonic Revolution.

The French were the first to exploit the potential for a military revolution that had been building for several decades prior to Napoleon's rise to prominence. During this period, thanks to the emerging Industrial Revolution, the French standardized their artillery calibers, carriages and equipment, and fabricated interchangeable parts. Other improvements in industrial processes allowed the French to reduce the weight of their cannon by 50 percent, thereby increasing their mobility while decreasing transport and manpower requirements dramatically.

The introduction of the levee en masse following the French Revolution helped to bring about another quantum leap in the size of field armies. Men proved much more willing to defend and fight for the nation than the crown. Consequently, France's revolutionary armies could endure privations, and attack almost regardless of the cost in men (since they could call upon the total resources of the nation). In battle, the individual could be relied upon; skirmishers and individually aimed fire could be integrated to great effect into the rolling volleys of artillery and musketry. Furthermore, armies became so large that they could now surround and isolate fortresses while retaining sufficient manpower to continue their advance and conduct field operations, thus largely negating the effects of the trace italienne and the Fortress Revolution.

The latter part of the eighteenth century also witnessed the creation of a new self-sufficient military organization—the division—and saw the growing importance of skirmishers in the form of light infantry, and cavalry as a reconnaissance, screening, and raiding force. A growing network of roads in Europe meant it was possible for an army to march in independent columns and yet concentrate quickly. Coordination was also improved through the availability of much more advanced cartographic surveys.

Napoleon's genius was to integrate the advances in technology, military systems, and military organizations (including his staff system) to realize a dramatic leap in military effectiveness over the military formations that existed only a short time before. Indeed, it took the other major military organizations of Europe at least a decade before they were able to compete effectively with the Grande Armee that Napoleon had fashioned to execute what one author has termed the "Napoleonic blitzkrieg."

Between the Napoleonic Wars and the American Civil War, the introduction of railroads and telegraphs, and the widespread rifling of muskets and artillery again dramatically transformed the character of warfare—the way in which military forces are organized, equipped, and employed to achieve maximum military effectiveness. The result was the Land Warfare Revolution. In the Civil War, both the Union and the Confederate forces used their rail nets to enhance greatly their strategic mobility and their ability to sustain large armies in the field for what, in the war's final year, was continuous campaiging. Their exploitation of the telegraph facilitated the rapid transmission of information between the political and military leadership and their commanders in the field, as well as among the field commanders themselves. The telegraph also dramatically enhanced the ability of military leaders to mass their forces quickly at the point of decision and to coordinate widely dispersed operations far more effectively than had been possible during the Napoleonic era.

The effects of rifling, which improved the range and accuracy of musketry and artillery, were not as quickly appreciated by the American military. Union and Confederate generals who clung to the tactics of the Napoleonic era exposed their men to fearful slaughter, as at Fredericksburg, Spotsylvania, and Gettysburg. The introduction of repeating rifles in significant numbers late in the conflict enabled the individual soldier to increase substantially the volume, range and accuracy of his fires over what had been possible only a generation or two earlier. One Confederate general is said to have observed that "had the Federal infantry been armed from the first with even the breechloaders available in 1861, the war would have been terminated within a year."[8] Still, both sides did adapt eventually.

The campaigns of 1864 and 1865 were marked by the proliferation of entrenchments and field fortifications. Indeed, by the time Sherman's men were marching from Atlanta to the sea in 1864, they lightened their packs by throwing away their bayonets—but they kept their shovels. Shelby Foote notes that the Confederate forces opposing Sherman had a saying that "Sherman's men march with a rifle in one hand and a spade in the other," while Union troops felt that "the rebs must carry their breastworks with them." Arguably, many of the major battles toward the war's end bore a greater resemblance to operations on the Western Front in the middle of World War I than they did to early Civil War battles like Shiloh or First Manassas.

Over the next fifty years this new military regime matured. The increases in the volume, range, and accuracy of fires were further enhanced by improvements in artillery design and manufacturing, and by the development of the machine gun. Again, military leaders who ignored, or who failed to see clearly, the changes in warfare brought about by technological advances and who failed to adapt risked their men and their cause. This myopia was induced partly by the fact that no large-scale fighting occurred among the great powers of Europe between 1871 and 1914. World War I provides numberous examples of this phenomenon, as the military regime that began with the mid-nineteenth century revolution in land warfare reached full maturity. One recalls here the mutiny of the French army after the futile and bloody Nivelle Offensive, the appalling casualties suffered by the British at the Somme and Passchendaele, and by the French and Germans at Verdun.

Just trailing this revolution in land warfare was the Naval Revolution. The Revolution of Sail and Shot had long since matured. The wooden ships that were powered by the wind and armed with short-range cannon that had dominated war at sea had not changed appreciably since the sixteenth century. But over the course of a few decades of rapid change from the mid-1800s to the first years of the twentieth century, these vessels gave way to metal-hulled ships powered by turbine engines and armed with long-range rifled artillery, dramatically transforming the character of war at sea. As persistent challengers to British naval mastery, the French consistently led the way early in the Naval Revolution.[9] In 1846 they pioneered the adoption of steam propulsion and screw propellers on auxiliary ships. In 1851 they launched the Napoleon, the first high-speed, steam-powered ship of the line. And in the late 1850s, France began constructing the first seagoing ironclad fleet. The British, however, quickly responded to these French innovations, taking the lead in applying these technologies. The mature phase of this revolutionary period found Britain attempting to sustain its position against a new challenger, Imperial Germany, by launching the first all-big-gun battleship, H.M.S. *Dreadnought*, in 1906. This period also saw the introduction of the submarine and the development of the torpedo. Indeed, the development of these two instruments of war led to the introduction in World War I of entirely new military operations—the submarine strategic blockade and commerce raiding, and anti-submarine warfare.

Toward that war's end, however, new operational concepts were developed to mitigate the effects of the dominant military systems and operational concepts. On land, massed frontal assaults preceded by long artillery preparations gave way to brief artillery preparation fires, infiltration tactics, and the use of the light machine gun as the dominant weapon of the German storm trooper assault. At sea, Great Britain and the United States established elaborate convoy operations to counter the U-boat threat that had transformed the nature of commerce raiding.

World War I both represented the mature stage of one military epoch, and presaged the rise of the Interwar Revolutions in Mechanization, Aviation, and Information. As the war progressed, the land forces of both the Allied and the Central powers found themselves employing new military systems based on dramatic advances in the fields of mechanization and radio. Following the war, improvements in internal combustion engines, aircraft design, and the exploitation of radio and radar made possible the blitzkrieg, carrier aviation, modern amphibious warfare, and strategic aerial bombardment. Entirely new kinds of military formations appeared, such as the panzer division, the carrier battlegroup, and the long-range bomber force. After a scant twenty years, the nature of conflict had changed dramatically, and those—like the British and the French—who failed to adapt suffered grievously.

Finally, in the mid-twentieth century, the Nuclear Revolution (especially after the coupling of nuclear warheads to ballistic missiles) brought the prospect of near-instantaneous and complete destruction of a state's economic and political fabric into the strategic equation. Here was a shift in technology so radical it convinced nearly all observers that a fundamental change in the character of warfare was at hand. Indeed, in the eyes of some observers, once nuclear weapons were stockpiled in significant numbers by the superpowers, they could no longer be employed effectively. Their only utility was in deterring war. Nevertheless, one also sees here the emergence of very different warfighting doctrines and military organizations among nuclear states (e.g., the U.S. nuclear submarine force; Soviet Strategic Rocket Forces).

Seven lessons

Reflecting on this record extending over seven centuries, it is possible to make some general observations about the character of military revolutions.

First, and to reiterate a point made earlier, emerging technologies only make military revolutions possible. To realize their full potential, these technologies typically must be incorporated within new processes and executed by new organizational structures. In the cases outlined above, all major military organizations fairly rapidly gained access to the emerging technologies. Failure to realize a great increase in military effectiveness typically resulted not so much from ignoring technological change as from a failure to create new operational concepts and build new organizations.

Perhaps the clearest example of the importance of organizational innovation occurred

370 Andrew F. Krepinevich

early in World War II. On the Western Front in 1940, British and French armored forces were roughly equal to the Germans' in size, and in quality. Both the allies and the Germans had modern aircraft and radios. In the interwar years, however, it was the German military that had identified both the operational concept to best integrate these new military systems and the organization needed to activate that concept. The result was a major increase in military effectiveness and the acquisition of a decisive comparative advantage. Germany defeated the allied forces and conquered France in six weeks. That victory was primarily due to the intellectual breakthroughs that led to new operational concepts and the organizational flexibility that allowed them to exploit these concepts.

A second lesson is that the competitive advantages of a military revolution are increasingly short-lived. Military organizations typically recognize the potentially great penalties for failing to maintain their competitive position. In early periods of military revolution, it was possible to maintain dominance for a relatively long period (witness the sluggish response of France to the Infantry Revolution and much of Europe to the Napoleonic Revolution). But since the Napoleonic era, it has been true that if a major military organization is to derive an advantage by having first access to new technologies it has to exploit those technologies quickly, before its major competitors copy or offset the advantage.

For example, the French innovations that sparked the nineteenth century Naval Revolution stimulated a furious British response that matched and then exceeded the French effort. Although the British were loath to introduce radical changes in ship design, they felt compelled to when faced with the French initiative, and retained a major advantage. What gave Britain its competitive advantage was its economic strength, its ability to tap into that strength through its financial system, and its ability to concentrate its resources on a naval competition in a way that France, a continental power, never could. As the revolution matured, France's fleeting opportunities evaporated.

By the end of the Naval Revolution, the tables were again turned. When the British launched H.M.S. *Dreadnought*, Germany quickly took up the British challenge, leading to the Anglo-German dreadnought arms race. Thus, the Royal Navy's lead in applying technologies to launch the first all-big-gun battleship designed to make all others "obsolete" produced only an ephemeral competitive advantage over Germany, and the other major navies of the world, which quickly constructed their own "dreadnoughts."

Indeed, in the last two centuries there do not seem to be any prolonged "monopolies" exercised by a single competitor in periods of military revolution. Fairly quickly, major powers who can afford the technology and who understand how to employ it, have it if they want it. Of course, one is immediately led to ask the question: Is "fairly quickly" quickly enough? After all, Admiral Alfred von Tirpitz, who directed Germany's naval buildup, viewed with alarm the period from 1906, when Britain launched *Dreadnought*, to 1910, when Germany's naval building program was able to offset partially the British advantage. It may be that although the period of competitive advantage appears to be fairly short there may be a potentially great advantage from being first, as the French discovered to their dismay and the Germans to their elation in the spring of 1940.

Having the initial competitive advantage in a period of military revolution—even if that advantage is considerable—is no guarantee of continued dominance, or even competitiveness. The list of military organizations that established an early lead, only to fall behind later, is long. Consider the history of the submarine: the French navy made much of the early progress in submarines in the late nineteenth century, but it was the Kaiser's navy that employed the new system to such devastating effect in World War I. In World War II, the United States quickly adopted many of Germany's innovations in mechanized air-land operations and in submarine commerce raiding. Or take military aircraft: the Americans were in the forefront of aviation in the first years of the twentieth century, but by the time of their entry into World War I had fallen substantially behind many European states. Or tanks: an American tank designed in the 1920s was adapted by the Soviets in the process of developing the T-34, one of the most effective tanks to emerge during World War II. The U.S. Army, on the other hand, was equipped during the war primarily with the inferior Sherman tank.

Even though monopolies may be fleeting, they are real and often decisive in war. The early years of World War II—in some respects like the Napoleonic era revolution in land warfare during the late eighteenth century—demonstrate what can happen when only one power is innovative and adaptive. In the run-up to that war, Germany proved far more adept than France, Britain, and Soviet Russia at operational and organization innovation on land. Although the Soviet Union, Great Britain, and the United States caught up to Germany's *blitzkrieg* in the span of a few years, France was unable to adapt quickly enough in 1940 to avoid disaster, while Soviet Russia suffered enormous devastation at the hands of the German war machine.

A third lesson of history is that asymmetries in national objectives and strategic cultures, as well as limitations on resources and the potential number and strength of enemies, allow for niche, or specialist, competitors. This phenomenon seems to be characteristic of recent periods of military revolution, where technological change has been broadening and accelerating, offering a potentially rich menu of military innovation. Furthermore, the cost of competing imposes strong limitations on how a military organization will pursue the competition. Again, the best example of this phenomenon occurred during the Interwar Revolutions in Mechanization, Aviation, and Information. With one exception, the period was characterized by selective competition among the military organizations of the great powers. For example, for a time Germany, traditionally a land power, became dominant in mechanized air-land operations. Soviet Russia quickly joined that competition to survive. Japan, an island nation, competed in naval aviation and modern amphibious operations, while the British developed strong capabilities in strategic aerial bombardment, strategic defenses, and (arguably) modern amphibious operations. Only the United States had the resources to complete in every major area of the interwar military revolution (save strategic defenses, for which it had no need), while simultaneously positioning itself to exploit the coming military revolution in nuclear weapons. Clearly the level and sophistication of human and material assets, and the unique strategic circumstances faced by each competitor, shape how competitors approach and attempt to exploit the opportunities inherent in military revolutions.

Fourth, the historical record suggests that war and revolution in warfare are quite separate entities. True, it took the test of World War II to convince the world's major army organizations (and, one might add, much of the German army itself) that Germany's blitzkrieg concept could produce great advantages for its practitioners. The war also convinced the U.S. Navy and the Imperial Japanese Navy that aircraft carriers would be the new centerpiece of battle fleets, and convinced everyone to recognize the revolution in naval warfare brought on by the use of submarines. But a confirming war is not essential for military organizations to seize opportunities. For instance, the revolution in naval warfare in the late nineteenth century, from wood, sail, and cannon to steel, turbines, and rifled guns, was widely accepted in the absence of war. The introduction of nuclear weapons is another obvious example of broad acceptance by military organizations that the competitive environment had changed radically.

Fifth, though most militaries will be quick to recognize a competitor's advantage, there are no certainties. Not even war will guarantee that all military organizations will recognize and exploit a military revolution, or understand a revolution in all its dimensions. Thus, in the American Civil War, both sides were relatively quick in exploiting the dramatic gains in strategic mobility and command, control, and communications made possible by the railroad and telegraph. But years passed before either side clearly realized how drastically the appearance of rifled guns and muskets in large numbers had invalidated the Napoleonic battlefield tactics. Again, despite the experience of World War I the world's major naval powers tended to discount the effectiveness of strategic warfare conducted by submarines. And even after the German campaign in Poland alerted the world to the potential of the blitzkrieg, the French army remained remarkably, indeed fatally, resistant to innovation.

More than anything else, it is perceptions of future contingencies and likely enemies that determine whether and when there is full exploitation of the advantages offered by the military revolution. Having a single enemy or challenger may ease a military organization's problem by making it more manageable. For instance, Britain had three major kinds of naval contingencies to prepare for in the interwar period: a war against a major continental power in Europe; a "small war" involving its imperial possessions; and a war against Japan. Conversely, the world's two other major maritime powers, the United States and Japan, saw each other as by far their most prominent challenger, and organized their naval forces around a single contingency—a Pacific war. As it turned out, the Americans and the Japanese exploited the revolution in naval aviation far more proficiently than did the British, in part because of their ability to focus more precisely. In competing during a period of military revolution it is clearly advantageous to be able to identify not only the nature of future conflict but specific contingencies and competitors. But if that is not possible, a premium should be placed on possessing both sufficient organizational agility and resources to adapt quickly if or when the picture clarifies.

A sixth lesson is that technologies that underwrite a military revolution are often originally developed outside the military sector, and then "imported" and exploited for their military applications. Thus, in the early fourteenth century, the Artillery Revolution was fueled by the discovery that the method being used to cast church bells could also be used for casting artillery—so that, as Bernard Brodie observes, "the early founders, whose task had been to fashion bells which tolled the message of eternal peace . . . contributed unintentionally to the discovery of one of man's most terrible weapons." The development of the railroad and telegraph, which helped to effect the Revolution in Land Warfare, and the rise of the commercial automotive and aircraft industry which led to the Interwar Revolution, are other obvious examples. Indeed, all the military revolutions of the last two centuries are in a real sense spinoffs from the Industrial and Scientific Revolutions that have been central, defining processes of modern Western history.

That said, having a substantially inferior economic and industrial base need not be an absolute barrier to competition in a military revolution. During the interwar period the Imperial Japanese Navy developed a first-rate naval aviation capability and modern amphibious forces, which they employed to devastating effect in the early months of their war with the United States. The Japanese accomplished this with a gross national product that was less than 20 percent (and perhaps closer to 10 percent) of that of the United States, its major naval competitor in the Pacific. Again, following World War II, the Soviet Union, despite a German invasion that destroyed much of its most productive areas, developed with relative speed a nuclear weapon strike force to rival that of the United States. This was accomplished even though the Soviet Union's GNP was much lower than that of the United

States, and it was burdened by war reconstruction costs and the maintenance of a far larger conventional military force. However, in neither case could this competitive posture be sustained indefinitely against a wealthier, equally determined rival.

In a sense, military revolutions may offer major opportunities for relatively small or "medium-sized" powers to steal a march on greater powers, or even for one great power to challenge an array of its peers. They do so by making it possible to substitute intellectual breakthroughs and organizational innovations for material resources. Examples are plentiful: Flanders exploiting the Infantry Revolution to challenge giant France; the Napoleonic Revolution that allowed France to challenge all of Europe; Germany's innovations (in mechanized airland operations) during the Interwar Revolution against France, Britain, the Soviet Union, and the United States; and Japan exploiting the Interwar Revolution (in naval aviation) against the United States and Great Britain. Indeed, as Geoffrey Parker has argued, the West's global dominance from 1500–1800 is but an instance of this phenomenon writ large.

A seventh and last lesson is that a military revolution does not ineluctably imply a quantum leap in the cost of maintaining military forces. To take one example, the Infantry Revolution of the fourteenth century that replaced heavy cavalry with infantry archers and pikemen actually lowered the cost of maintaining forces. Also, the Nuclear Revolution has been comparatively cheap. While the ability to employ such weapons to achieve political ends has been much debated, the fact remains that nuclear weapons appeared to offer those who possess them considerable "bang for the buck."[10]

The current revolution

Where are we now? Some believe that a revolution in warfare has already occurred, and cite the recent Gulf War as evidence. American military operations in that war, however, do not meet the historical criteria for revolutionary change. United States forces did not display any dramatic doctrinal changes in that war, nor any major new force structures or military organizations. One indication of how continuous with earlier practice the U.S. performance was is that during the U.S. "Linebacker" air operations in 1972, some nine thousand laser-guided bombs were dropped on Southeast Asia—roughly the same number as were dropped during the Gulf War. We are in a military revolution—but in its early stages.

What the Gulf War did was show us a glimpse of the potential influence of this revolution on military effectiveness. The Gulf War may be seen as a precursor war—an indication of the revolutionary potential of emerging technologies and new military systems. In this respect, it may be similar to the battle of Cambrai that took place on the Western Front in November 1917. There the British, for the first time, employed large numbers of planes and tanks in concert. They tried to integrate their operations, and those of the infantry and artillery, through the use of wireless communications. The British attack, spearheaded by nearly five hundred tanks, broke the German lines on a twelve-kilometer front within hours.

This breakthrough was as surprising to the senior British leaders as the one-sided Desert Storm operation was to senior American commanders. Indeed, the British had made no plans to exploit such a rapid rupture of the German front. In retrospect, one also realizes that the potential for far greater success at Cambrai was compromised by the immaturity of the new technologies and systems employed (tank breakdowns, limitations on aircraft bomb loads, and on wireless range, portability and reliability). To extend the analogy, we may be in the "early 1920s" with respect to this military revolution.

Where are we going? While precise prediction is out of the question, it is possible to speculate with some confidence on the current revolution's general path and nature. It appears certain that it will involve great increases in the ability of military organizations to detect, identify, track, and engage with a high degree of precision and lethality far more targets, over a far greater area, in a far shorter period of time, than was possible in the Cold War era. (No doubt it also will lead to systems and operations designed to degrade or offset these capabilities.) This aspect of the revolution will probably involve an improved ability to understand target systems and their relationship to operational and strategic objectives. The leverage obtained from such a capability is potentially enormous, since knowing which subset of targets to strike out of the many identified will be crucial to the effective employment of large numbers of precision weapons.

Furthermore, the growing importance of simulations—from computer-assisted design and manufacturing (CAD-CAM), to individual training simulators, to simulations of complex military operations involving high levels of systems and architecture integration—may witness a major increase in the ability of military organizations to extract the full potential of the human and material resources at their disposal.[11]

The transition rate to this revolution's mature stage will be a function of the level of military competition in the international system, the strategies for competition pursued by the competitors, and the four elements comprising a military revolution. It should also be appreciated that, as long as there are multiple competitors exploiting the potential of the emerging military revolution, the revolution itself will be likely to take several paths, if only because of the competitors' varying strategic goals, access to relevant resources, and strategic culture.

What it means for us

Perhaps, as many believe, the United States and the world's other great powers have an opportunity unparalleled in this century to construct an international system that will provide a stable, enduring era of relative peace. Even if there is time and even if the opportunity is grasped, the question will remain: Will it last? Is it possible to avoid, or even forestall, a resumption of the great power competition that has been a staple of the international system since the rise of nation-states? If history is any indicator, the United States will, at some point, find itself again in a military competition, in the midst of both a geopolitical and a military revolution. What can the world's dominant military power learn from the general lessons of the West's prior military revolutions?

First, the United States should anticipate that one or more competitors seeking to exploit the coming rapid and dramatic increases in military potential may soon arise. Remembering that monopolies are transient, the United States should ponder how to avoid such a competition, or how to postpone it for as long as possible. Or how to win it if necessary.

Second, continued American technological and operational leadership is by no means assured. During the Interwar Revolution, Great Britain held an initial dominant position in mechanized air-land and naval aviation operations that was quickly forfeited. Even when countries will not be able to compete in the full spectrum of military capabilities, some of them, by specializing, will become formidable niche competitors.

Third, it is by no means certain that competitors will follow the same path as the United States. Different security requirements and objectives, strategic cultures, geostrategic postures, and economic situations will likely lead different competitors in different directions. While there are those who believe that, given our current advantage, this military revolution will only progress at a pace and direction that the United States decides to give it, history suggests that this is a dangerous delusion.

Fourth, it is not clear that the United States can rely on the cost of competition acting as an effective barrier to others. Although most military revolutions have raised the cost of "doing business," sometimes dramatically, there have been significant exceptions—and in terms of direct and initial costs the Nuclear Revolution is one of them, and, with prolifer- ation very much at issue, this revolution is still very much with us. If much of the increase in military effectiveness in this emerging revolution stems from the so-called Information Revolution, which has dramatically lowered the cost of information-related technologies, competitors may find the barriers to competition relatively low. And given the history of military organizations adapting technologies initially developed in the commercial sector, the United States' ability to restrict access to these technologies, in the manner it attempted with nuclear fission and missile technologies, may be marginal at best.

In summary, the lessons of earlier revolutions seem to contradict much of the con- ventional wisdom with respect to the United States' prospective competitive military position. In a revolutionary epoch, long-term U.S. military dominance is not preordained. Indeed, one could argue that the prospects for continued U.S. dominance would be greater in a military regime that was entering early maturity, rather than in its early, most dynamic stages. If America wants to avoid or delay a resumption of military competition, it will have to identify a strategy for that purpose and pursue it energetically. If a competition cannot be avoided, the United States will begin with strong competitive advantages in terms of tech- nology and military systems. As we have seen, however, it is typically those military organiza- tions that are highly innovative and adaptive that seem to compete best in periods of military revolution. In those terms, it has yet to be clearly demonstrated that the United States military should be sanguine regarding its ability to respond effectively to the challenge that this revolution will likely pose.

Notes

1 Clifford J. Rogers, "The Military Revolutions of the Hundred Years' War," *The Journal of Military History*, April 1993, pp. 241–78.
2 At the Battle of Crecy, for example, the French lost 1,542 knights and lords, and suffered over 10,000 casualties among crossbowmen and other support troops, while the English lost two knights, one squire, forty other men-at-arms and archers, and "a few dozen Welsh." Bernard and Fawn M. Brodie, *From Crossbow to H-Bomb* (Bloomington, IL: Indiana University Press, 1973), pp. 39–40.
3 "Corning" involves mixing wet powder and allowing it to dry into kernels. It is purported to have been three times as powerful as the sifted form, and considerably less expensive. Other improve- ments included the introduction of the two-wheel gun carriage, trunnions, and iron cannonballs. See Rogers pp. 269–71.
4 Guicciardini, Francesco, *History of Italy* (New York: Washington Square Press, 1964), p. 153.
5 Rogers also notes that, although the technology and military weapon system had been perfected, when military organizations failed either to restructure effectively, whether through a lack of funds or organizational insight, they failed to achieve the benefits of a revolutionary increase in military effectiveness. For example, when the siege train was relatively weak, as was the case during the sieges of Guise (1424), Ferte-Bernard (1424), Torey Castle (1429), Chateau Gallard (1429), Laigny- sur-Marne (1432), and Harfleur (1440), the siege dragged on for from between three months to over a year.
6 Brodie, p. 64 and Geoffrey Parker, "The Western Way of War," lecture presented at the Johns Hopkins SAIS, February 17, 1994, p. 87. Parker goes on to note that the galley, while displaced as the centerpiece of naval warfare, did manage to survive, and even prevail on occasion, into the eighteenth century.
7 Gustavus Adolphus actually increased marginally the ratio of pike to shot when compared to the Dutch. However, he did it in such a way as to promote the integration of pike, shot, artillery,

and cavalry into combined arms operations. See Michael Roberts, "The Military Revolution, 1560–1660," *Essays in Swedish History* (Minneapolis: University of Minnesota Press, 1967); Geoffrey Parker also argues that a third military revolution (or perhaps more accurately, a third element of the military revolution) involved the radical increase in the size of armies that occurred in the latter part of the seventeenth century, or, more precisely, between 1672 and 1710.

8 Brodie, p. 136. Shelby Foote observes that the Sharp repeating rifles employed by Union troops late in the war gave a cavalry force of 12,000 more firepower than an entire corps of infantry. See Foote, *The Civil War: A Narrative* (New York: Vintage Books, 1986), Vol. III, p. 872.

9 For a discussion of the early period of this revolution, see Bernard Brodie, *Sea Power in the Machine Age* (Princeton: Princeton University Press, 1942), pp. 48, 52, 66–68, 75–76, 195; Terrence R. Fehner, *National Responses to Technological Innovations in Weapon Systems, 1815 to the Present* (Rockville: History Associates Incorporated, 1986), pp.7–14; and William H. McNeill, *The Pursuit of Power: Technology, Armed Force, and Society Since A.D. 1000* (Chicago: University of Chicago Press, 1982), pp. 227–28, 239, 291–92.

10 While this point is often made, its acceptance is far from universal. For example, the United States is just now beginning to face up to the enormous environmental costs associated with its nuclear weapons program. The cleanup costs are estimated to range from $150–200 billion over thirty years. The situation in the former Soviet states is considered to be far worse. See Government Accounting Office, *DoE Management: Consistent Cleanup Indemnification is Needed*, GAO/RCED-93-167 (Washington, DC: Government Accounting Office, July 1993). Still, it is not clear that long-term environmental costs will weigh heavily with the rulers of most of the countries that are now actively pursuing a nuclear capability.

11 For a more complete discussion, see Andrew F. Krepinevich, "La Revolution a Venir dans la Nature des Conflits: Une Perspective Americaine," in *Relflexions sur la Nature des Futurs Systemes De Defense*, Alain Baer, ed., (Paris: Ecole Polytechnique, November 1993); and Andrew F. Krepinevich, "Une Revolution dans les Conflits: une Perspective Americaine," *Defense Nationale* (January 1994).

20 From Kadesh to Kandahar

Military theory and the future of war

Michael Evans

Only the dead have seen the end of war.
PLATO

As the world enters the twenty-first century, it appears to be in the midst of revolutionary shifts in the character of international security, with the forces of information technology and globalization seemingly transforming the theory and practice of war. In retrospect, it is now possible to see the decade between the collapse of Soviet communism in August 1991 and the attacks on the Pentagon and the World Trade Center in September 2001 as an era of the unexpected. No one in the West expected, still less predicted, the fall of the Soviet Union; the Iraqi invasion of Kuwait and the Gulf War; the Asian financial crisis; the Indian and Pakistani nuclear detonations; or of course, the events of 11 September.

Over the past decade, armed conflict has not remained within the traditional parameters of conventional warfare between rival states. From Somalia through Bosnia to Kosovo, East Timor, and Afghanistan, the face of war has assumed bewildering expressions. Under new global security conditions, the postmodern has collided with the premodern, the cosmo-politan has confronted the parochial, while the Westphalian state system has been challenged by new substate and transstate forces. Conventional high-tech Western armed forces have had to come to terms with a world of failed states populated by ethnic paramilitaries, of rogue regimes equipped with ballistic missiles and poison gas; and of radical extremists embracing a philosophy of mass-casualty terrorism.

For Western policy makers and military professionals these are deeply perplexing times; war seems more dynamic and chameleon-like than ever before. There are pressing questions: What is the future of war in conditions of great flux? Can traditional ideas of military power continue to dominate in an age of both globalization and fragmentation? What is the meaning of Western military supremacy in an era when democratic civilization—as demonstrated by the events of 11 September—is highly vulnerable to unexpected and unorthodox threats?

This article seeks to provide some answers to these questions. It adopts an approach reflecting a conviction that while events are always impossible to predict, it is possible to undertake intelligent analysis of trends in order to make some interim judgments about the kind of military conditions that might emerge in the near future. The article explores four areas. First, the fragmentation of the international system in the 1990s is analyzed in an attempt to demonstrate how new political conditions caused a diffusion of conflict modes that in turn have brought great uncertainty to the world of military analysts. Second, the main theories of war that emerged in the 1990s and the complexity these brought to traditional military thinking are examined. Third, a snapshot is provided of some of the most important challenges facing the West in terms of the theory and practice of the military art over the next decade and a half. Finally, some of the likely characteristics of warfare over the next decade are identified and subjected to tentative analysis.

War in the 1990s: the diffusion of conflict

In the 1990s there appears to have been a major transition in international relations away from a mainly state-centered system toward one marked by greater interdependence and interconnectedness. This trend toward interconnectedness was propelled by the dual impact of globalization and its handmaiden, the information revolution. Together, these two forces appeared to have altered the context within which modern states operate, bringing about an apparent redistribution of power among states, markets, and civil society.[1]

From a military perspective, the globalization of the last decade is perhaps best described as a process in which space and time have been so compressed by technology as to permit distant actions to have local effects, and vice versa. The international system that emerged by the beginning of the twenty-first century was an interconnected world order in which regional and local military developments could be of global significance.

Defense analysts quickly discovered that conflict and disorder anywhere in the world could be quickly transmitted everywhere—and invested with crisis—by a pervasive global communications media, epitomized by the Cable News Network. It was also discovered that globalization is not a homogenous process but contains a striking paradox in that it brings about both convergence and divergence. The notion of interconnectedness and a heightened sense of global consciousness are paralleled by polarization and particularism. As President William Clinton put it in April 1999, the West finds itself engaged in "a great battle between the forces of integration and the forces of disintegration; [between] the forces of globalism and the forces of tribalism; [of the forces] of oppression against [those of] empowerment."[2]

In effect, by 2001 the contemporary international security system had bifurcated—that is, it had split between a traditional twentieth-century, state-centered paradigm and new twenty-first-century substate and transstate strata. The great change in the early twenty-first-century international system from that of the last quarter of the twentieth century is the transition away from a dominant state-centric structure toward one marked by a greater number of substate and transstate actors. With bifurcation came a reduction in the relative significance of strategic geography, simply because the globalization of the information era appeared no longer to allow any state or society to retreat behind physical or moral borders.[3]

It is very important to understand clearly what is meant by the "relative decline" of strategic geography. In no sense does such a phrase imply "the end of geography" in the same sense that Francis Fukuyama famously spoke of "the end of history."[4] In terms of logistics, campaign planning, and topographical analysis, geography remains fundamental to the art of war, while geopolitics remains an important component of statecraft.[5] Nonetheless, a shift away from territoriality toward connectedness has diminished the effect of strategic geography as a primary rationale for defining a nation's defense and national security postures. The process of this transformation—in which older forms of linear conflict have been supplemented by new forms of nonlinear conflict—has been recognized by both Western and non-Western strategists. For example, the leading American strategic analyst Phillip Bobbitt has observed, "National security will cease to be defined in terms of borders alone because both the links among societies as well as the attacks on them exist in psychological and infrastructural dimensions, not on an invaded plain marked by the seizure and holding of territory."[6] Similarly, two Chinese strategists have argued that we are entering an age of unrestricted warfare in which "there is no territory that cannot be surpassed; there is no means which cannot be used in . . . war; and there is no territory or method which cannot be used in combination."[7]

The result of globalization over the past ten years has been the development of an unpredictable and complex pattern of armed conflict. Under conditions of global strategic bifurcation the old distinctions—between civil and international conflict, between internal and external security, and between national and societal security—began to erode. It has become clear that in an era in which various transnational and substate forces were greatly empowered by technology, such issues as civil conflict, terrorism, and the proliferation of weapons of mass destruction could no longer be easily quarantined within states or regions. From the early 1990s onward, these phenomena emerged as global strategic threats precisely because they acted to blur the distinction between internal and external crises. Under new conditions, transnational and substate forces threaten not just states but entire societies and thus the fabric of international stability itself. Consequently, traditional ideas about warfare have come under challenge as the political, economic, and military dimensions of security have more closely merged and state-on-state war seems to have been supplemented by new forms of substate and transstate conflict.[8]

The changing character of conflict and war mirrored the bifurcation of the international security system in the 1990s. The various views expressed about the future of military conflict reflected the post-Cold War fragmentation of international security and the diffusion of contemporary war into a variety of different modes. War became at once modern (reflecting conventional warfare between states), postmodern (reflecting the West's cosmopolitan political values of limited war, peace enforcement, and humanitarian military intervention), and premodern (reflecting a mix of substate and transtate warfare based on the age-old politics of identity, extremism, and particularism).[9] It is important to note that none of these categories represents neatly divided compartments of activity; they overlap and interact with each other. The U.S. Marine Corps's recent doctrine of the "three-block war"—in which troops may be engaged in a conventional firefight, peace operations, and humanitarian relief simultaneously in a single small area—captures the essence of this complex interaction.[10]

However, if modern, postmodern, and premodern forms of war overlap with each other, each mode has distinctive features. Modern war remains symbolized by a classical doctrine of "encounter battles," collisions of rival states' armed forces moving on land, in air, and at sea. This is a mode of classical warfare that can be traced back to the first properly recorded battle in history, in which the Egyptians defeated the Hittites in a chariot and infantry battle at Kadesh in 1285 B.C. The most recent model (at this writing) of armed conflict by encounter battle is the 1991 Gulf War, when Western and Iraqi forces employing missiles, tanks, and mechanized infantry clashed in the deserts of Kuwait.

In the West's public consciousness, modern war is based on high technology and the conventional force-on-force warfare of the kind associated with the two world wars, Korea, and the Gulf. In contrast, postmodern war is mainly characterized by the extremes of Western risk aversion, since for the Western powers the stakes seldom involve issues of vital security or national survival. Postmodern war is based on high-tech aerospace power, casualty limitation, and cautious exit strategies, such as we saw during the Kosovo conflict of 1999. In many key respects, the war over Kosovo was the model of a postmodern conflict. It was, to borrow David Halberstam's ironic phrase, "war in a time of peace"—a conflict carefully calibrated, enabled by high-tech weaponry, with its course determined by Western opinion polls.[11]

However, postmodern conflict based around high-technology aerospace power has created its own antithesis—asymmetric warfare, including the threat of weapons of mass destruction, waged against Western society.[12]

For its part, premodern war is symbolized by the images of "blood and iron" the West now allegedly abhors. Premodern war is essentially social rather than technological in character; it is an expression of the existential rather than the instrumental aspect of warfare.[13] Those who wage such struggles may choose to sport middle-class suits and exploit the spread of advanced technology, but their mind-sets are mixtures of the antimodern, the millenarian, and the tribal. Such radicals embody what Pierre Hassner has called "the dialectic of the bourgeois and the barbarian."[14] Premodern conflict merges unconventional—to use the term du jour, asymmetric—warfare methods with the conventional or semiconventional military activities of failed states. The premodern model of conflict also tends to exploit the rise of nonstate actors, cultural identity politics, and ethnopolitical conflict. In many respects, pre-modern war represents a cultural revolt against the philosophy of Western liberal globalism; it is a conscious rejection of the universal values based on cosmopolitan democracy that followed Western victory in the Cold War. For many premodern radicals, the social order offered by globalization is anathema, it appears to them a facsimile of the secular, materia-listic, and trivial world inhabited by Homer Simpson. For millenarian radicals of political Islam like Osama Bin Laden, the West's alleged cults of hedonistic individuality and intel-lectual relativism threaten societies that seek to define themselves by collective spirituality and timeless cultural traditions.[15]

Premodern struggles embrace aspects of substate or intrastate civil conflict and ethnic cleansing ranging from Bosnia through Somalia to East Timor. Unlike the old national-liberation insurgents of the Cold War era, premodern radicals are more concerned with age-old cultural identity than the universal class ideology of Marxism, with a strategy of population displacement rather than winning popular support; and with sectarianism and secession rather than building inclusive model societies. One of the biggest changes in com-temporary military affairs, then, has been the obsolescence of the Cold War political model of unconventional warfare and, as a result, of much of the West's counterinsurgency theory.[16]

When distilled to basics, these three overlapping models of modern, postmodern, and premodern war provide us with two vividly contrasting images of future conflict—one that is mainly symmetric and one largely asymmetric. On one hand, we have the blend of modern and postmodern war seen in the 1991 Gulf War and waged in the air over Kosovo in 1999 to serve as a grim metaphor of Western supremacy in any conventional conflict. However, on another level, we are confronted with a strange mixture of premodern and postmodern con-flict—a world of asymmetric and ethnopolitical warfare—in which machetes and Microsoft merge, and apocalyptic millenarians wearing Reeboks and Raybans dream of acquiring weapons of mass destruction. To use a Hollywood analogy, it is as if the West's Buck Rogers were now lined up against assorted road warriors from the devastated society portrayed in the "Mad Max" films.

Military theory in the 1990s

The fragmentation of war has been mirrored in the world of strategic analysis. In the 1990s, military theory reflected the rapid diffusion of conflict following the end of the bipolar Cold War world. Multiple new theories of armed conflict appeared in the first half of the 1990s. At the beginning of the decade, the American analyst John Mueller gave us the "obsoles-cence of major war" theory, which argued that war in the advanced West was as outmoded as slavery and dueling.[17] The Israeli scholar Martin van Creveld followed Mueller by declaring that the Gulf War was a historical freak, a throwback to World War II rather than a vision of twenty-first-century war. Van Creveld argued that the long era of interstate war first codified by the Prussian philosopher Carl von Clausewitz in the early nineteenth century had ended. What he described as Clausewitzian "trinitarian war"—based on the nexus between people, government, and armed forces—was dead, and Western military theory derived from classical warfare had become obsolescent.[18]

The American futurists Alvin and Heidi Toffler then gave us the theory of "third wave" high-technology information warfare that helped initiate the "revolution in military affairs" debate.[19] According to the Tofflers and the information-age warfare theorists who followed them, the Gulf War provided a glimpse of postmodern war as the realm of high technology. Precision strike, "dominant battlespace knowledge," and stealth platforms would shape future conflict. In the 1990s RMA-style ideas dominated American force planning for a future based on fighting two major theater wars, as enshrined in the Pentagon's blueprint *Joint Vision 2010*.

In contrast, military writers like Robert Kaplan, Philip Cerny, and Ralph Peters proceeded to give us a vision of future war in which the form of social organization involved was far more important than the level of technology employed.[20] For Kaplan, the war of the future was the "coming anarchy" of a Hobbesian world of failed states; for Cerny it was the "neomedievalism" of warlordism and violent disintegration; and for Peters it was a struggle by Western forces waged against a world of warrior cultures and paramilitaries from Mogadishu to Grozny. In 1996 Samuel P. Huntington published his seminal study of a coming "clash of civilizations" in which conflict between world cultures and "fault-line wars" would dominate the geopolitical future.[21] Finally, in 1999, the British analyst Mary Kaldor put forward a theory of "new wars" in which identity politics and the privatization of violence would challenge the new global order.[22]

By the turn of the century, the West was awash in a world of competing ideas about the future of armed conflict. War and conflict had, in effect, split like an unraveling rope's end into a multiplicity of strands. War could be whatever one sought in the cookbook of theory: it could be desert combat in the Gulf, street fighting in Grozny, or something between the two. Armed conflict could be asymmetric or low-intensity style "fourth generation" conflict waged by guerrillas and terrorists against the West's conventional military supremacy. In addition, the ominous New Terrorism of nuclear, chemical, and biological warfare conducted by rogue nations and nonstate entities was also viewed by some analysts as representing a form of "nontraditional warfare."[23]

From theory to practice: the challenge of future war

Given the proliferation of military theory and uncertain political conditions, what are the possible contours of future warfare over the next decade? What cautious speculations can we make about emerging trends? In September 1999, the bipartisan U.S. (Hart-Rudman) Commission on National Security/Twenty-First Century stated:

> The future strategic environment will . . . be one of considerable turbulence . . . The international system will be so fluid and complex that to think intelligently about military issues will mean taking an integrated view of political, social, technological, and economic developments. Only a broad definition of national security is appropriate to such a circumstance. In short we have entered an age in which many of the fundamental

assumptions that steered us through the chilly waters of the Cold War require rethinking ... The very facts of military reality are changing, and that bears serious and
concentrated reflection.[24]

If the Hart-Rudman Commission's judgment about the facts of military reality changing
is correct—and many, including the present author, believe it is—those concerned with
preparing for armed conflict in the early twenty-first century must expect to confront a range
of old, new, and hybrid forms of armed conflict. During the Cold War, the West confronted
a unidimensional threat from the Marxist-Leninist Soviet Union—an adversary whose
motives were certain and whose moves were predictable. In the new century, such conditions
no longer apply. In the words of U.S. secretary of defense, Donald H. Rumsfeld, new
military thinking is now required to arm Western societies "against the unknown, the
uncertain, the unseen, and the unexpected."[25]

It has become imperative that all concerned with security issues pay greater attention to the
merging of previously discrete forms of war. The conceptual basis for the study of warfare in
the West must now be broadened to include a rigorous study of the interaction between
interstate, substate, and transstate conflict and of the diffusion of contemporary military
capabilities. We have to recognize that in an interconnected age, linkage and interdependence seem to pervade all aspects of armed conflict. Military analysts and force-structure
specialists need to concentrate on the multifunctional use of force in highly complex operations. In addition, military professionals must learn to embrace the challenges of proportion,
coercion, and dissuasion as well as the older tradition of battlefield destruction. In particular,
what the U.S. Hart-Rudman Commission has described as "the spectrum of symmetrical
and asymmetrical threats we anticipate over the next quarter century" must receive
increased attention from both military theorists and policy makers.[26] In short, the challenge
is to prepare for full-spectrum conflict.

The task will be much harder than many defense analysts realize. The notion of a spectrum of conflict is not a new idea, but for most of the Cold War the Western understanding
of war was based on generic intellectual categories of "conventional" (high-intensity) and
"unconventional" (low-intensity) conflict. Most in the field of strategic studies thought in
terms of separate worlds of conventional interstate (or high-intensity) and unconventional
intrastate (or low-intensity) military activity. Unfortunately, the spectrum of conflict that is
emerging in the early twenty-first century is distinguished by merged categories, multi-
dimensionality, and unprecedented interaction.[27]

In an era when all security issues are interconnected and when the national security of
Western states has become critically dependent on international security, single-scenario
strategies and rigid military force structures have become anachronistic. Traditional
concepts of deterrence and defense need to be supplemented by new doctrines of security
preemption, security prevention, and expeditionary warfare. Moreover, the clear separation
of peace and war must be supplemented by an acknowledgment that modes of war have
merged. In a new age marked by networks and instant communications, the need is for
advanced military forces with skills useful across a range of tasks that may involve preventive
deployment, preemptive strike, war fighting, peace enforcement, traditional peacekeeping
and peace building, and counterterrorism.[28]

However, the intellectual challenge facing military professionals is not, as Martin van
Creveld would have us believe, to consign Carl von Clausewitz and two thousand years of
Western military knowledge to the dustbin of history. Rather, the task is to learn how to fight
efficiently across the spectrum of conflict. No responsible Western military theorist can

accept at face value the thesis of the "obsolescence of conventional war" or the paradigm of asymmetric warfare as primary force planning or doctrinal determinants. In a dangerous and unpredictable world, military professionals and their political masters must prepare to fight in conditions of a "high-low mix"—to be ready to tame the big wildcats and not simply the vicious rodents, to be able to fight troops like Iraq's former Republican Guard as well as Taliban, al-Qaʻida militia, and terrorists. As every good operational commander knows, in the military art one can "trade down," but one can never "trade up." Moreover, all the evidence indicates that success in peace-support operations requires the kinds of conventional firepower, mobility and force protection available only to military establishments that are optimized for conventional warfighting.[29]

Readying ourselves for conventional war does not, however, absolve us from undertaking a major transformation in the way we think about the use of military force. The most pressing intellectual task at the crossroads of the old and new centuries is rapid adaptation to new and merging forms of conflict. In the West we have to reconcile how we would like to fight with how we might *have* to fight. We must try to synthesize relevant features from the massive literature on the classical Gulf War/RMA model of warfare with the changing reality of conflict—both conventional and unconventional—as it presents itself. We have to undertake an intellectual exploration of the growing interaction between interstate, substate, and transstate conflict and conduct a rigorous investigation of the phenomenon of merging war forms—internal, international, postmodern, modern, and premodern.

The merging of modes of armed conflict suggests an era of warfare quite different from that of the recent past. Fighting in the future may involve conventional armies, guerrilla bands, independent and state-directed terrorist groups, specialized antiterrorist units, and private militias. Terrorist attacks might evolve into classic guerrilla warfare and then escalate to conventional conflict. Alternatively, fighting could be conducted on several levels at once. The possibility of continuous, sporadic, armed conflict, its engagements blurred together in time and space, waged on several levels by a large array of national and subnational forces, means that the reality of war in the first decade of the twenty-first century is likely to transcend a neat division into distinct categories, symmetry and asymmetry.[30]

Indeed, it is arguable that the main reason for much of the intellectual confusion surrounding war at the turn of the century stems from the lack of a conceptual synthesis between the requirements of traditional conventional war and the emerging blend of interstate, transstate, and nonstate modes.[31] It is no accident that the most productive areas of military theory have been those that have attempted to concentrate on the expanding phenomenon of war. The most interesting new approaches have come from those who have endeavored to examine the growing complexity of conflict, its holistic yet multidimensional character, its sociological as well as technological dynamics. Conceptual progress has come from analytical work into war's connection to society as well as to the state; from assessing the convergence of modes of conflict and the growing requirements to control armed violence in an age of instantaneous media imagery; and from developing multipurpose forces that can wage warfare across the spectrum of conflict.

In short, it is the interactive character of war—Clausewitz's famous chameleon "that adapts its characteristics to the given case"—that has proven the most original avenue for analysis.[32] The immediate future of war lies perhaps in two key areas. The first is the realm of multidimensional theories of war and conflict that call for multifunctional forces for intervention missions; the second is the evolving theory of counterwar, or "mastery of violence," which may assist military practitioners and policy makers to understand and deal with armed conflict as a multifaceted phenomenon.

A multidimensional approach to war and conflict

As twenty-first-century war becomes, in the words of the prominent Russian military theorist Makhmut Gareev, "a multivariant," advanced armed forces need to develop multidimensional approaches to conflict.[33] The most interesting American and British military theory reflects a growing recognition that in a new age of multiple threats, discrete categories of conventional and unconventional conflict are eroding, along with corresponding legal and moral restraints.

Much of the West's preparation to meet an accelerating convergence of military challenges is shaped by three ideas. First, there is a general acceptance that armed forces must be able to adapt to differing modes of war, to become multifunctional. Second, as questions of both national and societal security merge and interpenetrate, reactive operational strategies alone become inadequate as means of deterrence. Security in the new era of liberal globalism also requires a willingness to undertake interventions, as well as, correspondingly, proactive military forces. Third, if global political and technological conditions permit radical groups and rogue states to use ballistic or biological weapons to inflict mass casualties on democratic societies, this new challenge must be met by military preemption in ways not seen since the late nineteenth century. In other words, those who espouse the mass murder of innocent civilians in cities and suburbs must be destroyed wherever and whenever preemption is possible. As President George W. Bush put it recently, it is necessary for the West to act decisively against the new threat emanating from "the perilous crossroads of radicalism and technology."[34] Specifically, the diffusion of advanced technology, from standoff missiles to commercial space systems to weapons of mass destruction, into the hands of smaller armies, paramilitaries, militias, and other armed groups puts a premium on Western expeditionary warfare.

Two leading American military theorists, Huba Wass de Czege and Richard Hart Sinnreich, have recently given an unequivocal view of the merging of conventional and unconventional conflict:

> Clear distinctions between conventional and unconventional conflicts are fading, and any future major conflict is almost certain to see a routine commingling of such operations. Similarly, once useful demarcations between front and rear or between theater and strategic operations will continue to evaporate as the instrumentalities of war become more interdependent and, as is increasingly true of communications and space systems, less easily separable from their civilian and commercial counterparts.[35]

As a result, the future requirement will be for joint forces designed for multidimensional, expeditionary-style operations—what the U.S. Army now refers to as "operational maneuver from strategic distance." Such operations are vital to control theaters where "high-low" threats and varied forms of conflict might be expected. Consequently, the main trends in contemporary Western military theory are toward operations with multinational and joint task forces with simplified headquarters structures—not simply corps and division, but increasingly force and formation. Smaller combat formations, such as the combined-arms brigades to serve modular building blocks for forces in the field, are needed.[36] Force structures will become more modular and capable of rapid task force organization from "golf bags" of varied military capabilities.[37]

In expeditionary warfare, the main need is to reconcile operational versatility with organizational stability. Western forces must be capable of undertaking joint, multidimensional missions ranging from shaping the environment to air-ground operational maneuver, to all-out conventional warfare. The demands of operational versatility are likely to place a premium on organizational change.

Multifaceted conflict: counterwar theory and mastery of violence

Recent trends in European-American military theory toward multidimensional operations have also been applied to what some European military thinkers now call "counterwar theory," or the "mastery of violence" as an operational military strategy.[38] In France, the development of counterwar theory reflects the perception that war in the twenty-first century has become "a mixture of phenomena." Some French military thinkers believe that in contemporary armed conflict it is largely impossible to treat war as merely a clash between rival forces; that the conventional cannot be separated from the unconventional; and that traditional lines of authority between military control and political responsibility are becoming blurred.

A military force may now be required to conduct intervention operations in conditions that correspond to neither classical warfare nor traditional peace-support operations. Extremely complex political conditions may arise in which law and order are lacking but the law of armed conflict must nonetheless, and at all costs, be upheld; in such a case a counterwar strategy, the disciplined control of violence, may have to be imposed. As French military analysts Brigadier General Loup Francart and Jean-Jacques Patry observe, "Military operations are now completely integrated with political, diplomatic, economic and cultural activities. Strategy is no longer simply a matter of defense. The problem is now, more than ever, *to conceive military operations in a political framework.*"[39]

General Wesley K. Clark, the American commander who prosecuted Nato's 1999 war against Serbia over Kosovo, has argued that politics in modern war now pervades all of the three levels of war—tactics, operations, and strategy. In the past, politics was mainly a factor at the strategic level, where statecraft guided the military instrument. However, in the early twenty-first century, politics also now impinges on the operational and tactical levels of war, Clark believes, to the extent that it may be necessary to speak of a "political level of war." If General Clark is right, the implications for future civil-military relations are profound.[40]

In an age of increased military-political integration and twenty-four-hour electronic media, the goal of force may be not annihilation or attrition but calibrated "elimination of the enemy's resistance" by the careful and proportional use of counterviolence. The use of armed force in a surgical manner—the rapier rather than the broadsword—would require that military thinking and action be politically sophisticated, legally disciplined, and ethically correct. These needs were among the main lessons of the Kosovo conflict.[41] As French military theorists have argued, the aim must be to ensure that the application of force in intervention operations—especially in an age of instant images—can be modulated and shaped by professional militaries to accomodate rapidly shifting politics and flexible operational and strategic objectives.

Warfare in 2015: a tentative analysis

Given the growing complexity of the military art and of the use of force in statecraft, what are the characteristics of warfare most likely to be over the next decade? Four basic sets can be tentatively offered. First, war is likely to remain a chameleon, presenting itself variously in interstate, transstate, and nonstate modes—or as a combination of these. However, a word of caution is necessary: it would be a serious mistake to dismiss the possibility of interstate conventional war. If in some areas of the world, such as Western Europe, it is highly improbable, in much of Asia and the Middle East it remains a distinct possibility.[42] Nonetheless, in general terms, the merging of modes of armed conflict does suggest an era of warfare in which national, transstate, and substate forces may coalesce or find themselves in mismatched confrontations. Moreover, the conventional and the unconventional, the symmetric and the asymmetric, may occur almost simultaneously, overlapping in time and space.

Second, advanced warfare will be largely joint-service in character. The revolution in information technology, especially as applied to command and control, long-range precision strike, and stealth, has so compressed time and space in military operations as to create an unprecedented nonlinear battle space characterized by breadth, depth, and height. During the 1990s, the concept of "battle space" replaced the linear battlefield that had defined armed conflict in the Western tradition from Alexander the Great to the Second World War. In essence, the concept of battle space has permitted a shift away from the organization of linear mass toward a simultaneous and "full-dimensional" concentration of *effects*.[43] This is especially significant with regard to the cumulative impact of missile firepower from air, ground, and sea.[44]

Third, most Western military experts believe that future operations will favor simultaneous attack by joint air-ground forces that are "situationally aware"—that have substantially complete and current views of the battlespace via computer and satellite. Advanced forces are also likely to be networked from "sensor to shooter"—that is, surveillance capabilities will be electronically connected to strike forces, and all of them to each other.[45] There will probably be fewer troops deployed on the ground, but the individual soldier—the "strategic corporal"—will have a greater potential impact on events. Growing weapons lethality and increased ability of soldiers to direct long-range precision "fires"—as seen in Afghanistan, where ground forces acted as highly effective sensors for air strikes—are likely to become features of warfare over the next decade.[46]

Fourth, the dominance of surveillance and strike means that joint operations by technologically advanced forces, capable of deep precision attack and quick maneuver, are likely to resemble large-scale ambushes. If an enemy can be remotely located, traditional movement to contact preceded by forward troops probing for the enemy will be replaced by well-prepared, deliberate, "deep" attacks using tactics that exploit rapid positioning for maximum effect. However, precision munitions are likely to be of limited use in close operations, in which infantry must be employed to finish off adversaries.[47]

In the close battle, armored forces and artillery are likely to remain extremely useful in applying suppressive fire in support of troops in action. In the recent campaign in Afghanistan, American forces put their faith in air cover at the expense of both artillery and tanks. It was soon discovered that while precision munitions delivered from high altitude are effective against known point targets, they are much less useful in area attack, as is necessary against forces that are scattered, not precisely located. The majority of American casualties (twenty-eight out of thirty-six) in Operation ENDURING FREEDOM came from enemy mortar fire that could have been suppressed by armor or artillery. The lesson learned from fierce combat in the complex terrain of Afghanistan's Shah-i-Kot region is that for area suppression, field guns and tanks remain essential in twenty-first-century warfare.[48]

The likely shape of war in the early twenty-first century essentially reflects the consequences of a bifurcated global system between an older state-centric world, on one hand, and new transstate and substate strata on the other. The West has entered a period in which classical interstate war has been supplemented by borderless threats from nonstate actors operating with the power of modern computers, ease of international travel, and, possibly, weapons of mass destruction, with which they can deal lethal blows to any society.

These trends, particularly the unholy alliance between new nonstate actors and advanced technology, collectively point to an urgent need for new strategic thinking. The shift toward connectedness and nonlinearity at the relative expense of territoriality and linearity has become perhaps the central reality of strategy in the opening years of the twenty-first century. Some international observers believe the strategic shift from territoriality to connectedness will be revolutionary in its consequences:

> We are at a moment in world affairs when the essential ideas that govern statecraft must change. For five centuries it has taken the resources of a state to destroy another state; only states could muster the huge revenues, conscript the vast armies, and equip the divisions required to threaten the survival of other states. . . . This is no longer true, owing to advances in international telecommunications, rapid computation, and weapons of mass destruction. The change in statecraft that will accompany these developments will be as profound as any that the State has thus far undergone.[49]

The great danger to Western countries is no longer the threat of military invasion of the nation-state but an assault on the very foundations of our networked society. Western societies are now most vulnerable not from external invasion but from internal disruption of the government, financial, and economic institutions that make up critical infrastructures.[50]

It was this great weakness that al-Qa'ida exploited with such devastating results on 11 September 2001. Increasingly, national security now depends on the protection of a specific set of social institutions and the information links between them. However, our reliance on critical infrastructures vastly exceeds our ability to protect them; it is therefore impossible to protect an entire society solely by "homeland defense."

To defend Western societies, the nation-state model of war based upon threat analysis and against defined enemies will have to be supplemented by new modes of strategic thought that concentrate on alleviating the vulnerabilities of modern states to new nonstate threats. As the French military analyst Phillippe Delmas has warned, "Today's world is without precedent. It is as different from the Cold War as it is from the Middle Ages so the past offers no basis for comparison. . . . Tomorrow's wars will not result from the ambitions of States; rather from their weaknesses."[51]

To meet the challenges of tomorrow's wars, Western countries will need highly mobile, well equipped, and versatile forces capable of multidimensional coalition missions and "mastery of violence" across a complex spectrum of conflict. They will need new national security apparatus for threat and vulnerability analysis and consequence management in the event of traumatic societal attack. They will need enhanced international intelligence and diplomatic cooperation to ensure that military force is employed with maximum efficiency. They will need new norms of international law that allow joint armed forces to be used, when the enemy can be located, in far-flung preemption operations.[52]

The reality of Western societal vulnerability in conditions of liberal globalism represents a strategic transformation that obliges defense experts and politicians to think rigorously about the kinds of war that might lie ahead. We are confronted with a challenge of finding new ways of using force in merged modes of conflict in an international system that must confront simultaneously both integration and fragmentation.

The problems facing policy makers, strategists, and military professionals in the early twenty-first century, then, have changed dramatically and decisively from those of the twentieth. Military power and capability have expanded into a network of transnational interconnections. As a result, preparing for armed conflict is no longer only a matter of simply assembling battlefield strength to destroy defined adversaries.

Increasingly, military power is entwined in politics—as an instrument that shapes, polices, and bounds the strategic environment, that punishes, signals, and warns. The task for strategists is now one of disciplining available military power into a broad security strategy—one that embraces also diplomacy, intelligence analysis, and law enforcement—in a calibrated, judicious, and precise manner. In the prophetic words, written over thirty-five years ago, of the British strategist Alastair Buchan, "The real content of strategy is concerned not merely with war and battles but with the application and maintenance of force so that it contributes most effectively to the advancement of political objectives."[53] At the dawn of a new century, of a new and uncertain era in armed conflict in a globalized yet deeply fragmented world, these words aptly describe the many dangerous challenges that lie ahead.

Notes

1 For a detailed analysis see Manuel Castells, *The Information Age: Economy, Society and Culture*, vol. I. *The Rise of the Network Society* (Oxford, U.K.: Blackwell, 1996), chaps. 5–7, and Philip Bobbitt, *The Shield of Achilles: War, Peace and the Course of History* (New York: Knopf, 2002), chaps. 10–12, 24–26.

2 President Bill Clinton, "Remarks by the President to American Society of Newspaper Editors," San Francisco, California, 15 April 1999, *Los Angeles Times*, 16 August 1999.

3 Jean-Marie Guèhenno, "The Impact of Globalisation on Strategy," *Survival* 40, no. 4 (Winter 1998–99), pp. 5–19; David Held and Anthony McGrew, "Globalisation and the Prospects for World Order," in *The Eighty Years Crisis: International Relations 1919–99*, ed. Tim Dunne, Michael Cox, and Ken Booth (Cambridge, U.K.: Cambridge Univ. Press, 1999), pp. 219–43.

4 Francis Fukuyama, "The End of History," *National Interest* (Spring 1989) and *The End of History and the Last Man* (New York: Free Press, 1992).

5 See John M. Collins, *Military Geography for Professionals and the Public* (Washington, D.C.: National Defense Univ. Press, 1998) and the essays in Colin S. Gray and Geoffrey Sloan, eds, *Geopolitics, Geography and Strategy* (London: Frank Cass, 1999).

6 Bobbitt, p. 813.

7 Qiao Liang and Wang Xiangsui, *Unrestricted Warfare* (Beijing: People's Liberation Army Literature and Arts Publishing House, 1999), p. 199.

8 For a useful discussion see Robert L. Pfaltzgraff, Jr., and Richard H. Shultz, Jr., "Future Actors in a Changing Security Environment," in *War in the Information Age: New Challenges for U.S. Security Policy*, ed. Pfaltzgraff and Schultz (Washington, D.C.: Brassey's, 1997), chap. 1.

9 This typology is drawn from Robert Cooper's excellent essay on the fragmentation of the international system and the implications for global security. See Robert Cooper, *The Post-Modern State and the World Order* (London: Demos, 1996), esp. pp. 38–47.

10 For views on the future of armed conflict see Makhmut Gareev, *If War Comes Tomorrow? The Contours of Future Armed Conflict* (London: Frank Cass, 1998); Mary Kaldor, *New & Old Wars: Organised Violence in a Global Era* (Cambridge, U.K.: Polity Press, 1999); Gwyn Prins and Hylke Tromp, eds. *The Future of War* (The Hague: Kluwer Law International, 2000); Mark Duffield, *Global Governance and the New Wars: The Merging of Development and Security* (London: Zed Books, 2001): Robert E. Harkavy and Stephanie G. Neuman, *Warfare and the Third World* (New York: Palgrave, 2001); Wesley K. Clark [Gen., USA, Ret.], *Waging Modern War: Bosnia, Kosovo and the Future of Combat* (New York: PublicAffairs, 2001); Andrew J. Bacevich and Eliot A. Cohen, eds. *War over Kosovo: Politics and Strategy in a Global Age* (New York: Columbia Univ. Press, 2001); Christopher Coker, *Waging War without Warriors? The Changing Culture of Military Conflict* (Boulder, Colo.: Lynne Rienner, 2002); William R. Schilling, ed., *Nontraditional Warfare: Twenty-first Century Threats and Responses* (Washington, D.C.: Brassey's, 2002); and Colin S. Gray, *Strategy for Chaos: Revolutions in Military Affairs and the Evidence of History* (London: Frank Cass, 2002).

11 David Halberstam, *War in a Time of Peace: Bush, Clinton and the Generals* (London: Bloombury, 2001),

esp. chaps. 39–43. The Kosovo conflict is well analyzed in Bacevich and Cohen, eds., *War over Kosovo.*

12 See Lloyd J. Matthews [Col., USA], ed., *Challenging the United States Symmetrically and Asymmetrically: Can America Be Defeated?* (Carlisle Barracks, Penna.: U.S. Army War College, Strategic Studies Institute, July 1998), and Steven Metz and Douglas V. Johnson II, *Asymmetry and U.S. Military Strategy. Definition, Background, and Strategic Concepts* (Carlisle Barracks, Penna.: U.S. Army War College, Strategic Studies Institute, January 2001).

13 For a discussion see Coker, chap. 7.

14 Pierre Hassner, "Beyond War and Totalitarianism: The New Dynamics of Violence," in Prins and Tromp, eds., p. 205.

15 See Bernard Lewis, *What Went Wrong? The Clash between Islam and Modernity in the Middle East* (London: Weidenfeld and Nicolson, 2002).

16 See Avi Kober, "Low-Intensity Conflicts: Why the Gap between Theory and Practise?" *Defense & Security Analysis* 18, no. 1 (March 2002), pp. 15–38, and Harkavy and Neuman, esp. chap. 5. See also Max G. Manwaring, *Internal Wars: Rethinking Problems and Responses* (Carlisle Barracks, Penna.: U.S. Army War College, Strategic Studies Institute, September 2001), pp. 25–34.

17 John Mueller, *Retreat from Doomsday: The Obsolescence of Major War* (New York: Basic Books, 1989).

18 Martin van Creveld, *The Transformation of War* (New York: Free Press, 1991).

19 Alvin and Heidi Toffler, *War and Anti-War: Survival at the Dawn of the Twenty-First Century.* (Boston: Little, Brown, 1993).

20 Robert D. Kaplan, "The Coming Anarchy," *Atlantic Journal*, February 1994, and *The Ends of the Earth: A Journey at the Dawn of the Twenty-First Century* (New York: Random House, 1996); Philip Cerny, "Neomedievalism, Civil War and the New Security Dilemma: Globalisation as Durable Disorder," *Civil Wars* 1, no. 1 (Spring 1998), pp. 36–64; Ralph Peters, *Fighting for the Future: Will America Triumph?* (Mechanicsburg, Penna.: Stackpole Books, 1999).

21 Samuel P. Huntington, *The Clash of Civilizations and the Remaking of World Order* (New York: Simon and Schuster, 1996).

22 Kaldor, esp. chaps. 4–6.

23 See for example, Walter Laqueur, *The New Terrorism: Fanaticism and the Arms of Mass Destruction* (Oxford, U.K.: Oxford Univ. Press), 1999; Kenneth F. McKenzie, Jr., *The Revenge of the Melians: Asymmetric Threats and the New QDR*, McNair Paper 62 (Washington, D.C.: Institute for National Strategic Studies, National Defense Univ., 2000); and the essays in William R. Schilling, ed., *Non-traditional Warfare.*

24 U.S. Commission on National Security/Twenty-First Century, *New World Coming: American Security in the Twenty-First Century, Supporting Research & Analysis, Phase 1 Report* (Washington, D.C.: U.S. Commission on National Security/Twenty-First Century, 15 September 1999), p. 57 [emphasis added].

25 Donald H. Rumsfeld, "Transforming the Military," *Foreign Affairs* 81, no. 3 (May–June 2002), p. 23.

26 U.S. Commission on National Security/Twenty-First Century. *Seeking a National Strategy:* A Concert for Preserving Security and Promoting Freedom, Phase II Report (Washington, D.C: U.S. Commission on National Security/Twenty-First Century, 15 April 2000), p. 14.

27 Robert L. Pfaltzgraff Jr. and Stephen E. Wright, "The Spectrum of Conflict: Symmetrical or Asymmetrical Challenge?" in *The Role of Naval Forces in Twenty-First Century Operations*, ed. Richard H. Shultz and Robert L. Pfaltzgraff, Jr. (Washington, D.C.: Brassey's, 2000), pp. 9–28.

28 Michael Rose, "The Art of Military Intervention," in Prins and Tromp, eds., pp. 241–50; Christopher Bellamy, *Spiral through Time: Beyond "Conflict Intensity,"* Occasional Paper 35 (Camberly, U.K.: Strategic and Combat Studies Institute, August 1998), pp. 15–38.

29 Ibid.

30 See Huba Wass de Czege and Richard Hart Sinnreich, *Conceptual Foundations of a Transformed U.S. Army.* Institute for Land Warfare Paper 40 (Washington, D.C.: Association of the United States Army, March 2002); and Bobbitt, chaps. 26–27.

31 For background see Eric Hobsbawm's stimulating essay "War and Peace in the Twentieth Century," *London Review of Books*, 21 February 2002, pp. 16–18.

32 Carl von Clausewitz, *On War*, ed. and trans. Michael Howard and Peter Paret (Princeton, N.J.: Princeton Univ. Press, 1976), p. 89.

33 Gareev, p. 94.

34 George W. Bush, "President Bush Delivers Graduation Speech at West Point," 1 June 2002, White House, www.whitehouse.gov/ news/releases/2002/0620020601–3.html.

35 De Czege and Sinnreich, p. 6.

36 See Brian Bond and Mungo Melvin, eds., *The Nature of Future Conflict: Implications for Force Develop-ment*, Occasional Paper 36 (Camberly, U.K.: Strategic and Combat Studies Institute, September 1998), and Brigadier C. S. Grant, "The 2015 Battlefield," *British Army Review*, no. 128 (Winter 2001–2002), pp. 5–13.

37 Huba Wass de Czege and Zbigniew M. Majchrzak, "Enabling Operational Maneuver from Stra-tegic Distances," *Military Review* 82, no. 3 (May–June 2002), pp. 16–20. See also Huba Wass de Czege and Antulio J. Echevarria II, "Insights for a Power-Projection Army," *Military Review* 80, no. 3 (May–June 2000), pp. 3–11.

38 Loup Francart [Brig. Gen., French Army] and Jean-Jacques Patry, "Mastering Violence: An Option for Operational Military Strategy," *Naval War College Review* 53, no. 3 (Summer 2000), pp. 144–84. See also George A. Bloch, "French Military Reform: Lessons for America's Army?" *Parameters: U.S. Army War College Quarterly* 30, no. 2 (Summer 2000), pp. 33–45.

39 Francart and Patry, p. 145 [emphasis added].

40 Clark, pp. 10–11. For a recent discussion of civil-military relations see Eliot A. Cohen, *Supreme Command: Soldiers, Statesmen, and Leadership in Wartime* (New York: Free Press, 2002).

41 For legal and ethical legacies of the Kosovo campaign, see Frederic L. Borch, "Targeting after Kosovo: Has the Law Changed for Strike Planners?" *Naval War College Review* 56, no. 2 (Spring 2003), pp. 64–81.

42 For a discussion see Paul Bracken, "The Military Crisis of the Nation State: Will Asia Be Different from Europe?" in *Contemporary Crisis of the Nation State?* ed. John Dunn (Oxford, U.K.: Blackwell, 1995), pp. 97–114, and Jeffrey Record, "Thinking about China and War," *Aerospace Power Journal* 15, no. 4 (Winter 2001), pp. 69–80.

43 Paul E. Funk [Lt. Gen., USA], "Battle Space: A Commander's Tool on the Future Battlefield," *Military Review* 73, no. 12 (December 1993), pp. 36–47; Frederick M. Franks [Gen., USA], "Full Dimensional Operations: *A Doctrine for an Era of Change*," *Military Review* 73, no. 12 (December 1993), pp. 5–10; and U.S. Army Dept., *Operations*, Field Manual 3–0 (Washington, D.C.: Department of the Army, June 2001), pp. 4–20 to 4–21.

44 Michael Russell Rip and James M. Hasik, *The Precision Revolution: GPS and the Future of Aerial Warfare* (Annapolis, Md.: Naval Institute Press, 2002), chaps. 11–13; and Ted Hooton, "Naval Firepower Comes of Age," *Jane's Defence Weekly*, 13 November 2002, pp. 17–28.

45 See the broad and growing literature on network-centric warfare, including Christopher D. Kolenda, "Transforming How We Fight: A Conceptual Approach," *Naval War College Review* 56, no. 2 (Spring 2003), which cites the basic sources, pp. 100–21.

46 Antulio J. Echevarria II, *Rapid Decisive Operations: An Assumptions-Based Critique* (Carlisle Barracks, Penna.: U.S. Army War College, Strategic Studies Institute, November 2001), pp. 14–18.

47 Huba Wass de Czege, "Maneuver in the Information Age," in Pfaltzgraff and Shultz, eds., pp. 203–24; Dick Applegate [Col., USA], "Towards the Future Army," in Bond and Melvin, eds., pp. 77–91; Grant, pp. 9–10.

48 U.S. Center for Army Lessons Learned, "Emerging Lessons, Insights and Observations: Operation Enduring Freedom" (Fort Leavenworth, Kans.: CALL, 1 August 2002), document in author's possession. A useful summary of this report can be found in Army Svitak, "U.S. Army, Navy Mull Lessons Learned in Afghanistan War," *Defense News*, 22–28 July 2002.

49 Bobbitt, p. xxi.

50 Ibid., pp. 776–823. A view recently reinforced by Stephen E. Flynn *et al.*, *America Still Unprepared— America Still in Danger: Report of an Independent Task Force Sponsored by the Council on Foreign Relations* (New York: Council on Foreign Relations, 2002).

51 Phillippe Delmas, *The Rosy Future of War* (New York: Free Press, 1995), p. 213.

52 For discussions see Adam Paul Stoffa, "Special Forces, Counterterrorism and the Law of Armed Conflict," *Studies in Conflict and Terrorism* 18, no. 1 (June 1995), pp. 47–66; Eric S. Krauss and Mike O. Lacey, "Utilitarian vs. Humanitarian: The Battle over the Law of War," *Parameters: U.S. Army War College Quarterly* 32, no. 2 (Summer 2002), pp. 73–84; and Bobbitt, chaps. 24–27.

53 Alastair Buchan, *War in Modern Society: An Introduction* (London: C. A. Watts, 1966), pp. 81–82.

21 Why strategy is difficult

Colin S. Gray

My aim is to relate the nature of strategy to the character of its artistic application and to the unknowable context of the twenty-first century. The immodesty, even arrogance, of this endeavor is best conveyed through an anecdote about a meeting between Hannibal Barca and an armchair strategist. Hannibal suffered from what in this last century has been the German failing—winning battles but losing wars. Hannibal won all of his battles in the Second Punic War except, sadly for a Carthage that did not deserve him, the last one, against Scipio Africanus at Zama in 202 BC. He is reported to have had little patience with amateur critics.

> According to Cicero (de Oratione), the great general when in exile in Ephesus was once invited to attend a lecture by one Phormio, and after being treated to a lengthy discourse on the commander's art, was asked by his friends what he thought of it. "I have seen many old drivellers," he replied, "on more than one occasion, but I have seen no one who drivelled more than Phormio."[1]

The theme of this article lurks in the ancient strategic aphorism that "nothing is impossible for the man who does not have to do it." When I was contributing to the *Defense Guidance* in the early 1980s its basic direction for the Armed Forces could be reduced to "be able to go anywhere, fight anyone, and win." To repeat my point, to those who do not have to *do* strategy at the sharp, tactical end of the stick, the bounds of feasibility appear endless.

True wisdom in strategy must be practical because strategy is a practical subject. Much of what appears to be wise and indeed is prudent as high theory is unhelpful to the poor warrior who actually has to do strategy, tactically and operationally. Two classic examples make the point.

Carl von Clausewitz advised us that there is a "culminating point of victory," beyond which lies a decline in relative strength.[2] Great advice—save, of course, that political and military maps, let alone physical terrain, do not come with Clausewitz's "culminating point" marked. Imagine that you are a German and that it is anytime between late June 1941 and late August 1942. You have read Clausewitz. Where is the culminating point—at Minsk or Smolensk, on the Dnieper, Don, or Volga? How can you find a culminating point of victory until adverse consequences unmistakably tell you where it was?

The other example of great strategic wisdom that is difficult to translate into practical advice is the insistence of Clausewitz (and Jomini) that "the best strategy is always to be very strong; first in general, and then at the decisive point."[3] Naturally the challenge is not to comprehend the all but sophomoric point that one needs to be very strong at the decisive point. Rather it is to know the location of that point. What did Clausewitz's advice mean for

Germans in the late summer and fall of 1941? Did they need to concentrate their dissipating strength on the Red Army in the field, on the road to Moscow, or both?

For a tougher call, consider the American military problem in Southeast Asia in the second half of 1965. General William Westmoreland somehow had to identify military objectives to match and secure the somewhat opaque political objectives. Mastery of the arguments in the classics of strategic theory was unlikely to be of much practical help.

The argument

Before expounding the central elements of my argument, which appear pessimistic, let me sound an optimistic note. Terrible though the twentieth century has been, it could have been far worse. The bad news is that the century witnessed three world wars—two hot, one cold. The good news is that the right side won each of them. Moreover, threats to peace posed twice by Germany and then by the Soviet Union were each seen off at a cost that, though high, was not disproportionate to the stakes nor inconsistent with the values of our civiliza-tion. Western statecraft and strategy in two world wars was not without blemish. One needs to remember the wisdom of Lord Kitchener who said during World War I: "We wage war not as we would like but as we must." Strategically, notwithstanding errors, the Western World did relatively well. Now for a darker view.

My key argument is organized around three reasons why it is difficult to do strategy well:

- its very nature, which endures through time and in all contexts[4]
- the multiplicity and sheer variety of sources of friction[5]
- it is planned for contexts that literally have not occurred and might not occur; the future has not happened.

This argument is essentially optimistic, even though that claim may appear unpersua-sive given that the high-quality strategic performance is always challenged by the nature of strategy—not only by its complexity but by the apparent fact that whatever can go wrong frequently does. Also, strategy can fall because it may apply the wrong solutions to incor-rectly framed questions because guesses about the future were not correct. If, despite this, the bad guys were beaten three times during the course of the twentieth century, there are grounds for hope.

Before explaining the many sources of difficulty for strategy, it is necessary to highlight the recurrence of a serious fallacy. Lest this point appear unfairly focused on the United States, I will sugar-coat the pill by citing an American who got it right, and two others—one American and one German—who got it wrong. Samuel Griffith, who got it right, was a scholar of Chinese military theory from Sun Tzu to Mao. He once observed that "there are no mechanical panaceas" when commenting on a *Newsweek* report in July 1961 about a fuel-air explosive to destroy bunkers.[6] The American and German, who got it wrong, allowed themselves to be seduced by the promise of "mechanical panaceas." One must hasten to add that these two warrior-theorists were exceptionally able men. The point is that, writing ninety years apart, they made almost the same mistake.

The issue underlying both views is whether much of the fog and thus friction that undoes applied strategy can be thwarted by modern technology. Writing in 1905, Lieutenant General Rudolf von Caemmerer, a member of the great general staff working under Field Marshal Alfred Graf von Schlieffen, offered this claim:

The former and actually existing dangers of failure in the preconcentrated action of widely separated portions of the army is now almost completely removed by the electric telegraph. However much the enemy may have succeeded in placing himself between our armies, or portions of our armies, in such a manner that no trooper can get from one to the other, we can still amply communicate with each other over an arc of a hundred or two hundred or four hundred miles. The field telegraph can everywhere be laid as rapidly as the troops marching, and headquarters will know every evening how matters stand with the various armies, and issue its orders to them accordingly.[7]

Caemmerer proceeded to admit that the telegraph might dangerously diminish the initiatives allowed to army commanders. The irony is that poor communications, lack of coordinated action, and a general loss of cohesion by the all important armies on the right wing of the German assault in early September 1914 allowed an Allied victory with the miracle on the Marne.[8] The telegraph was a wonderful invention, but it could not reliably dissipate the fog of war.

An American example of a functionally identical error is drawn from the magical "system of systems" invoked by Admiral William Owens, former Vice Chairman of the Joint Chiefs of Staff. In 1995 he wrote, "The emerging system . . . promises the capacity to use military force without the same risks as before—it suggests we will dissipate the fog of war."[9]

New technology, even when properly integrated into weapons and systems with well trained and highly motivated people, cannot erase the difficulties that impede strategic excellence. A new device, even innovative ways to conduct war, is always offered as a poisoned chalice. Moreover, scarcely less important, strategy cannot be reduced to fighting power alone.[10] Progress in modern strategic performance has not been achieved exclusively through science and technology.

Consider this argument: strategists today have at their disposal technological means to help dissipate the fog of war and otherwise defeat friction that previous generations could only imagine. Modern strategists can see over the hill, communicate instantaneously with deployed forces around the world, and in principle rapidly destroy enemy assets wherever they are located—at least in fine weather and provided no innocent civilians are colocated with the targets. The problem is that war can't be reduced simply to the bombardment of a passive enemy.

Despite electro-mechanical marvels it is no easier—in fact it is probably harder—to perform well as a strategist today than a century ago. Consider the utility of railroads, telegraph, radio, and aircraft to the strategist. The poison in the chalice of each is that other polities have acquired them; each has distinctive vulnerabilities and worse (recall the radio intercepts of World Wars I and II); and none of them can address the core of the strategist's basket of difficulties.

Strategy is not really about fighting well, important though that is. To follow Clausewitz, it is about "the use of engagements for the object of the war."[11] The fog of war and frictions that harass and damage strategic performance do not comprise a static set of finite challenges which can be attrited by study, let alone by machines. Every new device and mode of war carries the virus of its own technical, tactical, operational, strategic, or political negation.[12]

To tackle the fog and friction of strategy and war is not akin to exploring unknown terrain, with each expedition better equipped than the last to fill in blanks on the map. The map of fog and friction is a living, dynamic one that reorganizes itself to frustrate the intrepid explorer.

Why so difficult?

Field Marshal Helmuth Graf von Moltke—victor in the wars of German unification—had it right when, in *Instructions for Superior Commanders*, he wrote that "strategy is the application of common sense to the conduct of war. The difficulty lies in its execution . . ."[13] The elder Moltke was rephrasing the words of the master. Clausewitz advises that "everything in strategy is very simple, but that does not mean that everything is very easy."[14] Why should that be so? Five reasons can be suggested.

First, strategy is neither policy nor armed combat; rather it is the bridge between them. The strategist can be thwarted if the military wages the wrong war well or the right war badly. Neither experts in politics and policymaking nor experts in fighting need necessarily be experts in strategy. The strategist must relate military power (strategic effect) to the goals of policy. Absent a strategic brain—as was the case of the United States and NATO vis-à-vis Bosnia and Kosovo—one is left with an awkward alliance of hot air (policy statements) and bombardment possibilities (the world is my dartboard view of aerial strategists).[15] Strategy is difficult because, among other things, it is neither fish nor fowl. It is essentially different from military skill or political competence.

Second, strategy is perilously complex by its very nature. Every element or dimension can impact all others. The nature of strategy is constant throughout history but its character continually evolves with changes in technology, society, and political ideas. Success in strategy is not really about securing a privileged position in any one or more of its dimensions—such as technology, geography, or leadership—because it is always possible an enemy will find ways to compensate for that strategic effect from its special strengths. This is a major reason why information dominance in a technical-tactical sense cannot reliably deliver victory. Triumph in war does not correlate with superior technology nor mastery in any allegedly dominant dimension of conflict.

Third, it is extraordinarily difficult, perhaps impossible, to train strategists. Consider these words of Napoleon Bonaparte:

> Tactics, evolutions, artillery, and engineer sciences can be learned from manuals like geometry; but the knowledge of the higher conduct of war can only be acquired by studying the history of wars and the battles of great generals and by one's own experience. There are no terse and precise rules at all; everything depends on the character with which nature has endowed the general, on his eminent qualities, on his deficiencies, on the nature of the troops, the technics or arms, the season, and a thousand other circumstances which make things never look alike.[16]

Napoleon was in a position to know. Like Hannibal he was good at winning battles, but he failed catastrophically as a strategist. Like Imperial Germany, Nazi Germany, and the Soviet Union, Imperial France pursued political goals that were beyond its means. That is a failure in strategy.

Basic problems in training strategists can be reduced to the fact that no educational system puts in what nature leaves out, while the extraordinary competence shown by rising politicians or soldiers in their particular trades is not proof of an aptitude for strategy. The strategist has to be expert in using the threat or use of force for policy ends, not in thinking up desirable policy ends or in fighting skillfully.

Fourth, because strategy embraces all aspects of the military instrument (among others), as well as many elements of the policy and society it serves, the maximum possible number of things can go wrong. To illustrate, sources of friction that can impair strategic performance include those familiar to the military realm (incompatibilities among the levels of military activity and specialized functions such as operations, logistics, and weapons production) and, conceivably the most lethal of all, a mismatch between policy and military capabilities. In the world of strategists, as opposed to that of tacticians, there is simply much more scope for error.

Finally, it is critical to flag an underrecognized source of friction, the will, skill, and means of an intelligent and malevolent enemy. Andre Beaufre defines strategy as "the art of the dialectic of force or, more precisely, the art of the dialectic of two opposing wills using force to resolve their dispute."[17] Recall Clausewitz's dictum: "War is thus an act of force to compel our enemy to do our will."[18] Yet it is easier to theorize about new ways of prevailing than to speculate honestly and imaginatively about possible enemy initiatives and responses.

Further thoughts

There is a sense in which this article reinvents the wheel. It is no great achievement to appreciate that strategy is difficult to do well. Indeed, my point is not dissimilar from that made by Lawrence Freedman, who takes 433 pages in *The Evolution of Nuclear Strategy* to state that there is no truly strategic solution to the dilemmas of nuclear strategy.[19] When armchair strategists tell military practitioners that their task is difficult on the level of strategy, they should not expect much praise. After all, strategy does have to be done. Academics can vote undecided and write another book. Practicing strategists must make decisions regardless of the uncertainty.

Next, one must stress the strategic ignorance of even practical people. Clausewitz wrote:

> It might be thought that policy could make demands on war which war could not fulfill; but that hypothesis would challenge the natural and unavoidable assumption that policy knows the instrument it means to use.[20]

The challenge is that before undergoing trial by battle, no one really knows how effective military power will be. Every passage of arms remains unique. A capability that appears lethally effective in peacetime exercises will not translate automatically into a violent elixir to solve political issues. That the Armed Forces appear lethally potent against a conventional enemy in open warfare could prove irrelevant or worse in urban areas. In peacetime, militaries train against themselves, and that has to comprise a major source of uncertainty concerning future effectiveness.

It is vital to recognize potential tension in three sets of relationships: between politicians and commanders, between commanders and planners, and between commanders and theorists (recall Phormio's efforts to educate Hannibal). Military professionals must simplify, focus, decide, and execute. Politicians, by virtue of their craft, perceive or fear wide ramifications of action, prefer to fudge rather than focus, and like to keep their options open as long as possible by making the least decision as late as feasible. Although commanders are gripped by operational requirements, planners—especially if unschooled by real operational experience—are apt to live in an orderly world where a model of efficiency and compromise is acceptable, indeed is a driver.

The tension becomes acute when a soldier who is only a planner finds himself in a position of high command. The classic example is Dwight Eisenhower, a superb staff officer and military politician who lacked the experience and the aptitude for command, let alone supreme command.[21] As to the terrain between theorists and doers of strategy, the former are skilled in the production of complexity and are unlikely to enjoy the empathy for operational realities that makes strategic ideas readily useful. For example, the nuclear strategist might conceive of dozens of targeting options yet be unaware that his theory passed its "culminating point of victory"—actually its "culminating point of feasibility"—at a distinctly early stage. A President thoroughly uninterested in matters of nuclear strategy until suddenly confronted at dawn some Christmas with the necessity for choice can't likely cope intellectually, morally, politically, and strategically with many options. Probably he would find it useful to have alternatives: shall we go now, shall we go later, shall we go big, or shall we go small. But those broad binaries may be close to the limits of Presidential strategic thinking. Many strategists have presented seemingly clever briefings to policymakers and senior officers whose eyes crossed and brains locked at the sight of the third PowerPoint slide.

The many reasons why strategy is so difficult to do well can be subsumed with reference to three requirements. For strategic success:

- forces must be internally coherent, which is to say competently joint
- be of a quantity and provide a strategic effect scaled to the tasks set by high policy
- be employed coercively in pursuit of military objectives that fit political goals.

Competence cannot offset folly along the means–ends axis of strategy. Military history is littered with armies that won campaigns in the wrong wars.

Since the future is unforeseeable—do not put faith in the phrase "foreseeable future"—we must use only assets that can be trusted. Specifically, we plan to behave strategically in an uncertain future on the basis of three sources of practical advice: historical experience, the golden rule of prudence (we do not allow hopes to govern plans), and common sense. We can educate our common sense by reading history. But because the future has not happened, our expectations of it can only be guesswork. Historically guided guesswork should perform better than one that knows no yesterdays. Nonetheless, planning for the future, like deciding to fight, is always a gamble.

To conclude on a positive note, remember that to succeed in strategy you do not have to be distinguished or even particularly competent. All that is required is performing well enough to beat an enemy. You do not have to win elegantly; you just have to win.

Notes

1 J.F. Lazenby, *Hannibal's War: A History of the Second Punic War* (Warminster, UK: Aris and Phillips, 1978), p. 275.
2 Carl von Clausewitz, *On War*, edited and translated by Michael Howard and Peter Paret (Princeton: Princeton University Press, 1976), pp. 566–73. See also Antulio J. Echevarria II, "Clausewitz: Toward a Theory of Applied Strategy," *Defense Analysis*, vol. 11, no. 3 (December 1995), pp. 229–40.
3 Clausewitz, *On War*, p. 204; Antoine Henri de Jomini, *The Art of War* (London: Greenhill Books, 1992), p. 70.
4 This argument is the central theme of Colin S. Gray in *Modern Strategy* (Oxford: Oxford University Press, 1999).
5 Clausewitz, *On War*, pp. 119–21.
6 Samuel B. Griffith, *On Guerrilla Warfare* (New York: Praeger, 1961), p. 31.
7 Rudolf von Caemmerer, *The Development of Strategical Science During the Nineteenth Century*, translated by Karl von Donat (London: Hugh Rees, 1905), pp. 171–72.
8 Holger H. Herwig, *The First World War: Germany and Austria-Hungary, 1914–1918* (London: Arnold, 1997), pp. 96–106, is excellent.

9 Williamson Murray, "Does Military Culture Matter?" *Orbis*, vol. 43, no. 1 (Winter 1999), p. 37.

10 See Martin van Creveld, *Fighting Power: German and U.S. Army Performance, 1939–1945* (Westport, Conn.: Greenwood, 1982).

11 Clausewitz, *On War*, p. 128.

12 For lengthy musings, see Edward N. Luttwak, *Strategy: The Logic of War and Peace* (Cambridge: Harvard University Press, 1987). Luttwak argues that what works well today may not tomorrow exactly because it worked well today. Because Clausewitz insists war is essentially a duel, one may face an enemy capable of reacting creatively to one's moves and perhaps even anticipate them.

13 Caemmerer, *Strategical Science*, p. 276.

14 Clausewitz, *On War*, p. 178.

15 This is a fair reading of the underlying premise of airpower theory. See Giulio Douhet, *The Command of the Air*, translated by Dino Ferrari (New York: Arno Press, 1972), p. 50; and John A. Warden III, "Success in Modern War: A Response to Robert Pape's *Bombing to Win*," *Security Studies*, vol. 7, no. 2 (Winter 1997/98), pp. 174–85. To the air strategist targeting is strategy.

16 Caemmerer, *Strategical Science*, p. 275.

17 André Beaufre, *An Introduction to Strategy* (London: Faber and Faber, 1965), p. 22.

18 Clausewitz, *On War*, p. 75.

19 Lawrence Freedman, *The Evolution of Nuclear Strategy* (New York: St. Martin's Press, 1981), p. 433.

20 Clausewitz, *On War*, p. 75.

21 Dominick Graham and Shelford Bidwell, *Coalitions, Politicians and Generals: Some Aspects of Command in Two World Wars* (London: Brassey's, 1993), chapters 9–16, is pitilessly Anglo-Canadian in its critical view of Eisenhower as commander and serves as a partial corrective to the "patriotic" school of military history of the European campaign that finds undue favor among American writers such as Stephen E. Ambrose in *The Victors: Eisenhower and His Boys: The Men of World War II* (New York: Simon and Schuster, 1998).

22 The 'war on terror' in historical perspective

Adam Roberts

Today's international terrorism has assumed organisational forms and means of operating that are historically new. The shadowy entities labelled 'al-Qaeda' are different from earlier terrorist movements in the extremism of their aims, and in the far-flung, coordinated and ruthless character of their operations. No less novel is the contemporary US and international campaign against international terrorism. And yet, despite all the unprecedented aspects of this conflict, there are dangers in neglecting the history of terrorism and counter-terrorism. These dangers include the repetition of mistakes made in earlier eras.

President George W. Bush won the 2004 US presidential election partly on the basis of a clear line on terrorism. Despite its strengths and electoral appeal, the US doctrine on the 'war on terror' is vulnerable to the criticism that it takes too little account of the history of the subject. There is a need to articulate what might be called a British (or, more ambitiously, a European) perspective on terrorism and counter-terrorism – one that is more historically informed, encompassing certain elements distinctive from the US doctrine.

Defining 'terrorism'

The word 'terrorism', like many abstract political terms, is confusing, dangerous and indispensable. Confusing, because it means very different things to different people, and its meaning has also changed greatly over time. Dangerous, because it easily becomes an instrument of propaganda, and a means of avoiding thinking about the many forms and causes of political violence. Indispensable, because there is a real phenomenon out there that poses a serious threat. That threat, as indicated below, is especially to the societies from which it emanates.

'Terrorism' is used here mainly to refer to the systematic use of violence and threats of violence by non-state groups, designed to cause dislocation, consternation and submission on the part of a target population or government. This non-definitive definition is deliberately broad – essential if one is considering the history of terrorism over a long period.

The reference to non-state groups in this definition in no way excludes awareness that states, too, notoriously use terror – often systematically – and that states sometimes secretly sponsor non-state terrorist groups. Except where it has a bearing on the causes of, and action against, terrorist movements, such state terror is not a central focus of this essay. Most forms of terroristic state violence, whether against a state's own citizens or against foreigners, are prohibited in international law.

Attempts to define terrorism in recent years, especially since 2001, have reflected the fact that much contemporary terrorism is targeted against civilians. UN Security Council Resolution 1566 of 8 October 2004 comes close to a definition of terrorism when it refers to it as:

criminal acts, including against civilians, committed with the intent to cause death or serious bodily injury, or taking of hostages, with the purpose to provoke a state of terror in the general public or in a group of persons or particular persons, intimidate a population or compel a government or an international organisation to do or to abstain from doing any act, which constitute offences within the scope of and as defined in the international conventions and protocols relating to terrorism.

Similarly, the UN High-Level Panel on Threats, Challenges and Change, which issued its report in December 2004, focused on civilians in its suggested definition of terrorism:

any action, in addition to actions already specified by the existing conventions on aspects of terrorism, the Geneva Conventions and Security Council resolution 1566 (2004), that is intended to cause death or serious bodily harm to civilians or non-combatants, when the purpose of such an act, by its nature or context, is to intimidate a population, or to compel a Government or an international organization to do or to abstain from doing any act.[1]

These UN definitions may contain a basis for a formal international legal definition of terrorism. However, a limitation of both (and especially of the second) should be noted. The emphasis being quite largely on the threat to civilians or non-combatants, they might appear not to encompass certain acts such as attacks on armed peacekeeping forces, attacks on police or armed forces, or assassinations of heads of state or government. They might not include the attack on the Pentagon on 11 September 2001, but for the fact that it involved the hijacking of a civilian airliner.

There are traps in these or any other definitions of terrorism, and in the uses made of the term. The most serious is that the label 'terrorist' has sometimes been applied to the activities of movements which, even if they did resort to violence, had serious claims to political legitimacy, and also exercised care and restraint in their choice of methods. Famously, in 1987 and 1988 the UK and US governments labelled the African National Congress of South Africa 'terrorist': a shallow and silly attribution even at the time, let alone in light of Nelson Mandela's later emergence as statesman.

In certain circumstances, the repeated use of the term 'terrorist' to describe a particular class of adversaries can itself conceal key aspects of the political environment. In the 1960s many writers and journalists freely used the word 'terrorist' to describe a member of the Vietcong, the military arm of the National Liberation Front of South Vietnam. The Vietcong did undoubtedly use the weapon of terror ruthlessly and systematically against the South Vietnamese population. However, serious studies suggested that terror was not on its own an adequate basis of control: a sense of the moral justice of the cause was also present. The two factors were mutually reinforcing – and this helped to explain the capacity of the Vietcong to endure.[2]

What is perhaps easier to define than the grand abstraction of terrorism is *terrorist acts*. While still surrounded by a dense thicket of thorny problems, this term has the merit of keeping the focus on specific types of action. It encompasses certain violent acts that contravene national laws and, in some cases, specific international agreements on such matters as aerial hijacking. The term can also encompass acts that, in their targeting and manner of execution, contravene the basic principles of the laws of war. It is possible, at least sometimes, to draw a distinction between such acts and other types and forms of armed resistance.

Denial of history

Since 11 September 2001, statements by the principal Western leaders on the subject of the 'war on terror' have contained few references to the previous experience of governments in tackling terrorist threats, or to the ways in which certain international wars of the twentieth century were sparked off by concerns about terrorism. This appears to be true also of their inner deliberations, as revealed by Bob Woodward, Seymour Hersh and others. In particular, Woodward's *Plan of Attack* shows that there was little reference to historical precedents in the two years of decision-making leading up to the invasion of Iraq. An honourable exception occurred when Secretary of State Colin Powell, at a planning meeting on Iraq, asked sarcastically: 'Are we going to be off-loading at Gallipoli?'[3]

General Bernard Montgomery's first rule of warfare was 'Don't march on Moscow'.[4] Regarding terrorism and counter-terrorism there is no such straightforward rule. The history of these matters repays study, not because it offers a single recipe for action, but rather because it enriches our understanding of a peculiarly complex subject. It indicates a range of possibilities for addressing it, and a number of hazards to avoid. Historians are neither agreed nor infallible in addressing this subject, any more than are my own colleagues in the field of International Relations. A profession that encompasses both Professor Sir Michael Howard and Professor Bernard Lewis is not about to reach a unanimous party line on a subject as contentious as what to do about terrorism.

Yet it remains odd that since 2001 much writing on terror, particularly in the United States, has tended to neglect the long history of terrorism and counter-terrorism. This is true even of historians and historically informed writers: some, such as John Gaddis and Walter Mead, have written books about the war on terror that contain much important insight into US history and the US role in the world, but say almost nothing about the history of terror and counter-terror.[5] On the other hand, since 2001 there has been a good deal of writing touching on the history of these matters. A few works have covered only the last few decades.[6] Some works, however, have taken into account experiences of terrorism and counter-terrorism from the nineteenth to the twenty-first centuries – an excellent example being the work of Michael Ignatieff.[7]

In practice, the response of each country to the 'war on terror' has been deeply influenced by its own particular experience of terrorism and counter-terrorism. In the United Kingdom there has been frequent reference to the experience of countering terrorism in Northern Ireland. British ministers and officials, however, refrained from pointing out bluntly, and in public, that almost everything about the language and manner in which terror in Northern Ireland has been opposed, and about the attempts at underwriting its end through mediation and even negotiation, has been very different from the US approach to the 'war on terror'. Partly, of course, this is because the problems faced have been different: the IRA is far removed from al-Qaeda in ideology, in political goals and in methods. Yet the British may have been too reticent about their experience of terrorism.

The tendency to approach terrorism without benefit of history has, itself, a long history. Political debates about terrorism have perennially been ahistorical. Both terrorists and their adversaries tend to talk and write publicly about their campaigns with little reference to the centuries-long history of terrorism and counter-terrorism. This is not to say that they do not articulate a view of history more generally. Terrorists, for example, often focus on deep resentments based on perceptions of alien domination of the societies they claim to defend. When terrorists have put pen to paper, either at the time of their activism or subsequently, they have sometimes shown considerable awareness of international developments and the history of their own and earlier epochs.[8] At the same time, the long and tangled history of both terrorism and counter-terrorism is frequently airbrushed out of the picture. The publicly articulated world-view of terrorists and their adversaries is often a world of moral and political absolutes, in which terrorism, or the war against it, is seen as an essentially new means of ridding the world of a unique and evil scourge. On both sides, the favoured form of argument is phrased in terms of morality – and a relatively simple morality at that, in which the adversary's actions are seen as such a serious threat as to create an overwhelming necessity for the use of counter-violence.

Many specialists in counter-insurgency have seen their subject more as a struggle of light versus darkness than as a common and recurrent theme of history. A fine example of such an ahistorical approach to the subject is the French group of theorists writing in the 1950s and early 1960s about *guerre révolutionnaire*. These theorists denied the complexities—especially the mixture of material, moral and ideological factors—that are keys to understanding why and how terrorist movements come into existence. Colonel Lacheroy, a leading figure in this group and head of the French Army's *Service d' Action Psychologique*, famously stated: 'In the beginning there is nothing.'[9] Terrorism was seen as having been introduced deliberately into a peaceful society by an omnipresent outside force – namely International Communism. It is a demonological vision of a cosmic struggle in which the actual history of particular countries and ways of thinking has little or no place. These French theories – no doubt because they date from a period of failed military campaigns, attempted military *coups d'état*, systematic use of torture against insurgents, and a generally disastrous period in French history – are now almost entirely forgotten, even in France itself. They are also ignored in the United States, even though they, and the events with which they are connected, provide object-lessons in how not to conduct a counter-terrorist campaign.

If terrorists and counter-terrorists have often forgotten history, history has not entirely forgotten them. Many historians have written subtly and interestingly about the evolution of terrorism (which, like so much else, has significant European as well as extra-European origins), about its ever-changing philosophy, about its sociology and its consequences. Those historians who have combined historical analysis of terrorism with advocacy have tended to favour a tough line against terrorism, but biased more towards a strong police response than towards military interventions.[10]

In present circumstances there are powerful reasons to buttress the claim that the threat faced is totally new, and needs to be tackled in new ways. Today's terrorist incidents can involve a combination of elements, many of which are new: elaborate planning carried out far from the location of the attack; a suicide mission; an assault on a nuclear-armed power; the destruction of major buildings; and the killing of hundreds or even thousands of people, usually civilians. Such an attack may be on behalf of a movement many of whose demands are probably unachievable and certainly non-negotiable. Something new is undoubtedly happening, whether at the World Trade Center in Manhattan or at Beslan in North Ossetia. The difference between the scale of carnage now and what resulted from earlier phases of terrorism brings to mind the grim biblical statement that is inscribed on the Machine Gun Corps monument in London:

Saul hath slain his thousands
but David his tens of thousands.[11]

So sharp is the distinction from earlier eras that, from today's grim perspective, it would be easy to implore earlier terrorists: 'Come back: all is forgiven.' Former terrorists themselves, in the manner of old soldiers, have often deplored the terrible things that later generations of terrorists did, and the impurity of their motivations.[12] Because the changes have been so great, it would also be easy to brush aside earlier historical experience of terrorism on the grounds of diminished relevance – and this indeed appears to have happened in much contemporary analysis. It is a huge mistake.

Eight propositions based on earlier campaigns

At the risk of over-simplification, the following eight propositions can be drawn from the long history of terrorism, and action against it. These propositions all have a bearing on the conduct of, and language regarding, today's international campaign against terrorism.

1. Terrorist action often has unintended consequences

Most terrorist movements and individuals have notions of change with two main strands. Firstly, a spectacular act of violence will transform the political landscape, particularly by mobilising and radicalising the dormant masses. Secondly, a long terrorist campaign will wear down the adversary, leading to demoralisation, doubt and withdrawal. These are the terrorist equivalents of blitzkrieg and war of attrition.

Such movements have arisen in response to autocratic regimes, and (even in democracies) to one part of a population's dominance over another. They have also frequently arisen in response to foreign occupation. The common thread in the growth of suicide bombing since the attack on the US Embassy in Beirut in 1983 is not just religious extremism but the presence of foreign military occupation. As Robert Pape has written:

> the close association between foreign military occupations and the growth of suicide terrorist movements in the occupied regions should give pause to those who favor solutions that involve conquering countries in order to transform their political systems.[13]

There is no doubt that some terrorist campaigns have achieved significant objectives. Certain temporary international presences have proved vulnerable to terrorist campaigns, including especially those of over-stretched colonial powers, and, more recently, of international bodies such as the United Nations. The one sure consequence of a sustained terrorist campaign in a particular area is that it is bad for tourism – especially when, as has happened in several attacks in this past decade, from Egypt to Indonesia, it is the tourists themselves who are targets. Yet only rarely has the discouragement of tourism been the principal goal of a terrorist movement.

Other consequences of terrorist campaigns are much more unpredictable. For example, political assassinations have very seldom had the effects for which terrorists hoped, and more often have led to a strengthening of the regime against which they were fighting. An exhaustive study concentrating particularly on the effects of 56 assassinations of heads of government or state in the period 1919–68 concluded: 'We are dismayed by the high incidence of assassination indicated by our collected data ... We are also surprised by the fact that the impact of any single assassination, even of a chief executive or dictator, normally tends to be low.'[14]

Sometimes terrorist actions lead to major consequences that are different from what the terrorists anticipated. They may lead to vigorous political or military campaigns against the terrorists, and even to the outbreak of international wars, as in Europe in 1914. According to a friend who was close to him, Gavril Princip, the 19-year-old Bosnian Serb student who killed Archduke Ferdinand in Sarajevo in June 1914, had no idea that the result of the assassination would be war, let alone world war.[15]

In some cases terrorist action has been so callous that it has aroused antagonism even among the population that has some sympathy with, even involvement in, the terrorist cause. For example, in August 1949, when Communist terrorists in the Philippines murdered the popular widow of President Quezon, for the first time there was widespread popular wrath against the insurgents.[16] Such actions can contribute to the isolation of terrorist groups. Indeed, the terrorist dream of awakening the masses through their actions has almost never worked in the way in which terrorists have perennially hoped.

A terrorist leader may seek to provoke a repressive response from the adversary's regime, thus exposing its supposedly true nature – the iron fist inside the velvet glove. As Lawrence Durrell wrote in *Bitter Lemons*, his rich and subtle account of the Eoka insurgency in Cyprus:

> his primary objective is not battle. It is to bring down upon the community in general a reprisal for his wrongs, in the hope that the fury and resentment roused by punishment meted out to the innocent will gradually swell the ranks of those from whom he will draw further recruits.[17]

In some cases an aim may be to provoke not just government repression, but foreign military intervention. The possibility that these may be prime terrorist aims confirms the need for caution in crafting a counter-terrorist policy.

2. *Terrorism's endemic character*

One of the most pernicious aspects of terrorism is its capacity to become endemic in particular regions, cultures and societies. Because of its unofficial and clandestine character, and because of the extreme bitterness it engenders within and between communities, it easily becomes a habit. The experience of terrorism suggests that, after it has been taken up in one cause, it is adopted by others, and by splinter-groups, and how difficult it is to reach a definitive end to terrorist activities. Started by the Right, it gets taken up by the Left, or vice versa. Started by nationalists, it may get taken up by so-called religious fundamentalists. Started by the Stern Gang, it gets taken up by the PLO. Started by the high-minded, it gets taken up by criminals, drug-smugglers and mafiosi. Moreover, it can be difficult to call off terrorist struggles. A hard-core splinter group within a movement may refuse all compromise; and may be able to continue the struggle because the decentralised nature of terrorist organisation and action makes that easy.

This view of terrorism as damaging to the societies in which it takes place is confirmed by the history of the Middle East, Latin America, the Balkans and Ireland over the past two centuries. It forms an important buttress to moral condemnations of terrorism. An understanding of its destructive character within the societies that produce terrorist movements – which are of course the very societies that they purport to save – provides a better basis for securing international action against terrorism than do certain views of terrorism that focus on it as a threat principally to the democratic states of the West, or indeed to the United States in particular.

3. Capacity of counter-terrorism to achieve results

Contrary to myth, counter-terrorist activities and policies can sometimes succeed – at least in the sense of contributing to a reduction or ending of the activities of terrorists without yielding power to them. For example, the forces opposed to terrorists were successful in this sense in the long-running Malayan 'emergency' that began in 1948; in the Philippines at the same time; and against the 'Red Brigades' that were active in Italy and Germany in the early 1970s. Arguably, they have had a measure of success in Northern Ireland since 1969.

Perhaps 95% of the important action in any campaign against terrorism consists of intelligence and police work: identifying suspects, infiltrating movements, collaborating with police forces in other countries, gathering evidence for trials and so on. This underlying truth is far from denied by President Bush or other leading figures involved in the 'war on terror'. However, their rhetoric, being much more that of open war and of victory, has sometimes obscured this basic fact.

4. Need to address underlying grievances

While there is no simple formula for how terrorism can be undermined or defeated, the process often, perhaps even generally, requires action that is sensitive to the political environment. Where counter-terrorist strategies have succeeded, success has often been in combination with a political package that either responded to certain terrorist demands while rejecting others, or undercut the terrorists by reducing their pool of political support, or both. In Malaya, for example, the promise, and the actuality, of unqualified national independence was crucial to containing the terrorist threat.

Apropos the 'war on terror', John Gaddis has reminded us that during the Cold War it was perfectly well accepted that there was a need to address social issues on which Communist propaganda played:

> With the rehabilitation of Germany and Japan after World War II, together with the Marshall Plan, we fought the conditions that made the Soviet alternative attractive even as we sought to contain the Soviets themselves.[18]

It is sometimes suggested that making changes that respond in some way to terrorist demands constitutes appeasement, or at least implies recognition that a campaign of terrorism is justified. Such a suggestion is flawed. To say that a movement responds to real grievances – as for example over Palestine – is not to say that it is justified in resorting to terror, but it is to say that the terrorist movement reflects larger concerns in society that need to be addressed in some way. The exact way in which they are addressed may not be the way the movement is demanding. To refuse all changes on an issue because a terrorist movement has embraced that issue is actually to allow terrorists to dictate the political agenda.

5. Respect for a legal framework

Respect for law has been an important element in many operations against terrorists. One of the key figures involved in the Malayan campaign in the 1950s, Sir Robert Thompson, distilling five basic principles of counter-insurgency from this and other cases, wrote of the crucial importance of operating within a properly functioning domestic legal framework:

The government must function in accordance with law.

There is a very strong temptation in dealing both with terrorism and with guerrilla actions for government forces to act outside the law, the excuses being that the processes of law are too cumbersome, that the normal safeguards in the law for the individual are not designed for an insurgency and that a terrorist deserves to be treated as an outlaw anyway. Not only is this morally wrong, but, over a period, it will create more practical difficulties for a government than it solves.[19]

It is not only national legal standards that are important, but also international standards, including those embodied in the laws of war. A perception that the states involved in a coalition are observing basic international standards may contribute to public support for military operations within the member states; support (or at least tacit consent) from other states for coalition operations; and avoidance of disputes within and between coalition member states. In short, there can be strong prudential considerations (not necessarily dependent on reciprocity in observance of the law by all the parties to a war) that militate in favour of observing the laws of war.

There are some well-known difficulties in applying the laws of war to terrorist and counter-terrorist activities. Most terrorists do not conform to the well-known requirements for the status of lawful belligerent, entitled to full prisoner-of-war status. Further, few states could accept application of the law if it meant that all terrorists were deemed to be legitimate belligerents on a par with the regular uniformed forces of a government. However, application of the law does not require acceptance of either of these doubtful propositions. Rather it means recognition that, even in a war against ruthless terrorists, the observance of certain restraints may be legally obligatory and politically desirable – especially as regards treatment of detainees. Understandable doubt over the formal applicability of some provisions of existing law should not be turned into a licence to flout basic norms.[20]

6. Treatment of detainees

The treatment of detainees is an issue of crucial importance in the history of terrorism and counter-terrorism. Indeed, the defining moment in the birth of modern terrorism was an event in Russia in 1878 in response to the flogging of a political prisoner. This was what led a young woman, Vera Zasulich, to shoot and seriously wound General Trepov, the Police Chief of St Petersburg, who had had the prisoner flogged.[21] Walter Laqueur has said of this event: 'Only in 1878, after Vera Zasulich's shooting of General Trepov, the governor of the Russian capital, did terrorism as a doctrine, the Russian version of "propaganda by the deed", finally emerge.'[22] Likewise, torture meted out in Egyptian jails from Nasser's time onwards has often been cited as part of the explanation for the emergence of radical purportedly Islamic terrorism.

When fighting an unseen and vicious enemy, who may have many secret sympathisers, all societies encounter difficulties. In such circumstances, most states, even democratic ones, resort to some form of detention without trial. There are huge risks in such detentions. Firstly, a risk of arresting and convicting the wrong people; and secondly, maltreatment of detainees. Both tend to create martyrs and to give nourishment to the terrorist campaign.

The United Kingdom's long engagement against terrorism in Northern Ireland affords ample evidence for both these propositions, and it also points in the direction of a possible solution. This was one of many conflicts in which those deemed to be 'terrorists' were aware of the value, including propaganda value, of making claims to PoW status and publicising claims of ill-treatment. While denying that there was an armed conflict whether international or otherwise, and strongly resisting any granting of PoW status to detainees and convicted prisoners, the UK did slowly come to accept that they had a distinct status, and that international standards had to apply to their treatment. After initially using methods that were legally questionable and highly controversial, the UK used a different approach, in effect applying basic legal principles derived from the laws of war. This helped in the long and difficult process of taking some of the political sting out of the emotionally charged issue of treatment of detainees.[23]

The treatment of detainees and prisoners has been one of the major failures of the 'war on terror' ever since it began in late 2001. In January 2002 US Secretary of Defense Donald Rumsfeld infamously said of the prisoners in Guantanamo, 'I do not feel even the slightest concern over their treatment. They are being treated vastly better than they treated anybody else over the last several years and vastly better than was their circumstance when they were found.'[24] Needless to say, this and similar remarks were widely broadcast on radio and TV stations critical of the United States. The episodes of maltreatment and torture in Iraq since April 2003 have reinforced the damage. Those who suggest that humane treatment is a relatively unimportant issue – and those far fewer individuals who argue that torturing prisoners is a way to combat terrorism – do need to address the criticism that ill-treatment and torture have in the past provided purported justifications for the resort to terrorism, and also discredited the anti-terrorist cause.

7. Evil vs error

In the history of both terrorism and counter-terrorism there has long been a temptation to depict the adversary as evil. In terrorist movements, many otherwise decent and serious individuals have been seduced by the simple and attractive notion of the power of the deed: that a cleansing act of violence can rid the world of uniquely evil forces.

In counter-terrorist operations, the depiction of the adversary as evil, while it may faithfully reflect understandable feelings in a society under terrorist assault, poses severe practical problems. One hazard of treating terrorism as a problem of evil is that many people in the population from whom the terrorists come will know that such an explanation is too simple. They will have a broader idea of the mixture of characteristic traits that can make a terrorist: idealism, self-sacrifice, naiveté, hope, despair, ignorance, short-sightedness, thuggishness, hatred, sadism, cleverness and stupidity. The population may have sympathy with the cause for which the terrorists stand but not with the method. If the terrorist group is described as simply 'evil', the population will therefore be further alienated from the anti-terrorist cause, which they will see as depending on a caricature that they do not recognise.

In the struggle against terrorism, it may be most useful to conceive of terrorism as a problem, not so much of extreme evil (although it may be that), but rather of dangerously wrong conduct and ideas. The difference in approach – the view of terrorism more as a dangerous idea and as morally reprehensible than as absolute evil – has significant implications for how terrorist campaigns may be opposed, and how they may end.[25]

8. Similarities between terrorists and some of their opponents

A student of the history of terrorism cannot help being struck by certain similarities between terrorists and at least some of their opponents. Both share not only a vision of the world as a struggle of good versus evil, but also a belief that particular new weapons and tactics now give an opportunity to strike directly at the heart of the adversary's power. Russian terrorists in the nineteenth century believed that their new and quite accurate weapons – the pistol, the rifle and the bomb – could enable them to attack the source of all evil (namely the Tsar) directly and with limited side-effects.[26]

The similarity between so-called terrorists and their adversaries was noted by Régis Debray in his little-known novel *Undesirable Alien*. In this remarkably unsentimental view of his fellow revolutionaries in Latin America, he mocks his comrades in the struggle for having a taste for cowboy films, and suggests that red revolutionaries may be propounding nothing more than the ideology of the American western.[27] Sadly, events have moved on since then, and it is the Hollywood disaster movie that is emulated by Osama bin Laden and his colleagues.[28] The general philosophy of radical Islam also has Californian roots due to the presence there in the 1950s of its founding father, Sayyid Qutb.[29]

In the 'war on terror', a vision of clean and well-targeted war against dictatorial regimes has informed much US policymaking. As George W. Bush put it in his infamous (because premature) 'Mission Accomplished' speech on 1 May 2003:

> In the images of falling statues, we have witnessed the arrival of a new era. For a hundred of years of war, culminating in the nuclear age, military technology was designed and deployed to inflict casualties on an ever-growing scale. In defeating Nazi Germany and Imperial Japan, Allied forces destroyed entire cities, while enemy leaders who started the conflict were safe until the final days. Military power was used to end a regime by breaking a nation.
>
> Today, we have the greater power to free a nation by breaking a dangerous and aggressive regime. With new tactics and precision weapons, we can achieve military objectives without directing violence against civilians. No device of man can remove the tragedy from war; yet it is a great moral advance when the guilty have far more to fear from war than the innocent.[30]

This vision of the 2003 Iraq war as a more or less clinical excision of an evil regime looks to have been a desert mirage – just as many terrorist visions of achieving change through violence have also led to disappointment.

The 'war on terror'

The major pronouncements of what has been variously termed in official US speeches the 'war against terrorism' and the 'war on terror' have been self-consciously historic in character; they have enunciated historically novel and ambitious goals, but have contained only limited reference to the history of terrorism and counter-terrorism. In his address to Congress nine days after the destruction of the Twin Towers in New York, President Bush stated:

> Our war on terror begins with al Qaeda, but it does not end there. It will not end until every terrorist group of global reach has been found, stopped and defeated . . .
>
> Americans are asking: 'How will we fight and win this war?' We will direct every resource at our command – every means of diplomacy, every tool of intelligence, every instrument of law enforcement, every financial influence, and every necessary weapon of war – to the disruption and to the defeat of the global terror network.[31]

At the end of September 2001 President Bush added, in a radio address:

our war on terror will be much broader than the battlefields and beachheads of the past. This war will be fought wherever terrorists hide, or run, or plan. Some victories will be won outside of public view, in tragedies avoided and threats eliminated. Other victories will be clear to all.[32]

The term 'war' is not being used here in a purely rhetorical sense, as in the 'war on drugs' or 'war on poverty'. It has such a rhetorical side, but is being used to describe a notably broad and multi-faceted overall campaign of a type that is essentially new, and that includes major military operations (starting with Afghanistan) as one important aspect. In respect of both aspects of the war – the visible and the invisible – what is sought is 'victory'.

The most important subsequent articulation of the 'war on terror' was the February 2003 White House document, *National Strategy for Combating Terrorism*. This began by emphasising the unique nature of the current threat:

> The struggle against international terrorism is different from any other war in our history. We will not triumph solely or even primarily through military might. We must fight terrorist networks, and all those who support their efforts to spread fear around the world, using every instrument of national power – diplomatic, economic, law enforcement, financial, information, intelligence, and military.[33]

The oft-repeated claim of uniqueness has provided a justification for much of the rhetoric and strategic direction of the 'war on terror', and has provided, too, an implied justification for making little more than ritual reference to earlier history. However, the February 2003 document did contain at least a nod to history: 'Americans know that terrorism did not begin on 11 September 2001'. It continued: 'For decades, the United States and our friends abroad have waged the long struggle against the terrorist menace. We have learned much from these efforts.' In particular, past successes in destroying or neutralising various movements that had been active in the 1970s and 1980s 'provide valuable lessons for the future'.[34] However, the document was unclear about exactly what terrorist movements were being referred to, and about what lessons had been learned.

Subsequent articulations of US doctrine offered little further reference to the history of terrorism and counter-terrorism. The most extraordinary omission in most US statements in the 'war on terror' is the lack of reference to the existing US counter-insurgency doctrine, and the reluctance to embrace it even when faced with an insurgency in Iraq. By contrast, the UK military view tends to be that counter-insurgency doctrine is a principal basis of addressing terror.

Can military interventions be effective against terrorism?

In countries faced with terrorist attacks, there are often strong reasons for attacking terrorism at what is seen as its source. A state that allows terrorists to organise on its territory to wage operations elsewhere is naturally the object of suspicion, and may well be thought to deserve whatever it gets. Yet in the 'war on terror' the question of military intervention proved extremely divisive.

Counter-terrorist operations, when taking the form of open war and a conventional military response, have often led to tragedy. The First World War began when the assassination of Archduke Ferdinand in Sarajevo in June 1914 by a young Serbian nationalist led to an Austrian determination to root out the 'hornet's nest' that was Serbia. Similarly, Israel's disastrous intervention in Lebanon in 1982 was explicitly a response to a persistent and intense pattern of terrorist attacks on Israeli and Jewish targets not only in Israel but also internationally.

It is not surprising, therefore, that historians have generally been sceptical about waging war as a response to terrorist acts. However, they tend to be admirably discriminate: more sceptical than dogmatic. Two or three months after 11 September, the American historian Paul Schroeder wrote:

> Three lessons emerge from reasoning by historical analogy from the early summer of 1914 to the late summer of 2001. The first is that a great power must avoid giving terrorists the war they want, but that the great power does not want. The second is that a great power must reckon the effects of its actions not only on its immediate circum-stances, but also with regard to the larger structure of international politics in which it clearly has a significant stake. The third is that a great power must beware the risks of victory as well as the dangers of defeat. If it is not careful and wise, the United States could find itself enmeshed even deeper in the Middle East and Southwest Asia than it is today, and risk generating greater prospective dangers in the process of containing smaller near-term ones.[35]

He drew a crucial distinction between Afghanistan, where the war had a legitimate objective and was widely understood internationally, and other possible target countries, including Iraq.[36] Within 18 months of this warning, the United States was deeply involved in Iraq in exactly the way he had feared, with no prospect of an early exit. He was right that the two cases, and the nature of the US involvements in them, were very different, both in the justifiability of the intervention and in the consequences that followed.

Afghanistan: war and its aftermath

The first major engagement of the 'war on terror', *Operation Enduring Freedom*, which encompassed the US-led coalition military operations in and around Afghanistan that began on 7 October 2001, was widely viewed as a justifiable use of force – a term greatly preferable to the more familiar term 'just war'. It had a great deal of diplomatic support, and received significant legitimation from resolutions passed at the United Nations.[37] There appeared to be no other means of stopping the activities of al-Qaeda, protected as they were by the Taliban regime. The war did result in a victory – at least of sorts. By the end of the year, the Taliban regime had gone, replaced by the Afghan Interim Authority, and then in June by the Afghan Transitional Government. In the course of 2002 a total of 1.8 million Afghans, 1.5m of whom had come from Pakistan, resettled in Afghanistan. Although the return of refugees was not the main objective of the campaign – and the capture of the main al-Qaeda leaders, which was an objective, was *not* achieved – this huge refugee return was evidence that the 'war on terror' could achieve at least some positive effects, by helping to depose a reactionary, oppressive and thoroughly dangerous regime. The remarkably successful presidential election on 9 October 2004 provided a further small sign of progress in post-war Afghanistan.

On the first day of the US bombing campaign in Afghanistan, Donald Rumsfeld said of the Taliban: 'Ultimately they're going to collapse from within. That is what will constitute victory.'[38] That is what happened in November and December 2001. Some were critical of the fact that the main achievement was regime change. Richard Clarke, the White House counter-terrorism specialist, criticised the otherwise successful handling of the Afghan war on the grounds that 'we treated the war as a regime change rather than as a search-and-destroy against terrorists'.[39]

Three unique facts enabled the Afghan campaign to succeed. Firstly, the Taliban regime was weak both within Afghanistan and internationally. Secondly, the fanatical character of the bombing of the World Trade Center, and the persuasive evidence of links to Afghanistan, contributed to the Taliban's loss of allies, especially Pakistan, and also meant that the world accepted the legitimate element of self-defence in the US-led campaign. Thirdly, the role on the ground of the US-supported forces of the Northern Alliance enabled the US-led bombing campaign to be effective rather than merely punitive, and then provided a basis for post-war administration.

In respect of Afghanistan some historians doubted whether any positive result could be achieved in the US-led campaign in late 2001. They could and in some cases did point out, very reasonably, that Afghanistan is not a country in which foreign armed forces have ever had a happy time; that there is good reason to be cautious about the prospects of changing Afghanistan's violent political culture; and that there are problems in waging a bombing campaign against so devious and elusive a target as a terrorist movement.

Sir Michael Howard, former Regius Professor of History at Oxford, criticised the Afghan war during its opening phase, when its main aspect was bombing rather than support for ground forces. In a lecture in London on 30 October 2001 (and subsequently published in *Foreign Affairs*), he said that it would be 'like trying to eradicate cancer cells with a blow-torch'.[40] Three months later, in a thoughtful reappraisal, he said: 'I got it wrong, and I apologize.'[41] Yet in a broader sense he did not get it entirely wrong. Despite the achievement of results in Afghanistan, historians have good reasons to be sceptical about the efficacy of military interventions as a response to terrorist campaigns. Howard's vivid image of hazardous use of the blow-torch may fit other cases, including Iraq since 2003, better than it fitted Afghanistan.

Iraq: war and its aftermath

The Iraq war of 2003 provides a very different context for exploring the question of whether invasion of states believed to assist terrorism is an effective way to achieve the aims of a counter-terrorist policy. The rhetoric of the 'war on terror', with its emphasis on open war, may be part of the explanation of the US-led assault on Iraq in 2003. In his television address of 17 March 2003 presenting Saddam Hussein with an ultimatum to get out of Iraq within 48 hours, President Bush included the statement that Iraq had 'aided, trained and harbored terrorists, including operatives of al-Qaeda'.[42] Yet in reality Iraq's links to al-Qaeda up to March 2003 appear to have been very limited. There were some Iraqi connections with terrorists, especially those involved in the Arab-Israel conflict, but Iraq does not appear to have had any significant part in the ruthless campaign of international terrorist attacks for which al-Qaeda had been seen as responsible. Within the US government, there was already in early 2003 some official awareness that the accusation of the link between Iraq and al-Qaeda was weak. When on 20 March 2003 the US government gave to the UN Security Council a letter containing its justification for attacking Iraq, the letter dealt exclusively with Iraq's non-compliance with a range of UN Security Council resolutions on weapons issues. Terrorism was not even mentioned.[43]

Against this background, it is peculiar that the US government called the war in Iraq part of the 'war on terror', and issued medals for both the Afghanistan and Iraq campaigns which are called 'the Global War on Terrorism Expeditionary Medal' (for those who served in Afghanistan or Iraq) and 'the Global War on Terrorism Service Medal' (for those whose service was elsewhere). Naturally, critics objected that the administration was 'subtly using the single campaign medal to buttress its contention that the war in Iraq was undertaken as part of the worldwide battle against al Qaeda and other Islamic extremists'.[44]

Overall, the Iraq war has probably done more harm than good to the US and UK efforts to combat terrorism. The principal criticisms of the use of force in Iraq are that certain of the stated grounds for going to war (especially violations of the UN resolutions on disarmament) have proved to be weak; that the planning for the aftermath of war was so feeble; that the results of the war have proved so violent; and that a perception has arisen that Western countries seek to force Muslim populations into a single, externally imposed political template, a perception that damages attempts at coalition-building.[45] Historians were right to warn, as Michael Howard did in interviews in March 2003, that Iraq might be easy to defeat in a military campaign, but would be difficult to occupy and administer. At least in terms of the struggle against terrorism the results so far of the Iraq war appear to be distressingly negative. There is much force in the criticism of Robert Tucker and David Hendrickson:

> The pattern of the first Iraq war, in which an overwhelming victory set aside the reservations of most sceptics, has failed to emerge in the aftermath of the second. If anything, scepticism has deepened.[46]

The presence and role of foreign (mainly US) armed forces in Iraq is cited as justification for terrorist bombings, kidnappings and executions there, and also in other countries. Critics seized on this point. As Richard Clarke argued, Bush 'launched an unnecessary and costly war in Iraq that strengthened the fundamentalist, radical Islamic terrorist movement worldwide'.[47]

There are, to be sure, grounds for questioning the generally negative picture of the results of the Iraq war. Within Iraq, the removal from office of Saddam Hussein was widely welcomed, and some still retain the hope that a stable democratic order can emerge slowly from the twisted wreckage of his brutal regime. The elections in January 2005, with participation of close of 60% of those entitled to vote, strengthened hopes that something could be salvaged from the country's disasters. Outside Iraq, the war may have helped to induce an element of prudence in the conduct of policy of some governments.

One possible case is Libya. In December 2003 Colonel Gadhafi made his decision to bring Libya in from the cold, confirming his renunciation both of terrorism and of ambitions to develop nuclear weapons. Whether his decision owed anything to the Iraq war is debated. Although the process which bore fruit in December had begun long before the initiation of hostilities in Iraq in March 2003, it is possible that seeing a fellow Arab leader unceremoniously deposed may have helped to concentrate Gadhafi's mind. At the very least the Iraq War did not foreclose a highly significant policy development in Libya.

UK and US doctrine on military intervention

Iraq suggests a need to revisit the argument that attack is the best form of defence – an argument that had been expressed in two key documents of the 'war on terror', both issued in 2002. The UK *Strategic Defence Review: A New Chapter* says: 'Experience shows that it is better where possible, to engage an enemy at longer range, before they get the opportunity to mount an assault on the UK.'[48] *The National Security Strategy of the United States* commits the

United States to attack terrorist organisations by 'convincing or compelling states to accept their sovereign responsibilities'.[49] The implication here is that if states won't get rid of terrorists on their soil, the United States will do it for them. The argument is buttressed by the more fundamental ideas that lack of democracy is a principal cause of terrorism, and that a forcible intervention could lead to the growth of a stable democratic system.

In addition to the questions about the circumstances in which democracy can be imposed from outside, there are three serious grounds of criticism of the proposition that terrorism should be attacked at source rather than warded off defensively.

Firstly, *it is a false choice*. However desirable it may be to engage the enemy at longer range, there is no substitute for defensive anti-terrorist and counter-terrorist activities. Granted the imperfections of intelligence, the multiplicity of possible sources of attack and the hazards of taking military action against sovereign states, it may not always be possible, or sensible, to attack terrorism at source. Meanwhile, much can be done at home to reduce the risk of terrorist attack. The astonishing casualness of US airport security before 11 September 2001 illustrates the point.

Secondly, *the history of counter-terrorist operations suggests no such simple conclusion*. True, some counter-terrorist operations have involved military action in states perceived to be the sources of, or providers of support to, terrorist movements. However, by no means have all been successful. Furthermore, many counter-terrorist campaigns have been effectively conducted with only limited capacity to engage the enemy at longer range. For example, the UK and Malayan governments had to engage in the long struggle against terrorism without attacking the People's Republic of China, despite the fact that the PRC was aiding and abetting the communist terrorist movement in Malaya from 1949 onwards. Similarly, the UK government had to deal with terrorism in Northern Ireland without resorting to military action in the Republic of Ireland, despite claims that the Provisional IRA was deriving benefit from resources and support there – not to mention from communities in the United States.

Thirdly, *it is a recipe for a revival of imperialism*. Military intervention in states in order to eliminate the sources of terrorism must inevitably mean, in many cases, exercising external domination for a period of decades. This was the pattern of much European colonialism in the nineteenth century, including in Egypt. By a perverse paradox, external control, intended to stop terrorism in its tracks, frequently has the effect of provoking it and providing a ready-made justification for it.

Paul Schroeder has argued persuasively that the United States can legitimately and sensibly aim to exercise hegemony, but it is ill-advised to lunge, on the basis of blinkered historical ignorance, into the mirage of empire. His conclusion is that America's leaders, because they are ignorant of the past, are actually stumbling backwards into it:

> What they are now attempting therefore is not a bold, untried American experiment in creating a brave new world, but a revival of a type of nineteenth and early-twentieth century imperialism that could succeed for a time then (with ultimately devastating consequences) only because of conditions long since vanished and now impossible to imagine reproducing. Launched now, this venture will fail and is already failing. Its advocates illustrate the dictum that those unwilling to learn from history are doomed to repeat it.[50]

Any assessment of the US and UK doctrines of intervention in response to terrorism has to differentiate between cases. On both legal and prudential grounds, there was a stronger case for intervention in Afghanistan than in Iraq. In particular, there was a real chance of reducing by such means Afghanistan's involvement in terrorism. An assessment must also be provisional, as eventual outcomes will necessarily affect judgements of the interventions. However, what is clear is that there was a curious and historically uninformed optimism about the Iraq venture, which led to a lack of planning for those traditional consequences of distant empires – military occupation and counter-insurgency. Furthermore, the debate about intervention needs to be set in a larger context of an understanding of how terrorist campaigns end.

How do terrorist campaigns end?

The advocates of the 'war on terror' offer a limited vision of how the war might end. The focus is more on victory than other visions of possible endings, but it is victory of a special kind. Some elements of it were outlined in the White House *National Security Strategy* document of September 2002;[51] and they were further elaborated in the White House doctrinal statement of February 2003:

> Victory against terrorism will not occur as a single, defining moment. It will not be marked by the likes of the surrender ceremony on the deck of the USS Missouri that ended World War II. However, through the sustained effort to compress the scope and capability of terrorist organizations, isolate them regionally, and destroy them within state borders, the United States and its friends and allies will secure a world in which our children can live free from fear and where the threat of terrorist attacks does not define our daily lives.
>
> Victory, therefore, will be secured only as long as the United States and the international community maintain their vigilance and work tirelessly to prevent terrorists from inflicting horrors like those of September 11, 2001.[52]

In his State of the Union address on 3 February 2005, President Bush, while referring to the importance of 'eliminating the conditions that feed radicalism and ideologies of murder', reiterated the key central conception of offensive action as the main way to defeat terrorism: 'Our country is still the target of terrorists who want to kill many, and intimidate us all – and we will stay on the offensive against them, until the fight is won.'

Such glimpses of how victory might come about are essentially schematic and prescriptive rather than historical. They have an abstract and euphemistic quality. Because they leave little room for complexity, they have enabled some individuals to focus on the idea of destruction more than other possible mechanisms. When Timothy Garton Ash asked a very high US administration official how the 'war on terror' would end, he received the answer: 'With the elimination of the terrorists.'[53]

Such simple prescriptive views of how a terrorist campaign should end are also to be found in a book by two supporters of the Bush administration, David Frum and Richard Perle. Published in 2003, *An End to Evil: How to Win the War on Terror* is modestly described by its authors as 'a manual for victory'.[54] This paean of praise for Bush's anti-terrorist policy is also a diatribe against all those allies and bureaucrats who fail to support it properly: 'While our enemies plot, our allies dither and carp, and much of our government remains ominously unready for the fight.'[55] What does it say about how terrorist campaigns end? Virtually nothing. In true American fashion, this is a 'How to' book which is full of hectoring instruction but which gives no clue about how terrorist campaigns actually end.

How past terrorist campaigns ended

The talk of 'winning' and 'victories' suggests a decisive result. Yet such a result is seldom encountered in counter-terrorist struggles. There is a need for much broader understanding, based on historical evidence, of how terrorist campaigns do in fact end.[56] The processes – some of them deeply flawed – by which terrorist campaigns end are far more complex than is suggested by the language of the 'war on terror'. They usually include what is part and parcel of the 'war on terror': debilitating losses to the terrorist movement caused by military action, arrests and trials. However, they can also involve any or all of the following five elements.

Firstly, *awareness on the part of terrorist movements that they are being defeated politically, or at least are not making gains*. The actions of terrorists usually fail to arouse the masses: indeed, they frequently cause antagonism in the very population whose support is sought. Such failures can often lead to defections and splits, and to a political decision by all or part of a terrorist movement or its political allies to move to a different phase of struggle or of political action.

In November 2004 it was reported that six senior members of the Basque separatist group ETA had called on the organisation from their prison cells to lay down its arms. In their letter they stated: 'Our political-military strategy has been overcome by repression . . . It is not a question of fixing the rear-view mirror or a burst tyre. It is the motor that does not work.' This letter was 'the closest Eta members have come to recognising that, after more than 30 years in which it has killed more than 800 people, the group is facing defeat'.[57]

Secondly, *recognition by governments which organised or assisted terrorism that they must renounce this method of pursuing a cause*. Such recognition may sometimes (as in the case of Libya in 2003) be coupled with compensation to the families of victims of terrorist acts.

Thirdly, *the amelioration of conditions in order to weaken the strength and legitimacy of their support*. Such amelioration is something in which messianic terrorists have no interest. It may include a change in the political context, which side-steps some of the issues that provided grist to the mill of the terrorist movement, provides new opportunities for pursuing its aims in a different manner, or emphasises a new range of attainable goals of general appeal, for example in the field of human rights.

Fourthly, *the holding of genuine multi-party elections*. Democratic procedures, especially where there are safeguards for minorities, can undercut terrorist claims to speak for a specific nation or section of society.

Fifthly, *a shared awareness of stalemate, giving both sides a possible incentive to reach a negotiated or tacit settlement involving mutual concessions*. This may encompass a recognition by its adversaries that the terrorist movement, however criminal its actions, did represent a serious cause and constituency – leading to a reluctant acceptance that certain concessions should be made to some positions held by terrorists.

Sometimes terrorist campaigns wind down rather than end. They may degenerate into mafia-like activities, including kidnappings for ransom, drug trafficking and bank robberies. Or a few terrorist leaders, hidden in a jungle or a city, maintain their faith, even continue to plot or to detonate the occasional bomb, but lose completely their following and their impact.[58]

In some cases the combatants, or at least a proportion of them, may be retrained. This happened in Guatemala following the civil war of the 1980s and 1990s. The former Marxist guerrillas, who had been called terrorists by their enemies, received extensive retraining at a centre in Quetzaltenango. When I visited it in 1997, the work of the centre, supported mainly by European funds, appeared to be effective, the main concern being whether there would be jobs for the suitably retrained guerrillas.

Not all these processes whereby terror campaigns end are relevant to the current struggle against al-Qaeda and other terrorist movements. However, we do need a greater sense that terrorist campaigns, while they may go on for a long time, do eventually end; and do so not because every last terrorist is captured or killed, or because they are comprehensively defeated in military operations, or because there is a clear victory, but rather because terrorism is seen for what it is: a highly problematic means of bringing about change. It cannot be the sole basis for a movement, it often damages the very people in whose name it is waged, and it may burn itself out or backfire on its own authors.

UK policy to eliminate terrorism as a force in international affairs

On the ending of terrorist campaigns, UK policy is subtly different from that of the United States. It is also flawed, but in a different way. The key UK statement of doctrine about terrorism, published in July 2002, *The Strategic Defence Review: A New Chapter*, says that the goal of the government's efforts is 'to eliminate terrorism as a force in international affairs'.[59] This is a carefully thought-out phrase, and of course it is properly recognised that 'countering terrorism is usually a long-term business requiring the roots and causes to be addressed as well as the symptoms'.[60] Nonetheless, there are two main disadvantages to proclaiming as a goal 'the elimination of terrorism as a force in international affairs'.

Firstly, *terrorism is notoriously difficult to 'eliminate'*. The proclamation of this goal is not only unrealistic, but it also undermines one of the strongest arguments against terrorism – namely that, once started, it easily becomes endemic. The unofficial, decentralised and hydra-headed character of terrorism provides the main explanation for the difficulty of eliminating it.

Secondly, *if 'elimination' is the proclaimed goal, then every subsequent terrorist incident represents a victory for the terrorists*. The UK faced this problem in Northern Ireland. A number of government pronouncements in the 1970s and early 1980s had indicated the UK's aim was the complete ending of terrorist activity. Thereafter, every terrorist assault, including the IRA's mainland campaign, had a possible added bonus of 'proving' that the government had failed to achieve its proclaimed goal. Eventually the UK's aims were restated in more modest terms as being the reduction of terrorist activities: this was accepted by the public with remarkably little complaint, and may have helped in the slow winding down of the conflict in Northern Ireland.

Main lines of criticism

Any conclusions about how a historical perspective may affect views of the 'war on terror' must begin by acknowledging that this extraordinary 'war' is unique in having achieved something, however incomplete, in military operations in Afghanistan; in having put the full weight and ingenuity of the United States into the struggle; and in having involved a remarkable degree of international collaboration, much of which has survived the fall-out over Iraq. This struggle is not a single campaign, but is highly variegated. The responses to certain events, such as the Bali and Madrid bombings, have been much less military in character than the responses to other outrages. The overall verdict is not entirely negative.

Yet, against a background of the long historical record of the subject, six main lines of criticism of the US-led international campaign arise.

Firstly, the title and language of the so-called 'war on terror' is misleading. It conjures up the image and expectation of open war being a major and recurrent part of the action against international terrorist movements; and it suggests the unrealisable aim of the complete elimination of terrorist movements. There is a need for words to describe the overall policy with regard to terrorism that convey toughness but do not rely so heavily on the imagery of war. The core idea has to be a vigorous and sustained countering of terrorist threats, involving action at many levels, and aimed at achieving a significant reduction and marginalisation of terrorist activities. A better term, more accurate if less dramatic, would be 'international campaign against terrorism'. It may not be too late to use this term in at least partial substitution for 'war on terror'.

Secondly, the 'war on terror' risks becoming an exercise in latter-day imperialism. There is a need for intervention in certain societies, but it needs to be handled with extraordinary skill and care. The risk of stumbling into a colonial role is especially great because in US political culture there is a caricature vision of European colonialism of the nineteenth and twentieth centuries. In consequence it is believed, erroneously, that nothing the United States does today could remotely resemble such deplorable European practices. Yet to many the similarities are all too real. The irony of the situation is that foreign rule, especially foreign military occupation, is notoriously a producer of terrorist movements.

Thirdly, some official statements made in the course of the 'war on terror' have inadvertently credited terrorist movements with a greater capacity to achieve intended results than can be justified on the basis of the record. For example, in several passages the UK *Strategic Defence Review* states or implies that international terrorist attacks have 'the potential for strategic effect'.[61] This phrase is used for a good reason – to avoid implying that it is essential to tackle absolutely all terrorist movements everywhere simultaneously and with equal vigour – but it is flawed. It ignores the important distinction between *intended* and *actual* strategic effect. Although terrorist actions frequently have major effects, they are seldom those that the terrorists intended. It does not make sense to give terrorists more credit than they deserve for the size and capacity of their organisations, for the accuracy of their political calculations, or for the effectiveness of their actions.

Fourthly, the history of counter-terrorist operations in the twentieth century suggests that in the long struggle against terrorism, four assets are important:

- public confidence in official decision-making;
- public confidence in the intelligence on which that decision-making is based;
- operation with respect for a framework of law;
- a willingness to address some of the problems that have contributed to the emergence of terrorism.

Tragically, all of these assets risk being undermined by many events connected with the 'war on terror', especially the 2003 intervention in Iraq and the subsequent insurgency.

Fifthly, the torture and ill-treatment of detainees, of which there has been much evidence in the 'war on terror', is, to quote Talleyrand, worse than a crime: it is a mistake. Guantanamo and Abu Ghraib have provided propaganda gifts to adversaries.

Sixthly, the international campaign against terrorism stands in need of a more realistic vision of how terrorist campaigns end than the simple picture of the elimination or incarceration of terrorists.

On the basis of the historical record, some positive recommendations can be advanced about the most appropriate basic aims and character of the international campaign against terrorism. The struggle should be presented, not just as a fight against evil or as a defence of free societies, but also as a fight against tragically erroneous ideas. It should be seen as a means of ensuring that the societies from whence terrorism comes do not succumb to endemic violence. An important aim must be, not the capture of every last terrorist leader, but their relegation to a status of near-irrelevance as life moves on, long-standing grievances are addressed, and peoples can see that a grim terrorist war of attrition is achieving little and damaging their own societies. It needs to encompass close attention to after-care in societies that have been torn apart by terrorism.

The problem of terrorism can diminish over time. Such diminution will require continued resolution and toughness, including arrests, trials and a willingness to take military action where appropriate. It will also require a patient and more prudent approach that would mark a departure from certain major aspects of what we have seen so far in the 'war on terror'. Above all, the international campaign against terrorism needs to take account of the long history of terror and counter-terror – and of the way historians have understood it.

Acknowledgements

This text is partly based on the Emden Lecture, St Edmund Hall, Oxford University, 7 May 2004; and the Annual War Studies Lecture, King's College, London, 23 November 2004. A short extract from the latter appeared in *The World Today*, London, March 2005.

Notes

1 UN High-Level Panel on Threats, Challenges and Change, *A More Secure World: Our Shared Responsibility*, UN doc A/59/565, 2 December 2004, paragraph 164(d).

2 This is the conclusion, for example, of two exceptionally thorough and impressive US studies of the Vietcong published during the war: Douglas Pike, *Vietcong: The Organization and Techniques of the National Liberation Front of South Vietnam* (Cambridge, MA: MIT Press, 1966); and Nathan Leites, *The Vietcong Style of Politics*, Rand Memorandum RM-5487–1-ISA/ARPA (Santa Monica, CA: Rand, 1969).

3 Bob Woodward, *Plan of Attack* (New York: Simon & Schuster, 2004), p. 324.

4 General Bernard Montgomery said of US policy in Vietnam: 'The US has broken the second rule of war. That is, don't go fighting with your land army on the mainland of Asia. Rule One is don't march on Moscow. I developed these two rules myself.' Alun Chalfont, *Montgomery of Alamein* (London: Weidenfeld & Nicolson, [1976]), p. 318.

5 John Lewis Gaddis, *Surprise, Security, and the American Experience* (Cambridge, MA: Harvard University Press, 2004); and Walter Russell Mead, *Power, Terror, Peace, and War: America's Grand Strategy in a World at Risk* (New York: Alfred A. Knopf, 2004). See also John Lewis Gaddis, 'And Now This: Lessons from the Old Era for the New One', in Strobe Talbott and Nayan Chanda (eds), *The Age of Terror: America and the World After September 11* (Oxford: Perseus Press, 2001), pp. 1–22.

6 Bruce Maxwell, *Terrorism: A Documentary History* (Washington DC: CQ Press, [2003]). The documents in this book cover only a 30-year period, 'from 1972, when international terrorism bust into the public consciousness with live TV pictures of Palestinian terrorists holding Israeli athletes hostage at the Munich Olympics'. In some countries the public was aware of terrorism decades, or even centuries, earlier.

7 Michael Ignatieff, *The Lesser Evil: Political Ethics in an Age of Terror* (Edinburgh: Edinburgh University Press, 2004).

8 See e.g. David C. Rapoport, 'The International World as Some Terrorists Have Seen It: A Look at a Century of Memoirs', *The Journal of Strategic Studies*, vol. 10, no. 4, December 1987, pp. 32–58.

9 Col. Charles Lacheroy, 'La guerre révolutionnaire', talk on 2 July 1957 reprinted in *La Défense*

Nationale, Paris, 1958, p. 322; cited in Peter Paret, *French Revolutionary Warfare from Indochina to Algeria: The Analysis of a Political and Military Doctrine* (London: Pall Mall Press, 1964), p. 15. Paret comments that 'nothing', in this case, means 'the secure existence of the *status quo*'.

10 See e.g. Walter Laqueur, *The Age of Terrorism* (London: Weidenfeld & Nicolson, [1987]). Also Professor Michael Howard, 'What's in a Name? How to Fight Terrorism', *Foreign Affairs*, January/February 2002, pp. 9–13.

11 Monument 'erected to commemorate the glorious heroes of the Machine Gun Corps who Fell in the Great War (1914–1918)', Hyde Park Corner, London. As the monument's inscription notes, the Machine Gun Corps was formed on 14 October 1915, and its last unit was disbanded on 15 July 1922. The quotation is from 1 Samuel 18: 7.

12 A good example is Ratko Parezanin, a member of the Young Bosnia movement in 1914 and a friend of Gavril Princip, the assassin of Archduke Ferdinand in 1914. Parezanin's memoirs, published in 1974, are mentioned below (note 15).

13 Robert A. Pape, 'The Strategic Logic of Suicide Terrorism', *American Political Science Review*, vol. 97, no. 3, August 2003, p. 357.

14 Murray Clark Havens, Carl Leiden and Karl M. Schmitt, *The Politics of Assassination* (Engelwood Cliffs, NJ: Prentice-Hall, [1978]), p. 153.

15 See the remarkable and detailed memoir by a fellow-student in the Young Bosnia movement who was a friend of Princip, Ratko Parezanin, *Mlada Bosna I prvi svetski rat* [Young Bosnia and the First World War] (Munich: Iskra, 1974). The book was published on the 60th anniversary of the Sarajevo assassination. A useful short report is Iain Macdonald, 'Sarajevo: When a Teenager with a Gun Sent the World to War', *Times*, 28 June 1974, p. 18.

16 Robert B. Asprey, *War in the Shadows: The Guerrilla in History* (London: Macdonald and Jane's, 1976), p. 811; drawing on N.D. Valeriano and C.T.R. Bohannan, *Counter-Guerrilla Operations: The Philippine Experience* (New York: Praeger, 1962).

17 Lawrence Durrell, *Bitter Lemons* (London: Faber & Faber, 1956), p. 216.

18 Gaddis, 'And Now This', p. 20.

19 Robert Thompson, *Defeating Communist Insurgency: Experiences from Malaya and Vietnam* (London: Chatto & Windus, 1966), p. 52. From 1957 to 1961 the author was successively deputy secretary and secretary for defence in Malaya. As his and other accounts make clear, in the course of the Malayan Emergency there were certain derogations from human-rights standards, including detentions and compulsory relocations of villages.

20 For a fuller account, see Adam Roberts, 'The Laws of War in the War on Terror', in Paul Wilson (ed.), *International Law and the War on Terrorism*, US Naval War College, International Law Studies, vol. 79 (Newport, RI: Naval War College, 2003), pp. 175–230.

21 Roland Gaucher, *The Terrorists: From Tsarist Russia to the OAS*, trans. Paula Spurlin (London: Secker & Warburg, [1965]), pp. 10–11.

22 Laqueur, *Age of Terrorism*, p. 33.

23 The key document in this process was Lord Gardiner's minority report in *Report of the Committee of Privy Counsellors Appointed to Consider Authorized Procedures for the Interrogation of Persons Suspected of Terrorism*, Cmnd. 4901 (London: HMSO, March 1972). His minority report was accepted by the government, as announced by Prime Minister Edward Heath in the House of Commons on 2 March 1972.

24 Donald Rumsfeld roundtable with radio media, 15 January 2002, available at http://www.defenselink.mil/ transcripts/2002/to1152002111to115sdr. html.

25 The problematic character of defining the 'war on terror' as one of good vs evil is recognised in Talbott and Chanda, *The Age of Terror*, p. xiv.

26 Laqueur, *Age of Terrorism*, pp. 36–8.

27 Régis Debray, *Undesirable Alien*, trans. Rosemary Sheed (London: Allen Lane, 1978), pp. 121, 123 and 172. First published as *L'Indésirable* (Paris: Editions du Seuil, 1975).

28 This may be literally true, although reports of information by detainees given during interrogation need to be treated with extreme caution. According to numerous reports, Abu Zubaydah (a Palestinian captured in Pakistan in 2002 who was allegedly Osama bin Laden's chief of operations) told his interrogators in Guantanamo that terrorists might be taking clues from the film *Godzilla*, which had been remade in 1998 and showed a monster attack on Brooklyn Bridge and the Statue of Liberty. Timothy W. Maier, 'Has FBI Cried Wolf Too Often?', *Insight on the News*, 5 August 2002, available at http:// www.insightmag.com/news/2002/08/26.

29 On possible connections between southern California and religious radicalism see the brief references in Malise Ruthven, *Fundamentalism: The Search for Meaning* (Oxford: Oxford University Press, 2004), pp. 10 and 38. Sayyid Qutb (1906–66), when he was in California in the 1950s, was deeply influenced by the Western culture that he opposed as degenerate and corrupt.

30 President George W. Bush, remarks from the *USS Abraham Lincoln* at sea off the coast of San Diego, California, 1 May 2003.

31 President George W. Bush, speech to Congress, 20 September 2001.

32 President George W. Bush, radio address to the nation, 29 September 2001, available at http://www. whitehouse.gov/news/releases/2001/09/.

33 The White House, *National Strategy for Combating Terrorism* (Washington DC: February 2003), p. 1.

34 Ibid., p. 5.

35 Paul W. Schroeder, 'The Risks of Victory: An Historian's Provocation', *The National Interest*, no. 66, Winter 2001–02, p. 22.

36 Ibid., pp. 28–9. See also Schroeder's article warning against the likely effects of an attack in the Middle East, 'Iraq: The Case Against Preemptive War', *The American Conservative*, vol. 8, no. 20, October 2002, available at http://www. amconmag.com/1011121/iraq.html.

37 While no UN Security Council resolution specifically authorised the US-led military operations in Afghanistan, several resolutions passed both before and after 11 September 2001 provided a significant degree of support for such action. Resolution 1189 of 13 August 1998 had emphasised the responsibility of Afghanistan to stop terrorist activities on its territory. Resolution 1368 of 12 September 2001 recognised 'the inherent right of individual or collective self-defence in accordance with the Charter', condemned the attacks of the previous day, and stated that the Council 'regards such acts, like any act of international terrorism, as a threat to international peace and security'. It also expressed the Council's 'readiness to take all necessary steps to respond to the terrorist attacks of 11 September 2001, and to combat all forms of terrorism'. These key points were reiterated in Resolution 1373 of 28 September 2001, which additionally placed numerous requirements on all states to bring the problem of terrorism under control.

38 Donald Rumsfeld, cited in news report by Brian Knowlton, *International Herald Tribune*, 8 October 2001, p. 1.

39 Richard A. Clarke, *Against All Enemies: Inside America's War on Terror* (London: Simon & Schuster UK, 2004), p. 274.

40 Michael Howard, lecture in London on 30 October 2001, reported in Tania Branigan, 'Al-Qaida is Winning War, Allies Warned', *Guardian*, 31 October 2001. The lecture was the basis of Howard, 'What's in a Name?'

41 His reappraisal was in 'September 11 and After: Reflections on the War Against Terrorism', a lecture at University College London, 29 January 2002.

42 President George W. Bush, speech from the White House, 17 March 2003.

43 The stated reason for going to war in March 2003 was 'Iraq's continued material breaches of its disarmament obligations under relevant Security Council resolutions.' Letter dated 20 March 2003 from the Permanent Representative of the USA, John Negroponte, to the president of the UN Security Council.

44 Vernon Loeb, 'Medals Couple Two Conflicts: Critics Seek Separate Awards for Afghanistan, Iraq Fighting', *Washington Post*, 6 January 2004.

45 Jonathan Stevenson, *Counter-Terrorism: Containment and Beyond*, Adelphi Paper 367 (Oxford: Oxford University Press for the IISS, 2004), pp. 108–113.

46 Robert W. Tucker and David C. Hendrickson, 'The Sources of American Legitimacy', *Foreign Affairs*, vol. 83, no. 6, November/December 2004, p. 18.

47 Clarke, *Against All Enemies*, p. x.

48 UK Ministry of Defence, *The Strategic Defence Review: A New Chapter*, Cm. 5566 vols. I and II (London: HMSO, July 2002), vol. I, p. 9.

49 The White House, *The National Security Strategy of the United States of America*, Washington, DC, September 2002, p. 6.

50 Paul W. Schroeder, 'The Mirage of Empire Versus the Promise of Hegemony', in Paul W. Schroeder, *Systems, Stability and Statecraft: Essays on the International History of Modern Europe*, ed. David Wetzel, Robert Jervis and Jack S. Levy (New York and Basingstoke: Palgrave Macmillan, 2004), p. 305.

51 *National Security Strategy of the United States*, pp. 5–7.

52 *National Strategy for Combating Terrorism*, p. 12. This was the text under the heading 'Victory in the War against Terror'.

53 This answer was given by a senior administration official in Washington DC on 10 December 2002, as reported in Timothy Garton Ash, *Free World: Why a Crisis of the West Reveals the Opportunity of our Time* (London and New York: Allen Lane, 2004), p. 126.

54 David Frum and Richard Perle, *An End to Evil: How to Win the War on Terror* (New York: Random House, [2003]), p. 9.

55 Ibid., p. 4.

56 A useful distillation of conclusions on how terrorist campaigns end may be found in Adrian Guelke, *The Age of Terrorism and the International Political System* (London: I.B. Tauris, 1995), pp. 180–81.

57 Giles Tremlett, 'Old Guard Urges End to Eta Terror', *Guardian*, 3 November 2004, p. 15.

58 In 1987, nearly 40 years after the declaration of a state of emergency in Malaya, and over 35 years after the Malayan Communist Party decided to end the armed struggle (a decision that had been announced on 1 October 1951), some 600 guerrillas laid down their arms and started a new life as farmers in southern Thailand. Michael Fathers, 'Communist "Bandits" Lay Down Arms in Malaysia', *Independent*, 8 June 1987.

59 *New Chapter*, vol. I, pp. 4 and 7.

60 Ibid., p. 10.

61 Ibid., p. 7.

23 The lost meaning of strategy

Hew Strachan

On 19 November 2003, President Bush delivered a major speech on international relations at the Royal United Services Institute in Whitehall in London. The event was controversial; however, the speech was less so. Indeed, most British commentators welcomed it as a clear statement of United States foreign policy. 'We will help the Iraqi people establish a peaceful and democratic country in the heart of the Middle East. And by doing so, we will defend our people from danger,' Bush declared. He then went on: 'The forward strategy of freedom must also apply to the Arab–Israeli conflict.'[1]

This last sentence is puzzling. Strategy is a military means; freedom in this context is a political or even moral condition. Strategy can be used to achieve freedom, but can freedom be a strategy in itself? A fortnight after Bush's speech, on 2 December 2003, the British Foreign and Commonwealth Office published its first White Paper on foreign policy since the Callaghan government of 1976–79. Its focus was on terrorism and security; it was concerned with illegal immigration, drugs, crime, disease, poverty and the environment; and it included – according to the Foreign Office's website – 'the UK's strategy for policy, public service delivery and organisational priorities'. The punctuation created ambiguity (were public service delivery and organisational priorities subjects of the paper or objects of the strategy?), but the central phrase was the first one. It suggested that the Foreign Office now developed strategy to set policy, rather than policy to set strategy. The title of the White Paper was *UK International Priorities: A Strategy for the Foreign and Commonwealth Office*.[2] Introducing it in Parliament, the foreign secretary, Jack Straw, explained that 'the FCO strategy analyses the ways in which we expect the world to change in the years ahead'. There was no mention of diplomacy or foreign policy, the traditional domains of foreign ministries. Moreover, the timing of the White Paper's publication created wry, if cynical, comment. It managed – just – to put the horse before the cart: the Ministry of Defence's White Paper, *Delivering Security in a Changing World*, appeared a week later.[3] Those who wondered whether that too would establish a strategy for policy, as opposed to a policy for strategy, might point to the degree to which the Ministry of Defence had already come to set the foreign policy agenda. The key statement on British policy after the attacks of 9/11 was neither *UK International Priorities* nor *Delivering Security in a Changing World*, but the so-called 'New Chapter' to the Ministry of Defence's *Strategic Defence Review* published over a year previously, in July 2002.[4]

The confusion in Bush's speech and in the Foreign Office's White Paper embodies the existential crisis which strategy confronts. The word 'strategy' has acquired a universality which has robbed it of meaning, and left it only with banalities. Governments have strategies to tackle the problems of education, public health, pensions and inner-city housing. Advertising companies have strategies to sell cosmetics or clothes. Strategic studies flourish more verdantly in schools of business studies than in departments of international relations. Airport bookstalls carry serried ranks of paperbacks reworking Sun Tzu's *The Art of War*. Gerald Michaelson is a leader in this field: his titles are self-explanatory – *Sun Tzu: the Art of War for Managers – 50 Strategic Rules* (2001) and *Sun Tzu Strategies for Marketing: 12 Essential Principles for Winning the War for Customers* (2003). But strategic studies are not business studies, nor is strategy – despite the beliefs of George Bush and Jack Straw to the contrary – a synonym for policy.

Clausewitz defined strategy as 'the use of the engagement for the purpose of the war'.[5] He did not define policy. Clasusewitz's focus was on the nation and the state, not on party politics. Too much, therefore, can be made of the ambiguity created by the fact that the German word, *Politik*, means policy and politics: this may matter less for our understanding of *On War* than for our interpretations of later commentators. Clausewitz was at least clear that conceptually *Politik* was not the same as strategy, even if the two were interwoven. When he concluded that war had its own grammar but not its own logic, he implied that strategy was part of that grammar. By contrast policy provided the logic of war, and therefore enjoyed an overarching and determining position which strategy did not. Clausewitz's definition of strategy was therefore much narrower than that of contemporary usage. He too would have been perplexed by George Bush's 'strategy of freedom' and the Foreign Office's 'strategy for policy'.

The evolution of strategy

The word 'strategy' may have its roots in ancient Greek but that language preferred concrete nouns to abstract ones. Στράτηγος (*strātēgos*) meant 'general', but what the commander practised was more likely to be expressed by a verb. Moreover, for the Greeks, as for the medieval knights, what was done on the battlefield or in a siege was the conduct of war, and more a matter of what today would be called tactics.[6] The general's plans and his execution of manoeuvres in the lead-up to battle had no clear name until the late eighteenth century. The idea of strategy was a product of the growth of standing, professional armies on the one hand and of the Enlightenment on the other. In 1766 a French lieutenant-colonel, Paul Gideon Joly de Maizeroy, wrote: 'in an enlightened and learned age in which so many men's eyes are employed in discovering the numerous abuses which prevail in every department of science and art, that of war has had its observers like the rest'.[7] That book, *Cours de tactique, théoretique, pratique et historique,* as the title reveals, was about tactics, but over ten years later Joly de Maizeroy published his *Théorie de la guerre* (1777), in which he identified a second level to the art of war, a level which he called strategy, and which he saw as 'sublime' and depending on reason rather than rules:

> Making war is a matter of reflection, combination of ideas, foresight, reasoning in depth and use of available means . . . In order to formulate plans, strategy studies the relationship between time, positions, means and different interests, and takes every factor into account . . . which is the province of dialectics, that is to say, of reasoning, which is the highest faculty of the mind.[8]

The Napoleonic wars confirmed the distinction between tactics and strategy, between what happened on the battlefield and what happened off it. The introduction of conscription meant that field armies tripled in size within two decades. Their coordination and supply made demands of a general that were clearly different from the business of firing a musket or thrusting with a sword. Napoleon himself tended not to use the word strategy, but those who wrote about what he had achieved certainly did – not only Clausewitz, but also Jomini (the most important military theorist of the nineteenth century) and the Austrian Archduke Charles. The latter had proved one of Napoleon's most redoubtable opponents, fighting him to a standstill at Aspern-Essling in 1809. Charles was of the view that 'strategy is the science of war: it produces the overall plans, and it takes into its hands and decides on the general course of military enterprises; it is, in strict terms, the science of the commander-in-chief'.[9]

Jomini saw the campaign of Marengo in 1800 as the defining moment of the new era, the moment that 'the system of modern strategy was fully developed'.[10] He split the art of war into six parts, of which statesmanship was the most important and strategy the second. The latter he defined as the art of properly directing masses upon the theatre of war, either for defence or for invasion,[11] and wrote, 'strategy is the art of making war upon the map, and comprehends the whole theatre of operations'.[12]

Jomini's classification dominated land warfare in Europe until the First World War. His ideas were plagiarised by military theorists across the continent, and they provided the axioms inculcated in the military academies which proliferated from the turn of the eighteenth and nineteenth centuries. His emphasis on planning, cartography and lines of communication meant that his definition of strategy became the *raison d'être* of the general staffs which were institutionalised during the course of the nineteenth century. By 1900 military men were, broadly speaking, agreed that strategy described the conduct of operations in a particular theatre of war. It involved encirclement, envelopment and manoeuvre. It was something done by generals.

This was 'traditional' strategy – based on universal principles, institutionalised, disseminated and at ease with itself. It acknowledged, too, that strategy did not embrace the entire phenomenon of war. Strategy was only one of three components which made up war – the central element sandwiched between national policy on the one hand and tactics on the other. Each was separate, but the three had to be kept in harmony.

The problem that confronted traditional strategy lay not in its definition but in its boundaries with policy. Many generals came to believe, as Moltke the elder told Bismarck in the Franco-Prussian war, that once war was declared the statesman should fall silent until the general delivered the victory.[13] Friedrich von Bernhardi, writing in 1912, said that 'if war is resolved upon, the military object takes the place of the political purpose'. But Bernhardi should not be quoted selectively (as he so often was in Britain after the outbreak of the First World War). He fully recognised that the object could not be fixed from a purely military viewpoint, but had to take into account the reciprocal effects of military action on political affairs. The commander who demanded the right to set the object himself, without regard to the political purpose, had to be rebuffed. 'War is always a means only for attaining a purpose entirely outside its domain. War can, therefore, never itself lay down the purpose by fixing at will the military object.'[14]

Nor was this ambivalence about the dividing line between strategy and policy a symptom of Prussianism. A French general and one of the great military writers of his day, Jean Colin, declared in 1911 that 'once the war is decided on, it is absolutely necessary that a general should be left free to conduct it at his own discretion'.[15] Colin died in 1917, the year in which another French general, Henri Mordacq, became the military aide of Georges Clemenceau, the prime minister who not only united France's efforts in the prosecution of the First World War but also established most clearly the Third Republic's political primacy over the nation's army commanders. In 1912 Mordacq wrote a more nuanced discussion than Colin's on the relationship between policy and strategy in a democracy, one in which he stressed the need for the general to submit his plans for governmental approval to ensure that they conformed with the political objective. But he also reminded the government of its obligations: the civil power should indicate to the high command its political objective, and then it should let the soldiers get on with their job free of intervention. He quoted Moltke: 'strategy works uniquely in the direction indicated by policy, but at the same time it protects its complete independence to choose its means of action'.[16]

Strategy's propensity to replace policy was reflected at the institutional level. In the eighteenth and early nineteenth centuries policy and strategy were united in one man – the king or the emperor, Frederick the Great or Napoleon. In the states of the early twentieth century they could not be, however much Kaiser Wilhelm II may have believed they were. During the First World War, the machineries for the integration of policy and strategy either did not exist, as in Germany, Austria-Hungary and Russia, or emerged in fits and starts, as in Britain and France. Even in 1918, when the Entente allies appointed Ferdinand Foch their generalissimo, his principal task was the coordination of land warfare on the western front. He took charge of strategy traditionally defined. Less clear were the lines of responsibility between him and the Allied heads of state.

When the war was over, some strategic thinkers, most notably Basil Liddell Hart, would argue that it had been won not by land operations on the western front, but by the application of sea power through the blockade. Traditional definitions of strategy, those developed between, say, 1770 and 1918 by thinkers whom we would now classify as the classical strategists, were limited by more than just their focus on operations. They also neglected war at sea. The military historian needs to confront an existential question: why is there strategy on the one hand and naval strategy on other? Why is the use of the adjective 'naval' an indication that those who have written about the conduct of war at sea have not been incorporated into the mainstream histories of war?

'We are accustomed, partly for convenience and partly from lack of a scientific habit of thought, to speak of naval strategy and military strategy as though they were distinct branches of knowledge which had no common ground.' So wrote Julian Corbett, the first really important strategic thinker produced by Britain.[17] Corbett went on to argue that both naval and military strategy were subsumed by the theory of war, that naval strategy was not a thing by itself. His thinking in this respect was directly shaped by his reading of Clausewitz. In other words he located himself not in some maritime back-water but in the mainstream of classical strategic thought. His theory of war was that 'in a fundamental sense [war] is a continuation of policy by other means'.[18] He went on: 'It gives us a conception of war as an exertion of violence to secure a political end which we desire to attain, and . . . from this broad and simple formula we are able to deduce at once that wars will vary according to the nature of the end and the intensity of our desire to attain it.'[19]

When Corbett addressed the officers at the Royal Naval War College before the First World War, he distinguished between what he called 'major strategy' and 'minor strategy'. Plans of operations, the selection of objectives and the direction of the forces assigned to the operation were now not strategy but minor strategy. Major strategy

> in its broadest sense has also to deal with the whole resources of the nation for war. It is a branch of statesmanship. It regards the Army and Navy as parts of the one force, to be handled together; they are instruments of war. But it also has to keep in view constantly the politico-diplomatic position of the country (on which depends the effective action of the instrument), and its commercial and financial position (by which the energy for working the instrument is maintained).[20]

Corbett had therefore begun to apply the word 'strategy' to policy and to see the two as integrated in a way that Clausewitz had not. Corbett's title 'major strategy' prefigures what Britons came to call 'grand strategy' and Americans 'national strategy'. This unites him with his near contemporary, Alfred Thayer Mahan. Both then and since, however, commentators on the two founders of naval thinking have tended to polarise their views. Corbett argued that sea power was only significant when it affected events on land; Mahan was critical of amphibious operations. Corbett concerned himself with trade defence; Mahan was sceptical about cruiser war. Corbett doubted the importance of fleet action; Mahan was its greatest advocate. But Mahan, like Corbett, was working towards a theory of grand strategy. Like Corbett and Clausewitz, Mahan was rooted in the classical strategic tradition, in his case through Jomini. But Jomini's influence, although evident in what Mahan said about naval strategy narrowly defined, should not obscure the novelty and innovative quality of what he said about sea power more broadly defined. For Mahan, strategic arguments were based on political economy. Maritime trade was vital to national prosperity, and naval superiority was essential to the protection of the nation's interests. That naval superiority in itself depended on the seafaring traditions of the population, the nation's culture and the state's political structure.[21] There was therefore a symbiotic link between sea power, liberal democracy and ideas of grand strategy. All three elements seemed to have been required to achieve synergy – a point made clear if we look at the third great titan of naval thought, Raoul Castex.

Castex wrote a five-volume treatise on strategy in the inter-war period. He was a French admiral, and France was a liberal democracy which had been sustained during the First World War through British credit and Atlantic trade. But France saw itself as a land power before it was a sea power. Castex began his five volumes by defining strategy in terms identical to those of the pre-1914 military writers: 'Strategy is nothing other than the general conduct of operations, the supreme art of chiefs of a certain rank and of the general staffs destined to serve as their auxiliaries'.[22] He had not changed this formulation, originally written in 1927, a decade later. His discussion of the relationship between politics and strategy, and their reciprocal effects, treated the two as entirely separate elements, and concluded with a chapter entitled 'le moins mauvais compromis' ('the least bad compromise').[23] The key factor determining Castex's reluctance to embrace grand strategy as Corbett and Mahan had done was that France had vulnerable land frontiers. Its army was more important than its navy.

Sea-girt states, like Britain and the United States, freed – unlike France – from the need to maintain large standing armies for the purposes of defence against invasion, could develop along political lines that favoured individualism and capitalism. The prosperity thus engendered became the means to wage war itself – what Lloyd George, as Britain's chancellor of the exchequer in 1914, called the 'silver bullets'.[24] In 1923, these links – between peacetime preparation and the conduct of war itself, and between economic capability and military applications – prompted the military theorist, J.F.C. Fuller, to entitle a chapter of his book, *The Reformation of War*, 'The Meaning of Grand Strategy'.[25] He regarded the division of strategy into naval, military and now aerial components as 'a direct violation of the principle of economy of forces as applied to a united army, navy and air force, and hence a weakening of the principle of the objective'. Moreover,

> our peace strategy must formulate our war strategy, by which I mean that there cannot be two forms of strategy, one for peace and one for war, without wastage – moral, physical and material – when war breaks out. The first duty of the grand strategist is, therefore, to appreciate the commercial and financial position of his country; to discover what its resources and liabilities are. Secondly, he must understand the moral characteristics

of his countrymen, their history, peculiarities, social customs and system of government, for all these quantities and qualities from the pillars of the military arch which it is his duty to construct.[26]

Here, as in other respects, Fuller's ideas were aped and developed by Liddell Hart. Pursuing also the trajectory set by Corbett, Liddell Hart believed that Britain's strategy should be shaped not according to patterns of continental land war but in a specifically British context, conditioned by politics, geography and economics. He therefore distinguished between 'pure strategy' and 'grand strategy'. Pure strategy was still the art of the general. But the role of grand strategy was 'to coordinate and direct all the resources of the nation towards the attainment of the political object of the war – the goal defined by national policy'.[27]

Conflation of strategy and policy

Liddell Hart cast a long shadow forward, influencing both the allies' conduct in the Second World War and their subsequent interpretation of it. The political leaders of Britain, the United States and the Soviet Union coordinated their plans: they practised grand strategy, refusing to treat the theatres of war in isolation and settling the relationship of one theatre to another. The coping stone to the British official history of the Second World War was the six volumes of the deliberately titled 'grand strategy' series, two of them written by holders of Oxford's Chichele Chair in the History of War (as it is now dubbed), Norman Gibbs and Michael Howard. Although Howard's was the fourth volume in chronological sequence, it was the last but one to appear, and was published 16 years after the first. However, Howard found that the series' editor, J.R.M. Butler, had attempted no more helpful statement than to say of grand strategy that 'it is concerned both with purely military strategy and with politics'.[28] Howard therefore began his volume with a definition of grand strategy: 'Grand strategy in the first half of the twentieth century consisted basically in the mobilisation and deployment of national resources of wealth, manpower and industrial capacity, together with the enlistment of those of allied and, when feasible, of neutral powers, for the purpose of achieving the goals of national policy in wartime.'[29]

What had now happened – at least in Britain and the United States – was the conflation of strategy and policy. When Liddell Hart had himself defined grand strategy, he had admitted that it was 'practically synonymous with the policy which governs the conduct of war' and 'serves to bring out the sense of "policy in execution"'.[30] Edward Mead Earle, in the middle of the Second World War, defined strategy 'as an inherent element of statecraft at all times', and contended that grand strategy so integrated the policies and armaments of a nation that it could render the resort to war unnecessary.[31]

This conflation of strategy and policy has created particular problems for strategic theory shaped in the Anglo-American tradition since 1945, and particularly over the last 30 years. Earle was the dominant text up to and including the 1970s, a decade distinguished in 1976 by the publication of the English translation of Clausewitz's *On War* by Michael Howard and Peter Paret. Howard and Paret's edition gave the full text of Clausewitz a readership far larger than it had ever enjoyed before. Those readers, responding to Earle's injunction that strategy was an activity to be pursued in peace as well as in war, not least because the advent of nuclear weapons apparently gave them no choice, focused their attentions on chapter 1 of Book 1 of *On War*. That is of course the sole book of *On War* which is deemed to be fully finished, and it is the only book in which the idea of war's relationship to policy is fully developed. However, these new readers tended to interpret Clausewitz's understanding of policy and politics according to their own liberal lights, and not according to his. Policy was seen as controlling, guiding and even limiting war. The integration of strategy and policy was therefore a 'good thing' in a liberal and rationalist sense. But in Clausewitz's own day politics had the opposite effect – they removed the restraints on war. The French Revolution transformed the power of the state, and so transformed France's capacity to wage war. This is most evident not in Book I but in Book VIII of *On War*. 'As policy becomes more ambitious and vigorous, so will war, and this may reach the point where war attains its absolute form.'[32] In this passage Clausewitz seems clear in his own mind that the Napoleonic Wars had rendered real something that in Book I of *On War* he would treat as ideal, the notion of absolute war.

Moreover, the link between war and revolution suggests another reversal in the standard Anglo-Saxon interpretation of Clausewitz. War itself could effect domestic political change – the nation was constituted and defined through struggle. Clausewitz, for all that this article has quoted his definition of strategy, was not really concerned with definitions per se. He was interested in war as a phenomenon. War could be existential, not instrumental, its waging a social and moral catharsis. War could itself create a political identity.[33]

Clausewitz was a German nationalist who hated France and who often expressed himself in accents that link him to the so-called German *Sonderweg* and even to the Nazis. With Prussia defeated at Jena in 1806 and humiliated thereafter, war had become for Clausewitz not an instrument of policy but policy in its highest form. Prussia had to wage war to find its own identity: its readiness to sustain the struggle was an end in itself. The political declaration of February 1812, his response to Prussia's acceptance of Napoleon's demand that it contribute troops to the invasion of Russia, turned humiliation into defiance:

> I believe and confess that a people can value nothing more highly than the dignity and liberty of its existence. That it must defend these to the last drop of its blood. That there is no higher duty to fulfil, no higher law to obey . . . That even the destruction of liberty after a bloody and honourable struggle assures the people's rebirth. It is the seed of life, which one day will bring forth a new, securely rooted tree.[34]

Revolutionaries like Guiseppe Mazzini in the nineteenth century or Franz Fanon in the twentieth expressed themselves in comparable terms. So too did many Germans in the inter-war period, convinced by the defeat of 1918 that the army had been 'stabbed in the back'. Clausewitz the German nationalist was at times closer in his thinking to Erich Ludendorff, the German army's first quartermaster general of 1916–18, than we care to acknowledge or than Ludendorff himself did. In his post-war book, *Der totale Krieg*, Ludendorff wrongly claimed that Clausewitz's conception of politics was restricted only to foreign policy, and went on say that 'politics, at least during the [First World] War, ought to have fostered the vital strength of the nation, and to have served the purpose of shaping the national life'.[35] It was – and is – fashionable to see Ludendorff as deranged by 1935, if not before, but his prediction of the next war, that it 'will demand of the nation to place its mental, moral, physical, and material forces in the service of the war',[36] was not so inaccurate. Ludendorff was writing about what his English translators called totalitarian war, a conflict which would require the mobilisation of the entire population for its prosecution.

> War being the highest test of a nation for the preservation of its existence, a totalitarian policy must, for that very reason, elaborate in peace-time plans for the necessary pre-parations required for the vital struggle of the nation in war, and fortify the foundations

for such a vital struggle so strongly that they could not be moved in the heat of war, neither be broken or entirely destroyed through any measures taken by the enemy.[37]

As Carl Schmitt put it after the Second World War, only a people which can fight without consideration of limits is a political people.[38] The idea that politics could expand the way in which war was conducted was not just one entertained by fascists or Germans. Total war was a democratic idea. Clemenceau's government of 1917–18 had invoked the rhetoric of the French Revolution to summon the nation and Churchill spoke of total war in Britain in 1940–42. Definitions of strategy therefore broadened because of the ambiguity between the categories of war and of politics which world war generated. In the immediate aftermath of 1945 the powers assumed, as Clausewitz had tended to do in 1815, that the future pattern of war would pursue a trajectory derived from the immediate past. Total war would become the norm.

The Cold War and the strategy of dissuasion

The advent of nuclear weapons confirmed and consolidated those trends. If used, they would ensure that war was total – at least in its destructive effects. To obviate this, theories of deterrence were developed and employed, which themselves conflated strategy and foreign policy. Deterrence itself then became the cornerstone of a new discipline, strategic studies, but strategic studies were focused not so much on what armies did in war as on how nations used the threat of war in peace. By 1960 Thomas Schelling defined strategy not as 'concerned with the efficient application of force but with the exploitation of potential force'. Strategy itself therefore helped erode the distinction between war and peace, a trend confirmed by the high levels of military expenditure in the Cold War, and by the tendency to engage in proxy wars and guerrilla conflicts below the nuclear threshold.

The meaning of strategy had now changed. Conventional strategy was a strategy of action; it prepared for war and then implemented those preparations. Nuclear strategy was a strategy of dissuasion; it prevented war. Conventional strategy was built up through historical precedent. Nuclear strategy had no real precedents, beyond the dropping of the two atomic bombs on Japan. And so it focused on finding a new methodology, building scenarios and borrowing from mathematics and probability theory. Indeed methodology itself seemed on occasion to be the *raison d'être* of strategic thought. Nuclear strategy abandoned the focus on victory. It was, in the opinion of one French commentator, 'astrategic'.[39] Another Frenchman, General André Beaufre, demonstrated the impasse which strategy had reached. War, he declared, was total, and therefore strategy must be total. That meant that it should be political, economic, diplomatic and military. Military strategy was therefore one arm of strategy.[40] But what then was political strategy? Beaufre did not confront his own oxymoron.[41] Strategy without any adjective was for him both political and military, and therefore was about policy outcomes, not the use of force as the means to achieve them.

None of this was too problematic for the navies of the Cold War. Naval strategists had long seen strategy as operative in peace as well as war. Fleets and bases, even more than armies and fortifications, had to be prepared before a war broke out, and their shape and distribution moulded the strategy to be followed once hostilities began.[42] Those patterns provided their own forms of security in peace as well as in war: for example, they underpinned the notion of *pax Britannica*. But for the classical strategists of land war the notion of strategy in peace was inherently illogical. This had begun to change in the period before the First World War, when the attention given to war plans and peacetime military preparations led to arguments that these activities could properly be considered part of strategy. But the presumption was not that the end was the application of strategy in peacetime but its better use when war came. For the armies the end remained combat. For the navies the end might turn out not to be war at all.

Armies and their generals lost their way in the Cold War. The discipline of strategy, which defined and validated the art of the commander, the business of general staffs, and the processes of war planning, was no longer theirs – or at least not in the United States or in Britain. Beaufre wrote that 'the word strategy may be used often enough, but the science and art of strategy have become museum pieces along with Frederick the Great's snuffbox and Napoleon's hat'. Strategy, he concluded, 'cannot be a single defined doctrine; it is a method of thought'.[43] Edward Luttwak, writing towards the end of the Cold War, defined strategy as 'the conduct and consequences of human relations in the context of actual or possible armed conflict'.[44]

New words for old

Strategy was appropriated by politicians and diplomats, by academics and think-tank pundits, and it became increasingly distant from the use of the engagement for the purposes of the war. The latter activity was given new titles. Barry Posen distinguished between grand strategy and military doctrine. The former was 'a political-military, means–ends chain, a state's theory about how it can best "cause" security for itself'. The latter was a sub-component of grand strategy and concerned the means used by the military.[45] In the 1980s the American and British militaries responded to this crisis by embracing the operational level of war – sited between grand strategy and tactics. They even invented a spurious genealogy for it. If it had roots, they were Russian. Aleksandr A. Svechin, writing in 1927, placed operational art between tactics and strategy, and defined strategy as 'the art of combining preparations for war and the grouping of operations for achieving the goal set by the war for the armed forces'.[46] However, it proved more convenient for most commentators to locate the evolution of the operational level of war in Germany – perhaps because Germany was now an ally and perhaps because there was an Anglo-American conspiracy to laud Germany's military achievements in the two world wars despite their defeat in both.[47]

Most German generals before 1914 divided war into tactics and strategy, just like generals of every other state. The tasks and problems, which Schlieffen set the German General Staff while its chief between 1891 and 1905, were called '*Taktisch–strategischen Aufgaben*' (tactical-strategic problems), not operational problems. The First World War showed the generals of Germany, like those of every other state, that the conduct of war was not just a matter of strategy in an operational sense, but also involved political, social and economic dimensions. However, the veterans of the supreme command, the *Oberste Heeresleitung*, did not respond to this realisation as the British did: grand strategy figured neither as a phrase nor as a concept in the immediate aftermath of the armistice. Ludendorff entitled his reflections on the war, published in 1922, *Kriegführung und Politik*, 'the conduct of war and policy'. The title was significant on two counts.

First, the waging of war was kept separate from policy, although yoked to it. In 1916–18, the German supreme command under Hindenburg and Ludendorff had established de facto roles in areas of public life that were neither operational nor strictly military, even if they did indeed have implications for the conduct of the war. Ludendorff's conclusions from this experience were threefold. The first was to stress that operational matters, strategy as it was traditionally understood, were the business of professional soldiers; in many ways this was a reiteration of pre-war demands, and it was reflected in a number of works by former staff officers. The second was to blame the civil administration for not supporting the military as Ludendorff felt it should. The third conclusion was that government needed to develop mechanisms to enable it to resolve the tensions between the conduct of war and policy. For some that pointed to the creation of joint civil and military bodies, as in the Entente powers; for others it was an argument for the restoration of the monarchy; for Ludendorff it was a case for embodying the direction of policy and *Kriegführung* in a single leader, a *Führer*.[48]

The second point evident in Ludendorff's book was how little it said about strategy. Ludendorff had been contemptuous of strategy in 1917–18, and had as a result fought offensives in the west in the first half of 1918 that had succeeded tactically but had failed to deliver strategic outcomes. In 1922, he did no more than repeat the lapidary definition of the elder Moltke, that strategy was a system of expedients. Moltke himself had gone on to say that strategy is 'the transfer of knowledge to practical life . . . the art of acting under the pressure of the most difficult conditions'.[49] Such truisms conveyed little. German military thought in the inter-war period followed suit. Strategy dropped out of currency. In 1936–39, three massive volumes on the military sciences were published in four parts, the first appearing with an imprimatur from the minister of war, Werner von Blomberg. They had no separate entry for strategy, which was subsumed under *Kriegskunst*, or the art of war. What was said about strategy was new only in so far as it stressed that it was no longer simply a matter for the army, but now had to combine all three services. In other respects it remained what it had been before the First World War, a matter of operational direction:

> Thus strategy embraces the entire area of the military conduct of war in its major combinations, especially the manoeuvres (operations) and battles of armies and army components to achieve mutual effects and ultimately the military war aim.

The hierarchy of policy, strategy and tactics also remained intact:

> So strategy makes available to tactics the means for victory and at the same time sets the task, just as it itself derives both from policy.[50]

The relationship between war and politics was treated under a separate heading, '*Politik und Kriegführung*', and the latter word itself was now taken to mean not just the conduct of war in an operational sense but the combination of political and military factors by the supreme powers.[51] The domain of the army specifically was increasingly described not as strategy but in related terms, *as Militärische* or *Operative Kriegführung*. The achievements of the *Wehrmacht* in 1939–41 conformed to the expectations generated by these guidelines. They were the consequence of applied tactics more than of any overarching theory, and they confirmed – or so it seemed – that strategy was indeed a system of expedients, 'the art of acting under the pressure of the most difficult conditions'. The German army which invaded France in 1940 was doing little more than follow its own nose.[52] But after the event its victory was bestowed with the title *Blitzkrieg* and became enshrined in doctrine. Germany lost the Second World War in part for precisely that reason, that it made operational thought do duty for strategy, while tactical and operational successes were never given the shape which strategy could have bestowed.

This pedigree to the operational level of war, which is the focus for doctrine in so many Western armies, raises some interesting points. The first is an easy and largely true observation, that the so-called operational level of war is in general terms little different from what generals in 1914 called strategy. The second is that, like those generals, armed forces today are attracted to it because it allows them to appropriate what they see as the acme of their professional competence, separate from the trammels and constraints of political and policymaking direction. However, there is a crucial difference. In 1914, the boundary between strategy and policy, even if contested, was recognised to be an important one, and the relationship was therefore addressed. Today, the operational level of war occupies a politics-free zone. It speaks in a self-regarding vocabulary about manoeuvre, and increasingly 'manoeuvrism', that is almost metaphysical and whose inwardness makes sense only to those initiated in its meanings. What follows, thirdly, is that the operational level of war is a covert way of reintroducing the split between policy and strategy. Yet, of course the operational level of war determines how armed forces plan and prepare in peacetime, and therefore shapes the sort of war they can fight. The American and British armies developed their enthusiasm for the operational level of war in the 1980s, for application in a corps-level battle to be fought against an invading Soviet army in northern Europe. The successes of the 1991 Gulf War created the illusion that it was an approach of universal application. It is now applied in situations, such as peace support operations, in which the profile of politics is much higher than would have been the case in a high-intensity major war. One consequence for the United States military has been the disjunction between the kind of war for which it prepared in 2003 and the war in which its government actually asked it to engage. Thinking about the operational level of war can diverge dangerously from the direction of foreign policy.

Rediscovering strategy

Strategy should of course fill the gap. But it does not, because strategy has not recovered from losing its way in the Cold War. In the 1990s nuclear weapons and nuclear deterrence were deprived of their salience. The strategic vocabulary of the Cold War – mutual vulnerability, bipolar balance, stability, arms control – was no longer relevant. However, nobody wanted to revert to the vocabulary of traditional strategy. Strategic studies have been replaced by security studies. At times they embrace almost everything that affects a nation's foreign and even domestic policy. They require knowledge of regional studies – of culture, religion, diet and language in a possible area of operations; they require knowledge of geography, the environment and economics; they concern themselves with oil supplies, water stocks and commodities; they embrace international law, the laws of war and applied ethics. In short, by being inclusive they end up by being nothing. The conclusion might be that strategy is dead, that it was a creature of its times, that it carried specific connotations for a couple of centuries, but that the world has now moved on, and has concluded that the concept is no longer useful.

That would be a historically illiterate response. Classical strategy was a discipline based on history – based, in other words, on reality not on abstraction. Strategy after 1945 may have been materialist, in the sense that it responded to technological innovation more than it had in the past, and it may have used game theory and probability more than experience and principle. But that was not true of any major strategist writing before 1945. Such men used history for utilitarian and didactic purposes, some, like Liddell Hart, in ways that were blatantly self-serving. Even Clausewitz was more selective in his study of military history than he cared to admit. But he, like Jomini, or like Mahan or Corbett, wrote more history than theory. They all believed that strategy involved principles that had some enduring relevance. They mostly accepted that those principles were not rules to be slavishly followed, but they did believe that principles could give insight. Two obvious conclusions follow. First, history is necessary to put their theories in context. We have, for instance, to approach Clausewitz's discussion of the relationship between war and policy recognising that he was a product of Napoleonic Europe and not of the nuclear age. Secondly, a grasp of strategy traditionally defined is required if we are to appreciate the classical texts on the subject.

Strategy, however, is not just a matter for historians. It concerns us all. Strategy is about war and its conduct, and if we abandon it we surrender the tool that helps us to define war, to shape it and to understand it. Martin van Creveld, John Keegan and Mary Kaldor, among others, have argued that war traditionally defined, that is war between states conducted by armed forces, is obsolescent.[53] In so doing, they have pointed to a fundamental but under-appreciated truth, that war has its own primordial nature, independent of its political or social setting.[54] Moreover, the Western powers have unwittingly colluded in a process in which war is once again to be understood in its primitive state. War has been wrenched from its political context. In Hobbesian terms, the state's legitimacy rests in part on its ability to protect its citizens through its monopoly of violence, but the state's right to resort to war in fulfilment of its obligations has been reduced. One reason is that international law has arrogated the decision to go to war, except in cases of national self-defence, to the United Nations. Even states involved in a de facto war do not declare war, so as to avoid breaches of international law. Paradoxically, therefore, international law has deregulated war. The notion that waging war is no longer something that states do is particularly prevalent in America and Europe for three further reasons. First, enemies tend to be portrayed either as non-state actors, or, when they are not, as failed states (the description applied to Afghanistan) or rogue states (that deemed appropriate in the case of Iraq). Either way their political standing is compromised. Secondly, the armies of America, Britain and France are professional bodies, drawn from a narrow sector of the society on whose behalf they are fighting: such armies have become the role models in contemporary defence. But they represent their states more than their nations, their political leaderships more than their peoples. The same could be said of the private military companies, bodies without a formal national identity but on which even states with competent armed forces rely. Thirdly, and the logical consequence of all the preceding points, European states (thanks to 11 September this applies less to the United States) identify war with peacekeeping and peace enforcement. However, they are not the same. Peace support operations make problematic the traditional principles of war, developed for inter-state conflict. The objects of peacekeeping are frequently not clear, and the operations themselves are under-resourced and driven by short-term goals. On the ground command is divided, rather than united, and forces are dispersed, not concentrated; as a result the operations themselves are in the main indecisive.

War persists, but the state's involvement and interest in it are reduced. The issues raised by war too often seem to be ones not of their conduct and utility but of their limitation. The overwhelming impression is that they are initiated by non-state actors, that they are fought by civilians, and that their principal victims are not soldiers but non-combatants. The reality is of course somewhat different. States do still use war to further their national self-interest. The European members of NATO did so in Kosovo and the United States did so in Iraq. The infrequency of intervention despite the atrocities and humanitarian disasters in sub-Saharan Africa provides counter-factual evidence to support the point. Without perceived self-interest, the Western powers are reluctant to use military force.

The state therefore has an interest in re-appropriating the control and direction of war. That is the purpose of strategy. Strategy is designed to make war useable by the state, so that it can, if need be, use force to fulfil its political objectives. One of the reasons we are unsure what war is is that we are unsure about what strategy is or is not. It is not policy; it is not politics; it is not diplomacy. It exists in relation to all three, but it does not replace them. Widening definitions of strategy may have helped in the Cold War, but that was – ironically – both a potential conflict on a par with the two world wars and an epoch of comparative peace among the great powers. We now live in an era when there is perceived to be a greater readiness on the part of both the United States and the United Kingdom to go to war. Today's wars are not like the two world wars, whose scale sparked notions of grand strategy. Then big ideas helped tackle big problems. But today such concepts, loosely applied, rob the more localised wars that confront the world of scale and definition. Threats are made bigger and less manageable by the use of vocabulary that is imprecise. The 'war on terror' is a case in point. In its understandable shock after 9/11, America maximised the problem, both in terms of the original attack (which could have been treated as a crime, not a war) and in terms of the responses required to deal with the subsequent threat. The United States failed to relate means to aims (in a military sense) and to objectives (in a political sense). It abandoned strategy. It used words like prevention and pre-emption, concepts derived from strategy, but without context. They became not principles of military action but guidelines for foreign policy.

Britain's position is also instructive. Its assertion of the right to preemptive action was not first set out in *UK International Priorities* but in the Ministry of Defence's 'New Chapter' to the *Strategic Defence Review*. The Ministry of Defence, not the Foreign Office, was therefore articulating the policy which would guide Britain's decision to use force. One of the reasons why strategy has fallen into a black hole is that the government department most obviously charged with its formulation has expanded its brief into foreign policy, and that in turn is a consequence of widening definitions of war. Britain does not have an identifiable governmental agency responsible for strategy (despite the Foreign Office's apparent but perverse claim that that is its task). When the Falklands War broke out in 1982, Margaret Thatcher, as prime minister, had to improvise a war cabinet, a body that brought together the country's senior political and military heads: it has left no legacy, any more than has its prototype, the Committee of Imperial Defence, an advisory committee of the full cabinet set up in 1902.

When George Bush gave his London speech in November 2003, one possible challenger to his second term as president was Wesley Clark, who sought (but did not get) the Democrat nomination. Clark's career has been fashioned not by politics but by the army, and it culminated as Supreme Allied Commander Europe in the Kosovo war of 1999. The political and legal problems which that conflict generated undercut his military preparations, leading him to conclude: 'any first year military student could point to the more obvious inconsistencies between our efforts and the requirements posed by the principles of war'. Clark writes and lectures on waging modern war: he uses the word 'strategy' a great deal and he uses it with precision. His military experience is recent, but his refrain sounds familiar, even if old-fashioned: 'Using military force effectively requires departing from the political dynamic and following the so-called "Principles of War" identified by post-Napoleonic military writers a century and a half ago'.[55]

The point is not that generals should go back to what they were doing in the nineteenth century, but that politicians should recognise what it is that generals still do in the twenty-first century – and do best. If strategy has an institutional home in the United States or in the United Kingdom, it is located in the armed services. And yet in the planning of both the wars undertaken by the United States since the 9/11 attacks, those in Afghanistan and Iraq, professional service opinion, from the chairman of the Joint Chiefs of Staff downwards, has often seemed marginal at best and derided at worst. In 1986 the Goldwater-Nichols Act enhanced the authority of the chairman and made him the president's military advisor. This was the relationship played out between Colin Powell and George Bush senior in the first Gulf War in 1990–91. In 2001, the chairman answered less to the president than to the Secretary of Defense, Donald Rumsfeld. Rumsfeld was already at odds with his generals over the 'transformation' of the armed forces, and his subsequent reactions exposed the mismatch between his aspirations and their expectations. In the words of Bob Woodward: 'Eighteen days after September 11, they were developing a response, an action, but not a strategy.' The military 'had geared itself to attack fixed targets,' while the politicians were talking about doing a 'guerrilla war'. The military recognised that the consequence of the latter would be regime change, but the president refused to accept the probable consequences of his own policy, saying 'our military is meant to fight and win war', and denying that US troops could be peacekeepers.[56]

Kabul fell within 40 days. The United States had prevailed in Afghanistan (or so it seemed) without having had to formulate strategy. Action had generated its own results. The rapidity of the success bred more than surprise; it bred its own confidence, a 'can do' mentality which put more premium on taking the initiative than on learning lessons for the formulation of strategy. Planning for Iraq displayed a comparable under-appreciation of strategy. Clearly the US armed forces displayed their competence at the operational level of war in March–April 2003. They were also able to recognise the manpower needs of post-conflict Iraq and the requirement to cooperate with non-governmental organisations. Theoretically they could see the campaign in strategic terms, with a planning cycle that embraced four phases – deterrence and engagement; seizing the initiative; decisive operations; and post-conflict operations. But strategy was driven out by the wishful thinking of their political masters, convinced that the United States would be welcomed as liberators, and determined that war and peace were opposites, not a continuum. This cast of mind prevented consideration of the war's true costs or the implications of occupation, and the United States found itself without a forum in which the armed forces either could give voice to their view of the principles at stake or be heard if they did.[57]

* * *

Recent commentators have noted with dismay the under-funding both of the State Department in the United States and the Foreign and Commonwealth Office in Britain. They bemoan the readiness to militarise foreign policy rather than to use patient diplomacy. But the fault is not that of the military; it is the responsibility of their political masters.[58] They – not the soldiers – have used the armed forces as their agents in peace as well as in war. The confusion of strategy with policy is a manifestation both of the causes of this 'militarisation' and its consequences. President Bush's speech of November 2003 made clear that he had a policy. Indeed he has courted criticism precisely because it has been so clear and trenchant. But that is not strategy. The challenge for the United States – and for the United Kingdom – was, and is, the link between the policy of its administration and the operational designs of its armed forces. In the ideal model of civil-military relations, the democratic head of state sets out his or her policy, and armed forces coordinate the means to enable its achievement. The reality is that this process – a process called strategy – is iterative, a dialogue where ends also reflect means, and where the result – also called strategy – is a compromise between the ends of policy and the military means available to implement it. The state, and particularly the United States, remains the most powerful agency for the use of force in the world today. Lesser organisations use terror out of comparative weakness, not out of strength. The conflation of words like 'war' and 'terror', and of 'strategy' and 'policy', adds to their leverage because it contributes to the incoherence of the response. Awesome military power requires concepts for the application of force that are robust because they are precise.

Notes

1 See reports in *The Times* and the *Daily Telegraph*, 20 November 2003. What follows was delivered as my inaugural lecture as Professor of the History of War in Oxford on 4 December 2003.
2 CM 6052, December 2003.
3 CM 6041, December 2003.
4 CM 5566, July 2002.
5 Carl von Clausewitz, *On War*, ed. and trans. Michael Howard and Peter Paret (Princeton, NJ: Princeton University Press), p. 177, see also 128, 227.
6 Xenophon and Polybius both used στράτηγημά (*strātegemā*), or stratagem, to cover the art of the general. Xenophon uses στρατηγία (*strategiā*), or strategy, to mean plan in *Anabasis*, book II, chapter ii, 13; but contrast I, vii, 2, where a Persian council of war discussed 'how he [Cyrus] should fight the battle', and II, ii, 6, which speaks of the 'wisdom which a commander should have'. Onasander, Στρατηγικός (or *The General*) discussed 'the principles of generaliship' and 'the art of the general and the wisdom that inheres in the precepts' (Proemium, 3), but used the word 'strategy' in chapter XXXII, 5. I am grateful to Martin West and Brian Campbell for discussing these points with me.
7 Azar Gat, *The Origins of Military Thought from the Enlightenment to Clausewitz* (Oxford: Clarendon Press, 1989), p. 39.
8 Quoted by J.-P. Charnay, in André Corvisier (ed.), *A Dictionary of Military History and the Art of War*, English edition ed. John Childs (Oxford: Blackwell Reference, 1994), p. 769; see also Gat, *Origins of Military Thought*, p. 42.
9 Quoted by Charnay in Corvisier, *Dictionary of Military History*, p. 769.
10 Antoine-Henri Jomini, *Summary of the Art of War*, trans. G.H. Mendell and W.P. Craighill (Philadelphia: J.B. Lippincott, 1862), p. 137.
11 Ibid., p. 13.
12 Ibid., p. 69.
13 Gerhard Ritter, *The Sword and the Scepter: The Problem of Militarism in Germany*, 4 vols (London: Allen Lane, 1969–73), vol. I, pp. 187–260.
14 Friendrich von Bernhardi, *On War of To-day*, trans. Karl von Donat, 2 vols (London: Hugh Rees, 1912–13), vol. 2, pp. 187, 194.
15 Jean Colin, *The Transformations of War*, trans. L.H.R. Pope-Hennessy (London: Hugh Rees, 1912), p. 343.
16 Commandant [Henri] Mordacq, *Politique et stratégie dans une démocratie* (Paris: Plon, 1912), pp. 214, 237.
17 Julian Corbett, *Some Principles of Maritime Strategy*, ed. Eric Grove (Annapolis, MD: Brassey's, 1988; 1st ed. London, 1911), p. 10.
18 Ibid., p. 17.
19 Ibid., p. 30.
20 'The Green Pamphlet', printed as an appendix in ibid., p. 308.
21 Jon Tetsuro Sumida, *Inventing Grand Strategy and Teaching Command: The Classic Works of Alfred Thayer Mahan Reconsidered* (Washington DC: Woodrow Wilson Center Press, 1997), p. 27.
22 Raoul Castex, *Théories stratégiques*, 5 vols (Paris: Société d'Editions Géographiques, Maritimes et Coloniales, 1927–33); the quotation is from the revised edition of vol. 1, published in 1937), p. 9.
23 Ibid., vol. 3, p. 115.
24 Cameron Hazlehurst, *Politicians at War, July 1914 to May 1915: A Prologue to the Triumph of Lloyd George* (London: Jonathan Cape, 1971), p. 176.
25 J.F.C. Fuller, *The Reformation of War* (London: Hutchinson, 1923), p. 218.
26 Ibid.; see also Fuller, *The Foundations of the Science of War* (London: Hutchinson, [1926], pp. 105–107.
27 Basil Liddell Hart, *When Britain Goes to War* (London: Faber, 1928), p. 83; see also Liddell Hart, *Thoughts on War* (London: Faber & Faber, 1944), pp. 151–6.
28 J.R.M. Butler, *Grand Strategy*, 2 (London: Cabinet Office, 1957), p. xv.
29 Michael Howard, *Grand Strategy*, 4 (London: Cabinet Office, 1972), p. 1; see also Michael Howard, 'Grand Strategy in the Twentieth Century', *Defence Studies*, vol. 1, 2001, pp. 1–10.

30 Liddell Hart, *When Britain Goes to War*, p. 83.
31 Edward Mead Earle (ed.), *Makers of Modern Strategy: Military Thought from Machiavelli to Hitler* (Princeton: Princeton University Press, 1943), p. viii.
32 Clausewitz, *On War*, p. 606.
33 Herfried Münkler, *Über den Krieg. Stationen der Kriegsgeschichte im Spiegel ihrer theoristchen Reflexionenen* (Weilerswist: Velbrück Wissenschaft, 2002), pp. 91–115; Andreas Herberg-Rothe, *Das Rätsel Clausewitz* (Munich: Wilhelm Fink, 2001), pp. 31–4, 102–24.
34 Carl von Clausewitz, *Historical and Political Writings*, ed. and trans. Peter Paret and Daniel Moran (Princeton: Princeton University Press, 1992), p. 290.
35 Erich Ludendorff, *The Nation in Arms*, trans. A.S. Rappoport (London: Hutchinson, [1935]), pp. 19.
36 Ibid., p. 22.
37 Ibid., p. 23.
38 Münkler, *Über den Krieg*, p. 145.
39 Eric de la Maisonneuve, *Incitation à la réflexion stratégique* (Paris: Ed. Economica, 1998), p. 6.
40 André Beaufre, *An Introduction to Strategy* (London: Faber, 1965), pp. 14, 23.
41 Interestingly Bernhardi explicitly used the phrase 'political strategy' in *War of To-day*, vol. 2, p. 454, but only once and without defining it.
42 Castex, *Théories stratégiques*, vol. 1, pp. 17–18.
43 Beaufre, *Introduction to Strategy*, pp. 11, 13.
44 Edward Luttwak, *Strategy: The Logic of War and Peace* (Cambridge, MA: Belknap, 1987), p. 4.
45 Barry Posen, *The Sources of Military Doctrine: France, Britain, and Germany between the World Wars* (Ithaca, NY: Cornell University Press, 1984), pp. 13, 220.
46 Aleksandr A. Svechin, *Strategy*, ed Kent Lee (Minneapolis, MN: East View, 1992), p. 69.
47 On the Russian element, see Richard Simpkin, *Race to the Swift: Thoughts on Twenty-first Century Warfare* (London: Brassey's, 1985), pp. 37–53, and Shimon Naveh, *In Pursuit of Military Excellence: The Evolution of Operational Theory* (London: Frank Cass, 1997), pp.164–208. For a comparison, consider the German focus of the essays in Richard D. Hooker, Jr (ed.), *Maneuver warfare* (Novato, CA: Presidio, 1993).
48 Erich Ludendorff, *Kriegführung und Politik* (Berlin: E.S. Mittler, 1922), pp. 320–42; see also Otto von Moser, *Ernsthafte Plaudereien über den Weltkrieg* (Stuttgart: Belser, 1925), pp. 6–14; ein Generalstäbler, *Kritik des Weltkrieges. Das Erbe Moltkes und Schlieffens im grossen Kriege* (Leipzig: K.F. Koehler, 1920).
49 Daniel J. Hughes (ed.), *Moltke on the Art of War: Selected Writings* (Novato, CA: Presidio, 1993), p. 47.
50 Hermann Franke (ed.), *Handbuch der neuzeitlichen Wehrwissenschaften*, 3 vols in 4 (Berlin: Grenter, 1936–39), vol. 1, pp. 181–2; also p. 195.
51 Ibid., pp. 175, 549–53.
52 See, above all, Karl-Heinz Frieser, *Blitzkrieg-Legende. Der Westfeldzug 1940* (Munich: Oldenbourg Verlag 1995).
53 Martin van Creveld, *On Future War* (London: Brassey's, 1991; published in the US as *The Transformation of War*); John Keegan, *A History of Warfare* (London: Hutchinson, 1993); Mary Kaldor, *New and Old Wars* (London: Polity, 1999).
54 Stephen Launay, *La guerre sans la guerre: essai sur une querelle occidentale* (Paris: Descartes, 2003), p. 334.
55 Wesley Clark, *Waging Modern War: Bosnia, Kosovo and the Future of Combat* (Oxford: Perseus, 2001), p. 427.
56 Bob Woodward, *Bush at War* (New York: Simon & Schuster, 2002), pp. 174–6, 192; see also pp. 42–44, 84, 99, 128–9, 227, 245–6; Dana Priest, *The Mission: waging war and keeping peace with America's military* (New York: W.W. Norton, 2003), pp. 21–4, 34, 37.
57 James Fallows, 'Blind into Baghdad', *Atlantic Monthly*, January/February 2004, pp. 53–74; Anthony H. Cordesman, *The Iraq War: Strategy, Tactics and Military Lessons* (Washington DC: Center for Strategic and International Studies, 2003), pp. 153–71, 496–509. I am grateful for the comments on the last section of those who heard me speak at the Olin Institute of Strategic Studies, at Harvard, and at the Triangle Institute for Security Studies, North Carolina, in April 2005, and especially to Stephen Rosen, Peter Feaver, Richard Kohn and Jacqueline Newmyer. They forced me to sharpen my argument, even if they do not necessarily agree with it.
58 Priest, *The Mission*, pp. 11–19.

Index

Please note that references to Notes will have the letter 'n' following the note

An environmentally friendly book printed and bound in England by www.printondemand-worldwide.com

PEFC Certified

This product is
from sustainably
managed forests
and controlled
sources

www.pefc.org

PEFC/16-33-415

FSC

Mixed Sources

Product group from well-managed
forests, and other controlled sources
www.fsc.org Cert no. TT-COC-002641
© 1996 Forest Stewardship Council

This book is made entirely of chain-of-custody materials

#0291 - 101111 - C0 - 246/174/25 - PB